ROUTLEDGE HANDBOOK OF INTERNATIONAL STATEBUILDING

This new handbook offers a combination of theoretical, thematic and empirical analyses of the statebuilding regime, written by leading international scholars.

Over the past decade, international statebuilding has become one of the most important and least understood areas of international policy-making. Today, there are around one billion people living in some 50–60 conflict-affected, 'fragile' states, vulnerable to political violence and civil war. The international community grapples with the core challenges and dilemmas of using outside force, aid and persuasion to build states in the wake of conflict and to prevent such countries from lapsing into devastating violence.

The *Routledge Handbook of International Statebuilding* is a comprehensive resource for this emerging area in International Relations. The volume is designed to guide the reader through the background and development of international statebuilding as a policy area, as well as exploring in depth significant issues such as security, development, democracy and human rights Divided into three main parts, this handbook provides a single-source overview of the key topics in international statebuilding:

- **Part One:** Concepts and Approaches
- **Part Two:** Security, Development and Democracy
- **Part Three:** Policy Implementation

This handbook will be essential reading for students of statebuilding, humanitarian intervention, peacebuilding, development, war and conflict studies and IR/Security Studies in general

David Chandler is Professor of International Relations at the Department of Politics and International Relations, University of Westminster. He is a regular media commentator, founding editor of the *Journal of Intervention and Statebuilding* and the general editor of the Routledge book series Studies in Intervention and Statebuilding. He is the author or editor of over a dozen books.

Timothy D. Sisk is Professor at the Josef Korbel School of International Studies, University of Denver, and Director of the Center for Sustainable Development and International Peace (SDIP), a research and policy institute at the school. He is author or editor of three previous books.

ROUTLEDGE HANDBOOK OF INTERNATIONAL STATEBUILDING

Edited by David Chandler and Timothy D. Sisk

Routledge
Taylor & Francis Group
LONDON AND NEW YORK

First published 2013
by Routledge
2 Park Square, Milton Park, Abingdon, Oxfordshire OX14 4RN

Simultaneously published in the USA and Canada
by Routledge
711 Third Avenue, New York, NY 10017

First issued in paperback 2015

Routledge is an imprint of the Taylor & Francis Group, an informa business

© 2013 selection and editorial material, David Chandler and Timothy D. Sisk; individual chapters, the contributors

The right of the editor to be identified as the author of the editorial material, and o the authors for their individual chapters, has been asserted in accordance with sections 77 and 78 of the Copyright, Designs and Patents Act 1988.

All rights reserved. No part of this book may be reprinted or reproduced or utilised in any form or by any electronic, mechanical, or other means, now known or hereafter invented, including photocopying and recording, or in any information storage or retrieval system, without permission in writing from the publishers.

Trademark notice: Product or corporate names may be trademarks or registered trademarks, and are used only for identification and explanation without intent to infringe.

British Library Cataloguing in Publication Data
A catalogue record for this book is available from the British Library

Library of Congress Cataloging-in-Publication Data
Routledge handbook of international statebuilding / edited by
David Chandler and Timothy D. SiskSisk.
pages cm
Includes bibliographical references and index.
1. Nation–building. 2. Security, International.
I. Chandler, David, 1962–
JZ6300.R68 2013
355.02'8–dc23
2012040234

ISBN13: 978–1–138–93069–8 (pbk)
ISBN13: 978–0–415–67702–8 (hbk)

Typeset in Bembo
by Keystroke, Station Road, Codsall, Wolverhampton

CONTENTS

List of figures and tables   ix
Contributors   xi
Introduction   xix
Timothy D. Sisk and David Chandler

PART I
Concepts and approaches   1

1 Rethinking Weberian approaches to statebuilding   3
   Nicolas Lemay-Hébert

2 Corruption and statebuilding   15
   Dominik Zaum

3 Gender and statebuilding   29
   Clare Castillejo

4 Elites and statebuilding   42
   Jago Salmon and Catherine Anderson

5 Regulatory statebuilding and the transformation of the state   52
   Shahar Hameiri

6 Hiding in plain sight: The neglected dilemma of nationalism for statebuilding   64
   Stephen J. Del Rosso

7 Statebuilding, civil society, and the privileging of difference   83
   David Chandler

8	Hybrid polities and post−conflict polic *David Roberts*	94
9	History repeating? Colonial, socialist, and liberal statebuilding in Mozambique *Meera Sabaratnam*	106
10	The 'failed−state'effect: Statebuilding and state stories from the Congo *Kai Koddenbrock*	118
11	Failed statebuilding versus peace formation *Oliver P. Richmond*	130

PART II
Security, development, and democracy — 141

12	United Nations constitutional assistance in statebuilding *Vijayashri Sripati*	143
13	United Nations peacekeeping and the irony of statebuilding *Richard Gowan*	156
14	Statebuilding through security sector reform *Fairlie Chappuis and Heiner Hänggi*	168
15	Liberia: Security sector reform *Morten Bøås and Samantha Gowran Farrier*	185
16	Maintaining the police−military divide in policing peace *B. K. Greener and W. J. Fish*	196
17	Natural resource governance and hybrid political orders *Gilles Carbonnier and Achim Wennmann*	208
18	The political economy of statebuilding: Rents, taxes, and perpetual dependency *Berit Bliesemann de Guevara and Florian P. Kühn*	219
19	Political economy of post−conflict state uilding in Central America *Aaron Schneider*	231
20	Sharing power to build states *Anna K. Jarstad*	246
21	Elections and statebuilding after civil war: Lurching toward legitimacy *Timothy D. Sisk*	257

PART III
Policy implementation — 267

22 Intervention and statebuilding in Kosovo — 269
    Jens Stilhoff Sörensen

23 Bosnia: Building states without societies? NGOs and civil society — 281
    Roberto Belloni

24 Iraq: US approaches to statebuilding in the twenty-fist century — 293
    David A. Lake

25 'Liberal' statebuilding in Afghanistan — 304
    Péter Marton and Nik Hynek

26 Statebuilding after victory: Uganda, Ethiopia, Eritrea, and Rwanda — 315
    Terrence Lyons

27 Post–statebuilding and the Australian experience in Timor–Leste and Solomon Islands — 327
    Julien Barbara

28 Statebuilding in Palestine: Caught between occupation, realpolitik, and the liberal peace — 339
    Mandy Turner

29 EU police missions — 350
    Giovanna Bono

30 EU statebuilding through good governance — 362
    Wil Hout

31 The Security Council, R2P, and statebuilding — 375
    Thomas G. Weiss

32 Aid and fragility: The challenges of building peaceful and effective states — 387
    Alina Rocha Menocal

Index — 400

LIST OF FIGURES AND TABLES

Figures

19.1	Change in tax capacity in terms of revenue as a percentage of GDP	234
19.2	Tax trends in El Salvador	236
19.3	Direct and indirect taxation in Guatemala	241

Tables

2.1	Elite factionalization and violent conflict in highly corrupt countries	20
10.1	International funding amounts	127
14.1	SSR in statebuilding practice: Selection of cases for illustration	174
16.1	Military and police tasks in contemporary UN peace operations	203
29.1	EU police missions, 2003–2011	352
30.1	EU support strategies in six pilot countries	371

CONTRIBUTORS

Catherine Anderson is a public sector governance specialist with experience in fragile and conflict-affected settings in the Asia and Africa Regions. She has worked as staff and consultant for the World Bank, Bureau for Crisis Prevention and Recovery (BCPR), UNDP, DPKO and several international non-governmental agencies – including Revenue Watch Institute, Amnesty International, and Human Rights Watch. Catherine specializes in research, policy and programme management in the fields of public sector management, natural resource governance, justice and conflict. She holds an LLM (*with distinction*) in Law, Development and Governance, from SOAS, University of London, and a Bachelor of Political Science from Victoria University, Wellington, New Zealand.

Julien Barbara has worked on post-conflict statebuilding issues since 2001 as an Australian public servant and academic. Since 2008 he has worked for the Australian Agency for International Development (AusAID) on Solomon Islands issues including, from 2011 to mid-2012, as the Director of the Machinery of Government Program under the Regional Assistance Mission to Solomon Islands, based in Honiara. Prior to that he worked as an academic, publishing on post-conflict statebuilding issues, and on the East Timor desk in the Australian Departmen of Foreign Affairs and Trade. From 2002 to 2004 he was posted to Belgium and the European Union as an Australian diplomat.

Roberto Belloni is Associate Professor of International Relations at the University of Trento, Italy. He has written extensively on various aspects of international intervention in conflict areas including *State Building and International Intervention in Bosnia* (Routledge, 2007). With Anna K. Jarstad he has edited 'Hybrid Peace Governance', a special issue of *Global Governance: A Review of Multilateralism and International Organizations*, 18(1), 2012.

Berit Bliesemann de Guevara is Senior Lecturer at the Department of International Politics at Aberystwyth University, Wales. Before, she held a professorship at Bremen University's Institute for Intercultural and International Studies (InIIS). She earned her PhD at Helmut Schmidt University Hamburg with a work on intervention and statebuilding in Bosnia and Herzegovina, for which she was awarded the German Studies Award 2009. Her research focuses on statebuilding and stateness, formal and informal knowledge production in international intervention, causes and courses of intra–state violent conflict, as well as charisma and politics She is editor of *Statebuilding and State-Formation: The Political Sociology of Intervention* (Routledge, 2012).

Morten Bøås is Senior Researcher at Fafo's Institute for Applied International Studies. Bøås has published extensively on African politics and security, Liberia included. Among his works are *African Guerrillas: Rage Against the Machine* (Lynne Rienner, 2007, with Kevin Dunn) and *The Politics of Origin* (Zed Books, 2013, with Kevin Dunn).

Giovanna Bono is a Marie Curie Intra–EU Research Fellow at the University of St. Andrews in Scotland. She is the editor of *The impact of the 9/11 on EU foreign and security policy* (VUB Press, 2006) and *NATO's peace-enforcement tasks and policy communities: 1990–1999* (Ashgate, 2003). Her recent publications include 'The impact of the "politics of protection": The case of the EU and UN military and police mission in Chad (2007–2011)', *African Security*, 5(3–4), 2012 and 'The European Union and "supervised independence of Kosovo": A strategic solution to the Kosovo/Serbia conflict?', *European Foreign Affairs Review*, 35(2), 2010.

Gilles Carbonnier has been Professor of Development Economics at the Graduate Institute of International and Development Studies since February 2007. He obtained his PhD in Economics from Neuchâtel University. He has been editor–in–chief of *International Development Policy* since 2008, and is President of the board of directors of CERAH, the Centre for Education and Research in Humanitarian Action. His research and publications focus on the energy–development nexus and the governance of extractive resources, as well as on humanitarianism, the political economy of armed conflict and international development cooperation. Gilles Carbonnier has over 20 years of professional experience in international trade, development cooperation and humanitarian action.

Clare Castillejo is a senior researcher and research coordinator at FRIDE. Prior to joining FRIDE, Clare worked as a Social Development Adviser with the UK Department for International Development (DFID), as a researcher with Amnesty International, and as a Human Rights Specialist with UNDP. Clare has also worked as a researcher with the European Monitoring Centre on Racism and with the South Asia Human Rights Group. Clare has worked extensively in developing countries. She was based for four years in South Asia and has conducted research in West Africa, Southern Africa and China. She has a BA in Social Anthropology from the University of Sussex and an MA in Anthropology of Development from SOAS.

David Chandler is Professor of International Relations at the Department of Politics and International Relations, University of Westminster. He is founding editor of the *Journal of Intervention and Statebuilding* and the editor of the Routledge book series *Studies in Intervention and Statebuilding*. Professor Chandler is the author of a number of monographs, including *Freedom vs. Necessity in International Relations: Human-Centred Approaches to Security and Development* (Zed Books, 2013); *International Statebuilding: The Rise of Post-Liberal Governance* (Routledge, 2010); *Hollow Hegemony: Rethinking Global Politics, Power and Resistance* (Pluto, 2009); *Empire in Denial: The Politics of State-Building* (Pluto, 2006); *Constructing Global Civil Society: Morality and Power in International Relations* (Palgrave–Macmillan, 2004, 2005); *From Kosovo to Kabul (and Beyond): Human Rights and International Intervention* (Pluto, 2002, 2006); and *Bosnia: Faking Democracy after Dayton* (Pluto, 1999, 2000).

Contributors

Fairlie Chappuis is a Research Associate for the project 'Exporting the State Monopoly on Violence: Security Governance Transfers to Areas of Limited Statehood' at the Free University of Berlin, where she leads the case study on security governance and reform in Liberia. Before joining the Research Center SFB 700: Governance in Areas of Limited Statehood, she worked on security governance and reform issues within the Research Division at the Geneva Centre for the Democratic Control of Armed Forces (DCAF) 2006–2010. She is currently a doctoral candidate at the Free University of Berlin, where her research focuses on the challenges of security sector reform in post–conflict contexts. Her research interests include the link between securit and development, human security, governance processes, and post–conflict statebuilding and peace–building.

Stephen J. Del Rosso is director of the International Peace and Security program at the Carnegie Corporation of New York. A former career diplomat, Del Rosso served nearly 10 years in the Foreign Service with overseas assignments in Central America and the Caribbean during the height of US engagement in the region in the mid–80s. In Washington, he served in the operations center and on the executive secretariat staff of Secretary of State George P. Shultz, accompanying him on numerous overseas missions. Del Rosso holds a PhD in political science from the University of Pennsylvania, an MALD from the Fletcher School of Law and Diplomacy, where he was an Earhart Fellow, a diploma in international studies from the Bologna Center of the Johns Hopkins School of Advanced International Studies, and a BA in English from Tufts University.

Samantha Gowran Farrier has an MA in International Affairs, specializing in Peace and Conflict Studies from the Australian National University (ANU) in partnership with the Peace Research Institute Oslo (PRIO). She has previously worked at UNICEF Norway and worked as an intern at the Fafo Institute for Applied International Studies.

William J. Fish is Associate Professor in Philosophy at Massey University. His books include *Philosophy of Perception: A Contemporary Introduction* (Routledge, 2010) and *Perception, Hallucination, and Illusion* (Oxford University Press, 2009).

Richard Gowan is Associate Director for Crisis Diplomacy and Peace Operations at the Center for International Cooperation, New York University. He is a specialist in peacekeeping, multilateral security arrangements and the relationship between the UN and the EU. Formerly manager of the Europe Programme at The Foreign Policy Centre (London), he is also a Senior Policy Fellow at the European Council on Foreign Relations. He has broadcast widely – including the BBC, CNN and the Lehrer NewsHour – and frequently contributes to policy magazines and websites. He has worked with the OSCE Mission to Croatia, and published on the political philosophy of Raymond Aron.

Bethan K. Greener is a Senior Lecturer in International Relations at Massey University, New Zealand. Her book *The New International Policing* was published by Palgrave in 2009, and she has published articles in journals such as *International Relations, Policing and Society, International Peacekeeping,* and *Global Change, Peace and Security*.

Shahar Hameiri is an Australian Research Council Postdoctoral Fellow and Senior Lecturer in International Politics at the Asia Research Centre, Murdoch University, Australia. He is author of *Regulating Statehood: State Building and the Transformation of the Global Order* (Palgrave Macmillan, 2010), as well as of articles on statebuilding, regional governance, risk and security governance in leading journals, including *International Studies Quarterly*, *Political Studies*, *Review of International Studies*, and *The Pacific Review*.

Heiner Hänggi is Assistant Director and Head of Research at the Geneva Centre for the Democratic Control of Armed Forces (DCAF). He is also an Associate Professor of political science at the University of St Gallen, Switzerland, and associate faculty member at the Geneva Centre for Security Policy (GCSP). Prior to joining DCAF, he held a number of posts in research and journalism, including member of the task force responsible for establishing DCAF, senior research fellow at the Geneva-based Modern Asia Research Centre, and international affairs journalist and political editor for Swiss daily newspapers. Heiner Hänggi obtained his Doctorate and Licentiate in 'Staatswissenschaften' (Political Science, Economics, Law) from the University of St Gallen. He has served as a visiting scholar at the Institute of Southeast Asian Studies (ISEAS), Singapore, the Graduate School of Policy Science, National Saitama University, Urawa, Japan, and the Paul H. Nitze School of Advanced International Studies (SAIS), Johns Hopkins University, Washington, DC.

Wil Hout is Professor of Governance and International Political Economy at the International Institute of Social Studies, Erasmus University, Rotterdam. His research interests relate to international relations, development assistance and issues of ('good') governance. He is the author of *Capitalism and the Third World* (Edward Elgar, 1993), *The Politics of Aid Selectivity* (Routledge, 2007) and (co-)editor of a dozen volumes and special journal issues, most recently of *Governance and the Depoliticisation of Development* (with Richard Robison, Routledge, 2009) and *EU Strategies on Governance Reform: Between Development and State-Building* (Routledge, 2013). He has published articles in, among others, the *European Journal of International Relations*, *Third World Quarterly*, *Development and Change*, the *Journal of Development Studies*, *Critical Asian Studies*, and *Acta Politica: International Journal of Political Science*.

Nik Hynek is Research Leader at the Centre for International Security of the Institute of International Relations in Prague. He holds a PhD from the Department of Peace Studies at the University of Bradford. His publications have appeared in *Security Dialogue*, *Journal of International Relations and Development*, *International Journal*, *European Security*, *International Peacekeeping*, *Defence Studies*, *Contemporary Political Theory*, and *Communist and Post-Communist Studies*. He has recently published *Human Security as Statecraft* (Routledge, 2012), and co-edited *Statebuilding in Afghanistan* (Routledge, 2011), *Critical Approaches to Human Security* (Routledge, 2010), and *Canada's Foreign and Security Policy* (Oxford University Press, 2010).

Anna K. Jarstad is Associate Professor at the Department of Government, Uppsala University, Sweden. With Roberto Belloni she has edited 'Hybrid Peace Governance', a special issue of *Global Governance: A Review of Multilateralism and International Organizations*, Vol. 18, No. 1, 2012. With Timothy D. Sisk she has edited *From War to Democracy: Dilemmas of Peacebuilding* (Cambridge University Press, 2008). She has also published in journals such as *Conflict Management and Peace Science*, *Democratization*, *Africa Spectrum*, and *Civil Wars*. Her research covers conflict managemen in ethnically divided societies and the nexus of democratization and peacebuilding in war-torn societies, especially in Afghanistan, Bosnia-Herzegovina, Cyprus, Kosovo, Macedonia, New Zealand, and South Africa.

Kai Koddenbrock is a PhD candidate in International Relations at the University of Bremen. He was recently a visiting scholar at Columbia University's Department of Middle Eastern, South

Asian and African Studies. He is also a fellow at the Global Public Policy Institute, Berlin. His most recent publications include 'Recipes for intervention: Western policy papers imagine the Congo', *International Peacekeeping*, 19(5) and 'The international self and the humanitarianization of politics', in: Bliesemann de Guevara (ed.), *Statebuilding and state formation* (Routledge, 2012) and *Smart sanctions against failed states* (Vdm Verlag Dr. Müller, 2008). He has consulted with UN OCHA and GIZ. His research interests cover social and political theory, African politics and intervention.

Florian P. Kühn is Senior Lecturer and Researcher at Hamburg's Helmut Schmidt University. His PhD, entitled 'Security and Development in World Society. Liberal Paradigm and Statebuilding in Afghanistan', won the German Middle East Studies Association's (DAVO) dissertation award 2010. His research focuses on risk and resilience in international security and looks at South and Central Asia. He has published in *Journal of Intervention and Statebuilding*, *Canadian Foreign Policy Journal*, *International Relations*, and *International Peacekeeping* among others. Together with Berit Bliesemann de Guevara, he published *Illusion Statebuilding: Why the Western State is so Difficult to Export* (in German, edition Körber, 2010).

David A. Lake is the Jerri-Ann and Gary E. Jacobs Professor of Social Sciences and Distinguished Professor of Political Science at the University of California, San Diego. He has published widely in international relations theory and international political economy. Lake's most recent book is *Hierarchy in International Relations* (2009). In addition to over 70 scholarly articles and chapters, he is the author of *Power, Protection, and Free Trade: International Sources of U.S. Commercial Strategy, 1887–1939* (1988) and *Entangling Relations: American Foreign Policy in Its Century* (1999) and co-editor of 10 volumes including *Politics in the New Hard Times: The Great Recession in Comparative Perspective* (2013) and *The Credibility of Transnational NGOs: When Virtue is not Enough* (2012). The recipient of the UCSD Chancellor's Associates Award for Excellence in Graduate Education (2005), he was elected to the American Academy of Arts and Sciences in 2006 and a fellow at the Center for Advanced Study in the Behavioral Sciences in 2008–2009. He received his PhD from Cornell University in 1984 and taught at UCLA from 1983 to 1992.

Nicolas Lemay-Hébert is a Marie Curie Experienced Researcher at the International Development Department, University of Birmingham, and co-lead with Edward Newman of the cluster 'civil wars, intervention and statebuilding' at the Institute for Conflict, Cooperatio and Security, University of Birmingham. His research interests include peacebuilding and statebuilding, humanitarian interventions in post-conflict or post-disaster contexts, and local narratives of resistance to international interventions.

Terrence Lyons received his doctorate in international relations from the Johns Hopkins University School for Advanced International Studies and served as a Fellow associated with the Conf ict Resolution in Africa project at the Brookings Institution and as Senior Research and Program Leader for Conflict Resolution and Peacebuilding at the International Peace Researc Institute, Oslo. Lyons's research has focused on the relationships between protracted civil wars and processes of political development and sustainable peace, with a particular focus on Africa and on policy issues. Among his publications are *Demilitarizing Politics: Elections on the Uncertain Road to Peace* (Lynne Rienner, 2005), *Voting for Peace: Postconflict Elections in Liberia* (Brookings Institution, 1999), *Sovereignty as Responsibility: Conflict Management in Africa* (co-written with Francis M. Deng, Sadikiel Kimaro, Donald Rothchild, and I. William Zartman, Brookings Institution, 1996), and

Somalia: State Collapse, Multilateral Intervention, and Strategies for Political Reconstruction (co-written with Ahmed Samatar, Brookings Institution, 1995). He has also co-edited two books and several working papers, and published in a range of journals and policy-oriented publications.

Péter Marton is Assistant Professor at Corvinus University in Budapest. His research deals with Foreign Policy Analysis and the politics of statebuilding with special regard to issues of coalition burden-sharing. He has recently co-edited a book titled *Statebuilding in Afghanistan* (Routledge, 2011).

Oliver P. Richmond is Research Professor in International Relations, University of Manchester, UK. His publications include *Failed Statebuilding versus Peace Formation* (Yale University Press, forthcoming 2013), *A Short Introduction to Peace* (Oxford University Press, 2012), *A Post Liberal Peace* (Routledge, 2011), *Liberal Peace Transitions* (with Jason Franks, Edinburgh University Press, 2009), *Peace in International Relations* (Routledge, 2008), and *The Transformation of Peace* (Palgrave, 2005/7). He is the editor of the Palgrave book series *Rethinking Conflict Studies*.

David Roberts is Senior Lecturer in International Relations in the Department of Politics History and International Relations at Loughborough University. His books include *Political Transition in Cambodia 1991–99: Power, Elitism and Democracy* (Palgrave Macmillan, 2001); *Human Insecurity: Global Structures of Violence* (Zed Books, 2007); *Global Governance and Biopolitics: Regulating Human Security* (Zed Books, 2009); and *Liberal Peacebuilding and Global Governance: Beyond the Metropolis* (Routledge, 2011).

Alina Rocha Menocal is a Research Fellow in the Politics and Governance Programme, Overseas Development Institute, London. She has particular expertise in the challenges of democratization, linkages between state and society, and statebuilding. At ODI, Alina has been involved in a series of projects and assignments that seek to bridge the gap between research and policy in thinking about governance issues from a political economy perspective. Alina has built a considerable body of publications on many of these issues, including numerous reports, (peer-reviewed) journal articles, briefing and working papers, and blogs. She also has substantial experience of leading and managing projects.

Meera Sabaratnam is a Temporary Lecturer in the Department of Politics and International Studies at the University of Cambridge. She took her MSc and PhD in the Department of International Relations at the LSE; the PhD was completed in 2012. She is co-editor of *Liberal Peace? The Problems and Practices of Peacebuilding* (Zed Books, 2011) and *Interrogating Democracy in World Politics* (Routledge, 2010), and is currently Reviews Editor of the *Journal of Intervention and Statebuilding*.

Jago Salmon is a Crisis Governance Specialist in the Bureau for Crisis Prevention and Recovery, United Nations Development Program. He specializes in governance in conflict-affected countries and in policy formulation, program design, and capacity development. Jago has widespread experience in a variety of field settings in Africa, the Middle East and North Africa and extensive participation in internal United Nations and global policy-level discourses on aid for peacebuilding and statebuilding. Before joining UNDP, Jago worked with national and international civil society, including Small Arms Survey, International Crisis Group, the Overseas Development Institute. He earned a doctorate at the Humbolt-Universität zu Berlin with a dissertation on 'Militia Politics' focusing on Sudan (1985–2001) and Lebanon (1975–1991).

Contributors

Aaron Schneider is Leo Block Professor at the Josef Korbel School of International Studies, University of Denver. Previously a professor at Tule University, he is a specialist in the political economy of statebuilding with a regional specialization on Central and Latin America. He was previously a policy adviser to the Inter–American Development Bank, a Lecturer at the University of Sussex, and a special adviser to the President of Honduras. He has published widely in comparative politics, fiscal policies, and elite interactions in the Americas. He holds a PhD i Political Science from the University of California–Berkeley.

Timothy D. Sisk is Professor at the Josef Korbel School of International Studies, University of Denver and Director of the Program on Fragile States, a research and policy institute at the school. He specializes in electoral processes and conflict in fragile and post–war contexts. H is the most–recent former editor, with Tom Farer, of the journal of the Academic Council of the United Nations System (ACUNS), *Global Governance: A Review of Multilateralism and International Organizations* (published by Lynne Rienner). Sisk serves as an Associate Fellow of the Geneva Centre for Security Policy in Geneva, Switzerland. Professor Sisk's latest scholarly book is titled *International Mediation in Civil Wars: Bargaining with Bullets* (Routledge, 2009). Two other books for which he is the editor also recently appeared: *From War to Democracy: Dilemmas of Peacebuilding* (with Anna Jarstad, Cambridge University Press, 2008) and *The Dilemmas of Statebuilding: Confronting the Contradictions of Postwar Peace Operations* (with Roland Paris, Routledge, 2009).

Vijayashri Sripati is an adjunct professor and post–doctoral fellow at the Department of Political Science, University of Toronto. She took her doctorate in law from Osgoode Hall Law School, Canada. Her areas of specialization include the United Nations and global governance, international human rights law, Indian constitutional law, comparative constitutionalism, and legal education. She has published widely in journals in the United States, India, and the UK. An expert in United Nations Constitutional Assistance (UNCA), her artice 'UN Constitutional Assistance Projects in Comprehensive Peace Missions: An Inventory 1989–2011' (*International Peacekeeping*, Vol. 19(1), 2012) maps out the legal aspects of all the UNCA projects undertaken within the context of multidimensional peace missions and UNCA activities from the earliest projects in Namibia onwards.

Jens Stilhoff Sörensen is Lecturer in Peace and Development Studies at the University of Gothenburg and Research Fellow in the Swedish Institute of International Affairs. He has worked in and with the Balkans since the early 1990s, f rst for the Swedish Government (MFA/Sida) and international organisations (OSCE, EUMM) and then as a researcher. He is author of *State Collapse and Reconstruction in the Periphery* (Berghahn Books, 2009) and editor of *Challenging the Aid Paradigm: Western Currents and Asian Alternatives* (Palgrave Macmillan, 2010), as well as works in Swedish.

Mandy Turner is seconded to the Kenyon Institute in East Jerusalem (Council for British Research in the Levant) from the Department of Peace Studies, University of Bradford, where she was a lecturer in conflict resolution. She has been published in the journals *Conflict, Security and Development, International Peacekeeping, Democratization*, and *Journal of Intervention and Statebuilding*. She is co–editor (with Michael Pugh and Neil Cooper) of *Whose Peace? Critical Perspectives on the Political Economy of Peacebuilding* (PalgraveMacmillan, 2008/2011) and is assistant editor of the journal *International Peacekeeping*. Recent publications include *The Palestinian People and the Political Economy of De-development* (co–editedwith Omar Shweiki, Routledge, 2013) and

'Peacekeeping, Peacebuilding and Regime Change Wars', special issue of *International Peacekeeping* (co-edited with Florian Kuhn, October 2012).

Thomas G. Weiss is Presidential Professor of Political Science at The CUNY Graduate Center and Director of the Ralph Bunche Institute for International Studies, where he co-directed the UN Intellectual History Project (1999–2010). He was president (2009–10) of the International Studies Association and chair (2006–9) of the Academic Council on the UN System. His latest books are *Humanitarian Business* (2013) and *What's Wrong with the United Nations and How to Fix It* (2012). As Research Professor at Brown University's Watson Institute for International Studies (1990–98), he also held university administrative posts (Associate Dean of the Faculty, Director of the Global Security Program, Associate Director), was the Executive Director of ACUNS, and co-directed the Humanitarianism and War Project. Earlier, he was the Executive Director of the International Peace Academy (1985–9); a Senior Economic Affairs Officer at the UN Conference on Trade and Development in Geneva (1975–85); and held professional posts in the Office of the UN Commissioner for Namibia, the University Program at the Institute for World Order, the United Nations Institute for Training and Research, and the International Labor Organization. He has been a consultant for foundations and numerous inter-governmental and non-governmental organizations and was editor of *Global Governance* (2000–5) and research director of the International Commission on Intervention and State Sovereignty (2000–2).

Achim Wennmann is Researcher at the Center on Conflict, Development and Peacebuildin (CCDP) of the Graduate Institute of International and Development Studies in Geneva. At the CCDP, Dr Wennmann conducts research on the economic dimensions of peace mediation, hybrid political orders, the political economy of conflict and armed groups, and the natural resource management. He authored *The Political Economy of Peacemaking* (Routledge, 2011) and co-edited (with Mats Berdal) *Ending Wars, Consolidating Peace: Economic Perspectives* (Routledge, 2010). Dr Wennmann is also Executive Coordinator of the Geneva Peacebuilding Platform, an inter-agency network that connects the critical mass of peacebuilding actors, resources, and expertise in Geneva and worldwide.

Dominik Zaum is Reader in International Relations at the University of Reading. His publications include *The Sovereignty Paradox: The Norms and Politics of International Statebuilding* (Oxford University Press, 2007); *The United Nations Security Council and War: The Evolution of Thought and Practice since 1945* (Oxford University Press, 2008, with Vaughan Lowe, Adam Roberts, and Jennifer Welsh); *Corruption and Post-conflict Peacebuilding: Selling the Peace?* (Routledge, 2011, with Christine Cheng); and *Political Economy of State-Building: Power after Peace* (Routledge, 2012, with Mats Berdal).

INTRODUCTION
International statebuilding in war-torn societies

Timothy D. Sisk and David Chandler

The seismic shift in the international system in 1989, marked by end of the Cold War, produced significant new challenges and issues for international relations. First among them has been the reorganization and evolution of the international architecture for peace to address the threats to international peace and security that emanate from countries torn by violent, internal conflict within states, in contrast to the post–World War II architecture that primarily aimed to end the scourge of international war between states. Armed conflict within states has consistently pose the most realized, immediate threat to global peace, and from 1989 to 2012 the world has seen 137 armed conflicts worldwide; in 2011, 36 of the 37 conflicts recorded were intrastate as oppose to interstate (Themnér and Wallensteen, 2012: 566–567).

The threats to international peace and security from these conflicts involve tangible spillover of military insecurity that have direct, injurious consequences for neighboring countries and leading states globally. Within such conflicts, as well, there are grave violations of the core foundational norms of the international system after World War II, to include most poignantly the prevention and elimination of genocide. Today, there is equally concern with the human-security toll of conflict as more than 90 per cent of fatalities that result from such wars are civilian and they feature high rates of other types of injury to civilians, such as forced migration; moreover, countries affected by armed conflict also see high levels of armed violence (criminal and interpersonal violence, especially violence against women) (Geneva Declaration 2011).[1]

The problem of internal war and international security has created in turn a complex set of policy and implementation responses from the international system as a whole. Efforts to prevent such conflicts are now routine, with early warning and response units to stem violence integrate into the work of the UN and indeed many regional and sub-regional organizations. The UN has reorganized itself to intervene politically in such conflicts, particularly in the Department of Political Affairs, to have a standing capacity to mediate among domestic protagonists when political violence threatens or erupts and to encourage the parties to choose a negotiated settlement over fighting to the bitter end. Humanitarian aid responses have also evolved, reflecting the need to address th plight not just of refugees, but of the internally displaced as well and to address the exigencies of food insecurity, disease, and homelessness that conflict creates. Peacekeeping has also evolved, with new doctrines and practices in place for deployment of peacekeeping forces and a closer attention to the relationship between peacekeeping as such and progress toward consolidating a political settlement, and ostensibly more sustainable and context-appropriate responses over time.

But all these approaches, in and of themselves, are remedial of the symptoms of armed conflict and do not necessarily address the underlying drivers and capacity of governments worldwide to manage pressures stemming from such drivers. As such, these response mechanisms, in and of themselves, are ultimately insufficient. Over time, countries experiencing or emerging from conflict need sustainable, locally owned systems of governance through which the deep drivers that create social contestation and distributional conflicts can be resolved without resort to violent confrontations. This means that over the long term the strategic goal of international engagement (and especially post–conflict aid flows) in countries affected by conflict is to assist them in recovery of the state and the sealing of a new social contract in the wake of war. . . *statebuilding*.

Today, there are some 40–60 states in the international system, which together have a combined population of over a billion people, that are either in conflict or are just emerging from war (World Bank, 2011). Most of these countries have recently seen war before, whereas the dynamics of history, identity, economics, and demography – together with a weak state – leave others vulnerable to new escalations. Statebuilding has become the antithesis of state weakness, or 'fragility,' albeit without a clear, comprehensive understanding of the scope of the concept and of the conundrums that it presents for policy. In these volatile contexts, the international community today grapples with the core challenges and dilemmas of using outside force, development aid, and persuasion to build states in the wake of conflict and to prevent vulnerable countries from lapsing into devastating violence. The emerging field of statebuilding is highly complex, and there continue to be deep challenges for global actors such as the United Nations in trying to build internal peace using outside levers of power, money, and, in some cases, military force.

The goal of the handbook is to provide a comprehensive resource for core knowledge in this emerging area. Knowledge of the complex processes through which international engagement seeks to build states is just emerging. Whether the measures are peacekeeping, aid flows to fledgling regimes, or support for civil society to renew state–society relations, the approaches and methods of international engagement are either woefully inadequate or downright harmful. Thus, a review of statebuilding, which began in the tenuous wake of the post–Cold War era, will continue to be at the top of the international peace and security and development agendas for years to come.

Failed, weak, and 'fragile' states

One of the most recurring findings of scholarly research is that countries that have experienced episodes of internal conflict and violence are more likely to experience it in the future. Indeed, most of the new 'onsets' of civil war in the decade 2000–2010 occurred in countries that had previously experienced civil war. As well, some countries that may appear outwardly stable – such as Libya under the late autocrat Muammar Gaddafi, which remained a stable state for 40 years – are also deeply vulnerable to rapid collapse. When the state utterly fails, as it did in the Libya case during the civil war, or when states are weak or unable (or unwilling) to deliver essential services, the state itself becomes the prize in a violent interaction among competing social forces. Thus, the concept of fragility has evolved to describe those countries which, through the downward spirals of civil war, state collapse, and social dislocation, face recurrent or repeated cycles of conflict stemming from chronic poverty and inequalities (Stewart and Brown, 2009)

The fragility syndrome suggests that common to the so–called fragile states are deep structural vulnerabilities to violence. Scholars contend as to whether the deep drivers of conflict and fragility are primarily found in social relations – of ranked and unranked 'divided societies' in which identity-based groups are unable to share the state – or whether the causal drivers are rooted in economic factors such as relative inequalities, distributive rent-seeking, or chronic poverty. Equally, some suggest that demography may be a lurking underlying driver of conflict, particularl in those countries that feature large cohorts of educated but unemployed young men.

Others see the fragility syndrome of weak government, violent challenges, and poor delivery by the state of key public goods (particularly, economic management, education, and health care) as a function of the inadequacy of institutions to cope with underlying social stressors or that create incentives whereby elites and public officials have little incentive or see little value in providing an efficient state dedicated to the benefit of all. Theories of fragility therefore equal focus on the problem of 'elite predation' or the efforts of elites to capture the state for their own personal or narrow ethnic group or territorially based interests.

The syndrome of fragility suggests an inadequately consolidated state in terms of its ability to wield authority, or to achieve a monopolization of violence to use this only for justifiable o good ends (such as preventing aggression or fghting crime), its capacity (ability to formulate and implement policies), and its legitimacy (or justification of the 'right' of state elites to rule). In th fragile states, each of these domains is often seriously compromised. In terms of authority, armed non-stategroups (such as an ethnic militia) fill the security void of authority, sometimes throug the promulgation of local self-protection units, irregular forces, or, in the most extreme cases, sophisticated rebel groups. Fragile states with security vacuums often also see high levels of 'armed violence' or organizational and interpersonal crime, often fueled by an unregulated trade in weapons. Authority gaps also arise when the state has little capacity beyond the capital or if it fails in (or is prevented from) ruling throughout its territory and power is wielded by traditional authorities, dominant families, or warlords.

State capacity is compromised when ruling elites become corrupt, or when conflict over th state eviscerates ministries, empties offices of public servants, or disempowers local government Countries with weak capacity are often trapped in vicious cycles of natural resource or primary commodity dependency where rents from resources fuel conflict and not development, or wher the state fails to provide essential public services such as basic education, health care, or the macroeconomic stability needed for economic growth. Such capacity gaps especially arise in conflict-affectedcountries when the civil service and educated classes flee the violence or rapi regime change brings in new officials without the capabilities or training to make the state function.

Serial crises, which perpetuate fragility, often occur when a state lacks legitimacy. While legitimacy gaps are often seen even in consolidated states, the fragile states often lack the social cohesion needed for elites to construct and maintain the essential building blocks of the state: a political settlement. Political settlements lend legitimacy to the state when leading elites agree to the rules of the game of politics and work within them in representing contending social forces. Civil war and state fragility are very much about the absence of a core political settlement and continuous contention on what constitutes the legitimate rules of the game of politics and determines the way in which power is allocated. In these cases, ruling regimes come to power or are ousted but there remain tenuous relationships between the central state and peripheral or decentralized governance institutions. Consequently, a critical indicator of a state lacking such legitimacy is the effort of ruling elites to legitimate their rule through fraudulent electoral processes, appeals to extreme nationalism or ideology, or the hegemonic exercise of power through narrow ethnic networks.

At war's end, there is a narrow window of opportunity to rebuild the authority of the state (or, following secession or new grants of autonomy, to build the state from scratch) through security sector and rule-of-law reform, by regaining capacity through the revitalization of key ministries and restoration of local governance, and new-found legitimacy through political settlements (often reflected in new constitutions and institutions) and electoral processes. If th antonym to a fragile state is a consolidated one, then statebuilding is about expanding over time the autonomy, authority, legitimacy, and capacity of the state.

Conceptualizing international statebuilding

Historically, particularly in Western Europe, the consolidation of states has taken centuries and has, too often, involved violent processes of power consolidation, fixing of territorial boundaries and a mix of submissive and contractual approaches to expanding power. Statebuilding historically was also for the most part quite endogenous, such that the new forms of intervention in civil war (as above, to use the UN terminology of prevention, peacekeeping, peacemaking, and peacebuilding) have raised critical questions about how outsiders – through military force or the power of the purse – can and do engage in highly interventionist efforts to accelerate, shape, and indeed determine the outcomes of post–war statebuilding processes. In engaging to build states through military deployments, civilian capacity building, and development–aid flows, international actors have changed the nature of contemporary statebuilding such that any theoretical perspective on the issues of post–war recovery of authority, capacity, and legitimacy must be described in terms of a complex, multiple–level game in which outsiders try to affect the choices and behavior of insiders, and often the realities on the ground affect the strategies, goals, and purposes of outsiders.

The international–domestic interactions inherent to international statebuilding have challenged traditional theories of both international relations and comparative politics. No longer is the state absolutely sovereign, and international intervention has been the consequence both of 'liberal peace' efforts to expand democracy and free–market economic ideologies and of great–power intervention to pursue their own security interests. Likewise, when internationals are involved in choosing among local elites, in favoring one political faction over the other, or in helping determine the boundaries of the social contract, the theories of comparative politics also often fall short in explaining when statebuilding is consolidated or when fragility and conflict are likel to continue. This new theoretical terrain of statebuilding must simultaneously and complexly contend with various levels of interaction in global politics and must also in turn understand local dynamics, interests, cultures, and social forces.

This appreciation of international–domestic interactions and the complexity of global interventions in local settings has generated numerous assessments of the evolution of the international statebuilding regime and the 'lessons learned' from past interventions that inform future action. Initial collective international responses to such internal conflicts from leading international organizations, and especially the United Nations, centered on a formula that proved initially somewhat successful in instances such as Namibia, Mozambique, and El Salvador: the deployment of a UN peacekeeping mission, an internationally guided transition from war to peace (and toward democracy), and a fairly rapid exit of foreign forces following an electoral process that culminated in the restoration of full sovereignty to the newly legitimated regime.

However, this initial formula for success quickly ran aground in the messy post–war realities of civil wars in Angola, Cambodia, Somalia, and Rwanda which either relapsed into conflict o led to state capture by one party to the conflict (as in Cambodia), to state failure (as in Somalia) or to mass societal violence (as in Rwanda). Thus, the initial 'democratic transition' model of post–war recovery required critical rethinking, and the initial terminology of post–war 'peacebuilding' has been augmented by a focus on international assistance to rebuild (or, in some cases where new states have emerged, to build anew), the authority, legitimacy, and capacity of the state. International statebuilding evolved as a strategic approach to sustainable peace in post-war countries in the late 1990s as an explicit move toward a more long-term perspective on engendering peace, or what Roland Paris called the need for 'institutionalization before liberalization' (Paris, 2004).

The experiences of US-led intervention in Iraq and Afghanistan have also significantly affecte the international statebuilding debates. Despite heavy-footprint military interventions, exhaustive capacity-building initiatives (including especially equip-and-train approaches to security sector reforms), and massive aid flows designed to win hearts and minds and extend the authority, capacity, and legitimacy of nascent client (or thought to be client) states, the US significantl failed to build states in the wake of the Ba'athist dictatorship in Iraq (and subsequent sectarian and insurgent violence of the post-invasion period) and after the fall of the Taliban in Afghanistan in 2001. While many had raised the dilemmas and conundrums of outside efforts to build states internally, these two cases highlight the constraints and tensions of a domineering approach to statebuilding.

About this handbook

International Statebuilding is a handbook that provides a unique combination of theoretical, thematic, and topical analysis of the contemporary international statebuilding regime. This handbook is designed to guide the reader through the background and development of international statebuilding as a policy area, to isolate and consider some of the key conceptual and methodological debates, to give in-depth focus to key policy areas – such as security, development, democracy, and human rights – and to relate the research findings to policy formulation and implementation. The handbook aims to be a single-source overview of key topics addressed by leading scholars to serve as essential reference material for the interdisciplinary field of specialization on the statebuilding themes

Part I explores the underlying concepts and approaches to the field, including the intersection between international and local authority, formal and informal institutions, and the nexus between international and domestic economies and the creation and maintenance of viable states. Nicolas Lemay-Hébert shows in his contribution that there are fundamentally different theoretical points of departure for the statebuilding debates: one that focuses frst on institutions (which he defnes as a Weberian perspective) and one (following Durkheim) that argues for a greater focus on social cohesion as a prerequisite to effective state formation and consolidation. In Dominik Zaum's contribution, we learn that while anti-corruption efforts may be central to external agendas for statebuilding, in fact corruption can facilitate statebuilding by creating economic interdependencies and horizontal relationships across social groups.

Clare Castillejo shows how the statebuilding agenda is deeply transformative of gender relations within societies, and that external actors such as international organizations strategically use international norms to advance a gender-equality agenda during transitional times in which state institutions, policies, laws, and programs are being reconsidered. In their chapter, development practitioners and scholars Jago Salmon and Catherine Anderson argue the importance of a political settlement as a precondition for successful statebuilding, contending that in the absence of core consensus among a leading group of elites the rules of the political game are contested; they then analyze theories of elite bargains in two critical cases of statebuilding after war, namely South Sudan and Timor-Leste. This analysis leads them to call for a better understanding of the elite dynamics and what they term 'socially constituted development,' rather than a narrow focus by aid donors on technically oriented 'capacity development.' Sharhar Hameiri highlights that international statebuilding interventions have the effect of transnationalizing or regulating from afar the problems of violence such that statebuilding is an extension of global governance in managing the issues of interdependence in an interconnected world. Stephen Del Rosso analyzes perhaps the most important social factor in state formation and persistence, that of the development of a coherent national identity and associated nationalist narrative; in his view, the absence of a focus on national identity is a key missing element in the statebuilding debates. David Chandler analyzes how shifting discourses of race, culture, and difference inform interventionist strategies toward civil society in post-conflict countries, infusing them with vision of a grand, transformative social experiment.

David Roberts presents a contrarian view of post-conflict efforts to build Weberian states arguing that politics is as much about the persistence of pre-existing relationships and practices as it is about building from scratch institutions that are modern manifestations of what in ideal terms a state should be; in his view many of the newly created or newly emphasized institutions are essentially irrelevant to many people's lives in post-conflict countries, and therefore the international community should accept the reality of a hybridized 'institutional plurality' in these situations. Similarly, Meera Sabaratnam in her study of Mozambique argues that internal and external elites' unwillingness to address or restructure the fundamental relationships between the state and the population sustains the tensions generated by strategies of political rule and development. She argues that, in particular, 'liberal' statebuilding practices have tended to have distinctively 'conservative' effects in terms of state–society relations. Kai Koddenbrock takes the example of the Congo to argue that most current social analysis pathologizes the object of statebuilding – in this case, Congo's economy, society, and practices of government – while neglecting those modes of socio-political organization that do not fit the lens of failure and malevolence. In this way, he casts doubts on the self-evidence of statebuilding benefs and calls for a more nuanced approach to statehood and its analysis. This section concludes with Oliver Richmond's chapter, which argues that without incorporating a better understanding of the multiple and often critical agencies involved in peace formation, the states that emerge from statebuilding will remain as they are – failed by design, because they are founded on external systems, legitimacy, and norms rather than on a contextual, critical, and emancipatory epistemology of peace.

Part II explores three sets of statebuilding themes: the quintessential Weberian task of providing security, reconsidered today in terms of global, regional, domestic, and community and human security; economic recovery and development; and political transitions, to include democ – ratization pathways and the restoration of a minimum set of conditions for rule of law. The section begins with an analysis of the approaches and methods for United Nations assistance to constitution-makingprocesses; Vijayashri Sripati explores the policy and practices of assistance to constitution-making processes, arguing that such assistance has become highly normalized, and highly interventionist in terms of the ways in which international organizations like the UN are involved deeply in areas that were previously considered sovereign and endogenously sacrosanct. This is nowhere more true that when the UN intervenes militarily to keep the peace, and Richard Gowan's chapter explores the delicate linkages between peacekeeping, civilian or political engagement, and statebuilding as an exit strategy for such operations.

Security is the bedrock of statebuilding, and regaining or building anew the state's sole and legitimate use of violence is the subject of Heiner Hänggi and Fairlie Chapuis' chapter on security sector reform in post-conflict countries. Their analysis reveals the ultimate challenges of suc reform efforts and the practices that have evolved to address this perhaps key or most essential element in the statebuilding set of tasks early in the post-war period. Bethan K. Greener and W. J. Fish analyze the police–military divide in statebuilding, outlining the practical considerations that have led to military personnel being tasked with roles that, traditionally, would be squarely in the domain of civilian police. It then discusses both practical and theoretical reasons as to why this is a concerning trend and argues that the goals of peace and stability operations are more readily achievable if the traditional police/military divide is respected as much as possible. Morten Bøås and Samantha Gowran Farrier bring these debates to a country level with their look at what is often seen as an initial statebuilding 'success,' that of Liberia, highlighting the tensions between external and internal governance and the relationships between security sector reform and overall development of the institutions of rule of law and accountability that are intrinsic to building a modern, democratic state.

With many theories of conflict focusing on the capture of resources, rents, or external aid a a basis of fragility, post-war countries have urgently needed new mechanisms for natural resource management and for the sharing of wealth and management and distribution of rents from such resources. The chapter by Gilles Carbonnier and Achim Wennmann investigates current knowledge and practices of natural resource management in fragile post-war states, arguing that without a forward-looking, proactive attention to wealth-sharing and global governance mechanisms for addressing natural-resource-related conflict, the syndrome of 'fragility' will likel persist in many current conflict-affected countries. Berit Bliesemann de Guevara and Florian Kühn analyze the financing of international statebuilding and the political economy of dono and elite relations. Taking Bosnia and Herzegovina as a state relying on taxation at one end of a continuum, and Afghanistan as a licit and illicit rentier state at the other end as examples, they illustrate how the development and security dynamics stem from forms of finances. Aaron Schneider considers the political economy of post-conflict statebuilding in Central America, focusing on the challenges of raising revenues in El Salvador and Guatemala. He draws out an explanation for their diversity in success to trace broader lessons for statebuilding through the focus on the political economy of emerging sectors and the state in the two post-conflict countries.

In countries where the causal drivers or expressions of conflict are described in terms of ethni or identity differences, a common response of the international community has been to encourage the parties to adopt power-sharing institutions. However, Anna Jarstad shows that short-term power-sharingsolutions come at the price of undermining subsequent statebuilding, such that power-sharingshould be often, at best, transitional or interim and that over time the strategic goal of international statebuilding should be democratization. Timothy Sisk, in the fnal chapter of the section, explores the importance of electoral processes in statebuilding after civil war, and especially the ways in which the sequencing and form of elections reflect power relations an compromises, how elections can act in relation to social cohesion and contestation, and the role of external mediators and donors in shaping electoral outcomes in post-war countries.

Part III looks at implementation in key thematic areas in a number of pivotal cases and thematic areas. The contexts of Afghanistan, Kosovo, Liberia, and Iraq, among others, provide a look at the application of the concepts of statebuilding in practice in some of the most diffult cases. Jens Stilhoff-Sörensen describes the international engagement in Kosovo, which has emerged as a case-in-point of building up institutions of governance in a country that is not yet fully sovereign and whose very existence is deeply contested. Roberto Belloni assesses the vexed intervention of the international community in Bosnia, where he decries the approach of the international community as too top-down and driven by external imperatives and agendas rather than internal dynamics and preferences.

The case of US statebuilding in Iraq is an example of excessive international hubris in seeking to impose an order on a country made fragile by arguably ill-conceived intervention to effect 'regime change.' David A. Lake describes the statebuilding efforts as an 'utter failure' and in dissecting the approach shows how there are inherent theoretical tensions in the statebuilding-by-outsidersperspective when the intervention is driven more by the putative global interests of a great power to create a regional client state than by any kind of bottom−up approach.¹ Similarly, efforts to build an accountable state based on the rule of law have seen immense engagement, and limited, if any, success, in Afghanistan. Nik Hynek and Péter Marton consider the efforts to induce a 'liberal peace' in the very illiberal context of Afghanistan. In their chapter, they highlight that the existing literature on statebuilding in Afghanistan fails to transcend a one−size−fits−all approach based on liberal wishful thinking. They also analyze the possible motivations of countries and international organizations statebuilding in Afghanistan. Terrence Lyons analyzes the cases of Uganda, Eritrea, Ethiopia, and Rwanda, arguing that statebuilding faces specific circumstances after insurgent rebels win a civil war. In these cases new regimes are in a position of strength, less constrained by negotiated settlements or dependent on the interests of international interveners, often resulting in the consolidation of strong authoritarian regimes.

Julien Barbara considers the experiences of Australia in intervening in countries in its 'arc of instability' in the region, focusing on its extensive experience in statebuilding in Timor−Leste and the Solomon Islands, two of the region's best−known fragile−state contexts, showing how the incentives of local elites are critical and also addressing the conundrums that emerge when military intervention ends but statebuilding as such remains woefully incomplete. Mandy Turner analyzes international statebuilding efforts to establish the Palestinian Authority, an interim administration in the West Bank and Gaza Strip, and critically assesses the problems as a unique case study of neoliberal quasi−statebuilding in the highly securitized context of the Israel–Palestine conflict − at the foundation of which is a process of colonization

Giovanna Bono takes up an important mechanism in her analysis of the role of European Union (EU) police missions as a central approach to statebuilding by a more normatively driven actor. She, too, shows that international efforts are often not grounded in an understanding of local context and that even in these cases the interests of the outsiders often trump the perspectives of the local beneficiaries. Wil Hout also analyzes the EU perspectives on statebuilding in his insightful look at 'good governance' approaches and the support for state capacity development; yet these approaches are problematic because they assume that the end goal of such efforts is to create states that mirror those in the West, with the result that EU approaches are 'impotent' in the face of a set of local realities that are at odds with the social conditions that led to statebuilding historically in the West. Tom Weiss considers the relationship between the evolving global norm that states have the responsibility to protect their citizens, noting that the so−called R2P set of principles should be grounded not only on international reactions when the state fails to uphold such responsibility and perpetrates gross crimes against its own people. Instead, this principle also contains within it an international responsibility to rebuild war−torn states as an essential part of this newly developing norm. Finally, Alina Rocha Menocal examines the debates on aid effectiveness in post−war countries and the ways in which statebuilding has emerged as the leitmotif of traditional donor approaches to building up the capacity of states to govern; she addresses critically some of the new debates that have emerged around partnerships between donor countries and beneficiary regimes, arguing that while new approaches to dialogue on statebuilding goals are helpful, much work needs to be done to make aid more effective and to address the potential for doing more harm than good in using development aid as an inducement to develop sustainable domestic governing systems.

Note

1 For an analysis of current data tracking on civilians in armed conflict and forced migration, see Melande et al., 2009.

References

Stewart, F., and Brown, G. (2009). *Fragile states.* Oxford, UK: Centre for Research on Inequality, Human Security and Ethnicity (CRISE).

Geneva Declaration on Armed Violence and Development. (2011). *Global burden of armed violence 2011.* Available at: www.genevadeclaration.org

Melander, E., Öberg, M., and Hall, J. (2009). Are 'new wars' more atrocious? Battle intensity, genocide and forced migration before and after the end of the Cold War *European Journal of International Relations, 15*(3), 505–536.

Paris, R. (2004). *At war's end: Building peace after civil conflict.* Cambridge, UK: Cambridge University Press.

Themnér, L., and Wallensteen, P. (2012). Armed conflicts, 1946–2011. *Journal of Peace Research, 49*(4), 565–575.

World Bank. (2011). *World development report 2011: Conflict, security, and development.* Washington, DC: World Bank.

PART I

Concepts and approaches

1
RETHINKING WEBERIAN APPROACHES TO STATEBUILDING[1]

Nicolas Lemay-Hébert

Political sociology is key to understanding current debates on statebuilding. One's conception of what to rebuild – the state – will necessarily impact the actual process of statebuilding, whether consciously or unconsciously. Drawing upon the vast contemporary literature on state collapse and statebuilding that has emerged since Helman and Ratner's pioneer article in 1992–1993, this chapter analyzes the rise of the 'institutional approach' to statebuilding, strongly infuenced by the Weberian sociology of the state and legitimacy, and focusing on the capabilities of the state institutions to secure the state's grip on the society. Three practical implications of the institutional approach will be considered: (1) the claim of forecasting state collapse and the underlying equation between fragile states and 'underdevelopment'; (2) the hermetic distinction between state and society, which allows the differentiation between statebuilding activities and 'nation–building' ones; and (3) the 'more is better' approach that comes as a natural policy prescription – legitimizing intrusive interventions on the ground that they are more efficient for institutiona reconstruction. Finally, this chapter will highlight an alternative approach to the state and statebuilding, dubbed here the 'legitimacy approach,' more concerned with socio–political cohesion of the state than institutional reconstruction *per se*.

Every scholarly or policy–oriented contribution on statebuilding adopts, whether consciously or unconsciously, a definition of what it intends to reconstruct – that is, a definition of the stat In that regard, one striking aspect of current statebuilding debates is how little debate there is about what type of state major actors want to promote (Marquette and Beswick, 2011: 1706; Marquette and Scott, 2010: 9). As this chapter claims, the Weberian approach to statehood is the starting point for a number of analyses, having attained the status of orthodoxy in the mainstream literature. Following this 'institutional approach,' the state is equated with its institutions, state collapse is understood in terms of the collapse of state institutions, and statebuilding implies their reconstruction. While being portrayed implicitly as consensual and apolitical, the institutional approach to statebuilding carries specific consequences for scholarl and policy debates. First, this chapter looks at the Weberian influence on statehood and legitimacy, and the rise of the 'institutional approach' to statebuilding based on the Weberian approach. Three implications of the institutional approach are debated. First, by equating the strength of state with its institutional reach, the institutional approach amounts to equating state fragility with 'underdevelopment.' Second, the Weberian sociological approach of state autonomy leads researchers to conveniently distinguish statebuilding activities (understood in apolitical and technical terms) from 'nation–building' activities (linked to socio–political cohesion). This leads to the final implication of the institutional approach, related this time to policy prescriptions that stem from this discussion: if statebuilding is the reconstruction of state institutions, and if it is possible to isolate statebuilding from nation–building, then 'more is better' in terms of institutional reconstruction. The 'more is better' approach has already provided the normative foundations for international administration projects in Kosovo, Timor–Leste, and Iraq more recently (Lemay–Hébert, 2011b). However, there are alternatives to this specific reading of a Weberian lecture of statehood and statebuilding. In its last section, this chapter suggests a 'legitimacy' approach, more concerned with socio–political cohesion and the legitimacy central authorities can generate, and built around Emile Durkheim's sociology.

Weber, statehood, and statebuilding: the rise of the 'institutional' approach

Weber famously defines the state as 'a human community that successfully claims the monopoly of the legitimate use of physical force within a given territory' (Weber, 1948: 78). For Weber, the formation of modern Western states relied on the constant progression of their bureaucratic foundations over time. Hence, Weber saw administration and the provision of security as benchmarks according to which each state can be judged (Badie and Birnbaum, 1983). Besides security, which is certainly the central criterion of state strength, other criteria are also taken into account by various authors, all related to the capabilities of the state to secure its grip on the society. From this perspective, a weak state is a political entity that lacks the institutional capacity to implement and enforce policies; statebuilding is the creation of new government institutions and the strengthening of existing ones. Scholars adopting this 'institutional' approach tend to focus on the administrative capability of the state and the ability of the state apparatus to affirm its authority over the society.

The term 'failed state'[2] came to prominence in the contemporary academic and policy discourse with the publication of Gerald Helman and Steven Ratner's article, defining 'failed state' as 'a situation where governmental structures are overwhelmed by circumstances' (1992–1993: 5). Helman and Ratner's article constituted one of the first attempts to cope with the phenomenon in a post–Cold War world, an effort that coincided with the actual collapse of Somalia and the Socialist Federal Republic of Yugoslavia. It is also one of the first major post–Cold War works exemplifying the institutional approach, as their definition emphatically revolves around governmental institutions. Not only was Helman and Ratner's work pioneering, but it is still considered by many as authoritative (for example, Wilde, 2002–2003: 425). Unfortunately, Helman and Ratner do not go much deeper in their analysis of the collapsed state phenomenon and they do not provide any subsequent clarification, apart from a distinction between the degrees of collapse (Helman and Ratner, 1992–1993: 5).

Helman and Ratner's institutional focus has been developed by subsequent scholars who, in the purest functionalist tradition, assert that 'nation–states exist to provide a decentralized method of delivering political (public) goods to persons living within designated parameters.' For example, for influential US policy academic Robert Rotberg, 'it is according to their performances—according to the levels of their effective delivery of the most crucial political goods—that strong states may be distinguished from weak ones, and weak states from failed or collapsed' (Rotberg 2004: 2). Here, public goods encompass a list of state institutions and functions, including the supply of security, a transparent and equitable political process, medical and health care, schools and education, railways, harbors, and even a beneficent fiscal and institutional context, with which citizens can pursue personal entrepreneurial goals, thus framing his approach explicitly within the liberal peace paradigm (Chandler, 2004, 2010; Mac Ginty and Richmond, 2009; Paris,

1997). The institutional approach has had a profound impact on scholarly debates regarding state collapse and statebuilding. Interestingly, the institutional approach is so pervasive that even some authors who claim not to take a stance end up adopting it. For example, in *Making States Work*, Sebastian von Einsiedel asserts that:

> for present purposes, no attempt will be made at a final definition of the term 'fail state'. Much ink has been spilled on developing typologies of the forms of state failure, using either the degree of failure or its cause as a criterion. Instead, this volume treats state failure as a continuum of circumstances that afflict states with *weak institutions*.
> (von Einsiedel 2005: 16; emphasis added)

As one would expect, the Weberian approach to statehood and statebuilding has also found a large echo in the policy literature. Boutros Boutros–Ghali defines state collapse as 'the collapse of state institutions' (United Nations, 1995: 9), whereas the United Kingdom's Department for International Development (DFID) defines 'fragile states' as countries where 'governments cannot or will not deliver core functions to the majority of its people' (DFID, 2005). Similarly, the Organization for Economic Co–operation and Development (OECD) indicates that 'states are fragile when *state structures* lack political will and/or capacity to provide the *basic functions* needed for poverty reduction, development and to safeguard the security and human rights of their populations' (OECD, 2007: para. 3; emphasis added). These assumptions constitute the framework within which to understand the incorporation of legitimacy aspects, as constitutive of state strength, in the analysis provided by recent OECD reports (OECD, 2008).

Weber and legitimacy: a one-way process of legitimizing authority

If the (neo)Weberian approach to statehood has profoundly influenced the statebuilding literature, the same could be said of the Weberian legacy regarding legitimacy (Lemay–Hébert, 2013). If Weber is rightly regarded as one of the most influential thinkers in social science, his contribution regarding the concept of legitimacy has been deemed highly controversial. For David Beetham, for example, 'on the subject of legitimacy, his influence has been an almost unqualified disaster' (1991: 8). Weber defines legitimacy as 'the prestige of being considered exemplary or binding' (Weber, 1962: 72). Hence, for Weber, the claim of legitimacy is a bid for a justification of support and its success consists not in fulfilling normative conditions but rather in being believed. Weber conceives legitimacy as a necessary condition and a means for a government to exercise authority over society. This could be done by charismatic, traditional, or rational–legal principles (to take up the three well–known ideal types, presented in Weber 1947: 130). In this sense, legitimacy principles are in fact principles of legitimization of the central authority. However, according to Beetham and others, the main mistake is not Weber's but that of those social scientists – the neo-Weberians – who have reduced the explanation of beliefs to the processes and agencies of their dissemination and internalization (1991: 10; Hobson and Seabrooke, 2001).

Nevertheless, Weber's definition of legitimacy has not been exempt from criticisms in political sociology. It led Hanna Pitkin to argue that it was 'essentially equivalent to defining "legitimate as "the condition of being considered legitimate," and the corresponding "normative" definition comes out as "deserving to be considered legitimate"' (1972: 281). It is also on these grounds that Peter Blau states that Weber 'takes the existence of legitimate authority for granted and never systematically examines the structural conditions under which it emerges out of other forms of power,' while Carl Friedrich posits that Weber's analysis 'assumes that any system of government is necessarily legitimate' (Blau, 1970: 149; Friedrich, 1963: 186). Friedrich argues that Weber actually confuses the concepts of legitimacy and authority (1963: 216–246), a distinction made by Jürgen Habermas in his debate with Niklas Luhmann, for instance (Habermas and Luhmann, 1973: 243).

Weber's conception of legitimacy has been quite influential, leading many social scientists i the twentieth century to follow the Weberian definition of legitimacy as *belief* in legitimacy. For instance, Seymour Lipset defines the legitimacy of a political system as its capacity 'to engende and maintain the belief that the existing political institutions are the most appropriate ones for the society' (1959: 86), while Richard Merelman considers legitimacy as 'a quality attributed to a regime by a population. That quality is the outcome of the government's capacity to engender legitimacy' (1966: 548). Charles Tilly is also resolutely neo–Weberian when he states that 'legitimacy depends rather little on abstract principle or assent of the governed ... Legitimacy is the probability that other authorities will act to confirm the decisions of a given authority' (1985 171). Accordingly, scholars following the institutional approach to statebuilding, under the influence of Weber's pioneering work, tend to treat legitimacy either as a mere consequence of functioning institutions or as a process of legitimization. This naturally stems from the Weberian approach to legitimacy. As Robert Grafstein states, 'Weber virtually identifies legitimacy wit stable and effective political power, reducing it to a routine submission to authority' (Grafstein, 1981: 456).

This approach to legitimacy has had a remarkably enduring impact on the statebuilding literature. Rotberg's work is certainly a good example of the tendency to reduce legitimacy to a consequence of 'stable and effective political power.' Mentioning legitimacy only as a consequence of good delivery of public goods, he argues that public goods 'give content to the social contract between ruler and ruled' (Rotberg, 2004: 2–3). The author notes that 'there is no failed state without disharmonies between communities,' but considers these 'disharmonies' as consequences of the failure of state institutions (Rotberg, 2003: 4). Hence, legitimacy is treated as a natural by–product of successful state institutions. Institutional failure thereby produces a loss of legitimacy: 'a nation–state also fails when it loses legitimacy, that is, when its nominal borders become irrelevant and autonomous control passes to groups within the national territory of the state, or sometimes even across its international borders' (Rotberg, 2003: 9). The Weberian conception of the state could not be more crudely emphasized than in this framing.

Institutionalizing poverty, forecasting state failure

Conceiving state collapse as a breakdown of government institutions, as institutionalists contend, allows one to identify failed or failing states according to institutional strength. It therefore leads Francis Fukuyama to suggest a matrix that helps differentiate the degrees of stateness in a variety of countries around the world (2004: 7), and Robert Rotberg to propose a performance indicator comprising the functions that states perform (2004: 2). The *Political Instability Task Force*, formerly the *State Failure Task Force*, looks at state structures and claims to forecast state failure with a degree of exactitude of 80 per cent (Goldstone et al., 2010). Other indexes provide different lists of failing states, according to their own criteria for measurement of state performance (Fund for Peace, 2011; Rice and Patrick, 2008; World Bank, 2006).

It is also no coincidence that some use a diagnostic medical analogy to exemplify how we should be able to forecast state failure. For instance, after defining state failure in institutiona terms – inability to control its territory and guarantee the security of its citizens, incapacity to enforce the rule of law and deliver public goods to its population – the former UK Foreign Secretary Jack Straw stated in a speech that 'in medicine, doctors look at a wide range of indicators to spot patients who are at high risk of certain medical conditions – high cholesterol, bad diet, heavy smoking for example ... this approach does enable the medical profession to narrow down the field and focus their effort accordingly. We should do the same with countries' (Straw, 2002) Thus, it is a positivist approach that mixes a certain fascination for hard sciences with governmentality – some would see parallels here with the Foucauldian analysis of biopolitical social regulation (Foucault 2008; Chandler 2010). Other scholars have already unveiled the concealed assumptions that underlie the medical analogy and the failed state discourse, especially from a gender perspective (Manjikian, 2008).

What appears crucial here is that in the forecasting process, 'developed countries' of the West set the standard against which other states are measured. It reifies the 'Western state,' failing t see divergences between different OECD state models, while ignoring other means of provision of public goods, such as those provided by informal or traditional systems. In this regard, one can draw parallels with Edward Said's study of Orientalism, showing how the specific understanding of 'failed states' can be illuminating insofar as our understandings of those who use it are concerned (Wilde, 2002–2003: 428). 'Failed states' are thus understood as falling short of specific standards of social, political, and economic performance. In this context, the expression 'failed' or 'failing state' seem to be a convenient neologism describing nothing more than a state with low standards of living, a country that has not attained the same level of development – measured as the public goods provision of state institutions – as the 'developed world.'

Autonomizing the state from society and its impacts on statebuilding

A second implication of the institutional approach for statebuilding practices is related to the separation of the state from societal forces, known as the 'state autonomy' theory. Since in this conception the 'state' is synonymous with its institutions, the statebuilding process is defined a a strengthening process of government institutions. This division between state structures and societal forces leads to a distinction between statebuilding and nation–building, on the premise that it is possible to conduct *statebuilding* operations from the outside without entering into the contested sphere of *nation-building* (Lemay−Hébert,2009). In other words, it is possible to target the institutions of a given state, to reconstruct the state capabilities, without engaging in the realm of socio–political cohesion of 'society' in general.

Many prominent authors have promoted the 'state autonomy' theory on various levels (Stepan, 1978; Migdal, 1988). For Joel Migdal, 'the progress of statebuilding can be measured by the degree of development of certain instrumentalities whose purpose is to make the action of the state effective: bureaucracy, courts, military' (Migdal, 1988: 35). State capabilities include the capacities to penetrate society, regulate social relationships, extract resources, and appropriate or use resources in determined ways. Non−Western states are weak in relation to the strong societies they try to control.[3] Similarly, for Evelyn Davidheiser, the relative strength and autonomy of the state can be evaluated by looking at how the state influences and penetrates society and an evaluation of the forces countering autonomy through the infuence and penetration of the state by society (1992: 463).

This conception of the 'autonomous state' has long been equated with Weber's work, as publicized by such neo−Weberians as Theda Skocpol, Randall Collins, Michael Mann, and Charles Tilly (Skocpol, 1979; Tilly, 1990; Collins, 1986; Mann, 1988), and by historical realists in the international relations literature (Morgenthau, 1964). However, two caveats have to be kept in mind here. First, certain scholars argue that the 'autonomous state' theory is an inaccurate interpretation of Weber's work. For example, John Hobson and Leonard Seabrooke have emphasized that one of the reasons why this 'conception is equated with Weber is because it is deemed to be one of the *leitmotifs* of neo−Weberian scholarship' (2001: 256–257). Other authors have rightly asserted that we should understand Weber's political theory in conjunction with his other sociological works (Beetham, 1985: 151; Hobson, 1998: 288; Palumbo and Scott, 2008: 387; Weber, 1958). The second caveat stems from the necessity to understand the Weberian conception of the state in conjunction with the historical context in which Weber published his major works, especially his relation with the Marxist literature on the state. Weber's work is explicitly anti-Marxist on just this issue of the autonomy of the state, rejecting Marx's determinism in that regard (Nash, 2000: 10; Palumbo and Scott, 2008).

This distinction between the state on one hand and the society on the other fundamentally impacts on the conception and application of appropriate statebuilding measures, implying that it is possible to promote statebuilding without engaging in contested nation-building activities. It implies that it is possible to engage in technical statebuilding activities without getting involved in 'politics.' At the heart of this framework is the understanding of the state adopted. As Anthony Giddens observes, 'the "state" sometimes means an apparatus of government or power, sometimes the overall social system subject to that government or power' (1985: 17). Adopting a restrictive definition of the state – as state apparatus – will lead scholars to perceiv statebuilding as a scientific, technical, and administrative process. It is not surprising then tha the statebuilding literature strikingly neglects the question of politics; what is, in fact, a highly political process becomes depoliticized through a focus on state capacity-building, where concerns of stability and regulation are discussed in a narrow technical and functionalist framework (Chandler, 2006: 5–6).

More is better? Laying the theoretical foundations for international statebuilding

A third implication of the institutional approach's extensive influence over the statebuilding literature is the implicit prescription that 'more is better' in terms of statebuilding, where 'the more intrusive the intervention is, the more successful the outcome would be' (Zuercher, 2006: 2; Lemay-Hébert, 2011a). For Michael Doyle and Nicholas Sambanis, whose work has had an influential impact on the statebuilding literature, 'the deeper the hostility, the more the destruction of local capacities, the more one needs international assistance to succeed in establishing a stable peace' (2006: 4). Another example of this approach is the widely quoted RAND study on US-led statebuilding operations and their conclusion that a high level of economic assistance and high numbers of troops deployed for a long time were crucial for the success of the operations in Japan and Germany and can explain why recent operations showed little success (Dobbins et al., 2003). While the authors recognize, in another report on UN statebuilding, that the international organization has shown, *mutatis mutandis*, better results with a 'light-footprint' approach, they assert that 'the United States would be well advised to leave the small footprint, low prof le approach to the United Nations, and resume supersizing its nation-building missions' (Dobbins et al., 2005: 245). This, perhaps counterintuitive, prescription echoes Steven Ratner's remarks that 'interveners ought to err on the side of more rather than less even though the empirical evidence to date does not obviously support a more is better perspective' (Krasner, 2008: 23).

In this perspective, the term 'collapsed state' is not only a descriptive term but becomes 'a prescriptive term that is employed in connection with the contemplation and execution of international involvement' (Jackson, 2004: 22). Hence, for Fukuyama, 'the underlying problems caused by failed states or weak governance could only be solved through long-term efforts by outside powers to rebuild indigenous state institutions' (2006: 2), while for Rotberg, 'there is a great need for conscientious, well-crafted nation building – for a systematic refurbishing of the political, economic, and social fabric of countries that have crumbled' (2004: 31). Emblematic of the 'more is better' prescription, Helman and Ratner plead the case for a 'more systematic and intrusive approach' to statebuilding (1992–1993: 7). For them, the usual methods of strengthening governance in the developing world, such as providing aid and foreign support, will meet with scant success in failing states and will prove wholly inadequate in those that have collapsed. Thus, the conceptual basis for the international effort should lie in the idea of 'conservatorship.' The parallel with medicine, described earlier, is once again salient here, portraying the 'failed state' either as a homogeneous entity affected by a serious illness or as a helpless person who suffered a bad turn of fate: 'forms of guardianship or trusteeship are a common response to broken families, serious mental or physical illness, or economic destitution ... It is time that the United Nations considers such a response to the plight of failed states' (Helman and Ratner, 1992–1993: 12). Helman and Ratner's plea for conservatorship directly influenced the statebuilding debate in th 1990s, legitimizing the concept of international administration as the best solution to respond to 'institutional collapse' (Lemay−Hébert, 2011b).

The legitimacy approach: an alternative to the institutional approach

While accepting the institutional approach's focus on the security apparatus and state institutions, especially as a critical f rst step in statebuilding processes, the 'legitimacy approach' adds a layer of complexity in drawing attention to the state's underlying legitimacy. Hence, the strength of the state has to be defined in terms of 'the capacity of state to command loyalty—the right t rule' (Holsti, 1996: 82). One good example of this approach is Barry Buzan's work on the state, putting emphasis on the 'idea of the state,' assuming integration between the territorial, societal, and political aspects of the state. For Buzan, the state exists primarily on the socio−political rather than on the physical plane: 'the state is more an idea held in common by a group of people, than it is a physical organism' (Buzan 1991: 63). In this approach, the state is composed of three different elements, each crucial to understanding the strength of states: the physical base of the state (effective sovereignty, international consensus on territorial limits); the institutional expression of the state (consensus on political 'rules of the game' but also scope of state institutions); and the idea of the state (implicit social contract and ideological consensus pertaining to a given society) (Buzan, 1991: 64; Holsti, 1996: 98). The f rst two elements are subsumed within the institutional approach. But attention to the 'idea of the state' is the unique element of the legitimacy approach, and one with far−reaching implications. If a state cannot exist without a physical base, as the institutionalists stress, the reverse is also true: 'without a widespread and quite deeply rooted idea of the state among the population, the state institutions themselves have diff culty functioning and surviving' (Buzan, 1991: 64).

In sociological terms, one could say that this approach is more infuenced by a Durkheimian conception of the state than a strictly Weberian one. For Durkheim, the state 'is the very organ of social thought'; it comprises 'the sentiments, ideals, beliefs that the society has worked out collectively and with time' (Durkheim, 1957: 79–80; 1964: 79; 1986: 54). In Durkheimian terms, the collective conscience is distinct from individual consciences and, although it is diffuse in every society, it has specific characteristics that make it a distinct reality: 'it is, in effect, independent of the particular conditions in which individuals are placed: they pass on and it remains' (Durkheim, 1964: 80). For him, the division of labour and the development of organic solidarity paralleled the development of contract and the state. However, and contrary to Weber's conception of the state, Durkheim states that the coercive powers of the state could vary independently of the level of social development (Durkheim, 1973). The political society is primarily determined neither by possession of a fixed territorial area nor by density of population but by the act of 'coming together,' to use Durkheim's own words (1957: 45).

The purpose here is certainly not to portray Durkheim's sociology of the state in an uncritical light – it is well known that Durkheim indulged in an organicist thinking prevalent in the nineteenth century and his determinism in depicting an evolutionary conception of social transformation has already been criticized many times – but rather to demonstrate the wealth of sociological approaches existing on the state and to explore an alternative approach to the institutional approach dominant in the current thinking on statebuilding. One of the main differences between the two schools of thought identified in this chapter – the institutional an legitimacy approaches – stems basically from the conceptualization of the state. As mentioned above, the 'state' sometimes means an apparatus of government or power and sometimes the overall social system subject to that government or power. This difference in definitions is at th root of the distinction between the two approaches. In turn, this leads academics to adopt different conceptions of state collapse and reconstruction. Hence, one can argue that insisting on the political concept of legitimacy allows us to concentrate our attention on the state and society as distinct in terms of 'actors,' though not necessarily hermetic institutions and activities. As Alexander Wendt states, 'it seems impossible to define the state apart from "society". States an societies seem to be conceptually interdependent in the same way that masters and slaves are, or teachers and students; the nature of each is a function of its relation to the other' (Wendt, 1999: 199). In this regard, it appears crucial to understand state and society in their mutually constitutive relationship, where legitimacy conditions state strength and is, at the same time, an element of state strength. As Beetham argues, 'a given power relationship is not legitimate because people believe in its legitimacy, but because it can be justified in terms of their beliefs' (1991: 11)

The legitimacy approach has a number of implications for how we should regard state collapse. First of all, state collapse is not only driven by institutional collapse, but also by the collapse of the legitimacy of the central authority. The collapse of legitimate governance – a process parallel to but not a by-product of institutional collapse – opens the door to 'political entrepreneurs,' allowing them to mobilize the population on the basis of allegiances that displace national ones (Badie, 2000). Consequently, the strength of the state is defined as the 'capacity to comman loyalty' (Holsti, 1996: 82–83) in a political marketplace defined by political bargaining for loyalt (de Waal, 2009). In general, the legitimacy approach is more sociologically or anthropologically oriented, relativizing generalizing assumptions and emphasizing the particularities of each state and its societal context. This approach has been summarized by Edward Newman under the term 'transformatory peacebuilding' (2009: 47–48). The challenge of building and consolidating state institutions aside, one of the most important issues is for the indigenous institutions to define create, and solidify a viable collective identity in order to provide the social bond necessary for them to be recognized as legitimate by the citizens and, by extension, for the external actors to find efficient and unobtrusive ways to support this process. Rejoining the Durkheimian sociological tradition, this approach puts the emphasis on logics of social integration and solidarity and, *a contrario*, on logics of anomie,[4] not only upon the Weberian logics of state capacity, imposing a salutary contribution to debate in the f eld of statebuilding.

Conclusion

The argument, then, is to show how academic and policy-making conceptions of the state impact on their understandings of state collapse or weakness, and therefore the policies and practices of statebuilding. This contribution has highlighted how a specific reading of Max Weber's sociolog has come to dominate the statebuilding literature under what has been dubbed here the 'institutional approach.' Defining the state by its physical and institutional basis and its strengt by its institutional grasp over the society, the institutional approach equates state collapse with the collapse of state institutions, and statebuilding with institutional reconstruction. This approach has very tangible repercussions on major statebuilding debates. First, state institutions can be easily quantified, *de facto* opening the door to forecasting state failure and consciously or unconsciously equating state failure with 'underdevelopment.' Second, following a very specific reading of Weber, state institutions are autonomized from their societal moorings, allowing scholars to differentiate statebuilding from nation–building activities. Thus, statebuilding comes to be define as the technical and apolitical reconstruction of state institutions while nation–building is linked to the forging of a sense of common nationhood. From this stems the third repercussion of the institutional approach to statebuilding. If it is possible to avoid entering into much–debated socio–political debates, linked to the concept of nation–building, statebuilding operations ought to be 'stepped up,' following a Clausewitzian logic (Lemay–Hébert, 2011a: 1825). 'More is better' then becomes the natural policy prescription for international interventions in this context. In this regard, the mental conception interveners have of the concept of 'state collapse' will impact the actual intervention and the means deemed necessary by the international community to address statebuilding challenges (Lemay–Hébert, 2011b).

Showing that this orthodoxy can be contested, this chapter has sketched an alternative approach to the institutional approach, based on Durkheimian sociology. While recognizing the importance of the monopoly of the legitimate use of physical force and state institutions in any given statebuilding process, the 'legitimacy approach' adds a layer of complexity by looking at the nation–state as a constitutive whole, while focusing on socio–political processes of constitution – and collapse – of legitimate governance. Whether one decides to adopt the institutional or the legitimacy approach to statebuilding, it seems crucial to recognize the sociological corpus underlying each approach. For, to paraphrase John Maynard Keynes, with regard to the need to be aware of the underpinnings of policy by problematic economic theories, 'practical men, who believe themselves to be quite exempt from any intellectual influences, are usually the slaves o some defunct sociologist.'

Notes

1 This chapter is based on a paper presented at the Political Science Association Annual Conference in Edinburgh, 30 March 2010, under the title 'Trying to Make Sense of the Contemporary Debate on Statebuilding: The Legitimacy and the Institutional Approaches on State, State Collapse and Statebuilding.' The author would like to thank Bertrand Badie, Richard Batley, Danielle Beswick, David Chandler, Kalevi Holsti, Paul Jackson, and Heather Marquette for comments on earlier drafts.
2 The term 'failed state' is certainly not value–neutral. Endorsed originally by authoritative figures suc as the previous UN Secretary General, Boutros Boutros–Ghali, and the former US Secretary of State, Madeleine Albright, and widely used after September 11, the term can mislead if it is understood 'to imply a value judgment that there are specific standards of social, political and economic performanc and success to which all states should aspire . . . Moreover, the picture portrayed when "failed state" is used is one of societal failure. This automatically attributes the entire political responsibility and moral liability for state collapse to local communities – generating a moral justifation for outside intervention to assist those who have failed' (Yannis, 2003: 64).
3 However, Joel Migdal later came up with a different concept, the 'state–in–society' model, whereby he proposed to abandon the Weberian–inspired analysis of the state due to its disconnection of theory from practice (2001).
4 I refer here to Durkheim's second conception of anomie, elaborated in *Suicide*. His f rst conception in *The Division of Labor in Society* refers to anomie as inadequate procedural rules to regulate complementary relationships among the specialized and interdependent parts of a complex social system, while the second conception refers to a breakdown in moral norms, which 'springs from the lack of collective forces at certain points in society' (Durkheim, 1997: 382).

References

Badie, B. (2000). *The imported state: The Westernization of the political order*. Stanford, CA: Stanford University Press.
Badie, B., and Birnbaum, P. (1983). *The sociology of the state*. Chicago, IL: University of Chicago Press.
Beetham, D. (1985). *Max Weber and the theory of modern politics*. Cambridge, UK: Polity Press.
Beetham, D. (1991). *The legitimation of power*. Basingstoke, UK: Macmillan.
Blau, P. (1970). Critical remarks on Weber's theory of authority. In D. Wrong (Ed.)*Max Weber*. Englewood Cliffs, NJ: Prentice Hall.
Buzan, B. (1991). *People, states and fear: An agenda for international security studies in the post-Cold War era*. New York, NY: Harvester Wheatsheaf.
Chandler, D. (2004). Responsibility to protect? Imposing the liberal peace.*International Peacekeeping*, *11*(1), 59–87.
Chandler, D. (2006). *Empire in denial: the politics of statebuilding*. London, UK: Pluto Press.
Chandler, D. (2010). *International statebuilding: The rise of post-liberal governance*. London, UK: Routledge.
Collins, R. (1986). *Weberian sociological theory*. Cambridge, UK: Cambridge University Press.
Davidheiser, E. (1992). Strong states, weak states: The role of state in revolution*Comparative Politics*, *24*(4), 463–475.
Department for International Development (2005). *Why we need to work more effectively in fragile states*. London, UK: Department for International Development.
De Wall, A., 2009. Fixing the political marketplace: How can we make peace without functioning state institutions? Fifteenth Christen Michelsen Lecture, Bergen, Norway, 15 October.
Dobbins, J., Jones, S. G., Crane, K., Rathmell, A., Steele, B., Teltschik, R., et al. (2005)*UN's role in nation-building: From the Congo to Iraq*. Santa Monica: RAND report MG−304.
Dobbins, J., McGinn, J. G., Crane, K., Jones, S. G., Lal, R., Rathmell, A., et al. (2003). *America's role in nation-building: From Germany to Iraq*. Santa Monica, CA: RAND report MR−1753−RC.
Doyle, M., and Sambanis, N. (2006).*Making war and building peace: United Nations peace operations*. Princeton, NJ: Princeton University Press.
Durkheim, E. (1957). *Professional ethics and civic morals*. London, UK: Routledge.
Durkheim, E. (1964). *The division of labor in society*. New York, NY: Free Press.
Durkheim, E. (1973). The two laws of penal evolution. *Economy and Society*, *2*(3), 285–308.
Durkheim, E. (1986). The concept of state. In A. Giddens (Ed.)*Durkheim on politics and the state*. Cambridge, UK: Polity Press.
Durkheim, E. (1997). *Suicide: A study in sociology*. New York, NY: Simon and Schuster.
Foucault, M. (2008). *The birth of biopolitics*. London, UK: Palgrave−Macmillan.
Friedrich, C. (1963). *Man and his government: An empirical theory of politics*. New York, NY: McGraw−Hill.
Fukuyama, F. (2004). *Statebuilding: Governance and world order in the 21st century*. New York, NY: Cornell University Press.
Fukuyama, F. (2006). Nation−building and the failure of institutional memory. In: F. Fukuyama (Ed.), *Nation building beyond Afghanistan and Iraq*. Baltimore, MD: Johns Hopkins University Press.
Fund for Peace (2011). 2011 Failed States Index, *Foreign Policy*. Available at: www.foreignpolicy.com/failedstates
Giddens, A. (1985). *The nation-state and violence*. Cambridge, UK: Polity Press.
Goldstone, J. A., Bates, R. H., Epstein, D. L., Gurr, T. R., Lustik, M. B., Marshall, M. G., et al. (2010). A global model for forecasting political instability. *American Journal of Political Science*, *54*(1), 190–208.
Grafstein, R., 1981. The failure of Weber's conception of legitimacy: Its causes and implications.*Journal of Politics 43*, 456–472.
Habermas, J., and Luhmann, N. (1973). *Theorie der Gesellschaft oder Sozialtechnologie*. Berlin, Germany: Suhrkamp.
Helman, G., and Ratner, S. (1992–1993). Saving failed states. *Foreign Policy*, *89*, 1–20.
Hobson, J. (1998). Debate: The 'second wave' of Weberian historical sociology. *Review of International Political Economy*, *5*(2), 284–320.
Hobson, J., and Seabrooke, L. (2001). Reimagining Weber: Constructing international society and the social balance of power. *European Journal of International Relations*, *7*(2), 239–274.
Holsti, K. (1996). *The state, war, and the state of war*. Cambridge, UK: Cambridge University Press.
Jackson, R. (2004). International engagement in war−torn countries.*Global Governance*, *10*(1), 21–36.
Krasner, S. (2008). *Sovereignty and governance*. Lecture at the Legatum Prosperity Symposium, Brocket Hall, UK, 20–22 June.

Lemay-Hébert, N. (2009). Statebuilding without nationbuilding? Legitimacy, state failure and the limits of the institutionalist approach. *Journal of Intervention and Statebuilding*, *3*(1), 21–45.

Lemay-Hébert, N. (2011a). The bifurcation of the two worlds: Assessing the gap between the internationals and locals in statebuilding processes. *Third World Quarterly*, *32*(10), 1823–1841.

Lemay-Hébert, N. (2011b). The 'empty-shell' approach: The setup process of international administrations in Timor-Lesteand Kosovo, its consequences and lessons. *International Studies Perspectives*, *12*(2), 190–211.

Lemay-Hébert, N. (2013). Everyday legitimacy and international administration: Global governance and local legitimacy in Kosovo. *Journal of Intervention and Statebuilding*, *7*(1) (forthcoming).

Lipset, S. (1959). Some social requisites of democracy. *American Political Science Review*, *53*(1), 69–105.

Mac Ginty, R., and Richmond, O. (Eds.). (2009). *The liberal peace and post-war reconstruction: Myth or reality?* London, UK: Routledge.

Manjikian, M. (2008). Diagnosis, intervention, and cure: The illness narrative in the discourse of the failed state. *Alternatives*, *33*, 335–357.

Mann, M. (1988). *States, war and capitalism*. Oxford, UK: Basil Blackwell.

Marquette, H., and Beswick, D. (2011). State building, security and development: State building as a new development paradigm? *Third World Quarterly*, *32*(10), 1703–1714.

Marquette, H., and Scott, Z. (2010). *Marrying statebuilding and aid policy*. Paper presented at the SGIR conference, Stockholm, Sweden, 9–11 September.

Merelman, R. (1966). Learning and legitimacy. *American Political Science Review*, *60*, 548–561.

Migdal, J. (1988). *Strong societies and weak states: State–society relations and state capabilities in the Third World*. Princeton, NJ: Princeton University Press.

Migdal, J. (2001). *State in society: Studying how states and societies constitute each other*. Cambridge, UK: Cambridge University Press.

Morgenthau, H. (1964). *Politics among nations*. New York, NY: Alfred Knopf.

Nash, K. (2000). *Contemporary political sociology*. Oxford, UK: Blackwell.

Newman, E. (2009). 'Liberal' peacebuilding debates. In E. Newman, R. Paris, and O. Richmond (Eds.), *New perspectives on liberal peacebuilding*. Tokyo, Japan: United Nations University Press.

Organization for Economic Co-operation and Development. (2007) *Principles for good international engagement in fragile states and situations*. Paris, France: OECD.

Organization for Economic Co-operation and Development. (2008). *Concepts and dilemmas of state building in fragile situations: From fragility to resilience*, OECD/DAC Discussion Paper. Paris, France: OECD.

Palumbo, A., and Scott, A. (2008). Weber, Durkheim and the sociology of the modern state. In T. Ball and R. Bellamy (Eds.), *The Cambridge history of twentieth-century political thought*. Cambridge, UK: Cambridge University Press.

Paris, R. (1997). Peacebuilding and the limits of liberal internationalism.*International Security*, *22*(2), 54–89.

Pitkin, H. (1972). *Wittgenstein and justice*. Berkeley, CA: University of California Press.

Rice, S., and Patrick, S. (2008).*Index of state weakness in the developing world*. Washington, DC: The Brookings Institution.

Rotberg, R. (2003). Failed states, collapsed states, weak states: Causes and indicators. In R. Rotberg (Ed.), *State failure and state weakness in a time of terror*. Washington, DC: Brookings Institution Press.

Rotberg, R. (2004). The failure and collapse of nation-states: Breakdown, prevention, and repair. In R. Rotberg (Ed.), *When states fail: Causes and consequences*. Princeton, NJ: Princeton University Press.

Skocpol, T. (1979). *States and social revolutions*. Cambridge, UK: Cambridge University Press.

Stepan, A. (1978). *The state and society: Peru in comparative perspective*. Princeton, NJ: Princeton University Press.

Straw, J. (2002). *Failed and failing states*. Speech given at the European Research Institute, University of Birmingham, UK, 6 September.

Tilly, C. (1985). War making and state making as organized crime. In P. Evans, D. Rueschemeyer, and T. Skocpol (Eds.), *Bringing the state back in*. Cambridge, UK: Cambridge University Press.

Tilly, C. (1990). *Coercion, capital and European states, AD 990–1990*. Oxford, UK: Blackwell.

United Nations. (1995). *Supplement to an Agenda for Peace*. UN Doc. A/50/60 – S/1995/1, 3 January. New York, NY: UN.

Von Einsiedel, S. (2005). Policy response to state failure. In S. Chesterman, M. Ignatieff, and R. Thakur (Eds.), *Making states work: State failure and the crisis of governance*. Tokyo, Japan: United Nations University Press.

Weber, M. (1947). *The theory of social and economic organization*. London, UK: William Hodge.

Weber, M. (1948). Politics as a vocation. In H. Gerth and C. W. Mills (Eds.), *From Max Weber: Essays in sociology*. New York, NY: Oxford University Press.

Weber, M. (1958). *The Protestant ethic and the spirit of capitalism*. New York, NY: Scribner.
Weber, M. (1962). *Basic concepts in sociology*. New York, NY: Citadel Press.
Wendt, A. (1999). *Social theory of international politics*. Cambridge, UK: Cambridge University Press.
Wilde, R. (2002–2003). The skewed responsibility narrative of the 'failed states' concept. *ILSA Journal of International and Comparative Law, 9*, 425–429.
World Bank, The (2006). *Engaging with fragile states*. Washington, DC: The World Bank.
Yannis, A. (2003). State collapse and its implications for peace–building and reconstruction. In J. Milliken (Ed.), *State failure, collapse and reconstruction*. Oxford, UK: Blackwell.
Zuercher, C. (2006). *Is more better? Evaluating external-led state building after 1989*. CDDRL Working Paper no. 54, Stanford University, CA, April.

2
CORRUPTION AND STATE-BUILDING[1]

Dominik Zaum

Corruption has become a major preoccupation of the states and multilateral organizations engaged in statebuilding efforts in conflict-affected states. This is unsurprising given the centrality of questions of governance to international statebuilding efforts, and the apparent pervasiveness of the problem. Ample surveys of the populations in confict-affectedcountries identify corruption as a major concern, and anecdotal accounts of rampant corruption and embezzlement of foreign aid in statebuilding environments such as Afghanistan, Liberia, or Kosovo abound. Conflict-affected states have also consistently populated the bottom of corruption indexes such as Transparency International's Corruption Perception Index (CPI).[2]

Despite this, the evidence on the impact of corruption on statebuilding – let alone on the impact of statebuilding practices on corruption (both positively through governance and dedicated anti-corruptionefforts, and negatively by entrenching corruption) – remains rather thin. There are obvious methodological reasons for this. As corruption is a largely clandestine activity, data are inherently difficult to collect and to verify, and this problem is exacerbated in conflict-affect states where security concerns make the conduct of rigorous research difficult and dangerous especially research into the shadier practices of often very violent people.

However, it is also weak because of two inherently conceptual problems. First, in their examinations of the causal impact of corruption, most studies have focused on the scale of corruption in a country. This has arguably been fuelled by a proliferation of indices measuring corruption perception and experience, in particular the CPI but also other regional and global governance surveys, such as Afrobarometer or the Global Values Survey. Similarly, most surveys at the country level focus on the prevalence and scale of corruption. Despite some important methodological problems, in particular with measuring perception and aggregating data, these data can provide interesting findings that are relevant for statebuilding, such as the detrimenta impact of corruption on government legitimacy and on the quality of governance (Clausen et al., 2011; Seligson, 2002). However, they say little about*how* corruption affects governance and developments in fragile states, and through what pathways it impacts on statebuilding efforts. To better understand these causal pathways, this chapter argues, one needs to look at the organization of corruption, rather than its scale.

Second, most debates about corruption, fragile states and statebuilding root the corrosive impact of corruption in a particular understanding of the state and statebuilding that is problematically narrow, focusing almost exclusively on the impact of corruption on hierarchical state–society relationships, and the state's ability to provide basic public goods. This offers only a partial account of the state and the political and social relationships it entails, and consequently misses some of the more complex functions and challenges of corruption. The extensive literature in historical sociology and political economy on state formation highlights both the importance of a broader understanding of the state, which recognizes its role of managing relationships and power balances between different elites and social groups, and of the centrality of what one might call corruption to the resilience of orders that, while iniquitous, also successfully regulate and minimize violence (DiJohn, 2010; North et al., 2009; Reno, 2011). Statebuilding policies that do not recognize these functions of certain forms of corruption can undermine the consolidation of state authority and fuel renewed violence.

To examine the complex roles of corruption in statebuilding contexts, the remainder of this chapter is structured into four parts. The first section will very briefly outline how statebuildi is conceptualized in this discussion. The second section will examine the concept of corruption, and argue that the organization, rather than the scale of corruption, offers a better lens through which its impact can be analyzed. The third section will examine the complex relationship between corruption and statebuilding through the lenses of two key aspects of statebuilding – elite settlements, and the provision of public services – and will briefly discuss both the comple relationship between corruption and security, and the impact of aid on corruption in statebuilding environments. The fourth section concludes the chapter with a refection on the implications of the analysis for understanding contemporary statebuilding efforts and policy.

The state and statebuilding

Bar some important exceptions, much of the statebuilding literature – and key donor policy and practice papers (OECD/DAC, 2011; World Bank, 2010) – has for a long time focused pre-dominantly on two aspects of the state: its capacity to deliver basic public goods, in particular security, and the degree to which it is responsive and accountable, especially democratically accountable, to citizen demands. This is rooted in an understanding of the state as an actor autonomous from society, whose capacity needs to be strengthened to maintain its autonomy from special interests, and that needs to be held accountable to ensure that its exercise of power – coercive and otherwise – refects the needs and interests of the society which it rules (Mann, 1984). Linked to this conception of the state is a particular understanding of the origins of state fragility and conft that statebuilding efforts aim to address, rooting conflict in the weakness or even collapse of stat institutions, in particular their inability to provide basic public goods and services (see, for example, Ghani and Lockhart, 2008; Herbst, 1997; Rotberg, 2004; Zartmann, 1995).

This focus has shaped both approaches to statebuilding and the understanding and critique of statebuilding practices: for critics and proponents alike, the state remains the central provider of regulation and of public goods, and all invoke the notional social contract between state and society that needs to be strengthened through statebuilding efforts. Such an understanding of the state focuses attention on the 'vertical' dimension of statebuilding, emphasizing the strengthening of state capacity and democratic accountability of state institutions, and the character of the hierarchical state–society relationship embodied in a notional social contract. As the OECD/DAC's policy guidance on statebuilding argues, 'Statebuilding involves the ongoing negotiation of an unwritten contract between state and society' (OECD/DAC 2011: 13).

Importantly though, both the state and statebuilding also have an important horizontal dimension, as an institutional arrangement enshrining power balances in a society, and managing relations between different social groups (Englebert, 2002; Holsti, 1996; North et al., 2009; Papagianni, 2008). The focus on state capacity (or lack thereof) and state–society relations has distracted attention from the relationships between different groups within society, and the role of the state in structuring these relationships. It distracts from the different ways in which different social groups experience the state, and its apparent weakness or failure, and from the ways in which questions of allocation of resources – of jobs, of state services – by the state to different constituencies, rather than problems of rule and control (the lack of which is implicit in the state weakness argument), fuel conflict. It is often the character of inter–group relations, and the resulting marginalization of particular groups by state institutions, that have fuelled conflicts i places such as Bosnia, Lebanon, or Sudan.

Recognizing these two distinct dimensions of the state helps to explain why some states, despite very limited capacity to provide their citizens with public services and responsiveness to their needs, are very resilient and have not succumbed to violence and state collapse (DiJohn, 2010; Reno, 2011). Corruption can be an important part of the 'glue' that holds these states together, literally buying a degree of stability and support from relevant elites in what Alex de Waal has termed the 'neo–patrimonial marketplace' (de Waal, 2009; see also Menkhaus, 2006/2007). At the same time, corruption inhibits the development of stronger and more responsive state institutions, and the transition from 'limited access orders' to 'open access orders' (North et al., 2009). Furthermore, disrupting the structures and practices that underpin resilience risks fueling violence. When the state is not seen as a neutral arbiter and provider of public goods, interventions geared to reduce corruption and to strengthen its institutional capacity are perceived as partial and as influencing power balances in favor of those groups that control state institutions Such interventions aimed at strengthening a notional social contract by strengthening state capacity therefore risk upsetting the marketplace and undermining a reasonably stable order minimizing violence, as groups that feel marginalized by changes to the political order use violence to oppose it and to maintain their previous social and political positions and privileges.

Understanding the complex relationship between corruption and statebuilding therefore requires unpacking the state – and statebuilding – to be able to examine how it affects different aspects of these complex social constructs and practices. As the political economy literature suggests – and as will be explored in more detail below – what one could call 'vertical' and 'horizontal' statebuilding are impacted by corruption in different ways. Similarly, though, one needs to further unpack corruption, as different forms of corruption also have different implications for the relationships between the state and different social groups, and state institutions and their functions.

Understanding and measuring corruption

'Corruption,' as some observers have noted, 'is a phenomenon that seems to have obvious, intrinsic meaning when viewed from a distance but that differentiates increasingly, like an impressionist painting, as one comes closer' (Boucher et al., 2007: 1). A general, universally accepted def nition of corruption has remained elusive, as what constitutes corruption within a particular community or country reflects that community's specific norms that corruption transgresses. However, there is an 'objective core' of three characteristics of corruption that enables us to discuss and compare corruption across different cases (Sandholtz and Koetzle, 2000; Philp, 2011). These characteristics are

- administrative or political favors in exchange for inducements, financial or otherwis [3]
- the violation of shared norms of public offic
- the existence of a well–developed distinction between the public and private sphere, which breaks down in cases of corruption. In societies where the formal state competes with

alternative sources of authority and governance (i.e. tribal or religious), distinctions between public and private become blurred, and the distinction between corrupt acts and socially legitimate practices is often difficult to identify (see also Scott, 1969)

Most analyses of the causal impact of corruption focus on the scale of corruption; however, such a focus tells us little about the pathways through which corruption affects statebuilding outcomes, and similarly little about the areas where interventions could help to contain corruption, or insulate statebuilding practices from its consequences. Afghanistan and Myanmar might both have the same CPI score in 2011, but *how* corruption affects governance, economic development, and security, *what* its implications are, and *how* it is best addressed, differ between these countries.

The character of corruption and the ways it impacts political dynamics are shaped among other things by the wider social and political order, the resources and rents around which corrupt activities are organized, and the strength of the formal political and economic institutions that are compromised by corruption. Corruption in a country with large mineral wealth where one group emerged from conflict victorious (such as Angola) differs substantially from a country without major resource wealth where the main source of corruption is government procurement (e.g. Kosovo), or a country with a contested political settlement and large and easily accessible illicit resources (e.g. Afghanistan). To understand the impact of corruption, it is therefore necessary to focus more on the *organization* of corruption, and how it is embedded in the wider political economy, to gain better insights into its consequences and how to address it most effectively in statebuilding contexts (see also Johnston, 2005).

The organization of corruption

Discussions of corruption and statebuilding often pick up on a particular aspect of the organization of corruption, namely the distinction between grand and petty – or political and administrative – corruption (O'Donnell, 2007). Grand corruption takes place at the level of the political leadership, involving individuals who have the capacity to change and instrumentalize the institutions of the state toward their own private benefit. Petty corruption entails all the (mostly financial) demands from low- and mid-level offials to expedite a public service (such as issuing a licence or document) or to grant access to services (such as healthcare or education).

To analyze the impact of corruption on statebuilding, the distinction between grand and petty corruption is of limited use, for three reasons. First, the two forms of corruption are closely interrelated, and fuel each other: if for example politicians sell public offces in their jurisdiction (a form of grand corruption), those purchasing these off ces need to make that investment pay – through petty corruption. Second, it can be diffcult to determine where petty corruption ends and grand corruption starts, not least because administrative favors that would be classed as 'petty' corruption can involve sums and have wider implications that are anything but petty (e.g. bribes to police off cers to facilitate drug shipments). Third, such a distinction does not take account of the wider political–economic dynamics of which corruption is symptomatic. Whether it ties together a wide range of elites, and even non-elites, through extensive and stable patronage systems of mass corruption, or whether it fuels destabilizing and violent competition over resource rents among elites is not clear from this distinction. It is therefore worth unpacking the organization of corruption further, and examining different contexts, to better understand how it affects statebuilding outcomes.

Michael Johnston distinguishes between four types of corruption which are symptomatic of how power is organized in a society. They differ, first, with regard to the strength of the politica and economic institutions of a community, and second, with regard to participation in political and economic competition (Johnston, 2005). While the former gives an indication of the degree to which power is institutionalized, the latter describes the diffusion of power in a society, and the wider social and political dynamics into which corrupt exchanges are embedded. Two of these types of corruption are of particular importance for fragile and conflict-affected states, a they are organized around weak and contested institutions: 'official mogul' corruption and 'clan and oligarchs' corruption.[4] The key distinctions between them are the number of powerful and corrupt actors, and the degree to which corruption and control over state power and resources are concentrated or competed over. It is worth briefly examining these two forms of corruptio in a bit more detail, as they provide a useful analytical lens for the role of corruption in state-building environments.

'Official mogul' corruption

'Official mogul' corruption arises from political systems with weak states, where a small ruling elite has effectively 'captured' the state or parts of the state (i.e. specific sectors or provinces) an key aspects of the economy, dominating public life more or less unchallenged. With weak institutions, political and economic interactions are organized and governed by informal institutions and corruption, with the ruling elite's power resting on the ruler's personality and patronage networks. While corruption is likely to be endemic, it is also centralized, with the ruling elite controlling key resources and dispensing patronage. Potential challengers are either successfully suppressed or coopted into the elite.

While highly iniquitous, the hegemonic position of the ruling elite can make political systems characterized by 'official mogul' corruption very stable, especially if centralized patronage structures are interwoven with other social bonds, such as kinship or religious ties (Blundo and de Sardan, 2006; Jordan-Smith, 2009; Reno, 2011). Patron-client relationships tend to extend beyond elites and draw in large numbers of individuals into networks of corruption. This mass corruption, with its regular and predictable interactions between patron and clients, is likely to contain the most rapacious acts of corruption, as leaders need to maintain a degree of mass support to sustain their authority. Under certain conditions, such as a leadership with a long-term vision, and the existence of a competent bureaucracy in charge of economic management, centralized corruption is also compatible with what Tim Kelsall and David Booth (2010) have termed 'developmental neo-patrimonialism,' generating substantial economic growth and political stability over a prolonged period of time, as in Ethiopia or Rwanda.

'Clans and oligarchs' corruption

'Clans and oligarchs'-type corruption is associated with political orders characterized by weak institutions, but also by a divided political elite competing for access to power and control over resources. This decentralized form of corruption is relatively typical of post-conflict countries, especially those with peace agreements that involve power-sharing between different wartime groups. It is often associated with informal elite pacts (DFID, 2010: 43). Multiple, competing centers of political and economic power mean that this type of corruption tends to be characterized by physical, political, and economic insecurity.

Oligarchic corruption and insecurity not only fuel power struggles, but create opportunities for corruption and economic gain: control over resources such as alluvial diamonds or opium poppy crops by non-state actors, for example, is facilitated by insecurity (Goodhand, 2011). Oligarchic corruption also imposes substantial political and economic costs, and is likely to increase

Table 2.1 Elite factionalization and violent conflict in highly corrupt countrie [5]

Country	CPI score 2011	Elite factionalization	Violent internal conflict since 2006
Angola	2	7	No
Venezuela	1.9	7.3	No
North Korea	1	7.7	No
Turkmenistan	1.6	7.7	No
Burundi	1.9	7.9	Yes
Equatorial Guinea	1.9	8.2	No
Myanmar	1.5	8.6	Yes
Uzbekistan	1.6	8.7	No
Haiti	1.8	9	Yes
Libya	2	9	Yes
Afghanistan	1.5	9.4	Yes
DRC	2	9.5	Yes
Iraq	1.8	9.6	Yes
Somalia	1	9.8	Yes
Chad	2	9.8	Yes
Sudan	1.6	9.9	Yes

violence, as suggested by the correlation between elite factionalization and violent conflict i highly corrupt countries in Table 2.1. The latent insecurity even of powerful actors is both an incentive to expatriate prof ts from corruption, rather than plough them back into the economy or use them to build stable patronage networks, and an obstacle to institution–building and statebuilding.[6] As access to power and rents is often precarious and unpredictable, elites are more likely to engage in rapacious corruption as the opportunity for enrichment might not last long.

Focusing on the organization of corruption highlights that it is as much a collective action problem as it is a principal–agent problem, especially in fragile states where, as discussed further below, corruption and participation in patronage relationships can be a rational response to the constraints and challenges posed by confict and weak state institutions, and to deal with the vagaries of daily life. Such a perspective on corruption immediately raises questions about the efficacy of many of the traditional anti–corruption instruments, which mainly aim at either addressing information asymmetries (through auditing, transparency legislation, strengthening media and civil society) or strengthening sanctions against corrupt behavior (e.g. through better and tougher prosecution). Focusing on the organization of corruption also suggests that the different types of corruption identified above affect both horizontal and vertical aspects of statebuilding in different ways, and pose different challenges to addressing corruption in statebuilding contexts. These are examined in more detail in the following sections.

Corruption and statebuilding

This section looks in more detail at the complex relationship between corruption and statebuilding through the lens of two key statebuilding practices: the forging of an elite settlement (often referred to as a political settlement), which is a central aspect of 'horizontal' statebuilding; and strengthening the capacity of state institutions to provide basic public services, a central aspect of 'vertical' statebuilding. It also examines more generally the complex relationship between corruption and security, and corruption and aid, to assess how statebuilding practices can con–tribute to the entrenching of corruption in conflict–affected countries

Forging elite settlements[7]

Elite settlements are central to 'horizontal' statebuilding as they determine the relationships between different organized groups within society and how power is distributed and controlled, and express shared understandings of the organization and exercise of power (DFID, 2010; North et al., 2009; Parks and Cole, 2010). While elite settlements are distinct from peace agreements, a negotiated settlement has been part of most post–Cold War peace agreements. Corruption is part of the complex political realities that underpin the power structures that shape any negotiated elite settlement, and its role needs to be recognized when supporting the negotiation and implementation of any agreement (Cheng and Zaum, 2011). Importantly, it can support such settlements in two ways.

First, accepting a settlement where power is organized around corrupt relationships and opportunities for rent–seeking is often a way of literally buying support for reaching a settlement. Allowing wartime leaders to turn their military might into political power and rent–seeking opportunities has been a central element of a range of attempts to negotiate a settlement – though not always successful, and often at a high price. In Sierra Leone, for example, Revolutionary United Front (RUF) leader Foday Sankoh became not only vice–president but also chairman of the Commission for the Management of Strategic Resources (with authority over exploitation and trade in gold and diamonds) following the ultimately unsuccessful 1999 Lomé Peace Accord. In Liberia, the peace accord that ended the civil war in 2003 divided up cabinet posts between warring parties and effectively gave them the opportunity to maximize their returns from these offces over the two–year period of the transitional government. In the case of Afghanistan, the 2001 Bonn agreement has been described as 'an externally driven division of the spoils among a hand–pickedgroup of stakeholders who were on the right side of the War on Terror' (Goodhand and Sedra, 2010: S82) and provided an unstable, competitive elite settlement without the wider elements of a peace agreement between belligerents.

Second, corruption can be central to the maintenance of such an elite bargain. As Alex de Waal (2009) has argued, in societies with weak states, stability and political order is often provided not by public institutions autonomous from sectional interests, but by the most inclusive buy–in of elites in a 'neo–patrimonial marketplace.' Corruption can be central to sustaining patronage ties and the elite buy–in that stabilizes the settlement. There is ample evidence that corruption can be central to upholding elite settlements. The stability of the endemically corrupt regimes in Angola or Cambodia today, and in Liberia or Zaire during the Cold War, is witness to that. What these regimes have in common, however, is a relatively centralized form of corruption, and control over the key resources that sustain the patronage networks that supported stability in these countries. The contribution to the making and sustaining of a political settlement therefore comes almost exclusively from mogul–type corruption. Many of the post–war elite bargains stabilized by corruption, e.g. in Angola and Cambodia, are also cases where the settlement has been imposed by the victors, rather than negotiated, and where as a consequence a small elite has achieved hegemonic control over the country's political and economic life.[8] The failure of the Bonn settlement for Afghanistan is exemplary of the pitfalls of trying to 'buy' stability through accepting (and arguably fueling) oligarchic corruption.

However, it is worth noting two caveats. First, corruption can also undermine the emergence and maintenance of an elite settlement, in particular if it entrenches an exclusive settlement. As Charles Call (2012) has shown, exclusive elite settlements that marginalize important con–stituencies are a major reason for the recurrence of violence. If the patronage system underlying an elite bargain is excluding or marginalizing key organized groups within a society, they might work toward undermining the settlement and resort to force to overturn or change it. Even if such groups have no real political constituency, their ability to generate violence can undermine any statebuilding efforts. Both in Burundi and in the DRC, negotiations over a political settlement were accompanied by the emergence of such 'nuisance groups' (Uvin and Bayer, 2012). In Helmand, the post–Taliban order and its tribally based patronage system systematically excluded the previously powerful Ishakzai tribe from power, undermining the emergence of a stable political settlement in the province, making the Ishakzai more susceptible to overtures by the Taliban (Gordon, 2011). In addition, the prospect of rents from corrupt activities can fuel violence by actors excluded from the settlement, and hence the rents. In southern provinces of Afghanistan, for example, violence has been fueled by competition over control of drugs production and trafficking (Goodhand, 2011; Gordon, 2011)

Claims about the stabilizing impact of corruption and patronage (at least for the short and medium terms) (de Waal, 2009; LeBillon, 2011) therefore need to be qualified. If an elite settlement is accompanied by relatively centralized, mogul–type corruption, this corruption might well contribute to stabilizing the settlement. In orders characterized by oligarchic corruption, however, corruption might buy short–term stability, but the inherent competitiveness in the system is likely to undermine the emergence of a stable settlement.

Second, while inclusive elite settlements might be central to statebuilding, they also threaten to entrench corruption. Bringing into the settlement elites whose power is maintained with the help from rents from corrupt activities, limits the political will to address the resulting political iniquities and corruption. In Bosnia, for example, nationalist politicians lobbied successfully to extend the amnesty laws to economic crimes, and to cover not only the period of the war but go back to January 1991 when they assumed power (Belloni, 2007: 102). The lack of political will has often been identified as one of the major reasons for the failure of dedicated anti–corruption institutions.

Public service delivery

Corruption, in particular through its facilitation of black markets and informal service delivery, can help populations to access small–scale public goods and services. Generally, though, corruption is considered to have an overwhelmingly detrimental effect on the quality and access to public services, for two reasons in particular. First, it reduces funds available for the delivery of public services, reducing revenue collection by facilitating smuggling and VAT fraud at the border, or leading to the non–collection of taxes in return for bribes (Fjeldstad, 2005). Integrity Watch Afghanistan, for example, estimates that Afghans paid between $700 million and $1 billion in bribes in 2009, and suggests that the revenue lost from corruption may exceed the government tax intake (Gardizi et al., 2010: 7, Box 1). Second, corruption limits access to key services such as healthcare and education by imposing additional illegal user charges in the form of bribes. Unofficial user fees discourage poor people from using healthcare institutions (Hussman, 2011), for example. In the education sector, corruption limits access to schools and universities when places are awarded to the highest bidders, and undermines the quality of education through fueling teacher absenteeism (U4, 2006).[9]

Public service delivery is important for statebuilding for a range of reasons. The delivery of basic public services – including security – is generally deemed central to the local legitimacy of the institutions supported by statebuilding efforts. The declining or unequal provision of public services and the decline in state legitimacy can fuel renewed conflict, as in Sierra Leone (Keen 2005).[10] Ineffective and illegitimate institutions can also lead to the emergence of informal institutional alternatives to resolve disputes or deliver basic services, which in some cases might start to challenge formal state institutions. Corruption in public services that reinforces horizontal inequalities and excludes or marginalizes ethnic, religious, or tribal groups can fuel grievances and violence, as in Côte d'Ivoire, directly undermining statebuilding efforts.

However, key features of fragile and conflict–affected states can make it rational for both ruler and citizens more generally to engage in corruption (Khan, 2005). The small tax base and limited budgetary resources available to most governments in conflict–affected countries means that opportunities for building legitimacy through redistribution via public services are very limited. Patronage and provision of public services to selected clients is an effective way for rulers to target key constituencies necessary to sustain their authority. This makes it also rational for individuals at all levels of society to be part of patronage networks and engage in corruption (Khan, 2005), and both difficult and potentially destabilizing to address these forms of corruption

Corruption and security

The complexity of the relationship between corruption and security is highlighted by the lack of consensus in the literature on the impact of corruption on security. While much of the literature associates corruption with insecurity and violence (Rotberg, 2009), authors who approach the issue from a political economy and country–specific perspective often highligh corruption's stabilizing properties (Snyder 2006; Cheng and Zaum, 2011; North et al., 2009).

Those highlighting corruption as a cause of violence base their claim on two arguments in particular. The first, already discussed above, is that corruption provides incentives for the us of violence to capture the associated rents. The second argument advanced for the destabilizing consequences of corruption is that as it undermines the capacity and the legitimacy of state institutions, the ability of the state to demand compliance from its citizens diminishes, and people are more willing to accept violence as an instrument of political change (Clausen et al., 2011). As a study on Afghanistan for the UK's Department for International Development (DFID) puts it, 'Corruption has . . . become one of the few manners in which the State interacts with its citizens, thus conveying the widely adopted perception that the government is more a source of predation than protection' (Recovery and Development Consortium, 2008: 31). In such contexts, corruption becomes an important driver of insecurity (see, for example, Fishstein, 2010), inextricably linking the governance and security implications of corruption.

Violence and insecurity, however, are predominantly associated with oligarchic corruption. Indeed, as discussed earlier, there are clear examples of corruption having the effect of stabilizing political order and minimizing competition over power and violence. Historically, many highly corrupt regimes, as in Liberia or Côte d'Ivoire, were very stable and resilient to violence – as corruption predominantly took the form of centralized patronage, and patron–client networks often reinforced other social ties. The exclusive control over sources of patronage by the ruling elite made it diffcult to challenge it violently, and enabled rulers to buy off potential challengers.

Within a single country, different forms of corruption can have very different security–related outcomes. In southern Afghanistan, for example, the competitive and exclusionary nature of oligarchic corruption has been one of the drivers of violence and insecurity (Forsberg, 2010; Gordon, 2011). In contrast, in some northern provinces of Afghanistan the centralized, patronage–based form of rule established by some warlords has been central to maintaining a degree of security and stability. As Dipali Mukhopadhyay (2009) has shown, these warlords have entered a bargain with the Afghan central state which allows them to maintain their informal networks of power that have been integrated into the state – i.e. by allocating positions in the public sector, especially in security institutions, to members of these informal patronage networks. This gives these warlords (and by association the state) a higher degree of control over the societies they rule, providing a degree of governance and security (if not the rule of law) that also provides tangible benefits to the wider population. While some governors might in addition be buildin up formal governance institutions and strengthening their capacity, the key source of their power remains their informal patronage networks. Corruption is central to this bargaining process, and to the effective 'self−containment' of potential spoilers.

To the extent that corruption can contribute to security, this contribution has generally come from mogul−type corruption, and from supporting the cooption of potential spoilers into the state. It thus supports horizontal statebuilding, but does not strengthen the capacity of central state institutions to enhance security through the establishment of a monopoly of violence. As a result, there are two important caveats. First, corruption might contribute to security at the macro−level, but at the same time fuel insecurity at the level of communities and the individual. Patronage can ensure the literal buy−in of powerbrokers into the new political order, but if the price of this is a degree of impunity for these individuals within their jurisdictions, it can entrench persistent physical and economic insecurity, for example by encouraging violence or land grabs by individuals protected by patron−client relationships and crony−networks, or entrench organized crime.

Second, security based on patronage requires constant access to the resources that sustain the patronage network. Sudden shocks that undermine their availability (such as the withdrawal of external f nancial support, or rapid falls in the price of valuable natural resources) can quickly lead to insecurity and conf ict. The sudden decline in financial and military assistance to ruler in developing countries following the end of the Cold War deprived rulers of their ability to maintain patronage networks or coerce any opposition (Clapham, 1996), and fueled the rise in 'state failure' and conf ict, most notably in Somalia and Zaire/DRC. In Afghanistan, the decline of financial and military support for the Najibullah regime, following the collapse of the Sovie Union, both led to the fall of the regime and triggered a fundamental transformation of the Afghan political economy with the rapid expansion of the drugs trade, as military commanders had to open new avenues to generate revenue to finance their military efforts (Goodhand, 2011 149; Barfield, 2010: 248)

Aid and corruption in state-building contexts

Most statebuilding interventions involve substantial aid f ows, at times exceeding local GDP by multiples. This can substantially distort the economies of conflict−affected countries, especiall if it exceeds the countries' capacity to absorb these funds, fueling rent−seeking and providing incentives for corruption in the process (Collier and Hoeffler, 2004). Systematic evidence on th impact of aid on corruption, however, is lacking, mainly because of poor data especially from conf ict−affectedcountries, and because of the problems of meaningfully measuring corruption, and the difficulty of comparing different proxy variables used in country−specific corruption research.

More important with regard to statebuilding is the effect of the way in which aid money is spent, as this affects both the scale and the character of corruption (von Billerbeck, 2011). A detailed examination of the impact of different aid modalities on corruption is beyond the scope of this chapter, and the evidence on the impact of different forms of aid delivery (i.e. direct budget support or project−based aid) is inconclusive and highlights the importance of the specifi context (the strength and quality of institutions, existing levels of corruption, and the mechanisms donors have put in place to manage their aid and protect it against corruption). What the existing evidence highlights, however, is that in fragile states, aid spent off−budget and bypassing the state is often found to further weaken state authority (Ghani and Lockhart, 2008), undermining key statebuilding objectives. Research into the impact of aid and informal social service delivery by

NGOs or communities at the local level highlights that aid given directly to such non- and sub-state actors often revives and reinforces the patronage power of local elites who become the gatekeepers to aid and services (Jackson, 2005).

In statebuilding environments with only an informal elite settlement, where provincial and local powerbrokers compete over influence both in the provinces and with the center, financi or other assistance spent outside the budget and at the sub-state level can fuel and entrench this competitive political order and oligarchic corruption (see, for example, Gordon, 2011). An example of this has been the security-related contracting in Afghanistan. A US Congressional report on the $2.16 billion host-nation trucking program supplying the extensive US bases across Afghanistan found it characterized by poor monitoring and contracting practices, and fueling 'warlordism, extortion, and corruption, and it may be a significant source of funding for insurgents' (US House of Representatives, 2010: 2). In other words, it further entrenched decentralized, oligarchic corruption in Afghanistan. The use of private security companies, often with close links to local powerbrokers, to protect bases and projects has further strengthened this decentralization of power and corruption (Sherman and DiDomenico, 2009).

Conclusion

This chapter has advanced three arguments. While they have solid theoretical support, systematic empirical evidence to date remains weak. First, a more granular understanding of the complex roles of corruption in statebuilding contexts is best advanced through the lens of the organization of corruption. It suggests that different types of corruption differ in their impact on the political structures and dynamics in fragile states, and in their effect on statebuilding efforts. Generally, oligarchic corruption has a more detrimental effect on statebuilding efforts than mogul-type corruption.

Second, while the impact of corruption on statebuilding is largely negative, the effects across different dimensions of the state and of statebuilding efforts vary. In particular with regard to aspects of horizontal statebuilding, especially the forging and maintaining of an elite settlement, mogul-typecorruption can be supportive rather than detrimental, at least in the short and medium terms. While such corruption can thus contribute to quite resilient 'closed access orders,' it also obstructs the transition from resilient states based on highly personalistic rule toward more open, developmental societies, and the kind of liberal-democratic societies that are at the core of most statebuilding mandates but that have remained largely elusive.

Third, the character of corruption is a symptom of the wider organization of power and politics in a society, and is often central to the logic of a political system. This means that there is unlikely to be suff cient political will to meaningfully transform the political and social order to effectively contain corruption. This is not necessarily a consequence of a ruling elite's greed and desire to protect its position (this could be an exacerbating factor), but a structural problem rooted in the wider character of the political and social order. It also means that anti-corruption policies that challenge structures and practices that are central to the maintenance of the existing political order can reignite violence, as powerful actors resist these changes. This can undermine wider statebuilding efforts.

The issue of corruption crystalizes the fundamentally political nature of statebuilding, and the difficult moral and political trade-offs that it involves. Accepting corruption might buy stability in the short and medium terms, but might fuel grievances (and with them the risk of violence) in the long term. It might help to strengthen the resilience against violence, but at the same time become an obstacle to more substantive transformation. Actively pursuing the venal might satisfy our sense of justice, but undermine fragile political orders in conflict-affected states. This the highlights the need for a more differentiated discussion about corruption and its roles in state-building contexts. Considering it 'a powerful, all-consuming evil,' as proposed by Laura Underkuffler (2009: 37), deprives us of both analytical focus and precision, and ignores the political economy context that gives rise to corruption, and might make it a rational, even necessary choice for those dealing with the vagaries of daily life and survival in conflict-strew environments. It also highlights a need for greater reflection on how key contemporary statebuilding policies entrench and shape the character of corruption, and the role of external actors in shaping and perpetuating such orders.

Notes

1 This chapter draws on work conducted as part of an ESRC Public Placement Fellowship (ES/J00418/1) with the UK Stabilisation Unit, from October 2011 to March 2012, and research from the Power after Peace: the Political Economy of Statebuilding project, supported by the Carnegie Corporation of New York. The positions expressed in this chapter are the author's, and do not necessarily reflect the position of the Stabilisation Unit or its parent departments.
2 In the 2012 index, for example, 13 of the bottom 20 countries experienced conflict in the past fi years, according to the Uppsala conflict database
3 Thus, officials might offer favors in response to a threat of violence against them or a member of thei family.
4 The other two are influence markets and elite cartels. While the former characterizes corruption in free market democracies with strong political and economic institutions, the latter characterizes many transition countries with consolidated political and economic systems that none the less remain dominated by a narrow political and economic elite. All types are discussed in more detail in Johnston (2005).
5 Table 2.1 shows the degree of divisions within a country's elite, and whether a country has experienced internal conflict since 2006, for the countries identified as 'highly corrupt' in the 2011 Transparenc International CPI. Countries with a CPI score of 2 or lower are considered as 'highly corrupt.' Sources: Transparency International 2011 Corruption Perceptions Index; Fund for Peace Failed State Index 2012 (for factionalization data); and Uppsala Conflict Database (for violent internal conflict data)
6 According to a *Wall Street Journal* report, nearly $5 billion was taken out of Afghanistan in cash in 2011 through Kabul airport alone, suggesting that the real figure is much higher (Trofmov, 2012). To put this figure in context, the World Bank estimates Afghanistan's 2011 GDP at $30 billion (http://data.worldbank.org/country/afghanistan).
7 Some of the literature refers to political settlements, rather than elite settlements (Parks and Cole, 2010; Call, 2012; DFID, 2010). As political settlements often refer to both elite bargains (horizontal political settlements) and the strengthening of a social contract between elites and non-elites (vertical political settlements), here the more precise terms 'elite settlement' or 'elite bargain' are used.
8 In Cambodia, the original negotiated settlement of the 1991 Paris Peace Accord was overthrown by Hun Sen's military coup in 1997.
9 However, if public servants are lowly or irregularly paid, illegal user fees can be the only way to enable them to continue to provide a particular service such as education. In these cases, the detrimental corruption problem is the fact that resources allocated for their salaries are embezzled before they reach the intended beneficiary
10 The evidence for a close link between state performance (the output legitimacy of a state) and anti-state violence is only country-specific. I am not aware of strong systematic evidence for a close link bot between the provision of public services and state legitimacy, and between declines in public service delivery and violence.

References

Barfeld, T. (2010). *Afghanistan: A cultural and political history*. Princeton, NJ: Princeton University Press.
Belloni, R. (2007). *State building and international intervention in Bosnia*. Abingdon, UK: Routledge.
Blundo, G. and de Sardan, O. (2006). *Everyday corruption and the state: Citizens and public officials in Africa*. New York, NY: Zed.

Boucher, A., Durch, W., Midyette, M., and Terry, J. (2007) *Mapping and fighting corruption in war-torn states*. Stimson Center Report 61. Washington, DC: Stimson Center.

Call, C. (2012). *Why peace fails: The causes and prevention of civil war recurrence*. Washington, DC: Georgetown University Press.

Cheng, C., and Zaum, D. (2011). 'Selling the peace? Corruption and post–conflict peacebuilding,' in C. Cheng and D. Zaum (Eds.), *Corruption and post-conflict peacebuilding: Selling the peace?* Abingdon, UK: Routledge, pp. 1–25.

Clapham, C. (1996). *Africa and the international system: The politics of state survival*. Cambridge, UK: Cambridge University Press.

Clausen, B., Kraay, A., and Nyiri, Z. (2011). Corruption and confidence in public institutions: Evidenc from a global survey. *World Bank Economic Review*, 25(2): 212–249.

Collier, P., and Hoeffler, A. (2004). Aid policy and growth in post–conflict societies. *European Economic Review*, 48, 1125–1145.

de Waal, A. (2009). Missions without end? Peacekeeping in the African political marketplace. *International Affairs*, 85(1), 99–113.

DFID (Department for International Development). (2010). *Building peaceful states and societies: A DFID practice paper*. London, UK: DFID.

DiJohn, J. (2010). *State resilience against the odds: An analytical narrative of the construction and maintenance of political order in Zambia since 1960*. Crisis States Working Paper No. 75. London, UK: London School of Economics.

Englebert, P. (2002). *State legitimacy and development in Africa*. Boulder, CO: Lynne Rienner.

Fishstein, P. (2010). *Winning hearts and minds? Examining the relationship between aid and security in Afghanistan's Balkh Province*. Somerville, MA: Feinstein Center.

Fjeldstad, O.-H. (2005). *Revenue administration and corruption*. Bergen, Norway: U4–CMI.

Forsberg, C. (2010). *Politics and power in Kandahar*. Washington, DC: Institute for the Study of War.

Gardizi, M., Hussmann, K., and Torabi, Y. (2010). *Corrupting the state or state-crafted corruption: Exploring the nexus between corruption and subnational governance*. Kabul, Afghanistan: Afghan Research and Evaluation Unit (AREU).

Ghani, A., and Lockhart, C. (2008). *Fixing failed states: A framework for rebuilding a fractured world*. Oxford, UK: Oxford University Press.

Goodhand, J. (2011). 'Corrupting or consolidating the peace: The drug economy and post–conflict peacebuilding in Afghanistan. In C. Cheng and D. Zaum (Eds.), *Corruption and post-conflict peacebuilding: Selling the peace?* Abingdon, UK: Routledge, pp. 146–163.

Goodhand, J., and Sedra, M. (2010). Who owns the peace? Aid, reconstruction, and peacebuilding in Afghanistan. *Disasters*, 34(S1), S78–S102.

Gordon, S. (2011). *Winning hearts and minds? Examining the relationship between aid and security in Afghanistan's Helmand Province*. Somerville, MA: Feinstein Center.

Herbst, J. (1997). Responding to state failure in Africa. *International Security*, 21(3), 120–144.

Holsti, K. (1996). *The state, war, and the state of war*. Cambridge, UK: Cambridge University Press.

Hussman, K. (2011). *Addressing corruption in the health sector: Securing equitable access to healthcare for everyone*. Bergen, Norway: CMI/U4.

Jackson, P. (2005). Chiefs, money and politicians: Rebuilding local government in post–war Sierra Leone. *Public Administration and Development*, 25(1), 49–58.

Johnston, M. (2005). *Syndromes of corruption: Wealth, power, and democracy*. Cambridge, UK: Cambridge University Press.

Jordan–Smith, D. (2009). The paradox of popular participation in Nigeria. In R. Rotberg (ed.) *Corruption, global security, and world order*. Washington, DC: Brookings, pp. 283–309.

Keen, D. (2005). *Conflict and collusion in Sierra Leone*. Oxford, UK: James Currey.

Kelsall, T., and Booth, D. (2010). *Developmental patrimonialism? Questioning the orthodoxy on political governance and economic progress in Africa*. Africa Power and Politics Working Paper No. 9. London, UK: ODI.

Khan, M. (2005). Markets, states, and democracy: Patron–client networks and the case for democracy in developing countries. *Democratization*, 12(5), 704–724.

Le Billon, P. (2011). Corrupting peace? Corruption, peacebuilding, and reconstruction. In C. Cheng and D. Zaum (Eds.), *Selling the peace? Corruption and post-conflict peacebuilding*. Abingdon, UK: Routledge, pp. 62–79.

Mann, M. (1984). The autonomous power of the state: Its origins, mechanisms, and results *European Journal of Sociology*, 25(2), 185–213.

Menkhaus, K. (2006/2007). Governance without government in Somalia: Spoilers, state building, and the politics of coping. *International Security*, *31*(3), 74–106.

Mukhopadhyay, D. (2009). Disguised warlordism and combatanthood in Balkh: The persistence of informal power in the formal Afghan state. *Conflict, Security, and Development*, *9*(4), 536–563.

North, D., Wallis, J. J., and Weingast, B. (2009).*Violence and social orders: A conceptual framework for interpreting recorded human history*. Cambridge, UK: Cambridge University Press.

O'Donnell, M. (2007). Post-conflict corruption: A rule of law agenda? In A. Hurwitz and R. Huang (Eds.), *Civil war and the rule of law: Security, development, and human rights*. Boulder, CO: Lynne Rienner, pp. 225–259.

OECD/DAC. (2011). *Supporting statebuilding in situations of conflict and fragility: Policy guidance*. Paris, France: OECD/DAC.

Papagianni, K. (2008). Participation and state legitimation. In C. Call and V. Wyeth (Eds.), *Building states to build peace*. Boulder, CO: Lynne Rienner, pp. 49–71.

Parks, T., and Cole, W. (2010). *Political settlements: Implications for international development and practice*. San Francisco, CA: Asia Foundation.

Philp, M. (2011). Conceptualising corruption in peacebuilding contexts. In C. Cheng and D. Zaum (Eds.), *Corruption and post-conflict peacebuilding: Selling the peace?* Abingdon, UK: Routledge, pp. 29–45.

Recovery and Development Consortium. (2008).*DFID understanding Afghanistan: Strategic conflict assessment*. London, UK: DFID.

Reno, W. (2011). Anti-corruption efforts in Liberia: Are they aimed at the right targets? In C. Cheng and D. Zaum (Eds.), *Corruption and post-conflict peacebuilding: Selling the peace?* Abingdon, UK: Routledge, pp. 127–143.

Rotberg, R. I. (Ed.). (2004). *When states fail: Causes and consequences*. Princeton. NJ: Princeton University Press.

Rotberg, R. I. (Ed.). (2009). *Corruption, global security, and world order*. Washington DC: Brookings Press, 2009.

Sandholtz, W. and Koetzle, W. (2000). Accounting for corruption: Economic structure, democracy, and trade. *International Studies Quarterly*, *44*(1), 31–50.

Scott, J. (1969). The analysis of corruption in developing nations.*Comparative Studies in Society and History*, *11*(3), 315–341.

Seligson, M. A. (2002). The impact of corruption on regime legitimacy: A comparative study of four Latin American countries. *Journal of Politics*, *64*(2), 408–433.

Sherman, J., and DiDomenico, V. (2009). *The public cost of private security in Afghanistan*. New York, NY: Center for International Cooperation.

Snyder, R. (2006). Does lootable wealth breed disorder? A political economy of extraction framework. *Comparative Political Studies*, *39*(8), 943–968.

Trofimov, Y. (2012). Afghanistan targets flight of cash. *Wall Street Journal*, 22 February.

U4. (2006). *Corruption in the education sector*. U4 Issue Paper. Bergen, Norway: Christian Michelsen Institute.

Underkuffler, L. (2009). Defining corruption: Implications for action. In R. Rotberg (Ed.), *Corruption, global security, and world order*. Washington, DC: Brookings Press, pp. 27–46.

US House of Representatives. (2010). *Warlords Inc.: Extortion and corruption along the US supply chain in Afghanistan*. Washington, DC: US Congress.

Uvin, P., and Bayer, L. (2012). Burundi. In M. Berdal and D. Zaum (Eds.), *Power after peace: The political economy of post-conflict state-building*. Abingdon, UK: Routledge.

Von Billerbeck, S. (2011). Aiding the state or aiding corruption? Aid and corruption in post-conflict countries. In C. Cheng and D. Zaum (Eds.), *Corruption and post-conflict peacebuilding: Selling the peace?* Abingdon, UK: Routledge, pp. 80–96.

World Bank, The. (2010). *World Development Report 2011: Conflict, security, and development*. Washington, DC: The World Bank.

Zartmann, W. (Ed.). (1995). *Collapsed states: The disintegration and restoration of legitimate authority*. Boulder, CO: Lynne Rienner.

3
GENDER AND STATEBUILDING

Clare Castillejo

The international statebuilding agenda conceptualizes statebuilding as a deeply political process, concerned with the renegotiation of state–society relations and the allocation of power and resources. Despite this, there has been surprisingly little exploration of how statebuilding affects the gendered allocation of power and resources, or men and women's differing relationships to the state. There has also been little analysis of how international actors can integrate gender into statebuilding support, although this issue is moving up donors' agendas.[1]

Why gender and statebuilding?

Fragile states tend to be characterized by high levels of gender inequality.[2] Women are particularly disadvantaged by the extreme poverty and insecurity, weak state institutions and services, and dominance of informal power structures found in fragile states. Moreover, in these contexts women's relationship to the state is often extremely limited and in many cases entirely mediated by family or customary institutions.

Statebuilding can provide an important opportunity to address entrenched gender inequalities. Processes to renegotiate the social contract, redistribute power and resources and reform state institutions have the potential to strengthen women's political and economic power, rights, and relationship to the state. Moreover, conflict itself often transforms gender relations, as women take on new roles as household heads, community leaders, combatants, or peace-brokers. Post-conflict statebuilding processes can help maintain and expand this new space.

Countries such as Rwanda and Nepal provide examples of how the integration of gender in the statebuilding agenda can strengthen women's rights and political and economic power. However, in other contexts, such as Iraq, neither national nor international actors have prioritized gender equality within statebuilding, resulting in the reinforcement of discrimination and exclusion.

Not only is statebuilding an opportunity to promote gender equality, but a gender focus can also help international actors meet their statebuilding goals. For example, by promoting women's full participation in statebuilding processes international actors can help achieve inclusivity and strengthen the plurality of citizen voice. The promotion of gender equality can also significantly improve economic productivity and development outcomes (World Bank, 2011). Moreover, adopting a gender lens forces international actors to move beyond a default focus on technical institution building and engage with local and informal spheres and issues of accessibility and legitimacy.

The international community has made commitments to integrate gender into statebuilding support. United Nations Security Council Resolution (UNSCR) 1325 (2000) requires 'women's equal participation and full involvement in all efforts for the maintenance and promotion of peace and security.' The 2011 New Deal for Engagement in Fragile States (International Dialogue on Peacebuilding and Statebuilding, 2011) states that 'The empowerment of women . . . is at the heart of successful peacebuilding and statebuilding.' On a policy level, the OECD Policy Guidance on Statebuilding encourages external actors to support women's engagement in statebuilding, while many bilateral and multilateral agencies have their own policy commitments. However, in practice gender has been largely overlooked within international statebuilding support. A study on aid allocations for gender equality in fragile states demonstrates that the greater part of donor spending on security and governance in these contexts does not include any gender equality dimension and concludes that 'international commitments to increase the participation of women in decision−making are not being supported by donors' (OECD, 2010).

This failure to integrate gender into the international statebuilding agenda has a number of causes. Gender issues are often caught up in a broader dilemma between prioritizing stability by supporting elite−led processes and promoting genuine inclusion. In addition, work on gender equality frequently touches on sensitive issues related to family, tradition, and identity. This can provoke resistance from powerful local actors and raise uncomfortable tensions between supporting an endogenous statebuilding agenda and promoting normative values. Moreover, international support in fragile states focuses heavily on the center and on formal institutions, overlooking the informal and local realms where women act as citizens and the structural exclusion that they face.

Fundamentally, however, gender is mostly not seen by international agencies as a political issue to be integrated into the central frameworks of statebuilding. Instead gender tends to be sidelined to work in 'social' sectors, addressed through isolated projects that focus on women's special needs rather than gender power relations, and disconnected from broader efforts to analyze and respond to fragility. Greater understanding is required of how gender relates to the core politics of statebuilding in fragile contexts: in particular to political settlements and political governance; security and the rule of law; citizen voice and participation; and the informal nature of power. These issues are addressed throughout this chapter.

Political settlement

At the heart of statebuilding lies the political settlement. This is an agreement – mostly between elites – on 'the "rules of the game," power distribution and the political processes through which state and society are connected' (OECD, 2011). Post−conflict contexts can provide an opportunity to radically transform the political settlement. As the political settlement sets the statebuilding framework, the inclusion of women's interests in political settlements is critical if statebuilding is to deliver for women.

Evidence suggests that women are largely excluded from formal negotiations over the political settlement in fragile contexts. Key processes such as negotiating peace agreements and drafting constitutions are mostly controlled by male elites that resist women's demands for inclusion. A UNIFEM (2010) review of women's participation in 24 peace processes found that 'women are conspicuously underrepresented.' Even in contexts where women have played a significant rol in bringing about political change – as in South Sudan or Egypt – they have been marginalized from subsequent discussions over the nature of the state.[3]

Despite exclusion from the negotiating table, women frequently influence the formal political settlement from outside. This can involve intensive lobbying during peace negotiations and constitution drafting processes. For example, women activists in North and South Sudan successfully campaigned to get women's rights recognized in the interim constitutions that followed the end of conflict. Women have also used gender equality commitments in formal frameworks to press for a broadening out of the political settlement over time. For example, in Nepal, women used constitutional commitments to equality to campaign for changes to discriminatory citizenship and property laws.

The political settlement is not simply determined by formal frameworks. In fragile states informal 'rules of the game' play a crucial role and women typically have very little influence over these rules. Therefore, even where women's interests are included in the formal political settlement this may not be matched by a real shift in power relations. For example, in Guatemala an inclusive peace process resulted in comprehensive constitutional rights for women and a range of institutions to promote gender equality. However, there has been little change in exclusionary power relations within Guatemala, making this formal framework for gender equality in practice meaningless.

The statebuilding literature generally presents political settlements as gender-neutral. However, there can be a close connection between the distribution of political power and patterns of gender inequality. In such cases promoting a political settlement that includes women's interests is particularly challenging. A clear example is Afghanistan, where women's rights have historically been caught up in contests between different political forces and their international backers – from the Soviet-backed regime to the Taliban. Kandiyoti (2005) argues that the issue of women's rights 'continues to occupy a highly politicized and sensitive place in the struggles between contending political factions in Afghanistan.' Another example is Burundi, where elites blocked legislation to grant women inheritance rights, which is required to meet constitutional gender equality commitments. Burundian elites use land ownership to maintain power and buy patronage. Inheritance rights for women would significantly alter land distribution patterns and threaten a political settlement based on exclusionary land ownership (Gahungu and Kazoviyo, 2011). In both cases women's rights are presented as threatening 'tradition,' when in fact they threaten certain power interests.

There is increasing international focus on promoting 'inclusive' political settlements, as necessary for long-term stability. In practice international actors mostly have little influence over who shapes the political settlement. However, even where they do have influence, international actors often fail to promote women's inclusion in political settlement negotiations. This is partly because of an emphasis on 'bringing in' those who can threaten the state, as well as limited awareness of the importance of women's participation.

One such example is Kosovo, where the powerful United Nations Mission failed to promote women's participation in the peace processes or give women leadership roles within its own structures. This resulted in women's representatives being excluded from negotiations on the Comprehensive Proposal for Kosovo Status Settlement. However, where the international community does promote women's participation, this can make a significant difference. For example, high-level participation by women in the internationally supported Kenya National Dialogue and Reconciliation process led to the inclusion of women's views and interests throughout the process (McGhie and Wamai, 2011).

As international actors further develop their approaches to inclusive political settlements, women's inclusion is likely to move up their agenda. Existing experience provides some lessons for the international community on promoting political settlements that include women. Firstly it is clear that women's participation in top-level political settlement negotiations can make a real difference. It is important that international actors seek ways to incentivize elites to include women in negotiations, as well as support women's demands for inclusion. Moreover, formal expressions of the political settlement within peace agreements and constitutions establish the framework within which women can make future demands on the state. International actors can press for strong references to women's rights within these agreements and support activities to disseminate and implement them.

Beyond promoting women's formal participation, international actors should analyze the relationship between the political settlement, elite interests, and gender inequalities. This can help them to understand resistance and identify opportunities. However, it can involve asking uncomfortable questions about 'tradition' and whose interests it represents. Finally, it is important to recognize that women's formal inclusion can be meaningless if exclusionary informal 'rules of the game' are not addressed. While international actors inevitably focus on formal institutions, support for formal change must be accompanied by efforts to transform underlying power relations.

Political governance reform

Statebuilding in fragile contexts often involves political governance reform, frequently through internationally supported democratization processes. Democratization provides an opportunity to dramatically increase women's formal political participation, as seen in a wide range of contexts from East Timor to South Africa. However, it must be recognized that democratization is not automatically positive for women. In Egypt democratization has resulted in women being pushed out of public life and the empowerment of conservative political forces.[4]

The international community strongly promotes the adoption of parliamentary quotas for women within political governance reform. As a consequence many fragile states have comparatively high levels of female representation. In countries such as Rwanda and Nepal, where quotas are part of broader efforts to empower women, they have contributed to a more gender-responsive state.[5] However, in many contexts – from Pakistan to Uganda – women's increased political participation through quotas has not translated into substantive influence. Feminist critics increasingly question the international community's assumptions about the impact of quotas. For example, Goetz and Musembi (2008) call for a realistic assessment of what quotas can achieve in contexts of patronage.

There are various reasons why quotas fail to have policy impact. Despite increased numbers in the legislature, women are often not given decision-making roles within the executive or key committees. For example, women constitute 27% of the Afghan parliament but have very limited representation within cabinet and the high-level policy-making bodies that take decisions about security, counter-narcotics, and development (Borchgrevink et al., 2008). Evidence also suggests that women elected through quota systems often do not champion gender issues. This can be both because political parties deliberately select socially conservative female candidates and because new female parliamentarians are unwilling to challenge party leaders. As Cornwall and Goetz (2005) point out, 'winning and keeping office can be contingent on downplaying feminist sympathies.' However, it must be recognized that in many fragile contexts quotas have only recently been adopted and it may take time for their policy effects to be felt.

Despite these challenges, quotas are undeniably important in increasing women's political voice and changing perceptions about their public role, particularly given the serious structural barriers that prevent women from entering political institutions in many fragile states. These barriers often relate to the specific nature of post-conflict politics, where stakes are hi and politics is personalized and characterized by insecurity and patronage (Maley, 2004). In some fragile contexts women also lack political capacities and face social stigma for taking on a public role.

Political violence is common in fragile contexts, and women candidates are particular targets. For example, in Sierra Leone female candidates are harassed by male 'secret societies,' while in Afghanistan they face threats from male candidates and insurgents (Kellow, 2010; Human Rights Watch, 2010). Women are also disadvantaged by corrupt and clientist politics in many fragile states, as they have limited ability to offer financial bribes or mobilize patronage networks. Moreover, in contexts where customary leaders mobilize votes, their objection to women's political participation is a serious obstacle.

Political parties are a key gatekeeper to women's political participation. In fragile contexts political parties are typically highly personalized around male leaders and do business through informal networks that women cannot access. For example, Guatemalan female politicians describe how political parties are 'owned' by leaders, have no mechanisms for collective decision–making, and are continually reconstituted in response to new opportunities for power (Alamilla and Quintana, 2010). Women members are rarely given leadership roles within such parties. They are frequently sidelined within a 'women's wing,' whose role is to support male leaders rather than influence the policy agenda

Despite the problematic nature of political parties in fragile states and their critical role in mediating citizen engagement with statebuilding processes, they receive little international attention. Wild and Foresti (2010) note that donors are cautious about engaging in this highly sensitive area and that international support usually involves top–down technical assistance based on an ideal of what a political party should be. This typically includes promoting electoral quotas and providing capacity development for women members, but not addressing the exclusionary power structures and lack of internal democracy that keep women marginalized within parties.

In order to fully seize the opportunities provided by political governance reform, international actors must understand the specific gender challenges of politics in fragile contexts. They mus also move beyond a limited focus on quotas and elections and adopt a broader range of measures to promote women's political influence. These would certainly involve getting women elected but also equipping women to act effectively once in office, supporting coalition building amon women politicians, linking women politicians with women's civil society movements, and promoting the inclusion of women in the executive.

Critically, the international community should strengthen its engagement with political parties. This requires dialogue with male party leaders on gender equality issues; supporting women party members to promote a gender equality agenda; and addressing sensitive issues of party democracy and decision–making. Moreover, support for reform of political institutions should be combined with addressing the structural barriers to access that women face; for example, by addressing violence toward women candidates, the economic cost of participation, or stigma against women in public life.

Legal and justice reform

Establishing the rule of law is a statebuilding priority and significant international support is provided for legal and justice reform in fragile contexts. This support usually includes some measures to improve women's rights and access to justice. In order for such measures to be effective, an understanding is needed of how struggles over women's rights relate to broader power interests.

Constitutional reform often enshrines new rights for women, including to equality. However, such reform tends to create gaps between women's constitutional rights and the reality of national laws and justice institutions. Whether the state undertakes legal and justice reform to close this gap can depend on the relationship between gender inequalities and the broader political settlement. Closing this gap frequently requires expanding state jurisdiction over personal and family issues that are often delegated to customary or religious authorities. This means challenging the notion that these are 'private' or 'cultural' issues and redefining them as areas in which citizen have rights. International actors can provide critical support to women's campaigns for the realization of their constitutional rights.

Sierra Leone and Sudan provide contrasting examples of how women's rights can be related to broader power interests. In Sierra Leone women's rights are caught up in a power struggle between formal and customary authorities (Castillejo, 2008). In 2007 the government enacted legislation that gave women formal rights on a range of personal status issues previously under customary jurisdiction. This legislation both realized women's constitutional rights and was part of a broader agenda to extend formal state authority. Chiefs have resisted these reforms, which undermine their authority, revenue−raising ability, and the balance of power between formal and customary institutions.

While in Sierra Leone the extension of women's rights increased formal state power, in Sudan the restriction of women's rights serves the regime's interests. Since 1989 the regime has strengthened sharia as the main source of law and appointed highly conservative judges. Women's rights have been severely curtailed by this Islamicization of the law (Tønnessen and Kjøstvedt, 2010). The new interim constitution provides some limited rights for women, and women have used this constitution to lobby for the repeal of discriminatory laws. [6] However, the regime is unwilling to close this legal gap and is instead reinforcing conservative ideology to consolidate its power following the South's secession.

International statebuilding support often contains a strong emphasis on reforming justice institutions and improving access to justice. In fragile contexts women can face particularly severe barriers to accessing formal justice institutions because of their socioeconomic marginalization. These barriers include cost, language, travel, lack of education, limited awareness of their rights, and social stigma. In many cases they result in women using discriminatory customary justice institutions, even where reform has brought them new formal rights. International efforts to strengthen justice institutions therefore need to be combined with initiatives to address the socioeconomic barriers to access experienced by women. One option is the establishment of community−level paralegal committees, as seen in Nepal (El−Bushra et al., 2012). These have served women's basic justice needs, although there are questions over their sustainability and connection to formal justice institutions. Such initiatives must support women's access to formal justice rather than relegate their claims to informal justice mechanisms.

Even where significant international support is provided to the formal justice system, in many fragile contexts customary justice institutions continue to be the main provider. Justice reform programs must therefore engage with both formal and customary justice actors, promoting women's rights and seeking to strengthen links between the two arenas. There are some interesting examples of such internationally supported initiatives, such as Sierra Leone's Justice Sector Development Programme.

Security sector reform

Security sector reform (SSR) is a priority area for international statebuilding support. This support has traditionally focused on state security and paid little attention to gender issues. However, both UNSCR 1325 and the growth of human security approaches have led to an increasing international focus on the security of women citizens.

Men and women often have very different security needs in fragile contexts. For example, research in Liberia found that women's immediate security concerns relate to gender-based violence in the home and community (Onslow et al., 2010). Recent years have seen an increase in internationally supported initiatives to address women's security needs. According to El-Bushra et al. (2012), such initiatives typically involve increasing the number of women in security agencies, creating specific police facilities for women, addressing women's needs in DDR, an addressing displaced women's needs. However, Schoofs and Smits (2010) argue that women's security is still frequently marginalized within SSR. They describe how sexual violence has received little attention within SSR in Democratic Republic of Congo, despite being a major threat to women's security.

While SSR initiatives often improve security agencies' responsiveness to women, they rarely promote the inclusion of women in decision-making about security. For example, SSR in Kosovo included recruitment of women into the police and establishment of special police units to address domestic violence and trafficking. However, the Kosovo Security Council blocke women's civil society organizations (CSOs) from participating in drafting the Kosovo Security Strategy (Qosaj-Mustafa, 2010). Similarly, police reform in Burundi involved the recruitment of female police and the establishment of provincial-level gender focal points. However, women police officers face widespread harassment by male colleagues and are unable to enter senior management roles because they lack formal educational qualif cations.

International actors supporting SSR tend to address women's security through discrete projects rather than by mainstreaming gender throughout security analysis and planning. This can result in overlooking the ways that women's insecurity relates to gender power relations in society, as well as to the broader dynamics of fragility. For example, in Sudan domestic violence trends were linked to DDR processes and changing gender relations following conflict, but donor approache to domestic violence have not acknowledged this link (Domingo et al., 2011). Likewise, high levels of gender-based violence in Guatemala and Mexico are connected to broader patterns of fragility, including political and social exclusion, weak rule of law and widespread drug and gang crime. The response to this violence must therefore be situated within a holistic approach that addresses these multiple aspects of fragility.

The leading role taken by international actors in many SSR processes could offer an oppor-tunity to promote a gendered approach. However, awareness of gender issues remains limited within the male-dominated international security community. While progress is frequently made in strengthening security agencies' responsiveness to women, far more focus is required on transforming security institutions to allow women to enter decision-making roles. Increased atten-tion must also be given to the socioeconomic barriers that prevent women from accessing security services. Critically, international actors should integrate gender into security analyses and engage more with women's CSOs. This can improve their understanding of the relationship between women's insecurity and the broader context and their response to women's security needs.

Women's voice through civil society

Support to civil society is a central element of the international statebuilding agenda and international actors often provide significant support to women's CSOs. Ensuring that this suppor promotes a representative women's voice that can engage with broader statebuilding processes requires an understanding of the nature of women's civil society in fragile states and the impact external funding has on it.

Women frequently mobilize in unprecedented ways during conflict, to campaign for peac and for their interests to be included in post-conflict political settlements. In some contexts, suc as South Sudan, this can be the first time women have mobilized to make political demands. Women's civil society can also play a role in brokering peace, as the Mano River Women's Peace Network did in Liberia, Sierra Leone, and Guinea. However, women's activism often decreases substantially following the consolidation of peace. This appears to be both because the motivating factor of conflict has gone, and because women's activism becomes formalized into CSOs that compete for funds in the post-conflict aid environment. For example, although Kosovan women activists, politicians, and academics jointly lobbied to demand inclusion in negotiations on Kosovo's status, they no longer work together and their relationship is characterized by mistrust (Qosaj-Mustafa, 2010).

Cornwall and Goetz (2005) suggest that donor support for civil society creates 'new democratic spaces' in which women can pressure the policy process from outside formal political institutions. This seems to be particularly true in post-conflict contexts where there was previously little space for women's political activity. Castillejo (2011) describes how in Sierra Leone, South Sudan, and Burundi donor funding for civil society following conflict has provided women with resources, training, and networking opportunities and led to the development of a range of women's CSOs. Women's CSOs tend to play a variety of roles in fragile contexts including providing services; raising awareness on gender issues; mobilizing women to engage in political processes; representing women's interests in policy debates; and lobbying for political and institutional reform.

In some fragile contexts women can take on leadership roles within civil society without facing the hostility and obstruction found within formal politics. This is partly because civil society is a newer space with fewer links to traditional power and patronage relations, making women's participation less threatening. Civil society activism can therefore provide an important route for women to build up a political profile and enter formal politics without having to come up through political parties. For example in the Philippines, women's civil society alliances have provided a stepping stone for women to get elected and bring a feminist agenda to parliament (UNIFEM, 2008). The flourishing of post-conflict civil society as a space for women's political action often contrasts sharply with the exclusionary nature of formal politics.

A major challenge for international actors is that mainstream women's CSOs are often unrepresentative and dominated by elite women with little connection to grassroots communities. This is unsurprising, as in most fragile contexts only elite women have access to education and resources. However, in many cases more rooted, local-level women's organizations do also exist. These organizations tend to be less visible and attractive to international funders because of lack of connections, limited institutional capacity, and inability to speak 'donor language.' This situation can result in international support strengthening elite women's voice at the expense of other women's perspectives.

Issues of representativeness are particularly complicated when women's civil society is divided along the identity, ideological, and political cleavages that affect broader political society. This creates challenges for international actors in negotiating diverse women's agendas. For example, women's civil society activism in Nepal is largely based on community identity, with Dalit women mobilizing around caste discrimination, Madhesi women around language and customary practices, and Janajati women around access to services (El-Bushra et al., 2012). Through long-term engagement, donors have helped these diverse women's movements to build national-level advocacy coalitions. In contrast, donors in North Sudan have mostly not recognized the plurality of the women's movement and its relationship to wider ideological positions. Women's CSOs in North Sudan are divided into those with a secular pro-democracy agenda, those with an Islamic pro-democracy agenda, and those with a conservative Islamic agenda. However, international actors have mostly operated as though there were one unified women's voice and set of interest (Domingo et al., 2011).

International funding for civil society is undoubtedly vital in enabling women to mobilize and influence statebuilding in fragile contexts. However, the way that donors provide fundin can skew the priorities of women's activism, as informal women's networks become formal NGOs that respond to donor agendas. International actors are generally reluctant to provide core funding to women's CSOs, preferring to offer short–term project funding. This makes it difficul for CSOs to develop their organizational capacity or political agenda. Instead they develop projects that respond to donor priorities rather than constituents' interests and which are frequently both apolitical and unsustainable. Moreover, donors' preference for channeling funding through a handful of capital–based, English–speaking women's CSOs enables these CSOs to control the national women's civil society agenda.

International efforts to promote women's voice in statebuilding can be strengthened by greater engagement with the complexity of women's civil society. This involves listening to a range of women's perspectives and avoiding preconceived ideas of women's interests. It also requires combining support to elite women's CSOs with support to grassroots organizations that may not speak donors' language or share their agenda, but can genuinely represent local women. A priority for donors should be to link grassroots women's organizations into statebuilding debates and processes.

In order for women's civil society to flourish in fragile contexts, CSOs require sustained core funding that allows them to build political capacity and an independent political agenda and avoids diverting them into service delivery. Support is also required to strengthen alliances across different types of women stakeholders, including those alliances developed during conflict. Recognizing that civil society can provide an alternative route for women to enter formal politics, more emphasis is required on developing leadership skills and particularly political capacities among young non–elite women activists. In fragile contexts, where young people may have very different experiences and aspirations to current leaders, it is vital to develop a broader spectrum of future women leaders.

Informal power and customary institutions

The statebuilding literature acknowledges the importance of informal power in shaping political and social dynamics in fragile states. However, international actors rarely engage with the informal institutions and practices that are so central to both statebuilding processes and gender relations. This is unsurprising given their mandate, the sensitivity of work in informal arenas, and the limited entry points for such work. However, the result is to overlook the role of informal structures in mediating women's participation in statebuilding and limiting progress toward gender equality. Women's ability to act as citizens and engage with the state is particularly restricted by two different – but frequently related – types of non–formal power. These are the power of informal networks within formal institutions, and the power of customary institutions.

Formal political institutions in fragile states tend to be dominated by informal power relations and networks, with decision–making based on personal relationships rather than formal rules. Women are disadvantaged in multiple ways by such informality and patronage. First, women within formal institutions frequently find themselves excluded from the male networks and space where decisions are made. This prevents women from converting formal inclusion into actual influence. For example, in Kosovo and Burundi women politicians complain that important political decisions are made by small groups of male colleagues in bars (Castillejo, 2011). Second, women – and marginalized men – making claims on formal institutions are particularly disadvantaged when formal rules do not apply and patronage relations or informal payments are required to gain access or receive services. Third, informality poses a challenge for women's movements seeking to influence policy. For example, Tadros (2011) points out that in Jorda and Egypt, 'policy influence heavily relies on informal relationships rather than strictly forma citizen–state engagements.'

Building a state that is responsive to women requires engaging with the ways in which informality shapes formal institutions and the gendered impact of this. International support for institutional reform should go beyond formal structures and address practices of power within state institutions. This can include supporting women to highlight and challenge the informality they encounter within political, judicial, and administrative institutions. In addition, applying a gender lens to broader work on corruption, patronage, and accountability would be particularly valuable, as these governance challenges have specific implications for women

Customary institutions tend to be very powerful in fragile contexts and have particularly extensive control over women's lives. These institutions often play a central role in maintaining societal gender norms and have authority over issues of importance to women, such as personal status laws and access to community resources. In addition, they may be the only authority that women can access. Evidence suggests that many – although not all – customary institutions discriminate against women and maintain traditional patterns of social and economic exclusion (Economic Commission for Africa, 2007). This makes their substantial power problematic for an inclusive statebuilding agenda. However, it must be recognized that customary authorities can sometimes deliver outcomes that benefit women, such as rapid and accessible dispute resolution or customary leadership positions for senior local women.

Customary institutions can play a key role in mediating women's relationship to the state and participation in statebuilding processes. Customary leaders are often responsible for representing community interests in dialogue with formal state actors or international donors. Given the patriarchal nature of most customary institutions, this can result in women's interests being inadequately represented and their needs remaining unmet. Customary institutions can also be critical in facilitating or blocking women's access to state institutions and services. For example, in Liberia and Sierra Leone some customary authorities prevent women from seeking justice through formal courts, while in Afghanistan and Pakistan religious authorities sometimes prevent women from accessing education and health services.

The international statebuilding literature suggests that support for hybrid orders that combine formal and customary structures can enhance stability and state legitimacy in fragile contexts. However, such an approach can also formalize and further entrench the exclusion of women and other marginalized groups. While it is important that international actors engage more with customary authorities, this engagement must acknowledge the gender implications of customary power and seek to promote women's rights. There are some interesting examples of internationally supported initiatives to promote gender-sensitive reform of customary institutions, such as work with traditional leaders in Kenya to establish new customary land rights for women (Chopra, 2007).

There are often complex linkages between formal and customary power in fragile settings. Customary structures frequently dominate formal politics and can be the basis for informal patronage networks within formal institutions. In some fragile contexts customary institutions can determine who gets elected, in whose interests the law operates, and how state resources are allocated. This interdependency between formal and customary institutions has serious gender implications. It can result in the customary exclusion of women being carried into the formal sphere and in discriminatory customary institutions being strengthened through state support. International actors should therefore be cautious of any statebuilding processes that reinforce this customary–formal interdependence. For example, in Pakistan's Federally Administered Tribal Areas (FATA) the central state uses tribal leaders as an intermediary to maintain control over the population and represent state interests. This serves to reinforce these customary power structures, which are both highly discriminatory toward women and a source of deep local grievance (Vira and Cordesman, 2011).

Conclusion

It is clear that statebuilding can provide an opportunity to address deep-rooted gender inequalities within the state and in state–society relations. However, such change is often fiercely oppose by political and traditional elites, whose interests it can threaten. Evidence suggests that international actors are not taking full advantage of opportunities to promote gender equality within political, institutional, and social change processes in fragile states. While they frequently support a range of gender initiatives, these are mostly not linked to the broader statebuilding agenda, have a technical rather than political focus, and are discrete 'gender' projects rather than genuine mainstreaming.

The international statebuilding community needs to understand gender as a political issue. This involves asking how gender inequalities relate to the political settlement and broader patterns of power and resource allocation. It also involves examining how arguments about 'tradition' represent particular power interests and how gender inequalities relate to aspects of fragility such as violence, poverty, and corruption. Developing this understanding requires the adoption of a political economy approach to gender analysis, as well as greater integration of gender issues into existing political, conflict, security, and economic analyses. The development of gender awarenes across key statebuilding sectors – such as security – is critical.

It is vital that international actors champion women's interests with the most powerful actors and at the most critical moments in the statebuilding process, rather than making gender an 'add-on' after political deals are done. This involves proactively promoting women's participation in negotiations around the political settlement. The international community must also broaden and deepen its support for women's political participation. This requires addressing the multiple barriers women face to both access and influence within political institutions, as well as engagin more robustly with political parties. International work on gender in fragile contexts currently focuses heavily on institutional reforms, service delivery, and technical assistance. These are important, but their impact is limited if women cannot participate at the highest political levels or shape the policy agenda.

Economic, social, and cultural barriers emerge as a major factor preventing women from taking advantage of the new opportunities offered by statebuilding. These include barriers related to poverty, human capability, and social attitudes, as well as barriers related to the political culture in fragile states. International actors should therefore combine support for institutional reform with a focus on strengthening women's socioeconomic position and political capacities. A holistic approach to women's rights can highlight the ways in which women's lack of economic and social rights limits their access to civil and political rights in fragile contexts.

Sustained support for women's voice is critical if women are to inf uence the statebuilding agenda. Such support should foster broad coalitions across civil society, politics, and public institutions. It should also support these coalitions to develop their own policy agenda, to become effective political actors, and to engage with political and institutional change processes. This requires that international actors work with a much wider range of partners, including grassroots women's organizations. Donors also need to move beyond a model of technical support and project funding, to provide core funding and political capacity building in order to develop sustainable and politically effective women's organizations. Given the weakness of women's civil society in fragile settings, international actors must tread carefully to avoid dictating its agenda.

Perhaps the biggest challenge for the international statebuilding agenda is how to address the informality of power in fragile contexts. The promotion of inclusive statebuilding – and particularly women's inclusion – requires international actors to increase their work in this sensitive and difficult-to-access area. As a starting point the international statebuilding communit must enhance its understanding of how informal and customary power shape both statebuilding processes and gender inequalities in different fragile contexts. Ultimately, however, international actors need to take more risks in working with informal institutions, as well as provide greater support for women's political and civil society to engage with them.

Notes

1 There are some new initiatives under way to strengthen gender approaches within international statebuilding support, most notably by the OECD and DFID.
2 For example, all members of the G7+ group of conflict-affected countries included in the 2011 UND Gender Inequality Index rank extremely high, with the exception of Burundi.
3 In South Sudan women participated as fighters in the Sudan People's Liberation Army, while in Egypt women were active in the revolution that ousted the Mubarak regime. In both countries women were excluded from processes to draft the interim constitution that followed regime change.
4 Following the 2011 revolution Egyptian women were excluded from the committee to draft the interim constitution, parliamentary quotas for women were removed, and women participating in political protests are increasingly subjected to violent attacks.
5 In both Rwanda and Nepal post-conflict statebuilding involved a range of measures to promote gende equality, including economic empowerment, legal reform, and gender budgeting.
6 The 2005 National Interim Constitution states that 'The equal rights of men and women to the enjoyment of all civil and political rights and to all social, cultural and economic rights . . . will be ensured.'

References

Alamilla, I. and Quintana, M. (2010). *El fortalecimiento de la ciudadanía de las mujeres en el contexto de la construcción del estado*. Madrid, Spain: FRIDE.
Borchgrevink, K., Hernes, H., and Haavardsson, I. (2008). *Peacebuilding in Afghanistan: How to reach the women*. Oslo, Norway: International Peace Research Institute.
Castillejo, C. (2008). *Strengthening women's citizenship in the context of statebuilding: The experience of Sierra Leone*. Madrid, Spain: FRIDE.
Castillejo, C. (2011). *Building a state that works for women: Integrating gender into post-conflict state building*. Madrid, Spain: FRIDE.
Chopra, T. (2007). *Promoting women's rights by indigenous means: An innovative project in Kenya*. Washington, DC: World Bank.
Cornwall, A., and Goetz, A. M. (2005). Democratizing democracy: Feminist perspectives.*Democratization*, 12(5), 783–800.
Domingo, P., Elkarib, A., and Wild, L. (2011). *State-building and women's citizenship in conflict affected and fragile states: The case of Sudan (a focus on North Sudan)*. London: Overseas Development Institute.
Economic Commission for Africa. (2007).*Relevance of African traditional institutions of governance*. Addis Ababa, Ethiopia: Economic Commission for Africa.
El-Bushra,J., Lyytikäinen, M., and Schoofs, S. (2012).*Gender equality and statebuilding*. Draft Framing Paper for the OECD International Network on Conflict and Fragility, International Alert (unpublished)
Gahungu, G., and Kazoviyo, P. (2011).*The issue of inheritance for women in Burundi*. Madrid, Spain: FRIDE.
Goetz, A. M., and Musembi, C. N. (2008). *Voice and women's empowerment: Mapping a research agenda*. Brighton, UK: Pathways of Women's Empowerment.
Human Rights Watch. (2010). *Afghanistan: Unchecked violence threatens election*. Human Rights Watch Press Release, September 2010.
International Dialogue on Peacebuilding and Statebuilding. (2011).*A new deal for engagement in fragile states*. Accra, Ghana: International Dialogue on Peacebuilding and Statebuilding.

Kandiyoti, D. (2005). *The politics of gender and reconstruction in Afghanistan*. Geneva, Switzerland: UNRISD.

Kellow, T. (2010). *Women, elections and violence in West Africa: Assessing women's political participation in Liberia and Sierra Leone*. London, UK: International Alert.

Maley, M. (2004). *Enhancing women's participation in electoral processes in post-conflict countries*. New York, NY: United Nations.

McGhie, M. P., and Wamai, E. N. (2011). *Beyond the numbers: Women's participation in the Kenya National Dialogue and Reconciliation*. Geneva, Switzerland: Centre for Humanitarian Dialogue.

OECD. (2010). *Aid in support of gender equality in fragile and conflict-affected states*. Paris, France: OECD.

OECD. (2011). *Supporting statebuilding in situations of conflict and fragility: Policy guidance*. Paris, France: OECD.

Onslow, C., Schoofs, S., and Maguire, S. (2010). *Peacebuilding with a gender perspective: How the EU can make a difference*. Brussels, Belgium: Initiative for Peacebuilding.

Qosaj−Mustafa, A. (2010) *Strengthening women's citizenship in the context of statebuilding: Kosovo security sector and decentralization*. Madrid, Spain: FRIDE.

Schoofs, S., Nagarajan, C., and Abebe, L. (2010). *Implementing Resolution 1325 in Guinea, Liberia and Sierra Leone: Charting a way forward*. London, UK: International Alert.

Schoofs, S., and Smits, R. (2010). *Aiming high, reaching low: Four fundamentals for gender-responsive state-building*. The Hague, The Netherlands: Clingendael Conflict Research Unit

Tadros, M. (2011). *Working politically behind red lines: Structure and agency in a comparative study of women's coalitions in Egypt and Jordan*. Sydney, Australia: Developmental Leadership Program.

Tønnessen, L., and Kjøstvedt, H. G. (2010). *The politics of women's representation in Sudan: Debating women's rights in Islam from the elites to the grassroots*. Bergen, Norway: Chr. Michelsen Institute.

UNDP. (2011). *Gender inequality index*. New York, NY: UNDP.

UNIFEM. (2008). *Who answers to women? Gender and accountability*. New York, NY: UNIFEM.

UNIFEM. (2010). *Women's participation in peace negotiations: Connections between presence and influence*. New York, NY: UNIFEM.

United Nations Security Council Resolution 1325 on Women Peace and Security. (2000). New York, NY: UN Security Council.

Vira, V., and Cordesman, A. H. (2011). *Pakistan: Violence vs. stability: A national net assessment*. Washington, DC: Center for Strategic and International Studies.

Wild, L., and Foresti, M. (2010). *Support to political parties*. ODI Briefng Paper. London, UK: Overseas Development Institute.

World Bank, The. (2011). *World development report 2012: Gender equality and development*. Washington, DC: The World Bank.

4
ELITES AND STATEBUILDING

Jago Salmon and Catherine Anderson[1]

Since 1948 over 67 UN peace operations have been deployed to support post-conflict transitions. Bringing substantial resources to monitor military ceasefires and to address humanitarian needs these operations have increasingly also deployed resources to spur democratic governance and institutional development. The end of the Cold War triggered a dramatic expansion of these interventions as the balance of power has given way to an increasingly fragmented political world, and discredited models of economic and political government. In a few short decades, we have moved from a world of absolute sovereignty in which state intervention was intrusive [2] to one in which fragile and conflict-affected countries are themselves calling for improved international efforts to support statebuilding.[3] In the process, our understanding of statebuilding has changed.

Whether undertaken by member states in pursuit of their stated national interests, or more broadly justified 'to maintain international peace and security', intervention has always been avowedly political. At the same time, their legitimacy locally – like their economic equivalents of the structural adjustment era in the 1980s – has often rested on their technical persona. [4] Grounded in the work of Weber and Tilly, statebuilding has long been projected as a process that entails building three principal capacities – securing a monopoly on violence; mobilizing and managing revenues and resources; and providing public goods and services to the population. This model assumes, tacitly, that when placed side by side, rational bureaucratic forms of organizing power will command preceding systems and produce modern, capable states, that abide by international law and norms – even out of the rubble of war.

In practice, a growing body of fraught statebuilding experiences – Somalia, Kosovo, and Afghanistan – are causing the international community to question this model as successive interventions yield weak, not 'capable states,'[5] and peace agreements divvy-up the spoils of statehood, leaving an exclusive or predatory political settlement in place.

As the development community grapples to reconcile the basis for statebuilding's failure, and the 'capability approach' is increasingly questioned, the form and function of elite bargains is enjoying a resurgence of interest. Whether drawn from opposing sides of the battlefield, diaspora communities, ethnic and tribal fraternities, or political opposition parties, statebuilding and state transition are now widely seen to begin with some form of a political settlement, and to be heavily influenced by the ways in which elites act.

This chapter argues that giving prominence to elite settlements in statebuilding processes does not require an 'embrace [of] patronage politics – bribes and all' (de Waal, 2009) as the inevitable 'price of peace.' But, rather, the chapter acknowledges that institution-building is not a linear process; statebuilding processes produce winners and losers, and elites will invariably choose to buy into, oppose, or subvert the accumulation of capital, the means of violence and the projection of authority by the state. For statebuilding to work, it must account for the inexorable presence of elites and their interests; that it, statebuilding must be social constituted in a way that resonates with society experiences and expectations and socially negotiated conceptions of authority, fairness and equity in the evolution of institutional policies and practices. It further suggests that by enlarging the opportunity of elites to be part of and benefit from the state – by 'softening' th state – peacebuilding and statebuilding may be aligned.

Against this background, this chapter presents an initial overview of an evolving field, an aims to achieve three things. First it examines the new wave of statebuilding literature that is drawn from contemporary experience and focuses on the role of elites and the elite bargain in the transition process. Second, it applies this new wave of thinking to recent statebuilding experiences – in this instance those of Timor–Leste and South Sudan – to demonstrate the elite bargain at work; and finally, it begins to make the case for socially constituted development

Elites as 'state-makers'

In his seminal work of political sociology, Max Weber observed that as there 'is no conceivable end which some political association has not at some time pursued.' Yet, unlike other forms of organization, the modern nation–state is best defined by its ability to 'successfully uphold th claim to the monopoly of the legitimate use of physical force' (Weber, 1978: 54) over a specifi territory.

Taking Weber's definition often out of context, modern–day statebuilding has long been understood in functional terms. Although external interventions have never been blind to state politics, the internal mechanics of the statebuilding processes have largely been undervalued, as sovereignty is held up as necessary bedrocks of international peace and security. From the intervention of the United Nations Transitional Administration in Kosovo and East Timor in 1999 to the deployment of the United Nations Mission in South Sudan as recently as July 2011, statebuilding has been driven by the pursuit of rendering new states *capable* in key domains – securing a monopoly on violence, mobilizing and managing revenues and resources, and delivering public goods and services to the population.

In a deep reading of European history, Charles Tilly analyzed the origin of these capability functions, suggesting several important factors that are overlooked in practice today. The firs was that modern European states were formed not through a linear process of top–down creation but in part of the pursuit of wealth and power by 'coercive and self–seeking entrepreneurs' (Tilly, 1985: 169). Fueled by the need to meet the expanding costs of external wars, a long–lasting process of negotiation between state–makers and the emerging capitalist bourgeoisie 'created national states as a sort of by–product' (Tilly, 1990: 206). Second, elites saw their interests as best served by the centralizing core government functions and institutions, and did not seek the inverse; i.e. the disciplinary effects of government functions and institutions. In its most famous formulation, 'War made the state and the state made war' (Tilly 1975: 42).

Ultimately, contemporary statebuilding practice often assumes that the socio–political interaction that occurred to create states in modern Europe can be circumvented by external support and technical assistance.[6] Reconciling increasingly evident shortcomings in the existing 'capability' model has yielded several notable responses. One response has been that we need more of the same for longer, together with greater harmonization and alignment, better sequencing, and a commitment to avoid premature handover. Others emphasize soft norms of legitimacy, incentives, and authority – emphasizing that these are matters that require better understanding and management; while the still more radical approach has been to ramp up direct sovereign engagements or co-production (government-donor) of core government functions.

Within these debates, there has been a growing recognition that statebuilding processes are a source of intense contest, and that elite bargains lie at the heart of their success. This, in turn, is precipitating an impressive body of social and political science research as scholars and practitioners seek to better understand the ways in which elite interests interact and influence the state development process (Fritz and Menocal, 2007), and the reverse, the way in which external interests can influence and undermine the elite bargain – and generate further instability – in th pursuit of statebuilding. Di John and Putzel (2009) make the case that political settlements determine political and developmental outcomes. But more important, they suggest that elite bargains provide an explanatory framework for understanding trajectories of fragility and resilience, as well as how these relate to processes of development and poverty reduction.

In the section that follows, we examine the evolving literature on elite bargains and political settlements; then, applying what we learn, we examine two contemporary post-conflict transitions, Timor-Leste and South Sudan, to draw out the contours of the elite bargain at work.

The function of political settlements and elite bargains

As in any body of rigorous work, there are varying interpretations of what an elite bargain and political settlement actually are. In an early review of the literature for the UK Government's Department for International Development (DFID), Alan Whaites concluded that no singular formula for political settlements existed. At their core they consisted of 'common understanding, usually among elites, that their interests or beliefs are served by a particular way of organising political power' (Whaites, 2008).

In its simplest form, the term 'elites' in this instance, defines the parties at the negotiating tabl who must settle on a peace agreement and process. Whether crafted in mediated negotiations, constitutional deliberations, or the shadowy antechambers of power, elite agreements set the new rules of the game and 'write the history of the future' (Ghani and Lockhart, undated). In the words of UN special envoy to Syria, Lakhdar Brahimi, 'to build a state, there must be consensus on the type and shape of the state to be built and agreement between all parties as to the process that will be used' (2007: 7).[7] In this model statebuilding fows top-down. More recently, however, political settlements have been presented as spanning the continuum from negotiated peace agreements to long-term historical development, in the latter sense approaching the concept of a social contract (OECD, 2011: 9). An alternate view of the political settlement suggests that this interpretation downplays the f uid and adaptable bargaining that typically occurs among elites.

Khan (1995) suggests that the genuine political settlement is not made at the negotiation table but is established in the balance or distribution of power between contending social groups or social classes. By this account, peace agreements are discrete events, and mediation, collaboration or contests will continue to play out in key domains – e.g., security and coercion, the regulation of markets and capital, and around public appointments – well before and long after formal negotiations have ended.[8] This view cautions that rather than transforming state society relations, peace agreements can herald a redistribution of the spoils of statehood, while leaving an exclusive or predatory political settlement in place.

The recent works of North et al. (2007) further build on these ideas to examine the form and function of the elite bargain in fragile and transition contexts. In what they term 'limited access orders,' North et al. suggest that elites (or the political system) in fragile states manipulate the economy to create and distribute rents, favors, and opportunities as a means to maintain social and political order, to control inter-elite contests, and to pacify dissent to ensure stability.

This more nuanced view of elites and political settlements is leading to an expanding body of work which questions the relevance of the European experience to modern statebuilding. Also acknowledged is that, while the global order calls for states, external forces are today more significant and influential than they once were and actively disrupt elite incentives to centraliz and formalize power.

Several facets of this argument resonate. First, in post–conflict contexts, elites are legally anointed as state leaders often before de facto centralization of public authority has been achieved, and they 'receive their resources and legitimacy largely from without' reinforcing that authority before their legitimacy is why made out (Leander, 2004: 75). Second, that today control of capital is increasingly international, decentralized, and privatized and that statehood grants elites access to capital through credit, foreign direct investment (FDI), natural resource rents, and off–budget resources (i.e., drugs and weaponry) in a measure that vastly exceeds domestic tax revenues. And f nally, that instead of centralizing forces, the end of colonialism has yielded 'weakening, shrinking states,' and a dismantling and delegitimizing of formal administration. For all of these reasons, elites are incentivized to retain power; however, the historical incentives that existed for elites to centralize and consolidate effective administrative capacity to achieve wealth have altered, raising a new and unique set of challenges for statebuilders.

There is a good deal more, in both old and emerging literature, that contributes to our under standing of elite interests and patterns of behavior. This material variously highlights the salience of pre–existing regimes and contemporary elite coalitions as important, e.g., whether plural/competitive or coercive (Bratton and Van de Walle, 1994), together with the source of rents and revenues (Moore, 2004; Hesselbein, 2011). But our ambitions in this instance are modest – to highlight the influence of the elite bargain on transition success, and to explore the potentia contours of elite interests.

Applied to the recent transition experiences of Timor–Leste and South Sudan, we see both the shortcomings of the 'capable state' model and the function of elite bargains on the prospects for stability and sustainable development.

Elite bargains at work

Both Timor–Leste and South Sudan have experienced the full effects of the UN's 'liberal state' as a transition model, and both encountered severe social and political push–back – as elites acted to renegotiate what was seen to be an inequitable political bargain.

Foreign influence, particularly the unprecedented executive powers exercised under UN Transition Administration (UNTAET),[9] greatly inf uenced Timor–Leste's transition experience, and saw several def ning decisions and trade–offs made early on. The first Prime Minister, Mar Alkatiri, famously remarked,[10] 'we are between these two great expectations – that of the rich world that aids us and wants us to be diligent obedient boys and that of our people, living in extreme poverty waiting for results from the government to reap the benefts of independence.' But the political trade–off was sharper still than the social expectation of the population. Short–cuts to establish institutions, executive government, and a civil service were thought to have compromised the political settlement from the start. The then ruling party, Fretilin, dominated the legislative and executive branches of government and was reluctant to create space for open political participation. Popular participation in parliamentary appointment and constitutional negotiations was equally limited, and over the years, several factions (students, former veterans, opposition elites) expressed discontent through protests, demonstrations, and, in 2006, through violent social and political clashes that saw the ruling party removed from power (Chopra, 2000, 2002; Suhrke, 2001; Simonsen, 2006).

Within weeks of taking office in August 2007, the new government squared up to three sovereign credibility challenges[11] – to revitalise state administration, to act as primary source of economic and employment dividends, and to establish political legitimacy by showing that it could manage national wealth effectively and transparently, with high standards of discipline. By early 2012, and with the benefit of recently accumulated oil revenues, the government budget had increased t $1.7 billion (from $80 million in 2006) as the government took steps to renegotiate the local political settlement, ostensibly 'buying the peace,' and to correct the social and political 'short-circuiting' that had occurred in the previous years.[12] An immediate result was a sustained period of stability, though the record on the content and quality of spending, institutional performance, and standards of transparency and discipline varies widely and is overshadowed by a sharp upswing in allegations of corruption, and symptoms of the resource curse.

In a punctuated twist, what we see in Timor is that, whereas once external influences ha dictated a policy of economic austerity and the frst Timorese government assumed the unifying effect of the independence dividend, from 2006 onwards internal pressures (and extreme levels of poverty) and the threat of renewed instability drove social–political demands to renegotiate a political settlement and substantially scale-up spending. In part this reflects a healthy recalibratio of key institutional and policy arrangements to address needs that had gone unmet, and to galvanize a tenuous social and political compact. But, in some respects, the political settlement now emerging is less a renegotiation but rather a reproduction of durable features of the elite bargain that had existed prior to independence and involves social and political identity divisions and an internal political conflict that dates back to 1975. At the same time, the prospect of 'rentier state' and the corrosive path toward rent-seeking and institutional deterioration is becoming increasingly apparent.

After almost 25 years of regional, ethnic, and resource-based conflict in the Sudan, a Comprehensive Peace Agreement (CPA), signed in 2005 between the Sudan People's Liberation Army and the Government of Sudan, provided a roadmap for peace. On 9 January 2011 more than 99% of South Sudanese chose to secede from Sudan, and on 14 July the Republic of South Sudan joined the United Nations as its 193rd country.

During the six-year transition period from the signing of the CPA to independence, South Sudan achieved one of the fastest developments of public sector institutions in modern statehood. Thirty-sevenministries, 19 commissions, 10 state governments, a national parliament and 10 state legislatures were established. Rule-of-law institutions were created and the first steps i transforming the guerrilla army into a professional force were taken. Despite these achievements, South Sudan entered statehood with enormous challenges in the capacity of its institutions and its personnel, most of them the legacy of the long civil war. Nearly half of all civil servants have only a primary education.

It is rarely forgotten in South Sudan that this rapid development of state capacities took place in the shadow of the death of the political leader of the Sudan People's Liberation Movement, Dr John Garang de Mabior in 2005. Acknowledged as the leader of the revolutionary struggle, in fact the only leader the SPLM had known for 21 years, Garang had built few civilian structures or decision-making bodies. Replaced by two deputies, Salva Kiir Mayardit and Riek Machar, Garang's death allowed for the emergence of a new, more inclusive political settlement more appropriate to the challenges of state formation and political reconciliation.[13] Upon assumption of the presidency in 2005, Salva Kiir adopted a 'conciliatory posture, bringing warring Southern factions together in a fragile union premised on lowest common denominators' (International Crisis Group, 2011). Shortly after Garang's death, several reconciliation initiatives resulted in agreements between South Sudan's rival rebel factions, which had fragmented during the war; for example, the SPLM signed a deal with the South Sudan Defence Forces in 2006.

Despite a history of proxy wars and divisive politics, political groups and elites have remained cohesive in support of the SPLM—led government, which has championed a process of promoting political integration rather than tolerance for political opposition. The process of dialogue and political negotiation has been remarkable. Nevertheless it has not been sufficient to remove th risk of conflict, and the statebuilding process has revealed the extent of competition betwee elites at all levels of society.

Under the terms of the Comprehensive Peace Agreement, 70 per cent of the executive and legislative branches at both state and Government of Southern Sudan (GoSS) levels were put under SPLM control during the interim period. Elections in April 2010 introduced some degree of democratic activity, but were widely undermined by widespread irregularities. Allegations of fraud tainted final results in some areas and prompted standoffs, including in high—profile rac (International Crisis Group, 2011). A complex stew of political power, historical grievances, and competition over resources such as grazing land and water holes and tribal battles still exists.[4] In 2009, about 2,500 people were killed and about 400,000 displaced due to local conflicts an fighting. In 2010, 20 of the 79 counties had experienced some sort of violence including tribal battles, gang attacks, and others (Schomerus and Allen, 2010).

For several observers, this conflict was caused not only by the legacy of war, but by the pursui of a model of statebuilding based on reinforcing institutions. While GoSS made advances in establishing governing structures, adopting foundational legislation and initiating key reforms, these reforms reinforced the authority of a single party leading the powerful executive arm of government. Separate armed insurgencies led by Jonglei state gubernatorial candidate George Athor, South Sudan Legislative Assembly (SSLA) candidate Peter Gadet, David Yauyau from Jonglei's Pibor County, Gatluak Gai, who hoped to secure a county commissioner appointment in Unity State, and other Southern commanders all claimed to seek systemic changes to the Juba—based government or to overthrow it. The SPLA's at times indiscriminate attempts to crush the insurgencies have increased the deep—seated anger among many of the disenfranchised minority communities most affected by the violence (Small Arms Survey, 2011).

During South Sudan's preceding civil war when state institutions had failed, and in Timor—Leste's struggle for independence, social groups had turned to today's ruling elite for protection, and in return these leaders were to become the new leaders of state, coexisting with preceding organizations, often sharing resources but rarely ceding power. The leadership were almost all military, or linked by family or personal ties to the military, and many benefited enormousl from these connections. In South Sudan, competition over position or dispensations from the emergent state as the sole source of revenue and authority took the form of zero—sum games between those seeking to gain access and those rejecting state authority (Schomerus and Allen, 2010). The result was a state that was simultaneously unaccountable and frequently violent.

The elites in this context were a combination of political and military leaders who emerged from decades of struggle. These were men (certainly not women!) who wore pistols to meetings, and in the frst years of statehood struggled with the dilemmas of statebuilding, while often lacking access to even basic legal, administrative, and fnancial skills. While war, as defned by Tilly, was supposed to have encouraged centralization and a penetration of the state into society, in the case of South Sudan it had also decimated social structures, and fueled a proliferation of armed groups loosely affiliated with the central opposition movement

Recognizing the importance of elite settlements to stabilize the environment, largely as they remained unable to monopolize the use of force, in both Timor and South Sudan the governing class ultimately adopted a 'big tent' approach to politics, bringing potential opponents into the party and using political accommodation to address security threats (Dawkins and Gaere, 2012). In comparison to the exclusive/centripetal state structures that dominated Timorese and South

Sudanese territory before or – in the case of Timor–Leste – immediately after independence, the durable and underlying elite settlements that re–emerged demanded distributory reforms from the new Timorese and Southern Sudanese states. In the case of South Sudan, where the primary purpose was to legitimate the new ruling parties and ensure sustained peace, the ripple effect of the 'big tent' approach opened up the reins of governance to historically marginalized groups or in the case of Timor–Leste, to those more vulnerable, including the elderly and infirm. Not t be confused with liberal democracy, this was managed inclusion, as easily removed following perceived transgression as granted in return for loyalty.

In the cases of both Timor and South Sudan, elite settlements were driven by the need to include potential opponents and reward supporters, or 'buy the peace,' fueling a proliferation of ministries, para–statal organs and, in the case of South Sudan, extra–budgetary expenditure. In each case, state payrolls have rapidly expanded, and expenditures have increased through cash transfers and government contracts, granted through short–cut procedures and limited fiscal discipline. The absence of viable private sector economies in both South Sudan and East Timor have seen the state, its public assets, access to credit and aid become the primary source of economic opportunity.

In an unconscious reversal of Tilly's logic, in both Timor–Leste and South Sudan, elite bargains resulted not in the state centralizing resources, but in state elites agreeing to extract vast resources from state institutions and distribute these into private hands. In 2012, the president of South Sudan, Salva Kiir, stated in a letter to his government that at least $4 billion had gone missing over the previous five years, with later statements confirming that the primary culprits were under–secretaries, commissioners, and the SPLA.

Socially constituted development

South Sudan and Timor–Leste well reflect the incontrovertible fact that the durability of elit pacts are the underlying determinants of success in bringing about stability and preventing the renewal of conflict. The experience of Timor–Leste in the early years also speaks to the risks o ongoing fragility where a political settlement is exclusionary or seen to be privileging certain groups and interests.

We essentially draw two conclusions here. First is the need for development approaches in the aftermath of conflict to be based on a full understanding of the elite bargains and politica settlements that underlie the transition context. Recognizing that peace agreements are only part of the peace puzzle, statebuilding must not only respect and initially reflect the political settlemen but equally ensure that interventions reinforce stability in the long term. Without avenues to revisit entrenched networks of power and organizational systems, peace agreements themselves can become barriers to viable statehood rather than contribute to peaceful transitions. To avoid this, statebuilding interventions need to do more than reinforce functional capacities, and should acknowledge the need to reorient political power away from predatory exclusive groups.

Second, for statebuilding interventions to support sustainable peace, interventions need to not only rely on broadening the political settlement, as a means to alter the underlying terms of the elite bargain, but also to ensure that transition processes and institutional development are socially constituted, and consecrated on a durable social contract (United Nations Development Programme, 2012). Elites and peace settlements are hostages to a complex process, and must negotiate not only with each other, but with various constituents (e.g. social, ethnic, regional) over resources and power. Elite bargains struck in the public gaze are only part of the story and are themselves disputed and renegotiated in multiple loci and arenas. States are formed less by the fiat of elite groups or by legal process than by a layering of agreements, and a process of 'political sedimentation.' Even the grandest elite designs are contested and subverted, while populations contest and replace elites when challenged (Scott, 1998). It is the job of the international community to support nonviolent contests in ways that are socially durable and legitimate.

That development should be informed by social priorities is of course nothing new. But, by socially constituting the state, we do not suggest that successful transitions are those that are socially connected in conventional terms, i.e., through consultative, participatory processes, good governance, transparency, and accountability – although these factors are surely important. Rather, socially constituted development implies that the development community acknowledges and reflects legitimate and durable local social orders to ensure that authority is established, decisions are made, and accountability is enabled in a way that citizens understand, can accept, and safely contest. Not all social orders are equitable and legitimate, and in many cases there will be a need to avoid the excesses of local social or political practice or to evolve and adapt practices that already exist. At its most basic this requires that a state engage with those aspects of political organization most relevant to a society, respect its local economies and livelihoods, and relect socially negotiated concepts of authority, fairness and equity. The ambition over time may be transformative, that is, to evolve and adapt institutions into still more participatory, democratic models. But, in the f rst instance, development and statebuilding must explore, work with, and in some cases adopt, socially negotiated ideas and practices to build viable peace.

A state is socially constituted when society's or communities' experiences and expectations are reflected in the evolution of institutional policies and practices, and where social, political, and economic policies, in some measure, respond to socially articulated priorities. This is perhaps best highlighted by examples from the Ministry of Health and the Ministry of Social Solidarity (MSS) in Timor–Leste, where institutional development is, in many respects, seen to be a success. There is much nuance in these cases, but that the Ministry of Health was built from the ground up, that its institutional protocols and procedures were formed around the recorded practices and experience of local clinicians, and that the MSS adopted conflict resolution practices long used b local chiefs and communities to reintegrate IDPs are important lessons for effective development practice.

To conclude, we need to accept that in post–confict transitions elites will dominate or rule, and that the normative standards through which the international community bestows legitimacy on the state often stand in contrast to the norms and rules of elite pacts and their expectant constituencies. This highlights the importance of moving beyond simply focusing on building capacity and providing technical services to the state, and calls us to look more seriously at the state's social and political foundations, the implicit norms and rules that have previously enabled them to maintain stability and function, or those attributes that have caused the state to pull asunder. It requires integrating statebuilding and peacebuilding in developing institutions, rather than assuming that one is subsequent to or contingent on the other.

In many ways, this refection brings statebuilding thinking full circle. Max Weber highlighted that for power to move beyond a raw state, it must be institutionalized. In order to do so it must be viewed as legitimate, at least in part, by those who implement elite orders. Allowing then for the importance of elite settlements, while at the same time working to build socially constituted institutional structures and orders, requires that we move beyond building institutions to recognizing internal sources of legitimacy, which can enable both elites and the wider citizenry to grasp, govern, and participate in their own evolving societies.

Notes

1 The views expressed in this chapter are those of the authors and do not necessarily reflect the positio or policy of any organization. Many thanks to Doug Porter, Alison Hayes, and Tim Sisk for providing comments on previous drafts of this chapter.
2 Ironically, this view was perhaps most forcibly put by then Governor George W. Bush, in the October 2000 US Presidential debates, when rejecting the previous administration's intervention in Haiti. See www.pbs.org/newshour/bb/politics/july−dec00/for−policy_10−12.html
3 New Deal for Engagement with Fragile States, Fourth High−Level Forum on Aid Effectiveness, Busan, Korea, November 2012.
4 'Political' refers here to the fact that the decision on whether or not to intervene rests with individual member states, acting either collectively or bilaterally.
5 A rule−of−thumb estimate emerging from Collier et al.'s (2003) research is that approximately half of countries emerging from civil war return to violent conflict within five year
6 There is, of course, more to contemporary interpretations of statebuilding. The OECD−DAC, G7+, and development partners − DFID, World Bank, and UN agencies − add important nuances that variously emphasize the importance of institutions (WDR, 2011) and the soft norms of legitimacy, resilience, and responsiveness (OECD, 2011).
7 Recognizing that peace agreements are, nonetheless, only part of this puzzle, Brahimi (2007: 7) argued that by gaining elite buy−in 'through the patient development of a joint vision for the country's future' it is possible to develop buy−in for more justice, more equality, and increasingly better opportunities for upward social mobility.
8 Recent empirical work prepared as part of a suite of background papers for the World Bank World Development Report 2011, on Conflict Security and Development, drew a similar conclusion, an noted that power was vastly more important than institutions in determining outcomes in the immediate aftermath of conflict. Citing Rwanda and Mozambique, it also pointed to security and economy, an the opportunity to recruit loyal supporters into government as domains around which elite interests converged in their case study countries.
9 International agreements provided the UN Transition Administration of East Timor (UNTAET) with unprecedented executive powers of sovereignty, including control over national security and justice, all aspects of national and sub−national administration, and social recovery.
10 Mari Alkatiri, Remarks at Opening Session, Timor−Leste and Development Partners Meeting, 18 May 2004.
11 It would immediately revitalize *state administration*, to enable quick and visible conversion of petroleum wealth into services and direct benefits for its expectant citizens; it would become the prime mover o *economic activity*, to create employment opportunities; and it would establish its *political legitimacy*, by showing that it could manage national wealth effectively and transparently, with high standards of discipline and public accountability.
12 Government of Timor−Leste, IV Constitutional Government Program, 2007–2012, Presidency of the Ministers' Off ce, Democratic Republic of East−Timor (2007); Democratic Republic of Timor−Leste, Speech by His Excellency The Prime Minister, Kay Rala Xanana Gusmao, at the presentation of the bill on the State General Budget for 2008, National Parliament, 18 December 2007; and reiterated in National Priorities 2008, announced to TLDPM March 2008. National priorities were announced as follows: (i) public safety and security, (ii) social protection and solidarity, (iii) addressing the needs of youth, (iv) employment and income generation, (v) improving social service delivery, (vi) clean and effective government.
13 Both Salva Kiir and Riek Machar had publicly disagreed with John Garang's leadership style. In November–December 2004, shortly before the signing of the CPA, Salva Kiir had a high−profe clash with Garang over the lack of transparency and consultation in decision−making. Riek's role was even more controversial. He split from Garang and the SPLM in 1991, only to return after a high−profil reconciliation in 2001. Cf. International Crisis Group (2005).
14 'A multitude of issues feed into this conflict including population pressures, displacement, access to water, changing political loyalties, and a history of warlordism. Compounding these tensions is a lack of local authority resulting from the legacy of the conflict, a changing environment, a lack of infrastructure and a lack of broader political participation in the state−building endeavor. The complexity and intersection of issues above demonstrates that classifying conflicts as instances of tribal or ethni violence may produce an oversimplified understanding and obscure issues that require deeper consideration' (Schomerus and Allen, 2010: 24).

References

Brahimi, L. (2007). *State building in crisis and post-conflict countries.* Global Forum on Reinventing Government, 26–29 June 2007, Vienna, Austria.

Bratton, M., and Van de Walle, N. (1994). Neopatrimonial regimes and political transitions in Africa.*World Politics, 46*(4), 453–489.

Chopra, J. (2000). The UN's kingdom in East Timor. *Survival, 42*(3), 27–39.

Chopra, J. (2002). Building state failure in East Timor. *Development and Change, 33*(5), 979–1000.

Collier, P., Elliot, L., Hegre, H., Hoeffler, A., Reynal-Querol, M., and Sambanis, N. (2003).*Breaking the conflict trap: Civil war and development policy.* Washington, DC and New York, NY: The World Bank and Oxford University Press.

Dawkins, S., and Gaere, L. (2012). *Building the house of governance: Political accommodation in South Sudan.* Cambridge, MA: Conflict Dynamics International

De Waal, A. (2009). The price of peace. *Prospect*, November.

Di John, J., and Putzel, J. (2009).*Political settlements.* Governance and Social Development Resource Centre. Available at: www.gsdrc.org/go/emerging-issues

Fritz, V., and Menocal, A. R. (2007).*Understanding state-building from a political economy perspective: An analytical and conceptual paper on processes, embedded tensions and lessons for international engagement.* London, UK: Overseas Development Institute.

Ghani, A., and Clare, C. (undated). *Writing the history of the future: Securing stability through peace agreements.* Washington, DC: Institute for State Effectiveness.

Hesselbein, G. (2011). *Patterns of resource mobilisation and the underlying elite bargain: Drivers of state stability or state fragility.* Working Paper 88 (series 2), Crisis States Programme. London, UK: London School of Economics.

International Crisis Group. (2005). *Garang's death: Implications for peace in Sudan.* Crisis Group Africa Briefin No. 30, 9 August 2005.

International Crisis Group. (2011). *Politics and transition in the new South Sudan.* Africa Report No. 172, 4 April 2011.

Khan, Mushtaq. (1995). State failure in weak states: a critique of new institutionalist explanations. In J. Harris, J. Hunter and C. Lewis (Eds.), *The New Institutional Economics and Third World Development.* London: Routledge.

Leander, A. (2004) Wars and the un-making of states: Taking Tilly seriously in the contemporary world. In S. Guzzini and D. Jung (Eds.), *Conceptual innovations and contemporary security analysis.* London, UK: Routledge.

Moore, M. (2004). Revenues, state formation, and the quality of governance in developing countries. *International Political Science Review, 25*, 297–319.

North, D. C., Wallis, J. J., Webb, S. B., and Weingast, B. R. (2007). *Limited access orders in the Developing World: A new approach to the problems of development.* Policy Research Working Paper Series No. 4359. Washington, DC: The World Bank.

OECD. (2011). *Supporting statebuilding in situations of conflict and fragility: Policy Guidance.* Paris, France: OECD.

Schomerus, M.. and Allen, T. (2010). *Southern Sudan at odds with itself: Dynamics of conflict and predicaments of peace.* London, UK: LSE Development Studies Institute.

Scott, J. (1998). *Seeing like a state: How certain schemes to improve the human condition have failed.* New Haven, CT: Yale University Press.

Simonsen, S. (2006). The authoritarian temptation in East Timor: Nation-building and the need for inclusive governance. *Asian Survey, 46*(4), 575–596.

Small Arms Survey. (2011). *Fighting for spoils: Armed insurgencies in Greater Upper Nile.* Human Security Baseline Assessment, November 2011.

Suhrke, A. (2001). Peacekeepers as nation-builders: Dilemmas of the UN in East Timor. *International Peacekeeping, 8*(4), 1–20.

Tilly, C. (1975). *The formation of national states in Western Europe.* Princeton, NJ: Princeton University Press.

Tilly, C. (1985). War making and state making as organized crime. In P. Evans, D. Rueschemeyer, and T. Skocpol (Eds.), *Bringing the state back in.* Cambridge, UK: Cambridge University Press.

Tilly, C. (1990). *Coercion, Capital, and European States, AD 990–1990.* Oxford: Basil Blackwell.

United Nations Development Programme. (2012). *Governance for peace: Securing the social contract.* New York, NY: UNDP.

Weber, M. (1978). *Economy and society* (G. Roth and C. Wittich, Eds.). Berkeley, CA: University of California Press.

Whaites, A. (2008). *States in development: Understanding state-building.* DFID Working Paper. London, UK: DFID.

World Development Report (WDR). (2011). Washington DC: The World Bank. Available at econ.worldbank.org

5
REGULATORY STATEBUILDING AND THE TRANSFORMATION OF THE STATE

Shahar Hameiri

Despite the voluminous literature that has developed over the past decade to analyze, evaluate, and criticize statebuilding interventions (SBIs) in so-called fragile or failing states, the phenomenon – as well as its origins, drivers, and implications – remains for the most part poorly understood. Critical and policy-oriented scholars alike have tended to accept that these interventions are, or should be, about establishing a functioning and legitimate state of either the Weberian or neoliberal variant – an objective summarized by Fukuyama (2005) as 'getting to Denmark.' The main points of disagreement have therefore been over what kind of ideal–typical state should be preferred; whether SBIs are at all capable of helping the creation of such a state; and, if yes, how these interventions should be designed and implemented to attain this objective.

The centrality of the 'getting to Denmark' *problematique* forms part of a deeper malaise afflictin the statebuilding literature. It is perhaps surprising, even perplexing, that statebuilding scholars have shown very little interest in understanding the 'state,' despite its apparent place at the center of their research agenda. They have typically – and often implicitly – chosen to adopt ahistorical and static institutional, legal, and procedural conceptions of statehood, which are then used to benchmark the performance of real states. For example, after briefly mentioning studies that ref ect on the historical origins of postcolonial states, Robert Rotberg (2004: 28) claims:

> The remainder of this book takes the nation–state, whether appropriately or inappropriately so designated, as a given. Whatever their origins ontologically, states are the constituted repositories of power and authority within borders. They are the performers and suppliers of political goods recognized, strong or weak, by the international system.

This approach not only reifies problematic dichotomies between internal–external, state–society formal–informal, and public–private, but also masks the highly conflict-ridden and violent processes through which all states have been constituted, as well as the historical context in which commonly held perceptions of statehood and sovereignty have developed. It wrongly views the prototypical 'modern' state, to which particular, deficient, 'fragile' states are unfavorably compared, as the end–point of a now–concluded process, foreclosing the possibility that states – intervening and intervened – have in fact never stopped changing.

This is not just academic hair–splitting; the view of the state as a conceptually fixed entity a collection of institutions and actors governing a particular territory – carries serious consequences for the kind of research conducted and its analytical value. It has resulted in a field fundamentall preoccupied with observing what is *not* happening through SBIs, instead of seeking to explain these interventions and their effects in their own terms. All that many scholars of statebuilding end up doing is specifying the gap, as measured by a set of abstracted 'capacities,' between the intervened state they examine and an ideal–typical state that has in fact never existed. The analytical and practical value of such works is thus questionable. This is perhaps not surprising, as 'state failure' – the problem that SBIs are called upon to fix – is also similarly conceptualize in terms of what the states examined are not (Hameiri, 2007).

In contrast to these perspectives, the regulatory approach I advance here, and which I earlier laid out in detail in *Regulating Statehood* (Hameiri, 2010), seeks to explicitly interrogate what form of political rule is constituted by SBIs, without presupposing particular forms and capacities for the state. I examine the effects of SBIs not on some disembodied, normatively conceived, notion of state capacity, but on the distribution, production, and reproduction of political power in the intervened states, as well as in the intervening states. Rather than seeing the state as an 'empty vessel' amalgam of institutions and actors, I start from the premise that the state is fundamentally a site of social and political struggle and an expression of power. State institutions exist, of course, but the particular form that these institutions take and the way in which they privilege or marginalize particular interests in society is shaped by broader societal confcts, grounded mainly in the political economy (Poulantzas, 1978; Jessop, 1990).

Using this theoretical lens, I proceed to argue that SBIs represent a new mode of governance in the global political economy that is transforming the nature of statehood in both intervened and intervening states, leading to the emergence of a new kind of transnationalizing and transnationally regulated state. This complex and contested form of statehood does not find adequate expression within the International Relations and International Law perspectives that dominate the study of SBIs, but understanding its nature and the kinds of conflicts associate with its development is crucial for any meaningful analysis of SBIs and their outcomes.

That SBIs constitute attempts at state transformation is explained by their origination as a form of risk management in a world that is seen to be increasingly interconnected. Driven by the growing concern, within the world's major governments and international organizations, with managing the perceived risk posed to populations in the world's richer states and to global stability in general – by the growing interconnectedness between events in zones of poor governance and elsewhere – SBIs are intended to manage this risk by reshaping domestic governance environments in the countries from which risks are seen to originate, to secure particular political outcomes. But rather than ruling the intervened states directly, SBIs are aimed at achieving these outcomes by circumscribing the spectrum of political choices available to domestic leaders and populations in the intervened states. This is attempted by shifting important aspects of domestic policymaking into transnationalized or transnationally regulated spaces of governance opened within or near the domestic governance apparatus of these states and into the hands of actors – technocrats and experts – who are typically not popularly or politically accountable. I use the term 'transnational' here in preference to 'international' to emphasize that there is a wide range of state and non–state actors involved in SBIs and that these interventions encompass a range of scales exceeding, though not necessarily circumventing, the intergovernmental level. At the same time, the formal sovereignty of intervened states and their governments is rarely challenged. As a result, SBIs are typically found simultaneously inside and outside the state – they are regulatory and intergovernmental at the same time. Understanding the manner in which this 'multilevel' mode of governance functions and the kinds of conflict engendered through this kind of intervention is essential for understanding the effects of particular interventions.

Crucially, the kind of statehood generated through SBIs is not restricted to localized, isolated cases of lapsed governance in post–conflict 'failed' states in Africa, the Balkans, or the Pacif Islands region. The European Union's response to the debt crisis of member states, Greece and Italy in particular, manifests striking similarities with SBIs. In both instances, democratic politics is essentially viewed with suspicion as threatening to the attainment of desired political outcomes, and their marginalization through the empowerment of technocratic forms of rule is seen as essential for global stability. Indeed, contemporary SBIs – whether successful or not in achieving their stated objectives – are associated with the emergence of increasingly authoritarian, hierarchical, and anti–competitive forms of political rule within and between states.

Below I briefly explain why prevalent approaches are problematic, and then introduce m own regulatory approach to the study of statebuilding.

Institutionalism and the fetishization of state capacity

The study of SBIs has to date been dominated by approaches, both mainstream and critical, that primarily seek to evaluate the effects of these interventions on the capacity of the intervened states to perform the role of a modern state. This has in practice meant comparing the observed functionality of the governing institutions of these states to the particular variant of prototypical state favored by the observer, and the kind of capacities this state's institutions should possess. Indeed, the concept of state capacity has been at the core of the study of statebuilding, while the notion of capacity development has been at the heart of statebuilding practice. Although the effects of interventions on immediate issues, such as humanitarian crises or violent conf ict, have not been entirely ignored, both practitioners and scholars have tended to emphasize the significance of stron state capacity, and thus of capacity development by interveners, for the eventual emergence of peaceful, self–governing states – the ultimate stated aim of SBIs. Two main conceptions of state capacity have permeated the literature – neoliberal institutionalism and neo–Weberian institutionalism. While differing in their respective framing of state capacity in some important ways, both essentially denote normative preferences for a social and political order of a particular kind, rather than a way of explaining SBIs and their effects. Therefore, to the extent that such versions of capacity are seen to be missing in the states examined, before or after intervention, this tells us little more than that the social and political power relations that make such 'capacities' possible are lacking there (Hameiri, 2009). The debate between proponents of these differing views of state capacity over SBIs' effects has therefore been largely unproductive, because both neoliberal and neo–Weberian perspectives on the relationship between capacity development and statebuilding ultimately provide a *negative* explanation of the effects of statebuilding: rather than telling us what is occurring and why, they constantly focus on what is *not* occurring. While this does facilitate a normative debate over what form of statehood and sovereignty is most desirable and the role of international interventions within this vision, it does not explain the effects of interventions as such.

The emphasis on measuring the effects of SBIs on the capacity of intervened states has another unfortunate side–effect. It creates a dichotomy between external and domestic that is not only empirically problematic, but also leads to the under–theorization of the interventions themselves. This is because SBIs are essentially viewed as a delivery device for state capacity thus conceived. They are seen as little more than a grouping of 'outside' actors, organizations, agencies, and contractors, working with varying degrees of coordination and success 'inside' the territorial borders of another state, to 'build' its governing capacities. Important questions pertaining to the way in which SBIs transform these states, as well as their effects on the very nature of social and political struggles and the institutional and spatial arenas where these are played out, are thus completely elided.

Below, I briefly examine the core assumptions of the neoliberal and neo-Weberian institutionalist approaches to state capacity and their problematic lineages within debates on statebuilding. The two approaches have been distinguished for analytical purposes, but it is possible to find them conflated within the same policy document or the work of a single scholar. Th conflation is in fact another manifestation of the muddled thinking about the state that inheres in much of the literature.

Neoliberal institutionalism has been a particularly dominant approach to understanding state capacity within the actual practice of statebuilding because of its ideological hegemony among multilateral and Western bilateral development assistance organizations (Craig and Porter, 2006; Carroll, 2010). The approach has a history that predates the more recent concern with the security implications of 'poor' governance, dating back to earlier research in the 1990s by international development specialists on the links between development outcomes and 'good governance' institutional environments (see World Bank, 1997; Burnside and Dollar, 1997). The strong purchase of neoliberal institutionalism within statebuilding practice, which is directly related to its longer history within development orthodoxy and practice, could be evidenced by the very early shift in Iraq, following the 2003 'coalition of the willing' invasion, from anti-statist neoconservative rhetoric to the adoption of a neoliberal program of statebuilding by Paul Bremer's transitional administration (Dodge, 2009).

Neoliberal institutionalism, which has its intellectual origins in neoclassical economics and new institutional economics (see North, 1995), combines the overarching neoliberal normative preference for extending liberal market-based relations into ever-expanding spheres of social, economic, and political life, with an emphasis on creating and strengthening the capacity of institutions in state and society to provide conditions seen to be supportive of the effective functioning of liberal markets. It is this emphasis on institutions as preconditions for market-led development that marks the distinction between this approach and the structural adjustment-style, rapid marketization shocks associated with earlier humanitarian interventions in the 1990s (Paris, 2004). State capacity, from this perspective, combines the adequate public provision of institutions, such as property rights and rule of law, that are said to underpin market-led economic growth with the capacity to marginalize the influence of 'vested interests' in state and society who are seen to distort markets for personal benefit. The absence or weakness of such institutional structures is seen to make predation and conflict more likely (Collier, 2000). Because functioning liberal markets are viewed as an inherent public good, this approach renders contending ideological and political positions illegitimate and even dangerous.

In the field of statebuilding, neoliberal institutionalism is particularly expounded by practitioners and consultants, often working within or on behalf of major governments and international organizations. Because of the emphasis on the links between security and development, defined through neoliberal, technocratic notions of functioning statehood, proponents have tended to agree that SBIs have rarely met their objectives in practice, but that this has had more to do with poor implementation and insufficient resources devoted to defeating spoilers and vested interests than with the desirability and feasibility of these interventions' objectives as such (OECD, 2006; Brinkerhoff and Brinkerhoff, 2002; Morgan et al., 2005). More recently, there has been a discernible shift within this camp on the part of some development agencies, the UK Department for International Development (DFID) and the World Bank in particular (Leftwich, 2005; Parks and Cole, 2010; World Bank, 2008), toward the incorporation of political economy insights into capacity development approaches. Nevertheless, these donors are still basically wedded to the idea of market-led development as a public good, and view some actors' resistance to it as either illegitimate or amenable to financial compensation on the path to 'good governance' (Hughes and Hutchison, 2012). Thus, despite their apparent shift away from purely technical notions of state capacity, observers remain fixed on the extent to which these interventions hel intervened states attain levels of governance associated with the ideal–typical neoliberal state.

While neoliberals have adopted the concept of state capacity relatively late, for neo–Weberian scholars it has been important for some time. Originally, the notion of state capacity was used as a way of contesting pluralist and Marxist social and state theories, which, according to trailblazing neo–Weberianscholars such as Theda Skocpol (1985), paid insufficient attention to the state i its own right, seeing it merely as a reflection of society. Skocpol thus argues

> States conceived as organizations claiming control over territories and people may formulate and pursue goals that are not simply reflective of the demands or interests o social groups, classes, or society. This is what is usually meant by 'state autonomy' . . . Pursuing matters further, one may then explore the 'capacities' of states to implement off cial goals, especially over the actual or potential opposition of powerful social groups or in the face of recalcitrant economic circumstances.
>
> (Skocpol 1985: 9)

This 'horizontal' notion of state capacity – its capacity to control society – is similar in principle to the neoliberal perspective mentioned above. The main difference is that here state intervention in markets to shape economic outcomes is seen as legitimate and even desirable (Weiss, 1999).

But state capacity here also has a vertical component, comparing state capacity with a Weberian ideal–typical state providing coherent and rational governance. Well–functioning states are evaluated not only in terms of their capacities to enforce their will on society, through whatever means possible, but also through their capacity to provide legitimate governance and leadership. Because the neo–Weberian camp is more pluralistic than the neoliberal group mentioned above, there is some disagreement over what precise kind of functions states should perform adequately, although most agree that security is the main function all states should provide (see Milliken and Krause, 2003; Rotberg, 2004).

In terms of the literature on statebuilding specifically, scholars adopting a neo–Weberian perspective on state capacity have ranged from those, such as Rotberg (2004) and Zartman (2005), who are in favor of interventionism and view the construction of legitimate and well–functioning state institutions as mainly dependent on the political will of interveners, to critical scholars, such as Chandler (2006), Bickerton (2007), and Ottaway (2003), for whom interveners are inherently incapable of producing legitimate institutions. Others, such as Richmond (2009) and Boege et al. (2009), would like to see interveners assist states to approximate more traditional and hence supposedly more legitimate forms of governance. Here too, apart from the adoption of a problematic distinction between 'modern' and 'traditional,' or 'western' and 'indigenous,' the underlying concern with attaining a particular social and political order through improved state capacity remains in place. Thus, despite the apparent diversity, the overarching emphasis on evaluating state capacity, in terms of the effectiveness of authority structures and the state's capacity to assert itself within a particular territory over societal forces, means that the neo–Weberian approach also fails to provide an analytic lens through which to examine states, societies, and the effects of statebuilding on these. Rather, it embodies a normative preference for social order and stability of a particular kind.

We have therefore seen that the bulk of the statebuilding literature, whether policy–focused or critical, tends to approach the study of SBIs in terms of what these interventions are not achieving – a legitimate and well–functioning state of a particular, preferred kind – and seeks essentially to identify the gap between observed states and an ideal–typical one. The 'modern' state is viewed as a conceptually fixed entity and to the extent that changes in statehood are countenanced, this is typically done by critics of 'liberal peacebuilding' (for example, Richmond, 2009) to advocate more 'traditional' forms of governance, which are viewed as more suitable to non–Western, non–liberal societies (for a critique, see Chandler, 2010). The resulting research makes for an interesting normative debate over the most desirable form of statehood and governance, but does little to shed light on actual SBIs and their implications in terms of the distribution, production, and reproduction of power within and between states. It is toward this objective that I now turn my attention.

Multilevel regimes and the regulation of statehood

As indicated by the above critical review of the literature on statebuilding, what is required to overcome the current impasse of the debate over SBIs and their effects is an approach that from the outset seeks to historicize and problematize the state and that provides the requisite conceptual vocabulary and theoretical tools to make sense of the unique manner in which SBIs relate to the state and change it. By looking at SBIs not simply as a delivery device for state capacity, but as constituting a new form of political rule manifesting as a transformation of intervened states, we can finally rid ourselves of problematic presuppositions regarding what states *should* be like and focus on explaining what is actually happening and why.

As mentioned in the introduction, my approach draws on a particular branch of materialist state theory, mainly associated with the work of Poulantzas (1978) and Jessop (1990), in which the state is viewed as an expression of power. The particular form that state institutions assume and their functioning, in terms of privileging or marginalizing particular interests or forms of conflict, reflects the historically specific and contingent outcomes of struggles between dynam coalitions of interests, rooted primarily in the political economy – classes, class fractions, and other groups (Hewison et al., 1993: 4–5; Jayasuriya and Rodan, 2007). Crucially, the emergence of such interests is viewed here not as a direct derivative of rigid social structure determined by the nature of capitalist development, but as a product of particular historical processes through which group and class identity and agency are formed, also shaped by ideology, mobilization, and cooption (see Wood, 1995). Furthermore, the interests and coalitions that shape the use of state power in particular cases can, and often do, extend beyond these states' borders.

The notion of state transformation, from this perspective, refers to an institutionalized or routinized transformation in the manner in which political power is distributed, produced, and reproduced in particular states and societies. There are three dimensions to this transformation – shifts in the *location* of state power, meaning the institutions in which state power is exercised and the mechanisms through which it is exercised; shifts in the kinds of *actors* that exercise state power; and shifts in the *ideological* justif cation for the exercise of state power (Hameiri, 2009). SBIs constitute attempts to transform all three dimensions, but because social and political conficts relating to patterns of economic development are integral to every society and polity, state transformation is never a complete project, but rather a continuous process.

To understand how and why state transformation is attempted in the context of statebuilding, it is essential to relate the origination of these interventions to the emerging concern in the post–Cold War era and after 9/11 in particular with the potential security implications of poorly governed states, which previously were generally seen mainly as a development or humanitarian issue, not as a security problem. This shift was most clearly expressed in the September 2002 National Security Strategy (NSS) of the Bush administration in the US, which stated: 'America is now threatened less by conquering states than we are by failing ones' (White House, 2002: 1). This NSS paper and others that followed, as well as similar documents by the United Nations (High–LevelPanel on Threats, Challenges and Change, 2004) and the European Union (2003), to name but a few, reflected the incorporation of the risk management paradigm within the hear of the security agenda for the world's most powerful states and international organizations. What is novel about the securitization of state fragility is that these states are seen as threatening not in and of themselves, but due to the *potential* for other 'non−traditional' security problems – terrorism, crime, environmental degradation, irregular migration, and more – to emerge there and then spill over across borders to endanger societies far away. Because the security problems associated with state fragility tend to be conceived as potential, partly unknown, dangers – risks – the way in which this security problem is engaged is through the establishment of environments seen as less hospitable to the origination or proliferation of risk, what in the world of criminology has been called 'situational risk management' (Clapton, 2009). In turn, the specific way in whic 'risky' environments have been defined and evaluated, as well as the proposed solutions, has bee based on the kinds of neoliberal or neo−Weberian institutionalist conceptions of state capacity mentioned above, with the neoliberal variant being particularly dominant.

Crucially, managing the perceived risk of poor governance has not meant directly governing these so−called fragile states and their populations. It has rather involved a range of interventions within their bureaucratic and public policymaking apparatuses in particular, as a way of circumscribing the range of political choices available to leaders and people there. Hence, SBIs represent not a return to earlier forms of trusteeship or neo−colonialism (see Bain, 2003), as such, but an attempt to transform states from within, by changing the nature and functioning of strategic parts of their governing apparatuses, based on the idea that particular forms of governance would help minimize the risks associated with state fragility. More specifically, SBIs constitute attempt to transform the intervened states by shifting policymaking authority toward regulatory, non−majoritarian institutions (or spaces of governance) into the hands of managers and experts in specific areas, who are not usually politically or popularly accountable, and with the justificatio of providing 'good governance' for both economic development and social and political stability.

At the same time, the formal sovereignty of the intervened countries is rarely challenged, and even when it is temporarily usurped by international administrations, as in Iraq and East Timor, for example, this is only for a very short time, until authority is officially handed over to domesti governments. This is because, as already indicated, SBIs are fundamentally reluctant, defensive exercises aimed at managing the risks of state failure, but without assuming responsibility for governing unstable states and their populations (see Chandler, 2006), not a manifestation of liberal hubris and will to govern, as some critics suspect (see Duffield 2003; Richmond and Franks 2007). As a result, SBIs tend to have a dual existence, both within and outside the state. International organizations and intervening governments will often sign formal legal agreements with the governments of the intervened state to facilitate SBIs, but these agreements mainly aim to establish the broad parameters shaping interventions within the bureaucracy, demarcating the space within which independent regulatory authority is to be exercised by experts of various kinds. The task, then, is to both conceptualize this complex mode of governance and theorize its potential effects on the distribution, production, and reproduction of power within the intervened states.

The concept developed here to describe this complex existence is 'multilevel regime.' Following the insights of Pempel (1998) and Jayasuriya and Rosser (2006), it is important to highlight the value of viewing regimes as constellations of social and political forces, institutions and ideologies of public authority. The relationship between these components is understood here as a kind of pyramid, with social and political coalitions at the bottom, institutions in the middle, and ideas at the apex, meaning that institutions and ideas are fundamentally anchored in the social and political coalitions present (Jayasuriya and Rosser, 2006). Unlike the traditional notions of regime in comparative politics and International Relations, multilevel regimes are neither domestic nor international and not even transnational. This is because rather than seeking to circumvent or replace the governing institutions of the intervened states, SBIs are dependent on and inherently linked to these. Therefore, these regimes constitute mechanisms for state transformation, rather than a category that could be easily accommodated within existing, prevalent notions of national and international governance.

Multilevel SBI regimes have two unique characteristics. First, as already mentioned, they are associated with the establishment of coordinated transnational spaces of regulatory governance within or beside the governing apparatuses of intervened states. Second, they have a multilevel governance structure that is integral to regime rules and functions. But rather than manifesting the creation of levels of governance above or below the state, the entire multilevel structure is present simultaneously within the transnational spaces of governance being established. In other words, through these regimes state spaces are being substantively reconfigured. This notion o multilevel governance is premised on Hooghe and Marks' (2003) distinction between Type I and Type II multilevel governance. Type I is akin to a traditional notion of federalism, whereby territorial units of various sizes are contained within one another. Type II refers to flexible, task specific forms of governance, combining a range of actors, both governmental and non-governmental, at various scales. In Type II-style arrangements, the inter-scalar power relations tend to be less determined and heavily contested. This means that fundamental questions of political rule – who gets to govern what and how, and who gets to participate in decision-making and on what basis – are more open-ended and disputed than in Type I arrangements. Therefore, examining the relationship between various scales, in the context of specific governance arrangements, is a crucial part of analyzing how SBIs actually operate.

To see what this means in practice, we can look at the Australian-led Regional Assistance Mission to Solomon Islands (RAMSI). Since July 2003, RAMSI has been deployed in the small Pacific archipelago state of Solomon Islands with the explicit objective of restoring law and order and rebuilding the country's governance capacity. This intervention was negotiated between the Solomon Islands government and the Australian government, and is legally enabled through an intergovernmental regional agreement and through the annual ratification of the Facilitation o International Assistance Act by the Solomon Islands Parliament. RAMSI comprises three main pillars – law and justice, economic governance, and machinery of government. These pillars are coordinated through the Special Coordinator's offce, which is also responsible for coordinating the relationship between RAMSI, the Solomon Islands government, and the Pacific Islands Forum. In effect, however, the pillars operate independently within Solomon Islands, and are primarily responsive to the government department in Canberra with the most relevant expertise, such as the Australian Treasury, or the Attorney-General's Offce. RAMSI personnel are nearly all seconded to work within the Solomon Islands public service in key roles, or act as advisors to local counterparts, although in reality the distinction between the two roles is blurry. Furthermore, many of RAMSI's advisors are in fact employees of large companies, such as GRM, which specialize in identifying and recruiting specialists in particular areas of international development and capacity building.

Many of RAMSI's programs have been designed to support 'good governance' in the neoliberal mold in Solomon Islands, by attempting to quarantine important aspects of policymaking within strategic parts of the bureaucracy. For example, RAMSI personnel have established and populated many of the positions within the Economic Reform Unit (ERU) at the Solomon Islands Ministry of Finance and Treasury. The ERU has since 2003 played a key role in drafting the national budget, thus placing considerable pressure on the capacity of elected politicians to use public funds to support local-level patronage networks as they had done since independence.

The example above shows that it is not only the intervened states that are being transformed through SBIs. The internationalization of the Australian Treasury, for example, or of the Australian Federal Police (AFP), which has gone from a domestic law enforcement agency to a transnational police force, reflects a broader transformation in the nature of Australian statehoo and governance. Securing Australia no longer means simply protecting its borders from aggressors, but providing support for an adequate level of governance in Australia's neighboring countries, through a range of interventions within these countries' governing apparatuses in a variety of areas.

Nevertheless, although SBIs, in the form of multilevel regimes, attempt to transnationalize parts of the domestic governance apparatus of intervened states so as to limit the range of political choices available to people and leaders there, success is far from guaranteed. Intervention regimes tend to coexist and come into conflict with other regimes within the state, which have differen support bases and ideological underpinnings. Confict between regimes within the state tends to shape not only the nature of statehood, but also the regimes themselves. In other words, the apparent power imbalance between interveners and domestic actors does not mean that the former get their way. This is because of the dynamic nature of the social and political coalitions assembled within and around the spaces of intervention. It is also, however, because the necessity of maintaining the support of the governments of intervened states, which as mentioned earlier are usually still officially in charge, along with the overarching concern with managing the potential emergence and proliferation of risk, means that interveners often act pragmatically and scale down their objectives where serious resistance is met.

For example, in Solomon Islands, despite the strong neoliberal overtones of RAMSI's objectives, the highly contentious issue of land privatization has never been seriously countenanced. This is despite strong objections from right-wing commentators, who argued that land reform would be essential for market-led growth (Sodhi, 2008). Furthermore, although RAMSI's interventions within the bureaucracy have helped render the ransacking of the state's coffers much harder than before, the distribution of patronage remains essential for the attainment of political power. Many Solomon Islander politicians rely on formal and informal payments from foreign-owned logging companies, the biggest economic players in the country, as well as on Taiwanese foreign aid, to build support bases locally and political coalitions nationally. RAMSI has stabilized the security environment and has made foreign direct investment easier. Both of these objectives are good for the logging industry and have thus been supported by logging-backed politicians. Indeed, the highly unsustainable logging sector has gone through a massive boom period in the RAMSI years, until the onset of the global financial crisis, reaching a pea of 1.5 million cubic meters of timber exports in 2008, about double the peak of the previous logging boom of the 1990s and six times the estimated sustainable yield (Hameiri, 2012). Nonetheless, the current accommodation between the RAMSI-backed technocrats in the public service and the politicians that depend on logging rents for their political survival will surely be tested with the imminent exhaustion of commercial logging in Solomon Islands, currently estimated to occur by 2015.

Conclusion

Statebuilding has become one of the most important practices of our time in world politics. For the most part, however, it remains poorly understood. This is because the dominant approaches in the statebuilding literature, whether critical or policy-focused, tend to accept the premise that statebuilding should be understood and evaluated in terms of whether it leads to the emergence of an ideal-typical state, of either the neoliberal or neo-Weberian kind. As I have shown in the first section of this contribution, the two conceptions of state capacity, while far from identical, remain essentially normatively infused projections of preferred governance and statehood, rather than frameworks for explaining the effects of statebuilding in their own terms. Such approaches tend to tell us the extent to which SBIs are *not* leading to the emergence of an ideal–typical state of one kind or another, rather than what is actually happening through these interventions. Because of the reification of the ideal–typical, ahistorical 'state' to which intervened states ar compared, the interventions themselves also remain under-theorized, understood as little more than 'external' actors and organizations operating 'inside' other countries to build their governing capacities.

In contrast, the framework I have briefly outlined in the second part of the paper, and whic I have laid out in detail in *Regulating Statehood* (Hameiri, 2010), seeks to avoid presupposing the state, instead focusing on the manner in which SBIs transform the state, by seeking to shift governance to newly established, transnational or transnationally regulated spaces of governance within the intervened states, and into the hands of experts and managers who are typically not politically or popularly accountable. This process is justified through the association of 'poor governance, which is defined in relation to either neoliberal or neo-Weberian notions of 'good governance, with the emergence and potential proliferation of a range of non-traditional security risks within the borders of these states. I have offered the concept of 'multilevel regime' to refct the complex manner in which SBIs exist simultaneously inside and outside the state, linking socio-politicalcoalitions, institutions, and legitimating ideologies, as well as a variety of governance scales, within the spaces of governance being established. The particular political outcomes of SBIs, understood in this way, are far from determined and are shaped by ongoing struggles between different regimes within the state.

This framework allows us to see SBIs, not for what we would like them to be – vehicles for building 'effective' states – but for what they are – a novel and dynamic mode of governance within the global political economy, concerned with the reorganization of political rule both within and between states.

References

Bain, W. (2003). *Between anarchy and society: Trusteeship and the obligations of power*. Oxford, UK: Oxford University Press.

Bickerton, C. J. (2007). State-building: Exporting state failure. In C. J. Bickerton, P. Cunliffe, and A. Gourevitch (Eds.), *Politics without sovereignty*. London, UK: University College Press, pp. 93–111.

Boege, V., Brown, A., Clements, K., and Nolan, A. (2009). Building peace and political community in hybrid political orders. *International Peacekeeping*, 16(5), 599–615.

Brinkerhoff, D. W., and Brinkerhoff, J. M. (2002). Governance reforms and failed states: Challenges and Implications. *International Review of Administrative Sciences*, 68(4), 511–531.

Burnside, C., and Dollar, H. (1997). Aid, policies and growth. Policy Research Working Paper No. 1777. Washington, DC: The World Bank.

Carroll, T. (2010). *Delusions of development: The World Bank and the post-Washington consensus in Southeast Asia*. Basingstoke, UK: Palgrave Macmillan.

Chandler, D. (2006). *Empire in denial: The politics of state-building*. London, UK: Pluto Press.

Chandler, D. (2010). *International statebuilding: The rise of post-liberal governance*. London, UK: Routledge.

Clapton, W. (2009). Risk and hierarchy in international society. *Global Change, Peace and Security*, 21(1), 19–35.

Collier, P. (2000). *Economic causes of civil conflict and their implications for policy*. Washington, DC: The World Bank, June15.

Craig, D., and Porter, D. (2006). *Development beyond neoliberalism? Governance, poverty reduction and political economy*. London, UK: Routledge.

Dodge, T. (2009). Coming face to face with bloody reality: Liberal common sense and the ideological failure of the Bush Doctrine in Iraq. *International Politics*, 46(2), 253–275.

Duffield, M. (2003). Social reconstruction and the radicalization of development: Aid as a relation of global liberal governance. In J. Milliken (Ed.), *State failure, collapse and reconstruction*. Malden, MA: Blackwell, pp. 291–312.

European Union. (2003). *A secure Europe in a better world: European security strategy*. Paris, France: The European Union Institute for Security Studies, December.

Fukuyama, F. (2005). *State-building: Governance and world order in the twenty-first century*. London, UK: Profil Books.

Hameiri, S. (2007). Failed states or a failed paradigm? State capacity and the limits of institutionalism.*Journal of International Relations and Development*, 10(2), 122–149.

Hameiri, S. (2009). Capacity and its fallacies: International state building as state transformation.*Millennium: Journal of International Studies*, 38(1), 55–81.

Hameiri, S. (2010). *Regulating statehood: State building and the transformation of the global order*. Basingstoke, UK: Palgrave Macmillan.

Hameiri, S. (2012). Mitigating the risk to primitive accumulation: State–building and the logging boom in Solomon Islands. *Journal of Contemporary Asia*, 42(3), 406–425.

Hewison, K., Rodan, G., and Robison, R. (1993). Introduction: Changing forms of state power in Southeast Asia. In K. Hewison, R. Robison, and G. Rodan (Eds.), *Southeast Asia in the 1990s: Authoritarianism, democracy and capitalism*. Sydney, Australia: Allen and Unwin, pp. 2–8.

High–LevelPanel on Threats, Challenges and Change. (2004). *A more secure world: Our shared responsibility*. New York, NY: United Nations Department of Public Information.

Hooghe, L., and Marks, G. (2003). Unraveling the central state, but how? Types of multi–level governance. *American Political Science Review*, 97(2), 233–243.

Hughes, C., and Hutchison, J. (2012). Development effectiveness and the politics of commitment. *Third World Quarterly*, 33(1), pp. 17–36.

Jayasuriya, K., and Rodan, G. (2007). Beyond hybrid regimes: More participation, less contestation in Southeast Asia. *Democratization*, 14(5), 773–794.

Jayasuriya, K., and Rosser, A. (2006). Pathways from the crisis: Politics and reform in South–East Asia since 1997. In G. Rodan, K. Hewison, and R. Robison (Eds.),*The political economy of South-East Asia: Markets, power and contestation* (3rd ed.). Melbourne, Australia: Oxford University Press, pp. 258–282.

Jessop, B. (1990). *State theory: Putting the capitalist state in its place*. Cambridge, UK: Polity Press.

Leftwich, A. (2005). Politics in command: Development studies and the rediscovery of social science.*New Political Economy*, 10(4), 573–607.

Milliken, J., and Krause, K. (2003). State failure, state collapse and state reconstruction: Concepts, lessons and strategies. In J. Milliken (Ed.),*State failure, collapse and reconstruction*. Malden, MA: Blackwell, pp. 1–24.

Morgan, P., Land, T., and Baser, H. (2005).*Study on capacity, change and performance: Interim report*. Discussion Paper No. 59A, April. Maastricht, The Netherlands: European Centre for Development Policy Management.

North, D.. (1995). The new institutional economics and Third World development. In J. Harriss, J. Hunter, and C. M. Lewis (Eds.), *The new institutional economics and Third World development.*. London, UK: Routledge, pp. 17–26.

OECD. (2006). *Whole of government approaches to fragile states*. Paris, France: Organisation for Economic Co–operation and Development.

Ottaway, M. (2003). Rebuilding state institutions in collapsed states. In J. Milliken (Ed.)*State failure, collapse and reconstruction*. Malden, MA: Blackwell, pp. 245–266.

Paris, R. (2004). *At war's end: Building peace after civil conflict*. Cambridge, UK: Cambridge University Press.

Parks, T., and Cole, W. (2010).*Political settlements: Implications for policy and practice*. San Francisco, CA: The Asia Foundation.

Pempel, T. J. (1998). *Regime shift: Comparative dynamics of the Japanese political economy*. Ithaca, NY: Cornell University Press.

Poulantzas, N. (1978). *State, power, socialism*. London, UK: Verso.

Richmond, O. P. (2009). Beyond liberal peace? Responses to "backsliding". In E. Newman, R. Paris, and O. P. Richmond (Eds.), *New perspectives on liberal peacebuilding*. Tokyo, Japan: United Nations University Press, pp. 54–77.

Richmond, O. P., and Franks, J. (2007). Liberal hubris? Virtual peace in Cambodia.*Security Dialogue*, 38(1), 27–48.

Rotberg, R. I. (2004). The failure and collapse of nation–states: Breakdown, prevention and repair. In R. I. Rotberg (Ed.), *When states fail: Causes and consequences*. Princeton, NJ: Princeton University Press, pp. 1–45.

Skocpol, T. (1985). Bringing the state back in: Strategies of analysis in current research. In P. B. Evans, D. Rueschemeyer, and T. Skocpol, *Bringing the state back in*. Cambridge, UK: Cambridge University Press, pp. 3–37.

Sodhi, G. (2008). *Five out of ten: A performance report on the Regional Assistance Mission to the Solomon Islands*. Issue Analysis No. 92, January. Sydney, Australia: Centre for Independent Studies.

Weiss, L. (1999). *The myth of the powerless state*. Ithaca, NY: Cornell University Press.

White House. (2002). *National Security Strategy of the United States*. Washington DC: White House, September.

Wood, E. M. (1995). *Democracy against capitalism: Renewing historical materialism*. Cambridge, UK: Cambridge University Press.

World Bank, The. (1997). *World Development Report: The state in a changing world*. Washington, DC: World Bank Group.

World Bank, The. (2008). *Public sector reform: What works and why? An IEG evaluation of World Bank support*. Independent Evaluation Group. Washington, DC: World Bank.

Zartman, I. W. (2005). "Early" and "early late" prevention. In S. Chesterman, M. Ignatieff, and R. Thakur (Eds.), *Making states work: State failure and the crisis of governance*. Tokyo, Japan: United Nations University Press, pp. 273–295.

6
HIDING IN PLAIN SIGHT
The neglected dilemma of nationalism for statebuilding

Stephen J. Del Rosso

Reflecting on the state of the world after the end of the Cold War, the renowned political philosopher Isaiah Berlin observed that 'in our modern age, nationalism is not resurgent; it never died' (Berlin, quoted in Moynihan, 1993: 141). Defying the overly conf dent assumptions of Marx and Engels, and the latter–day predictions (or hopes) of a number of scholars and political commentators at the end of the 20th century (Breuilly, 1994; Guehenno, 1995; Hobsbawm, 1990; Ohmae, 1992–1993), nationalism has persisted as one of the most powerful, consequential and over–determined forces in contemporary world affairs. Even a cursory scan of today's newspaper headlines provides further evidence that, in its many forms, nationalism – although the term itself may not always be used – is an increasingly salient factor in global developments and the practice of domestic and foreign policy. Ethnic fissures in a host of 'fragile states' have raise questions about the continued viability of some multinational polities, while even in a more stable Europe, which has undergone a decades–long drive toward economic and political integration, nationalism's stubborn persistence remains a puzzle to some and a comfort to others. From a reassertive Russia and rising China, to a United States grappling with its relative decline, competition among various forms of 'state–led' nationalism is creating new tensions in an increasingly multi–polar world. Especially in the Middle East, but also in South Asia and, ever more so, in Africa, nationalism's complex interrelationship with religion has added yet another volatile dimension to the challenge. Perhaps most signifcant, as well as perplexing, has been the interplay between nationalism and the integrative, culturally homogenizing, technologically driven imperatives of a globalizing world, which upon close examination can both magnify and dampen its appeal. In sum, nationalism's effect on contemporary international and domestic politics is as inescapable as it is significant

It is therefore surprising that the subject of nationalism, with only rare exceptions (such as Laremont, 2005; Lemay–Hébert, 2009), has been given such scant scholarly attention where it would appear to have particular relevance – in the study of statebuilding. There is a lively and vibrant literature on nationalism, much of it featured at the annual convention of the Association for the Study of Nationalities and in its f agship publication, *Nationalities Papers*, and in the study of civil war and its termination, but this interest has not transferred to scholars focusing specifally on statebuilding.[1] This neglect seems especially evident as it relates, per OECD/DAC guidance on statebuilding, to the importance of 'building the legitimacy of the government in the eyes of the society' (cited in USAID, 2011: 2). Given nationalism's well–chronicled ability to bind together a society through a common identity, often based on ascriptive criteria, tapping into nationalist sentiment would seem to be a necessary step for gaining such legitimacy, even as modern manifestations of this sentiment play out in diverse and uneven ways. The recent, long overdue acknowledgment by international development agencies that statebuilding is 'an inherently endogenous process . . . driven by state–society relations' is of special relevance to nationalism, whose 'ability to affect outcomes' – arguably even more so than other aspects of this process – 'naturally rests with the host [country]' and the societal groups within it (cited in USAID, 2011: 2).

As part of a new wave of scholarly analysis on statebuilding, Roland Paris and Timothy Sisk describe the key contradictions underpinning this complex process and the dilemmas they imply for international actors engaged in post–war peace operations. Citing the well–recognized inadequacies of these operations during the past two decades and the 'muddling through' that has typically characterized their implementation, the authors call for a more nuanced and realistic recognition of the inherent nature of these contradictions and risks in addressing contemporary statebuilding challenges. Paris and Sisk's framework is a useful corrective to approaches to statebuilding that fail to adequately problematize the intrinsically vexing assumptions on which this process is based. Integrating recognition of these factors into policy and practice can, they argue, highlight the necessary tradeoffs among various externally driven strategies for rebuilding war–torn states while improving their prospects for success (Paris and Sisk, 2009).

Following Paris and Sisk, this chapter will posit nationalism as yet another dilemma for statebuilding that is also implicated, to varying degrees, in the dilemmas these authors describe. But, as suggested by Andrew Gilbert, dilemmas of statebuilding should be considered as subjects for interrogation, as starting points rather than end points for research (Gilbert 2010: 9). As such, the dilemma of nationalism examined below will be suggestive of a research agenda that warrants further elaboration. The central argument is that nationalism is playing an important role in statebuilding that goes largely unnoticed or unacknowledged. Its ability to 'hide in plain sight' – as reflected in its relatively rare invocation in contemporary scholarly analyses on statebuilding and even more infrequent citing in policy pronouncements and debates – has important implications for policy and practice. As suggested below, this lacuna can be attributed to nationalism's wavering and multiple meanings and its complex and insufficiently understood interaction with broader developments in the contemporary world.

In making this case, this analysis will refer selectively to some of the most noteworthy 'classical' texts in the large and diverse body of nationalism literature, as well as cases from the recent and more distant past, whose relevance may not always seem apparent to contemporary statebuilding challenges, but which still resonate in important, if insufficiently appreciated, ways. As Gilber further notes in commenting on Paris and Sisk's approach to statebuilding, 'you do not have to be a dialectical materialist to see that contradictions [and dilemmas] are a fact in all social (and political) formations, and that the friction they create and their management are a primary cause of motion, change and development in the world' (Gilbert 2010: 8–9). The same holds true for nationalism. Notwithstanding the terminological and conceptual confusion surrounding this historically freighted term, shining a light on nationalism's complicated role in statebuilding is a necessary (if also insufficient) step for managing the frictions caused by modern expressions of this particular – and particularly redolent – social and political formation.

Semantic and conceptual slippage

Commonly linked to the notion of popular sovereignty that animated the French Revolution and provoked a subsequent 'nationalist' reaction to Napoleon's expansion inflamed by the German Romantics, nationalism's origin and trajectory have long been a subject of scholarly inquiry. And yet, despite the depth and breadth of attention to this subject, it remains one of the most ambiguous concepts in the vocabulary of political and analytical thought, lacking both a single, universal theory (Hall, 1993: 1) and a canonical text (Anderson 1991: 5). From the focus of such scholars as Anthony Smith and Liah Greenfeld on its premodern origins, to the claims of Ernest Gellner, Karl Deutsch, and Eric Hobsbawm of its more recent emergence as a natural byproduct of industrialization, and its postmodernist dismissal by Rogers Brubaker as an 'empty, contingent signifier' constructed from a dense web of social interactions, nationalism continue to resist definitive explication (Brubaker, 1996; Deutsch, 1966; Gellner, 1983; Greenfeld, 1992 Hobsbawm, 1990; Smith, 1993). Among its many meanings, it has been invoked to describe the quest of a minority ethnic group for greater political control over its affairs through increased autonomy or, more commonly and problematically, in the form of a 'state of one's own,' as well as the continued exercise and expansion of 'national' power, both internally and externally, after statehood has been achieved. It is considered by some as an ideology that 'prioritizes the nation' combined with 'a strategic plan of action for putting [it] into practice' (Sutherland, 2012: 7), and by others as 'a set of "nation"–oriented idioms, practices, and possibilities that are commonly and continuously available or endemic in modern cultural and political life' (Brubaker, 1996: 7). While some have extolled nationalism's ability to 'manifest concern for fellow citizens . . . discourage cheating . . . and promote trust' (De Las Casas, 2008), Albert Einstein famously derided it as an 'infantile disease' (Einstein, 1929), and George Orwell assailed its 'habit of assuming that human beings can be classified like insects and . . . of identifying oneself with a single nation or other unit, placing it beyond good and evil and recognizing no other duty than that of advancing its interests' (Orwell, 1945).

At the heart of these contending interpretations of nationalism is the related lack of unanimity surrounding the root concept of 'nation,' derived from the Latin *natio* (to be born – which suggests, at least semantically, a congenital condition). In seeking to cut through the definitiona Gordian knot surrounding this term, Walker Connor, drawing on Max Weber, describes the nation as simply 'the largest grouping of people who believe they are ancestrally related,' and nationalism, in its most basic form, as 'identification and loyalty to' (Connor, 1995: 104) thi human collectivity. This subjective approach dispenses with the laundry list of contested nationhood criteria that runs the gamut from Ernest Renan's intangible 'spiritual community, endowed with a past and wish to uphold it through a "daily plebiscite"' (Renan, cited in Dahbour and Ishay, 1995: 153) to Joseph Stalin's more formulistic notion of 'a historically constituted, stable community of people formed on the basis of common language, territory, and economic life, and psychological makeup manifested in a common culture' (Stalin, cited in Dahbour and Ishay, 1995: 192). It also circumvents the recurrent epistemological debate among 'primordialists,' 'ethno–symbolists,' 'modernists,' 'constructivists,' and 'post–modernists' over the extent to which nations are predestined, 'imagined' (in Benedict Anderson's well–known formulation; Anderson, 1991), rationally chosen, or socially constructed.

But, notwithstanding the parsimony and ostensible clarity of Connor's approach, it also leaves many questions unanswered about the growth and trajectory of the nation, and the circumstances under which it trumps other objects of identity. Compounding this persistent conceptual muddle is the popular practice, especially (but not solely) among Americans, of equating 'the nation' with 'the state' – another 'essentially contested subject' (Gallie, 1962) in its own right that has been conjoined with the nation in the vaunted, if empirically elusive, ideal of the nation–state. While there are more mundane reasons for the continuation of this practice, in some ways it can be seen as an etymological relic of the initial melding of the two concepts in the French Revolution's assertion that governing power rests with the people. The United Nations itself is perhaps the most prominent institutionalized expression of this interchangeability, while the term 'international' persists in common parlance, even if the dynamic it describes is more accurately described as 'inter–state.' The synonymous use of state and nation also extends to the related terms 'statebuilding' and 'nationbuilding,' particularly by American officials (Hillary Clinton cited in Crabtree, 2011) and think–tank experts (Dobbins, 2003, 2007, 2008), who, as Francis Fukuyama maintains, tend to reflect America's 'national experience and history, in which cultura and historical identity was heavily shaped by political institutions like constitutionalism and democracy' (Fukuyama, 2004: 99).

In the scholarly literature, however, analytical distinctions between nation and state are legion, even if terminological slippage persists (perhaps most conspicuously in the International Relations field, whose name itself reflects this slippage). While, of the two terms, 'nation' has generate the greater number of contending definitions, beginning with Plato's notion of the ideal state i the *Republic*, through its rendering by Thomas Hobbes as an order–imposing Leviathan and by Hegel as 'the highest embodiment of the Divine idea on earth' (Hegel's Philosophy of Right, 2012), scholars have long modified and expanded the meaning of the state in distinctive ways Although early philosophical considerations of the state ranged from the abstruse to the more concrete, all embodied the essential problematic of channeling individual impulse for collective purpose. Later social theorists built on these venerable insights as they continued to wrestle with this challenge. Beyond Max Weber's oft–quoted early 20th century notion of the bureaucratic modern state as 'a human community' (by which he meant a bureaucratic staff) that can sustain the claim 'to the legitimate monopoly of control over the means of violence in a given territory' (Weber 1948),' a host of related roles and competencies have long been attributed to the state, whether in its authoritarian, democratic, capitalist, or socialist form (see North, 1981; Seton–Watson, cited in Ma, 1992: 294; Marx and Engels, in Dahbour and Ishay, 1995: 178–182). Despite the state's current status as the world's preeminent political organizing principle, it long competed with a raft of alternatives, from city–state to empire. But, as Krasner (1988) explains, 'Path dependent patterns of development [ensured that] once Europe was committed to [this] form of political organization . . . other possibilities were foreclosed' (Krasner, 1988: 90) for the continent and the world in general. Thus, noted Bertrand Badie (2000), the Western–inspired 'imported state' became the dominant template for diverse non–Western political elites who tried to emulate their former colonial rulers when they assumed the reins of power. In the process, they reframed the colonial divide between ruler and population in domestic, and often ethnic and tribal, terms, and, over time, invented their own practices of the state that transformed the original model (Badie, 2000) – for both good and ill.

In whatever way the state has been defined and come to dominate world politics, for muc of its history it has also been beleaguered, particularly in its imported form. Challenged from below by restive groups that have bridled under its rule and from above by the disparate forces of 'globalization' that have undermined its sovereignty and core capacities, the viability of the modern state has, in certain instances, seemed in question (although, as Stephen Krasner (1999) reminds us, sovereignty – even among the most established states – has always been com – promised). In response to an apparent wave of 'state failure' after the end of the Cold War, the CIA funded an effort to specify the elements of this seemingly growing phenomenon as a f rst step in improving 'early warning' and prevention capacities (Gurr, 2000). A post–9/11 security imperative linking state viability to terrorist threats fueled a surge in policy research that expanded on earlier efforts and created multiple indices of 'weak,' 'fragile,' 'failed,' 'failing' states or, in the World Bank's initial formulation, 'Low Income Countries Under Stress' (Center for Global Development, 2004; Fund for Peace, 2004–2012; Patrick and Rice, 2008; World Bank Group, 2002). While nationalism formed the implicit backdrop to much of this analysis, its contribution to the rise and fall of contemporary states was never explored explicitly.

The collective impact of the many challenges recounted in the 'fragile states literature' echoed Robert Jackson's earlier work on 'quasi–states.' Jackson differentiated between a state as a repository of 'juridical [or external] sovereignty,' reflecting the Westphalian notion of derivin its status from having its independence and territorial integrity recognized by other states, and its 'empirical [or internal] sovereignty,' denoting its ability – or lack thereof – to assert supreme authority within its territorial boundaries (Jackson, 1991: 21). Later, internationally normative conceptions of internal sovereignty led to the additional criterion that a state should provide for the basic needs of its population, and later still, that it should protect its citizens from mass atrocities.

But it is the often problematic relationship between nation and state in the melded form of nation–statethat highlights nationalism's ability both to support and to challenge the foundations of statehood. At its core, this relationship echoes the contending, normatively infused views of two towering 19th century political theorists, John Stuart Mill and Lord Acton. Mill maintained that, 'It is in general a necessary condition of free institutions that the boundaries of the government should coincide in the main with those of nationality' (cited in Dahbour and Ishay, 1995: 100), while Acton warned against the dangers of one dominant ethnic group casting 'the shadow of a single authority' (Acton, cited in Connor, 1995: 6) over a minority population. The wielding of majoritarian authority posed a particular challenge for minorities trapped on the 'wrong side' of newly established, territorially defned state borders, in which nations were nestled within other nations like so many Russian *matryoshka* dolls.

From the post–colonial proliferation of states in early 19th century Latin America to the statebuilding efforts of the latter half of the century's most skillful political entrepreneurs, Otto von Bismarck and Camillo Cavour, the idea that national and political borders should coincide gained prominence. At the same time, the task of converting 'peasants into Frenchmen' (Weber, 1976), or mutually unintelligible residents of the Italian peninsula into Italians, proved as demanding as it was enduring. A mid–20th century variation on this challenge was taken up by the newly independent states of Africa and Asia, whose inherited colonial borders were drawn with little regard for local tribal or ethnic interests but, with rare exception (such as Singapore and Malaysia, Pakistan and Bangladesh, Eritrea and Ethiopia, and, most recently, Sudan and South Sudan), were left unchanged. It is these post–colonial states, particularly in Africa, where the 'imported' concept of the nation, as with the state, often exists uneasily beside more deeply rooted forms of identity, and where the ability to keep diverse polities together and meet their basic needs through 'effective, legitimate and resilient' rule (OECD/DAC, 2008: 2) forms the crux of the contemporary statebuilding challenge.

The continuing diffculties of reconciling state with nation reflect the fact that, in most cases 'the state is larger than the "nation" – that is, the juridical limits of the state extend considerably beyond the area settled by its *Staatsvolk*, the German term (with no exact English language equivalent) for the state's dominant . . . founding ethnic group which is the source of its principal culture' (Ra'nan and Mesner, 1991: 5). The nation extends well beyond the territorial boundaries of the state in cases such as Hungary, post–Soviet Russia, North and South Korea, and Armenia, to name only a few, or, as in the case of the Kurds, may overlap several states but lack one of its own (for a discussion of 'state–nations' see Stepan et al., 2011). As Connor (1995: 29–30), among others, has pointed out, 'national' homogeneity in a state is exceedingly rare in the contemporary world, despite a century of often sanguinary efforts to achieve this goal, ranging from 'ethnic cleansing' and the adjustment of borders through war or secession to less violent, if often still wrenching, reliance on migration and assimilation. Charles Tilly applied *reductio ad absurdum* to this goal when he warned that, if taken to its logical extreme, 'the world would splinter . . . in[to] thousands of satellite entities, most of them tiny and economically nonviable'

(Tilly, 1990: 3). When Woodrow Wilson famously championed the cause of 'national self–determination' at the end of the First World War, he never clearly specified who the 'self' wa or the limits on what was to be determined, which planted the seeds of later discord that precipitated the next world war (Kedourie, cited in Ra'nan and Mesner, 1991: 227).

It is this still–salient clash of the presumed right of self–determination and the sanctity of existing international borders that raises the question of whether nationalism is essentially state–destroying or statebuilding. Connor's treatment of nationalism also implies that, since 'most states consist of more than one nation, and there are difficulties transferring primary allegiance from nations t states, the real effect of nationalism is "nation–destroying" not "nationbuilding"' (Ma, 1992: 294). However, such a judgment remains incomplete since so much depends on the nature of what Connor (and Wilson before him) leaves unspecified. Reiterating a core theme of this chapter nationalism, in practice, can take many forms and, depending on how it is manifested, may contribute in multiple and, at times, contradictory ways to statebuilding. It can also emerge as a byproduct of state–directed action. As Charles Tilly and, earlier, Otto Hintze (Hintze, cited in Giddens, 1987: 26–27), pointed out, the imperatives of war–making that reinforce the fundaments of the state can also serve to inculcate and buttress a cohesive national sentiment. Not only, in Tilly's much–cited phrase, do 'wars make states, and vice versa' (Tilly 1990: 67), but marshaling the resources and commanding the obedience of a diverse population in wartime can help forge a nation (or nations) into a state.

Recurrent themes

The expansive literature on nationalism reflects a wide range of historical examples of the divers effects of nationalism on statebuilding. In each case, the way that nationalism has been character–ized and has played out empirically represents distinct facets of this phenomenon that correspond – notwithstanding the notable contextual differences – to elements of more recent statebuilding challenges. Comparing historic cases with examples drawn from contemporary times and the recent past underscores the necessity of avoiding ahistoricism in statebuilding analysis and of treating each putative expression of nationalist sentiment *de novo*, instead of a modern mani–festation of a recurrent phenomenon with deep links to the past.

In light of nationalism's inherently mutable nature, scholars have long sought to distinguish its many seemingly distinct forms (Hechter, 2000, among others), which invariably coexist with one another. Drawing on a number of these diverse but related scholarly classifications, national ism can be grouped under the following general headings with examples compared across eras.

State-led nationalism

The '*Risorgimento* nationalism' that led to the creation of modern Italy is a form of 'integrative' or 'unif cation' nationalism that also played out in 19th century Germany and France. In these cases, state–led programs were implemented to construct common or shared identities once state borders were defined and involved, among other assertions of centralizing authority, the development of 'national' educational curricula and efforts to promote linguistic standardization among polyglot populations. Post–Ottoman Turkey under Kamal Ataturk is one of the early 20th century's paradigmatic examples of this form of nationalism. While the borders of many more recently established states were imposed by external powers, the essential dynamic of strengthening, sometimes forcefully, the bonds between presumptive nation and state has, in a number of cases, resembled the experience of earlier statebuilders. Recent examples include India, which continues to counter centripetal forces among its multiethnic, multisectarian democratic polity through concerted, if only partially effective, central state action, and Afghanistan and Iraq, where ongoing efforts to bind together sometimes fractious national groups, who have, at times, identified with a transcendent, state-led national identity, have been complicated by the recent history and ongoing effects of large-scale wars. And, although cloaked in the language of liberalism and exceptionalism, the United States is no stranger to concerted, state-led efforts to create a *unum* from its *pluribus*. State-led nationalism in Africa has had a mixed record. While in the conflict-ridden, seemingly fissiparous Democratic Republic of Congo there is a surprising degre of identification with the central state among contending 'national' groups (Weiss and Carayannis in Laremont, 2005: 162–165), in other African countries, as Jeffrey Herbst (2000) has pointed out, nominal state leaders have had little interest in promoting an overarching centralizing, nationalist vision. In the latter case, their 'greed' (as Paul Collier and Anke Hoeffler (2000) described the quest for personal economic gains from the extraction of natural resources) has trumped any ambition to extend their reach throughout the entire state, while also fueling the 'grievances' (the other factor that Collier downplayed by comparison) of national groups that believe they are not getting their fair share of the state's riches.

Sub-state nationalism

Variably characterized in the literature as 'peripheral,' 'minority,' 'sub-state,' and, in its more extreme forms, 'secessionist,' this type of nationalism involves efforts by self-identified 'national groups – from Basques and Catalans in Spain to Polisario rebels in the Western Sahara – to, in Ernest Gellner's famous formulation, 'render the boundaries of the nation congruent with those of its governance unit' (Gellner, 1983), up to and including the achievement of independent statehood. While the granting of territorial autonomy within an existing state has been a common means of addressing this challenge in a number of Western states (for example, Spain, the United Kingdom, Belgium, and, less successfully, in the Former Yugoslavia), in the African context it has been tried far less frequently since 'claims to [this form of autonomy] are invariably perceived as challenges to the central state' (Kirkby and Murray, 2010: 115). Rwanda's experience in the early 1990s provides a tragic example of the complete breakdown of efforts to deal peacefully with sub-state nationalism, while, more recently, Burundi has had success in managing this challenge. South Sudan's break away from Sudan (which also faces a secessionist threat in Darfur) is the latest example of secession in Africa, which may or may not presage further state fragmentation on the continent and elsewhere.

Irredentist nationalism

A variation on sub-state nationalism involves efforts by one nation-state to integrate an 'unredeemed,' primarily contiguous region that is part of another nation-state, into its own. The attempt by some early 20th century Italian nationalists to claim the Istrian peninsula and other Italian-populated regions formerly under Austro-Hungarian rule, and Nazi Germany's later machinations to absorb the Czech Sudetenland and achieve *Anschluss* with Austria, are classic examples of this form of nationalism. Much more common in more recent times has been the threat of incipient irredentism, the possibility that agitation by a neighboring state (what Rogers Brubaker (1996) calls the 'homeland state') on behalf of its presumably beleaguered national kin – such as Russians in the 'near abroad' – will lead it to absorb the territory inhabited by its nationals into its own. This form of nationalism remains rare in practice, although its potential in diverse contexts, including Hungarians in Romania and Slovakia, Russians in Moldova, Azeris in Iran, Khmer in Southern Laos, Chinese in Mongolia and the Russian Far East, and Kurds in Turkey,

Iraq, Syria, and Iran, who yearn to regain their unredeemed territory in an independent Kurdistan, can exert a powerful psychological effect on affected states and national groups alike. The porosity of borders in much of contemporary Africa and the transborder nature of many tribal and sub-state groups, such as various Somali clans living in Ethiopia, Kenya, and Djibouti in the East, and the Mende, Gola, Kissi, and Vai living in and around Sierra Leone and its neighbors in the West, present an ongoing irredentist threat to existing nation-states, however latent.

Decolonizing nationalism

Forms of 'post-colonial' or 'post-imperial' nationalism involve the establishment or, in some cases, reestablishment of new nation-states from the shards of weakening or disintegrating empires or multinational states. In Africa, in particular, early decisions by new leaders to maintain the sanctity of existing colonial borders under the customary law principle of *uti possidetis juris* could not obscure the incongruity between these borders and the multiplicity of identities of the peoples within them. From Sierra Leone to Kenya, post-colonial African states still wrestle with the task of knitting together diverse groups within their borders that were often played off against each other by colonial powers. Clearly, since the last wave of decolonization ran its course, this form of nationalism as a catalyst to statebuilding has receded. However, in many parts of the world, nation-statesare still addressing the unfnished business left in its wake. The imposition over the past two decades of internationally run 'transitional administrations' (Chesterman, 2003) on post-conflict states-in-the-making (or remaking), such as Kosovo, Timor-Leste, and Sierra Leone, has revealed the inherent tensions involved in attempting to nurture a positive conception of decolonizing nationalism among peoples who had achieved (and need assistance in maintaining) their independent status through outside intervention.

Civic and ethnic nationalism

Hans Kohn's mid-20th century differentiation between more 'liberal, civic Western [European]' nationalism, based on allegiance to democracy and freedom, and 'illiberal, ethnic Eastern [European]' nationalism, tied to blood, descent, and history, was reflected in much of the subsequent nationalism literature (Kohn, 1958). Post-Cold War versions of this analytical framework were also applied to the Balkans in the writings of political commentators such as Robert Kaplan (1993), Michael Ignatieff (1993), and William Pfaff (1993), and in the pronouncements of Western policymakers, such as US Secretary of State Warren Christopher (1993). But, as Will Kymlicka (2001: 24) has pointed out, this binary dichotomy ignores the strong cultural component of the 'civic' nationalism practiced in the United States and France, among other liberal nation-states whose Enlightenment roots ostensibly make such components anathema. Contra Liah Greenfeld's evocative claim that 'nationalism was the form in which democracy appeared in the world, contained in the idea of the nation as a butterfy in a cocoon,' others have argued that divisions of class, gender, and status have prevailed over nationalism's presumed egalitarian impulses. Furthermore, as George Schopf in notes, 'ethnic particularism often trumps civic universalism in times of stress (immigration, foreign wars, terrorism)' (Schopflin, cited in Kuzio, 2001). The equation of civic nationalism with democracy further breaks down in the case of Latin America, where states with longstanding traditions of civic nationalism were also, for much of their history, undemocratic (Kymlicka 2001, p.26, footnote 20). More prevalent throughout history has been the melding of civic and ethnic elements in mature and consolidating democracies, as well as in more autocratic states, from Eastern and Central Europe to Africa and Asia.

Diaspora or long-distance nationalism

The ability of nationalist bonds to connect geographically dispersed peoples across territorial boundaries has complicated statebuilding efforts both in states where immigrant groups have settled and in their ancestral homelands. Not only have new arrivals, whether or not entering legally, presented major integration challenges for state−led nationalists in their host countries, but they also have injected themselves into domestic developments in the lands they left behind. For example, far−flung diasporas of Greeks and Armenians, among others, actively agitated fo the independence of their co−nationals living under Ottoman and Austro−Hungarian imperial rule, and the nation−states that succeeded them, throughout the 19th and early 20th centuries. Driven by the exigencies of violent conflict and economic deprivation in their homelands, post 1990 diaspora groups emulated more established settlers in sending remittances, and sometimes arms, to assist ethnic kin abroad in meeting their basic needs and waging their struggles against oppressive centralized states dominated by rival ethnic groups. Enabled by advances in communications and transport, the role played by diaspora groups of Irish, Kurds, Armenians, Jews (if, in this case, religion is considered a basis for nationalist identity), and, more recently, Eritreans and Tamils, in challenging state−led nationalism in their countries of origin is well documented. A World Bank study (Collier, 2003) highlighted the risk factors associated with diaspora engagement in home state affairs, while a 2007 USIP report found that diasporas can play both peacemaking and 'peacewrecking' roles, sometimes simultaneously (Smith and Stares, 2007). In Liberia, diaspora nationalism has taken a novel turn, as the government there actively seeks the cooperation of diaspora groups to testify in its Truth and Reconciliation Commission (Liberia Truth and Reconciliation Commission Project, 2012).

Supranationalism

Efforts to create a form of shared identity that transcends particularism and the borders of subsidiary political, 'national' units were inherent features of empires from Persia and Rome to Austria−Hungary and the Soviet Union. When the ideal type of the nation−state became the world's preeminent, large−scale political organizing principle, such efforts continued in the form of colonialism and other overt, as well as less formalized, modes of 'neo−imperial' domination, from Soviet control of its Eastern European satellite states to the power exerted by the United States over its allies following World War II. The more benign 'liberal nationalism' espoused by Giuseppe Mazzini in the mid−19th century (Dahbour and Isahay, 1995: 87–97) and later championed by scholars such as Yael Tamir (1993), links exclusive nationalist claims to geographically more expansive and inclusive identities that, in various ways, delink the nation from the state. Marxism's dismissal of nationalism as a retrograde impediment to the ultimate establishment of world socialism was, according to Tom Nairn, its 'great historical failure' (Nairn, 1981: 329), but this did not prevent Lenin and Stalin from tactically exploiting nationalism to serve longer−term strategic ends. The development of the Europe Union (EU) over the past six decades, notwithstanding its recent travails, represents the most notable example of an ongoing project of 'transcending the nation.' But as one 'Eurocrat' recently observed, even if 'European integration has already gone too far for national authorities to control its workings . . . by most measures, national . . . loyalties remain entrenched' (Marquand, 2012). Pan−Africanism as a form of supranational nationalism foundered for similar reasons in the 1960s, as also appears to be the case with the Pan−Arabic appeal of the ongoing 'Arab Awakening,' notwithstanding the additional element of the border−spanning links of the Islamic*Unmah*.

Reflecting the multiplicity of forms that nationalism can take, the above typology is far from exhaustive. It highlights, however, some of the key overlapping imperatives and interconnections across and between these forms, and the tendency for the seeds of one to be implanted in the other. For example, not only does statebuilding nationalism often incite and clash with sub–state varieties, but other forms, such as decolonizing nationalism, over time, typically assume statebuilding nationalist characteristics that begin a cycle of competing nationalisms at both the intrastate and interstate levels. A similar dynamic also plays out in cases of supranationalism, which, through efforts to transcend particularism, can actually magnify the potency and appeal of more narrow conceptions of nationalism in reaction to the perceived imposition of a less familiar or attractive, homogenizing identity.

While recognizing the unique characteristics of the individual cases cited above, this comparative excursion into history is designed to highlight the similarities that have faced statebuilders in their varied encounters with nationalism over time. In short, nationalism has always presented a dilemma for statebuilding, even as its current role goes largely unrecognized or unacknowledged by scholars of statebuilding and the policymakers and practitioners they seek to influence. Commenting on current statebuilding challenges, the OECD/DAC acknowledge that while 'the contextual histories of the state–formation process must inform statebuilding policy in specific contexts . . . there are some general patterns from the [ongoing] contemporary state–formation process that inform our understanding of' its causes (OECD/DAC, 2008: 5). This analysis concurs with this insight but adds the corollary that general patterns can also be discerned from cases from different eras and regions that ostensibly have no relationship to contemporary statebuilding challenges but can still illuminate the variable roles that nationalism has played in different times and places. Such historically informed analysis can put current cases into perspective and provide a basis for drawing and applying potentially useful lessons from the past. Moreover, apropos of Paris and Sisk's stated objective of addressing the operational challenges of statebuilding in terms of the 'visible manifestations of deeper tensions' (Paris and Sisk, 2009: 16), nationalism, as history attests, is the embodiment of a deeper tension *par excellence*.

The case for nationalism as a sixth dilemma for statebuilding

Beyond its historical role in statebuilding, nationalism's claim to separate status in Paris and Sisk's 'dilemmas framework' also rests on its particular relevance to the broad body of recent policy–oriented analysis that gives prominence to the institutions of governance in a state and 'their relationship to a territory's citizens or population' (Call, 2008: 61). Recalling the work of late 19th and early 20th century political sociologists Max Weber and Emile Durkheim, this focus on 'state–society' relations emphasizes the essential role of legitimacy in a state's formation and sustainability. Although 'there is no international consensus around the dimensions of legitimacy' (Jones and Elgin–Cossart, 2011: 19), the importance of establishing and strengthening domestic institutions that can buttress state legitimacy is increasingly seen as an essential task in statebuilding by the national and international agencies charged with addressing state fragility (Zoellick, 2009; OECD/DAC, 2008; USAID, 2011; World Bank, 2011).

Elsewhere in this volume and in his other work, Nicolas Lemay–Hébert cogently examines the two schools of thought ref ected in the seminal writings of Weber and Durkheim as they relate to the question of legitimacy and its implications for contemporary statebuilding. He compares the Weberian–inspired 'institutional approach' (p. 23), in which a state's legitimacy derives from its 'administrative capability,' with the Durkhemian–based 'legitimacy approach,' in which this attribute is a function of a state's ability to 'command loyalty . . . and [promote] socio–politicalcohesion' (Lemay–Hébert, 2009: 23–24). While acknowledging the importance of strong institutions that allow a state to 'perform the functions of statehood,' Lemay–Hébert cautions against an over–reliance on technocratic statebuilding interventions that give short shrift to 'the realm of ideas and sentiment' where the 'fate of states is primarily determined' (Kalevi Holsti, cited in Lemay−Hébert, 2009: 24).

As noted at the beginning of this chapter, the issue of legitimacy has become a leitmotif for national and international agencies involved in statebuilding. Reflecting the institutional approac described by Lemay−Hébert, the OECD/DAC refers to a state's 'domestic legitimacy,' which is based on its ability 'to meet its citizens' expectations.' This form of legitimacy is 'embedded in historical forms' (OECD/DAC, 2008: 7) that can influence those expectations and resist manipu lation from the outside. When these expectations are tied to competence and service delivery, they represent what Michael Scharpf calls 'output legitimacy' (Scharpf, cited in OECD/DAC, 2008: 24), which is primarily concerned with meeting societal expectations in terms of practical problem−solving. Reflecting the Durkheimian approach, Scharpf also cites what he calls 'inpu legitimacy' (Scharpf, cited in OECD/DAC, 2008: 24), which reflects the participatory natur of the decision−making process in a state. Input legitimacy is more abstract and normative, based largely on the subjective belief that a governance system is fair to the extent that it gives sufficien voice and agency to self−defined societal groups

This focus on legitimacy in statebuilding is in many ways overdue, since its roots in sociological thought can be traced back to the 19th century. Building on this early work, successors of Weber and Durkheim continued to examine the complex relationship between state and society. While 'society' is composed of many elements, this chapter argues that groups inspired by nationalism are particularly salient members of society. When mobilized, their influence on the maintenanc or dissolution of state legitimacy can be especially significant. For example, when sub−state groups such as Hezbollah in Lebanon or Boko Haram in Nigeria − who exhibit a form of religious nationalism − assume some of the problem−solving functions of the state, 'output legitimacy' is necessarily undermined.

Rejecting Weber−inspired, neo−statist notions of a state's 'autonomous' functioning, an important strand of scholarship on state−society relations has emphasized both the role of state power and the contributions that society can make in the political arena. As characterized by Joel Migdal, this perspective views a state's effectiveness as variable depending on its mutually reinforcing relationships with various social forces and its ability to empower them, as it itself is empowered (Migdal, 1994). The cases cited previously in this chapter highlight that groups motivated by nationalist impulses embody a mélange of social forces at the sub−state level that have often played outsized roles in both statebuilding and 'state−destroying.' They, in turn, have been affected by the nature and goals of the nationalist agenda of the state, which can run the gamut from liberal multiculturalism that acknowledges and supports subnational diversity to more authoritarian forms of forced assimilation that seek to stif e expressions of political or cultural particularism.

Again with reference to Lebanon, Hezbollah's recent success in augmenting its informal influence by gaining political power through the ballot box − however suspiciously viewed by other elements of Lebanese society − indicates a dialectical state−society relationship that also implies an evolving notion of state power. In the case of Nigeria, the dialectic may be less apparent, since it is obscured, in part, by Boko Haram's avowed maximalist goal of establishing a caliphate. However, both this group and the state that tries to meet the challenge it poses are inevitably changing − just as sub−state groups and the states they have challenged and interacted with have changed, in distinct ways, throughout history.

The essence of this aspect of the dilemma of nationalism for statebuilding is reflected in th degree to which contending state−society nationalist agendas are each implicated in the other, and in the diverse and unanticipated ways they can play out. This dynamic recalls the post−colonial theory of hybridity, which explains how 'values imposed by external actors are received, interpreted, challenged and resisted in a variety of ways' (Stamis, 2010: 13–14). However, in the case of the dilemma of nationalism, rather than imposed by external actors in post–conflict peac operations, the interacting nationalist values in question are generated primarily internally by the host state and society (although they can be shaped to some extent by their encounters with the nationalism of external actors).

Significantly and unsurprisingly, this variation of the process of hybridity often revolves around questions of power and how it is wielded. 'Power in the modern world,' maintains John Breuilly (1994) in his comparative analysis of nationalism and the state, 'is principally about control of the state.' But such control does not necessarily have to be total, by either the state or national groups. A great deal depends on how each articulates and presses for its goals, and how each adjusts its expectations accordingly. The quest for partial control that falls short of maximalist national claims – for example, on the part of the state, for something less than ethnically dominated authoritarian rule and, on the part of national groups, for self–determination that does not require independent statehood – opens up a range of possibilities for statebuilding that reflect the multiplicity and malleability of the state and society (*qua* nation).

Much of the recent analysis on statebuilding has stressed the importance of 'the social contract' – whether codified or less formally agreed to – that embodies the process through which, a articulated by the OECD/DAC (2008: 9), 'the social/political .. . and power relation[s] between holders of state power and organized groups in society are negotiated and managed.' Representing a tangible expression of the choices made by each side, the durability of such compacts depends on the degree to which initial expectations continue to be met or change over time. While the state–society dynamic sometimes exists in precarious balance, nationalism can provide a powerful means of either stabilizing or destabilizing this relationship, depending on the particular form in which it is expressed. For example, a state's ability to convince its citizenry that it has a rightful claim to govern is a key factor in establishing and maintaining its viability, as well as an important dimension of the state–society dynamic noted above. Historically, nationalism's role in undergirding this claim has been inextricably linked to the development of this concept over time, which, as Craig Calhoun describes, involved 'the idea – and eventually the taken–for–granted, gut–level conviction – that political power could only be legitimate when it reflecte the will . . . of the people subject to it' (Calhoun, 1997: 69). The greater the extent to which 'the people' share or accede to the nationalist project of the state, the more likely it is that this legitimacy will be established. Conversely, when elements of the polity have differing or conflicting visions of their respective nationalist claims, the legitimacy of the state is put into question – at least by some groups – and political agitation or violent conflict can result. Althoug the state has various means and opportunities at its disposal to demonstrate the fairness of the system, this task, which is an essential component of 'input legitimacy,' is facilitated – as in other statebuilding processes – when there is a degree of correspondence between the nationalist visions of the state and society, even if not fully harmonized.

In a much–cited 2010 report, the UK's Department for International Development (DFID 2011) elaborates on the idea of a social contract in terms of what it calls 'political settlements . . . the types of formal and informal political bargains that can end confcts and bring sustainable peace, promote reform and bring poverty reduction.' While the report acknowledges the role played by this type of bargaining between the state and organized groups in a society in achieving 'effective accountable public authority,' it also clarifies that this process and the 'forging of common understanding' it entails 'usually take place between elites' (DFID, 2011: 8). As Mushtaq Khan points out, these 'elite pacts' are key to sustainable statebuilding because 'if powerful groups are not getting an acceptable distribution of benefits from an institutional structure, they wil strive to change it' (Khan, cited in DFID, 2011: 8). This emphasis on the crucial role of elites in statebuilding resonates strongly with a major stream of analysis in the nationalism literature describing how elites throughout history have promoted and manipulated nationalism to serve their statist and personal ends. Representing diverse perspectives on nationalism, scholars including Brubaker (1996), Breuilly (1994), Gellner (1983), and Hobsbawm (1990), among others, have described the machinations of elite political entrepreneurs in inciting and channeling nationalist sentiment. Although the political settlements and nationalism literatures each treat elites in distinctive ways, statebuilding researchers could benefit from further research that explore the intersection of these two approaches.

Nationalism's role in the other dilemmas of statebuilding

As the preceding analysis suggests, nationalism deserves pride of place as a separate dilemma for statebuilding. Expanding on a reference at the beginning of this chapter, it also can play an important role in the other dilemmas described in Paris and Sisk's framework.

The authors define the 'footprint' of a peace operation as 'its degree of intrusiveness in th domestic affairs of the home state.' This dilemma is a function of the size and breadth of the tasks of the international presence, as well as 'the assertiveness of the external actors in pursuing these tasks' (Paris and Sisk, 2009: 307). Whether described in economic, military, or political terms, the footprint dilemma stems from the fact that, 'although a dominant international presence ("a heavy footprint") may be required to maintain security and initiate political and economic reforms, a less intrusive international presence ("a light footprint") may be required to allow local political, social, and economic life to achieve a post−conifct equilibrium on its own terms' (Paris and Sisk, 2009: 307). While a number of contributors to Paris and Sisk's volume describe how this dilemma plays out in diverse settings, the specific role of nationalism in these cases is no analyzed in depth. To his credit, David Edelstein, in describing the case of Kosovo, alludes to the 'nationalist resistance to the presence of foreign military forces' that may be accelerated by a large number of foreign troops with an 'assertive mandate' (Edelstein, in Paris and Sisk, 2009: 90). And Astri Suhrke, in commenting on the negative connotations of foreign−directed statebuilding efforts in Afghanistan, refers to 'the distinct core' of Afghan nationalism, which is 'def ned by pride in a country that was never colonized and a people that repeatedly has driven out foreign invaders' (Suhrke, in Paris and Sisk, 2009: 242). But, in both cases, the passing (and, in other instances, implicit) invocations of nationalism raise more questions than they answer. For example, how does the 'distinct core' referred to by Suhrke complicate or facilitate efforts by Afghanistan to relate to its neighbors, given current regional dynamic and other competing state−lednationalisms? Or, how does the Taliban's Pashtun identity complicate current efforts, following over three decades of war, to reinforce a pan−ethnic Afghan national identity? This is not a criticism of either author, whose incisive chapters have broader purposes in mind, but rather a suggestion that an examination of the multifaceted role of nationalism as it relates to the size and scope of foreign statebuilding efforts in Kosovo and Afghanistan could add additional nuance and explanatory power to these accounts. This is true in many other cases, such as Haiti, where the explicit role of Haitian nationalism in response to a succession of foreign−led statebuilding efforts, of the mostly 'heavy' footprint varieties, has not figured prominently in scholarly an policy−orientedanalyses (see Crane et al., 2010). Similarly, in Bosnia−Herzegovina (and, indeed, in the entire Balkans), where nationalism's role in precipitating and sustaining conflict has lon been a subject of scholarly inquiry (see Kennan, 1993), nationalist responses to the very large footprint of external statebuilding efforts are also worthy subjects for deeper analysis.

A similar, nationalist−inspired dynamic can play out in local responses to the 'duration dilemma,' which involves the problems that arise the longer a post−conflict operation endures

As Paris and Sisk explain, 'over time, local actors tend to grow increasingly irritated by – or even hostile towards – the continued presence of outside actors.' The 'countervailing pressures' that they say 'mitigate against a prolonged or open–ended international deployment' (Paris and Sisk, 2009: 306–309) can be generated, in no small way, by both state–led and sub–state nationalist imperatives. Again, these are alluded to in the examples cited above, but not examined comprehensively. For example, in the case of Afghanistan, the responses to the extended presence of NATO forces, and Western aid agencies and NGOs, by Pashtun, Tajik, Hazara, and Uzbek sub–state national groups are likely to be different – both from each other and from those of the state–led central government. In the case of Iraq, the differential nationalist reactions by sub–state groups, especially the Kurds and Turkmen, to both the heavy and (since the recent withdrawal of the bulk of Western forces) light footprint statebuilding efforts also warrant further study. In the Paris and Sisk volume, David Edelstein compares UN–authorized external intervention and statebuilding efforts in Timor–Leste with the UN– and NATO–led missions in Kosovo (Paris and Sisk, 2009: 84–90). In Timor–Leste, the UN mission drew down its presence before 'intense resistance built up against' it. Arguably, it was concern among international interveners about generating a duration dilemma that contributed to the drawdown decision (along with other compelling budgetary and political factors). When rioting broke out in the country's capital, Dili, in February 2006, questions were raised about the wisdom of what was viewed, in retrospect, as a premature and needlessly hasty international withdrawal. While this case has been addressed by a number of scholars (Chesterman, 2003; Chopra, 2002), again, the specific role of 'post colonial' and 'state–led' nationalisms in initial and ongoing statebuilding efforts has not been sufficiently analyzed. This is especially pertinent in light of the new state's internationally facilitated independence from Indonesia and its more recent leadership role in the OECD–affiliated International Dialogue on Peacebuilding and Statebuilding's 'New Deal for Engagement in Fragile States,' which calls for 'country–led and country–owned transitions out of [state] fragility' (OECD/DAC, 2011). In Kosovo, the more prolonged nature of the UN mission 'generated considerable resistance among the Kosovar Albanian population' and came to be seen by Kosovars as 'an impediment to the ultimate goal of national self–determination' (Edelstein, in Paris and Sisk, 2009: 89). Again, this single reference to an imperative closely tied to nationalism suggests that there is something here that could benefit from further study. The Kosovo case also involves issues of both irredentist and diaspora nationalisms, in terms of the Albanian majority's relationship with its ethnic kin in Albania (which, as Donald Horowitz (1985: 285), has pointed out, is more complicated than might be assumed) and the Kosovo Serb minority's relationship with Serbia.

Closely related to the above two dilemmas is the 'dependency dilemma,' which involves the 'danger of fostering dependency among local elites and the general population of a host state on the international presence' (Paris and Sisk, 2009: 308). Again, the complications posed by this dilemma are magnified in the context of nationalism. As described by Edelstein, Kosovars unde an internationally run transitional administration were torn between their need for external assistance that also undermined their ability to stand on their own, and a nationalist desire for self–determination in the form of independent statehood (Edelstein, in Paris and Sisk, 2009: 88–89). Also evident in this and other statebuilding cases is the 'participation dilemma' – involving the participation of 'factional leaders' who 'do not necessarily represent the population[s] of their countries, yet . . . are typically individuals who are involved in peace negotiations and therefore remain central political actors in the period immediately following the conflict' (Paris and Sisk 2009: 307–308) – which is similarly suitable to a nationalism frame. When factional leaders claim to represent distinct national groups, which is often the case in statebuilding (such as in Bosnia–Herzegovina or Sudan), their potential role as exponents or spoilers of peace agreements and post−conflictstatebuilding is heightened because of the power of nationalism that underpins their claims, even if they are motivated primarily by greed. As noted above in the reference to political settlements, their role as elites gives them special purchase in this process. Finally, there is the 'coherence dilemma,' which relates to the difficulty of achieving 'coordination among the myria international actors involved' in statebuilding efforts (Paris and Sisk, 2009: 308–309). Although nationalism's role in this dilemma of statebuilding is less apparent than in the others, it has a potentially consequential link to the motivations and actions of these international actors, particularly when one country takes the lead (such as the US in Iraq and Afghanistan, the UK in Sierra Leone, Nigeria in Liberia, and Australia in Timor−Leste) despite the distinctive nature of each operation).

Conclusion

This chapter has sought to demonstrate that nationalism's longstanding role in statebuilding continues apace in a contemporary context, despite its apparent neglect by scholars of state−building. Any research agenda addressing this issue should also take account of the way that nationalism, in its multiplicity of forms, continues to evolve. Specifically, it should examine ho this multifaceted phenomenon has responded to a wide range of 21st century challenges that have cultural, political, and ethical dimensions. Clair Sutherland has dubbed these challenges 'cosmopolitan,' to evoke the term's original reference to those ancient Greeks whose identity extended beyond the boundaries of their city state or 'polis' to the world or cosmos. Particularly relevant to the theme of this chapter, Sutherland cites 'the dual, often contradictory roles of contemporary [states]' in enabling 'participation in global society,' while also 'protect[ing] national society − or select groups − from destructive competition' (Sutherland, 2012: 173). In this characterization, state−led nationalism interacts both with sub−state nationalism and with certain forms of supranationalism. In varying degrees, this has been a common feature of states since their advent, but, as Sutherland notes, because 'the increase in the density, diversity, intensity and speed' of interchange under the rubric of globalization is 'qualitatively different' (Sutherland, 2012: 4) from earlier eras, so too has been this nature of the intersection among contending nationalisms.

  The profound changes that Sutherland and others have described as having taken place in the modern world obviously cannot be fully understood without an appreciation of what came before them. The same holds true for nationalism in its current role and, specifically, the dilemma i poses for statebuilding. It may be the case, as Sutherland maintains, that 'contemporary national−ism evolves in very different circumstances to the 19th century European context that Gellner described' (Sutherland, 2012: 27), but many of the dynamics Gellner addressed, such as the disorienting movement of agricultural workers into urban environments and nationalism's ability to promote a sense of belonging among them, have their analogs in contemporary examples of statebuilding in the developing world. Similarly, while the 'grids of communications flows' described by Deutsch involving telephones, mail, and highway systems that promoted national assimilation during the process of industrialization in Europe (Deutsch, 1966) may be out of date, new forms of information technology can serve the same purpose in modern societies − or can undermine assimilation and integration when they readily connect national groups in one nation−state to co−nationals in another, or to fellow 'cosmopolitans' who adhere to more expansive notions of nationalism not centered on any single territorial state. The generic mechanism may mirror Deutsch's in both instances but technological advances have altered the nature of its specific form and impact. And finally, but by no means exhaustively, Anthony Smith account of the way nationalist appeals have been based on 'myths of common ancestry, shared memories and cultural traditions' (Smith, 1999: 9) – regardless of their veracity – expressly links past and present cases.

Clearly, nationalism is only part of the story, but, as described above, it can have an inordinate influence on prospects for success or failure in statebuilding. This is not to argue that national identity should be 'essentialized or reified' (Brubaker, 1996: 7), as Lemay–Hébert recounts wa the case in Kosovo, where the international community's misguided efforts to promote inter-ethnic reconciliation by the use of affirmative action ('positive discrimination') served to 'increas [hostility], instead of improve relations' (Lemay–Hébert 2009: 31). Rather, it is to make the case that scholars of statebuilding need to look through the lens of nationalism, even if it reveals a host of other problems that complicate the task. All these problems exist regardless of whether we admit to seeing them, but acknowledging them is a necessary first step in the search for solutions.

In commenting on the dismal record of post–conflict peace operations, Simon Chesterma remarked that 'just as generals are accused of planning to fight the last war,' international agencies leading these efforts have reflected only gradual learning; to wit, 'Kosovo got the operation tha should have been planned for Bosnia four years earlier, East Timor got that which should have been sent to Kosovo' (Chesterman, 2003: 11). To increase the prospects for success in statebuilding, both external interveners and their local partners – as well as the scholars and analysts who scrutinize and critique them – need to look further back beyond the most recent cases to the nationalist theories, empirical records, and 'myths' of earlier times. Without a starting point, a baseline to compare with current developments, statebuilding analysis efforts can resemble exercises 'in planting cut f owers' (Billington, cited in Gregorian, 1999: 2). But understanding what works and what does not work, as Paris and Sisk remind us, 'will require more than lists of lessons learned.' Responding to Isaiah Berlin's post–Cold War message dispelling rumors of nationalism's premature demise, the fundamental task for addressing the dilemma of nationalism for statebuilding is one of discovering, not of inventing, and of learning, not of disregarding, what has been there all along.

Acknowledgments

The author thanks Tanisha Fazel at Columbia University and Susan Woodward of the City University of New York for their insightful comments and feedback on earlier versions of this chapter.

Note

1 Fazel, T. (2012). Email correspondence, 13 July 2012.

References

Anderson, A. (1991). *Imagined communities: Reflections on the origins and spread of nationalism*. New York, NY: Verso and New Left Books.
Badie, B. (2000). *The imported state: The Westernization of the political order*. Stanford, CA: Stanford University Press.
Breuilly, J. (1994). *Nationalism and the state*. Chicago, IL: University of Chicago Press.
Brubaker, R. (1996). *Nationalism reframed: Nationhood and the national question in the new Europe*. Cambridge, UK: Cambridge University Press.
Calhoun, C. (1997). *Nationalism*. Minneapolis, MN: University of Minnesota Press.
Call, C. (2008). Building states to build peace? A critical analysis. *Journal of Peacebuilding and Development*, 4(2), 60–74.

Center for Global Development. (2004). Commission on Weak States and US National Security, *Final Report*. Center for Global Development, Washington, DC, 8 June.
Chesterman, S. (2003). *'You the People': The United Nations, transitional administrations and statebuilding*. Final Report of Project on Transitional Administrations, International Peace Institute, November.
Chopra, J. (2002). Building state failure in East Timor. *Development and Change, 33*(5), 979–1000.
Christopher, W. (1993). Opening statement at press conference, 'New Steps toward Conflict Resolutio in the Former Yugoslavia,' 10 February.
Collier, P. (2003). *Breaking the conflict trap: Civil war and development policy*. Washington, DC: World Bank.
Collier, P., and Hoeffler, A. (2000). *Greed and grievance in civil wars*. Washington, DC: World Bank Development Research Group.
Connor, W. (1995). *Ethnonationalism: The quest for understanding*. Princeton, NJ: Princeton University Press.
Crabtree, S. (2011). *In Afghanistan, nation-building by any other name is still nation-building*. Available at: tpmdc.talkingpointsmemo.com
Crane, K., Dobbins, J., Miller, E., Ries, C. P., Chivvis, C. S., Haims, M. C., et al. (2010). *Building a more resilient Haitian state*. RAND National Security Division, the Rand Corporation, Santa Monica, CA.
Dahbour, O., and Ishay, M. (Eds.). (1995). *The nationalism reader*. Atlantic Highlands, NJ: Humanities Press International.
De Las Casas, A. (2008). Is nationalism good for you? *Foreign Policy Magazine*, 19 February. Available at: www.foreignpolicy.com
Deutsch, K. (1966). *Nationalism and social communication: An inquiry into the foundations of nationality*. Cambridge, MA: MIT Press.
DFID. (2011). *Politics of poverty: Elites, citizens and states. Findings from ten years of DFID-funded research on governance and fragile states*. London, UK: Department for International Development.
Dobbins, J. (2003). *America's role in nation-building: From Germany to Iraq*. Los Angeles, CA: RAND Corporation.
Dobbins, J. (2007). *The beginner's guide to nation-building*. Los Angeles, CA: RAND Corporation.
Dobbins, J. (2008). *After the Taliban: Nation-building in Afghanistan*. Washington, DC: Potomac Books.
Einstein, A. (1929). What life means to Einstein: An interview by George Sylvester Viereck *Saturday Evening Post*, 26 October.
Fund for Peace. (2004–2012). Failed State Index 2006–2012. Available at: www.fundforpeace.org/global/?q=fsi
Fukuyama, F. (2004). *State-building: Governance and world order in the 21st century*. Ithaca, NY: Cornell University Press.
Gallie, W. (1962). Essentially contested subjects. In M. Black (Ed.), *The importance of language*. Englewood Cliffs, NJ: Prentice Hall.
Gellner, E. (1983). *Nations and nationalism*. Ithaca, NY: Cornell University Press.
Giddens, A. (1987). *The nation-state and violence*. Berkeley, CA: University of California Press.
Gilbert, A. (2010). *On the methodological advantages of contradiction in foreign state-building*. Paper presented at Workshop on Research on State–Building in the Western Balkans: Comparative Methodologies, London School of Economics, London, UK, 10 December.
Greenfeld, L. (1992). *Nationalism: Five roads to modernity*. Cambridge, MA: Harvard University Press.
Gregorian, V. (1999). *New directions for Carnegie Corporation of New York: A report to the board*. Carnegie Corporation of New York, February.
Guehenno, J. M. (1995). *The end of the nation-state*. Minneapolis, MN: University of Minnesota.
Gurr, T. (2000). *State Failure Task Force Report: Phase III findings*. McClean, VA: SAIC.
Hall, J. (1993). Nationalism: Classifed and explained. *Daedalus, 122*, July.
Hechter, M. (2000). *Containing nationalism*. Oxford, UK: Oxford University Press.
Hegel's Philosophy of Right, Third Part: Ethical Life iii. The State. Available at: www.marxists.org
Herbst, J. (2000). *States and power in Africa: Comparative lessons in authority and control*. Princeton, NJ: Princeton University Press.
Hobsbawm, E. (1990). *Nations and nationalism since 1788*. Cambridge, UK: Cambridge University Press.
Horowitz, D. (1985). *Ethnic groups in conflict*. Berkeley, CA: University of California Press.
Ignatieff, M. (1993). *Blood and belonging: Journeys into the new nationalism*. London, UK: BBC Books and Chatto & Windus.
Jackson, R. (1991). *Quasi-states: Sovereignty, international relations and the Third World*. Cambridge, UK: Cambridge University Press.
Jones, B., and Elgin–Cossart, M. (2011). Development in the shadow of violence: A knowledge agenda for

policy 2011. *Report on the future of investment in evidence on issues of fragility, security and conflict.* International Development Research Council, Ottawa, Canada, 22 September.

Kaplan, R. (1993). *Balkan ghosts: A journey through history.* New York, NY: St Martin's Press.

Kennan, G. (Ed.). (1993). *The other Balkan Wars: A 1913 Carnegie Endowment Inquiry in retrospect.* Washington, DC: Carnegie Endowment for International Peace.

Kirkby, C., and Murray, C. (2010). Elusive autonomy in Sub−Saharan Africa. In M. Weller and K. Nobbs (Eds.), *Asymmetric autonomy and the settlement of ethnic conflict.* Philadelphia, PA: University of Pennsylvania Press, pp. 97−120.

Kohn, K. (1958). *The idea of nationalism,* New York, NY: Macmillan.

Krasner, S. (1988). Sovereignty: An institutional perspective. *Comparative Political Studies, 2,* April.

Krasner, S. (1999). *Sovereignty: Organized hypocrisy.* Princeton, NJ: Princeton University Press.

Kuzio, T. (2001). Nationalizing states or nation−building: Critical view of the theoretical literature and empirical evidence. *Nations and Nationalism, 7*(2), April.

Kymlicka, W. (2001). *Politics in the vernacular: Nationalism, multiculturalism, and citizenship.* Oxford, UK: Oxford University Press.

Laremont, R. R. (Ed.). (2005). *Borders, nationalism and the African State.* Boulder, CO: Lynne Rienner.

Lemay−Hébert,N. (2009). Statebuilding without nation−building? Legitimacy, state failure and the limits of the institutional approach. *Journal of Intervention and Statebuilding, 3*(1), 21−45.

Liberia Truth and Reconciliation Commission Project. (2012). Available at: www.theadvocatesfor humanrights.org

Ma, S. Y. (1992).Nationalism: State−building or State−destroying?*Social Science Journal, 29*(3), 293.

Marquand, D. (2012). Europe's missing union. *New York Times,* 8 July, p. 28.

Migdal, J. (1994). Introduction: Developing a state in society perspective. In J. Migdal, A. Kohli, and V. Shue (Eds.), *State power and social forces: Domination and transformation in the Third World.* Cambridge, UK: Cambridge University Press.

Moynihan, D. (1993). *Pandemonium: Ethnicity and international politics.* Oxford, UK: Oxford University Press.

Nairn, T. (1981). *The break up of Britain: Crisis and neo-nationalism.* London, UK: Verso.

North, D. (1981). *Structure and change in economic history.* New York, NY: W. W. Norton.

OECD/DAC. (2008). State building in situations of fragility: Initial findings. Paris, France: OECD/DA Publishing.

OECD/DAC. (2011). *A new deal for engagement in fragile states 2011.* International Dialogue on Peacebuilding and Statebuilding (IDPS), OECD/DAC. Available at: www.oecd.org

Ohmae, K. (1992−1993). The rise of the region state. *Foreign Affairs,* Winter, 78−87.

Orwell, G. (1945). Notes on nationalism. Available at: http://orwell.ru/home.html

Paris, R., and Sisk, T. (Eds.). (2009).*The dilemmas of statebuilding: Confronting the contradictions of postwar peace operations,* New York, NY: Routledge.

Patrick, S., and Rice, S. (2008). *Index of state weakness in the developing world.* Washington, DC: Brookings Institution.

Pfaff, W. (1993). *The wrath of nations: Civilization and the furies of nationalism.* New York, NY: Simon and Schuster.

Ra'nan, U., and Mesner, M. (1991). Nation and state: Order out of chaos. In R. Ra'nan et al. (Eds.),*State and nation in multi-ethnic societies.* Manchester, UK: Manchester University Press.

Smith, A. (1993). *National identity.* Reno, NE: University of Nevada Press.

Smith, A. (1999). 'Ethno−symbolism' and the study of nationalism. In A. Smith, *Myth and memories of the nation.* Oxford, UK: Oxford University Press.

Smith, H., and Stares, P. (2007). *Diasporas in conflict: Peace-makers or peace-wreckers?* Tokyo, Japan: United Nations University Press.

Stamis, E. (2010). Values, context and hybridity. *Working paper: The future of the peacebuilding architecture project.* Centre for International Policy Studies, University of Ottawa, Ottawa, Canada and the Norwegian Institute of International Affairs, Oslo, Norway.

Stepan, A., Linz, J., and Yadev, Y. (2011). *Crafting state-nations: India and other multinational democracies.* Baltimore, MD: Johns Hopkins University Press.

Sutherland, C. (2012). *Nationalism in the twenty-first century: Challenges and responses.* Basingstoke, UK: Palgrave Macmillan.

Tamir, Y. (1993). *Liberal nationalism.* Report for the Institute for Philosophy and Public Policy, School of Public Affairs, University of Maryland, College Park, MD, Special Issue, winter/spring.

Tilly, C. (1990). *Coercion, capital, and European states: AD 990–1992,* Cambridge, MA: Blackwell.

USAID. (2011). *Statebuilding in situations of fragility and conflict: Relevance for US policies and programs.* Washington, DC: United States Agency for International Development.

Weber, E. (1976). *Peasants into Frenchmen: The modernization of rural France, 1870–1914.* London, UK: Sage.

Weber, M. (1948). Politics as a vocation. In H. H. Gerth and C. Wright Mills (Eds.), *From Max Weber: Essays in sociology.* London, UK: Routledge.

World Bank, The. (2011). Conflict, security and development. *The World Development Report 2011,* Washington, DC: The World Bank.

World Bank Group Report on Low Income Countries Under Stress: A Task Force Report. (2002)., Washington, DC: World Bank Group.

Zoellick, R. (2009). Fragile states: Securing development. *Survival,* 50(6), International Institute for Strategic Studies, London, UK.

7
STATEBUILDING, CIVIL SOCIETY, AND THE PRIVILEGING OF DIFFERENCE

David Chandler

This chapter seeks to draw out an understanding of the role of narratives and discourses of cultural difference and of civil society development, within international statebuilding, through the location of the discourse of culture as a transitional stage between interventionist and regulatory discourses of race and of civil society. It particularly seeks to highlight that the discourse of civil society is key to understanding the statebuilding discourses of intervention and regulation that have developed in the past decade. In drawing out the links between the framings of cultural divides and of civil society, this chapter seeks to explain how the discourse of civil society intervention has been reinvented on the basis of the moral divide established and cohered through the discourse of culture and how the discourse of civil society contains a strong apologetic content, capable of legitimizing and explaining the persistence of social and economic problems or political fragmentation while simultaneously offering potential policy programmes on the basis of highly ambitious goals of social transformation.

In the policy framings of international statebuilding, the concept of civil society is used very differently to how the concept was deployed in traditional political discourses of liberal modernity. This chapter will clarify some of these differences and highlight that, whereas for traditional conceptions of civil society autonomy was seen as a positive factor, in the international state – building discourse autonomy is seen as a problematic factor and one that necessitates regulatory intervention. Civil society discourse highlights the problematic nature of autonomy, understood as irreducible differences, which risk conflict if not regulated via the correct institutional mechanisms. In the distinctive use of difference in this context of external engagement, the concept of civil society is used in ways which reflect and draw upon pre–modern concepts o difference, especially the pre–existing colonial and post–colonial discourses of race and culture.

Civil society will be understood less as a really existing set of institutions and practices, or as a sphere of policy intervention, than as a discursive framework capable of producing meaning, i.e., as a policy paradigm through which the problems (and solutions) of statebuilding intervention are interpreted. The cultural paradigm established a moral divide between formally equal polities in the West and in the post–colonial world, suggesting that the political subject of non–Western orders was less capable of acting in a rational or autonomous manner. This problematization of the post–colonial subject and moral framing of difference was reproduced in the paradigm of civil society, which reproduced the apologia of essentialized differences at the same time as under-standing irrational or sub–optimal social, economic, or political outcomes on the basis of rational choices made by autonomous subjects. The civil society framework views post-colonial societies from the standpoint of self-governing individuals (as in the liberal-democratic model) rather than as submerged and subjugated by collectivities of race, nation, or religion (as in the framings of race and culture) and, to this extent, may appear to be more progressive. However, as argued below, this would be misleading.

The differentiation of culture

After World War II, overt articulations of racial understandings of international divisions were largely discredited by the experiences of Nazism, the successes of anti-colonial struggles, the decline of the European colonial powers and the Cold War competition of the Soviet Union. However, the inequalities of the international sphere were not overcome. In many ways, the arguments of racial distinction were taken over through the replacement of the concept of race by the concept of culture (Malik, 1996). This discourse of apology in the essentialization or reification of difference took the form of discourses of cultural difference. Cultural differences were given the same determining weight as earlier distinctions of race, on the basis that cultures were separate, homogeneous, and with their own paths of development. Path dependencies were key to understanding culture in reified terms of dependency upon the past rather than as reflective of the social relations of the present. The hold of the past over the present thereby enabled a moral rather than a racial critique of the capacity of the colonial (and post-colonial) Other.

As Edward Said noted in *Orientalism*, social and political movements of non-Western societies were interpreted in cultural rather than political terms by colonial theorists. These interpretations always highlighted the psychological and non-rational underpinnings of demands and protests, which were seen to express the hold of tradition or the need to express identity, often in reaction to the civilizing impact of the colonial project (Said, 1985: 236). This moral critique of the non-Western subject was based upon a culturalized framing of the subject as less rational than the liberal rights-subject of Western democracy. Culture played an important role as apologia for colonial power and the limits to which colonial authorities were able to marginalize resistance to their rule. In this context, opposition was understood to be the product of a clash of cultures rather than as a product of colonial frameworks of domination. This understanding of a clash of cultures took its sharpest form in the theorization of the problems of 'transition' or of 'hybridity' as an inevitable consequence of Western influence

Hybridity was seen to be a problematic consequence of colonial influence undermining traditional forms of social relations without establishing Western norms and values. Instead, the clash of cultures was seen to result in a 'spiritual,' 'moral,' or 'cultural' vacuum (Furedi, 1994a: 123). Colonial intervention had resulted in the dilemma or contradiction of creating a maladjusted society, lacking the stability of either traditional society or modern society. It was in the discourses of imperial apologia in the late 1940s that much of the statebuilding and statebuilding discussions of transition (in the 1990s) and hybridity (in the 2000s) have their intellectual roots.

One of the key concepts denoting the problematic nature of this clash of cultures was that of 'marginal man': the product of both colonial intervention and traditional culture, but a hybrid product, inhabiting neither culture but exhibiting the problems of this cultural clash. The theory of marginal man was first explored by Robert Ezra Park, one of the leading American sociologist in the interwar years and a former President of the American Sociological Society (Furedi, 1994b: 52–53). Park explicitly raised questions about the moral integrity of the marginal man, developing the notion that an individual suspended between two cultural realities is marginal, resulting in difficulties in establishing a stable identity. His work on the problems of hybridity was more fully developed, in the colonial context, by his student Everett Stonequist, who explained different reactions to colonial domination as the product of maladjustment (Stonequist, 1961).

Where the discourse of race expressed the confidence of imperial rule and the essentializin of difference, the discourse of culture expressed the decline of the imperial project and a defense against the shifting international norms, which expressed more sympathy for the claims of the colonial subject. The elitist assumptions of Western superiority were no longer reproduced in the discourse of race, but those of the psychological problems of (post−)colonial transition and of cultural hybridity: these moral, psychological, and cultural frameworks reflected the shift fro naturalizing and legitimizing external rule to ways of negotiating imperial withdrawal, suggesting that the limited progress made to democracy and self−government and in terms of economic and social progress could be explained through the path−dependencies of culture and the irrational outcomes of the cultural clash between the 'liberal' West and the traditional values and beliefs of the colonial Other. This discourse of culture as apologia can be drawn out in relation to the three key themes of what will become the statebuilding discourse: development, conflict, an democracy.

Culture and development

In the post−1945 world, the international agenda was dominated by decolonization and while the concept of culture played a similar role to that of race, the questions of controversy were less those of rule and the justifications for political inequality than those of economic and wealt division between the former colonial powers and the post−colonial world. By the 1970s and the end of the post−war economic boom of European reconstruction, the economic and social divisions between the 'developed' and the 'developing' world had become greater and were the subject of a number of critiques that understood the problem to be that of the world market system which reproduced the inequalities of power and opportunity despite the formal equalities of the international states−system (for example, Wallerstein, 1976; Gunder Frank, 1967).

Douglass C. North developed the framework of institutionalism as a direct apologetic defence of the status quo, asserting that, rather than capitalism, culture was the key to understanding developmental inequalities. North tackled the framings of the critics of underdevelopment directly through the assertion that there was no such thing as the logic of capitalism, but rather many capitalisms, dependent on their institutional and cultural context (North 1990; see also Foucault, 2008: 164–165). The important point to highlight is that culture came to the fore along with disillusionment with the extent of economic and social progress in the post−colonial world. The shift from economic and social explanations to the realm of the cultural ref ected the lowering of policy horizons, as culture operated as a limiting factor for international intervention. For North, there was little that international intervention could do, as even institutional reform at the level of state policy would only have a limited impact unless the informal values and norms of post−colonial societies were in line with these policy goals. There was therefore little that could be done to externally assist post−colonial development, as 'informal constraints that are culturally derived will not change immediately in reaction to changes in formal rules' and it was this 'tension between altered formal rules and the persisting informal constraints' that produced counterproductive outcomes (1990: 45).

Culture, conflict, and democracy

During the Cold War, the apologetic framing of the problems of the post−colonial world was defensive, attempting to exculpate the colonial powers and explain the reproduction and institutionalization of inequalities independently of the impact of the workings of the world market. This culturalized framing of difference and inequality was given greater weight in the first decade after the end of the Cold War as the end of superpower rivalry opened up the post–colonial world to more extensive international intervention.

Culture was a vital framing justifying new frameworks of intervention in the 1990s. However, culture operated as a way of legitimizing intervention, in an international context where traditional views of sovereignty and non–intervention were formally dominant, rather than as a comprehensive framework for international engagement in the paradigm of international statebuilding. In this respect, culture already appeared to be a limiting framing in the 1990s. Perhaps the best examples of 1990s discussions of the role of cultural difference can be seen in Mary Kaldor's conception of 'New Wars' and Francis Fukuyama's views of the role of culture in relation to civil society in democratic transitions. Here we see culture play the role of legitimizing external international engagement but also limiting it.

Kaldor developed the concept of 'New Wars' to describe conflicts in the post–colonial worl in ways that constructed a moral divide between the understanding of war and conflict in th West and in the non–West. The binary of old and new war has little to do with the spatial framing of conflict as intra–state rather than inter–state; for example, the US or Spanish civil wars woul be construed as old wars rather than new wars (Kaldor, 1999: 13–30). Following Kalevi Holsti's analysis of 'wars of the third kind' (Holsti, 1996: 19–40), Kaldor drew a moral distinction where old wars were rational, constitutive of a collective or public interest, and politically legitimate, whereas new wars were understood to be irrational, driven by private interest, and politically illegitimate. This moral divide then enabled Kaldor to argue that illegitimate political repre – sentatives had no right to hide behind the rights of sovereignty and that external humanitarian intervention was morally necessary and legitimate, casting international interveners as interest-free enforcers of emerging international legal norms rather than as undermining international law.

Like Kaldor, Fukuyama also used a culture paradigm, in the 1990s, to explain the limits to democratic transition and the restrictive nature of international recognition and institutional integration, suggesting that those former–Soviet states that were not being engaged with (such as Belarus, Ukraine, and Russia) lacked the cultural preconditions for transition. In calling for a lowering of expectations about the speed and extent of post–communist reform, he advocated an apologia based on the problem of underestimating the cultural gap:

> [S]ocial engineering on the level of institutions has hit a massive brick wall: experiences of the past century have taught most democracies that ambitious rearrangements of institutions often cause more unanticipated problems than they solve. By contrast, the real diff culties affecting the quality of life in modern democracies have to do with the social and cultural pathologies that seem safely beyond the reach of institutional solutions, and hence of public policy. The chief issue is quickly becoming one of culture.
>
> *(Fukuyama, 1995: 9)*

Fukuyama stressed that while civil society may be a precondition for democratic transition, 'civil society in turn has precursors and preconditions at the level of culture' (1995: 7). For Fukuyama, the understandings needed to explain the slowness of cultural change require the expertise of sociologists and anthropologists rather than political theorists (1995: 7).

The reinvention of civil society

Culture played a similar role to race in essentializing difference during the Cold War and early 1990s, in that it acted as apologia for differential treatment. Central to the continuity of discourses of race and culture and those of the more extensive interventionist frameworks of international statebuilding would be this privileging of difference over universality. The extension of international statebuilding is dependent upon the dismissal of universal social, economic, or political frameworks of understanding. The precondition for the reinvention of civil society as both explanatory factor and sphere of policy–making is the understanding that the problems of post–colonial or post–conflict society are a product of difference located within the historic path dependencies of social structures and institutions: there is thereby no universalizing logic within which we can understand the actions and political expressions of these societies within the same framings as those of the Western liberal–democratic subject, held to be capable of rational political and economic choices.

The key to understanding the role of the concept of civil society in the framing of international statebuilding is in how post–colonial or post–conflict societies come to be understood as open to manipulation or change through policy–intervention. In fact, the institution–building at the heart of international statebuilding is focused on a reframing of traditional liberal democratic conceptions of civil society rather than any shift in the formal understanding of the operation of state–level institutions. For this reason it is important to spend a little time on what could be called the post–liberal framing of civil society and the governance framing of policy objectives that accompanies it (see Chandler, 2010).

The first point to establish is that the shift from cultural framings of the problems of colonia and post–colonial societies to a civil society framing operates on two levels: (1) that of ideas or understanding, the comprehension of the nature of the problems themselves, and (2) the practical or policy level, of the kinds of external policy responses that might be appropriate to address these problems. On both these levels, it would be wrong to understand the civil society framing of problems or policy interventions as being narrowly focused on something that we might seek to describe as civil society, as a real sphere or set of relations. Foucault's work on biopolitics usefully draws our attention to the transformation of civil society framings as both ideational (operating as a 'network' or 'grid' of 'intelligibility,' i.e., as a way of understanding the problematic of post–colonial or post–conflict society) and as facilitating a set of practices, making possible series of policy interventions, which follow from civil society becoming a sphere of statebuilding intervention (becoming 'governmentalizable') (Foucault, 2008: 252).

The second point, which Foucault also draws our attention to, is that this framing of civil society depends on inverting or transforming the classical liberal doctrine of civil society as a sphere in which the autonomous subject interacts. For Enlightenment theorists, civil society was conceived in political and juridical terms; as Foucault notes, 'civil society is absolutely indistinguishable from political society,' for example, in classic liberal framings such as John Locke's *Second Treatise of Government* (Foucault, 2008: 297). This view of the rights–bearing autonomous subject of civil society is also clear in the classical treatment in Adam Ferguson's *Essay on the History of Civil Society*, in which civil society is the political reflection of Adam Smith' economic analysis in which the autonomous interaction of rational interest–bearing individuals results in the collective development of the social good.

The foundational basis of the classical rights–based liberal framing of civil society is the autonomous interaction of subjects free from governing intervention. The rights– and interest– bearing subject of liberal theorizing exists prior to the institutions of government, and civil society is understood to be grounded in human nature as an indispensable and constant factor of human existence (Foucault, 2008: 298–299). The difference between civil society and political society is not in the subjects constituting it but in the lack of a formal contract establishing or constituting sovereignty; the reciprocal relations are the basis of market relations and liberal–democratic forms of political–legal relations, but exist independently and prior to these.

The subject of civil society – the autonomous rational individual – is the foundational subject of both halves of the liberal equation of government, the subject of both rights and interests. With regard to both, the individual subject's pursuit of self–interest coincides with the collective good as interests converge either through the market mechanism or through the reasoned debate of the political sphere. The liberal subject is not open to government intervention, but rather establishes the rationality of *laissez-faire* (Foucault, 2008: 270). This subject is very different from the post–colonial or post–conflict subject who is assumed to be unable to pursue their interest or rights in a civic way, which contributes to the collective good of society. In this framing, the problems of post–conflict or post–colonial societies are understood as problems with the frameworks or institutional contexts of these societies, as reflected in the choices made by individuals. This enables these choices to become understood as being amenable to policy intervention.

The third crucial point to highlight is that the policy interventions, which can impact on these choices, do not necessarily have to be restricted to the narrow sphere of what might be described as civil society in 'reality.' In the civil society paradigm of international statebuilding, international policy practices assume that the rational choices made by post–colonial and post–conflict subject are irrational due to the institutional context and that this institutional context can be reformed in specif c ways to facilitate the choosing of different choices. In this way, the divisive context of policy–making hierarchies can be legitimized (as in racial and cultural understandings) but the problem of the autonomy of the post–colonial subject is brought to the fore. In the civil society approach there is no assumption that external interveners can make policies on behalf of the post–conflict subject

The task of international statebuilding intervention, in this paradigm of understanding, is that of the indirect influencing of outcomes through institutional means. The framework of civil society enables management at a distance, where intervention is understood as necessary but never as suff cient as the post–colonial subject is the means and ends of intervention. Civil society will only have been achieved when this subject makes the 'right' or 'civil' choices revealing a rationality and maturity with regard to collective interests. The task of international intervention is to help facilitate this through policy intervention at the level of institutional frameworks facilitating the compatibility of individual choices with collective outcomes.

Civil society becomes central to the international statebuilding paradigm of understanding only when this classical liberal framing is transformed: when civil society becomes a sphere of external or international policy–intervention rather than an unproblematic sphere of autonomy as under rationalist framings of the liberal polity. Civil society becomes a way of understanding social problems and policy interventions on the basis of reconceiving cultural discourses, which understood problems as deeply rooted and not amenable to policy intervention. In fact, policy intervention only becomes possible with the expansion of civil society as a framework for understanding and managing social problems. By removing civil society from the political–juridical framing of rights–based liberalism it opens up 'a new object, a new domain or field' fo policy intervention (Foucault, 2008: 295) on the basis of which post–colonial and post–conflic society can become the object of policy.

Foucault points toward how civil society is transformed. Whereas cultural understandings (as racial framings before them) understood social problems as being the product of collective identification and belonging, the civil society framework privileges the individual and under–

stands social outcomes as the products of individual choices. Civil society becomes the mediating link in which individuals respond to 'environmental variables' (Foucault, 2008: 269). Methodologically, the shift from the collective of race, ethnicity, or culture to the privileging of the individual enables civil society to be formulated as a sphere of intervention.

The statebuilding policy framework depends on the relationship between the state and society being inversed. Rather than society being natural and the state as the product of societal relations, the state is prior and society and social relations are seen to be the product of state–shaped institutions at both formal and informal levels. In this way, society (of interest–pursuing individuals) is held to be highly malleable. This malleability is based on viewing social and political outcomes from the viewpoint of individual choices. As Foucault notes, in the shift from culture to civil society 'we move over to the side of the individual subject' but not as the subject of rights; rather as an object open to policy interventions (2008: 252).

The transformation of cultural framings of confict in post–colonial or post–conflict societie into civil society framings can be highlighted through a comparison of Kaldor's 1990s New Wars thesis with the 'greed and grievance' framework developed by Paul Collier and Anke Hoeffle in the mid–2000s (Collier and Hoeffler 2004; Collier et al., 2009). It could be argued that th intention of the Collier thesis is little different from Kaldor's: that of morally delegitimizing political actors in contexts of post–colonial confct; however, Collier's reconstruction of confict in the rational choice framework of institutionalist approaches facilitates a much broader or more holistic range of policy interventions than does Kaldor's.

Rather than morally distinguish the post–colonial context from that of the West, making it seem merely 'irrational' or 'backward,' the rational choice framing of Collier seeks to develop an understanding of post–colonial societies in the universalist terms of economic frameworks of individual choices. In their critique of theorists who sought to understand conflict in the rationa terms of political rights (struggles over grievances), Collier and his Oxford University–based team sought to understand conflict in terms of individual economic interests. In this framing, grievanc no longer becomes explanatory or a legitimating factor; it is the opportunity for rebellion that has explanatory value. Essentially, if finance is easily available (for example, due to easy access t primary commodity exports) and there is little opportunity cost (i.e., few other avenues to earn income, if access to secondary education is low and the economy is stagnant) then conflict 'entrepreneurs' will arise who do not necessarily have any stake in furthering the interests or needs of their alleged constituents (Collier and Hoeffler, 2004)

Conflict is entirely removed from the political–juridical framing of modern liberal understandings. For Collier's project, 'where rebellion is feasible, it will occur without any special inducements in terms of motivation' (Collier et al., 2009: 19); 'motivation is indeterminate, being supplied by whatever agenda happens to be adopted by the f rst social entrepreneur to occupy the viable niche' (Collier et al., 2009: 20). Once conf ict is understood as the product of the choices of individuals, within an economic (rather than a political) framework of understanding, the possibility of reshaping the institutional context, and therefore the outcome of decision–making, arises. This approach of indirectly infuencing the conduct of individuals on the basis of this shift from a rights–based to an economic or rational–choice framework of understanding is the civil society approach which has displaced cultural framings within the policy–practices of international statebuilding.

To reiterate, the civil society framework can best be understood as an ideational paradigm or discourse, facilitating a certain 'governmental rationality.' This perspective is rather different from those that have a narrower focus on civil society as a reality. Intervention in the narrower fiel of civil society is just one set of policy interventions within this framework and often is not the most important. For example, in the work of Collier and his team, who have been highly influential in the policy developments of the World Bank, this civil society framing leads to a range of policy interventions, of which work in and upon civil society itself is not the key concern. Bearing in mind the framework of opportunities, rather than political or ideological concerns, policy is organized around minimizing the opportunities and raising the costs of rebellion. Such policies might include the development of international regulatory institutions concerning the trade in primary goods, preventing rebel groups having easy access to world markets; the sharing of sovereignty or international institutional control of income sources to prevent state capture being the source of aggrandizement; policies that prevent barriers to job creation or educational opportunities, thus raising the opportunity costs of engagement in rebel activities; and external support to enhance the capacity of the state military to more easily deter rebel movements, etc.

Civil society and the problem of autonomy

Whereas the liberal–democratic tradition argues that social conflicts can be resolved through rational deliberation and societal engagement, the statebuilding paradigm does not assume that conflicts within civil society can be resolved through democratic processes and therefore opens up the sphere of civil society to policy intervention in order to structure institutional frameworks that can contain conflicts. This active, interventionist approach to civil society argues that external intervention by government or external actors is necessary to challenge or disrupt irrational or counterproductive forms of political identification through the process of multiplying frames o political identification. In this respect, interventionist civil society policy has become central to international statebuilding as a framework in which political and social collectivities are understood and engaged with as products of irrational mindsets shaped by the past but as open to transformation.

In this framing, civil society intervention is often presented as a way of challenging criminal, ethnic, regional, or nationalist conceptions of political identity and providing a policy framework through which these identifications can be substituted with a variety of alternative identications, such as those of women, youth, unemployed, small businesses, the precondition being that these alternative identities transgress and cross-cut those that are considered to be irrational and problematic. This multiplication of political identities is then held to pluralize the political process, with barriers to progress in statebuilding goals overcome through the means of civil society intervention.

As Audra Mitchell and Stephanie Kappler highlight, this framing of civil society as a sphere of policy intervention draws upon internal Western discourses critiquing liberal rationalist approaches (much as earlier colonial discourses drew upon internal Western elite concerns) (Mitchell and Kappler, 2009). Concerns with difference and the inability of the liberal–democratic process to overcome particularist and conflicting identities have been expressed clearly by critic of the rationalist assumptions of modern framings of the political. Perhaps most infiential in this respect have been agonistic frameworks, which suggest that conflict is inevitable and that differences are irreconcilable through liberal–democratic frameworks (Honig, 1993), but that conflict can be accommodated and transformed through civil society intervention with the goal of multiplying political identifications. This has been expressed by, for example, William Connolly in terms of the development of 'agonistic respect' (Connolly 2002), or by Chantal Mouffe through reviving the left/right distinction (Mouffe, 2005). The key point about the agonistic critique of rationalist approaches to democracy was that civil society becomes problematized as a sphere of irreconcilable difference at the same time as it becomes transformed into a sphere of policy intervention. Transferred to the sphere of international intervention, in the statebuilding policy framework, a whole set of policy practices opens up, based on the thesis that through engaging with and transforming uncivil post–colonial or post–conflict societies, irrational antagonistic conflict can be transformed into rational agonistic contestation. Throug institutionalist practices, external intervention is held to be able to build or constitute civil societies as a basis on which the problems of societal development, inclusion, and security can be resolved.

As noted above, with regard to the moral or cultural understanding of the problem of post–colonial society, the starting assumption is that civil society lacks the rational or civic qualities of civil society in the West. The focus of policy analysts is on group, ethnic, religious, or regional identifications, which are understood to be products of the past or path–dependencies of conflict, or colonial or Soviet rule. Civil society is understood to be hybrid in the sense of reflecting th divisions or traditions of society but as open to intervention and transformation through informal institutional change (change of the norms and values of society). The statebuilding discourse of civil society intervention is very different from that of the 1980s and early 1990s, where writers and commentators tended to juxtapose civil society as a sphere of pristine values and civic norms *vis-à-vis* the sphere of formal politics and state power, which was seen to be self–seeking and exclusionary. Civil society as a sphere of external intervention is necessarily hybrid and the fiel of both strategic calculation and tactical engagement, as Timothy D. Sisk notes:

> Strategically, the promotion of civil society cannot occur in a platitudinous fashion that sees all civil society as an inherent good for peace and democratization. Quite the contrary, there needs to be a sharp strategy of differentiation in civil society promotion by which international donors are quite discriminating in identifying three types of non–stateactors to support: those that cross–cut identity lines or fissures of conflict . those that are moderate but reflecting primarily one perspective or protagonist socia group, and those that are more extreme but which, through coaxing and inclusion, can become moderate.
>
> *(Sisk, 2008: 255)*

In the statebuilding literature, the goal of external intervention is to transform civil society forms of voluntary association from existing and divisive forms (of bonding social capital) to pluralist and inclusivist forms (of bridging social capital) (Putnam, 2000). The clash of cultures, in the self–understanding of international statebuilders, is played out in the policy interventions that attempt to transform traditional (non)civil society into a civic polity in which social and political divisions are submerged, mitigated, or disappear. For this reason, civil society cannot be left to its own devices: 'effective international action requires identifying and working diligently against those civil society groups that are deemed not constructive to peacebuilding aims, either because of their irredeemably extreme nature and positions or because they have other interests or activities ... that work against progress toward peace or democracy' (Sisk, 2008: 255–256).

Civil society is seen as the sphere capable of generating the solutions to problems of conflct, the barriers to development or to democracy. The focus on civil society rather than social or economic transformation builds on the moral and cultural discourses of empire with their emphasis of maladjustment and psychological framings of social and political questions. The problems are perceived to be in the hold of the past over the minds of post–colonial subjects rather than the social relations of the present. The precondition of civil society intervention is the assumption of the irrationality of the informal institutional frameworks – of the mindsets – of post–colonial subjects.

These irrational mindsets are held to be capable of transformation through policy intervention; it is held that irrational values and identities can be challenged by education and social interaction which encourages the pluralization of political identities. It is for this reason that (in this narrower framing) civil society intervention takes two main forms (Belloni, 2008). First, there is support for 'democracy groups,' NGOs engaging in policy advocacy or civic education, which directly promote the politics of inclusion and civic principles. The second group of internationally funded NGOs are those that, while not directly advocating democracy and civic values, attempt to pluralize political identification on the basis of ascribed identities held to be capable of breakin down primary collective affiliations, such as those of women, youth, or small and medium business enterprises. In post-conflict situations, often any framework for engaging people acros ethnic or ideological divides is considered productive for changing people's mindsets and breaking them from the hold of dominant and problematic political identities (Chandler, 1999: 40).

Despite being a framework making a broad range of policy interventions both possible and legitimate, the discourse of civil society is flexible enough to also offer an understanding of th limits to policy success or to societal transformation (as with the previous discourses of race and of culture). As Carothers and Ottaway note, civil society intervention, as a key framing of policy-making, evolved with the extension of statebuilding mandates and goals in response to the perceived failures of democratic transition in the mid-1990s (2000: 7). During the Cold War there was no discussion of civil society intervention as part of democracy-promotion; intervention was limited to indirect support for economic development or support for moderate political parties against political extremes. There was little support for societal movements, which were often seen to be too much under the influence of leftist programs. The exception was in Easter Europe, where social protest opposed communist rule. The end of the Cold War enabled greater societal intervention as well as associating civil society movements with democratic transition.

Civil society becomes a focal point of international intervention and the statebuilding project because it posits a framework in which international engagement can be legitimized on the basis of the autonomy of the post-colonial subject. Cultural frameworks posit autonomy as problem-atic and act as apologias for the limited success of external intervention but cannot provide a framework of legitimacy for intervention or for a set of policy prescriptions. In civil society interventions, the autonomy of the post-colonial subject is both apologia and means and the goal of intervention. Intervention in civil society is seen to be the precondition for the autonomy of the subject, with civil society – harmonious or conflict-free interaction – as the goal of intervention.

Conclusion

International statebuilding is increasingly operating on a holistic paradigm of preventive intervention and indirect regulation, external intervention not to control states or societies but to enable them to manage their autonomy. The discourse of culture, which replaced that of race as an essentializing explanation for inequality, fits uneasily with the interventionist framewor of international statebuilding. The emphasis on differential cultures provides an apologia for economic and social inequalities but provides little purchase for regulatory intervention. It is only once cultural differences are understood as social constructs, which can be shaped and reshaped through institutional intervention, that civil society becomes a central concept within the international statebuilding policy framework.

The focus on civil society maintains the role of race or culture in rationalizing difference and inequality on the basis of distinctive 'path dependencies' created in specific contexts of interactio between states and societies, but also – through positing these differences as the rational choices of the individuals within those societies – opens up society as a sphere of external policy intervention. Civil society enables difference and inequality to be articulated and explained but locates these distinctions as products of the choices of these societies themselves. In taking over a modern liberal concept, which had a positive framing of individual autonomy, the statebuilding discourse tends to be much more judgmental and moralistic about drawbacks to policy inter − ventions at the same time as expanding the interventionist policy remit of international statebuilding beyond that possible through the framework of cultural division.

References

Belloni, R. (2008). Civil society in war−to−democracy transitions. In A. K. Jarstad and T. D. Sisk (Eds.), *From war to democracy: Dilemmas of statebuilding*. Cambridge, UK: Cambridge University Press.
Carothers, T., and Ottaway, M. (2000). Introduction: The burgeoning world of civil society aid. In M. Ottaway and T. Carothers (Eds.), *Funding virtue: Civil society and democracy promotion*. Washington, DC: Carnegie Endowment for International Peace.
Chandler, D. (1999). *Bosnia: Faking democracy after Dayton*. London, UK: Pluto.
Chandler, D. (2010). The EU and Southeastern Europe: The rise of post−liberal governance. *Third World Quarterly*, *31*(1) 69–85.
Collier, P., and Hoeffler, A. (2004). Greed and grievance in civil war*Oxford Economic Papers*, *56*, 563–595.
Collier, P., Hoeffler, A., and Rohner, D. (2009). Beyond greed and grievance: Feasibility and civil war *Oxford Economic Papers*, *61*, 1–27.
Connolly, W. (2002). *Identity/Difference: Democratic negotiations of political paradox*. Minneapolis, MN: University of Minnesota Press.
Foucault, M. (2008). *The birth of biopolitics: Lectures at the Collège de France 1978–1979*. Basingstoke, UK: Palgrave.
Fukuyama, F. (1995). The primacy of culture. *Journal of Democracy*, *6*(1), 7–14.
Furedi, F. (1994a). *Colonial wars and the politics of Third World nationalism*. London, UK: I. B. Tauris.
Furedi, F. (1994b). *The new ideology of imperialism: Renewing the moral imperative*. London, UK: Pluto Press.
Gunder Frank, A. (1967). *Capitalism and underdevelopment in Latin America*. New York, NY: Monthly Review Press.
Holsti, K. (1996). *The state, war, and the state of war*. Cambridge, UK: Cambridge University Press.
Honig, B. (1993). *Political theory and the displacement of politics*. Ithaca, NY: Cornell University Press.
Kaldor, M. (1999). *Old and new wars: Organized violence in a global age*. Cambridge, UK: Polity Press.
Malik, K. (1996) *The meaning of race: Race, history and culture in Western society*. Basingstoke, UK: Macmillan.
Mitchell, A., and Kappler, S. (2009). *Transformative civil society and the EU Approach to peacebuilding*. Paper presented at the *Millennium: Journal of International Studies* conference 'After Liberalism', London School of Economics, London, UK, 17–18 October.
Mouffe, C. (2005). *On the political*. London, UK: Routledge.
North, D. C. (1990). *Institutions, institutional change and economic performance*. Cambridge, UK: Cambridge University Press.
Putnam, R. D. (2000). *Bowling alone: The collapse and revival of American community*. New York, NY: Simon & Schuster.
Said, E. (1985). *Orientalism*. London, UK: Penguin.
Sisk, T. D. (2008). Peacebuilding as democratization: Findings and recommendations. In A. K. Jarstad and T. D. Sisk (Eds.), *From war to democracy: Dilemmas of peacebuilding*. Cambridge, UK: Cambridge University Press.
Stonequist, E. V. (1961). *The marginal man: A study in personality and culture conflict*. New York, NY: Russell and Russell.
Wallerstein, I. (1976). *The modern world system*. New York, NY: Academic Press.

8
HYBRID POLITIES AND POST-CONFLICT POLICY

David Roberts

> Democratization is not something that one people does for another. People must do it for themselves or it does not happen.
>
> *(Ake, 1991: 38)*

In the field of statebuilding (as the means of building peace through liberal institutionalization) hybridity refers to the outcome of conjoining internal and external beliefs about state management. In terms that apply to the modern process of globalization, of which statebuilding can be seen as but one element, Nyoongah Mudrooroo refers to hybridity as 'part of the contestational weave of cultures' (1990: 24), recalling the permanence throughout history of different people and cultures seeking hegemony in different ways. Hybridity is a constant in regime change and has been thoroughly debated in the literature on democracy and development, to name but two areas of research (Diamond, 2002; Migdal, 1974). Despite this, its appearance in the postconflic statebuilding literature has caused something akin to a rumbling. What was being suggested was that statebuilding did not happen on a *tabula rasa*; that there was something already there that may either resist what is privileged in international statebuilding, or at least adapt or manipulate it. This notion seemed to take some liberal commentators by surprise. Certainly, the limited reference to how local actors react to global influences in the orthodox literature suggests that i was not a matter being taken seriously. This material tends to be more concerned with the technical aspects of developing statebuilding and peacebuilding intervention and refining existing assumptions and practices, rather than confronting data that substantially challenge the legitimacy of hegemonic approaches and wisdom. But hybridity has always been with us and is here to stay, and the purpose of this chapter is to review where we have come from and where we are going, to adapt a Cambodian aphorism, with the meaning and consequences of hybridity in international statebuilding.

What is hybridity?

As with many social sciences concepts, hybridity has been purloined from the natural sciences. Hybridity in biology, for example, refers to the consequences of successful mating of two distinct breeds. It became well known in the social sciences because of the racial connotations to be found in colonial discourses, where it suggested racial mixture and binary representations of the Imperial and the Other. The resultant miscegenation was considered to produce something even more inferior than the colonized people, leading to a fear of the dilution of the imperial European races in 'cross-breeding' (Bhabha, 1994; Young, 1995). However, such assumptions are rarely given any credence these days. It is widely acknowledged that changes occurring through mixing of cultures and peoples work both ways. Most importantly, it was clear to the earlier scholars that local cultures were rarely, if ever, eliminated in their entirety, instead adopting and adapting as local agency, will, and capacity determined. Indeed, it is often the rule that the fusion of differing forms creates a stronger force; the process of hybridization is heterotic and the outcome may be stronger and more suited to local conditions.

The outcome of such hybridization has been typologized by Christian Reisinger, who identifies three forms of multiple, coexisting, and often overlapping power in what he calls 'institutional multiplicity.' These are 'government, informal powers, and external actors' (2009: 485), and are the component parts of hybrid regimes. They include the state as appointed through formal democratic elections, normally instigated and executed by international actors; cronies rewarded by newly elected elites for loyalty, bypassing the formal democratic process; existing traditional powers, sometimes in the rural areas, whose positions and policies are beyond the effective reach of metropolitan forces; the international institutions charged with extending liberalism and the formal Weberian state through the act of statebuilding; the constabulary who attend security sector reform (SSR) retraining while continuing to extract bribes using weapons and means of physical restraint supplied by international 'partners'; existing informal institutions of governance that remain embedded in the formal institutions meant to replace them and which disburse policy, patronage, and power behind a patina or nomenclature of democratic exhibitionism; new formal state institutions that manipulate society in informal and extra-democratic ways while announcing their conversion to democracy; elites who adopt liberal rhetoric while enhancing and preserving their positions using traditional structures, passages, and clients; and an almost unending series of combinations of the above, enacted according to local preferences.

After peacebuilders leave, institutions evolve to serve local intent that is often entirely at odds with liberalism. In parts of Africa, for example, 'the civil service often continues to suffer from a mix of ethnic/regional and political clientelism ranging from the creation of additional ministries to accommodate important support groups to the abuse of civil servants to rally support for incumbents during pre-election periods' (Menocal et al., 2008: 35). In Cambodia, hundreds of new administrative posts were created as rewards to political allies rather than as a means of serving the public, an outcome that was largely missed by most of the international peacebuilders there (Roberts, 2001). What evolves often has the appearance of democracy because local elites are able easily to hoodwink gullible international observers by applying the nomenclature and physical facades of the new. But behind such facades persist the very ways such reformation is designed to eliminate. Such institutions are commonly understood better by local people than by international agents. Another example familiar to many is 'the incorporation of warlords and militia commanders in government in post-Taliban Afghanistan' (Mac Ginty, 2010: 405). This is hybridity in statebuilding: the synthesis of the formal and informal, the old and the new, the local and the global.

Hybrid peace?

It is not the only consideration of hybridity, however. Roger Mac Ginty refers to the idea that the peace itself rather than, or in addition to, the statebuilding process is also a hybrid. Conceptually it bears much similarity with hybridity in statebuilding. However, he explicates a 'fusion peace' (2010: 397) that mixes the broader interests in peace as an outcome of exogenous and indigenous interactions. Some internal preferences might be dominant and others might be subalterns to exogenous determinism. Thus, 'we might see how local mores hold sway on issues of reconciliation, while international norms and practices prevail in relation to the structure of the economy. The result is a hybridized peace that is in constant flux, as different actor and processes cooperate and compete on different issue agendas' (Mac Ginty, 2010: 397). Mac Ginty notes four elements to hybridization in peacebuilding. These involve:

> The compliance powers of the liberal peace; the incentive powers of the liberal peace; the ability of local actors to resist, ignore or subvert the liberal peace; and the ability of local actors to formulate and maintain alternatives to the liberal peace. All of these variables are interdependent and occupy a space partially constructed by the other variables.
>
> *(Mac Ginty, 2010: 392)*

In short, there are external carrots and sticks that internal actors and institutions receive in different ways. Mac Ginty describes the outcome as 'a whirr of hybridity,' wherein 'different factors prevail in different contexts, on different issues, at different times. It is not the case that there is a discrete liberal peace that is then hybridized. Instead, the liberal peace is already hybridized, by dint of the complex multidimensional environment in which it exists' (Mac Ginty, 2010: 404).

What we may reasonably conclude from noting both expressions of hybridity is that they involve the same forces but expressed both in terms of institutional interaction and broader social relations. They may both be understood in terms of Joel Migdal's dictum regarding the consequences of the old meeting the new (1974). In both arenas, while there is external propulsion of preferences, there is also an internal reaction that may be favorable, disinclined, or disinterested. This may be unorganized or institutional in its identity and formation, but it appears as a reactive and dynamic dichotomy that disguises a more complex series of interactions and groupings all concerned with the maintenance, adaptation, or elimination of the status quo. People and institutions react to demands for the substantial cultural, political, social, and economic changes explicit in liberal interventions, one way or another. As the evidence from various case studies shows (above), the hybrid polity is as remarkable for manipulating liberalism as the mainstream literature is for turning a blind eye to this form of reform and resistance. This is a broadly generalizable notion and requires more acute and nuanced consideration in statebuilding and peacebuilding. Not to do so would result in only partial understanding of, and ability to improve, contemporary statebuilding and peacebuilding.

Hybrid political order?

This hybridity was quite thoroughly and specifcally explored and developed formally by a team of researchers from the Berghof Foundation in 2009. The publication that came out of that research is currently considered authoritative, original, and part of an emerging discourse on the matter of what to call polities in so-called 'failing,' 'failed,' and 'post-conflict' spaces, since increasingly it is these 'zones' that form the focus of Western security discourse, praxis, and intervention (Kaldor, 1999; Duffield, 2001). The Berghof Report reminded scholars an practitioners of the long pre-existing social structures such as neo-patrimony, patronage, and clientelism, and presidentialism, to name but a few, that characterize post-conflict terrains (Boeg et al., 2009), and considered hybridity in terms of the outcome of statebuilding meeting neo-patrimony, although technically, an earlier round of hybridization produced neo-patrimony, or the outcome of the hybrid fusion of imperialism and the local. Peacebuilding interventions then reproduce the process of colonization in which the old and the new are grafted onto one another. And Trutz von Trotha noted that all polities are hybrids: mixes of various forms. This prompted him to ask 'whether the postmodern word–coinage is really necessary ... since hybridity is not a peculiarity of the postcolonial order or indeed of postmodernity' (2009: 42).

After reviewing the evidence in a variety of places, especially in Africa, Boege et al. conclude that the best way to describe such phenomena is to build on the earlier debate regarding hybridity. To this evolving lexicography they added the term 'hybrid political orders,' which implies to the authors 'a new type of statebuilding' (Boege et al., 2009: 16). As a precursor to this revision of statebuilding methods, the report sketches the political topography of post–conflict spaces (among others that included 'failed' and 'failing' states) in ways that identify an array of political agencies that complement state actors and institutions. It is a key point of the report that even though the state may often not have penetrated all the areas of a geography, this does not mean that there exists no authority, or that the region is 'stateless.' Instead, and importantly, the report scopes parallel informal sources of authority that enjoy degrees of legitimacy normally associated with formal, Weberian structures. It declares that 'the state's "outpost"' is mediated by 'informal' indigenous societal institutions that follow their own logic and rules within the (incomplete) state structures (Boege et al., 2009: 20). The report lists 'customary law, traditional societal structures (extended families, clans, tribes, religious brotherhoods, village communities) and traditional authorities (such as village elders, headmen, clan chiefs, healers, *bigmen* [and] religious leaders' as examples of such informal power (Boege et al., 2009: 20).

This was not the frst time such parallel structures had been identified. Various peacebuilding anthropology, and development scholars have been busy describing such formations for at least two decades, since post–Cold War liberal peacebuilding began with early operations in Namibia and Cambodia. But it represents an important stage in the post–conflict peacebuilding narrativ that acknowledges the existence, diversity, and role of such extra–formal bodies, considers how these actors and institutions blend with external forces, and discusses how this could shape more sophisticated peacebuilding interventions. This intellectual process reflects the reality of the situation, following the experience in Africa where democratizing African elites have incorporated traditional structures into contemporary polities in recognition of the role they play beyond the metropolis and in the absence of effective centralized state institutions, rather than attempting to exclude them. As Boege et al. remark:

> In recognition of the relative weakness of state institutions and the relative strength of traditional communities and authorities, governments have come to rely on the latter for performing certain state functions, thus contributing to a resurgence of customary rule, albeit in (partly) new forms and with new functions.
>
> *(2009: 22)*

The formal state is in this sense manipulating customary actors and rendering them unpopular (as tax collectors, for example) and undermining the authority they depend on to govern at the peripheries. At the same time, however, it confers legitimacy on others, whose status is accepted, and therefore endorsed, by central state authorities.

The topography of power is further complicated by additional groupings that have arisen perhaps independently of either contemporary peacebuilding or traditional governors. These may not be new institutions and practices; they may have been in existence for decades and even centuries before. But the position of actors such as 'warlords and their militias in outlying regions, gang leaders in townships and squatter settlements, vigilante–type organisations, ethnically–based protection rackets, millenarian religious movements, transnational networks of extended family relations, organised crime or new forms of tribalism' needs to be considered carefully in the statebuilding debate (Boege et al., 2009: 22). This is because to various degrees in different places, they fill the vacuum of competency left by the ineffective state that usually characterizes post conflict spaces. They also remind, importantly, that what liberal statebuilding privileges is often not considered relevant to local people, who turn instead to actors and institutions that respond to their will. It is routinely the case that whosoever provides for people, be it traditional 'security' through powerful armed militias or 'non−traditional' security like basic needs, may well garner and share legitimacy and authority in parallel with the rhetoric and propaganda of older or newer centralized state institutions. People will likely confer more legitimacy on institutions and actors that look out for them than on those that do not.

International superimpositions of democratic practice cannot substitute for or replace, in the short term, national political behaviors derived from needs, experiences, histories, and evolutions quite different from those from which Western democracy is derived. Returning momentarily to Cambodia to illustrate this, we may recall how political stability broke down the moment the election results were released. Foreigners expected the inevitable and long−running contest for political authority in Cambodia to be managed peaceably through the formal structures, institutions, and mechanisms involved in the democratization process. In reality, the ongoing competition for power was conducted through the informal rules, bodies, and contrivances that have traditionally been used to settle disputes. The two coexisted, but the latter enabled power to be managed in ways more familiar to the dominant elite, and all parties paid lip service to democratic rules. Indeed, the feuding continued until it was settled by force, four years after the peacebuilders left, and resulted in the ousting of the electoral victor but greater political stability than the NGO sector there could recall in the previous five years (Roberts, 2001). This kind o messy miasma will likely remain the norm as long as the informal element retains utility to local parties in such scenarios. Such expectations are rooted deeply in previous modes of behavior that are frequently considered legitimate locally; their recasting as inappropriate by democratization does not mean their execution will be eliminated. As Menocal et al. argue, 'in these regimes, commitment to the rules of the game is at best "instrumental" (i.e. based on performance) and not [liberally] "principled" (i.e. based on political attributes)' (2008: 32).

However, others are less impressed. Some take the view that referring to governance in post−conflict and other unstable spaces as 'hybrid political orders' brings little new to the table that we didn't already understand and is dangerous because it implies that there is 'order' in place in the sense that it is understood from a liberal perspective (Hoffman, 2009). Hoffman is sympathetic to the attempts to think outside the liberal box, especially with regard to terminology that can mislead the ill−informed. However, he takes issue with the idea of 'order,' suggesting that this title gives 'the false impression to the world that order does indeed exist' where in fact such spaces to which the term 'hybrid political orders' is applied are in fact places where 'violence and suffering continue unhindered and create a situation characterized by disorder and lawlessness' (2009: 80). Perhaps more signif cantly, the use of 'order' does nothing to tell us about conditions in such places; Hoffman asks: strong order, weak order, what kind of order? His point is one of differentiation: applying a term that can be so broadly interpreted disallows any form of disaggregation of conditions and experiences, which in turn disallows focused policy−making. Hoffman argues that Boege et al.'s expression of hybridity, in parallel with that of other scholars who have written independently and earlier on the subject, does not offer anything new, when most peacebuilding operations are as a matter of course combinations of top−down actions and bottom up−reactions.

The absence of such debate on hybridity from mainstream scholarship and international public policy suggests that such explication and theorizing is indeed much needed. Such topographical complexity as conveyed through serious discussions of hybridity is what constitutes the political landscape in which statebuilding and peacebuilding operate. Yet some take the view that these are necessarily 'bad' things that must be changed. For democracy to deepen and hybrid composition to be replaced by democracy, 'the democratic process needs to be viewed as the only legitimate means to gain power and to channel/process demands' (Menocal et al., 2008). The problem with this is that too often, what peacebuilding and statebuilding privilege is not what local people want, and thus does not *earn* legitimacy. The provision of elite institutions, fancy cars and offices in metropolitan centres, regular elections, and recognition at the UN i not necessarily what a majority of regular folk consider to be important. This is not to claim that democracy is a bad thing; it is to suggest that liberal peacebuilding's infatuation with elite institutions and democracy–building is not what will make an intervention, and the elites it heralds, legitimate. For any political order to surface, it must be seen as legitimate by the people over whom it seeks authority to rule.

Hybridity, inevitability?

Hybridity, then, exists before statebuilding attempts formal norms change, and exists throughout and afterwards. Hybridity represents the meeting point of indigenous perpetuity and exogenous reformation, where neo–patrimonial processes, attached to elite functions and privilege, persist through a combination of convention and the cooption and manipulation of newer liberal systems. Hybridity describes in some ways Marina Ottaway's notion of the 'raw power state,' in which transition occurs from a 'dysfunctional' polity to one run through indigenous institutions (2002: 1004). However, the concept of hybridity engages more with the ways in which democracy is accepted, as well as circumvented, manipulated, or rejected. It is a 'halfway house' between what orthodox peacebuilding seeks and what indigenous will permits. The hybridities under discussion here are characterized by a 'rhetorical acceptance of liberal democracy' (Ottaway, 2003: 3), distinguishing them from traditional polities that refuse to tolerate in any form at all the idea of pluralism. But they also reflect people's engagement with aspects of democracy the value. In the process of hybridization, the rhetoric, vernacular, and symbols of the imported legal–rational model of government and state appear intact and are in some limited ways adopted, but this also serves to disguise the extent to which pre–existing systems remain authoritative, authoritarian, socially penetrative, and legitimated to varying degrees. In essence, hybridization occurs as the process of catachresis appropriates and manipulates democratization according to local interests. Catachresis refers to 'the process by which the colonized take and reinscribe something that exists traditionally as a feature of imperial culture' (Ashcroft et al., 1998: 34). In the statebuilding and peacebuilding context, it is the process whereby the local rewrites what it is given to f t its own needs, accepting, interrupting, and/or redirecting the intended impact of orthodox peacebuilding.

The outcome is closer to a reconf guration of politics wherein the prevalence and nomen – clature of a rhetorical state disguise the persistence and entrenchment of neo–patrimony. The prowess of the new is more chimerical than substantial beyond the totemic and symbolic, and an unwillingness to recognize this, aided by retrenchment in Northern research epistemologies, conceals the persistence, legitimacy, and prevalence of the old. In this contest for hegemony, it is not the case that the newer automatically overwrites the older. It is not even the case that the two coexist simultaneously and equally side by side. Indeed, Marina Ottaway argues that in the short term, neo–patrimonial 'power trumps [liberal] institutions' (2002: 1015). When neo–patrimony readjusts to peacebuilding, the evidence strongly suggests that the outcome is asymmetrical primarily because local systems are tuned to local needs, mass or elite, which are poorly served in the short to medium term by the liberalizing agenda. The old ways retain relevance, efficacy, and legitimacy. Asymmetrical hybrid formations will persist, because the technocratic emphasis of orthodox peacebuilding is ontologically divergent from the concerns, interests, priorities, and problems of local people in the post–conflict state, be they mass or elite What matters most to outsiders in peacebuilding may well not be what matters most to insiders who must manage their compromised and often volatile environment. Fred Mutesa remarks that orthodox peacebuilding will either 'undermine neo–patrimonial tendencies and push the . . . agenda forward or the political system [will] adapt to the new measures in a way that still perpetuates old practices, albeit under modified conditions' (2005: 2). It is the case normally tha the second clause carries. As Timothy Donais writes:

> The reality is that the capacity–building rhetoric of peacebuilding, and its assumptions about the creation of new institutional structures that are either indifferent to, or deliberately distinct from, domestic political culture, obscures the extent to which successful capacity building relies on a broader process of norms transmission that have proven exceedingly difficult to achieve within conventional peacebuilding time frames
>
> *(2009: 16)*

In reality, the norm trumps the nomenclature. In orthodox peacebuilding discourses, nomen clature assumes to trump norms. Ministries of Justice, Defence, and Internal Affairs (for example) may be built or renovated on main streets, and titular posts of office–holding may be announce in national newspapers to give the appearance of the rule of law, but political elites routinely bypass these institutions and expectations because they do not serve core interests such as retaining or attaining power. Further, elites may award official posts to key allies and/or enemies to sustai and placate them. After the elections in Cambodia in 1993, both main parties awarded posts to loyal followers that served the purpose not of enhancing democratic practice but of rewarding loyal supporters, fending off potential and real enemies, and ensuring that their own lieutenants could reward those far lower down the ranks on whom the pyramid of neo–patrimony depends to varying degrees for sustenance. It was widely reported, for example, that 'the price list quoted by FUNCINPEC [opposition] off cials for jobs in the administration ranges from 200 USD to 3,000 USD, depending on how good the position will be for extracting bribes.' This was 'bound to happen [as] . . . FUNCINPEC is more vulnerable to corruption because they come with empty hands and they need houses' (Roberts, 2001; Ashley, 1998).

Such practices are common in post–conflict polities. Such public offices associated with peacebuilding reformation, then, are often nominal before they are functional; Patrick Chabal and Jean–Pascal Daloz call them 'a decor, a pseudo–Western facade masking the realities of deeply personalized political realities' (2005: 15–16). Rather than being impartial bodies, state institutions are quite normally 'owned' by supporters of elite politicians and serve their personal and political needs. Again, there is precedent for thinking about this behavior in the development literature. Robert Jackson and Carl Rosberg, widely credited and respected scholars of African development, write that 'the most important spoils of factional struggle . . . are government and party off ces' (1982: 52). Positions in 'public' institutions are normally hived off after elections in languages few foreign observers speak well enough to understand or stay long enough to hear. Entire political institutions with democratic labels are created in order to satisfy and pay off political opponents and, crucially, their supporters, while leaving an impression of democratic practice and the built state. Thomas Carothers has typologized such practices as 'dominant–power politics,' whereby the superficiality of democracy is evident in the continued domination of the politica scene by pre–pluralism elites and their appointees (2002). Although Joakim Ekman argues that in hybrid polities, 'parliaments . . . may function as potential platforms for the Opposition' to democratically regulate such behavior (2009: 9), Michael Bratton considers that in reality, most opposition parties are conspicuous in their absence once past elections (Bratton, 2007). In reality, their presence may be conspicuous but their impact will likely be negligible, as Carothers maintains.

Our longest case study of such evolution, Cambodia, confirms this pattern. The 'strongman of Cambodia, Prime Minister Hun Sen, has seen off innumerable contenders who have vied for power using the democratic process through longstanding pyramids of supporters who are paid or otherwise manipulated in his service – according to deeply inscribed and widely understood political practices (St. John, 2005). This is not to condone or condemn such practices, but to make the point that peacebuilding compromises processes considered locally legitimate and necessary to maintain conventions that serve existing hierarchies well. There is no good reason to expect they will all simply stop functioning because outsiders would prefer they do something different. For a new political ideology to take root and grow, it must be more relevant than that which it seeks to dismiss; the idea of 'culture contact' resulting in the adoption of the new has long been dismissed (Migdal, 1974). Since democracy cannot and does not satisfy key elite interests in the immediate and short terms, we should not be surprised if commitment to its consolidation turns out to be minimal.

The f rst goal of competing elites is to take or retain power, and democracy may be considered irrelevant and/or detractive to that purpose except where it can be manipulated to an advantage; democracy is not the only game in town. Making this point, Menocal et al. suggest that for democracy to consolidate, 'the democratic process needs to be viewed as the only legitimate means to gain power and to channel/process demands' (2008: 32). It is not, since what it offers as substitute does not provide what many elites need to maintain or challenge the status quo. This is not to say that democracy is necessarily wrong, but it is to suggest that it may not serve elite preferences. In Katherine Fierlbeck's well–chosen words:

> The fundamental attraction of democracy is that it permits the diffusion of power within . . . a social environment. [But] if certain actors . . . retain for themselves the ability to def ne what is or is not open for collective decision–making... then democracy simply cannot function as an effective mechanism to diffuse power and it becomes a meaningless reflection of its original purpose
>
> *(1998: 2)*

This has a substantial impact on society's view of the institutional emphases attendant on peacebuilding. Menocal et al. note that 'in hybrid regimes many formal institutions that are crucial to make democracy work suffer from a lack of credibility and/or trust' (2008: 33). This is because their primary objective serves a longer–term purpose, in the form of the instauration of political and economic rights and values that are sometimes – perhaps even often – less important and relevant to local priorities but more important to liberal interventionists. Bratton concludes that 'because the performance of all formal institutions systematically falls short of popular expectations . . . people will plug ensuing institutional gaps with informal ties,' perpetuating the hybrid mix (2007: 8). The legitimacy of a polity, democratic or otherwise, rests in substantial part on its relevance to people and their needs. As long as the new forms of political and economic organization fail to provide what older forms do, the older forms will persist and the idea of the neoliberal peace is rearranged through hybrid reformation. Accordingly, powerful traditions persist that enjoy local legitimacy and that are at odds with the expectations and diktat of orthodox peacebuilding. As Timothy Kelsall puts it:

> The reality is that these practices ... are both necessary and illegal: they are necessary because politicians for reasons of traditional legitimacy must deliver resources through personalised clientelistic networks, and illegal because they contravene an imported ideological, legal and governmental system founded on a strong separation between public and private that has never existed [in most postconflict places]
>
> *(2008: 636)*

It is thus illegal and ideologically problematic only when outsiders say that it is. As Vito Tanzi writes:

> To argue that the personal relationships that come to be established between public sector employees and individuals who deal with them reflect a 'corrupt' society ma be correct in a legalistic sense, but it misses the point that these relationships simply reflect different social and moral norms
>
> *(1995: 25)*

Trying to replace or outlaw informal practices, the prevalence, necessity, and legitimacy of which are misunderstood in peacebuilding practice and misrepresented or denied in peacebuilding literature, is a Sisyphean, and ultimately pointless and wasteful, task. They will coexist with liberal evolutions, especially as younger generations of politicians and activists outside traditional or successful networks of patronage use democratic institutions as a means of challenging the old order, often attracting external patronage as they go.

Ways forward?

A more nuanced and sophisticated imaginary of what statebuilding engages with, wittingly or unwittingly, is essential if we are to understand what is happening in post–conflict spaces, wh it is so often bypassed, ignored, or rejected, making for wastefulness, and how liberal interventions could be reformed. Indeed, it is the view of some that such institutions will be inevitable as long as external interventions fail to recognize the local scope and legitimacy of the informal (Mac Ginty, 2010; Roberts, 2011). Given the logics of such competing groups in their own contexts beyond the ken of most peacebuilding strategies, the relevance, necessity, and legitimacy of those groups to large numbers of people, and the enormous costs of intervening frequently, and frequently unsuccessfully, it seems reasonable to explore how peacebuilding and statebuilding might adapt to and take advantage of such scenarios, rather than ignoring, denying, or refuting them. Such an approach, declare Boege et al.,

> entails perceiving community resilience and customary institutions not so much as 'spoilers' and problems, but as assets and sources of solutions that can be drawn upon in order to forge constructive relationships between communities and governments, and between customary and introduced political and social institutions. For example, instead of denouncing kinship–based societal formations as sources of corruption and nepotism, and hindrances to accountability and transparency, one can also look at them as valuable social support networks which have their own checks and balances.
>
> *(2009: 30)*

The prevailing model is wasteful of resources and potential, and too frequently does not develop local capacity. Not everything local is necessarily good and helpful for building peace, but much that is good and helpful is missed. Identifying the existence and nature of the hybrid polity is a first step in seeing a bigger picture with more components, and then seeing how thos can be developed for the wider benefit of the societies in whose name peace is built. It remain a key concern of much liberal scholarship that where polities are messy mixes of political orders, 'institutional multiplicity needs to be replaced by one common institutional framework' (Helling, 2009). Such thinking suggests that 'different institutional universes are necessarily in competition, even conflict, with one another,' leading to the conclusion that 'consolidated governance struc tures cannot take shape unless a unified institutional framework is first worked out' (Mallet 2010: 80; Van Biljert et al., 2009). But this is narrow and prejudiced thinking that perpetuates a Eurocentricity redolent of imperial assumptions of superiority. Other ways can work. Thus, for Richard Mallet, 'it is not the type of institutional set-up per se that determines political outcomes, but the ongoing interactions between the various institutions and organisations' (2010: 80).

From this perspective, there is an opportunity in future peacebuilding to stop going against the grain and work in conjunction with existing combinations and modes of local and national governance to stabilize peace and begin reconstruction. Such an angle has been discussed in development circles (Kelsall, 2008). It reflects the notion that two different systems do not hav to be mutually exclusive, but might work in conjunction with one another and reflect a path o least resistance based around accepting a plurality of preferences and priorities that determine the shape and nature of a variety of institutional formations. Mallett suggests that such 'institutional multiplicity involves a continual and dynamic process of reordering and renegotiation of the institutional arrangement . . . resulting in complex outcomes which are neither exclusively detrimental nor benef cial' (Mallett, 2010: 80). I would add at this point that this combination and fluidity around local preferences is all but inevitable where two cultural attitudes to huma organization are forced to coexist by the hegemony of liberal peacebuilding and prevailing assumptions about the Liberal Peace and the associated cosmopolitan universalism that is embedded in and sustains such beliefs. Thus, liberal peacebuilding is itself responsible for the evolution of institutional multiplicity. It is a normal internal reaction to external intervention, and should be treated as such. This is not to say that institutional development is paralyzed in binary form; rather this is what will happen in liberal peacebuilding in the short, medium, and even longer terms, as arrangements in Cambodia two decades after intervention attest.

It appears to be, once more, a question of legitimacy: the persistence of the view that liberalism should predominate among institutions leaves unaddressed the narrowness, selectivity, elitism, and paucity of liberal provision that serves as the rationale for the persistence of the hybridity that counters such inadequacy. Liberal hegemony will not be realized – leaving aside the matter of whether it should or should not – as long as it neglects the political, social, and economic priorities of populations and, in so doing, leaves the door open for, indeed necessitates, alternative provision through old ways and 'illiberal' institutions.

Conclusion: What to do?

The upshot of this is that statebuilders and peacebuilders need to decide what their priority is: liberal institution-building or peacebuilding? The former has been ineffective and the latter has not been achieved. As is well documented elsewhere, nearly half of the interventions backslide into war within five years (Krause and Jutersonke, 2005) and of the remainder, there is littl evidence of deeply embedded democracy and liberalism. No conscious international peace-building policy actively recognizes and reforms around the opportunities and challenges presented by natural hybridization. By natural hybridization, I mean the inevitable reactions of elites and masses to the elements of peacebuilding they favor and resent. No peacebuilding is absolutely dominant or hegemonic; sites of resistance spring up everywhere in accordance with the relevance of an intervention to local people's preferences, reforming the incoming actors' and institutions' intentions through local agency and capacity. The inevitability, and power, of such challenges, and the messy reality of hybrid reformations, is not something that has been placed high on the agenda of orthodox literature and mainstream international policy, yet. For this reason, it is safe to say that research and scholarship as it stands on hybrid political orders does make a contribution to the discourse and through this, potentially, to praxis. A key priority of research in statebuilding and peacebuilding is to alert policymakers to complexity and failure where ignorance is undermining the efficacy of practice. The study, description, and theorizing of hybridity is centra to understanding how to manage the 'institutional multiplicity' that characterizes post−conflict 'failed,' and 'failing' spaces. Accepting the vitality and inevitability of hybridity in statebuilding for peace is the first step in reforming the intervention process so it is less inclined to collaps under the weight of its own hubris.

References

Ake, C. (1991). Rethinking African democracy. *Journal of Democracy*, 2(1), 32–44.
Ashcroft, B., Griffths, G., and Tiffin, H. (1998). *Key concepts in post-colonial studies*. London, UK: Routledge.
Ashley, D. (1998). The failure of confict resolution in Cambodia. In Z. Brown and D. Timberman (Eds.), *Cambodia and the international community: The quest for peace, development and democracy*. Singapore: Asia Society.
Bhabha, H. (1994). *The location of culture*, London, UK: Routledge.
Boege, V., Brown, A., Clements, K., and Nolan, A. (2009). Undressing the emperor: A reply to our discussants. In M. Fischer and B. Schmelze (Eds.), *Building peace in the absence of states: Challenging the discourse on state failure*. Berlin, Germany: Berghoff Research Centre.
Bratton, M. (2007). Formal versus informal institutions in Africa. *Journal of Democracy*, 18(3), 96–110.
Carothers, T. (2002). The end of the transition paradigm. *Journal of Democracy*, 13(1), 5–21.
Chabal, P., and Daloz, J.-P. (2005).*Africa works: Disorder as a political instrument*. Bloomington, IN: Indiana University Press.
Diamond, L. (2002). Elections without democracy. *Journal of Democracy*, 13(2), 21–36.
Donais, T. (2009). Empowerment or imposition? Dilemmas of local ownership in postconflt peacebuilding processes. *Peace and Change*, 34(1), 3–26.
Duffield, M. (2001). *Global governance and the new wars: The merging of development and security*. London, UK: Zed.
Ekman, J. (2009). Political participation and regime stability: A framework for analyzing hybrid regimes. *International Political Science Review*, 30(1), 7–31.
Fierlbeck, K. (1998). *Globalizing democracy: Power, legitimacy and the interpretation of democratic ideas*. Manchester, UK: Manchester University Press.
Helling, D. (2009). *Anatomy of a 'political chameleon': Re-examining fluid shapes and solid constants of nationalism and nation-building*. CSRC Discussion Paper 17. London, UK: Crisis States Research Centre.
Hoffman, B. (2009). Are hybrid political orders an appropriate concept for state formation? Timor–Leste revisited.In M. Fischer and B. Schmelze (Eds.),*Building peace in the absence of states: Challenging the discourse on state failure*. Berlin, Germany: Berghof Centre.
Jackson, R., and Rosberg, C. (1982). *Personal rule in Black Africa: Prince, autocrat, prophet, tyrant*. Berkeley, CA: University of California Press.
Kaldor, M. (1999). *New and old wars*. Cambridge, UK: Polity Press.
Kelsall, T. (2008). Going with the grain in African development*Development Policy Review*, 26(6), 627–655.
Krause, K., and Jutersonke, O. (2005). Peace, security and development in postconflict environments. *Security Dialogue*, 36(4), 447–462.
Mac Ginty, R. (2010). Hybrid peace: The interaction between top−down and bottom−up peace. *Security Dialogue*, 41(4), 391–412.
Mallett, R. (2010). Beyond failed states and ungoverned spaces: Hybrid political orders in the postconflic landscape. *eSharp*, 15, 65–91.
Menocal, A., Fritz, V., and Rakner, L. (2008). Hybrid regimes and the challenges of deepening and sustaining democracy in developing countries. *South African Journal of International Affairs*, 15(1), 29–40.

Migdal, J. (1974). *Peasants, politics and revolution: Pressures toward political and social change in the Third World.* Princeton, NJ: Princeton University Press.

Mudrooroo, N. (1990). *Writing from the fringe: A study of modern aboriginal literature.* Melbourne, Australia: Hyland House.

Mutesa, F. (2005). Poverty reduction in a political trap? The PRS process and neopatrimonialism in Zambia. In W. Eberlei, P. Meyns, and F. Mutesa, *The nexus between public resources management reforms and neopatrimonial politics.* Lusaka, Zambia: UNZA Press.

Ottaway, M. (2002). Rebuilding state institutions in collapsed states. *Development and Change, 33*(5), 1001–1023.

Ottaway, M. (2003). *Democracy challenged: The rise of semi-authoritarianism.* Washington, DC: Carnegie Endowment for International Peace.

Reisinger, C. (2009). A framework for the analysis of post–conflict situations: Liberia and Mozambiqu reconsidered. *International Peacekeeping, 16*(4), 483–498.

Roberts, D. (2001). *Political transition in Cambodia, 1991–1999: Power, elitism and democracy.* London, UK: Curzon Routledge.

Roberts, D. (2011). *Liberal peacebuilding and global governance: Beyond the metropolis.* London, UK: Routledge.

St. John, R. B. (2005). Democracy in Cambodia — One decade, US$5 billion later: What went wrong? *Contemporary Southeast Asia, 27*(3), 406–428.

Tanzi, V. (1995). Corruption, governmental activities, and markets. *Finance and Development*, December, 24–26.

Van Biljert, M., van Lieshout, P., and Went, R. (2009). Imaginary institutions: State–building in Afghanistan. In M. Kremer, P. van Lieshout, and R. Went (Eds.), *Doing good or doing better: Development policies in a globalizing world.* Amsterdam, The Nedtherlands: Amsterdam University, pp. 157–176.

von Trotha, T. (2009). The Andersen principle: On the difficulty of truly moving beyond state–centrism In M. Fischer and B. Schmelzle (Eds.), *Building peace in the absence of states: Challenging the discourse on state failure.* Berlin, Germany: Berghof Research Centre.

Young, R. (1995). *Colonial desire: Hybridity in theory, culture and race.* London, UK: Routledge.

9
HISTORY REPEATING?
Colonial, socialist, and liberal statebuilding in Mozambique

Meera Sabaratnam

This chapter looks briefly at three successive attempts at statebuilding in Mozambique and draw out interesting elements of continuity between them in terms of political authority, political economy, and public administration practices. These are the colonial *New State* from 1930 to 1974, the socialist post–independence state from 1975 to 1989, and the liberal post–conflict restructuring from 1990 onwards. Mozambique has counted among one of the major early 'success stories' of post–conflict peacebuilding in that it brought formerly warring parties into generally peaceful and regular electoral cycle, its central government has expanded its provision of public services, and it has had high year–on–year economic growth since the end of the war in the early 1990s. Yet it is also the case that the attempted 'liberal' statebuilding practices have tended to have distinctively 'conservative' effects in terms of state–society relations, often reproducing rather than transforming power and authority. The chapter will focus on three central themes: political authority, political economy, and public administration. These are dimensions of statebuilding that overlap and have tended to mutually reinforce one another. The discussion will trace approaches to statebuilding in each period before analyzing them together.

External statebuilders have been notoriously bad at making sense of the historical experiences and trajectories of state–society relations. As such, there is often the working assumption that externally driven post–confict statebuilding is substantially changing the dynamics of rule in a polity through the import of liberal ideas. Yet, very often, this does not seem to be the case. Recent academic literature on statebuilding has moved towards a more 'sociological' analysis of the state based on the classic approaches of Weber and Durkheim to the phenomenon of statehood (see Chapter 1, this volume). This important turn flags up the dangers of attemptin to import authority and legitimacy in a hurry and without relevant institutions. However, there is also a need to reflect on the historic patterns of establishing rule and authority in particula places. Such an analysis, grounded in an alternative analytic sensibility around the historic objectives of statebuilding in the global South (see Mamdani, 1996; Scott, 1998), raises deep questions about the idea of 'state failure', the nature and politics of statebuilding, the values and objectives it supports, and the tensions that it tries to overcome.

Colonial statebuilding: the New State (*Novo Estado*), 1930–1974

Portugal had been embarrassed at the Berlin Conference of 1884–5. Its ambitions to be equal to other European imperial powers in Africa were threatened by its lack of control over the territories to which it laid claim. Powerful African groups fought back, the slave trade was still present, and the concession companies were disorganized and unproductive (Vail and White, 1980: 200–230). Proposals were made to have the colonies taken over by Britain or Germany, which Portugal resisted. The fascist dictatorship that emerged in 1926 soon developed the project of the New State (*Novo Estado*) to consolidate the chaotic administration of the First Republic in Portugal, and to consolidate imperial rule abroad. These were articulated in the Colonial Act (1930) and the Organic Charter (1933).[1] These two acts laid the foundation for the first moder 'statebuilding' project across the entire territory of what is now bordered as Mozambique, consolidating it as a single political entity incorporated into Portugal.

The Organic Charter redesigned colonial public administration within Mozambique, emulating strategies of native administration elsewhere (see Mamdani, 1996). Colonial companies were disbanded, and passed into the control of the state, which installed state administrative posts throughout the country. The territory was marked out into around 100 administrative divisions, which sometimes followed the boundaries of the old concession company territories. The enforcers of the colonial companies – the *cipais* (i.e., sepoys) – were recruited instead by the state directly as native police. Another layer of native administration was created via *régulos*; these were 'traditional leaders' whom the state recognized as intermediaries for rural populations, and who raised the Portuguese flag. This was critical in terms of expanding the state's visibility, surveillanc practices and economic reach over the population as a whole.

Also codified in the Organic Charter was the *indígenato* system, formalizing a racial division between subject 'native' *indígenas* and citizen 'non–natives' in law and the political economy. 'Citizens' could own property, move freely, participate in various public institutions, and had no labor obligations. 'Natives' on the other hand were excluded from colonial social and political life, taxed heavily and compelled to offer 'contract' – essentially forced – labor (called *chibalo*) (O'Laughlin, 2000). Within this, a category of the 'assimilated' (*assimilados*) was also created. These would be those natives who had sufficiently 'advanced' in their adoption of Europea culture, religion, and language to be treated under the same legal codes. These *assimilados* were crucial in Portugal's attempt to buttress and legitimize its political authority in the colonies as leading a civilizing multiracial lusophone community.

The same Charter established an autarchic imperial economy in which colonies would supply foreign exchange, taxes, and raw materials for industrialization in Portugal, such as cotton, sugar and copra. As discussed by Isaacman (1995), these practices often led to widespread malnutrition among the peasantry. Yet for the colonial authority, these were justified as necessary for the 'development' of the colony and imperial system overall. However *chibalo* and famine accelerated economic migration into the South African mines, where wages were higher and conditions slightly better.

The colonial statebuilding project in Mozambique under the New State was thus radical and ambitious – establishing a national centralized bureaucratic authority and decentralized forms of public administration, patterns of agricultural production and cheap labor export, and a civilizing, developmentalist rationale for the colonial state. This statebuilding project aimed, largely successfully, to concentrate administrative capacity and power in the hands of a relatively small group of people loyal to the colonial state. This same group also largely controlled the export–oriented political economy. Overall, its aims were to pacify and profit from the peoples and territories within Mozambique through the apparatus of a bureaucratic state, which was visible, centralized, and planned. Yet both its methods of rule and its distributive outcomes were widely unpopular. The next section will explore the attempt to overturn these in the period after independence.

Socialism and post-independence statebuilding, 1975–1989

Independence was hard fought in Mozambique, eventually coming in 1975 following a coup in Lisbon. Decolonization was both unexpected and rapid, leading to a near collapse of state functions. State power was handed over to the Frelimo movement, which had been fighting a anti-colonial guerrilla war; it had to find ways of building up state functions, authority, and capacity from a low baseline. Much of the human capital, in the sense of people with secondary education and administrative experience, had left the country. Although sympathetic *cooperantes* from other countries were sometimes used to fll these positions, they did not always match the vacancies. During the first years following independence, those with any training at all worke in several posts simultaneously. This was especially the case in education and healthcare, which the government was keen to rapidly expand, to develop the country and cement its authority.

In response to this context, and a radical turn in the movement, Frelimo moved in 1977 to establish a socialist one-party state and a series of revolutionary reforms. The aim of the Party was to dismantle colonial power and institute forms of collective modernization and development. The old racialized divisions of the colonial state were to be replaced by a *Homem Novo* (New Man) ideal of citizenship based on scientific socialism, literacy, equality, and the rejection of superstition (Mosca, 1999). Frelimo also set about creating political structures throughout the country to connect with the population. A hierarchical network of Party cells, based on colonial administrative divisions, became the engine for the spread of its influence, which also becam highly fused with the structures of local state administration.

In principle, these sought to be inclusive, participatory and democratic in deliberative and decision-making structures. As such, this marked in theory a substantial departure from colonial rule. However, in many places these reproduced and connected with existing forms of social authority (Harrison, 2000). Yet elsewhere, these new structures disrupted authority – for example, allowing populations the space to humiliate and marginalize *régulos* who had collaborated more enthusiastically with the colonial state. The party also sought to embed itself deeply into the state bureaucracy, particularly under the charismatic authoritarianism of President Samora Machel. He was convinced that the vestiges of the colonial bureaucracy were reactionary, and sought to undermine them as an independent force (Egerö, 1987). Thus the Party was a primary shaper of public administration and political life at both a central and a local level, based on a combination of inclusion and hierarchical order.

The state also needed to reconstruct an economic basis for its existence, which it did through an ambitious programme of state intervention in the economy. In terms of physical capital, at independence assets had been stripped, booby-trapped, or destroyed to prevent further use. Trading networks and shops closed down. The government's programme of rapid nationalization of industries and shop networks was a logical reaction to this collapse (Pitcher, 2002: 38–39; Hanlon, 1984). Simultaneously, the new government attempted to industrialize rapidly and extensively imported heavy machinery from both the West and Eastern Bloc countries, although few people knew how to use or maintain it. In terms of the rural economy, the government promoted the development of gigantic state farms and co-operatives that peasants were encouraged – and sometimes compelled – to work at or join, often producing the same crops as under colonialism. In the first few years of independence these measures collectively resulted i appreciable economic growth, although by the early 1980s many had failed through poor design, drought, armed sabotage (as discussed below), or simple over-ambition. It was also increasingly difficult to import food. Due to Frelimo support for the ANC, Mozambique lost much of the foreign exchange its workers earned in South African mines. Due to the imports and the loss of foreign exchange, Mozambique went quickly from having virtually no foreign debt in 1980 to becoming very heavily indebted by 1984.

Overall, then, the post-independence statebuilding project sought explicitly to be revolutionary and to overturn colonial rule through new ideas for political authority, public administration and the political economy. Yet despite these radical ambitions, there were often striking continuities with dynamics of hierarchy in social relations. Marshall (1993) argues, for example, that literacy programmes in factories tended to reinforce structures of authority in management and social class, make onerous, unpaid demands on workers' time, and reinforce the status of Portuguese as the language of political participation. As such, literacy programs – at the heart of the government's vision for a modern, empowered, developed population – often ended up producing or reproducing forms of alienation between the ruling elites and masses. Other elements of the government's new programme, such as the creation of communal villages, cooperatives, and collective production, showed similar tendencies, often including physical compulsion, creating tensions between state and peasantry (Bowen, 2000).

The biggest threat to post-independence statebuilding was, however, Renamo's deliberate and widespread programme of state destruction.[3] It is broadly agreed that the group came about when the Rhodesian security services (and, after 1980, the South African security services) extensively funded, trained, and supported a group of disgruntled ex-Frelimo to deliberately destabilize the new Frelimo regime (Vines, 1995; Manning, 2002; Cabrita, 2000). At later stages, support was received from right-wing groups within the United States and Europe as part of Cold War anti-communist infiltration

Renamo deliberately targeted infrastructure such as roads and railway lines, particularly those linking Southern Rhodesia to Mozambique in the Beira corridor and those supplying productive industries, as well as any symbols of state power, including communal villages, health and education posts, and the bureaucratic apparatus (Young, 1990). The impact of these attacks was pervasive and substantial, both through damage caused and reduced activity due to fear among civilians. Various eyewitness accounts testify strongly to the brutality of the war, which produced displacement of up to four million people and caused hundreds of thousands of deaths and mutilations (Magaia, 1988; Nordstrom, 1997). Yet despite the seemingly senseless character of the atrocities, in places Renamo did come to a *modus vivendi* with populations through tapping resistance to Frelimo's statebuilding program (Geffray, 1990; Hall, 1990). In this sense, the outcome of Renamo's violence exactly cohered with its intentions – to destabilize the state and make normal life unviable, and to challenge Frelimo's attempts at 'modernist' social transformation and thus the establishment of its political legitimacy.

The 15 years after decolonization thus saw Mozambique's second ambitious statebuilding project in the 20th century, based in the attempt to push the territory and population along a socialist developmental pathway away from colonialism. To a certain extent there were very important changes and successes, such as a halving of illiteracy, and indeed the fact of political independence. Yet, as will be discussed further below, elements of the statebuilding programme reproduced some of the same antagonistic dynamics and distributions of power that had caused resistance to the colonial order, which Renamo fed off during its sabotage campaign. The next section will explore how the turn to a liberal statebuilding agenda in the 1980s onwards may only have minimally disturbed some of these antagonistic dynamics.

Liberalization and post-war statebuilding, 1989–present

Although elements of liberalization were put in place from the 1980s, it was from the 1990s onwards that a third and largely 'liberal' post–war programme of statebuilding in Mozambique was undertaken, under the close watch of the IFIs and European donors who exerted considerable influence (see Hanlon, 1996). The guiding principles for these reforms were economic and political liberalization, technical assistance, renewed framings for development policy, good governance, and capacity–building. In design, these principles were intended to remake the relationship between state and citizenry along liberal and democratic lines, and thus reduce violence.

On the political front, the move to multiparty elections and the funding of Renamo as a political party were enough to secure a peace deal, backed by solid financing for the talks an for demobilization programs from the UN and Italian government. The government of Mozambique had anticipated this by changing the Constitution accordingly in 1989 (Munslow, 1990; Hall and Young, 1991; Mendes, 1994). There were a series of delays in setting up an acceptable National Electoral Commission and process but elections were f nally held in 1994. Subsequent parliamentary and presidential elections have been held regularly, if not always smoothly, every five years. Under lobbying from the Mozambican journalist community, th press and broadcast media were also increasingly liberalized (Jone, 2005) in the post–war period. Various small– and not–so–small–scale civil society organizations have also emerged with the help of international sponsorship. As such, the public arena itself is visibly wider and less coercive than under the post–independence regime.

The macroeconomic liberalization programme that had begun in the 1980s with the IMF, progressively removing state intervention from the economy, also continued in the 1990s. In 1984 the government approved a structural adjustment programme in return for debt rescheduling. Official cooperation with the World Bank and EEC under the Lomé Conventio also began. This assistance was conditional on measures such as the removal of prices of production inputs and exchange controls on the currency, but developed into much wider programs of privatization, subsidy withdrawal, and divestiture in the 1990s. Famously, several industries such as the cashew industry suffered heavy losses of jobs and profits following the withdrawal of state pricing and exposure to competition from subsidized markets elsewhere (see Cramer, 1999). This project in particular led to substantial backtracking. Elsewhere, however, public spending has been deeply curtailed.

Another round of debt cancellation occurred in 1999 under the Highly Indebted Poor Countries Initiative, whereby Mozambique had most of its outstanding debt cancelled in return for adherence to Poverty Reduction Strategy Papers (PRSPs) agreed with Western donors, particularly the World Bank. These PRSPs upheld central elements of structural adjustment but also included an emphasis on Millennium Development Goals indicators such as numbers living on less than $1 per day and access to public services. These papers continue to form a central part of the negotiating framework for future budget support for the government and thus are an ongoing constraint on state action in the present.

In order to undertake these reforms and restructure state institutions, central and local government also received substantial forms of 'technical assistance' in terms of either donor agency employees seconded from embassies or people contracted as consultants, as part of the 'capacity–building' and 'knowledge transfer' agenda. This was often the only option available for ministries, whose capacity to pay civil servants' salaries was limited. A few were long–term appointments, but the majority carried out short–term analysis or restructuring projects, often around planning and budget capabilities. Increasingly, there developed 'revolving doors' between ministries, consultancies, and donor agencies, as the agencies hired talented Mozambican nationals out of ministries. As such, it is fair to say that any improvements in public administration in this period were uneven and often short-lived, subject to a range of competing interests and agendas.

Beyond interventions in the organs of the state, there was a large influx of aid, which wa administered directly to the population by external groups. These included (mostly European and North American) bilateral aid agencies, multilateral aid agencies and NGOs, carrying out a massive range of humanitarian and developmental missions, often setting up parallel structures to those of the state and in competition with each other. By 1989 the population was heavily reliant on food aid from donors, and by 1994 foreign aid overall counted for 60 per cent of Gross National Income (Batley, 2005: 417). In recent years this has substantially reduced, and increasing quantities go directly to central government as part of the statebuilding agenda. However, overall it still constitutes just under half of the government's budget.

The liberal statebuilding project undertaken during and after the war thus, like its predecessors, attempted to radically reshape state functions and the state–society relationship through an alternative vision of the role of the state in society, which combined liberal ideas about the state–society relationship with a New Public Management (i.e., pro–market and outsourcing) approach to public administration. In areas such as the push for political freedoms and macro-economic liberalization, it has broadly succeeded in its aims. Yet, just as each new regime attempts to define itself against the failures of previous regimes, each statebuilding project has also reproduced or only slightly modified some broad contours of rule in Mozambique. The nex section offers an assessment of the various changes and continuities in three dimensions of statehood: political authority, political economy, and public administration.

Continuities and changes in statebuilding, 1930–present

Political authority

To discuss the sources of political authority in statebuilding projects is to discuss how regimes claim their right to rule and legitimize the choices made on behalf of subjects. It is signif cant that in Mozambique across all three statebuilding projects discussed, political authority has been continuously constituted and reconstituted through ideologies of 'development', resting on a diagnostic of Mozambican 'underdevelopment'. It is also significant that political authority ha had to reconstitute itself in response to resistance by trying to liberalize or coopting dissenting voices.

For the colonial regime, there was a combination of ideas of moral and spiritual development through the Catholic Church, coupled with the 'progressive' political and economic effects of colonialism on 'backward' races. These provided an overall rationale for the colonial state, and justifications for particularly strong exercises of its power in forcing labor towards 'public works'. For Frelimo after independence, the core critique of colonialism was that it had led to underdevelopment and backwardness in Mozambique, thus requiring a very wide-scale program of social, political, and economic change, to be advised by those sufficiently knowledgeable and educated within the regime. Mahoney (2003) has commented in particular on the similarities between the colonial 'New State' and Frelimo's 'New Man' authoritarian and modernizing developmental ideologies. Both regimes used this justification to exercise tight control over political institutions and the political economy.

In the period since the end of the war, the goal of pursuing 'development' continues to provide political authority with its central justification, both for the state and for donor interventions This has reinforced and maintained the basic didactic hierarchies established by development, and in particular has facilitated the concentration of political decision-making into the hands of development experts and officials.[4] The integration of Millennium Development Goals and other markers of 'development' into statebuilding is not, however, a departure from the basic rationale of the state. Unsurprisingly, the Poverty Reduction Strategy Papers, a primary instrument of liberalization interventions, are tied to the authority of development actors, as well as required to show 'developmental' outcomes such as reductions in absolute poverty. As with the previous regimes, however, the designation of what is developmentally necessary has effectively closed off political contestation and reinforced the power of state actors vis-à-vis the population. Mkandawire (1999) has called such states 'choiceless democracies'. Moreover, although aspects of ideology such as the necessity of state intervention have apparently changed, others have not. For example, contemporary agricultural interventions continue to presume the undifferentiated subsistence character of a smallholder peasantry (Cramer, 2006: 261–262; Duffield, 2007 Chapter 4).

Albeit stable and enduring, developmental political authority has often had to make liberalizing moves to ward off dissenters. For example, the colonial regime was forced in the 1960s to permit various kinds of reform to try to stay in power, such as the nominal abolitions of the *indígena* category and of *chibalo*. Equally, Frelimo was required from the late 1980s to allow forms of political and economic liberalization to contain the internal (Renamo) and external (donor) forces of opposition. Since the end of the war, the transition from the Chissano to the Guebuza government can be seen as another such form of retrenchment, following a nearly lost 1999 presidential election (Sumich, 2010). In substantive terms, however, none of these retrenchments resulted in forms of change within the core personnel of the regime, nor their ability to exercise power through the state.

Indeed, only two small elites have wielded state power since 1930. Yet on the surface these liberalizations seemed to be signs of substantive political change; indeed, both the regularity of elections and Chissano's 'voluntary' step-down have been seen to be signs of the health of Mozambique's democracy. Overall, however, in all cases, we have seen periodic returns to the centralization of power. Currently, this is based in a reassertion of the Party within institutions of the state and a reinvigoration of Party structures as organizational vehicles.

Political economy

The persisting centrality of the state elite is made clearer when we consider the political economic relationship between the state and large companies in recent years. Reading off critiques of liberal statebuilding, we would expect the enforced liberalization and privatization of state enterprises to constitute a radical departure from forms of prior ownership. Pitcher (1996, 2002) has, however, analyzed particular elements that suggest some continuities on the basic ground of cooperation between the state and large enterprises.

The colonial state, as mentioned, sought first to operate through large colonial companies, before taking them over directly as instruments of the state under the New State. This was to secure monopolistic control of production, which propped up the state and its export-oriented political economy. The post-independence government's policy was essentially one of continuation with this structure of ownership, in terms of investment coming from the state and profit being returned to the state. While the state itself was much more oriented towards the needs of the population than the colonial regime, there were nonetheless continuities in the mutually supportive relationship between the state and large enterprise, which operated monopolistically.

Today, the processes of privatization and liberalization that have taken place in the post-independence period have largely transformed state monopolies into private monopolies or oligopolies across a range of sectors. Although nominally 'private', almost all large enterprises now must have a fairly direct relationship with the regime either via the state or via commercial partnership with members of the Frelimo*nomenklatura*. Thus, for example, the president controls large stakes in the 'privatized' public utilities sector, the former president has significant interest in mining, and even the party itself has an investment arm (Hanlon, 2009). Investment laws require foreign investors to partner with a national investor, who is usually connected with the Party somehow. This is more obviously true of the so—called 'mega—projects', such as Mozal (Mozambique Aluminium), which are half—owned by foreign investors and half—owned by the state. Monopolistic structures of industry also persist in many markets; although legally permitted, competition between the companies of the state elite is generally minimal.

As Pitcher argues, this signals that privatization in Mozambique has not been the wholesale reorientation of public enterprise towards the private sector, but has contended with and reinforced structures of political power. The recent re—emergence of colonial—era companies such as Sena Sugar Estates – this time co—owned by the state and Mauritian investors, and backed by World Bank guarantees rather than the colonial state – is perhaps a more obvious reminder of such continuities (Multilateral Investment Guarantee Agency, 2011). These continuities may be particularly obvious to rural populations, some of which have endured compulsory land evictions under all three regimes to serve large plantation agriculture.

These large estates can also shape opportunities for wage labor in the central provinces where many operate, which often represent generational continuities for workers and their families. Although this is now not *chibalo* or war labor, and workers are entitled to various minimum wages, these wages are often inadequate and very strongly eroded by inflation. Such generational continuities are also obvious in the ongoing patterns of migrant labor to South Africa from the southern provinces, cash—cropping in the northern provinces, and the structure of Mozambican Indian ownership of businesses across the country.

These forms of continuity – close collaboration between the state elite and large enterprises, geographical patterns of wage labor and income generation, and the role of the Indian merchant community – are indications of the extent to which liberal statebuilding has reproduced the broad structures of the political economy under the colonial and socialist regimes. There are important additives to this, including the influx of development aid, although often the distribution and effects of that money remain limited to the development industry in the capital city. Overall, however, the national political economy remains shaped by a concentration of ownership in small elites and an extraverted and export—oriented approach to rural development and regional traditions of income generation. This continuity strongly interacts with the developmental basis of political authority, which can allow the state to defer responsibility for the lack of change in economic conditions while also reinforcing the need for top—down direction[5]

Public administration

Public administration practices have also shown interesting forms of continuity as well as change. Critical accounts of statebuilding have emphasized that neoliberal policies have served to 'hollow out' the state, making it simply a regulatory agency rather than a substantive distributor and arbiter of political goods (Chandler, 2010). Intuitively the claim seems plausible, and fits with the genera story about the character of contemporary statebuilding.

However, the actual practices of public administration seem to have worked in some contrary ways. For example, both the colonial state and the socialist state were marked by substantial planning architectures in order to integrate the political reach of the state with the desired economic outcomes concerning production and autarchy. Salazar's Five Year Plan for

Mozambique and Machel's Ten Year (later Five Year) Plans for addressing developmental problems were thus a significant feature of their regimes. One would expect that liberalizatio would thus reduce the size and scope of national planning architectures as the country was moved away from a planned economy.

Yet the opposite seems to have happened; planning architectures and processes within Mozambique are now, perhaps more than ever, the central activity of politics and political life, across not just the state but public organizations and agencies. For example, the government continues to present its Five Year Plan (*Plano Quinquenial do Governo*), which is now the apparent basis for the Action Plan for the Reduction of Absolute Poverty (PARPA), which fulfils PRS planning requirements. Each sector is also required to develop a Sector–Wide Action Plan (SWAP), with implementing agencies also required to produce strategic plans at the level of the organization. Local governments, and now even administrative districts, have multiple regular planning exercises.

These plans are important because their negotiation is an interface of visibility between government and donors, and perhaps because they represent a concrete output of cooperation. Although *what* is planned has to a substantial extent altered from production targets to development targets, the bureaucratic practice and culture of planning have not diminished *per se*. Indeed, the establishment of a *more* powerful planning ministry in Mozambique – the Ministry for Planning and Development – indicates the centrality of this activity to the state, as well as reflecting the increasing desire of the Mozambican state to have as much influence over the outcome of planning processes as possible.[6]

Another policy of liberal administration is 'decentralized' governance, which is articulated as countering the dysfunctional, centralized bureaucratic post–colonial state. Yet, as West and Kloeck–Jenson(1999) have shown, these efforts have in places been greeted and treated as, variously, the reinvigoration of the colonial *régulo* system, the reappointment of Frelimo Party representatives, the re–recognition of Renamo*nambo* representatives, or the recognition of other traditions of decentralized authority. Some of the former *régulos* who have been involved have requested to have powers over local taxation and labor returned, as well as uniforms, flags, an transport with which to project their authority. This indicates that decentralization practices have been received as resonant with earlier forms of native administration and Party organization. Nor is this necessarily a misperception. For example, in the recent presidential campaigns, many complained that decentralized budgets were being diverted towards the projects of people affiliated with the Frelimo Party or their relatives (Langa, 2011; Serra, 2009). The local distribution of power and goods in this sense functions to ensure the longevity of the regime's project, as did previous systems.

Beyond planning and decentralization, there are even resonances in the resurrection of the 'villagization' idea via the Millennium Development Villages constructed recently. One in Gaza province was opened by Jeffrey Sachs, who arrived with 500 mosquito nets, a plough, and four yokes (AIM, 2006). In the colonial era, the peasantry were herded into *aldeamentos* (villages) to keep them separated from the rebels. These promised access to water and other infrastructure within the context of counter–insurgency (Jundanian, 1974). Frelimo essentially repeated the strategy with the *aldeias communais*, which served security functions during the Renamo conflic as well as developmental ones. These are not remembered particularly fondly either. Clearly, in the present day, there is a far lesser threat of widespread violence from either the state or an insurgency, and the population is not physically compelled to remain there. These are important differences. What is interesting, however, is the continuity in the administrative imagination, which gives rise to the enduring appeal of the model village as a vehicle for progress, development and better administration.[7]

This historical reading of statebuilding practice suggests that there is much in the way of continuity in the state–society relationships established, including in the discourses that govern political authority and legitimize the state, the ownership and orientation of the political economy, and the modalities and personnel in public administration. Clearly, this does not indicate that *nothing* has changed. As noted in this section, important changes include the diminution of widespread physical violence and compulsory free labor, and the shift away from economic autarchy, which are important features both of everyday life and in the relationships between state and society. Yet these are not by and large *as* central to forms of rule as some of the elements discussed, which pertain to the issues concerning the claiming, distribution, and structuring of political power, wealth, and control. The conclusion will reflect on the significan of this for how scholars, practitioners and citizens might approach the issue of statebuilding.

Conclusions: why we must think historically about statebuilding

The history of statebuilding in Mozambique shows that this is not a recent phenomenon driven by novel policy but a repeated phenomenon, with variations, incorporated into structures of global modernity. As the chapter has argued, although different regimes appear to institute radical change, dynamics of political authority, political economy, and public administration continue and substantially repeat previous strategies of rule.

This is crucial to remember on many levels. From the perspective of external practitioners, it puts into perspective the non–novel character of many contemporary interventions, and might even encourage a close examination of previous failures. For example, current donor agricultural policy in Mozambique is based on support for cooperatives with no substantive account of why they previously failed in this context. For scholars, both critical and supportive, this should encourage deeper reflection on the status, effectiveness, and logic of contemporary statebuilding which has often been held up as 'liberal' or 'neoliberal' in character. Looking at the problem historically suggests that dynamics of statebuilding are embedded substantially in particular dynamics that long pre–date the past 20 years. For citizens, historical awareness and consciousness of former statebuilding strategies offers a terrain for reflection on the present, as many in Mozambique have already recognized around the issue of state corruption.

Duffield has argued that post–war liberal intervention represents a 'radical developmental agenda of social transformation' (2001: 10–11). However, at least for Mozambique, this is to obscure the very *anti-radical, socially and politically conservative* dimensions of its effects on structures of power, wealth, and authority in the country. From this perspective, which uses history as a counterpoint, reforms have allowed for an entrenchment of power and modalities of rule, while appearing to increase their contestability. In this sense, intervention has provided the background and means for the elite to retrench without being substantially disturbed – indeed, with the increased possibility of cementing their position within society more generally.

This historical perspective finally also allows us to see that dissent in Mozambique is not necessarily suppressed for long. There was substantial discontent with the election results of 1999, which triggered opposition demonstrations. The recent social unrest, triggered by rises in food (February 2008) and fuel prices (September 2009), in major cities has demonstrated that there is an increasing sense of dissatisfaction with the government. This took it very much by surprise, and the government is trying desperately to respond through appeals to its historic mission and to the value of 'peace' in establishing 'development', thus rearticulating and reasserting a long–standing rationale for government in Mozambique. Yet it is unclear how long it will be able to maintain this under the present structures of power and wealth, which have sharpened inequality and centralization in Mozambique, as in many other places in the world.

Acknowledgment

This research was generously funded by the ESRC Studentship ES/F005431/1.

Notes

1. For more details on the reforms, see Newitt (1995), Chapters 15 to 17.
2. Frente de Libertação de Moçambique/Mozambique Liberation Front.
3. Resistência Nacional Moçambicano/Mozambican National Resistance.
4. See Ferguson (1990) for the most famous account of these dynamics.
5. See arguments in Chandler (2006) about statebuilding and political responsibility.
6. Interview with senior civil servant, Ministry for Planning and Development, Maputo, 28 August 2009.
7. Scott's discussion (1998: Chapter 7) of the functions served by villagization in Tanzania as providing a way of capturing and reading the peasantry influences the analysis here

References

Agência de Informação de Moçambique. (2006) *Millennium villages to reach Millennium Goals*. AIM Reports No. 323, 4 July, Maputo.
Batley, R. (2005). Mozambique: the costs of 'owning' aid. *Public Administration and Development*, *25*(5), 415–424.
Bowen, M. L. (2000). *The state against the peasantry: Rural struggles in colonial and postcolonial Mozambique*. Charlottesville, VA: University Press of Virginia.
Cabrita, J. M. (2000). *Mozambique: The tortuous road to democracy*. Basingstoke, UK: Palgrave.
Chandler, D. (2006). *Empire in denial: The politics of state-building*. London, UK: Pluto Press.
Chandler, D. (2010). *International statebuilding: The rise of post-liberal governance*. London, UK: Routledge.
Cramer, C. J. (1999). Can Africa industrialize by processing primary commodities? The case of Mozambican cashew nuts. *World Development*, *27*(7), 1247–1266.
Cramer, C. J. (2006). *Civil war is not a stupid thing: Accounting for violence in developing countries*. London, UK: Hurst & Co.
Duffield, M. R. (2001). *Global governance and the new wars: The merging of development and security*. New York, NY: Zed Books.
Duffield, M. R. (2007). *Development, security and unending war: Governing the world of peoples*. Cambridge, UK: Polity.
Egerö, B. (1987). *Mozambique: A dream undone: The political economy of democracy, 1975–84*. Uppsala, Sweden: Nordiska Afrikainstitutet.
Ferguson, J. (1990). *The anti-politics machine: "Development," depoliticization, and bureaucratic power in Lesotho*. Cambridge, UK: Cambridge University Press.
Geffray, C. (1990). *Les causes des armes au Mozambique: Anthropologie d'une guerre civile*. Paris, France: Karthala.
Hall, M. (1990). The Mozambican National Resistance Movement (Renamo): A study in the destruction of an African country. *Africa: Journal of the International African Institute*, *60*(1), 39–68.
Hall, M., & Young, T. (1991). Recent constitutional developments in Mozambique.*Journal of African Law*, *35*(1/2), 102–115.
Hanlon, J. (1984). *Mozambique: The revolution under fire*. London, UK: Zed Books.
Hanlon, J. (1996). *Peace without profit: How the IMF blocks rebuilding in Mozambique*. Oxford, UK: James Currey.
Hanlon, J. (2009). *Mozambique's elite: Finding its way in a globalised world and returning to old development models*. Crisis States Research Centre Seminar, London School of Economics, London, UK.
Harrison, G. (2000). *The politics of democratisation in rural Mozambique: Grassroots governance in Mecúfi*. Lewiston, NY: Edwin Mellen.
Isaacman, A. F. (1995). *Cotton is the mother of poverty: Peasants, work and rural struggle in colonial Mozambique, 1938–61*. Portsmouth, NH: Heinemann.
Jone, C. (2005). *Press and democratic transition in Mozambique, 1990–2000*. Johannesburg, South Africa: IFAS Research.
Jundanian, B. F. (1974). Resettlement programs: Counterinsurgency in Mozambique. *Comparative Politics*, *6*(4), 519–540.

Langa, J. (2011). Sete Milhões, Tesouro e... Mondlane. *O País,* Maputo, 26 March.
Magaia, L. (1988). *Dumba nengue, run for your life: Peasant tales of tragedy in Mozambique; historical introduction by Allen Issaacman.* Trenton, NJ: Africa World Press [Trans. M. Wolfers].
Mahoney, M. (2003). Estado Novo, Homem Novo (New State, New Man): Colonial and anticolonial development ideologies in Mozambique, 1930–1977. In D. C. Engerman (Ed.), *Staging growth: Modernization, development, and the global cold war.* Amherst, MA: University of Massachusetts Press, pp. 165–198.
Mamdani, M. (1996). *Citizen and subject: Contemporary Africa and the legacy of late colonialism.* Princeton, NJ: Princeton University Press.
Manning, C. L. (2002). *The politics of peace in Mozambique: Post-conflict democratization, 1992–2000.* Westport, CT: Praeger.
Marshall, J. M. (1993). *Literacy, power and democracy in Mozambique: The governance of learning from colonization to the present.* Boulder, CO: Westview Press.
Mendes, J. (1994). *A nossa situação, o nosso futuro e o multipartidarismo.* Maputo, Mozambique: UEM.
Mkandawire, T. (1999) Crisis management and the making of 'choiceless democracies' in Africa. In R. Joseph (Ed.), *The state, conflict and democracy in Africa.* Boulder, CO: Lynne Rienner.
Mosca, J. (1999). *A experiência socialista em Moçambique (1975–1986).* Lisbon Portugal: Instituto Piaget.
Multilateral Investment Guarantee Agency. (2011). *Project Brief, Companhia de Sena S.A.R.L.* Washington, DC: MIGA.
Munslow, B. (1990). Mozambique: Marxism–Leninism in reverse, the ffth congress of Frelimo. *Journal of Communist Studies and Transition Politics,* 6(1), 109–112.
Newitt, M. D. D. (1995). *A history of Mozambique.* London, UK: C. Hurst.
Nordstrom, C. (1997). *A different kind of war story.* Philadelphia, PA: University of Pennsylvania Press.
O'Laughlin, B. (2000). Class and the customary: The ambiguous legacy of the Indigenato in Mozambique. *African Affairs,* 99(394), 5–42.
Pitcher, M. A. (1996). Recreating colonialism or reconstructing the state? Privatisation and politics in Mozambique. *Journal of Southern African Studies,* 22(1), 49–74.
Pitcher, M. A. (2002). *Transforming Mozambique: The politics of privatization, 1975–2000.* New York, NY: Cambridge University Press.
Scott, J. C. (1998). *Seeing like a state: How certain schemes to improve the human condition have failed.* New Haven, CT: Yale University Press
Serra, C. (2009). Sobre os sete milhões em Catembe. *Diário dum Sociólogo.* Available at: http://oficina desociologia.blogspot.com
Sumich, J. (2010). The party and the state: Frelimo and social stratification in post–socialist Mozambique *Development and Change,* 41, 679–698.
Vail, L., and White, L. (1980).*Capitalism and colonialism in Moçambique: A study of Quelimane District.* London, UK: Heinemann.
Vines, A. (1995). *Renamo: From terrorism to democracy in Mozambique?* London, UK: James Currey.
West, H. G., and Kloeck–Jenson, S. (1999). Betwixt and between: 'Traditional authority' and democratic decentralization in post–war Mozambique.*African Affairs,* 98(393), 455–484.
Young, T. (1990). The MNR/RENAMO: External and internal dynamics. *African Affairs,* 89(357), 491–509.

10
THE 'FAILED-STATE' EFFECT
Statebuilding and state stories from the Congo

Kai Koddenbrock

Foreign attempts at building the Congolese state require a circumscribed understanding of two things: the state and the Congo. Statebuilders need to know what they are building. This basic prerequisite plays out in interesting ways. Congo analysts, for example, like to question the Congo's entire existence in the opening phrase. 'They call it a country, in fact it is just a Zaire-shaped hole in the middle of Africa' (*Economist*, 1995: 37) and 'The Democratic Republic of Congo does not exist' (Herbst and Mills, 2009: 2) are two prominent examples of this. Rhetorical hooks pay reference to expectations of the public. Among this public, whether the Congo exists at all seems to be in doubt.

Yet what does this lack of existence refer to exactly? Does it refer to the Congo as a country, nation, state, territory, or society? Since the rise of concepts such as 'failed state' and 'weak state' in the early 1990s, and their importance as global security threats after 9/11 and the war in Afghanistan, places like the Congo tend to be categorized according to their level of statehood. Failed-stateindicators abound and inform policy-making (Bueger and Bethke, 2012). Concepts and practice interact. Failed-state and statebuilding analysis functionally support each other because failed states make statebuilding necessary, while practices of statebuilding influence th understanding of places such as the Congo and keep state terminology intact.

Since the late 1990s, the DR Congo has seen numerous international interventions and support efforts: diplomatic negotiations during the peace process, leading to the Government of National Unity in 2002; a steadily growing peacekeeping mission, MONUC (now MONUSCO), whose mandate turned from military observer mission to a stabilization mission, including a robust mandate with the aim of fighting alongside government forces; two militar EU missions, in 2002 and 2006; massive elections support in 2006; and the common plethora of aid sectors funded by Western donors, from infrastructure to education, and from agriculture to health and sanitation. Furthermore, since the refugee crisis in eastern Congo after the Rwandan genocide in 1994, humanitarian aid has constituted an important share of the overall aid effort.

These interventions are attempts at statebuilding because they strive to create stability, build administrative institutions and occasionally to increase social welfare. They aim to construct 'legitimate, effective governmental institutions' (Paris and Sisk, 2007: 1). On paper at least, some key governmental institutions have been built over the past few years. Presidential and legislative elections have taken place, in 2006 and 2011, and a new constitution was passed in 2007, containing provisions for decentralization and a working balance between the central government in Kinshasa and the rich provinces in the center and east of the country (World Bank, 2011b: 29). The government pursued an ambitious agenda of the *cinq chantiers* (five pillars) toward development. However, the Congo continues to feature heavily as a failed state and policy analysis is replete with descriptions of the Congolese government's pathologies.

This chapter seeks to highlight the important point that the state concepts used in statebuilding, as both policy practice and academic sphere of reflection, predetermine what problems are identified and shape what solutions are sought. Analysis of statebuilding in the Congo has tended to summarize the evolution of international efforts there and to underline the problematic status of the Congolese state and government (Paddon and Lacaille, 2011). This chapter by contrast will adopt a theoretical perspective that does not take the state as the self-evident *telos* of social organization but rather as a 'principle of intelligibility' (Foucault, 2009: 287) that serves to read the state into existing social practice and simultaneously understands these practices as enacting the state itself. Using this perspective introduces a more ref exive perspective on statebuilding, as readers, analysts, and practitioners of statebuilding are shown to engage in 'ontological politics' (Law and Urry, 2004: 396) when they take the state as a given and continuously employ a vague notion of the state that stabilizes the Congo's international status as a 'weak' or 'failed' state.

The usefulness of this perspective for the study of statebuilding is demonstrated by the analysis of three Congo stories, showing how the 'failed' state can – but does not necessarily have to – be read into existing social processes. I use the term 'story' to indicate that these accounts of historical and contemporary processes are open to interpretation and by no means constitute *ipso facto* evidence that the Congo is, in fact, best understood as a failed state. The three stories presented are f rst, a historical analysis of the rise and decline of the Congolese state; second, a contemporary policy story of weak state and government capacity; and third, a story told by a 2004 survey on Congolese attachment to the Congo as a state and nation. These stories serve to argue that the state, as the objective of statebuilding, is indeed a quite fluid conception, whic is in constant need of re-production by analysts, readers, and practitioners alike. Taking this more seriously can open up possibilities for dealing with the Congo in a more reflective way, mor attuned to reflection on the impact and adequacy of international statebuilding

Enacting the state in statebuilding analysis

Thanks to the reigning two-pronged approach of external and internal statehood (Orford, 2011), the Congo's external statehood is secured. International law believes in the Congo. It is internationally recognized; it has ambassadors and a president who is accepted in international forums. The Congolese state is a recognized personality in international law. On the other hand, the dominant conception of the state as an actor with capacities means that its internal statehood is commonly seen as weak or failed. This lack of internal statehood legitimizes statebuilding in the eyes of statebuilders.

Although the failed- or weak-state concept has been under fire for almost a decade, it continues to be widely used in statebuilding policy discourse (Bilgin and Morton, 2002). These concepts refer to a state as an actor with specifc capacities. The actor-ness of the state is evident in terms such as 'the state *has* a monopoly of violence,' 'it *is* able to provide security,' etc. The understanding of the state implicitly used in this narrative is one of state strength. The state's strength and comprehensiveness rise and decline. The state is personified; it has an 'essential subjectivity' (Mitchell, 1991: 86).

Michel Foucault has attempted to engage in a history of the government of people and societies without taking the state as actor for granted. By contrast, he analyzed how the concept and institutions of the state came about and began to be seen as self-evident. In this theoretical perspective:

> The state is therefore a schema of intelligibility for a whole set of already established institutions, a whole set of given realities ... Second, the state functions as an objective in this political reason in the sense that it is that which must result from the active interventions of this reason or rationality. The state is therefore the principle of intelligibility of what is, but equally of what must be.
>
> *(Foucault, 2009: 286–287)*

In this view, the concept of state operates as a presupposed principle of intelligibility while simultaneously serving as the uncontested goal or result of social organization. Despite the growing prominence of governmentality-inspired research in the social sciences, this theoretically challenging proposition regarding the state itself has rarely been made resonate to statebuilding scholarship. Studying the state in this way was pioneered in the late 1970s (Abrams, 1988[1977]; Foucault, 2009) and introduced into American political science in the early 1990s (Mitchell, 1991) and is now being slowly taken up by statebuilding scholars (Kosmatopoulos, 2011; Heathershaw, 2012; Dunn, 2009; Koddenbrock, 2012). Timothy Mitchell starts from this theoretical vantage point and argues that:

> We should not ask 'Who is the state?' or 'Who dictates its policies?' Such questions presume what their answers pretend to prove: that some political subject, some *who* preexists and determines those multiple arrangements we call the state. The arrangements that produce the apparent separateness of the state create the abstract effect of agency, with concrete consequences.
>
> *(Mitchell, 1991: 90–91; emphasis in original)*

This means that the state, as an agent separate from social practices, is an effect of arrangements and abstractions. While a citizen is free not to think of the police or the parliament building as embodiments of the state, various arrangements exist that compel her to do so. Parliamentary debates are replete with allusions to the well-being of the nation-state and its national population and stabilize the imaginary of the state through this practice. The requirement to carry ID cards to be able to show them during police controls and the fnes or jabs resulting from failing to do so quite forcefully make the state appear as something separate, although the citizen victim could just as well blame the individual police officer as a simple representative of an organization tha carries guns (and is thus not linked to the state) for her pain! The practice of seeing through the violent police officer to see the state at work through him can be seen as the process of abstractio involved in every social encounter where the state is at stake. The state effect is thus an intertwined process between practices that try to embody the state and practices that ascribe the state concept to these practices.

To look at the production of the 'failed-state' effect, the following three Congo stories focus on the conception of the state as an 'effect' originating in the continuous production of the concept 'state' when naming governmental technologies. In this view, there is no *thing* like the state that we can partake in, although we can engage in practices that contribute to the production of the state effect. From the perspective adopted here, you can take part in *enacting* the state, not in the state *itself*.

This performative approach to the state is intimately linked to research on state imaginaries and the symbolic dimensions of the state (see further Schlichte, 2005; Ong and Collier, 2005; Gupta and Sharma, 2006). For example, writing about state imaginaries in the Congo, Michael Schatzberg argues that the concepts of 'state as family, Mobutu as father' dominated the state imaginary of early post-independence Congo and made it legitimate. Building on pre-colonial conceptions of kinship, Christian missions and Belgian paternalist colonialism, this repertoire was ably used by President Mobutu to make his rule and authority appear self−evident and legitimate (Schatzberg, 1988: 82–88, 93–98).

Looking at state imaginaries brings in the performative perspective that what people imagine the state to be does indeed shape what the state *is* in a specific social and historical situation Statebuilder conceptions of a 'failed' and 'weak' state thereby may enact a different 'state' from that seen from other perspectives, of those living in these areas. The three Congo stories presented below enable the reader to interrogate the state imaginaries at play among these statebuilding stories. The thrust of these stories is decidedly not to reveal what the state in the Congo *really* was or is, but to demonstrate different ways of producing the state as an *effect* of analysis and of other concrete practices.

Congo story I: the historical rise and decline of the Congolese state

Many attempts at establishing institutionalized forms of political order can be seen as statebuilding – from the Kongo kingdom to Belgian colonialism, from Mobutu Sese Seko's reign to UN peacekeeping starting in 1999, or the financing of the 2006 elections because 'any powerful grou struggling to institutionalize its power as a legitimate form of state rule can be framed as an agent of statebuilding' (Bliesemann de Guevara, 2012). This approach, of a historical sociology of statebuilding and state formation, takes statebuilding to be a 'conscious effort at creating an apparatus of control' and state formation as 'an historical process whose outcome is largely unconscious' (Berman and Lonsdale, 2002). From this perspective, current international state − building efforts can be situated in a historical process of the ups and downs of the state in the Congo and have to be thought of as complementary to the government's own efforts at state− building. Over time, different actors tried to consciously shape this process despite its unconscious undercurrents. This perspective also allows us to go beyond a merely Western−centered focus.

When exactly statebuilding and state formation in the Congo began is an open question. Some may argue they started hundreds of years ago; others could argue they have not even properly started yet. The Congo was populated by a large number of kingdoms long before Portuguese imperialism and Belgian colonialism. The Kongo kingdom, the Luba or the Lunda 'Empire,' as Ndaywel è Nziem calls them (1998), were only some of the myriad political orders. The Kongo Kingdom extended from the 15th to the 18th century across Western Congo, Congo Brazzaville and present day Northern Angola (Ndaywel è Nziem, 1998: 80–103). The Kongo kingdom's history was intertwined with that of Portuguese imperialism from the 15th century. The Luba and Lunda kingdoms dominated the South and a highly centralized mode of organization had prevailed in the Great Lakes region around Lakes Kivu and Edward (Ndaywel è Nziem, 1998: 212). For Michael Schatzberg, 'modal forms of political organization, centralized administration and small−scale autonomy, were thus present well before the colonial era' (Schatzberg, 1988). Whether scholars read these histories as evidence of *state* formation or of alternative political orders depends on how they understand the state and on how self−evident the state form is for them.

Nominally and legally, the Congo became a state once King Leopold II of Belgium managed to secure legal title to the Congo Free State as his personal property during the Berlin conference 1884–1885 (Nzongola−Ntalaja, 2002). The Belgian parliament was forced to turn the Congo from royal possession to a colony proper in 1908 because humanitarian advocacy movements had created outrage among the European public over the practices employed by Leopold's underlings to extract as much profit as possible from the territory (Hochschild, 1998)

Statebuilding, in Berman and Lonsdale's framing (2002), intensified when the imposition o Belgian governmental technologies and administration gathered pace during World War I.

Belgium pursued a highly motivated policy of creating both unified 'natives' and a system o total control. According to Schatzberg, they came closer to this aim 'than either the French or the British' (Schatzberg, 1988: 137; see also Young, 1965). The state came to be called 'Bula Matari,' the smasher of rocks (Nzongola−Ntajala, 2002: 16).

The increasing strength of the decolonization movement and the realization in the West that economic profits could just as well be extracted from formally independent states through trad had resulted in a wave of independence across Africa. Congo became independent in 1960 and held its first democratic elections. Belgium, however, actively boycotted the elected governmen led by Patrice Lumumba and, in concert with the CIA, contributed actively to his assassination in late 1960.

The first ever UN peace enforcement mission, ONUC, played a dubious role in Lumumba' demise because it pretended to be neutral between an elected government and the Katangan rebels supported by Belgium and the US (Orford, 2011). Although there was an elected government and parliament, Dag Hamarskjöld was not shy to proclaim that the situation 'had revealed the special possibilities and responsibilities of the Organization in situations of *vacuum*' (quoted in Orford, 2011: 84; emphasis added).[2]

President Mobutu Sese Seko's reign, promoted by Belgium and the US, lasted from 1965 to 1997. His way of dealing with the political order inherited from colonialism is usually portrayed in two phases: a successful and expansive phase until 1973 and the successive disintegration of the Congolese state in the 1970s and 1980s (Young and Turner, 1985), followed by its utter disappearance in the long years of the civil wars from 1997 to 2002. After the Rwandan genocide, Mobutu lost his grip on power for good. Supported by Rwanda and Uganda, Laurent Kabila's rebel movement swept across the country to end Mobutu's rule in mid−1997.

Laurent Kabila's reign, however, was short lived. His four−year rule, until his assassination in 2001, constituted a break with Mobutu's former allies. His first overseas trips as president wer to China, Libya, and Cuba. Kabila planned to create people's councils and a social democracy and wanted to pursue a pan−African foreign policy (Zacharie, 2009). For this 'unreformed communist' (Prunier, 2009: 335), this required the prevention of multi−party democracy (Stearns, 2011). This approach, in concert with his apparent lack of engagement in stopping the Hutu f ghters in Eastern Congo from threatening Rwanda, made him lose international and regional support, facilitating his murder at the height of the second Congo war in 2001. His successor and son Joseph Kabila, in turn, trod more carefully and strove to hold the middle ground between the interests of the regional and international power−brokers and the desires of the people.

The disintegration of the Congolese state peaked during the two Congo wars. The first Cong war took place in 1997; the second lasted from 1997 to 2002. The second war is also known as 'Africa's World War' (Prunier, 2009) because a large number of African states intervened to support the various warring parties. The east of the country to this day remains unstable, although the Joseph Kabila government has increasingly consolidated its power since 2002. Despite regular rebellions in the east, led by Laurent Nkunda between 2005 and 2008 and Bosco Ntaganda in 2012, Kabila easily won his second elections in 2011, amid allegations of massive fraud that did not suff ciently tarnish his reputation either inside or outside the country.

The state story distilled from this overview could be that various political orders have existed since the 15th century that could be termed 'state,' depending on the meaning of this term. Belgians imposed their administration between 1914 and 1960 and contributed to a strong state that, after a short period of struggles until Mobutu was firmly in place in about 1967, 'rose' eve further just to 'decline' from the mid−1970s onwards (Young and Turner, 1985). In 2012, during Joseph Kabila's now decade−long reign, the Congo regularly features as one of the most failed states worldwide in influential lists, such as the *Foreign Policy* 'Failed States Index.' However, a recent World Bank flagship report (2011b) sets a more optimistic tone and identifies progre and hope. Rise and decline continue to operate in a cyclical fashion; what remains constant is the practice of reading these cycles as expressions of *state* strength and weakness.

Congo Story II: lack of government capacity and benevolence

Convictions in Europe and the US about what the Congo needs have been fluctuating over tim (Dunn, 2003). Government, economy, and society are seen as the key objects of analysis and the social entities to be worked on and improved by both Congolese and international intervention. In 2012, policy and academic debate on Congolese government, economy, and society zeroes in on circumscribed characteristics that are, however, not self−evident. The economy is portrayed as a mining economy only and society is seen as inherently violent or struck by episodes of barbarism (Koddenbrock, 2012; Autesserre, 2012).

The status of state and government, in turn, is paramount for legitimizing different components of international intervention. The deficits of the Congolese polity are entry−point for intervention. In line with weak state *capacity*, the Congolese government is mostly portrayed as unable to enforce Congolese laws, provide security and other state functions. It is in general seen in terms of absence rather than presence (Institut Français des Relations Internationales, 2009; International Crisis Group, 2010; International Peace Institute, 2011). Nevertheless, there is a countervailing analysis focusing on the destructive or questionable acts of the Congolese government and its lack of legitimacy. Since its partnership with China and the Kabila govern− ment's increasing willingness to oppose Western prescriptions, this focus on state weakness as malevolence is gaining ground (see Paddon and Lacaille, 2011). Being destructive, however, requires means of influence. How tensions like this one between apparent weakness and malevolence play out with regard to mining management, secret deals with Rwanda, and the controversial movement of internally displaced people is the focus of the following section. The way these tensions are dealt with serves to highlight the role this mode of policy analysis plays in enacting the Congolese state as 'failed.'

Assuming the Congolese government is powerless or even inexistent can lead to surprises that do not f t this assumption. As a prelude, a quick summary of the most important actors: the Forces Armées de la République Démocratique du Congo (FARDC) are the Congolese armed forces. Numerous waves of integrating various rebel groups have left its lines of authority and cohesion quite unstable. The Conseil National pour la Défense du Peuple (CNDP) is a rebel group that rose to prominence after the 2006 elections and threatened to occupy the Kivu in 2008. The Rassemblement Congolais pour la Démocratie (RCD) did occupy the east until 2002 and is the cradle of much of CNDP (ex−)personnel. The Forces de Libération du Rwanda (FDLR) was founded in the aftermath of the Rwandan genocide. It roams the Western parts of Kivu, vows to topple the Rwandan government and was an ally of the Congolese government until 2008, when the Rwandan and Congolese governments suddenly decided to jointly f ght it.

Tension 1: mining control

When President Kabila announced a mining ban in the fall of 2010, which was to stop all mining activities in the Kivu and Oriental Province, the FARDC troops that were frequently regarded as beyond Kinshasa's reach swiftly left the important Bisie mine. A similar process had occurred when Kabila ordered the non−integrated 85th brigade to leave in 2008 when the deal with Rwanda was struck (United Nations, 2009), replaced by the 1st brigade, mostly composed of former CNDP rebels (United Nations, 2010). In early 2011, Global Witness reported that there were no armed groups near the mine, only the mining police. The UN Group of experts, by contrast, asserted this was not yet the case (United Nations, 2011). What is more, customary authorities are said to have an important role in distributing mining and land rights in the area (International Peace Information Service, 2010).

Taken together, these pieces of analysis indicate that the government may indeed shape mining control but that its exact geographies and hierarchies remain hard to understand. There is considerable research, too, on the elite networks spanning from the Kivus to the Congolese capital Kinshasa or the Rwandan capital Kigali, but who controls whom where has not been convincingly shown yet. Analysis fluctuates between ascribing a destructive 'politics of the belly' (Bayart, 1993) to the Congolese government and showing that they are just utterly unable to exert authority over these mines and the resulting trade. This ambivalence should give analysts pause when using the lack of so-called 'resource governance' as a straightforward call for Western statebuilding initiatives.

Tension 2: Congolese deals with Rwanda

In November 2008, the Congolese and Rwandan governments decided to leave their competition aside in order to pacify the Congo's east and to provide a more fertile ground for President Kabila's re-election in 2011. They agreed to arrest the CNDP rebel leader Laurent Nkunda, who had nearly occupied Goma, the capital of North Kivu, and to integrate the CNDP rebel forces into the Congolese army and join forces to fight the FDLR. The FDLR is openl hoping for regime change in Rwanda and is still regarded as a threat by the Rwandan government. This deal with Rwanda constituted a major step towards better cooperation and ensuing military operations temporarily weakened the standing of the FDLR.

Although Congolese President Kabila had used similar tactics in 2005, when he surprisingly sided with the Rwandan-supported RCD rebels to secure votes in the 2006 elections, some influential Western analysts were caught off guard by these developments (International Crisis Group, 2010: i). They could believe neither that agreements were found behind their back nor that cooperation between former supposed enemies was possible. These political moves showed the extent to which the Congolese government can be seen as able to act and shape Congolese politics, if strategic interests are at stake.

Among the Western policy world, this deal was read as unfavorable for the Congolese government. It was assumed that tough concessions had to be made because the government was believed to have negotiated from a position of weakness. The CNDP rebels were given guarantees that they would not to be taken to court for crimes committed, that they could retain their parallel administration structure over parts of North Kivu, they were awarded control over important mining areas, and Tutsi refugees in Rwanda were to be allowed to eventually return to the Congo. The International Crisis Group bemoaned in this regard 'that commitments had also been made regarding access to grazing land in North Kivu for thousands of cows belonging to Congolese Tutsis and Rwandan military' (International Crisis Group, 2010: 32–33), a rare glimpse into another important pillar of the Kivu economy beyond mining (see further Koddenbrock, 2012; Autesserre, 2012).

The logic of these deals remains highly opaque and there is a sense of respect for how ably the Kabila government has kept Western donors at bay in this (Paddon and Lacaille, 2011). This does not prevent some think-tanks from making specific recommendations toward the respectiv governments and international organizations. The International Crisis Group, for example, reacted to these surprising developments with a call for more transparency but did not argue as to *why* secrecy cannot contribute to solving complex diplomatic challenges: 'A strategy based on secret presidential commitments, however, will not bring peace to the Kivu: the present approach must be re-evaluated and broadened in order to engage all local communities and prepare the future of the region in a transparent dialogue that also involves neighbouring countries' (International Crisis Group, 2010: i). Experts of diplomacy might well assure this ICG analyst that secrecy has at times played a fundamental role in moving international relations forward.

Again, there is a fundamental tension in policy reporting: the urge to paint the state and government as incapable or malevolent leads to prescriptions that lack rigor. Diplomatic deals that might be seen as strategic and constructive are made to seem weak and useless without proper substantiation.

Tension 3: moving internally displaced people

The third and last example of 'facts' that serve to enact the state as failed can be seen in the way the Kabila government is reported to have managed the displaced populations in and around Goma. In this case, the government is described as indecent and destructive rather than unable. In the eyes of the analysts, this has more or less the same effect on their perception of state and government capacity.

Prior to the 2011 elections, Kabila possibly wanted to convey the impression that the region was getting more stable. He thus told the IDPs around Goma to go home because it was purportedly safe. Tens of thousands immediately did. The international representatives in Goma were outraged by this display of governmental power because they argued that it wasn't safe (Human Rights Watch, 2010). But they could not do anything but acknowledge the fact that most of the camps were suddenly empty.

At key moments, the government is reported to make announcements, issue decrees, or order some of their citizens to move, and this shows important results. These signs of authority and influence would, in theory, make the use of state failure terminology more difficult. Yet th implications of these incidents are not dealt with. These events are presented as episodes, so the overall narrative remains one of state weakness and lack of governmental capacity.

Congo story III: measuring state and nation

The following reading of survey data collected by American scholars underlines that swiftly linking concepts such as state and nation to survey statements or messy social life is a challenging endeavor. It is the exception rather than the rule to acknowledge this. Longstanding USAID official Tony Gambino was an exception when he wrote in a recent World Bank report: '[Making] sense of Congolese reality is a humbling, daunting intellectual undertaking. This . . . implies that various actors, even those most knowledgeable, regularly miscalculate, further tangling this already near-impenetrable analytical web' (World Bank, 2011a: 19). Analytical restraint, however, would make reports and recommendations appear less convincing.

Interpretation of the Congo does not always employ the pathologizing failed-state register. There is also a more positive variant of using the state as a principle of intelligibility at play in Congo analysis. This research strand tends to stress the surprising resilience of the state in the Congo (for example, Englebert, 2003). This argument does not necessarily stabilize the need for international statebuilding in the Congo but partakes in the 'ontological politics' of taking the state as self-evident entity and as the sole aim of social organization.

For their publication entitled *The Enduring Idea of the Congo* (2004), Herbert Weiss and Tatiana Carayannis interviewed Congolese citizens from f ve major Congolese cities and highlighted multiple connotations connected to the idea of the 'unity of the Congo,' among others. While 'brotherly love' and 'territorial integrity' feature on top of the list with 10–35 per cent of respondents, 'Mobutu's Zaire' and the 'Belgian Congo' are less prominent with about 11–27 per cent and a generally smaller acceptance rate (2004: 162).

With the help of high response rates to the insinuating statement 'The Congo must be unified even if the use of force is necessary to achieve this,' Weiss and Carayannis deduced a strong commitment among the Congolese to national unity and the idea of the Congo. Countering popular assumptions that ethnic tensions were one of the main reasons for conflict in the Cong at the time, they argue that Congolese identity trumps ethnic identity in all of the cities surveyed: 'Put very simply, the survey data presented here clearly shows that a national consciousness and identity has been emerging in the Congo' (Weiss and Carayannis, 2004: 163). They credit Mobutu for kick-starting this national consciousness. According to them, there was more separatism than nationalism during independence but since Mobutu's authenticity campaign national pride and consciousness had been instilled (Weiss and Carayannis, 2004: 159; also Prunier, 2009).

What about the state in this? In their survey, Weiss and Carayannis pose one question about the state and several about service provision. Asked about the state's institutional form, respondents are quite equally divided among the 'federal state,' 'unitary state,' and 'decentralized unitary state.' Service provision in roads, security, health care, and education is seen as rather unsatisfactory but at times surprisingly less so. Health care, for example, boasts satisfaction rates of up to 50 per cent, a result quickly dismissed by the authors on the basis that people must have become used to very low standards (Weiss and Carayannis, 2004: 167).

The combination of these survey data serves to measure 'elements of unification and identification with the state and nation' (Weiss and Carayannis, 2004: 174). However, this short glimpse into the most widely quoted survey on Congolese nationalism and state-identifcation tells us more about the conceptual apparatus employed by the analysts than about state and nation imaginaries among the Congolese. Their opinions on federal structures or service provision do not reveal what they associate with the state. Letting interviewees choose between six terms such as 'brotherly love' and 'Mobutu's Zaire' to get at their conception of Congolese unity is highly constraining.

A more productive approach might have been to ask the Congolese about their conceptions of political order, about their assessments of the political role and legitimacy of the parliament, the president, or chiefs in their area. Asking about the state by proposing three constitutional terms that include the term 'state' indicates the extent to which Weiss and Carayannis take it as a given.

Contemporary forms of statebuilding

Most current forms of intervention and statebuilding attempt to tackle the problem of 'reconstructing state authority' in the Congo (Autesserre, 2012: 2). The frequent and seemingly arbitrary changes of priorities and programs over the years, however, implicitly allude to a challenge: what the Congo needs or is requires meticulous analysis. It also shows that Congolese realities are not only out there but are also made because the Congo changes less quickly than some of the aid programs. The concepts used shape the problems identified and the measures taken

A recent euphoric World Bank report on the *Resilience of an African Giant* is a major step in realigning Congo images in the statebuilding community (2011b). Much policy thinking is still dominated by the reductionist analysis of weak state, mining economy, and brutalized society (Koddenbrock, 2012; Autesserre, 2012). However, sovereign government decisions are increasingly accepted – for lack of another choice, perhaps – and the Congo is seen as a country of potential. Economic Partnership agreement negotiations between the EU and the DRC have not been concluded and the World Bank's new Poverty Reduction Strategy Paper is not public yet although it has been in place since 2011. These are signs of an increasingly assertive Congolese 'counterpart.'

Dominant narratives play an important role in shaping the forms of statebuilding interventions but they do not prevent them from being varied and multifaceted. Aid and statebuilding in the Congo is also costly. Table 10.1 gives an overview of OECD member state aid to the Congo and the costs of MONUC and MONUSCO.

Contrary to the dominant mining economy narrative, for example, the Agence Belge de Développement now focuses its support on agriculture because it contributes 56 per cent of GDP (2010: 3). Infrastructure and health are its other priorities. DFID distributes £130–250 million per year to various sectors from humanitarian, governance, and security, health and sanitation to HIV and malaria prevention and treatment (DFID, 2011). The EU Commission has a similar portfolio, as has the World Bank, which describes its work as focused '69 per cent on sustainable development (infrastructure, water, energy, agriculture, and forests/environment), 9 per cent on governance and the private sector, and 23 per cent on human development (education, health, and welfare services)' (World Bank, 2011b). The multi-billion peacekeeping mission MONUSCO offers a comparable variety. MONUSCO's bureaucratic sections and respective activities include, among others, human rights, political affairs, civil affairs, disarmament, child protection, HIV, and, crucially, its large military wing.

However, policy debate revolves mostly around security sector reform, mineral certificatio schemes, and the protection of civilians as remedies to the deficient state, economy, and societ identified in policy debate (Koddenbrock, 2012). Focus and clarity are essential for policy analysis of the Congo. Clarity, however, comes at a price. This contribution has tried to show that analysis would profit from a deeper interrogation of the theoretical premises involved, thereby makin the enactment of the state as 'failed' far less self-evident.

Conclusion

The stories presented in this chapter send potentially mixed messages: the Congo has a history but it does not exist. Its state is weak but its government is authoritarian. Nationalism is deeply rooted but the Congo is not a nation. The Congo's identity and the character of its institutions are clearly a matter of insecurity and debate. This is a formidable challenge for external statebuilding efforts in the Congo because they need to base their work on clear concepts.

Disbursing aid, sending EU troops or UN peacekeepers to the country, or trying to convince the government to engage in specific policies are not necessarily futile endeavors. Their unpredictable results (Veit, 2010) and their arbitrary analytical basis, however, deserve more attention than current policy analysis and policy prescriptions are willing to acknowledge. The uncertainty of impact and analysis calls for a notion of 'political ethos' that combines assuming

Table 10.1 International funding amounts

	2003	2004	2005	2006	2007	2008	2009	2010
All donors including multilateral	5416	1919	1881	2197	1356	1765	2356	3541
MONUSCO	508	665	940	1078	1135	1129	1222	1351
Total (US$m)	5925	2584	2822	3275	2492	2895	3579	4892

Sources: http://stats.oecd.org; www.un.org/en/peacekeeping/missions/monusco/facts.shtml; www.un.org/en/peacekeeping/missions/monuc/facts.shtml

responsibility for the 'perhaps' at the basis of statebuilding (Campbell, 1998) with openness toward critique. This chapter has sought to set out an example of analysis from this starting point.

There are very few analysts who do not place their analysis in the convenient frame of state failure or government malevolence, although some have attempted to take a harder look at the logics at play within the institutions commonly associated with the failed state, such as the police or the army (Baaz and Stern, 2008; Baaz and Olsson, 2011: 224). Statebuilding results would not necessarily be better if this more curious approach were adopted more widely. Yet analytical variety and contestation would certainly allow more space for creativity among all those involved.

Note

1 See Latour's brilliant juxtaposition of burglars and the police in *The Making of Law* (2010: 257–258).
2 MONUC and MONUSCO's progressive loss of neutrality and alignment with the Congolese Armed Forces is an interesting reversal of the role played back in the early 1960s. The 'vacuum' trope, by contrast, continues to be deployed in the same manner. As the analysis in this chapter shows, state failure in the Congo is often discursively framed as a 'power vacuum' despite observable government action and regulation.

References

Abrams, P. (1988[1977]). Notes on the difficulty of studying the state. *Journal of Historical Sociology*, 1(1), 58–89.
Agence Belge de Développment. (2010). *Le Partenariat RD Congo-Belgique: Faits et Chiffres et Stratégie 2010–2013*. Avalable at: www.btcctb.org
Autesserre, S. (2012). Dangerous tales: Dominant narratives on the Congo and their unintended consequences. *African Affairs* (in press).
Baaz, M. E., and Olsson, O. (2011). Feeding the horse: Unoffcial economic activities within the Police Force in the Democratic Republic of the Congo. *African Security*, 4(4), 223–241.
Baaz, M. E. and Stern, M. (2008). Making sense of violence: Voices of soldiers in the Congo (DRC)*Journal of Modern African Studies*, 46(1), 57–86.
Bayart, J.–F. (1993). *The state in Africa: The politics of the belly*. London, UK: Longman.
Berman, B., and Lonsdale, J. (2002). *Unhappy valley: Conflict in Kenya and Africa*. Oxford, UK: Currey.
Bilgin, P., and Morton, A. D. (2002). Historicising representations of 'failed states': Beyond the Cold–War annexation of the social sciences? *Third World Quarterly*, 23(1), 55–80.
Bliesemann de Guevara, B. (Ed.). (2012). *Statebuilding and state-formation: The political sociology of intervention*. London, UK: Routledge.
Bueger, C., and Bethke, F. (2012). Actor–networking the 'failed state' – An inquiry into the life of concepts. *Journal of International Relations and Development* (in press).
Campbell, D. (1998). *National Deconstruction: Violence, identity and justice in Bosnia*. Minneapolis, MN: University of Minnesota Press,.
DFID. (2011). *Operational Plan 2011–2015 DFID Democratic Republic of Congo*. London, UK: DFID.
Dunn, K. C. (2003). *Imagining the Congo: The international relations of identity*. New York, NY: Palgrave Macmillan.
Dunn, K. C. (2009). Contested state spaces: African national parks and the state. *European Journal of International Relations*, 15(3), 423–446.
Economist, The. (1995). A hole in the map of Africa, 8 July.
Englebert, P. (2003). *Why Congo persists: Sovereignty, globalization and the violent reproduction of a weak state*. Working Paper 95, Queen Elizabeth House Carnegie Project, Oxford, UK.
Foucault, M. (2009). *Security, territory, population: Lectures at the Collège de France 1977–78*. Basingstoke, UK: Palgrave Macmillan.
Global Witness. (2011). *Congo's minerals trade in the balance: Opportunities and obstacles to militarization*. London, UK: Global Witness.
Gupta, A., and Sharma, A. (Eds.). (2006). *Antrhopology of the state*. Oxford, UK: Blackwell.
Heathershaw, J. (2012). Conclusions – Neither built nor formed – The tranformation of post–conflict state and international intervention. In B. Bliesemann de Guevara (Ed.), *Statebuilding and state-formation: The political sociology of intervention*. London, UK: Routledge, pp. 246–259.

Herbst, J., and Mills, G. (2009). There is no Congo. *Foreign Policy*. Available at: www.foreignpolicy.com

Hochschild, A. (1998). *King Leopold's ghost: A story of greed, terror, and heroism in Colonial Africa* (1st ed.). Boston, MA: Houghton Mifflin

Human Rights Watch. (2010). *Always on the run: The vicious cycle of displacement in Eastern Congo*. New York, NY: Human Rights Watch.

Institut Français des Relations Internationales. (2009). *How to reform peacemaking in the Democratic Republic of Congo: When peace processes become international "systems of organized action"*. Paris, France: Institut Français des Relations Internationales.

International Crisis Group. (2010). *Congo: No stability in Kivu despite raprochement with Rwanda*. Brussels, Belgium: International Crisis Group.

International Peace Information Service. (2010). *The complexity of resource governance in a context of state fragility: The case of Eastern DRC*. Antwerp, Belgium: International Peace Information Service.

International Peace Institute. (2011). *Renewing MONUSCO's mandate: What role beyond the elections?* New York, NY: International Peace Institute.

Koddenbrock, K. (2012). Recipes for intervention – Western policy papers imagine the Congo.*International Peacekeeping*, *19*(5), 549–564.

Kosmatopoulos, N. (2011). Toward an anthropology of state failure: Lebanon's Leviathan and peace expertise. *Social Analysis*, *55*(3), 115–142.

Latour, B. (2010). *The making of law: An ethnography of the conseil d'Etat*. Cambridge, UK: Polity.

Law, J., and Urry, J. (2004). Enacting the social. *Economy and Society*, *33*(3), 390–410.

Mitchell, T. (1991). The limits of the state: Beyond statist approaches and their critics. *American Political Science Review*, *85*(1), 77–96.

Ndaywel è Nziem, I. (1998). *Histoire générale du Congo: De l'héritage ancien à la république démocratique*. Brussels, Belgium: Duculot.

Nzongola−Ntalaja, G. (2002). *The Congo from Leopold to Kabila: A people's history*. London, UK: Zed Books.

Ong, A., and Collier, S. (Eds.). (2005). *Global assemblages*. Oxford, UK: Blackwell.

Orford, A. (2011). *International authority and the responsibility to protect*. Cambridge, UK: Cambridge University Press.

Paddon, E., and Lacaille, G. (2011). *Stabilising the Congo*. Oxford, UK: Refugee Studies Centre.

Paris, R., and Sisk, T. (2007). *Managing contradictions: The inherent dilemmas of postwar statebuilding*. Ottawa, Canada: Research Partnership on Postwar Statebuilding.

Prunier, G. (2009). *Africa's world war: Congo, the Rwandan genocide, and the making of a continental catastrophe*. Oxford, UK: Oxford University Press.

Schatzberg, M. (1988). *The dialectics of oppression in Zaire*. Bloomington, IN: Indiana University Press,.

Schlichte, K. (Ed.). (2005). *The dynamics of states: The formation and crises of state domination*. Aldershot, UK: Ashgate.

Stearns, J. K. (2011). *Dancing in the glory of monsters: The collapse of the Congo and the great war of Africa*. New York, NY: Public Affairs.

United Nations (2009). *Interim report of the Group of Experts on the Democratic Republic of Congo*. New York, NY: United Nations.

United Nations (2010). *Final report of the Group of Experts on the Democratic Republic of Congo*. New York, NY: United Nations.

United Nations (2011). *Interim report of the Group of Experts on the Democratic Republic of Congo*. New York, NY: United Nations.

Veit, A. (2010). *Intervention as indirect rule: The politics of civil war and state-building in Ituri*. Frankfurt−on−Main, Germany: Campus−Verlag.

Weiss, H. F., and Carayannis, T. (2004). The enduring idea of the Congo. In R. R. Larémont (Ed.)*Borders, nationalism and the African State*. Boulder, CO: Lynne Rienner.

World Bank, The. (2011a). *World Development Report 2011: Background case study Democratic Republic of Congo*. Washington, DC: The World Bank.

World Bank, The. (2011b). *Resilience of an African giant*. Washington, DC: The World Bank.

Young, C. (1965). *Politics in the Congo: Decolonization and independence*. Princeton, NJ: Princeton University Press.

Young, C., and Turner, T. (1985). *The rise and decline of the Zairian state*. Madison, WI: University of Wisconsin Press.

Zacharie, A. (2009). De la dette au développement: Un chemin semé d'embauches. In T. Trefon (Ed.), *Réforme au Congo (RDC): Attentes et désillusions*. Paris, France: L'Haramattan, pp. 103–118.

11
FAILED STATEBUILDING VERSUS PEACE FORMATION[1]

Oliver P. Richmond

This chapter is a future-oriented framing exercise that sets out to establish a set of perspectives from which the limits of statebuilding can be understood in terms of the interrelationship between statebuilding and peace formation. It thereby outlines the often countervailing forces and norms of state formation, statebuilding, and peacebuilding according to their associated theoretical approaches, concepts, and methodologies. It introduces a new concept of 'peace formation' which counterbalances the previous concepts' reliance on internal violence or external institutions' agency in terms of pushing reform and the use of operational conditionality. Without incorporating a better understanding of the multiple and often critical agencies involved in peace formation, the states that emerge from statebuilding will remain as they are – failed by design, because they are founded on external systems, legitimacy, and norms rather than upon a contextual, critical, and emancipatory epistemology of peace. Engaging with the processes of peace formation may aid international actors in gaining a better understanding of the roots of a conflict, how local actors may be assisted, how violence and power-seeking may be ended or managed, and how local legitimacy may emerge. It may also provide an understanding of how newly forming peaces may influence international order and the liberal peace

Failure by design

Statebuilding, like liberal or neoliberal peacebuilding, is failed by design. This is f rstly because the institutional frameworks are externally designed with a European or northern, developed, rational, and individualistic context in mind, do not include urgent responses to economic needs, and fail to provide public services quickly enough to undercut currents of violence and root causes of conflict. Second, liberal forms of peacebuilding also follow this pattern in that the normative universe they operate from (institutions, donors, or INGOs based in New York, Washington, Geneva, Brussels, Paris, London, Tokyo, etc.) is rarely commensurate with that of the specific context they are applied in (currently mostly in developing, post-conflict settin outside of the global north, with the exceptions perhaps of a few cases such as Bosnia or Kosovo). This has also been the case with the closely allied modernization approaches aiming at development, which have also suffered from ideological prescriptions that are widely thought to undermine any short-term peace dividend (enabling material and power inequality instead). Third, and as a result of these problems, both statebuilding and liberal peacebuilding strategies fail to connect with their target populations, end up buttressing problematic elites and their often chauvinistic, nationalistic, or personal interests, and so lack a connection in context, on the ground, among populations that have their own understandings of identity, sovereignty, institutions, rights, law, and needs according to their own socio–historical and cultural traditions. Finally, while analysts are keen to focus on the normative and technical processes of such forms of intervention, they are rarely keen to consider the global as opposed to regional or local power structures in which they take place (particularly the unintended consequences of global capitalism on already marginalized states and their citizens). This dominant form, which for a while in the 1990s looked to be hegemonic, might be called the liberal peace, though at times its liberalism and its contribution to peace have been very questionable (Doyle, 1986). Despite this there has been a common consensus that statebuilding is crucial for broader peace and security, and there have been many theoretical and policy contributions to improving its tools and mechanisms (Kapur, 1998: 4; World Bank, 1997; Chibber, 1997: 17; US National Security Strategy, 2002; European Security Strategy, 2003; US Department of Defense, 2008; Fukuyama, 2004: 17; OECD–DAC, 2007).

This chapter begs to differ from the mainstream consensus, which came about long before the empirical evidence could be broadly assessed, was partly colored by post–Cold War triumphalism, rested on a crude form of capitalism and the erosion of citizens' classical liberal rights and needs – and therefore resulted in building states around a marginalized political subject whose main role was to be pacified, to produce, to respect private property, and to vote in a procedura manner. This subject was to be subordinate to international expertise, as with the colonial subject's relationship to the metropolitan center during previous Western anthropological engagements with political power structures in the early 20th century (Asad, 1973: 17). Indeed, many of these debates came about because of policy objectives to create a sustainable peace, but ironically without the involvement of the subjects of that peace, in its many theaters around the world. These subjects may be termed the 'children' of Western interventionism and humanitarianism (Paris, 2002).

Alternative approaches are now emerging, driven partly by local, peaceful forms of agency (though often critical and resistant): 'peace formation' processes would see political subjects as formative of the state, economy, society, and international community rather than as their subjects. A crucial dilemma that needs to be addressed is whether peace formation processes, as seen in many post–conflict situations (and even in the current 'Arab Spring'), and which ofte coexist with violent state–formation processes, will create parallel structures to the neoliberal state internationals persist in trying to produce from Bosnia to Afghanistan, or whether the peace–building and statebuilding projects of the international community can be brought into line with such expressions of local agency.

This chapter outlines the state formation and statebuilding arguments as well as the contours of the critique of liberal statebuilding/peacebuilding that has since emerged. It outlines the preliminary issues with local forms of peacebuilding or 'peace formation' (Richmond, 2011). These four concepts represent in fairly clear terms the contours of the relationship between different forms of conf ict and peace. By looking at the smaller scale and often invisible local attempts at peacebuilding and peace formation it attempts to provide some answers to the pressing question of how large–scale peacebuilding, often aimed at statebuilding, can be significantly improved and made more representative of the lives, needs, rights, and ambitions of its subjects – meaning the many citizens, individuals, and communities in post–conflict environments aroun the world. It aims not to speak on their behalf, but to investigate ways in which their voices and life worlds may become more visible.

State formation, statebuilding, peacebuilding, and peace formation

State formation debates offer a negative peace mainly maintained through power–sharing and balance of power arrangements within and between states, dictated by a security dilemma and the relative power of various factions (Tilly, 1985). They offer a crude version of conflict management in first–generation form (Richmond, 2008: 40–57). Thus state formation is a constantly contested process and the negative peace that emerges represents a victor's peace or an uneasy truce, meaning that it is inherently unstable. Peace is made by local elites who desire, often for predatory reasons (social, political, economic, and international), the capacities the state offers to them. This process occurs within and between states at the regional level.

Statebuilding approaches offer a more sophisticated concept of peace than the negative and realist versions that state formation offers. This is still a first–generation conflict management approach but it sees the possibility of a status quo that is fairly solid as long as the state is suffiently well designed and prosperous. Statebuilding approaches offer the possibility of achieving a liberal peace, but they are more concerned with institutional and legal design as well as market access and are less concerned with the normative architecture of peacebuilding (Kapur, 1998: 12; Chandler, 2010: 15). Peace is made via collaboration between a range of international actors, concerned with regional stability rather than normative agreement or standards, and local elites who maintain control of the state often to pursue and satisfy personal or family agendas. This approach to making peace is also inherently unstable because the state rests on international support and elite compromise, lacking local legitimacy in many cases because the state does not provide welfare or services designed to offer a material peace dividend. Instead it focuses on rights and markets.

Liberal peacebuilding is a third–generation approach that offers a peace built with twin anchors in international norms, law, and institutions, and the liberal democratic and 'marketized' concept of the state. It offers a liberal peace that may range from conservative (relying on external support and internal power–sharing) to orthodox (which as envisaged by the UN rests on human rights, civil society, democracy, and the rule of law) to a more ambitious emancipatory version (where issues of social justice and identity are the focus) (Richmond, 2005). Peace is made internationally within this framework, with as much local participation as possible, but this is not necessarily its driving force. This peace, it is argued, should be extremely stable, though in practice it is often complex, prone to stalemate and to elite hijack. It is also prone to limitations brought about by a lack of coordination and consensus among its international supporters, and a lack of their material support for its range of programs and innovations.

It has long been clear that the international 'liberal peace' project – now often called statebuilding – has been undermined by a series of crises (Richmond, 2005; Chandler, 2006; Pugh, 2008; Pugh et al., 2008; Cooper, 2007; Jahn, 2007; Duffield, 2007; Mac Ginty, 2008 Mac Ginty and Richmond, 2007). These have emerged in its application to many post–conflict countries since the end of the Cold War. 'Failed statebuilding' has been the result. By this I mean that states have come into being as a result of a mixture of local and international dynamics and interventions that are effectively failed by design. Such states lack core capacity (as defined b the World Bank, 1997) in many crucial areas, partly because neoliberalism dictates this or because their standards and norms are ill suited, causing potentially fatal flaws in their design and weaknesses in their local legitimacy, peace dividend, and redistributive capacity.

However, there have been some unanticipated and very interesting consequences, not least in the redevelopment and evolution of the Western backed and propagated (by key donors, the UN system, international NGOs and agencies, and international financial institutions such as the World Bank) liberal peace project itself (Richmond, 2011: 186–216). In response, local actors, often in association with select international actors, have begun to design their own versions of peacebuilding relevant to their own locations, states, cultures, histories, needs, and expectations. This process has been difficult to describe and the policy and academic literatures have struggle to find an appropriate language to capture its variety, not least because it stands as a challenge t many of the policy instruments and concepts many hold dear. It has often been called 'grassroots peacebuilding,' 'civil society oriented,' and 'donor supported.' This area of peace activity has become so important that such terminology no longer does justice to its significance, especiall in relation to external policies and goals and the emergence of new donors. I call this 'new' area 'peace formation' (it is of course not new, but instead is an attempt to unite a scattered range of significant efforts in this direction that already exist). The agency it rests on is varied and complex. It has not been the result of direct resistance or action, such as violent demonstrations, but more a result of quiet capacity drawing on locally resonant social practices and critical discourses, understandings of peace drawing on history, myth, religion, social and customary institutions, and patterns of governance. It sometimes expresses itself via resistance, opposition, civil disobedience, foot dragging, flight, non–compliance, limited cooperation, rhetorical resistance or other 'hidden acts of resistance' that have represented a lack of local legitimacy for a particular strategy, or stymied its progress (Scott, 1985). In some cases direct opposition has emerged as with the 'Kosovanization,' 'Timorization,' and 'Afghanization' campaigns against encroaching international trusteeship (Richmond, 2011: 66–91). Women's groups are often at the forefront of attempts to organize local peacebuilding initiatives in a wide range of areas, especially if peace formation mobilizes in the style that liberal understandings of civil society expect. In general, it can now be taken as read that wherever a peace process, peacebuilding, statebuilding, or development occurs, attempts to localize it will also occur.

Peace formation can operate as hidden and individual attempts to maintain everyday life, its security, economic, and political, social, and customary needs, as well as some form of modern–ization or progress. This can be in the form of refusal or what has become widely known as hidden forms of resistance, as Scott has termed these processes (Scott, 1985). This private (to Western/Northern eyes at least) transcript has unexpected impacts as it is often multiplied across a wide range of different actors and contexts. More obvious forms of mobilization through various groups involved in civil association also add to its repertoire, whether through customary governance and law or customary conflct resolution processes, church or religious groups, trade unions, sports or social associations, or political parties, newspapers, lobbying organizations, and a range of CSOs and NGOs, which involve significant constituencies that political leaders an internationals must reach for legitimacy to be maintained. Political and civil association offers similar opportunities for refusal, cooptation, modifcation, and acceptance, in disaggregated and private spaces or, more broadly, in terms of more recognizably organized forms of mobilization. Private and passive resistance to more active resistance, lobbying, and social displays have an impact as forms of representation on administrative and political actors involved in statebuilding, especially where they offer platforms for discussions of a broader peace, even if elites f nd such requests impracticable (for example, requests for equality, or for a revision of customary practices not in line with human rights).

These dynamics of peace formation may have been spurred on by the slow progress, sometimes inability, sometimes reluctance, of statebuilding to engage with deep–rooted causes of conflict including indigenous issues, the need for dignity, ideological opposition to the liberal peace or neoliberal markets between local factions or international agendas, inequality and poverty, custom and culture, land tenure and ownership, identity or religious divisions, or elite predation. Increasingly, as earlier during the Zapatista rebellion in Mexico, there has been a perception that international intervention, whether for security, peacebuilding, development, or statebuilding, does not provide self-determination, is not pluralist in its engagement with difference on the ground, does not provide social justice, and rejects local autonomy. It may not even be very democratic if local consensus is blocked in this way (Harvey, 1998).

This critique is not merely based on a view of understanding how to further spread democracy, the rule of law, free trade, or civil society. Peacebuilding and statebuilding themselves also need to be more accountable, democratic, and law-governed, with higher ethical and methodological standards than at present, meaning they should be drawn from its subjects, not from its managers. As importantly, we also need to understand how civil society (and what lies beyond this often Westernized social artifice) makes peace at its own level, but also how the small-scale and ofte low-level efforts made beneath state, often in hidden or marginal spaces, have actually been silently modifying the grand liberal peace and liberal statebuilding project. Peace formation may lead to different political forms, rights, and institutions, which need to be understood, accommodated, and mediated. This indicates the need to evaluate what such 'hidden' modifications to the liberal peace mean for understanding peace itself in its multiple forms, and whether they offer greater sustainability for the liberal peace, or other and alternative types of peace, or may be sowing the seeds of future conflict by deviating from the liberal peace, or from the goal of socia justice. To achieve this requires a political sociology and ethnography of peace formation, drawing on a range of examples from around the world to address the following questions.

1   What do local voices suggest is inadequate about liberal peace and statebuilding projects they have been the subjects of and how they respond? How does their political subjectivity develop as a result of such contact?
2   Do local actors (NGOs, social and labour movements, customary institutions or groups, religious or identity actors) work to modify the liberal peace or donor strategies, to make them more democratic, accountable, ethical, or do they resist them and mount their own counter-effortsto make peace? What does this version of peace represent? A clear alternative or hybridity?
3   How successful have these strategies been, with what effect on local forms of peace and on the international liberal peace project itself?
4   What are the dynamics of peace formation and how do they encounter the liberal peace, and the emerging new donors (including BRICs/MIST actors)?[2]

Peace formation draws on second-generation conflict resolution approaches and fourth-generation approaches, with the latter seeking to empower local agency and international enablement of a hybrid form of peace. Peace and justice are intertwined, difference and social justice are enabled, and different life worlds meet (Boege and Curth, 2011). This creates a contextual legitimacy via a set of relationships and networks that has so far been lacking for the liberal peace system in some of its aspects at least (especially dealing with non-Western cultures, in its advocacy of capitalism, and its construction of rights, the state, and norms in the international rather than the contextual sphere). Peace is made locally in this framework, perhaps individually in hidden and public spaces across a wide range of everyday life activities, but may be 'enabled' internationally. This support would engage with political, social, economic, and identity needs and rights as they are both locally and internationally understood. It might be thought that because of its contextual legitimacy such a peace might be inherently stable. Though this may be true, it is often at this level that the roots of the conflict are most acutely experienced. Furthermore peace formation is necessarily small-scale and so large-scale mobilization to shape norms, law, and the state, and procure resources and security, as well as international recognition, does not arise quickly or directly. Yet without doubt this level is quietly influential of other levels of th peacemaking process, in that it provides the raw agency, legitimacy, consensus, and capacity that make them coalesce into the state, norms, law, government and governance, institutions, and international organizations necessary for a wide-ranging peace.

Local agency

It is important to note that 'local agency' should be seen in relation to peacebuilding in a complex way. The local might be seen as transnational, transversal (grassroots to elites), traditional and modern, liberal and non-liberal, simultaneously (Appadurai, 1996: 178; Massey, 1994). It represents fluid identities and movement, rather than static and fixed identities. 'Agency' refe to capacity related to critical, discursive agency and social praxis (Foucault, 1976: 184). It is often critical, hence the term 'critical agency' whereby discourses encounter the politics of peace and attempt to shape them (Richmond, 2011: 1–21). This might be of individuals to help themselves and to shape their political environment, to negotiate with international actors, to take on international norms, to operate the liberal state, to form their own contextual institutions of peace, and so forth. It might imply large-scale and organized political mobilization. It might also imply individual, community, and alternative forms of civil society organizations (in a 'local–local' context below the Western-induced artifce of 'civil society'; Richmond, 2011: 13), and their ability to act. Both imply a mutual construction of the local, state, and international.

This may be hidden and disguised from potential sanctions from predatory elites; it may be fragmented, atomized, and not representative of mobilization on a large, industrial scale. Yet it is well known in anthropology, ethnography, and sociology, as well as in more radical versions of political theory that small, hidden, often individual actions, not coordinated in any way, add up to a sum that is greater than its parts even if they are not the product of large-scale and coordinated mobilization (Scott, 1985). Thus, peace formation can represent significant mobilization of local actors or it may be small-scale and fragmented, hiding itself to escape sanction. It may take place in traditional, customary, religious, or other culture venues. It may be simultaneously liberal and modern and localized and contextual (not to introduce a some- what artificial dichotomy between tradition and modernity) (Boege, 2011: 433). It implies mediation between its different facets, and also with the 'international.' In this way the might of international statebuilding is modifed by the actions of its many recipients in diverse contexts, from Afghanistan to Timor-Leste, where peace formation is inevitably occurring. Many of these recipients also now construct international and local peacebuilding simultaneously. This may represent non-compliance (or stagnation) as in Bosnia or more outright resistance as in parts of Central America. It may also lead to wholesale adoption of international agendas, with a twist, as in the 'authoritarian democracies' that have emerged in Namibia, Mozambique, and Rwanda. It modifes those agendas via the introduction of concepts such as 'local ownership' and participation in World Bank, IMF, and UN policies (Richmond, 2012a). It is certainly political.

The international approach, in terms of peacebuilding and statebuilding as defned by its liberal norms, laws, and institutions, harks back to liberal internationalism in the 20th century, and the liberal institutionalism which represents the UN, humanitarians, donors, and other international agencies. This also defines its social dynamics. Its economic dynamics are mainly neoliberal i its intent for post-conflict states, though of course its exercise of material resources via centralize institutions and donors is more in the view of centralized economic planning. This underpins the liberal peace, and its security, institutional, constitutional, and civil dynamics, formulated within the framework of states and their liberal domestic character, and their membership of an 'international society.'

The mediation of local and liberal pits modern aggregations of material and epistemic power against local and atomized resistant and critical agencies. Yet this 'dark matter' has a significan capacity to influence, modify, resist, coopt, accept, and ultimately hybridize the liberal peace representing as it does both the forces of conflict, and peace formation and external interventio (Richmond, 2011: 186–216). Its aim is not merely to create a liberal peace where it has clear deficiencies, but also to lead an advance in peace formation more generally, toward a more emancipatory and empathetic form of peace in both local and international contexts (Richmond, 2008). In this way it is a form of critical agency and resistance that goes beyond the production of new meta-narratives, based on social practices, autonomy, and self-determination (Pickett, 1996: 445–447), pointing toward liberal–local hybrid forms of peace.

Formation versus building

Peace praxis and theory have certain problem-solving limitations and 'local' blockages built into their own theoretical and methodological biases and into their very concrete dimensions in practice. On one hand, no longer is 'peace' an abstract concept that cannot be created other than through historical chance, but on the other its very construction is fraught with pitfalls. This has underlined the conceptual limitations of a literature now dominated by peacebuilding, statebuilding, and state formation concepts. Statebuilding has not become the antidote to state formation dynamics of violence; nor has peacebuilding in its liberal form connected with local forms of political legitimacy, with their social, cultural, political, and economic requirements. Failed statebuilding has been the result of externalized states being based on blueprints determined by decontextualized and depoliticized agendas for states that provide security, political rights, and institutions, and market access but little in the way of political rights. Nor have they been proficient at developing a social contract, meaning they have led to virtual forms of peace. This 'failed by design' type of statebuilding has also come about because of confusion in the literature, which has fed expediency in international policy toward post-conflict, post-development contexts. This can be rectified by disaggregating and examining the relationships of state formation, statebuilding, peacebuilding, and peace formation, as follows.

1 *State formation* describes the formation of the state through indigenous or internal violence between competing groups and their agendas, which often turn the state into a criminal and predatory elite racket *à la* Tilly (1985). This perhaps leads ultimately to internal balances of power and power-sharing arrangements. Through this process of shifting alliances and force often associated with forms of identity, parochial or national, the nature of the resultant state is determined often in the favor of authoritarian elites.
2 *Statebuilding* is an externalized process focused on the role of external actors, organizations, donors, IFIs, agencies, and INGOs and their key role in building liberal institutions for security, democracy, markets, and creating basic infrastructure. This role rests on international technical expertise and capacity. They also attempt to persuade or force local elites to comply with liberal institutions as they are under construction. It is normally aimed at producing the basic framework of a neoliberal state in a procedural and technocratic sense, and less interested in norms or civil society. It is ideologically biased toward neoliberalism and self-help in the economic realm, meaning a small state, though it requires significant security capacity also This combination means the state that comes into being is externally dependent.
3 *Peacebuilding*, especially in its liberal guise, focuses on external support for liberally oriented, rights-basedinstitutions with an especial and legitimating focus on norms, civil society, and

a social contract via representative institutions embedded in a rule of law. This support is legitimized by international norms. In its earlier form it was more focused on localized dynamics of peace. However, its contemporary neoliberal variation, now dominant, highlights the importance of free markets and capitalism, liberal property rights, freedom, and competition. It parallels statebuilding but is normatively broader, more focused on peace than singular understandings of security and sovereignty though they are inevitably intertwined. The two alternative modes of liberal peace lead to different types of state in theory – the liberal mode implies social democracy and so a strong/large and interventionist state focused mainly on material redistribution and rights while the neoliberal mode focuses on a weak state supported by private enterprise, globalized capital, and rights, except in the realms of its security where it is often very able (or dependent on outside provision).

This much has been extensively theorized in the literature. There is a missing link in all of this, however, arising from the inherent biases of Northern, rational, compliance-oriented, problem-solvingtheory. If statebuilding and state formation represent different ends of the same spectrum and liberal peacebuilding parallels statebuilding, all resting on the application of force, liberal interventionism, or softer forms of external agency, such as conditionality, then this points to an obvious omission in an emerging four-sided matrix representing the architecture of both the contemporary state and peace praxis. This implies the following.

4 *Peace formation* processes can be defined as one where indigenous or local agents of peace-building, conflict resolution, development, or in customary, religious, cultural, social, or local political or local government settings find ways of establishing peace processes and the dynamics of local forms of peace, which are also constitutive of state, regional, and global hybrids. They may do so in relation to local understandings of politics and institutions, welfare and economics, social and customary resonance and identity, law and security, framed also by external praxes of intervention. This occurs through non-violent, politicized processes, representing resistance and critical agency, as well as cooptation and compliance. They offer some socio-historical continuity but are also aimed at transformation, drawing on external influences. This is not to romanticize the local or its related peace formation processes, of course (Richmond, 2009).

In an agonistic way these four cornerstones of this matrix, representing several phases of an interdisciplinary and inter-methodological dialogue spanning at least 40 years about the state and peace, point to the same thing – peaceful order rather than one resting on structural violence and identity discrimination, or even a benign hegemony. Sociology, anthropology, development studies, post-colonial and subaltern studies, as well as economics, politics, and international relations all have played a role in this debate and its interwoven methodologies (Geertz, 1973; Asad, 1973; Escobar, 1995; Bhabha, 1994; Spivak, 1988; Kapoor, 2008). It points to a hybridized epistemology for peace in simple terms. Which one of these four cornerstones determines the character of that order, the state it creates, and the quality of the 'peace' that emerges? Understanding peace formation in its relation to the other three dynamics is key to the sustainability of any peace and state that emerges, yet it is also the most challenging aspect of the whole process of creating a viable and legitimate order or peace. A peace dominated by the processes of peace formation also connected to externalized peacebuilding is likely to be more viable, particularly if each actively shapes the other – as many current examples show. One that is dominated by statebuilding or state formation is likely to be very conservative, security-oriented, and is unlikely to survive in the long term because it will lack both international and broad local legitimacy and resonance (because the state will tend to be elite—dominated and authoritarian). A peace dominated by liberal peacebuilding is likely to rest on external support and international rather than local legitimacy.

Political mobilization around the liberal state project differs in scale, scope, and ambition to the smaller scale, localized political projects that are now emerging in post—conflict polities. Thes are also transnationally networked via critical agency forming an emerging post—colonial civil society (Richmond, 2012b). The latter has the potential to make a more locally resonant and sustainable form of peace, even if on a smaller scale, and contradicting or weakening the Western notion of a rational, strong, productive, and secure state. Indeed the Western notion of the state, when exported, has only really attracted the interest of predatory elites who were able to exploit its weak points with little accountability to their citizens or to internationals. Political and civil society actors have often been attracted by liberal reforms but internationals have not offered sensitive and long—term support. So the process under way of designing local forms of political institutions, accountability, prosperity, security, and law, with reference to local and international standards, should be supported rather than ignored. At the moment many such efforts are wasting time and energy trying to combat the heavy—handed unsuitability of liberal statebuilding. Instead the international community could be seeking out local peace agencies in a wider range of areas, and becoming involved in extended and supportive relationships with them, using action and ethnographic methodologies and advanced ethical guidelines. They should be much more focused on improving the everyday life and potentials for individuals and communities in post—conflic states. This raises a range of important issues, in which local agency, needs, capacity, and expec— tations would need to be treated: including supporting local—local political, legal, social, cultural, class, and economic systems, norms, processes, and institutions, especially in the realms of needs, rights, culture, identity, and religion. The support of such processes in order to stabilize the polity would also engender contact, reform, and modification of both local and international processes so as not to compromise each other's standards, and ultimately shape the state.

Conclusion

Local peace formation agencies operate in parallel or related to, or even despite, the liberal statebuilding project of mainly Western donors and the UN system, raising two key issues. The first is what type of peace emerges in each context via the interplay of international and local processes of peacebuilding. The second relates to what impact international and local approaches have on each other. Over the past 20 years the contact between them has significantly modifi the international liberal peacebuilding/statebuilding project and the local contextual projects for peace. Post—liberal forms of peace represent (unequally) both liberal and local contexts in a hybrid form. Each has been pushed hard to examine, comply with, and advance the other's standards, norms, processes, institutions, and objectives. Sometimes the outcomes have been retrogressive, seeming to support warlords, patriarchy, and isolation, but more often this mediation of local contexts and global ambitions has had positive and mutually transformative implications.

Peace formation connects with more grounded versions of security, implicit in the human security concept which has become mainstream (even if mainly rhetorical). This concept has faced much resistance at the international level, but it has been very difficult to dislodge becaus it ties into local expectations of security that engages with military, welfare, identity, and rights issues, rather than just 'hard security' regional or state—level matters. Hybrid notions of law and transitional justice have also emerged. Democracy has advanced from the previous international focus on elections to more of a participatory, grounded ethic and framework for long—term politics. Human rights frameworks have engaged with questions of context and dignity beyond externalized legal shells. Development and marketization have been forced to confront and engage with local poverty, lack of access to resources and facilities, and structural inequality, not least in the global political economy and North–South relations. Concepts such as local ownership, participation, human security, Responsibility to Protect, sustainable development, and 'do no harm' have emerged. They illustrate the legitimacy, agency, and capacity of the local in relation to the supposedly hegemonic liberal peace model, and represent glimmers of the emerging post–liberal peace, which will be heavily contextualized in a local, transversal, transnational sense; will develop new international and local standards; will differ from place to place; and makes peacebuilding clearly a political act, rather than a potentially colonial process. Such concepts also represent international responses to their own failures or weaknesses on the ground, indicating a confluence of interest, local and international, in reconstituting peacebuilding and the state, not to mention international strategies for peace and development. This represents the birth of the post–liberal peace in response to post–colonial forms of civil society now emerging. It is crucial to the current effort to increase the legitimacy and sustainability of peacebuilding and statebuilding in the context of addressing global structural inequities, which often undermine attempts at making peace even as they gather pace. Only then will the critical agencies of peace formation, the state, and international peacebuilding converge on a more plausible and pragmatic peace process.

Notes

1 Thanks to Annika Bjorkdahl, Yiannis Tellidis, and Sandra Pagodda for their helpful comments. All errors are the author's alone.
2 BRICS = Brazil, Russia, India, China. MIST = Mexico, Indonesia, South Korea, Turkey.

References

Appadurai, A. (1996). *Modernity at large.* Minneapolis, MN: University of Minnesota Press.
Asad, T. (Ed.). (1973). *Anthropology and the colonial encounter.* New York, NY: Humanity Books.
Bhabha, H. (1994). *The location of culture.* London, UK: Routledge.
Boege, V. (2011). Potentials and limits of traditional approaches to peacebuilding. In *Berghof Handbook II: Advancing conflict transformation.* Berlin, Germany: Berghof Conflict Research
Boege, V., and Curth, J. (2011). *Grounding the responsibility to protect: Working with local strengths for peace and conflict prevention in the Solomon Islands.* ISA Asia Pacifica Conference, Brisbane, Australia, 29–30 September.
Chandler, D. (2006). *Empire in denial: The politics of statebuilding.* London, UK: Pluto Press.
Chandler, D. (2010). *International statebuilding: The rise of post-liberal governance.* London, UK: Routledge.
Chibber, A. (1997). The state in a changing world. *Finance and Development,* September, 17–20.
Cooper, N. (2007). Review Article: On the crisis of the liberal peace. *Conflict, Security and Development,* 7(4), 605–616.
Duffield, M. (2007). *Development, security and unending war.* London, UK: Polity.
Doyle, M. W. (1986). Liberalism and world politics. *American Political Science Review,* 80(4), 1151–1169.
Escobar, A. (1995). *Encountering development.* Princeton, NJ: Princeton University Press.
European Security Strategy (2003). Brussels, Belgium: European Union.
Foucault, M. (1976). *The history of sexuality, Vol. 1: The will to knowledge.* London, UK: Penguin.
Fukuyama, F. (2004). The imperative of statebuilding. *Journal of Democracy,* 15(2), 17–31.
Geertz, C. (1973). *The interpretation of cultures.* New York, NY: Basic Books.
Harvey, N. (1998). *The Chiapas Rebellion: The struggle for land and democracy.* Durham, NC: Duke University Press.
Jahn, B. (2007). The tragedy of liberal diplomacy: Democratization, intervention and statebuilding. *Journal of Intervention and Statebuilding,* 1(2), 87–106.
Kapoor, I. (2008). *The post-colonial politics of development.* London, UK: Routledge.

Kapur, D. (1998). The state in a changing world: A critique of the 1997 World Development Report. *WCFIA Working Paper No. 98-02*. Cambridge, MA: Weatherhead Center for International Affairs.

Mac Ginty, R. (2008). Indigenous peace–making versus the liberal peace. *Cooperation and Conflict*, 43(2), 139–163.

Mac Ginty, R., and Richmond, O. P. (Eds.). (2007). Myth or reality? The liberal peace and post–conflic reconstruction. Special Issue of *Global Society*.

Massey, D. (1994). *Space, place and gender*. Minneapolis, MN: Minneapolis University Press.

OECD–DAC (April 2007). *Principles for good international engagement in fragile states and situations*. Vienna, Austria: OECD–DAC.

Paris, R. (2002). International peacebuilding and the 'mission civilisatrice'. *Review of International Studies*, 28(4), 637–656.

Pickett, B. L. (1996). Foucault and the politics of resistance. *Polity*, 28(4), 445–466.

Pugh, M. (2008). Corruption and the political economy of liberal peace. Presented at the International Studies Association Annual Convention, San Francisco, CA, 26–28 March.

Pugh, M., Cooper, N., and Turner, M. (2008). *Whose peace?* London, UK: Palgrave.

Richmond, O. P. (2005). *The transformation of peace*. London, UK: Palgrave.

Richmond, O. P. (2008). *Peace and international relatons: A new agenda*. London, UK: Routledge.

Richmond, O. P. (2009). The romanticisation of the local: Welfare, culture and peacebuilding*International Spectator*, 44(1), 149–169.

Richmond, O. P. (2011). *A post-liberal peace*. London, UK: Routledge.

Richmond, O. P. (2012a). Beyond local ownership and participation in the architecture of international peacebuilding. *Ethnopolitics* (in press).

Richmond, O. P. (2012b). Critical agency, resistance, and a post–colonial civil society. *Conflict and Cooperation* (in press).

Scott, J. C. (1985). *Weapons of the weak: Everyday peasant resistance*. New Haven, CT: Yale University Press.

Spivak, G. C. (1988). Can the subaltern speak? In C. Nelson and L. Grossberg (Eds.), *Marxism and the interpretation of culture*. Basingstoke, UK: Macmillan.

Tilly, C. (1985). War making and state making as organised crime. In P. Evans, D. Rueschemeyer, and T. Skocpol (Eds.), *Bringing the state back in*. Cambridge, UK: Cambridge University Press.

US Department of Defense. (2008). *National Defense Strategy*. Washington, DC: DOD.

US National Security Strategy. (September 2002). Washington, DC: The White House.

World Bank, The. (1997). *The state in a changing world*. Washington, DC: The World Bank.

PART II

Security, development, and democracy

12
UNITED NATIONS CONSTITUTIONAL ASSISTANCE IN STATEBUILDING

Vijayashri Sripati

In 2011, the United Nations (UN) Secretary–General described UN Constitutional Assistance (UNCA) – a key tool of international statebuilding – as 'potentially a high–return investment' (UNSG, 2011: 4). The 'biggest returns' are seen to come not just in lives saved but also in the promotion of economic growth and wellbeing (UNSG, 2011: 4). Indeed, the UN has long deployed constitutional assistance as a conflict–prevention strategy in post–conflict and develo ment assistance contexts. Consequently, UNCA has today developed into an established field o statebuilding intervention in which practice has far outstretched theory.

After the overthrow of Colonel Gaddaf , in 2011, Libya became the 14th state to receive Security Council–mandated constitutional assistance. The statebuilding mandate of the UN Support Mission in Libya (UNSMIL) included assisting the (Libyan) National Transitional Council to 'ensure a consultative inclusive political process . . . to agree on a constitution and holding of free and fair elections' and 'ensure the full and equal participation of women and minorities' in the discussions about the political transition (UNSC, 2011a). Since 1989 the Security Council has mandated statebuilding missions to assist states in writing new constitutions in Burundi, Democratic Republic of Congo (DRC), Namibia, Rwanda, Somalia, Sudan, South Sudan, Afghanistan, Cambodia, Timor–Leste, Nepal, Iraq, and Kosovo (Sripati, 2010, 2012). UNCA also covers support offered to rebuild post–conflict states such as Sierra Leone and Liberi by reforming their existing constitutions (Sripati, 2012). A broader def nition of statebuilding covers the 'political processes through which social/political relations and power relationships between holders of state power and organized groups in society are negotiated and managed' (OECD–DACD,2008: 2). Reflecting this broader understanding of state–building, UNCA no even extends to helping restore fractured constitutional orders in states such as Guinea, Madagascar, Fiji, Niger, Mauritania, Togo, and Kyrgyzstan (Call, 2011).

A key statebuilding actor in UN constitutional assistance, the UN Development Program (UNDP), offers constitutional assistance to 'build the capacity of government institutions and processes to improve their performance' (UNDP–South Sudan, 2011). Under the UNDP paradigm, UNCA constitutes a key means of driving sustainable development and achieving inclusive economic growth. It also spurs fulf lling the Millennium Development Goals such as women's empowerment (Luwanga, undated). According to the UNDP, its efforts in forging a participatory constitutional process for Swaziland helped create the enabling environment for restoring the rule of law and speeding its socioeconomic development (UNDP, 2005). It has implemented constitutional support programs in Bhutan, Ecuador, Eritrea, Gambia, Guyana, Malawi, Maldives, Nauru, Solomon Islands, South Sudan, Swaziland, Tokelau, Zambia, and Zimbabwe (Sripati, 2012). In all these states, the UNDP has intertwined its constitutional support with development assistance.

However, the UN has long used the generic term 'electoral assistance' to cover for constitutional assistance, thereby indicating that it has merely a facilitating rather than a directing or overseeing role. More significantly, in this way, it has obscured the potentially paternalistic nature of constitutional assistance – affecting the very heart of sovereign self-government – and failed to clarify the relationship of authority and accountability at play. Finally, it has obscured its exact role and the power relations in play, by nowhere mapping out its constitutional assistance projects, as implemented in both the peace operations and the development assistance context. This chapter therefore situates UNCA center-stage in the analysis. It summarizes the (standard-setting) policy-practices of UNCA and its implications for our understanding of constitutional development as a key platform of international statebuilding interventions. By offering constitutional assistance, the UN ostensibly claims to have a technical or institutionalist set of techniques and expertise which are universally applicable in the promotion of peace, security, democracy, and human rights and in the elimination of corruption and other obstacles to the development of the rule of law. But as the commonalities in UN-assisted constitutions illustrate, these attempts to institutionally manage or correct social, economic, and political conflicts involve the UN acquiring large degree of influence over constitutional processes and constitutional outcomes (Sripati, 2010) In the post-colonial era, domestic control over constitution-making was seen as the *sine qua non* of sovereign status, involving a domestic consensus over the state's social and politico-economic order. Today's international statebuilding frameworks, which legitimize and facilitate UNCA and the consequent internationalization of constitution-making, therefore merit critical examination.

The evolution of UNCA

When and why did the UN f rst engage with constitution-making? Although the UN Charter spoke of freedom and self-determination, Western colonial powers continued to clutch onto most of their colonies at the time of ratification (1945). Mandated by the Charter to assist wit decolonization, the UN first helped to free Trust territories (UN, 1945). For instance, it helpe liberate Libya and drafted its first constitution (Pelt, 1970). However, following the Cold War it continued rebuilding many sovereign and conf icted states; it assisted them in sculpting new constitutions and building new political institutions. It offered constitutional assistance to resolve their conf icts and build peace.

During the 1990s, many states, including Angola, Burundi, Liberia, Mozambique, Sudan, Somalia, Rwanda, and the Democratic Republic of the Congo, erupted in conf ict. The UN therefore shifted its energies from the peaceful settlement of disputes to 'conf ict prevention' (UNSG, 2001). It stepped up its efforts to attack 'the root causes of conflict' and devised 'nationally owned' strategies to strengthen state capacities (UNSG, 2001). The UN considers a 'good' constitution to be central to a successful peace settlement; that is, one that is forged in a participatory way and fulfills certain criteria, capable of resolving conflicts and building peac and promoting democracy, human rights, security, and development (Sripati, 2012; UN, 2009). In short, a good constitution generates good internal governance. Accordingly, constitutional assistance gained increasing traction in UN policy circles (UNSC, 2005; UNSG, 2006). According to the UN Secretary General:

A carefully crafted constitution can provide a society with the tools to manage and resolve disputes peacefully, while a flawed constitution can exacerbate existing problem ... External support for the drafting of constitutions is available but could be more coherent and strategic; to that end, I welcome the support of Member States for strengthening United Nations activities in this area.

(UNSG, 2001: 16)

In 1996, in its 'Agenda for Democratization,' a milestone in statebuilding, the UN stated that:

The peace–keeping mandates entrusted to the United Nations now often include both the restoration of democracy and the protection of human rights. United Nations departments, agencies and programmes *have been called upon to help States draft constitutions*, create independent systems for the administration of justice, provide police forces that respect and enforce the rule of law, depoliticize military establishments and establish national institutions for the promotion and protection of human rights.

(Boutros-Ghali, 1996: 2; emphasis added)

But almost a decade later, it had blended its constitutional assistance into its 'core' Charter activities:

The UN worked tirelessly around the globe throughout the year to prevent and resolve conflicts and to consolidate peace. From Afghanistan to Burundi, from Iraq to the Sudan, from Haiti to the Middle East, the tools employed were as diverse as the circumstances. My envoys used their good offices in seeking peace agreements or i trying to prevent disputes from violently escalating. Peacekeepers deployed to conflic zones in record numbers and in complex multidimensional operations working not only to provide security . . . and to help war–torn countries, *write constitutions,* hold elections and strengthen human rights and the rule of law. United Nations agencies, funds and programmes tailored their assistance to the special needs of post–conflict societies.

(UNSG, 2005: 3; emphasis added)

Meanwhile UN global conferences and summits held from 2000 onwards, such as the Millennium Declaration (UN, 2000a) and the World Summit Outcome (UN, 2005), began to endorse the importance of its constitutional assistance in a number of different ways. Consequently, now the UN offers these ostensible purposes for its constitutional assistance: not to speed the process of decolonizing, but to prevent conf icts, build peace, empower women, and protect the rule of law. More importantly, it now showcases its constitutional assistance for its supposed ability to address the manifold problems seen to beset its member states:

The United Nations has taken important steps towards transforming the political landscape to empower women worldwide, adopted institutional changes, and advocated for policy changes that tackle gender discrimination in politics . . We have . . . assisted Member States with numerous difficult political transitions and sensitive elections. W have championed human rights and the rule of law . . . In Kenya, the United Nations maintained support for the review process that led to the adoption of a new constitution with enhanced checks and balances . . . In Somalia, the United Nations worked . . . to further the implementation of transitional tasks, including constitution–building . . .

The United Nations undertook successful efforts to help countries return to constitu‐
tional order following unconstitutional changes of Government in Guinea, and the
Niger. In Kyrgyzstan, the United Nations contributed to the adoption of a new
constitution.

(UNSG, 2011: 5)

Emergence of UNCA policy

UN constitutional assistance first received high‐level policy attention in the Report of the Brahimi panel on peacekeeping reform (UNSG, 2000). However, constitutional assistance was not raised explicitly in terms of its centrality to statebuilding until 2005 – long after the organization had first begun supporting constitution‐making (see Security Council Report, 2007). In 2009 the UN Secretary‐General released a guidance note on UN Assistance to constitution‐making projects. This key policy paper on UNCA endorsed constitutional assistance as a conflict prevention and peace‐building mechanism and articulated its key policy function in terms of 'standard‐setting' (UN, 2009).

The momentum on the policy‐making front rippled outward to strengthen the institutional basis for and the UN's constitutional assistance capacities. Determined to 'make a difference on the ground,' the UN supported the establishment of a broader range of actors equipped with a wider array of tools (UNSG, 2011). The Peacebuilding Commission, an intergovernmental body, appeared first. Now actively involved in Burundi, the Central African Republic, Guinea, Guinea Bissau, Liberia, and Sierra Leone, it offers constitutional assistance so as to boost economic reconstruction and strengthen governance capacities (UNSG, 2011).

The Mediation Support Unit (MSU) came next. It offered a 'rapid response' to finding solutions to political disputes. Positioned to deploy within 72 hours of a conflict erupting, it stand‐byexperts could rapidly be dispatched into a conflict zone to advise negotiators on peac process design, constitution‐making, gender issues, power‐sharing, and natural resources‐sharing (UNSG, 2011).

The Special Advisers on the Prevention of Genocide and the Responsibility to Protect were added to the UN's conflict prevention portfolio in 2007. These envoys help defuse tensions and resolve problems in the context of constitutional and electoral crises, reunifcation negotiations, peace talks, and a range of other cross‐cutting issues. As Ivorian armed forces and militia groups backed opposing camps and thousands of Ivorians fled to neighboring countries, Edward Luck the Special Adviser on the Prevention of Genocide, urged the Security Council to reinforce the 9000‐strongUnited Nations Operation in Côte d'Ivoire (UNOCI) with additional troops (UN, 2011). New troops would prevent mass atrocities from occurring. When asked 'How respon ‐ sibility to protect values could be refected from within a country itself?' Luck referenced UNCA in Namibia, Mozambique, and Angola as examples (Luck, 2009).

Finally, the Office of the High Commissioner of Human Rights (OHCHR) sponsors constitution‐makingconferences and prepares 'tools' (analytical guides and materials) to bolster the UN's efforts in achieving tangible results in the f eld (OHCHR, 2010).

UNCA policy: Standard-setting

Statebuilding involves manifold tasks from disarming armed groups to sculpting new constitutions and from designing economies and speeding up foreign investment to formulating new national development frameworks for combating corruption and promoting good governance. Standard‐ setting for constitution‐making first began when peace agreements – both the processes by whic they were negotiated and their substance – drew international law's normative attention. Since its earliest projects in Namibia, the UN has expanded the programmatic scope and policy agenda of its constitutional assistance (Sripati, 2012). Right from the start, the UN has conceived its constitutional assistance to meet perceived challenges to its policy successes caused by the conduct of local constitution–makers and policy actors on the ground, acting without UNCA and the content of the resulting constitution.

The images of Balkan women raped as a policy of war and of the Taliban publicly executing Afghan women concentrated public media and elite–policy attention. In response, the UN Security Council passed resolution 1325 (UNSC, 2000) on 31 October 2000. It urged stakeholders to protect the human rights of women and girls when negotiating and implementing peace agreements. A follow–up study recommended engendering constitutional processes and the constitutionalization of women's rights (UN 2000c). These developments sparked the UN's transparent, inclusive, and participatory constitution–making standard. Soon, after broad public consultations through questionnaires, internet submissions, and public meetings, UNIFEM's training for women and minorities and public education activities appeared on the UNCA agenda (UN, 2009; Sripati, 2010). Indeed, they became UNCA's signature feature. Implemented from Afghanistan, Bhutan, Timor–Leste, Eritrea, and Iraq to Kosovo, Malawi, Maldives, Zimbabwe, Rwanda, Somalia, Swaziland, and Nepal, they signaled that there could be little deviation from UN 'standard setting' in the making of constitutions (Sripati, 2010; Constitution of the Islamic Republic of Afghanistan, 2004; The Kingdom of Bhutan Constitution, 2008). More recently, the UN underscored a new standard to govern peace processes, human rights, and peace agreements and resulting constitutions: freedom from sexual violence (UNSC, 2009).

Universal standard–setting has continued apace into other areas of policy. In the wake of the 9/11 attacks, the UN has regarded terrorism as hindering the peaceful settlement of disputes, and battling it was considered a conflict prevention technique. It therefore nudged Afghanistan, Iraq and Bhutan to constitutionalize anti–terror provisions (Sripati, 2012).

UNCA has also played a key role in universalizing financial standards set by the Internationa Financial Institutions (IFIs) such as the World Bank and the International Monetary Fund (IMF). Since IFIs drive post–conflict reconstruction and development assistance (del Castillo, 2009), th UN places them at the center of statebuilding (UNSC, 2011b) and thereby of internationalalized constitution–making(UNSC, 2011a). For example, the Rwandan Arusha Agreement (2000) prescribed crafting a new constitution rooted in the principles of equality, non–discrimination, and democracy to solve Burundi's ethnic conflict (Sripati, 2012). It designated the UN to monito its implementation. Implementing Arusha's internationally conceived solution hinged on IFI and international donor support. Indeed, the Arusha Agreement underscored this (Arusha Peace Agreement, 2000: art.9).

The IFI conditionalities (financial standards) cover designing and implementing fiscal and monetary policy and institution–building (Gong, 2002; Stewart and Wang, 2010). These standards include free market reforms, private property rights coupled with fair judicial mechanisms for their enforcement, trade liberalization, protection of intellectual property, privatization, and general accounting principles (Gong, 2002; Stewart and Wang, 2010). More signifcantly, they constitute today's 'civilized' financial standards (Gong, 2002). Michael Camdessus, then IM Director, offered the first stirrings of that view in 1999

> A consensus is clearly crystallizing ... on the need to establish at the international level the discipline that has progressively come to prevail in domestic markets . ... that governments had not devoted enough attention in order to secure such a *civilized environment* ... Consequently, tremendous effort is under way to establish *standards and*

codes of good practice at the international level that build on and offer the potential to globalize the standards that exist *within the most advanced nations.*

(Camdessus, 1999: vi; emphasis added)

The IMF's conditionalities, presented as neutral standards for good economic governance, shone the spotlight on improving the efficiency and accountability of the public sector, promotin transparency, and curbing corruption (IMF, 2010). Understandably, they grafted onto the UN's (implicit) standards for constitutional content (Sripati, 2012). These standards aimed at achieving 'good economic governance,' which converged with the UN's ideas about political governance and development. For instance, according to the UN Secretary–General:

Good governance and development . . . also depend on and reinforce each other. That is one of the main lessons the United Nations has drawn from its vast and varied experience throughout the world. Without the rule of law and respect for human rights; without transparency and accountability; and unless governments derive their power legitimately, through the ballot box, the path to prosperity is likely to be more difficult and gains could remain fragile and reversible.

(UN-OHRLLS and UNDP, 2006: Preface)

Consequently, programs in educating locals in financial governance, in drafting and reviewin anti–corruption laws, achieving ratification of anti–corruption treaties, and other forms of institutional support merged into UNCA (Sripati, 2012; UN–OHRLLS and UNDP, 2006). The idea that local constitution–makers lacked the capacity to address their economic challenges and that this lack of capacity had governance implications underpinned these activities (UN–OHRLLS and UNDP, 2006). And so we have the UN building legitimate institutions in Bhutan (Royal Government of Bhutan and UNDP, 2006), Maldives (Republic of Maldives: The President's Office, 2006), Cambodia, Côte d'Ivoire (IMF, 2009a), Central African Republic (IMF, 2009b), Timor–Leste(Boon, 2006), Afghanistan, Iraq, Liberia, Kosovo, Malawi (UNCT–Malawi, 2006), and Sierra Leone (Sripati, 2012).

As the next section demonstrates, UNCA standard–setting infltrates the realm of development assistance. By slipping its constitutional assistance into its wider development framework, the UN avoids treading the inflammatory path of discounting sovereignty and instead supposedl works in lockstep with it.

Constitutional assistance intertwined with development assistance

The UNDP chief representative, the UN Resident Coordinator (UNRC), gears her humani – tarian and development tasks toward preventing conflict. For instance, the UN encourages he to carve out political space allowing national actors to participate in the shaping of post–confct constitutional frameworks (UN, 2000b). Alternately, she can nudge the government to erase gender–basedinequalities through constitutional reform (UNSG, 2010). The UN expects even UNRCs functioning in states lacking a peace mission, such as Guinea, to ratchet up their conflict prevention role. For example, in 2008 the UN supplied the UNRC there with mediation advice and electoral assistance to bolster his efforts in helping Guinea return to constitutional order peacefully.

The UN Development Assistance Frameworks (UNDAFs) and Poverty Reduction Strategy Papers (PRSPs) – two ostensibly technocratic processes – open up two key 'entry points' for the UNDP to offer its 'capacities' for constitutional support. They are thus deeply political. UN

Country Teams (UNCTs) primarily assist governments in shaping their priorities on a par with their human rights obligations (UNDG, 2007). They prepare UNDAFs to assist countries to strengthen their capacity in all spheres. 'Major changes in government' signaled 'either through elections or a new constitution' offer them a 'significant opportunity' to strategically lever themselves in a state's development context (UNDG, 2010: 18–19). For instance, the UNDP pushed Malawi to reform its constitution on the grounds that speeding its development goals required harnessing its governance capacities and political accountability (UNCT−Malawi, 2006).

PRSPs afford UNCTs an opportunity of supporting the interventions therein. Started by the World Bank and the IMF in 1999, they articulate the economic and social poverty−reduction programs that countries seeking debt−relief under the Heavily Indebted Poor Country (HIPC) debt reduction process must produce (IMF, 2011). In short, their prescriptions tie up to governance reforms. Since PRSPs also address the consequences of conflict and implementatio of peace agreements, IFIs have hugely infuenced post−conflict recovery in Africa (Obwona an Guloba, 2009). The PRSP process has locked in more than 65 low−income countries – virtually all UNCA recipients – in the tight grip of IFIs (World Bank, 2010). This is troubling since scholars have exposed the detrimental role IFIs play in Third World countries (for example, Pahuja, 2011).

As previously mentioned, since the UN considers good economic governance critical to attaining good (political) governance, constitution−making moments offer opportunities for the philosophies underpinning the IFIs and the UNDP to converge. In fact, they are encouraged to do so (UNDG, 2007). For example, the UN−mediated Lome Agreement prescribed good governance reforms in Sierra Leone's constitutional and f nancial sectors (Lome Peace Accord, 1999). The UN's 'joint vision' for consolidating peace in Sierra Leone comprised a mixture of initiatives by the UNDP and IFIs (UNSG, 2008). The UNIPSIL supported Sierra Leone's constitutional review process and the UNDP and IFIs implemented building its anti−corruption commission (UN Integrated Peacebuilding Mission in Sierra Leone and UN Country Team, 2009).

As shown above, the UNDP may initiate constitutional assistance or apply its leverage by targeting an ongoing constitution−making process. Meanwhile, the Bureau of Crisis Prevention and Recovery (BCPR) provides another thrust to UNDP's fast widening role in constitutional assistance. As one of UNDP's most inf uential Bureaus on matters related to constitutionalism, it endorses the idea that sustainable development hinges on crisis prevention (UNDP−BCPR, 2007). It therefore concentrates on putting in place institutions and systems of a durable nature, following breakdowns. This places it at the center of national constitution−making efforts.

UNCA: internationalizing public law and policy

Promoting women's political participation and the rule of law, crushing corruption, and other ostensible purposes animate UNCA. I will now examine how the UN justif es its supposed use of UNCA to these ends in terms of implementing certain elements of public international law and policy.

According to the UN, it tools its 'collective security' system with a 'conflict−preventive activity': UNCA (UNSG 2011: 3; 2006: 40). UNCA prevents conflict, builds peace, and pro motes the rule of law (UN, 2009). However, I suggest that from a broader perspective, the UN's views about a 'good' constitution offer the starting point to understand how UNCA fits into th international law and policy framework (hereafter 'Framework') (UN, 2009). The UN considers a constitution, fulfilling certain criteria – that is a 'good' constitution – capable of promotin democracy, human rights, peaces, security, and sustainable development (UN, 2009). In short, a 'good' constitution radiates 'good governance.' UNCA equates to assisting a state to write such a constitution, and this is how it (UNCA) simultaneously serves to implement international law and policy.

According to the UN, 'democracy in international law' flows from the Charter; indeed, 'democracy is one of the universal and indivisible core values and principles of the UN' (UN Office in Vienna, 2008: 3). Since UNCA serves to 'guide national efforts towards consolidating democracy,' it promotes international law (UN Office in Vienna, 2008: 11). How might a goo constitution strengthen democracy? Emerging from a participatory process, it opens out to women and indigenous groups, allowing them to infuse their rights into it – an opportunity long shut off to them (UN, 2009: 2). In this way, it fosters democracy's two 'essential elements': freedom of expression and women's rights to political participation (UN Office in Vienna, 2008 2). The UN concedes that the Charter remains silent about democracy. However, it suggests that these two essential elements fow from the evocative phrase 'we the peoples' in its preamble (UN Office in Vienna, 2008: 2)

Neglecting to notice UNCA, scholars suggest that the UN supports democracy but leaves its content 'vague' (Bowden and Charlesworth, 2008: 95). Indeed, I suggest that today political participation of women and indigenous groups constitutes the additional criteria that have supposedly become determinative of 'democratic (internal) governance' (UN, 2009: 3). For instance, Ban Ki-Moon, the UN Secretary-General, recently alluded to the norms that state-building should prioritize in the Middle East and North Africa:

> Whenever I had an opportunity of speaking or meeting with Arab leaders, *I made it quite pointedly*, this role of women. When they create a certain committee for reform or when they were *drafting constitutions* or regulations, or enacting law, then there must be a clear provision on protecting the human rights as well as providing equal opportunities to women and also youth groups.
>
> *(UN Press Release, 2011: 1; emphasis added)*

How else does the promotion of participatory rights by UNCA contribute to promoting international law? Consider the UN Security Council's explanations for mandating UNCA in Nepal. Nepal is home to 59 groups of *Adivasi Janajatis* (indigenous peoples) such as Magar, Tharu, and Rai. The Security Council tasked the UN Mission in Nepal (UNMIN) with 'paying special attention to the needs of women, children and traditionally marginalized groups in the peace process' (UNSC, 2007: 1). UNCA ostensibly brought home to Nepal's *Adivasis* their rights of participation and consultation articulated in the UN Declaration on the Rights of Indigenous Peoples (UN, 2007: art. 41). Indeed, the UN aff rms that:

> The UN should address the rights that have been established *under international law* for groups that may be subjected to marginalization and discrimination in the country, including *women*, children, minorities, *indigenous peoples*, refugees, and stateless and displaced persons.
>
> *(UN, 2009: 4; emphasis added)*

Meanwhile, the late Thomas Franck had famously declared the 'right to democratic governance' as 'emerging' in international law (Franck, 1992: 46). Franck first articulated this thesis in 1992 His idea marked the supposed triumph of liberal (market) democracy over the totalitarianism of the Soviet Union and African dictatorships (Franck, 1992: 49; del Castillo, 2009: 34). Can we consider UNCA to be promoting democratic governance as a right? Yes. Beginning from the

1990s, UNCA projects have burgeoned, straddling Africa, Asia, Asia–Pacific, and now the Middl East and North Africa. They have all promoted the internationally designed solution for preventing conflict and promoting peace: constitutional market democracy

How does UNCA fit into the international public polic structure? If we may recall, it sets in place institutional barriers to corruption. In this way, it accelerates 'realizing the international ideals of free markets, democracy, rule of law, peace, and broad prosperity' (UN Office for Dru Control & Crime Prevention, 2002: Foreword). Moreover, some scholars argue, 'a democratic society operating under a market economy has a strong predisposition towards peace' (Franck, 1992: 88). This notion helps the UN explain UNCA's role in dismantling threats to the free market as a means of promoting another international ideal: peace. UNCA promotes international law and policy in these myriad ways.

UNCA also implicates a key doctrine conceptualized in international public policy and international law: 'strengthening state sovereignty' (UNSG, 2001: 3). A multidimensional concept, sovereignty underpins the international systems. In its external form, it stands for constitutional independence. However, the UN redefines sovereignty as a variable capacity an as a responsibility. These notions trigger a hierarchy of strong (more sovereign) and weak (less sovereign) states (Chandler, 2009: 15). However, was it not to avoid this very unequal combination of states that the UN General Assembly affirmed that 'all peoples have the right to self–determination; by virtue of that right they freely determine their political status and freely pursue their economic, social and cultural development' and that 'inadequacy of political, economic, social or educational preparedness should never serve as a pretext for delaying independence'? (UN, 1960: 1 (para 2); Chandler, 2009: 23).

Chandler laments the recasting of sovereignty as capacity and responsibility because it masks external intervention – in internal affairs – disguised as 'partnership' (Chandler, 2009: 21):

> By associating sovereignty with a sliding scale of capacities, rather than political and legal rights of equality, not only is a new international hierarchy legitimized but inter–vention can be framed as supporting 'sovereignty' at the same time as it is undermining the rights of self–government.
>
> *(Chandler, 2009: 23)*

Commencing from where Chandler stops, I argue that the UN situates UNCA squarely at the core of this discourse about sovereignty. Consider the UN's three influential reports reversin the concept of sovereignty.

The 2009 UN Report on the implementation of the responsibility to protect states that:

> the responsibility to protect is an ally of sovereignty, not an adversary. It grows from the positive and affirmative notion of sovereignty as responsibility, rather than from th narrower idea of humanitarian intervention. By helping states to meet their core protection responsibilities, the responsibility to protect seeks to *strengthen sovereignty*, not weaken. It seeks to help States to succeed, not just to react when they fail.
>
> *(UNSG, 2009: 7; emphasis added)*

An earlier report of the Secretary–General on *The Prevention of Armed Conflict* states that:

> Early action taken nationally to alleviate conditions that could lead to armed conflict with international assistance, as appropriate, can help to *strengthen* the sovereignty of states . . . The United Nations peace–building support offices can be instrumental, i

supporting and closely collaborating with the country teams and non-resident United Nations agencies/offices, in developing multifaceted programmes that address many root causes of conflicts. Examples of this include improving support for democratic principles such as ... security sector reform, promoting tolerance and respect for human rights and *providing technical assistance for the constitution* and national institutions

(UNSG, 2001: 3, 20; emphasis added)

Finally, the 2004 Report of the High Level Panel on Threats, Challenges, and Change states that:

Successful international actions to battle poverty, fight infectious disease, stop trans national crime, rebuild after civil war, reduce terrorism and halt the spread of dangerous materials all require capable, responsible States as partners. *It follows that greater effort must be made to enhance the capacity of States to exercise their sovereignty responsibly*. For all those in a position to help others *build that capacity*, it should be part of their responsibility to do so.

(UN, 2004: 18)

What might this mean for the swath of 'post-conflict' and Least Developed Countries (LDCs) subject to UN constitutional assistance? How might sovereignty as 'capacity' and 'responsibility' transform constitution making in LDCs? First, sovereignty no longer stands for these states' self-determination. Rather, it now refers to their capacity to create 'good governance.' They can supposedly strengthen their sovereignty by sculpting a good constitution. Conversely, they can weaken their sovereignty by neglecting to do so and risk another round of international intervention.

Second, when sovereignty becomes responsibility, it yokes LDCs with responsibilities they do not determine freely or unilaterally. Rather, those responsibilities arise from supposed 'partnership' with the UN. Now sovereignty stands 'co-produced' (Chandler, 2009: 24). Consequently, the UN deploys UNCA to define those responsibilities. In simple terms, UNC influences both the constitution-making process and the outcome. However, it is framed as building state capacity to exercise (state) sovereignty 'responsibly.' Constitution making in the LCDs then stems not from the people's free will but rather from the dictates of the 'UN family' including the IFIs. How does such a process end? It throws up the 'good' constitution embodying the UN's standards – but lacking autochthonous validation.

Finally, does this co-produced sovereignty shield states from the perilous grip of international regulations? No. It pushes them deeper into their clutches.

Conclusion

We have now experienced more than two decades of UNCA. It has essentially played out in the more impoverished and politically weaker sections of the globe; the Least Developed Countries (LDCs). Most significantly, it has come to stay. Indeed, the UN asserts that 'it is likely to be called upon in the future to assist other countries in their constitution-making processes' (UN, 2009: 2). By offering constitutional assistance, the UN predetermines both constitution-making *processes* and their constitutional *outcomes*. The commonalities in UN-assisted constitutions – international human rights, gender equality provisions, National Human Rights Institutions (NHRIs), market economy clauses, anti-corruption commissions, and anti-terror provisions – attest to this (Sripati, 2010). Therefore, its assertion that it offers merely technical assistance conceals more than it reveals. True, UNCA may have forced up the presence of women in constituent assemblies and broadly engendered constitution–making. However, the neoliberal brand of democracy it exalts and promotes potentially undermines the full realization of universal rights including gender equality. Furthermore, the question of how its coercive external influence masked as standard–setting – supposedly rejected by the post–World War II right to self–determination – continues today merits interrogation. Despite its profound implications, UNCA slumbers in deep sleep. It remains essentially uncharted and only tangentially remarked upon in technocratic discussions that view it solely as a post–conflict phenomenon. This chapter therefor aims to situate it center–stage to provide a platform for further debate about it.

Acknowledgments

A very special thanks to David Chandler for his encouragement and support. I benefited immensely from discussions with Professors Martin Doornbos and Craig Murphy. I thank them for their advice and guidance.

References

Arusha Peace Agreement. (2000, 28 August). Available at: https://peaceaccords.nd.edu
Boon, K. (2006). 'Open for business': International f nancial institutions, post–conflict economic refor and the rule of law. *Journal of International Law and Politics*, 15(4), pp. 513–581.
Boutros–Ghali, B. (1996).*An agenda for democratization*. New York, NY: United Nations.
Bowden, B., and Charlesworth, H. (2008) Defining democracy in international institutions. In H. Charlesworth and J. Farrell (Eds.), *The role of international law in rebuilding societies after conflict*. Cambridge, UK: Cambridge University Press, pp. 90–110.
Call, C. T. (2011). Political missions and departures from constitutional orders. In R. Gowan, *Review of political missions*. New York, NY: Center on International Cooperation, pp. 8–16.
Camdessus, M. (1999). *Excerpts from selected addresses by Camdessus: From crisis to a new recovery*. Washington, DC: IMF.
Chandler, D. (2009). Great power responsibility and "failed states": Strengthening sovereignty. In J. Raue and P. Sutter (Eds.), *Facets and practices of state building*. Amsterdam, The Netherlands: Brill/Martinus Nijhoff, pp. 15–30.
Constitution of the Islamic Republic of Afghanistan. (2004). In G. Flanz (Ed.), *Constitutions of the countries of the world* (Vol. II). Dobbs Ferry, NY: Oceana Publications, pp. 1–32.
Del Castillo, G. (2009). *Rebuilding war-torn states: The challenge of post-conflict economic reconstruction*. Oxford, UK: Oxford University Press.
Franck, T. (1992). The emerging right to democratic governance*American Journal of International Law*, 86(1), 46–91.
Gong, G. (2002). Standards of civilization today. In M. Mozaffari (Ed.),*Globalization and civlization*. London, UK: Routledge, pp. 77–94.
Kingdom of Bhutan Constitution, The. (2008). In G. Flanz (Ed.), *Constitutions of the countries of the world* (Vol. II). Dobbs Ferry, NY: Oceana Publications, pp. 1–39.
International Monetary Fund. (2009a). *Côte d'Ivoire: Poverty Reduction Strategy Paper*. Available at: www.imf.org
International Monetary Fund. (2009b). *Central African Republic: Poverty Reduction Strategy Paper*. Available at: www.imf.org
International Monetary Fund. (2010). *Factsheet: The IMF and good governance*. Available at: www.imf.org
International Monetary Fund. (2011). *Factsheet: Poverty Reduction Strategy Papers*. Available at: www.imf.org
Lome Peace Accord. (1999, 7 July). Available at: www.sierra–leone.org/lomeaccord.html
Luck, E. (2009). *Implementing the responsibility to protect at the United Nations*. Presentation at the Asia–Pacifi Centre for Responsibility to Protect. Available at: www.globalr2p.org/centres/asia–pacific.ph
Luwanga, F. (undated). *Statebuilding in South Sudan: The UNDP experience*. New York, NY: UNDP–South Sudan.
Obwona, M., and Guloba, M. (2009). Poverty reduction strategies during post–conflict recovery in Africa *Journal of African Economies*, 18(1), i77–i91.

OECD–DACD. (2008). *Statebuilding in situations of fragility – Initial findings*. Paris, France: OECD.
OHCHR. (2010). *High Commissioner's Strategic Management Plan 2010–2011*. Geneva, Switzerland: OHCHR.
Pahuja, S. (2011). *Decolonizing international law*. Cambridge, UK: Cambridge University Press.
Pelt, A. (1970). *Libyan independence and the United Nations: A case of planned decolonization*. New Haven, CT: Yale University Press.
Republic of Maldives: The President's Office. (2006). *Roadmap for the Reform Agenda*. Available at: www.un.int/maldives/Roadmap.pdf
Royal Government of Bhutan and UNDP. (2006). *Technical assistance for institutional and human capacity building of the Anti-Corruption Commission*. New York, NY: UNDP.
Security Council Report. (2007). *Special Research Report No. 2: Peacebuilding Commission*. New York, NY: United Nations.
Sripati, V. (2010). *United Nations constitutional assistance: A 'Third World approaches to international law' (TWAIL) perspective*. PhD thesis, Osgoode Hall Law School, Toronto, Canada.
Sripati, V. (2012). UN Constitutional Assistance Projects in comprehensive peace missions: An inventory 1989–2011. *International Peacekeeping*, 19(1), 93–113.
Stewart, F., and Wang, M. (2010). Poverty Reduction Strategy Papers within the human rights perspective. In P. Alston and M. Robinson (Ed.), *Human rights and development: Towards mutual reinforcement*. Oxford, UK: Oxford University Press, pp. 447–476.
UN. (1945). *Charter of the United Nations*. New York, NY: United Nations.
UN. (1960). *Declaration on the Granting of Independence to Colonial Countries and Peoples*. GA Res. 1514 (XV). New York, NY: United Nations.
UN. (2000a). *Millennium Declaration*. GA Res. 55/2. New York, NY: United Nations.
UN. (2000b). *Report of the Panel on Peace Operations* A/55/305–S/2000/809, New York, NY: United Nations.
UN. (2000c). *Women, peace and security: Study submitted by the Secretary-General pursuant to Security Council Resolution 1325*. New York, NY: United Nations.
UN. (2004). *A more secure world: Our shared responsibility – Report of the Secretary-general's High-Level Panel on Threats, Challenges and Change*. New York, NY: United Nations.
UN. (2005). *World Summit outcome*. New York, NY: United Nations.
UN. (2007). *UN Declaration on the Rights of Indigenous Peoples*. GA Res. 61/295, A/61/L.67 and Add. 1. New York, NY: United Nations.
UN. (2009). *Guidance note of the Secretary General: UN Assistance to constitution-making projects*. New York, NY: United Nations.
UN. (2011). *Press conference by Secretary-General's Special Advisers on Responsibility to Protect, Genocide, in connection with situation in Côte D'Ivoire*. New York, NY: United Nations.
UN Press Release. (2011). *Press conference by Secretary-General Ban Ki-moon at United Nations Headquarters*. SG/SM/14021. New York: United Nations.
UNCT–Malawi.(2006). *Role of the UN Malawi in a changing aid environment: A position paper by the UN Country Team*. Lilongwe, Malawi: United Nations.
UNDG. (2007). *Common Country Assessment and United Nations Development Assistance Framework: Guidelines for UN Country Teams on Preparing a CCA and UNDAF*. New York, NY: United Nations.
UNDG. (2010). *How to prepare an UNDAF – Part III: Technical Guidance for UNCT*. New York, NY: United Nations.
UNDP. (2005). *Executive Board of the UNDP and of the UN Population Fund – Draft Country Programme Document for Swaziland (2006–2010)*. Dp/DCP/SWZ/1. New York, NY: United Nations.
UNDP–BCPR. (2007). *Bureau Strategy 2007–2011*. New York, NY: UNDP.
UNDP–SouthSudan. (2011). *Support to the Ministry of Legal Affairs and Constitutional Development – Providing Technical Assistance*. New York, NY: UNDP.
UN Integrated Peacebuilding Mission in Sierra Leone and UN Country Team. (2009)*Joint Vision for Sierra Leone of the United Nations' Family*. Freetown, Sierra Leone: UNIPSIL.
UN Office for Drug Control and Crime Prevention. (2002). *Global Programme against Corruption – Anti-Corruption Tool Kit*. Vienna, Austria: UNODCCP.
UN Office in Vienna. (2008). *Democracy & the United Nations*. Vienna, Austria: United Nations.
UN–OHRLLSand UNDP. (2006). *Governance for the future: Democracy and development in the Least Developed Countries*. New York, NY: United Nations.
UNSC. (2000). *Security Council Resolution 1325*. S/Res/1325. New York, NY: United Nations.
UNSC. (2005). *Security Council Resolution 1625*. S/Res/1625. New York, NY: United Nations.

UNSC. (2007). *Security Council Resolution 1740*. S/Res/1740. New York, NY: United Nations.
UNSC. (2009). *Security Council Resolution 1888*. S/Res/1888. New York, NY: United Nations.
UNSC. (2011a). *Security Council Resolution 1996*. S/Res/1996. New York, NY: United Nations.
UNSC. (2011b). *Security Council Resolution 2009*. S/Res/2009. New York, NY: United Nations.
UNSG. (2000). *Report of the Panel on United Nations Peacebuilding Operations*. A/55/305–S/2000/809. New York, NY: United Nations
UNSG. (2001). *Report of the Secretary-General on the prevention of armed conflict*. A/55/985. New York, NY: United Nations.
UNSG. (2005). *Report of the Secretary-General on the work of the organization*. A/60/1. New York, NY: United Nations.
UNSG. (2006). *Progress Report of the Secretary-General on the prevention of armed conflict*. A/60/891. New York, NY: United Nations.
UNSG. (2008). *Sixth Report of the Secretary-General on the Integrated Peacebuilding Office in Sierra Leone*. S/2008/281. New York, NY: United Nations.
UNSG. (2009). *Eighteenth Progress Report by the Secretary-General on the United Nations Mission in Liberia*. S/2009/896. New York, NY: United Nations.
UNSG. (2010). *Report of the Secretary-General on peacebuilding in the immediate aftermath of conflict*. A/64/866–S/2010/386. New York, NY: United Nations.
UNSG. (2011). *Report of the Secretary-General on preventive diplomacy: Delivering results*. S/2011/552, New York, NY: United Nations.
World Bank, The. (2010). *Board presentations of JSANs on country-owned PRSPs as of 29 February 2012*. Washington, DC: The World Bank.

13
UN PEACEKEEPING AND THE IRONY OF STATEBUILDING

Richard Gowan

In February 2010, the London *Guardian* accused the UN peacekeeping force in the Democratic Republic of Congo (MONUC) of signing a 'pact with the devil' (Smith, 2010). The supposedly Satanic f gure involved was Bosco Ntaganda, a former militia commander being pursued for war crimes by the International Criminal Court. Ntaganda had, however, agreed to integrate his forces into the Congolese army and now held the rank of general. While the army was already notorious for its indiscipline and appalling human rights record, MONUC continued to give it support. While the mission's leadership insisted that it did not have contact with Ntaganda, the *Guardian* warned that its cooperation with a military that included such a man was 'another shameful chapter in UN peacekeeping that ranks alongside the impotent displays in Srebrenica and Rwanda.' The Special Representative of the Secretary–General (SRSG) in the Congo, Alan Doss, penned a rebuttal. He argued that it was wrong to 'assume that when peacekeepers are invited into a troubled country, all shortcomings and responsibilities for law and order default to the United Nations' (Doss, 2010):

> Governments remain responsible for their security forces, civilian protection and the integrity of borders, natural resources and public institutions. We assist the DRC in many of these areas, but we cannot impose our will on the government.

Bosco Ntaganda remained at large, going on to cause considerable further instability and trauma in the eastern Congo. But Alan Doss's defense of MONUC in 2010 offers a useful starting point for considering how UN peace operations have tackled the dilemmas of statebuilding in recent years. His invocation of Congolese sovereignty was simply an adaptation of the opening paragraphs of the Security Council mandate then in force for MONUC, which affirmed the government's 'primary responsibility' for national security and civilian protection. Similar language can be found in the preambles to the mandates for other recent large–scale UN missions. Critics of UN operations question the sincerity of these words. But Doss and other UN mission leaders have struggled to balance their commitment to building up fragile states' sovereignty with concerns about how governments exercise their sovereign powers.

This is troubling, because peacekeeping has increasingly been equated with statebuilding over the past decade. As Jake Sherman has shown, many peacekeeping mandates not only promise respect for sovereignty but charge peacekeepers to help governments 'extend state authority' –

a phrase first applied to the UN peacekeeping operation in Sierra Leone (UNAMSIL) in 200 (Sherman, 2012, 13–14):

> In certain cases, the extension of state authority has been geographic, i.e. extending the territorial writ of the government. In other cases, it entails strengthening the capacity, effectiveness, and legitimacy of state institutions in key sectors, such as assisting the state to obtain a monopoly on the use of force. Most often, extension of state authority involves a combination of these aspects.

This chapter reflects on how UN peacekeeping has evolved, and sometimes failed to evolve to manage these tasks. In doing so, it draws on the author's work on the *Annual Review of Global Peace Operations* – a volume first published by the Center on International Cooperation in 200 – and the work of other scholars associated with the *Review*, especially Sherman and Ian Johnstone.[1] Nonetheless, it largely describes the UN's operations in Africa – which, it argues, have become the organization's strategic center of gravity – and does not cover all recent UN missions. The UN Assistance Mission in Afghanistan and its counterpart in Iraq, although technically political missions rather than peace operations, are notable omissions here. And the chapter's thematic focus is also deliberately narrow, concentrating on military operations and high politics of peacekeeping. This inevitably excludes important aspects of UN missions, such as the role of international police in maintaining public order. But this narrow focus has a purpose: to explore the connections between force and politics in peace operations and to show why UN military deployments have had unintended and sometimes tragic consequences.

As peacekeepers have taken on increasing security roles in support of weak governments – often in tandem with ill–trained, abusive, or politically divided security forces – the UN has had to sustain large–scale operations for unexpectedly long periods. In 1998, the UN had only 12,000 troops in the field. As of late 2011, it had over 80,000 military personnel and 14,000 police officers deployed worldwide. The vast majority of these were serving in missions with 'extension of state authority' in their mandate. Yet, as the chapter demonstrates, this has proved problematic. Some of the largest operations – including MONUC, which had over 20,000 troops in 2010 – have been less effective than the raw data about their size imply. And, as the Bosco Ntaganda controversy suggests, UN off cials have often been deeply frustrated by the governments that they are authorized to assist. In some cases, the UN appears to have been engaged in strengthening state structures that are dangerous to citizens. Weak governments have repeatedly threatened to withdraw their consent from UN missions – and some have carried through on this threat. This chapter aims to explain how these problems have arisen, and concludes by suggesting that they may be an unavoidable part of all statebuilding projects.

Peacekeeping: Expanding yet struggling?

To understand how UN operations stumbled into these diffculties, it is f rst necessary to survey the way in which peacekeeping grew so rapidly from 1999 onwards. The speed of this growth threatened the UN with overstretch from the mid–2000s onwards, laying the seeds for future challenges to operations. Yet in the mid–to–late 1990s, it seemed very unlikely that blue–helmeted peacekeeping had any future at all, let alone one characterized by rapid expansion. The disasters of Somalia, Bosnia, and Rwanda were still very fresh memories. The crises in Kosovo and Timor–Leste marked a turning–point, however, as the Security Council mandated UN civilian official to administer the two territories. These episodes did not necessarily signal a significant expansio of UN *military* operations. In Kosovo, NATO deployed ground forces while in Timor–Leste an

Australian-led force undertook the initial stabilization operation (although it then handed responsibilities to UN troops). Instead, a new set of peacekeeping missions in Africa from 2000 onwards created the conditions for the UN to re-emerge as a military actor.

The first of these African missions was in Sierra Leone. The Security Council initially mandated 6,000 troops to deploy in 1999 to replace an earlier West African force. The UN mission deployed slowly and was 'far too patchy to be effective; many troops were inexperienced and unmotivated; logistics were poor; and even maps were out of date' (Adebajo and Keen, 2007: 262). In May 2000, rebels launched an offensive that threatened to overwhelm the mission – 500 UN troops were taken hostage – until a British intervention restored order. The Security Council approved a major expansion of the mission, which eventually numbered over 17,000 personnel. After this episode, UN officials and Security Council diplomats began to rethink th military dimension of UN operations. The Council mandated larger UN forces and asked them, as Ian Johnstone noted in 2006, 'to use force for a range of purposes beyond self-defense, including the protection of civilians and maintenance of public security' (Johnstone, 2006: 2).

By the time Johnstone wrote, there were just over 62,000 UN military personnel worldwide (Center on International Cooperation, 2006: 138). Fifty thousand (82%) were deployed in Africa, where numerous missions had mandates involving the extension of state authority, including those in Sierra Leone, Liberia (launched in 2003), Côte d'Ivoire (2004), and Burundi (2004). But the primary test of the UN's capability to provide military support to a weak state lay in the Congo, to which MONUC deployed in 1999.

MONUC was initially a small force, primarily devoted to monitoring. The Congo was emerging from an appalling civil war that had involved its neighbors and by some estimates claimed over three million lives. The government of President Joseph Kabila had little or no control of much of the country, where militias roamed freely. By the end of 2002, the UN still only had 4,300 troops on the ground. Over the year that followed, the mission shifted toward a far more assertive military posture, in part in response to an upsurge of violence in the eastern province of Ituri in the second quarter of the year (Boshoff, 2004: 140–141). MONUC was unable to cope, and the Security Council mandated the short-term deployment of a European Union (EU) rapid reaction force to restore order. Although the EU operation was a success, it withdrew after three months and MONUC was given a new mandate and extra troops to maintain stability in Ituri. By the end of the third quarter of 2003, the mission had over 10,000 troops in the field, including a 4,800-strong 'Ituri Brigade.' This new formation's commande warned that his troops were 'now enforcing peace, as opposed to keeping peace' and 'the brigade's capacity is enormous' (Boshoff, 2004: 142). The ground forces were backed by attack helicopters. MONUC expanded the range of its robust operations to other provinces in the eastern Congo – notably North and South Kivu – and the mission would eventually surpass 20,000 personnel.

As we will see in the next section, these numbers were deceptive: MONUC was sometimes too thinly spread to have a decisive impact. This would prove true of other missions, such as that in Darfur. Nonetheless, UN peace operations had not merely been resurrected after the failures of the 1990s but had also begun to adopt a new attitude toward providing security in weak states. Beyond Africa, UN missions contributed to the extension of state authority in a variety of ways. In Haiti, Brazilian-led forces used the mandate as the basis for anti-gang operations in the slums of Port-au-Prince. After the 2006 war between Israel and Hezbollah in southern Lebanon, the Security Council instructed the UN Interim Force in Lebanon (UNIFIL) to 'take all necessary action in areas of deployment of its forces and as it deems within its capabilities' to help the government 'exercise its authority throughout the territory.' This was a code for a crackdown on Hezbollah, which proved impossible to put into practice. Nonetheless, the deployment of nearly 15,000 troops – primarily but not solely from Europe – did manage to stabilize the

Israeli–Lebanese border. By the mid-2000s, therefore, the UN had re-established its credentials as a credible military actor, in spite of numerous setbacks along the way.

This was accompanied by an increasing emphasis on peacebuilding and especially institution-building in the security and justice sectors. There was a focus on developing 'integrated missions' and integrated planning processes, giving the SRSGs in charge of peacekeeping operations the power to coordinate UN funds and agencies. This initiative, supported by Secretary-General Kofi Annan but distrusted by many UN humanitarian and development officials, resulted in innumerable bureaucratic turf wars and almost as many policy seminars on better integration. In late 2005, Barnett R. Rubin quipped that 'the main instruments of strategic planning often remain endless "coordination" meetings among rival organizations, and the stapler, which serves to assemble those organizations' programs into a single "plan"' (Rubin, 2005: 93). But if improvisation was often the norm in the field, the Department of Peacekeeping Operations (DPKO) in New York began to place greater emphasis on learning and collating lessons across missions, and even released a peacekeeping doctrine in 2008. The goal of this endeavor, which encountered considerable resistance from DPKO old-timers, was to develop 'uniform practices and procedures' to guide day-to-day UN work (Benner et al., 2011: 44).

The new generation of heavy UN military operations thus offered a framework for improving and coordinating civilian contributions to post-conflict peacebuilding. A central civilian and military concern for almost all new peace operations was the management of post-conflict elections. UN officials were haunted by early post-Cold War operations, notably that in Angola where peacekeepers had overseen elections but then withdrawn, precipitating more violence. Nonetheless, the Security Council continued to insist on national elections as an operational priority, and DPKO now calculates that the UN has overseen votes in countries 'with populations totaling over 120 million people, giving more than 57 million registered voters the chance to exercise their democratic rights' (UN, 2012: 2). These polls included presidential elections in Sierra Leone (2002), Liberia (2005), Burundi (2005), Haiti (2006), and the Democratic Republic of Congo (2006). Although UN peacekeepers deserve a great deal of credit for securing these processes – especially where, as in Haiti and the Congo, there was serious unrest associated with the polls – they frequently resulted in new political challenges for the UN.

Recalling previous failures such as Angola, the UN secretariat now assumed that the success of initial post-conflict elections did *not* guarantee lasting stability. The Security Council was willing to keep operations in place rather than risk a return to war. In most cases, the UN was also able to persuade newly elected leaders to acquiesce to this arrangement. For many of them, the peacekeepers represented a source of political and personal security. The main exception was Burundi, where the election winners believed that the UN mission (ONUB) had supported their opponents and duly maneuvered to have it withdrawn in 2006. Yet even where governments accepted the UN's continued presence in theory, relations were not always easy in practice. As the veteran UN envoy Lakhdar Brahimi and DPKO official Salman Ahmed argued in 2008 there was likely to be 'an inverse relationship between the longevity of the peace operation and the room for it to play an effective political role' (Brahimi and Ahmed, 2008: 4). Leaders were able to use their fresh popular mandates to gain leverage over international officials. Johnstone concludes that peace operations often rest on bargains with political elites that have 'built-in obsolescence' as conflicts recede and domestic politics develop (Johnstone, 2011: 174–175)

> Typically, the UN starts out dealing with weak transitional governments, as in Haiti, Burundi and the DRC. The governments need the UN (and other external actors), especially for security and development assistance, and are therefore willing to tolerate significant external interference in exchange. But as the host becomes stronger, it

becomes less tolerant of international tutelage – content to accept a small peacebuilding presence if that means greater economic aid, but less interested in a military presence and governance advice.

As Johnstone concludes, 'it is ironic that consolidating sovereign capacity to exercise authority throughout the state is seen as a desirable end–state in a peace process, but the stronger the host government gets, the less leverage outsiders have to ensure it does so in a legitimate and sustainable manner.' This proved to be a particular problem in the Congo. After winning the 2006 elections, President Joseph Kabila became an increasingly difficult partner for the UN, courting Chines investment and implying that he no longer needed the support of Western powers and international organizations (although he temporarily moderated his stance during the financia crisis, when the Congolese state almost went bankrupt and China cut back its offers of financia support). Kabila also insisted on launching ill–advised offensives against anti–government militias in the east of the country. These often involved brutality against civilians.

The Congolese military was poorly equipped and the UN provided logistical support. UN officers admitted that this was a morally complex enterprise, but argued that they had a greater chance of restraining the army from committing abuses if they remained involved. This strategy went badly wrong in 2008, when a rebel counter–offensive routed the army and threatened to overwhelm MONUC forces. As criticism of the UN's complicity with the Congolese army mounted, the Security Council approved a 'conditionality policy' for MONUC in 2009, directing the mission to withdraw support from units led by commanders with a history of human rights abuses (Reynaert, 2011: 19). Although the UN did manage to vet a number of Congolese officers, MONUC was still unable to bring figures such as Bosco Ntaganda to justic

In the face of such dilemmas, UN officials began to re–evaluate the principles of peacebuildin and statebuilding. If the initial expansion of operations after 1999 had fostered a technocratic approach to peacebuilding – emphasizing 'integration' and 'uniform practices and procedures' – the setbacks of the later 2000s stimulated greater interest in the specific political dynamics o post–conflictcountries and the behavior of their elites. (Long–time UN mediators such as Lakhdar Brahimi had never really caught the technocratic bug anyway.) This new focus on elite politics has been perceptively summarized by Alan Doss since he retired from UN service. Between 2000 and 2010, Doss had served in a cross–section of the UN's new generation of African peace operations, first as deputy head of mission in both Sierra Leone and Côte d'Ivoire and then a SRSG in Liberia and the Congo. In a blunt paper published in 2011, he reflected on how th characters of the leaders in each country had affected the UN's work. He contrasted Presidents Ahmad Tejan Kabbah of Sierra Leone and Ellen Johnson Sirleaf of Liberia with Joseph Kabila in the Congo (Doss, 2011: 3). The f rst two had been constructive partners to the UN:

> Both Kabbah and Johnson Sirleaf were at ease (although often frustrated) in working with the international community. They developed good support networks, within and outside the region, which proved highly valuable for mobilizing debt relief (for Liberia) or, in times of trouble, military assistance (Sierra Leone's case), which helped in turn to reinforce their political positions at home. Johnson Sirleaf has been particularly effective in working with non–governmental and business groups, which has broadened her appeal in and beyond the donor community.

Conversely, Doss found little to praise in Kabila's personality or track record. In contrast to his defense of Congolese government sovereignty in the *Guardian*, he now made his feelings clear:

There has been progress (much of the country is relatively stable and some human development indicators show significant improvement) but Kabila has yet to overcom an impression of presidential ineffectiveness. He is not at ease in the media spotlight and is a reluctant communicator, even with his own people. He too is more comfortable with incremental approaches rather than grand strategy, responding to rather than leading events. This has been especially evident in his handling of the security situation in the East and other critical concerns, notably security sector reform and endemic corruption. He has been very anxious not to alienate the security forces and has only belatedly spoken out and taken (some) action against notorious human rights violators.

Doss concludes that his experiences in peace operations suggest that institution–building is still essential in post–conflict environments, but 'strong institutions also require strong men an women capable of making a qualitative difference to the way those institutions function' (Doss, 2011: 5). This raises the policy question of how UN officials should deal with strong leaders wh aim to disrupt or undermine international peacekeeping or peacebuilding activities. Doss warns that SRSGs will sometimes need to be assertive. In their 2008 paper, Brahimi and Ahmed advocate a quieter approach: 'the ground should be prepared with the host government . . . to assure them that the objective remains for the peace operation to phase out, as quickly as possible, including on the political front, and that mediation assistance can be provided in more discrete ways that pose no threat to the government's authority' (Brahimi and Ahmed, 2008: 3).

Yet in the mid–2000s, some UN missions found that host governments wanted to erase their political role completely. A case in point was Côte d'Ivoire. The UN sent a mission (UNOCI) to the country to support a fragile peace process in 2004 (this paragraph largely follows Piccolino and Karlsrud, 2011: 453–459). The Security Council initially mandated a force of 7,000 personnel to monitor the peace agreement – far fewer than had been required to pacify the much smaller Sierra Leone, and only half the number of troops the UN had sent to neighboring Liberia. This was partially offset by the fact that France kept a military presence in its former colony. But the UN had a weak base from which to promote reconciliation, and both the French and the UN found it extremely difficult to work with President Laurent Gbagbo (a 'Machiavellian temporizer according to Doss). More broadly, the second SRSG in charge of the mission – Pierre Schori, a former deputy foreign minister of Sweden – reported that he was revolted by 'the gap between the misery and powerlessness of the poverty–stricken majority and the glaring riches and arrogance of the ruling classes' (Schori, 2009: 27). Gbagbo and his supporters returned this disdain. Planned national elections were postponed in 2005. UN forces were harassed after the French clashed with government forces in 2005, and in early 2006 pro–Gbagbo protestors surrounded UNOCI positions. Nervous peacekeepers killed five civilians. The government launched a successful political campaign to neuter the UN mission, initiating direct talks with its foes:

> Ivorian actors insisted that the peace process was now 'nationally owned'. Diplomats close to the Gbagbo regime were candid in admitting that one of the objectives of the direct dialogue was 'to keep the UN out' and it seems that the total marginaliza– tion of UNOCI was what the Ivorian authorities had in mind and the UN feared. Eventually, the Ivorian presidency seemed to be satisfied with a solution that implie curtailing UNOCI's political influence. The role of UNOCI was redefined as one providing financial, and to some extent technical, support to an internally defined process – according to the meaningful French expression, *accompagner le processus de paix.*
>
> (Piccolino and Karlsrud, 2011: 455–456)

The poor relations between UNOCI and the Gbagbo government exploded into violence in late 2010, when the long-delayed national elections were finally held – and Gbagbo narrowl lost. We will return to this episode near the end of the chapter, as it brings operational problems experienced by other UN missions into extremely sharp focus. However, the neutering of UNOCI in the early years of its deployment is also illustrative of larger trends troubling the UN in the mid-2000s (although it is unusual in that the Ivorian government used its leverage to avoid elections, rather than exploiting electoral victory to gain leverage over the UN, as in Congo). UN officials faced the prospect of declining influence in a significant number of the countr where peacekeepers remained deployed. Looking back on this period, readers may ask two questions. First, if so many UN operations faced deteriorating political conditions, why did the Security Council not use its diplomatic leverage to reinforce the peacekeepers? Second, if the UN had invested so much in developing its military capacities since 2000, why did the missions not gain more political benefts from the large number of troops they fielded

The answer to the first question is that the Security Council was far from completely passive but it often struggled to bring its political weight to bear against recalcitrant governments. The rush of new missions in the early 2000s – and the need to review their mandates regularly – meant the Council had to juggle multiple crises. 'The pressure for these political peacemaking missions has to come from the Security Council,' the UN's Under-Secretary-General for Peacekeeping Operations, Jean-Marie Guéhenno admitted in 2007, 'but there is only so much time that the key leaders of the world can devote to an issue' (Mascolo, 2007).

In many cases, Council members were happy to let one or two powers manage policy toward a specific mission. Britain, for example, was generally agreed to have oversight of its former colony Sierra Leone, while France played a similar role on Côte d'Ivoire and the US took the lead on Liberia. If this saved time and energy, it could have curious results: French and American diplomats often bickered over the relative importance of the Liberian and Ivorian missions, for example, despite the fact that the fates in the two neighboring countries were obviously intertwined. Studies by the Center on International Cooperation have also emphasized that Council members often lose sight of the complex political realities in post-confict countries, instead focusing on process issues in New York (Gowan with Whitfield, 2011; Novosseloff an Gowan, 2012). Although the UN launched a new Peacebuilding Commission in 2006 to take some pressure off the Security Council and develop long-term strategies to help countries emerging from conflict, it failed to gain traction. Moreover, the Security Council has frequentl had to bargain with regional organizations such as the African and European Unions over details of peace processes and peace operations, reducing the UN's political autonomy. In many cases, including Côte d'Ivoire, China and Russia have insisted as a matter of ideological principle that UN officials must respect national sovereignty (Piccolino and Karlsrud, 2011: 456)

Although the Council has spent a huge amount of time debating peace operations, therefore, the political results have often failed to match the amount of diplomatic energy expended. There are exceptions: we have noted that the Council imposed a 'conditionality policy' on MONUC's support to the Congolese military, for example. But some governments – including those of Burundi in 2006, Eritrea in 2008, and Chad in 2010 – have risked the wrath of the Council and demanded that UN forces leave their territory altogether. The UN's room for maneuver has frequently proved remarkably limited, and missions have shut down. If this demonstrates the Council's *political* flaws, the UN has also had to tackle *military* limitations.

Overstretch

We have seen that the UN responded to crises in weak states such as Sierra Leone and the Congo in the early 2000s by expanding military operations. But if this process restored the UN's credibility after the failures of the 1990s, it soon brought the risk of operational overstretch. As the overall number of troops under UN command continued to rise, the organization found it increasingly difficult to persuade governments to provide sufficient numbers of specialized milita assets – including helicopters and other air assets, engineering units, and field hospitals – to kee all its operations running smoothly. In 2004, Jean–Marie Guéhenno warned the General Assembly that operations were at a 'crossroads' and severe resource shortages loomed (Gowan, 2008: 456). When the UN began to deploy a new operation to South Sudan in 2005, it was delayed by a lack of engineers to build facilities and protection units to guarantee the safety of the nascent force. By 2008, the organization seemed to be near a 'systemic crisis' in which the range of demands on peacekeepers could no longer be sustained (Gowan, 2008).

This concern was compounded by doubts over the quality and commitment of many of the forces available to the UN. In the wake of the Balkan wars, Western generals and politicians remained deeply skeptical of deploying under UN command. Although European troops have consistently played a prominent role in blue helmet operations in the Middle East (and were readily available to ship out to Lebanon in 2006), they have generally not deployed to Africa. There have been exceptions – Ireland and Sweden sent a joint rapid reaction force to Liberia, for example – but in many years European troops represent between 1% and 2% of all UN forces in Africa (Gowan, 2009). Similarly, Latin American countries with well-trained militaries focused on the UN mission in Haiti through the 2000s rather than spreading their contributions more widely. The vast majority of UN troops in Africa have come from the continent itself or from South Asia. The quality of contingents from both regions has varied considerably. Some units have simply lacked basic equipment. In mid–2010, the UN came under renewed criticism for its performance in the Congo when it was revealed that a militia had undertaken mass rapes 30 km from a peacekeeping base. A UN investigation of the incident revealed that the company at that base 'had only one Congolese interpreter, an ambulance and two jeeps':

> Its 80 peacekeepers, who had recently been deployed without any special training on the protection of civilians and best practices, were unfamiliar with the terrain, circumstances and the armed groups involved. Furthermore, its response capacity was further constrained by other operational constraints.[2]

These operational constraints included 'the lack of military logistics and telephone coverage': the UN had not even had sufficient communications equipment to keep track of events

Journalists investigating the story learned that the UN was unable to maintain a sufficientl consistent presence to deter militias. 'When the peacekeepers approached a village, the rebels would run into the forest,' one interviewee explained, 'but then the Blue Helmets had to move on to another area, and the rebels would just return.'[3] This was not surprising. We have noted that the UN set up a sizeable brigade to maintain peace in Ituri province in 2003, but it has often been unable to concentrate its forces so effectively in the Congo. Benjamin Tortolani and this author previously compared the scale of the UN's deployment in Sierra Leone in 2001–2002 to MONUC's presence in 2008 (when, as we have noted, the mission came under particular pressure from militia attacks). At its peak, UNAMSIL had mustered 17,500 troops, which represented one soldier for every 343 members of the population or, on another ratio, one for every 1.7 square miles of territory (Gowan and Tortolani, 2009: 51). By contrast, MONUC had one soldier for 3,748 Congolese citizens and 54 square miles of territory. When the 2008 crisis in Congo almost spiraled out of control, and there were calls for the EU to send a rapid reaction force as it had in 2003, European leaders were shocked to discover that MONUC had only 800 troops in the strategically important eastern town of Goma.

In spite of its earlier expansion, MONUC's military presence was thus less impressive than it appeared on paper. A similar situation would emerge in the Sudanese region of Darfur, a case that dominated debates about the effectiveness of UN operations in the later 2000s. While war broke out in Darfur in 2003, the African Union initially attempted to manage the crisis. Although an AU peacekeeping force did manage to ease the crisis on its first deployment, it was soon overwhelmed by the sheer scale of the region and the complexity of the conflict. The Securit Council discussed deploying a peacekeeping force in 2006 and 2007, eventually approving a joint UN–AU force (UNAMID) that was formally launched in January 2008. It was ultimately to involve some 25,000 personnel. But UNAMID suffered from a mix of military defects and political problems. The Sudanese government went to great lengths to hamper the mission's deployment – one standard tactic was to refuse permission for UN aircraft, located at Sudanese air bases, to fly. Khartoum also exploited a loophole in the mission's mandate to stop Wester countries sending contingents (unusually, some European countries *did* want to contribute on this occasion) and insisted that as much of the force as possible should consist of African units. This forced DPKO to search for additional military contributions from African armies that were already heavily engaged in other peace operations. The result was a force that was even less well-resourced than other UN missions, and militias and criminals preyed on its personnel. UNAMID lost 28 members to 'malicious acts' between 2008 and 2011 – the UN mission in Liberia recorded just two fatalities of this type from 2003 on (CIC, 2012: 231 and 283).

In both the Congo and Darfur, UN forces were effectively overwhelmed by their operational environments. UN officials sometimes claim that these two cases are not representative of peacekeeping as a whole: they distract from the organization's successes in cases such as Liberia and Sierra Leone. This is a partially fair defense. However, military flaws have brought mission elsewhere close to disaster too. To illustrate this, we can return to Côte d'Ivoire. We have already seen that the Gbagbo government placed significant constraints on the mission there, UNOCI in the mid–2000s and repeatedly postponed elections. When the polls f nally took place at the end of 2010, Gbagbo suffered a surprise defeat to a long–time rival, Alassane Ouattara. Gbagbo's supporters went on a rampage, killing many of Ouattara's allies in the main city of Abidjan. A contingent of Bangladeshi peacekeepers distinguished themselves by securing the Abidjan hotel compound in which Ouattara was staying, ensuring that he was not also a fatality. Yet much of the rest of UNOCI performed poorly. 'Pro–Gbagbo regular army forces, youth militia, foreign mercenaries and special forces have blocked U.N. food and fuel deliveries,' th*Washington Post*'s UN correspondent reported, 'torched vehicles, heaved Molotov cocktails at U.N. installations, [and] shot and kidnapped U.N. peacekeepers' (Lynch, 2011). He added that 'in many cases, the U.N. responded to challenges to its freedom of movement by returning to base.'

While UN officials queried this negative reporting – highlighting occasions on which UNOC units had managed to protect civilians – it was also rumored that frightened UN staff in Côte d'Ivoire were failing to keep UN headquarters fully informed of events, and that some local UN employees were colluding with Gbagbo's forces. The crisis culminated in late March and April 2011, when the Security Council authorized both UNOCI and French forces in Côte d'Ivoire to use force to protect civilians under heavy weapons fire in Abidjan. Pro–Ouattara forces swep into the city and took Gbagbo prisoner. Although Russia accused the UNOCI of taking sides, the Security Council's decision was celebrated as a potential turning point for the UN operations: not only had UNOCI stood up to Gbagbo but it had used force effectively, if only at the last moment. But as UN officials readily conceded, it has been a close run thing: they were luck that a large number of peacekeepers were not killed. In 2012, seven soldiers from Niger serving with UNOCI were murdered in an ambush on the increasingly volatile Ivorian–Liberian border.

Conclusion

The resolution of the Ivorian crisis was one of a series of successes for UN operations in early 2011 that arguably redeemed peacekeeping after an extremely difficult period (for DPKO, thi had been compounded by the loss of highly regarded UN staff in the 2010 earthquake in Haiti). These included facilitating an independence referendum in South Sudan and overseeing further presidential elections in Haiti and Liberia. But serious challenges remained. In 2010, President Kabila had pushed the UN to submit a proposal for pulling its forces out of Congo. Although he eventually agreed to let the UN stay on under a new mandate – with an increased emphasis on supporting the government – the future of the UN presence in the country remained uncertain. The mission's military resources were 'sharply curtailed' to such an extent that Secretary–GeneralBan Ki–moon concluded that it was 'no longer able to implement critical parts of its priority mandated tasks' including protecting civilians and dealing with armed groups (CIC, 2012: 46). In 2011, Congo held patently f awed presidential elections that Kabila won – once again, the UN was criticized for its ties to the president. In 2012, Bosco Ntaganda turned against Kabila. Forces loyal to him launched new offensives in the eastern DRC that – at the time of writing in late 2012 – left the national army and UN peacekeepers on the defensive.

The UN's woes were not conf ned to Congo. South Sudan's secession was complicated by repeated clashes over the demarcation of its border with the north, while UN forces within South Sudan itself (lacking helicopters) struggled to damp down ethnic violence. In the spring of 2012, the Syrian crisis created a new challenge for DPKO, which had to deploy military observers in the midst of a deteriorating conflict – UN officials were relieved when the mission withdr four months later without sustaining any fatalities. UN peacekeeping remained in a state of both high activity and frequent confusion. The mission in Darfur, almost universally agreed to have been a costly and ugly failure, began to downsize.

By 2012, UN off cials predicted that the overall number of peacekeepers was also likely to shrink gradually in the years ahead – unless new large missions upset their plans. There was a general sentiment that countries such as Liberia and Haiti had reached a 'good enough' level of stability, and that the continued presence of peacekeepers was unnecessary. Policy–makers in the UN secretariat – from Ban Ki–moon down – now also questioned whether it would be wise to launch large military missions on the Congo or Darfur models in future (Gowan, 2011). There was a new emphasis on UN civilian political missions as a lighter alternative to peacekeeping, and even stalwart DPKO staffers highlighted the non–military aspects of their work (CIC, 2011).

The era of peacekeeping that began in 1999 and 2000 thus seems to be waning, even though tens of thousands of peacekeepers remain deployed worldwide. Many academic experts have already tried to write that era's epitaph. Alex de Waal has made an especially resonant effort to summarize what has happened to peacekeeping in Africa – and what went wrong. He posits that 'the Sierra Leone conflict was resolved through an international military and financial presen that was so large, relative to the small size and even tinier economy of the country, that it became the principal source of patronage' (de Waal, 2009: 107). Such a peacekeeping force becomes 'the Leviathan that enforces its will, leading to peace.' But in more challenging environments such as the DRC or Sudan, a UN mission 'becomes just another buyer and seller in the auction of loyalties, and usually a rather inept one, readily manipulated or bypassed by the better–endowed and cannier national players' (de Waal, 2009: 108).

This chapter has largely confirmed this diagnosis, while also echoing Ian Johnstone's emphasi on the 'ironic' dimension of statebuilding: UN peacekeepers, and international actors more generally, invest in securing and supporting governments that then reject outside interference. The chapter has also underlined the tragic implications of this irony by focusing on the political, ethical, and operational dilemmas that arise when peacekeepers work alongside weak and unstable governments. While scholarship on statebuilding continues to focus on technocratic issues, the recent history of UN peacekeeping suggests that equal attention should be given to human factors that ensure that all efforts to build up a state go more or less wrong eventually.

Notes

1. The chapter also shows the influence of other scholars involved with the *Review*, including Bruce D. Jones, A. Sarjoh Bah, Benjamin Tortolani, Victoria DiDomenico, Andrew Sinclair, Megan Gleason, and Morgan Hughes. It refers to a sister publication, the *Review of Political Missions*, on which the author worked with Alischa Kugel and Teresa Whitfield. None of these experts are to blame for this chapter' flaws
2. Available at: www.ohchr.org
3. Available at: www.startribune.com

References

Adebajo, A., and Keen, D. (2007). Sierra Leone. In M. Berdal and S. Economides (Eds.), *United Nations interventionism, 1991–2004*. Cambridge, UK: Cambridge University Press.

Benner, T., Mergenthaler, S., and Rotmann, P. (2011). *The new world of UN peace operations: Learning to build peace?* Oxford, UK: Oxford University Press.

Boshoff, H. (2004). Overview of MONUC's military strategy and concept of operations. In M. Malan and J. Gomes Porto (Eds.), *Challenges of peace implementation: The UN Mission in the Democratic Republic of the Congo*. Pretoria, South Africa: Institute for Security Studies.

Brahimi, L., and Ahmed, S. (2008). *In pursuit of sustainable peace: The seven deadly sins of mediation*. New York, NY: Center on International Cooperation.

Center on International Cooperation. (2006). *Annual review of global peace operations 2006*. Boulder, CO: Lynne Rienner.

Center on International Cooperation. (2011). *Review of political missions 2011*. New York, NY: Center on International Cooperation.

Center on International Cooperation. (2012). *Annual review of global peace operations 2012*. Boulder, CO: Lynne Rienner.

de Waal, A. (2009). Mission without end? Peacekeeping in the African political marketplace. *International Affairs*, 85(1), 99–113.

Doss, A. (2010). Response: The UN Mission in Congo has not signed a 'pact with the devil'. *The Guardian*, 23 February.

Doss, A. (2011). *After the fall: Leaders, leadership and the challenges of post-conflict peacebuilding*. Geneva, Switzerland: Geneva Centre for Security Policy.

Gowan, R. (2008). The strategic context: Peacekeeping in crisis, 2006–08. *International Peacekeeping*, 15(4), 453–469.

Gowan, R. (2009). The EU should do more to support UN peacekeeping in Africa. *Center for European Reform Bulletin*, No. 66.

Gowan, R. (2011). Floating down the river of history: Ban Ki-moon and peacekeeping, 2007–201 *Global Governance*, 17(4), 399–416.

Gowan, R., and Tortolani, B. (2009). Robust peacekeeping and its limitations. In J. Nealin Parker (Ed.), *Robust peacekeeping: The politics of force*. New York, NY: Center on International Cooperation.

Gowan, R. with Whitfield, T. (2011). *Security Council working methods and UN peace operations: The case of UNMEE*. New York, NY: Center on International Cooperation.

Johnstone, I. (2011). Managing consent in contemporary peace operations. *International Peacekeeping*, 18(2), 168–182.

Lynch, C. (2011). Laurent Gbagbo's guide to crippling a U.N. peacekeeping mission. *Foreign Policy* online, 1 April. Available at: http://turtlebay.foreignpolicy.com

Mascolo, G. (2007). The way we operate is dangerous and problematic. *Der Spiegel* online, 2 August. Available at: www.spiegel.de

Novosseloff, A., and Gowan, R. (2012). *Security Council working methods and UN peace operations: The case of Chad and CAR, 2006–2010*. New York, NY: Center on International Cooperation.

Piccolino, G., and Karlsrud, J. (2011). Withering consent, but mutual dependency: UN peace operations and new African assertiveness. *Conflict, Security and Development, 11*(4), 447–471.

Reynaert, J. (2011). *MONUC/MONUSCO and civilian protection in the Kivus*. Antwerp, Belgium: IPIS.

Rubin, B. R. (2005). Constructing sovereignty for security. *Survival, 47*(4), 93–106.

Schori, P. (2009). Leadership on the line: Managing field complexity. In C. Clement and A. C. Smith (Eds.), *Managing complexity: Political and managerial challenges in United Nations peace operations*. New York, NY: International Peace Institute.

Sherman, J. (2012). Peacekeeping and support for state sovereignty. In Center on International Cooperation, *Annual review of global peace operations 2012*. Boulder, CO: Lynne Rienner.

Smith, D. (2010). The Congo conflict: 'The Terminator' lives in luxury while peacekeepers look on. *The Guardian*, 5 February.

United Nations. (2012). *Background note: United Nations peacekeeping*. New York, NY: UN.

14
STATEBUILDING THROUGH SECURITY SECTOR REFORM

Fairlie Chappuis and Heiner Hänggi

While statebuilding under international auspices is a relatively new agenda, security sector reform (SSR) is an even newer concept within it, having first emerged in the late 1990s. Three mai developments have contributed to the rise of SSR as an important policy concept. These include the growing recognition among the donor community of security as a developmental issue; the appreciation of SSR as an important element of democratization, as most recently shown in the context of the political transitions initiated by the revolutions of the 'Arab Spring'; and, f nally, the involvement of international stabilization operations in post−confl ct security sector (re)construction. Thus the SSR concept increasingly shapes international development cooperation, democracy assistance, and peacebuilding efforts. It has also become a centerpiece of international efforts to restore state authority in post−conflict contexts, as demonstrated, fo example, by the integration of SSR support across the United Nations system. SSR has become central to international support to statebuilding in post−conflict contexts because the theoretica argument for SSR is compelling in the context of the liberal paradigm based on democratic governance, the rule of law, and respect for human rights. Yet looking back over a decade of interventions of this kind, examples of unqualified success are difficult to   nd. Despite many isolated instances of impressive transformation, SSR remains an inherently challenging reform agenda.

SSR also represents a rupture with conventional visions of security. It is driven by the normative understanding that an ineffective or unaccountable security sector represents a decisive obstacle to sustainable development, democratic consolidation, and domestic and international peacebuilding. Moreover, the term 'security sector' represents a broader, more holistic under−standing of security concerned with the security not only of the state but also of its population. Going beyond a more conventional, narrow vision of external state security and military affairs, the security sector comprises all the structures, institutions, and personnel responsible for security provision, management, and oversight, concerned with both internal and external security. This includes core security forces such as the armed forces, police, border guards and intelligence, as well as management and oversight bodies, such as relevant government ministries, the legislature, and civil society organizations. Judicial institutions and non−statutory security forces may also be included. Reform of the security sector thus refers to all efforts to change the security sector so that security for both the state and its population can be provided effectively and efficiently withi a framework of civilian, democratic governance and respect for human rights. From this perspective it should be clear that SSR is a political process through which a country seeks to enhance the effectiveness and accountability of its security institutions. SSR is therefore also an incontrovertibly normative agenda.

The purpose of this chapter is to introduce SSR as a general concept, with special emphasis on its relevance for post–conflict statebuilding. The first section focuses on the conceptual coherence that makes SSR the expression in policy of a vision of security governance that is fundamentally rooted in the liberal statebuilding paradigm. The next section outlines the general nature of externally assisted SSR programs, while the following section, the core of this chapter, focuses on a range of typical examples of SSR in post–conflict statebuilding. The final secti discusses some of the challenges and opportunities SSR raises as a facet of statebuilding.

Statebuilding, security, and good governance

From a statebuilding perspective, SSR is the expression in policy of the specific concept of governance and state authority that liberal peacebuilding is based on. State authority – the ability of the state to make rules and have them followed – is based on the extent to which the state can control who uses force, where, when, why, and how. While there are many possible answers to these questions, there is only one within the framework of statebuilding as part of the wider liberal peacebuilding strategy: the state must monopolize violence effectively and efficiently, and in a legitimate way. The legitimacy of the state's monopoly on the use of force, and some would say the state itself (see Chappuis and Hänggi, 2009), therefore hinges on assuring that the use of force is subject to the rule of law and functions within a framework of respect for human rights. SSR is a normative agenda because it aspires to subject the security sector to certain standards of good governance that are based on a specific vision of legitimacy of the state and its relationshi to the population.

Good governance of the security sector is achieved within this model by a framework of civilian, democratic control that provides for accountability and transparency in who uses force, when, where, why, and how. There are specific institutional prescriptions usually associated wit this vision, which are based on the structures and models that have characterized security sector governance in wealthy democracies in the post–World War II era. However, the idea that the legitimacy of a state's rule depends on its responsibility to provide security for individuals and communities is an older idea firmly rooted in the development of modern statehood in Wester Europe and starting as far back as the 18th century (see further Krause, 2006). The separation of internal from external security tasks and the subjugation of military to civilian power are two elements of what is now thought of as good governance of the security sector. These developments were instrumental in shaping the modern vision of a legitimate state monopoly on the use of force (Krause, 2006: 6–13).

Good governance of the security sector in this context depends on democratic control because it is the only way to ensure that security is provided in the interests of the population and not against their interests. Democratic control means that elected representatives are responsible for defining security priorities and translating them into national policy. While every system of democratic control is only as robust as the democracy that sustains it, a functional system of oversight needs to provide for a separation of powers and several layers of checks and balances. Typically this includes different layers of accountability within the services and their ministries as administered by the executive, as well as robust oversight provided by the legislature, the judiciary, independent statutory authorities, and civil society, including the media.

Good governance of the security sector also requires civilian control. While security personnel may be technically proficient in the provision of security, ensuring that the use of force by th state is legitimate means protecting against abuse of power and conflicts of interest that may resul when non-civilians are too intimately involved in security policy-making. Security professionals must provide advice to ensure robust and well-informed policy-making, but their involvement needs to be limited. The typical arrangement for good security sector governance keeps top security officials from policy-making by several layers of institutional separation (e.g., throug national security councils, joint advisory mechanisms, etc.). By the same token, the involvement of civilians in the internal organization and management of the security forces also needs to be limited, both to protect the security forces from politically motivated interference by civilians and to ensure that the security forces are managed by professionals with a full understanding of their technical requirements. The goal of civilian democratic control is therefore to create a separation of powers that ensures that force can be used by the state without being subject to either the particular interests of civilian political leaders or members of the security forces.

Good governance of the security sector also depends on security forces that function both effectively and efficiently. This means that security forces must be adequately trained and equipped to fulfill their mandates. It was often hoped in the years following the end of the Cold War tha the reduction of spending on security forces would yield a peace dividend that could be redirected to other fields of public policy. However, what the radical downsizing of security sectors showe in a number of cases was that a genuine need for security provision cannot be met by overly small or poorly resourced forces. The need to provide adequate resources for the security sector must be balanced against the need for efficiency, meaning that the security forces should com petently execute their missions without squandering public resources. Ensuring that an affordable level of public funds is put to maximum use in security provision offers the best chance to ensure that security is provided without undue cost to the state's other areas of responsibility.

Efficiency, equity, and accountability are standards of good governance that ought to apply to public sector service delivery as a whole within the liberal statebuilding paradigm. Thus an important tenet of good security sector governance holds that the security sector and the use of force should also be subject to these standards. As logical as this proposition may be, it is a requirement that ought to be read against the frequent tendency among decision-makers to treat security matters as beyond the realm of public debate or to handle security actors with an inappropriate degree of deference. This tendency has seen security sector management reserved for security professionals or so-called 'experts,' with discussions of threat and response elevated to the realms of high politics and handled with excessive secrecy. The exceptional status given to security matters not only creates opportunities for actors to exercise inappropriate degrees of influence, but also opens the door to overly sensationalized and militaristic responses to security challenges. Thus the assertion that the security sector should 'be subject to the same standards of eff ciency, equity and accountability as any other [public] service' as made by the United Nations Secretary-GeneralKof Annan in 1999, represents a departure from conventional conceptions in many places of the appropriate role and status of the security sector among other state functions (Annan, 1999: 5).

In sum, liberal statebuilding as an international undertaking includes a normative agenda for the security sector expressed in the idea of good governance. The concept of good governance applied to the security sector includes specific prescriptions for subjecting the use of force to th rule of law and ensuring respect for human rights. On this basis it should be recognized that SSR is less a security agenda than a governance agenda. The point of SSR as a policy agenda is not just to ensure that the state alone has the ability to use violence; that is, to eliminate all violent challenges to the existing political order from non-state actors. Indeed every dictatorship monopolizes violence successfully. The point is also not to make the security forces more effective in how they use violence: every repressive state is backed by security forces that are very effective in the use of force. Instead the central importance of SSR is in changing the way the state uses its monopoly on violence by making it legitimate and accountable according to the precepts of good governance that are part of the liberal statebuilding paradigm. Programs that do not aim to establish good governance of the security sector – for example focusing exclusively on the effectiveness of the security forces without regard for how they are controlled and to what end – cannot be rightly described as SSR, even though they may entail changes to the security sector that may be entitled 'reform.'

Security sector reform as a statebuilding policy agenda

As a policy agenda, SSR consists of a number of activities that are designed to restore to the state a legitimate monopoly on the use of force, and enable the government to provide security to the state and its people in an effective and efficient way, subject to both the rule of law and respect for human rights. While a great variety of interventions and programs may serve this overall goal, in practical terms the nature of reform will be determined by the context that frames it. Thus despite the roots of the SSR agenda in the liberal state paradigm, and the Western provenance of the concept of good governance of the security sector, it is generally acknowledged that no common model of SSR exists. In principle every country engaging in SSR constitutes a special case and hence a different reform context, and there can be no one-size-ts-allsolution to the challenges of governing the security sector. This insight has become the basis in practice for the imperative to ensure that every SSR process is adapted to the requirements of its specifi context. However, considering the similarity of challenges they face, a certain number of SSR contexts may be broadly distinguished for analytical purposes. Acknowledging that in most cases the problems countries face will cut across categories, three SSR contexts emerge as typical when the overarching purpose of the reform agenda is taken as a point of departure. These are the context of socioeconomic development, democratization, and (post-conflict) peacebuilding.[2]

The developmental context refers to SSR as a means to improve the conditions for, or remove obstacles to, national socioeconomic development. This may mean ensuring that the security sector is made more efficient and held to higher standards of economic accountability, thereby freeing u resources for other developmental goals. It may also involve signaling to potential investors and the business community that the dangers of political interference and arbitrary intervention have been addressed through a strengthening of rule of law, transparency, and accountability.

The democratization context refers to SSR as a means of strengthening democratic transition and consolidation in states emerging from authoritarian rule. In these contexts reform will tend to focus on strengthening democratic civilian control and accountability to ensure that democratic rule is not endangered by praetorian intervention or the undue infuence of security actors. This will often entail changing the way that security policy is decided, including removing political levers of influence at the disposal of the security sector. The nature of a transition as pacted o not is likely be a def nitive factor in shaping the degree of inf uence the security forces retain following a transition to democracy.

The post-conflict context refers to SSR as an instrument of peacebuilding through state-building. The rationale for SSR as an element of peacebuilding stems from the idea that weak and fragile states unable to control the use of force are a risk both to other states and to their own populations. Ensuring that the state controls the use of force in an effective and efficient way subject to the rule of law and with respect for human rights, is seen as a lever of conflict preventio and a contribution to peace. While other types of SSR may be driven by strong internal political and technical support, the post-conflict context is likely to be marked by extensive internationa involvement in reform.

In each of these contexts SSR may comprise a number of different dimensions. For analytical purposes, these can be understood as touching on elements of internal and external security provision, which reflects the origins of the SSR agenda in the models of Western statehood Historically in Europe the internal/external division of security enabled the military elements of the security sector to constitute themselves as institutions designed to direct force beyond the state. At the same time, a parallel process of centralization and increasing political control allowed other elements of the security sector (and most notably the police) to specialize in the internal provision of law and order. As norms bounding the legitimate use of force developed alongside the state's practical ability to control territory and project force, the internal/external division of labor in security provision hardened to the point where it defined the appropriate roles and mandates of each element of the security sector (Krause, 2006: 8–11). These respective roles and responsibilities have become a central part of the prescription for good governance of the security sector and as a result def ne the SSR agenda.

- *Elements of external security:* These aspects of the SSR agenda include reforms focusing on the agencies responsible for territorial defence and national security, including the branches of government and the civil service charged with their oversight and accountability. This may include reform of military, intelligence, and border agencies, whether to improve effciency, effectiveness, or democratic civilian control. This type of reform may also entail changes to national security policy–making and the institutional architecture that governs relationships among the security forces, the executive and legislative branches of government, as well as the judiciary and civil society.
- *Elements of internal security:* This type of reform targets the agencies charged with ensuring law, order, and justice, including mechanisms for their management and oversight. Typically such reforms focus on the police, justice sector institutions, ministries, and other government branches such as the legislature or independent statutory oversight bodies. They may also involve relations with the media and civil society. Reforms may range from improvements in training and equipment through to thorough institutional changes in management, structure, and mandate.

While this distinction between external and internal security is useful in analytical terms considering the different character of the security institutions involved in the respective tasks, it should be noted that the distinction between these two realms of security is often heavily blurred. This is especially true of post–conflict contexts. It is, for example, typical that post–conflict S will be largely devoted to disentangling internal and external security mandates inherited from politicized and abusive regimes. This task is made all the more complicated by the fact that the security sector may have been more or less obliterated in the course of confict. This means that SSR in such contexts is often less a matter of reform of existing institutions than of rebuilding new institutions from scratch. Moreover, SSR in such contexts generally takes place alongside a number of related policy agendas that are also seeking to (re–)establish a legitimate state monopoly on the use of force.

- *SSR-related activities specific to post-conflict contexts:* International actors have developed programs to deal with many of the specific security challenges typical of the post–conflict context: disarmament, demobilization, and reintegration (DDR), small arms and light weapons programs (SALW), humanitarian demining, armed violence reduction (AVR), and transitional justice are all processes that involve SSR in so far as they aim to restore the state's legitimate monopoly on the use of force either by targeting non–state actors who threaten violence (e.g.,

DDR, SALW, AVR) or by establishing the state's right to use violence exclusively and strengthening the rule of law (e.g., transitional justice). However, implementing so many different programs all at once can cause problems in reform by making it more complicated and difficult to coordinate: a common example comes from the challenges of integrating ex combatants into the security forces. At the same time, however, the various linkages between these different issue areas also raise opportunities for leveraging influence and positive improvements in one area against another. Coordination and cooperation among international actors are essential to realizing this potential, though functional examples of such coordination remain few.

While SSR and related activities typically focus on transforming the internal security dynamics of the state undergoing reform, the blurring of internal and external security spheres makes the necessity of linking these reform agendas clear: for example, in West Africa the cross-border illicit trade in small arms and light weapons has regional security implications but is facilitated in large part by the failure of states to capably control their own internal security spheres and adequately police their borders, a problem that could be addressed in each state through SSR. In a similar way each aspect of SSR is vulnerable to delays and setbacks in other areas: for example, the process of domestic law and order reform that is part of SSR can be all too easily undermined by failures in other areas, such as transnational fows of illicit goods and people, or the failure to deal with ex-combatants and veterans, among others.

To summarize, it is clear that SSR is a broad agenda that can serve different purposes according to the reform context. While each case of SSR is unique, certain reform contexts do possess marked characteristics. Among these contexts, statebuilding as part of post-conflict peacebuildin distinguishes itself both by the scale of the task of reconstruction at hand, and by the degree of international involvement in supporting that process. As a result the specific elements of the reform agenda and the way the process unfolds will be strongly influenced by the modalities o cooperation and coordination that exist between external and internal actors. From this per - spective international assistance to SSR in post-conflict statebuilding, although a relatively recen phenomenon,[3] is also rather diverse, with a multitude of external actors – ranging from multi- lateral organizations to bilateral donors and various non-state actors – engaged in a wide variety of support activities.

Security sector reform in statebuilding practice

The following section offers a brief overview of the range of international interventions in which SSR has f gured, in order to show how each of these configurations presents particular challenge and opportunities for SSR as an element of statebuilding. Across the different cases, it is clear that certain challenges common to SSR in the post-conflict context express themselves differentl depending on how international actors approach the task of statebuilding in each case. As is often said of SSR policy, there is no one-size-fs-all model and thus surveying a number of different cases provides the best way to grasp the nature of the challenges and opportunities involved when SSR is part of statebuilding under international auspices.

All of the following examples are drawn from cases within the past 10–12 years as this time frame coincides with the emergence of SSR as a defined policy agenda and its subsequent incorporation into several existing missions.[4] Most of the following are UN-led missions though some missions have been led by other international actors, namely the European Union (EU), the North Atlantic Treaty Organization (NATO) and individual powers such as the US, with varying degrees of input from other actors. The scope of international engagement in statebuilding generally, and SSR in particular, inevitably varies from case to case, yet in practice three distinct types of engagement can be distinguished across a spectrum of degrees of international involvement in SSR and statebuilding (see Table 14.1). Although not exhaustive, the selection of cases is illustrative of the varying extents to which SSR has featured in different instances of statebuilding.

The middle range of the spectrum reflects situations of complex, multidimensional UN−le peacekeeping operations with a range of peacebuilding tasks. This is arguably the most typical conf guration for external interventions in post−conflict contexts and usually involves an extensiv SSR component with significant international input into the reform agenda. Because of the extent of international involvement in this type of operation, we refer to it as the 'heavy footprint' variation of SSR in statebuilding. At the more interventionist range of the spectrum is the 'heavier footprint,' which reflects all of the same characteristics of the typical heavy footprint but wit

Table 14.1 SSR in statebuilding practice: Selection of cases for illustration

Categories	Characteristic features	Examples
Heavy footprint	• Strong international presence • Extensive external involvement in SSR though working together with a national authority • The most typical case: Complex, multidimensional peacekeeping missions with peacebuilding tasks	Bosnia−Herzegovina (1995–1997) Sierra Leone (1999–2006) Afghanistan (2001–present) Timor−Leste (2002–2005/2006–present) Democratic Republic of Congo (2002–present) Liberia (2003–present) Solomon Islands (2003–present) Haiti (2004–present) Burundi (2004–2006) Iraq (2004–2011) Côte d'Ivoire (2004–present)
Heavier footprint	• Very strong international presence, if not an actual occupying force • External actors assume all or part of powers of government under an executive mandate • External actors tend to dominate SSR • Relatively rare type of intervention	Bosnia−Herzegovina (1997–present) Timor−Leste (1999–2002) Kosovo (1999–2008) Iraq (2003–2004)
Lighter footprint	• Small international presence, limited in some cases to only a few individuals • External actors support national actors in developing and implementing SSR agenda • Often follows heavy footprint operations or occurs where more comprehensive intervention is infeasible	Timor−Leste (2005–2006) Guinea Bissau (2006–present) Sierra Leone (2006–present) Burundi (2007–present) Central African Republic (2007–present) Chad (2007–2010) Kosovo (2008–present)

All cases have been dated according to the first year of deployment of a major international operation usually a UN mission.

even greater involvement of external actors through the instrument of an executive mandate, whereby external actors take on some or all of the powers of government (Doyle, 2001: 529).[5] As a result, external influence tends to dominate SSR agendas in such contexts. These types o mission are relatively rare and are often focused on achieving stabilization such that external involvement can be curtailed. At the opposite end of the spectrum is the 'lighter footprint,' whereby the scope of reform may remain just as complex and multidimensional as in other cases, but the extent of international involvement in statebuilding, and in SSR in particular, will be much less. This variation usually reflects much smaller missions and a reduced role for externa actors in supporting SSR agendas: typical examples include UN peacebuilding offices and E civilian missions.

The logic of a spectrum might suggest a linear evolution from the heaviest types of intervention toward the lightest. Indeed, such a progression is usually the explicit goal of the most interventionist types of mission, which aim to move from complex peacekeeping and stabilization towards statebuilding and peacebuilding. However, it is important to note that while some cases may evolve in this way, there is no necessary linear relationship between the categories, and cases may fall into any of the categories at different times, depending on the prevailing political situation and the extent of international engagement.

A heavy footprint: SSR in the typical post-conflict intervention

As the most typical type of intervention, these missions are generally very large in scale, ambitious in mandate and also involve a diverse cast of external multilateral and bilateral as well as non-state actors. The classic example of this kind of mission is complex, multidimensional UN peacekeeping operations with peacebuilding tasks. However, such interventions usually occur in a context where a local political authority exists, and international mandates inevitably involve supporting that national authority in the implementation of reform. Recent cases of this type of mission include assistance missions such as those in the Democratic Republic of the Congo (DRC), Liberia, Sierra Leone, Haiti, as well as Timor-Leste after the end of the mission's executive mandate.

Missions of this kind are frequently deployed with the goal of implementing the terms of a peace agreement, often including support for a transitional or new political authority through statebuilding. As a result, SSR assistance may focus on increasing the ability of the state to provide security through direct reform of the security forces, as well as improving their institutional features. This can include, for example, measures to rationalize organizational structures and management in the security sector, such as payroll or human resource reforms, leadership training, or internal disciplinary mechanisms. Improving the governance of these forces should also be an important element of SSR and reform will often focus on supporting the ability of the state to decide on security policy; for example, through adjustments to the legal framework or training for government staff and parliamentarians on technical aspects of security policy and oversight. A paradigm example of this kind of support comes from Sierra Leone, where the UK and other external actors provided support to the reform of the military and police organizations and the wider justice sector, as well as a new institutional setting for security governance.[6]

Local authorities in these contexts are generally extremely weak at developing reform plans and implementing them, or may be lacking the political will to engage in such reforms. This can mean that external actors provide relatively high levels of direct support, a situation that can imply substantial power asymmetries between external and local actors. Striking a delicate balance between local ownership and external assistance in these situations is a matter of constant political negotiation. One feature of this effort is that a greater proportion of external assistance may be devoted to building capacity among local authorities so that they can take over themselves. Capacity building has thus become central to the SSR agenda in a number of contexts: UN support for police reform in Liberia since 2004 provides a typical example, whereby assistance began with UNPOL staff training Liberian police recruits directly while also preparing Liberian police trainers to eventually take over this task.

Problems of coordination and cooperation among international actors may be compounded in this kind of mission context because the scope of activities is so great, yet it is unlikely that there will be a strong central authority to impose a specific direction on reform (neither a stron national authority nor an international actor with an executive mandate). This can introduce problems of incoherent support and create opportunities for arbitrage among local actors. Despite these problems, however, high levels of support are likely to increase the relative benefits of coordination if a mechanism can be worked out, for example, through such measures as donor trust funds or the inclusion of SSR in national development strategies or peace agreements, which subsequently provide strategic direction for reform: for example, SSR has been written into national poverty reduction strategies in Sierra Leone (2005), the DRC (2006), and Haiti (2007), and into the 2008 national development strategy of Afghanistan. SSR was also made a condition of peace accords in Sierra Leone (Lomé Accords, 1999), Burundi (Arusha Accords, 2000), and Liberia (Comprehensive Peace Agreement signed in Accra, 2003) among others.

The external nature of the SSR concept is likely to make local ownership a key concern, especially where capacity is relatively weak among local political authorities (Caplan, 2004: 221). This problem is well recognized in SSR policy, and the strategies designed to surmount this challenge have included participative approaches to dialogue about SSR and security as well as technical assistance, working in facilitation roles, and capacity building through training and co-locations and co-deployments (see further Nathan, 2007). Early in the post-war transition in Liberia, for example, UNPOL staff were deployed together with Liberian police officials in orde to provide on-the-job training and guidance while also assisting in the provision of security (United Nations, 2004: 7).

The highly sensitive political nature of SSR is also likely to be visible in such cases, as often those with substantial influence over the reform agenda will be the power-brokers who ma stand to lose as a result of reform. This presents challenges for external actors who will need to seek out allies in reform among local power-brokers while raising awareness in general of the potential benefits reform may present. This may turn out to be difficult in practice if there is transitional government with limited credibility; if there is a lack of political will to engage in reform on the part of the local government; or if the government's ideas on SSR deviate from the approach preferred by international actors. Burundi provides an example of a trade-off between local (governmental) ownership and the need for a holistic approach to SSR: the national authorities rejected the UN mission's proposal for a comprehensive SSR programme and instead insisted on a piecemeal approach, where police, defence, and intelligence reforms were undertaken separately from one another.

Finally, this type of intervention is likely to refect substantial intersections between SSR and other security-related activities, most notably DDR (see further Scherrer and Bryden, 2012). While in some contexts entirely new security forces are re-established and the old dissolved (for example, the military in Liberia and Iraq), more usually ex-combatants are folded into the reformed forces (as in DRC, Sierra Leone, and Burundi, among others). Several reasons explain this: integrating formerly warring parties may prevent a security dilemma developing as a result of factions giving up arms. Integrating ex-combatants or veterans into new forces may placate political partisans while also offering a way to provide jobs and livelihoods for individuals who are otherwise well equipped to use violence for criminal or political ends. However, despite the potential positive synergies between DDR and SSR, this kind of undertaking also raises certain challenges. It may be that the security or economic rationales for determining force size generate a number substantially different to what would be needed to satisfy political considerations. Establishing the right size for the post−conflict security sector therefore inevitably involves trade offs. Moreover, adapting training to reflect very different levels of education and experience excluding human rights abusers through vetting and lustration, and dealing adequately with veterans and families are all issues that pose significant challenges. The political challenges associated with such a strategy are also substantial: for example, ensuring control over the new force, avoiding the creation of patronage networks, reliably breaking old command chains, and generating public trust.

A heavier footprint: SSR under executive mandates

At the most interventionist end of the spectrum are those missions that aspire to transform the security sector as part of a comprehensive effort to build or rebuild the state. These missions generally include large numbers of external actors from multilateral, bilateral, and non−state institutions and are typically characterized by ambitious mandates that aim at comprehensive reform across a number of government functions and social spheres. This may imply the establishment of a new government, a new electoral system, and new public services. Such an ambitious agenda usually includes extensive SSR touching at least on the military, the police and the justice sector, as well as security policy−making and legislative frameworks, if not the security sector in its entirety. SSR in such contexts will also take place beside a full range of other security−related post−conflict activities, including extensive DDR.

Most importantly, the ability of external actors to implement the reform agenda is buttressed with the executive powers of the state itself. In these relatively rare situations external actors literally supplant the national authority for the purposes of establishing a functional basis on which sovereign executive powers may eventually be returned to the legitimate national authority. Recent and notable cases where external actors have assumed executive authority for a certain period of time include Kosovo, Timor−Leste, Bosnia−Herzegovina, and Iraq. Each mission was confgured slightly differently: in Kosovo and Timor, for example, the UN was charged directly with executive powers; in Bosnia−Herzegovina and in Iraq interim authorities were established under international auspices of varying legitimacy. In all cases, SSR was a cornerstone feature of the task of statebuilding, whether implicitly or explicitly expressed in the mandates of each operation. However, the nature of the executive mandate and the scope of broader efforts at state−building in these contexts raised both specifc challenges and opportunities for conducting SSR.

In all of these cases the scope of SSR was relatively comprehensive, aiming to reform to some extent a wide range of justice and security actors, such as the military, border guards, the judicial system, police, and prisons. Reform efforts also included broader governance−focused elements, including, for example, drafting new security sector legislation or establishing or strengthening oversight mechanisms. Attempts were also made to change the conditions of security governance through reform of government ministries responsible for management and oversight: for example, targeting the ministries of interior/internal affairs, defence, and justice.

Across these cases the institutions of the security sector had either become dysfunctional (Iraq) or were to be reconstituted under a new national entity (Timor−Leste, Kosovo, Bosnia−Herzegovina). As a result, in each case the security sector or parts of it were largely reconstituted from scratch, and establishing entirely new security institutions posed special challenges. In Kosovo the police was newly established, as was also the police in Timor−Leste and to some extent the defence force. In Iraq the military was controversially disbanded and replaced with a new force while attempts were made to reform the existing police force. In Bosnia—Herzegovina the armed forces were recomposed from other fighting forces to form an essentially new entity

Establishing entirely new security institutions is an especially challenging task in post—conflic contexts. To give one example, new forces lack experienced personnel who can provide leadership and direct the organization strategically. Accelerated training for potential new leaders is one possibility for overcoming this problem, although such training can never fully make up for lack of actual operational experience. Another possibility is to have foreign personnel fill strategic positions, although this contravenes the desire for local self—determination and ownership that is important in most reform efforts. Alternatively, personnel from the defunct security institutions can be brought in to fill the void; however, besides leadership skills and experience they may potentially bring with them all the bad habits of the previous security institutions. In Timor—Leste,for example, the defence forces were established as a new institution but integrated personnel from the informal forces that had fought for liberation against Indonesia. While they brought with them leadership experience and the respect of the people for whom they had fought, these cadres also brought their old chains of command, directly challenging the hierarchy of the new institution.

These cases of ambitious statebuilding missions with executive mandates also reflect the variet of mission conf gurations within which SSR may take place. While multilateral missions under UN auspices may garner the most international legitimacy, comprehensive missions with executive mandates may take place in other statebuilding contexts, as demonstrated by the case of Iraq. The legitimacy of international engagement can be a key factor in determining both the overall political dynamics and the way in which assistance is perceived and received by local parties. Each of these executive mandates enjoyed varying degrees of international legitimacy, yet in none of these cases was this international legitimacy sufficient to satisfy internal demand for legitimacy. Indeed, in all of these cases international actors were accused of neglecting the rights of the population to self—determination and of failing to adequately include local actors in SSR decision—making processes.

A lack of local ownership over SSR negatively impacted reform at a number of points in each case, and even a comprehensive approach cannot substitute for that fundamental lack of legitimacy. For example, while statebuilding in Iraq was based on an approach that was very broad in scope, reform inevitably suffered as a result of the lack of legitimacy that accompanied the reform agenda. This lack of legitimacy was exacerbated by the nature of the intervention as part of a larger post—9/11 US security strategy. This meant that SSR assistance in Iraq (and also in Afghanistan) became a matter, not only or even firstly, of securing the safety of the local population and the state, but of preventing the resurgence of forces that might threaten the security interests of intervening states. These conficting reform prerogatives and an increasingly violent context made the chances for successful SSR in Afghanistan and Iraq extremely bleak.

A lighter footprint: SSR in limited support missions

Although SSR is frequently an essential component in comprehensive statebuilding initiatives, it is not limited to these contexts. Indeed at the opposite end of the spectrum, where external involvement is most limited, SSR may be a key feature of the lighter footprint variation of international efforts at statebuilding. Such missions tend to be much smaller in both size and scope compared to more comprehensive statebuilding agendas: they may for example include a smaller international presence and focus more narrowly on specific statebuilding issues, and SS may only be implicit in mission mandates. While such missions still involve a variety of multilateral, bilateral, and non—state actors in providing assistance and mandates remain both complex and multidimensional, the scope of direct international input into reform is likely to be much less. International support in such contexts primarily consists of supporting an existing national authority with expertise and financial resources while direct implementation and decision-making are left to national stakeholders.

These kinds of intervention may arise in a variety of contexts; UN peacebuilding offices o EU civilian missions would be typical examples. Frequently a smaller mission will be left behind after a larger international mission completes its initial mandate and winds down. The UN Mission in Sierra Leone (UNAMSIL), for example, was authorized in 1999 with a maximum strength of up to 17,500 personnel. When it was deemed to have completed its mandate six years later it was closed and replaced by a different kind of assistance mission, United Nations Integrated Office for Sierra Leone, which began its work in 2008 with a staff of approximately 70 (UNIPSIL, 2012). Both missions were tasked with supporting the process of SSR in Sierra Leone under a comprehensive and ambitious mandate. However, the role of international actors in the reform process obviously changed substantially as a result of the differing capacity levels between the two missions.

This kind of assistance responds to the fact that SSR as an element of statebuilding is a long-term task. This is due, on the one hand, to the scale of the transformation that SSR aspires to: it takes a long time to build functional institutions. On the other hand, it is also due to the fact that progress can often create new reform needs: for example, improvements in civil-military affairs as marked by the absence of military personnel on the streets may increase demand for police patrols; improved police effectiveness may increase strain on the judicial system; improved independent or parliamentary oversight may generate demand for more capacity building. Thus as larger, more comprehensive missions complete initial mandates and scale down, or when they must leave for other reasons, they are frequently replaced with more limited support missions that seek to continue the reform process.

In challenging contexts where reform may be too politically difficult to attempt on a large scale, a limited support mission may nonetheless be acceptable. While a comprehensive approach requires thinking of reform in holistic terms, this does not mean that reform across the entire security sector needs to occur simultaneously. Thus while military or intelligence reform is often too sensitive an issue for external actors to engage in directly, support to other areas such as the justice sector or police may be acceptable. This kind of support can create entry points for more comprehensive reforms later on through the same kinds of linkages that make comprehensive and long-term approaches to SSR desirable.

An advantage in this kind of mission is that leadership and control of the reform agenda sit squarely with national actors. This raises fewer problems in terms of assuring local ownership of the reform agenda; however, it also means that external actors are less able to infuence the path of reform, which can sometimes be held hostage to local political dynamics. In Guinea-Bissau, for example, external support to SSR has proved ineffectual over a period of several years and the military remains a major power-broker in an unstable political landscape. However, at the same time the case of Guinea-Bissau also demonstrates the relatively high degree of inf uence that external actors may have even in the context of the most limited assistance missions, as the dependence of Guinea-Bissau on foreign assistance has translated into a strong degree of external influence over political dynamics (see further International Crisis Group, 2012)

A further context wherein external assistance to SSR will be minimal is when a national authority seeks explicitly to limit the scope of external engagement in reform. This may occur for political reasons or if the context itself is such that more extensive engagement is infeasible for security or other reasons. In some cases national actors have put an end to external assistance, as for example in Chad in 2010 when the UN Mission in Central African Republic and Chad

(MINURCAT), which had been responsible for supporting a very limited SSR program, was requested to leave.

Conclusion

The preceding overview of the range of external assistance to SSR gives a sense of some of the challenges and opportunities that SSR as a component of statebuilding presents. However, such a necessarily brief summary inevitably over-simplifies the dynamics of reform and the specific nature of each context. Nevertheless, across the different configurations of international assistance to SSR in the context of statebuilding, several key features emerge as common to all.

Across all of the cases mentioned above, poor security sector governance figured as a root cause of conflict and frequently an exacerbating factor. Where a long legacy of mismanagement and poor governance of the security sector has caused conflict, attempts to change that system inevitably threaten the power bases of those who still control, or seek to retain control over, the system. This can make reform extremely sensitive and therefore difficult. However, at the same time, recognition of the fact that poor security governance has been a cause of conflict can also create strong public demand, and therefore political pressure, for improvement. The inclusion of SSR in a number of peace agreements reflects both how sensitive and how important this issue is for statebuilding.

The legacy of poor security sector governance is often a lack of foundations on which to rebuild future institutions. In post-conflict security sectors the military has frequently become politicized and even a faction in the conflict, while the personnel of the police and other security agencies tend to abandon their posts, leaving the institutions to wither. Thus SSR in post-conflict contexts often requires starting from nothing in terms of institution building: all staff must generally be verified, vetted, (re)trained, and even the simplest resources supplied from outside the country. This poses immense challenges for international actors in terms of the degree of assistance that may be required. It also poses challenges for local actors in terms of the degree of international involvement that must be tolerated in order to implement reform. However, starting from nothing can also be a boon to the reform process if it provides an opportunity to establish new, better institutional cultures without having to inherit poor past practices.

Whether institutions are rebuilt from scratch or reformed on the basis of existing forces, transforming security governance will always be a long-term endeavor. The legacy of conflict and poor security provision, as well as the scale of change that is necessary to transform a post-conflict security sector according to the vision of good security sector governance, means that SSR in post-conflict contexts will inevitably take a very long time. Even the first 10 years after the arrival of peace – the time frame typically designated as 'post-conflict' – is a relatively short time-horizon for SSR, and it is often said that 'it takes a generation.' This long time-frame is a challenge to international assistance due to bureaucratic project deadlines within agencies and the short attention spans of international actors when it comes to crises. However, the long time-frame of reform also offers opportunities in so far as it can signal to all involved that change is robust, while also generating more demand for further improvements as new systems increasingly take root.

Establishing security in post-conflict contexts is generally the first priority for international actors, especially given that most local security forces are defunct as a result of the conflict. This poses a challenge to reform in so far as the tasks of providing security directly and enabling local security agencies to provide security can become confused. The temptation for international actors is to have local forces take over responsibility for security provision as soon as possible so that they may reduce their own commitment and thereby avoid the risk and expense of longer term engagements. This pressure can drive international actors to provide assistance that targets training and equipment transfers while neglecting the institutional reforms and norms that will ensure that improvements in effectiveness do not result in abuse. At the same time, however, this pressure to establish security quickly and transfer responsibility can work in favor of the reform process if it provides an incentive for international actors to involve local actors in the reform agenda and to ensure that they are ready to take responsibility faster.

Related to the urge among international actors to confuse security reform with security provision is the fact that the goals of reform for external actors may differ from the interests of the state subject to reform. This is the case with interventions based on Western security imperatives associated with the post–9/11 era, as in Afghanistan and Iraq, where external actors have sought to secure the state as a bulwark against challenges from non–state forces hostile to Western interests. However, this justification for SSR interventions often glosses over the fac that the kind of security apparatus or reform priorities that may be in the interests of those who intervene (for example, strong counter–terrorism or counter–narcotics capabilities) may be prioritized over those reform needs that would best serve local security interests: for example, law and order reform including prisons, justice, and police or governance reform.

SSR is often an idea that comes from outside a post–conflict context and is promoted ther by external actors and locals who decide to support the agenda. This can pose challenges in several ways: f rst, it means that a number of external actors may be promoting an SSR agenda, and experience has shown that lack of coordination and cooperation can be a problem. Second, it means that it may not always be locals that are in control of the reform agenda: this may be because of a lack of skill or experience in a certain area, or because programs are primarily financed from outside agencies who have their own agendas and priorities. Third, it can also mean that outsiders promote reform models and practices that are poorly adapted to the exigencies of local social, cultural, or political contexts. In all cases, a failure to make sure reforms are led and implemented by local actors, with the full coordinated support of international actors, is likely to mean that reforms will not be sustainable in the long term.

Ultimately SSR and the concept of good governance of the security sector on which it is based reflect a great deal of conceptual coherence within the liberal statebuilding paradigm, an this conceptual coherence is also what makes SSR a normative agenda. The normative aspects of SSR can make it politically sensitive and as a result some have described SSR as neo–colonialism, imperialism, paternalism or ahistorical social engineering (see for example Egnell and Haldén, 2009). Yet questions of the overall legitimacy of the approach are inherently bound to views on the legitimacy of the liberal statebuilding paradigm itself, which has faced similar criticisms (see for example Duffield, 2001, 2007; Chandler, 2007; Paris, 2002). Within this paradigm it is important to remember that SSR is a normative and hence highly political agenda that concerns fundamental questions about how a polity governs itself. Framing SSR in these terms highlights the stark contrast with concepts that would paint SSR as a neutral or apolitical matter of technical changes to the workings of the security forces. In practice the political and the technical visions of SSR are frequently conf ated in statebuilding interventions. On the one hand, politically sensitive SSR questions can be more effectively dealt with when they are presented in terms of less threatening, supposedly technical changes. On the other hand, security assistance of questionable motives (for example within the post–9/11 paradigm) may be rendered more acceptable by adopting the language around SSR as a legitimizing concept. This confusion in terms and usage has led to a situation where not all that is termed 'SSR' is in fact SSR,[8] and not all that is SSR is called so.[9]

Notes

1. For a critical discussion of the concept of liberal peacebuilding see Paris (2004).
2. For an earlier version of this categorization see Hänggi (2004: 9–15).
3. Although having been involved in supporting reforms in the security sector since the 1990s, key international actors such as the United Nations (UN) and the European Union (EU) had begun to conceptualize their own approaches to SSR support by the mid-2000s. On the development of SSR within the UN, see Hänggi and Scherrer (2008). On SSR in EU policy, see Spence and Fluri (2008).
4. The analysis and examples provided in this section draw principally on the following small but representative sample of case-based literature on SSR: Albrecht and Jackson (2009) (Sierra Leone); Baker (2007) (Sierra Leone, Liberia); Banal and Scherrer (2008) (Burundi); Bernabéu (2007) (Kosovo); Boshoff (2004) (DRC); Centre d'Alerte et de Prévention des Conflits et le Centre de Recherche d'Etudes e de Documentation en Sciences Sociales – CENAP/CREDESS–Bdi (2012) (Burundi); Chandler (2004) (Bosnia–Herzegovina,Iraq); Chappuis et al. (2012) (Timor–Leste, Liberia); Clément (2009) (DRC); Ebo (2006) (Sierra Leone); Ebo (2008) (Liberia); Funaki (2009) (Timor–Leste); Giustozzi (2008) (Afghanistan); Goldsmith and Dinnen (2007) (Solomon Islands, Timor–Leste); Hansen (2002) (DRC); Hood (2006) (Timor–Leste); International Crisis Group (2008) (Timor–Leste); International Crisis Group (2012) (Guinea–Bissau); Malan (2008) (Liberia); McDougall (2009) (Solomon Islands, Timor–Leste); Mobekk (2008) (Haiti); Mobekk (2009) (DRC); N'Diaye (2009, 2012) (CAR); Observatoire de l'Afrique (2008) (Guinea–Bissau); Ouattara (2011) (Côte d'Ivoire); Peake (2009) (Timor–Leste); Peake and Brown (2005) (Solomon Islands); Perdan (2008) (Bosnia–Herzegovina); Rumin (2012) (Burundi); Scherrer (2012) (DRC); Scheye (2008) (Kosovo); Sedra (2006, 2012) (Afghanistan); Sedra (2007) (Afghanistan, Iraq); Solhjell et al. (2010) (Chad); Woodward (2003) (Kosovo, Bosnia–Herzegovina).
5. Similar terms include 'administrative authority,' 'executive authority,' 'supervisory authority,' and 'transitional authority.' On different forms of executive mandates, see Chesterman (2004: 56–57).
6. This included a new national security architecture based on a national security council and a new legal framework within which it would function. See further Albrecht and Jackson (2009).
7. On the inclusion of SSR in poverty reduction strategies, see further Garrasi et al. (2009).
8. For example, security assistance that fails to consider the governance dimension of how violence will be used and controlled.
9. For example, implicit SSR mandates that are framed in other terms but constitute attempts to ensure that the use of force is subject to the legitimate monopoly of the state within a framework of rule of law and respect for human rights.

References

Albrecht, P., and Jackson, P. (2009). *Security system transformation in Sierra Leone 1997–2007*. Birmingham, UK: The Global Facilitaton Network for Security Sector Reform (GFN–SSR).
Annan, K. (1999). *Address of the United Nations Secretary-General to World Bank Staff, 'Peace and Development – One Struggle, Two Fronts'*. 19 October, Washington, DC.
Baker, B. (2007). Post–war policing by communities in Sierra Leone, Liberia, and Rwanda.*Democracy and Security*, 3(2), 215–236.
Banal, L., and Scherrer, V. (2008). ONUB and the importance of local ownership: The case of Burundi. In H. Hänggi and V. Scherrer (Eds.), *Security sector reform and UN integrated missions: Experience from Burundi, the Democratic Republic of Congo, Haiti and Kosovo*. Münster, Germany: Lit Verlag, pp. 29–60.
Bernabéu, I. (2007). Laying the foundations of democracy? Reconsidering security sector reform under UN auspices in Kosovo. *Security Dialogue*, 38(1), 71–92.
Boshoff, H. (2004). Overview of security sector reform processes in the DRC.*African Security Studies*, 13(4), 61–66.
Caplan, R. (2004). Partner or patron? International civil administration and local capacity–building. *International Peacekeeping*, 11(2), 229–247.
Centre d'Alerte et de Prévention des Conflits et le Centre de Recherche d'Etudes et de Documentatio en Sciences Sociales – CENAP/CREDESS–Bdi (2012)*Etude en besoins de sécurité au Burundi*. Bujumbura, Burundi.
Chandler, D. (2004). Imposing the 'rule of law': The lessons of BiH for peacebuilding in Iraq.*International Peacekeeping*, 11(2), 312–333.

Chandler, D. (2007). The security–development nexus and the rise of anti–foreign policy. *Journal of International Relations and Development*, *10*(4), 362–386.

Chappuis, F., and Hänggi, H. (2009). The interplay between security and legitimacy: Security sector reform and state–building. In J. Raue and P. Sutter (Eds.), *Facets and practices of state-building*. Leiden, The Netherlands: Martinus Nijhoff.

Chappuis, F., Kocak, D., and Schroeder, U. (2012). *Security governance transfers to areas of limited statehood: Comparing security sector reform in the Palestinian Territories, Liberia and Timor-Leste*. SFB Working Paper. Berlin, Germany: Freie Universität Berlin.

Chesterman, S. (2004). *You, the people: The United Nations, transitional administration, and state-building*. Oxford, UK: Oxford University Press.

Clément, C. (2009). SSR in the DRC. In H. Born and A. Schnabel (Eds.)*Security sector reform in challenging environments*. Münster, Germany: Lit Verlag, pp. 89–117.

Doyle, M. W. (2001). War making, peace making, and the United Nations: The United Nations' post–Cold War record. In C. Crocker, F. O. Hampson, and P. Aall (Eds.), *Turbulent peace: The challenges of managing international conflict*. Washington, DC: United States Institute of Peace, pp. 529–560.

Duff eld, M. (2001). *Global governance and the new wars: The merging of development and security*. New York, NY: Zed Books.

Duffield, M. (2007). *Development, security and unending war: Governing the world of peoples*. Cambridge, UK: Polity Press.

Ebo, A. (2006). The challenges and lessons of security sector reform in post–conflict Sierra Leone – Analysis *Conflict, Security & Development*, *6*(4), 481–501.

Ebo, A. (2008). Local ownership and emerging trends in SSR: A case study of outsourcing in Liberia. In T. Donais (Ed.), *Local ownership and security sector reform*. Münster, Germany: Lit Verlag, pp. 149–168.

Egnell, R., and Haldén, P. (2009). Laudable, ahistorical and overambitious: Security sector reform meets state formation theory. *Conflict, Security & Development*, *9*(1), 27–54.

Funaki, Y. (2009). *The UN and security sector reform in Timor-Leste: A widening credibility gap*. New York, NY: Center on International Cooperation.

Garrasi, D., Kuttner, S., and Wam, P. E. (2009).*The security sector and poverty reduction strategies.*.Washington, DC: Social Development Department.

Giustozzi, A. (2008). Shadow ownership and SSR in Afghanistan. In T. Donais (Ed.), *Local ownership and security sector reform*. Münster, Germany: Lit Verlag, pp. 215–232.

Goldsmith, A., and Dinnen, S. (2007). Transnational police building: Critical lessons from Timor–Leste and Solomon Islands. *Third World Quarterly*, *28*(6), 1091–1109.

Hänggi, H. (2004). Conceptualising security sector reform and reconstruction. In A. Bryden and H. Hänggi (Eds.), *Reform and reconstruction of the security sector*. Münster, Germany: Lit Verlag, pp. 3–18.

Hänggi, H., and Scherrer, V. (2008).*Security sector reform and UN integrated missions: Experience from Burundi, the Democratic Republic of Congo, Haiti and Kosovo*. Münster, Germany: Lit Verlag.

Hansen, A. (2002). *From Congo to Kosovo: Civilian police in peace operations*. Adelphi Papers. London, UK: Oxford University Press.

Hood, L. (2006). Missed opportunities: The United Nations, police service and defence force development in Timor–Leste, 1999–2004.*Civil Wars*, *8*(2), 143–162.

International Crisis Group. (2008). *Timor Leste: Security sector reform*. Asia Report 143. Brussels, Belgium: ICG.

International Crisis Group. (2012). *Beyond compromises: Reform prospects in Guinea-Bissau*. Africa Report 183. Brussels, Belgium: ICG.

Krause, K. (2006). *Towards a practical human security agenda*. DCAF Policy Paper 26. Geneva, Switzerland: DCAF.

Malan, M. (2008, March). *Security sector reform in Liberia: Mixed results from humble beginnings*. Strategic Studies Institute, U.S. Army War College, Pennsylvania.

McDougall, D. (2009). The failure of security sector reform to advance development objectives in East Timor and the Solomon Islands. In H. Born and A. Schnabel (Eds.), *Security sector reform in challenging environments*. Münster, Germany: Lit Verlag, pp. 171–197.

Mobekk, E. (2008). MINUSTAH and the need for a context–specific strategy: The case of Haiti. In H. Hänggi and V. Scherrer (Eds.),*Security sector reform and UN integrated missions: Experience from Burundi, the Democratic Republic of Congo, Haiti and Kosovo*. Münster, Germany: Lit Verlag, pp. 113–168.

Mobekk, E. (2009). Security sector reform and the UN mission in the Democratic Republic of Congo: Protecting civilians in the East. *International Peacekeeping*, *16*(2), 273–286.

Nathan, L. (2007). *No ownership, no commitment: A guide to local ownership of security sector reform*. Birmingham, UK: University of Birmingham.

N'Diaye, B. (2009). Security sector reform in the Central African Republic. In H. Born and A. Schnabel (Eds.), *Security sector reform in challenging environments*. Münster, Germany: Lit Verlag, pp. 39–66.

N'Diaye, B. (2012). The Central African Republic. In A. Bryden and V. Scherrer (Eds.), *Disarmament, demobilization and reintegration and security sector reform: Insights from UN experience in Afghanistan, Burundi, the Central African Republic and the Democratic Republic of the Congo*. Münster, Germany: Lit Verlag, pp. 143–180.

Observatoire de l'Afrique. (2008). *Security sector reform (SSR) in Guinea-Bissau*. Africa Briefing Report, 2 January. Brussels, Belgium: Observatoire de l'Afrique.

Ouattara, R. (2011). Cote d'Ivoire. In A. Bryden and B. N'Diaye (Eds.), *Security sector governance in francophone West Africa: Realities and opportunities*. Münster, Germany: Lit Verlag, pp. 73–94.

Paris, R. (2002). International peacebuilding and the 'mission civilisatrice'. *Review of International Studies*, 28(4), 637–656.

Paris, R. (2004). *At war's end: Building peace after civil conflict*. Cambridge, UK: Cambridge University Press.

Peake, G. (2009). A lot of talk but not a lot of action: The difficulty of implementing SSR in Timor-Leste In H. Born and A. Schnabel (Eds.), *Security sector reform in challenging environments*. Münster, Germany: Lit Verlag, pp. 213–238.

Peake, G., and Brown, K. S. (2005). Policebuilding: The international deployment group in the Solomon Islands. *International Peacekeeping*, 12(4), 520–532.

Perdan, S. (2008). Bosnia: SSR under international tutelage. In T. Donais (Ed.), *SSR and local ownership*. Münster, Germany: Lit Verlag, pp. 253–272.

Rumin, S. (2012). Burundi. In V. Scherrer and A. Bryden (Eds.)*Disarmament, demobilization and reintegration and security sector reform: Insights from UN experience in Afghanistan, Burundi, the Central African Republic and the Democratic Republic of the Congo*. Münster, Germany: Lit Verlag, pp. 71–114.

Scherrer, V. (2012). The Democratic Republic of Congo. In V. Scherrer and A. Bryden (Eds.)*Disarmament, demobilization and reintegration and security sector reform: Insights from UN experience in Afghanistan, Burundi, the Central African Republic and the Democratic Republic of the Congo*. Münster, Germany: Lit Verlag, pp. 143–177.

Scherrer, V., and Bryden, A. (Eds.). (2012). *Disarmament, demobilization and reintegration and security sector reform: Insights from UN experience in Afghanistan, Burundi, the Central African Republic and the Democratic Republic of the Congo*. Münster, Germany: Lit Verlag.

Scheye, E. (2008). UNMIK and the signifcance of effective programme management: The case of Kosovo. In V. Scherrer and H. Hänggi (Eds.), *Security sector reform and UN integrated missions: Experience from Burundi, the Democratic Republic of Congo, Haiti, and Kosovo*. Münster, Germany: Lit Verlag, pp. 169–228.

Sedra, M. (2006). Security sector reform in Afghanistan: The slide towards expediency. *International Peacekeeping*, 13(1), 94–110.

Sedra, M. (2007). Security sector reform in Afghanistan and Iraq: Exposing a concept in crisis. *Journal of Peacebuilding & Development*, 3(2), 7–23.

Sedra, M. (2012). Afghanistan. In V. Scherrer and A. Bryden (Eds.), *Disarmament, demobilization and reintegration and security sector reform: Insights from UN experience in Afghanistan, Burundi, the Central African Republic and the Democratic Republic of the Congo*. Münster, Germany: Lit Verlag, pp. 31–70.

Solhjell, R., Karlsrud, J., and Lie, J. H. S. (2010). *Protecting civilians against sexual and gender-based violence in Eastern Chad*. Oslo, Norway: Norwegian Institute of International Affairs.

Spence, D., and Fluri, P. (Eds.). (2008). *The EU and security sector reform*. London, UK: John Harper.

UNIPSIL (2012). *About UNIPSIL – History*. Available at: http://unipsil.unmissions.org

United Nations. (2004). *Second progress report of the Secretary-General on the United Nations Mission in Liberia*. 22 March. S/2004/229. New York, NY: United Nations.

Woodward, S. L. (2003). In whose interest is security sector reform? Lessons from the Balkans. In G. Cawthra and R. Luckham (Eds.), *Governing insecurity: Democratic control of military and security establishments in transitional democracies*. London, UK: Zed Books, pp. 276–302.

15
LIBERIA
Security sector reform

Morten Bøås and Samantha Gowran Farrier

Since the end of the Liberian civil war in 2003 the international community has been involved in various attempts at rebuilding the Liberian state. This process is regularly presented as a success and a showcase for what the United Nations (UN) and the international community can achieve together with local partners. It is, for example, argued that not only is the United Nations Mission in Liberia's (UNMIL) approach to security sector reform (SSR) a success as far as the technical benchmarks set by the international community have been met and that the country has been peaceful since the arrival of UNMIL, but also that the most successful aspects of the mission have been the political will for reform, local ownership and technical expert capacity (see interview with Rory Keane, UNMIL advisor on SSR, in Stadelmayer, 2011). The Liberian SSR has therefore supposedly taken place in partnership with the Liberian government. However, as a growing body of independent third-party research has shown, there is in fact little if any local ownership in this process (Ebo, 2005, 2007; Loden, 2007; Stig, 2009; Bøås and Stig, 2010; Andersen, 2010).

As a result, the democratic aspects of SSR in Liberia have become subordinated to an external governance of statebuilding, leading to a technical approach to statebuilding and SSR. In essence, what is taking place is that the international community is assuming governing functions, making the distinction between external and internal governance blurred for those not directly involved in the process. Furthermore, this is also blurring the obstacles to break, the dilemmas to be solved, and the historical background that should be considered in the SSR process. This is crucial as it leads to a lack of clarity concerning the measures that must be taken. In addition, it means that SSR becomes more of a concern for the international community than for the Liberian government and the country's population, as the international community assumes core state functions. These are, therefore, not only technical problems but fundamental issues that must be solved if we are to achieve a qualitatively better SSR in the form of democratic control of the process of reform of the Liberian police and army, and legitimate, trust-based rule of law in the security sector.

In practice, this means that, even if the SSR in Liberia has swiftly been moving forward, the degree of parliamentarian control and civil society involvement in the process is minimal. Institutions are built but the strengthening of local capacity to oversee and regulate the process and the new institutions being built has, to a large extent, been neglected. It is an ironic paradox that the international community expects local actors to govern in accordance with the principle of participatory democratic rule, while they themselves do not feel obligated to adhere to the very same principle.

This chapter will therefore show how the lack of transparency, accountability and participation of local actors leads to an alienation of the beneficiaries in the implementation phase of the SSR. This is highly problematic in itself, and particularly due to the Liberian history of social, economic and political exclusion and the prevailing polarized nature of the country's polity. The chapter elaborates on the consequences of this type of external governance, and how it affects the attempted statebuilding process. Based on this, we discuss why a people–centered approach is crucial if the obstacles to a better SSR are to be broken and the many dilemmas that must be confronted in such a process subsequently solved. There is undoubtedly a problem of local capacity as well as a lack of an incentive structure for local participation, and the national government of Ellen Johnson–Sirleaf should have been more proactive in putting in place a framework for this. However, this does not remove the responsibility of the international community to incorporate local actors into the SSR process, as it is, in essence, an integral part of the mission's mandate. Prior to these discussions we offer an introduction to the Liberian civil war and the Comprehensive Peace Agreement (CPA) that constitutes the background for the current international engagement in Liberia, as there is always a historical context that should be reflected in the implementation of SSR. Unfortunately for Liberia, the country's complicated past has by and large been neglected by the international agencies that have occupied the driver's seat in the SSR process.

Finally, it should also be noted that in spite of much talk about an end to the UNMIL mandate, it was extended yet again prior to the national elections in 2011. This time the extension was until 30 September 2012, with a total force of 9,206 uniformed personnel. Yet the withdrawal of UNMIL is related to the success of the SSR. Thus, the extension of the mandate only emphasizes the weaknesses within the reform of the security sector and the lack of sustainability due to issues of local ownership and capacity–building.

Understanding post-conflict Liberia: A historical context to be considered

To understand the context in which the peacebuilding operation and the subsequent SSR are taking place, it is necessary to comprehend the underlying dimensions that led to the civil war in 1989. The Liberian civil war is not an example of a 'new war.' Rather, its root causes are deeply embedded in its history (Bøås, 2010). It is a history of the destruction of both the state and social communities, gradually deteriorating during a struggle for recognition and inclusion in the national political economy. The war was brutal and destructive, but it also represented a possibility of freeing oneself and one's identity group from the state of exclusion that resulted from not being part of the groups in power (Huband, 1998; Ellis, 1999; Bøås, 2005; Utas, 2003). The war was therefore framed according to questions concerning how the country should be governed and resources distributed. During the rule of the True Whig Party (TWP), who governed the country exclusively as a one–party state for all but six years between 1870 and 1980, ethnicity was polarized and politicized, resulting in ethnic cleavages that further widened during the struggle for state power in the civil war (Huband, 1998; Ellis, 1999; Bøås, 2005).

The civil war has been analyzed through different perspectives, highlighting youth (Utas, 2003), elite manipulation and religion (Ellis, 1999), and belonging and identity related to citizenship and land rights (Bøås, 2005, 2008, 2010). This chapter follows primarily the latter perspective on the civil war – seeing conflicts over belonging, inclusion and exclusion as th primary underlying dimension of the war.

The Liberian conflict was therefore not just one war, but a series of conflicts tangled up each other, as Taylor's rebellion against Samuel Doe's dictatorship pushed the Liberian state over the edge and into the abyss. This 'nationalization' of local conflicts created a 'logic of the war that dramatically affected the course of the conflict and the subsequent militia formation (se Bøås and Hatløy, 2008). Even prior to the war, Liberia was characterized by corruption, political and economic violence, identity crises, generational and other group clashes, and widespread poverty. Local chiefs were incorporated into the structure of the TWP through a combination of brute force and neo-patrimonial indirect rule through district commissioners. This created a rural elite that cemented ethnic differences that through fosterage and intermarriage previously had a relatively flexible nature (see d'Azevedo, 1989). The result was a highly competitive patrimonial environment where various local elites were locked into struggles over state resources, often but not exclusively built on ethnic affiliation and exclusionary practices that formed th politics of control of state institutions as a zero-sum game (Bøås, 2009).

Such a neo-patrimonial system can be remarkably stable as long as the resources necessary to maintain the system are available. Until the 1970s, this was the case in Liberia. However, when President Tubman died in office in 1971, and the vice-president William Tolbert succeeded him, it became obvious that TWP's hegemony was becoming increasingly insecure. Tolbert's regime was just as corrupt as that of his predecessor, but lacked the ability and willingness to use coercion and patronage. Thus, when riots broke out in 1979, the stage was set for a regime change – which came in the form of a military coup led by Samuel Doe, a young officer of Krahn origin Initially the coup was well received among ordinary Liberians. However, it soon became obvious that the soldiers who had assumed control of the state were not able or willing to even attempt to dismantle the neo-patrimonial state. On the contrary, they themselves became captives of this logic. The result was a competitive relationship within the military regime, cementing the ethnicization of Liberian politics that had started with the administrative boundaries established by the TWP. Ethnicity therefore became even more politicized and polarized as the social construction of difference between the various groups increased. Samuel Doe's rule is most aptly summed up as a story of corruption, grand theft of state resources, murder, rape, torture and other human rights abuses. This prepared the ground for the civil war that started on Christmas Eve 1989 when the National Patriotic Front of Liberia (NPFL), a small rebel army led by Charles Taylor, crossed the border to Liberia from Côte d'Ivoire. Although the political economy of conflict that the war established created its own logic – in which war was both a way of life and a mode of production – the confict lines around which the war initially started remained present throughout the war and into the post-war period. Specif cally, the questions concerning what set of rights and obligations should underwrite a common Liberian identity remained a focal point for militia formation, and, as the elections in 2011 showed only too well, these issues have still not been properly addressed (Bøås, 2012).

Calling for international assistance and SSR: the blurring of the external and the internal

The framework for the Liberian SSR is constituted by articles VII and VIII in part four of the CPA and by UN resolution 1509 of 19 September 2003 (Jaye, 2006; Stig, 2009). Article VIII requested the UN police (UNPOL) to undertake the training of a new Liberian National Police (LNP), while article VII is concerned with the reconstruction of the Armed Forces of Liberia (AFL). The latter article stated that the Economic Community of West African States (ECOWAS), the UN, the African Union (AU), the International Crisis Group (ICG), and the United States (US) should be involved in the reconstruction of the army. However, as important as the reform of the army and the police was for the SSR process, it was the Liberian disarmament, demobilization, and reintegration (DDR) program that was the starting point of the SSR process even though the two components were not sufficiently linked

The DDR

In a post—conflict country, SSR and DDR should ideally be seen as interlinked components o the statebuilding project. In Liberia they have been approached as two separate processes (Bøås and Stig, 2010). Instead of taking the local context and the root causes of the conflict into seriou consideration, international actors have implemented an off—the—shelf solution to both DDR and SSR. In Liberia, the DDR should have laid the foundation for the SSR, but the failure to imple— ment this has heightened security threats due to unsuccessful reintegration (Bøås and Stig, 2010).

Thus, a fragmented approach to DDR has left gaps in the process. The initial UN estimate of ex—combatants identified to undergo the DDR process was 38,000. However, the actual number disarmed was 103,018, of whom only 13,873 participated in the reintegration and rehabilitation programmes (Jennings, 2007). Despite vocational training in the reintegration process, most ex—combatants are still unemployed. This is at least partly related to the poor vocational training offered to ex—combatants, as the skills they gained left them prepared for jobs that did not exist (Bøås and Bjørkhaug, 2010). Yet, despite the severe lack of trained security forces to meet the security threats in Liberia, the thousands of ex—combatants that already possess the skills needed for the security forces have not been used. The DDR program has therefore left many ex—combatants in a vulnerable position, and 'this suggests that DDR approaches are in dire need of a rethinking that links them more directly to programmes aimed at social cohesion and societal security' (Bøås and Bjørkhaug, 2010: 16).

The AFL

The US was asked to play the leading role in the reconstruction of the army. However, the intention was not that the US should take exclusive control of the process, as was the end result. The US outsourced the reform of the AFL to DynCorp, a private military company. This decision can clearly be questioned, as this type of privatization of security changes not only who controls the process of reform, but also by which means the reform is conducted (Avant, 2008). The reconstruction of the AFL by a private military corporation has to a large degree undermined the democratic credentials of the reform, excluding not only civil society and the legislature, but also the elected government (see also ICG, 2009). In line with the contract, DynCorp is only accountable to the US (Loden, 2007; Stig, 2009). Thus there is a situation whereby the private military corporation is not even accountable to the state for which it is reforming the military forces. This clearly represents a democratic deficit in the SSR. In addition, it raises question concerning the lack of transparency in the process since not even the Liberian Ministry of Defence has seen a copy of the contract.

However, in practice, the issue of promoting democratic governance in a post—conflict countr such as Liberia is not as easy as it may seem in theory. The Ministry of Defence, the legislature, and civil society have all had opportunities to involve themselves more in the reform than they have done, suggesting that the reform is proceeding as less of a closed process than previous research on the SSR has argued (Loden, 2007; Ebo, 2005, 2007). For example, during the process of recruitment, DynCorp met with civil society groups at the various locations of recruitment, and despite opportunities to join DynCorp on its recruitment tours, the Ministry of Defense took part only in the last recruitment tour, in May 2008. This is noteworthy since the recruitment process started in January 2006. Part of the explanation is the lack of incentives for local actors to follow the process more closely. Such a structure was simply not put in place, as it was assumed that this would happen automatically.

We also have to recognize the historical relationship between Liberia and the US. Compared to other countries, where private military corporations have been involved in similar processes, the involvement of DynCorp is not viewed as a democratic problem by the Liberian government or by the majority of the country's civil society organizations. From the government's point of view, the choice of the US to outsource the reform to a private company should not be questioned as it represents an opportunity to strengthen ties to the US so that Liberia can benefi from US military support in the future (Stig, 2009). Both the government and the people are insecure about the future and consequently express a dependency on external assistance to secure the peace. However, if US–Liberia history is a guide to the future this seems more a desire to remake Cold War elite linkages of patronage than a genuine belief that the US will come to the rescue if conflict arises again

Initially an AFL force of 6,000 soldiers was recommended. This number was later adjusted to 4,000, followed by the US decision to lower the benchmark further to 2,000, an estimate based on what American analysts believed the country could sustain economically (Ebo, 2005). The recruitment and training of a new 2,000–member Liberian army was completed in December 2009 (Human Rights Watch, 2011). Yet reports of misconduct and desertions due to poor living conditions for the soldiers are already emerging, raising concerns about the quality and sustainability of this part of the SSR. There are repeated reports of human rights abuses conducted by soldiers, and the poor salaries and the lack of a clear incentive structure seem to have eroded the commitment of some of the newly trained troops. In fact, it has been argued that many AFL members would not hesitate to leave the force if better opportunities became available elsewhere (ICG, 2011). If this is correct, it is worrying as the Mano River region is still volatile, as the aftershocks of the 2010 election crisis in Côte d'Ivoire and the flood of refugees into Liberi testify (see also Bøås, 2012).

The LNP

As previously mentioned, the reform of the LNP was stipulated in article VIII of the CPA that requested the UN police (UNPOL) to undertake the recruitment and training of a new LNP together with the Liberian government. UNPOL therefore has a half executive mandate; it is responsible for the recruitment and training of the LNP, while the government is responsible for appointing the leadership of the force.

UNPOL has in fact exceeded its technical benchmark of training a force of 3,500. As of August 2011, there were 4,153 newly trained police officers; however, UNPOL had to lowe its criteria for recruitment to reach this target,[1] and despite the benchmark being exceeded, the visibility of the LNP is still very low. Much of the focus has been concentrated on Monrovia, and the effectiveness of the force varies widely. Particular rural areas are still not only vulnerable to threats of violence and insecurity, but are also *de facto* without an operational police force. As a consequence, the new LNP is seen as little improvement in the eyes of many Liberians, and public confidence in the force remains low

The question of enhancing local ownership in the reform of the LNP is not straightforward. The leadership of the LNP is seen as the main problem in the institution today and, as previously highlighted, this is 'supposed' to be the responsibility of the Liberian government (Stig, 2009). As with the reform of the AFL, the focus has been on the technicalities of training a new force within a certain timeframe. The technical aspects of the SSR are addressed through external actors, while the political aspects have been left to the government. This corresponds to the mandate of the mission, but at the same time it is increasing the perception of intrusiveness by the international engagement since the political aspects have still not been properly addressed. It represents what seems to be a general tendency in international peacebuilding operations of prioritizing the efficiency of outputs over the effectiveness of output (Chandler, 2006; Nathan, 2007; Stig, 2009).

It is generally claimed by the international community that SSR can be successfully achieved in four to five years. However, building up an institution to contain both a new force and democratic governance takes longer. Since the 1990s, SSR has been an important activity in international statebuilding operations. As the Liberian case illustrates, SSR has come to resemble both a first and a last step in international statebuilding. Constructing new security forces is important in a country destabilized by years of civil war; it is an effort to stabilize the country and the state institutions that are being built. However, it is also an exit strategy for the international community, and, as pointed out in the 2008 UN progress report on Liberia, the withdrawal of UNMIL is related to success in the SSR.

Through the CPA of 2003, the UN was called on to facilitate a consolidated mission to Liberia (see CPA, 2003). The mandate for the operation was therefore authorized by the UN, but with the consent of the CPA. Thus, the fact that international actors had been called upon to exercise a degree of administration without being explicitly authorized to do so corresponds to how Chesterman (2004) defines a 'light footprint' model of intervention. This model implies that th intervention will not be too intrusive in form, but rather a partnership between the intervening powers and the national authorities. Yet, as we have seen, the intrusiveness of the international engagement is high in Liberia, even though it was supposed to be a light footprint mission.

This is problematic as the formal responsibility for the outcome lies not with the intervening powers that are conducting the reforms, but with the national authorities whom they have been called upon to assist (Chesterman, 2004; Stig, 2009), thus releasing the external actors from the criteria of participatory democratic governance. Most of the contemporary debate on external statebuilding operations is based on external interventions of a theoretically more intrusive nature (see Caplan, 2005; Chandler, 2002, 2006; Chesterman, 2004), yet the lack of local ownership and a people-centered approach in the SSR in Liberia suggests that the level of intrusiveness has become quite high. This is an intriguing aspect since the mandate of the mission frees the external actors involved in the SSR from the criteria of accountability for the outcome.

Conducting reforms that are accountable and transparent and include the beneficiaries of reform is crucial both for the future of self-government and as a means to ensure that the government of Liberia will be more inclusive in its future policy-making. As Nathan (2007) argues, local ownership has two imperatives in regard to the SSR. First, the reform should ensure that it reflects local needs and dynamics, and second, it should enhance the chances of con – solidating peace and democracy.

The obstacles and the dilemmas of external governance

As Bryden and Hänggi (2004) suggest, there are two core normative elements defining the concept of SSR: the creation of security bodies capable of providing security for the state and its people; and the development of democratic governance. This is in accordance with the def nition of peacebuilding that has been applied since the 1990s (see Boutros-Ghali, 1992; Paris, 2004). It combines the normative task of promoting democratic governance with statebuilding. However, in practice, instead of promoting democratic governance through the SSR in Liberia, the democratic aspects have rather been subordinated to external governance in the international community's approach to the reform process. This is making the type of democracy being promoted similar to what Mkandawire (1999) calls 'a choiceless democracy' and it is a way for the international community to avoid dealing with the root causes of conflict. This is a consequence of both the duration aspect of the mission and the mandate that followed with it. Thus, what was supposed to be a partnership of governance between the government of Liberia and external actors has developed into an uneven partnership.

The international community has followed a highly technical approach to SSR, where the political aspects have supposedly been left to the government. Still, it is the international actors that are defining what the competences of the state are – usually a tactic of governance reserve for the state (Foucault, 1991). This has made the partnership of governance more artificial, an blurs the distinction between the roles of the government in question and the external actors, making it difficult for the local actors to recognize who is actually governing what in the refor process. The government is getting the political blame for a policy that has not been particularly inclusive, in spite of the fact that the partnership of governance has been an uneven partnership for the government as well (Stig, 2009). This is due to a lack of knowledge of the governance structure of the SSR and it is connected to the lack of transparency in the reform process, indicating that the partnership of governance between the international community and the government to a large extent is a tacit one. This is a consequence of both the external approach to the SSR and the lack of local capacity.

Approaching SSR as a technical requirement, where elements in the process can be counted and quantified, corresponds theoretically with the hallmark of a light footprint mission, wher the degree of intrusiveness should be as minimal as possible. Yet the approach in Liberia has an intrusive character as it neglects the political reality of the context in which the international engagement is taking place. Reconstructing security institutions is an important aspect of security reform; it is vital for securing not only the state but also its people. However, as has been argued by UNPOL representatives, one needs someone at the receiving end that is capable and willing to take over the responsibility when the international community starts its withdrawal (Stig, 2009). Currently this capacity is lacking but at the same time, by not promoting local capacity in the government and legislature and among community leaders and civil society, the dependency on external actors has increased (Stig, 2009). This has undermined the capacity of the international community to provide incentives for local actors to get involved in the reform – incentives that should have been in place from the very beginning.

The lack of transparency, accountability, and participation of local actors has led to alienation of the very beneficiaries of the reform. Our argument is not that local actors immediately woul develop good practices, but they need to be empowered for the outcome to have any chance of being sustainable in the long run (Nathan, 2007; Stig, 2009). There is a lack of capacity at all levels of society that needs to be addressed to secure democratic self-governance after the international community's withdrawal. This fact underscores the importance of focusing not only on the technicalities of reform, but also on the political aspect of conducting transparent, accountable, and inclusive reforms, aiming at building the capacity of the leadership that is going to govern these institutions as well as the civil society to holds them accountable. Theoretically, a peacebuilding operation becomes more intrusive when external actors take on a political dimension as well. Yet, in the Liberian context, the peacebuilding operation seems to have become more intrusive through the very lack of a well-defined political agenda

Even though there are both technical and political problems in the security institutions, it is the political problems that risk undermining the institutions, and thereby also the entire peacebuilding process. These are political problems of democratic governance, related to the experiences of actors in different communities in post-conflict Liberia, which are not heard o listened to. These ideas and experiences are not necessarily political in the traditional Western sense, but they are certainly political in the local communities (Bøås, 2008). This is a crucial dimension to be aware of since there is a significant difference between the formal reality o rebuilding security institutions and the informal reality in which they are being rebuilt (Stig, 2009). The problem is that Liberia has never existed as a prototypical Western state. As Bøås and Jennings (2005) have pointed out, trying to rebuild something that never existed is problematic, especially when the approach does not comprehend the context in which it is being implemented. Trying to achieve this with a state is extremely difficult when a people−centered focus is missing Liberia is still highly polarized, and the root causes of the civil war have not been adequately addressed. If the capacity to govern the reformed institutions is not built, not much will have been achieved, and if the polarized nature of society, and the divisions that led to the outbreak of civil war in the first place, are not addressed, these divisions will continue to represent a securit challenge.

In the UN−led peacebuilding operation, there is a gap between how the institutional focus of the SSR is being implemented and how the security situation is experienced on the ground. There are still severe security challenges in need of being addressed since the root causes of the conflict are still apparent, especially the experience of alienation and insecurity in local com− munities − particularly in the hinterland. In a society like Liberia, where it historically has been impossible to rely on the state as an impartial provider of security, informal security arrangements have been established (see also Utas, 2012). These arrangements are more evident in the rural areas as compared to Monrovia, and they are to a large extent based on social constellations of identity. This is problematic, since this feeds land disputes that are following ethnic and tribal lines, reinforcing identity as a potential dimension for future conflict. It increases the importanc of addressing the security challenges in these communities and including these local actors in the development of the new security architecture. By alienating local actors from the process of reform, their socioeconomic basis of security is also weakened, thus increasing the importance of informal security arrangements (Obi, 2005; Stig, 2009).

SSR in a post−conflct setting is supposed to be a part of the development of an effective and overarching governance framework (Bryden and Hänggi, 2004). However, the SSR in Liberia lacks a holistic perspective, which is needed especially since the identity dimension − so apparent in the local communities − is also causing problems in the LNP and the AFL. Civilians, especially in the hinterland, are still experiencing discrimination by police officers on the basis of ethni group, and ethnic tensions have surfaced between recruits in the new army (Stig, 2009). No real change seems to have taken place in the new LNP, and the results of the reform of the AFL are, as we have seen, none too promising. The SSR has focused on rebuilding legitimate forces by reconstituting the AFL and vetting and reconstructing the LNP. However, legitimate forces cannot be achieved by exclusively focusing on these institutions. The problems go upward to the leadership and downward to the communities from where the recruits are drawn, leading to the conclusion that the SSR is undermining itself as a peacebuilding activity by its lack of focus on the local perspective of security and the political reality in which the reform is taking place. In accordance with Nathan's (2007) two imperatives of local ownership, a higher degree of local involvement in the process could have improved the correspondence between the SSR and local needs and dynamics. It could have diminished the gap between the external approach of the SSR and the civilian experience of security and it could have made the process of policy imple− mentation more transparent. Furthermore, it would improve the chances of consolidating peace and democracy. Instead, the peacebuilding operation is at risk of resulting in a virtual peace, since the notion of security − and thereby what secures the peace − is considered differently by local actors and the international community (Richmond, 2004; Stig, 2009).

A feeling of dependency on international actors is felt in Liberia, based on the acknowledgment that the root causes of conflict still exist. These must be addressed if one is to ensure that th problems of the past do not return to haunt the future. The argument by Chandler (2002), Ignatieff (2003), and Richmond (2004) that governance has evolved into a notion of peace as governance corresponds to how the international presence is experienced as securing the peace. This is not positive for the long−term sustainability of the Liberian peace, as it only prolongs the dependency on external actors, thus underscoring our argument that the level of intrusiveness caused by the international engagement is high, contradicting its aim of being a light footprint mission.

Conclusion

Security sector reform is supposedly part of a broader peacebuilding framework, yet in practice it is being approached in an isolated fashion. In Liberia, the SSR lacks the holistic orientation that is needed for success to be possible. The reform has reached its technical benchmarks of reforming the forces; however, the political aspects of the reform have been neglected and a people−centeredapproach is totally missing. Even though the international community expects the government of Liberia to govern in accordance with the principles of democratic governance, these principles are lacking in the SSR. Yet the formal responsibility for the outcomes lies not with the international actors, who are conducting the reforms, but with the national authorities they have been called to assist. What was supposed to be a partnership of governance between the international community and the government has become uneven. The SSR has not proceeded as a transparent, accountable, and inclusive process, making the governance structure unclear for those who are not involved in it. The lack of local capacity to be involved in the process underlines the importance of conducting reforms that are transparent, accountable, and facilitate civic engagement, in addition to participation of the government and the legislature. By not conducting transparent and inclusive reforms, the statebuilding operation is fostering the very same experience of exclusion and polarization that has charactezised the Liberian state since its foundation.

Even though the institutions of the LNP and the AFL have been reformed, the main challenges to the SSR remain the same. As we have argued throughout this chapter, the main problems in the LNP and the AFL exist both at the leadership level and on the community level, where the new police force and army are recruited. The same problems that are manifested in the communities are reflected in the new institutions. The root causes that led to the civil war i the first place are still present, increasing the perception of insecurity and maintaining the polarize nature of Liberian society. The UN mandate in Liberia has been extended several times, but sooner or later the UN will start its full withdrawal, leading us to the conclusion that Liberia will be left to its own destiny with the root causes of the civil war mainly ignored.

Plans were made for Liberia without considering the situation on the ground – subsequently, the policy implementation of the SSR has proceeded in the same manner. The efficiency o output has been prioritized, while the effectiveness of output has been neglected. This has affected how the peacebuilding operation – supposed to be a light footprint model – has become quite intrusive, enhancing the dependency of the external engagement and causing problems for the future sustainability of self−reliant democratic government and governance. The Liberian government could have undoubtedly done more to become involved in the process, but in a country like Liberia such involvement cannot be taken for granted, meaning that the international community bears a strong responsibility for not providing the framework for genuine local participation in the SSR.

Note

1   This includes 620 Police Support Unit off cers and 332 Emergency Response Unit off cers. Female members of the LNP currently stand at about 16 per cent.

References

Andersen, L. R. (2010). Outsiders inside the state: Post−conflict Liberia between trusteeship and partnership. *Journal of Intervention and Statebuilding*, *4*(2), 129–152.

Avant, D. (2008). *Opportunistic peacebuilders? International organizations, private military training and state-building after war*. Discussion draft for Research Partnership on Postwar State−Building. Available at: reliefweb.int

Bøås, M. (2005). The Liberian civil war: New war/old war? *Global Society*, *19*(1), 73–88.

Bøås, M. (2008). Funérailles pour un ami: des luttes de citoyenneté dans la guerre civile libérienne. *Politique Africaine*, *112*, 36–51.

Bøås, M. (2009). Making plans for Liberia – A trusteeship approach to good governance. *Third World Quarterly*, *30*(7), 1329–1341.

Bøås, M. (2010). Militia formation and the nationalisation of local conflict in Liberia. In K. Mulaj (Ed.) *Violent non-state actors in contemporary world politics*. London, UK: Hurst, pp. 257–276.

Bøås, M. (2012). Liberia: Elections – No quick fix for peacebuilding. *New Routes*, *1*, 15–17.

Bøås, M., and Bjørkhaug, I. (2010). *DDRed in Liberia*. Brighton, UK: MICROCON.

Bøås, M., and Hatløy, A. (2008). Getting in, getting out: Militia membership and prospects for re−integration in post−war Liberia. *Journal of Modern African Studies*, *46*(1), 33–53.

Bøås, M., and Jennings, K. M. (2005). Insecurity and development: The rhetoric of the failed state. *European Journal of Development Research*, *17*(3), 385–395.

Bøås, M., and Stig, K. (2010). Security Sector Reform in Liberia: An uneven partnership without local ownership. *Journal of Intervention and Statebuilding*, *4*(3), 285–303.

Boutros−Ghali, B. (1992). *An agenda for peace: Preventive diplomacy, peacemaking and peace-keeping*. Report by the UN Secretary−General. New York, NY: United Nations.

Bryden, A., and Hänggi, H. (2004). *Reform and reconstruction of the security sector*. Münster, Germany: LIT Verlag.

Caplan, R. (2005). *International governance of war-torn territories*. New York, NY: Oxford University Press.

Chandler, D. (2002). *From Kosovo to Kabul: Human rights and international intervention*. London, UK: Pluto Press.

Chandler, D. (2006). *Empire in denial: The politics of statebuilding*. London, UK: Pluto Press.

Chesterman, S. (2004). *You, the people: The United Nations, transitional administration and state-building*. Oxford, UK: Oxford University Press.

CPA (2003). *Comprehensive Peace Agreement between the Government of Liberia and the Liberians United for Reconciliation and Democracy (LURD) and the Movement for Democracy in Liberia (MODEL) and Political Parties*. Accra, Ghana, August 18. Available at: www.usip.org

d'Azevedo, W. (1989). Tribe and chiefdom on the windward coast. *Liberian Studies Journal*, *14*(2), 90–116.

Ebo, A. (2005). *The challenges and opportunities of security sector reform in post-conflict Liberia*. Occasional Paper no. 9. Geneva, Switzerland: Geneva Centre for Democratic Control of Armed Forces.

Ebo, A. (2007). Liberia case study: Outsourcing SSR to foreign companies. In L. Nathan (Ed.), *Local ownership of security sector reform: A guide for donors*. Commissioned by the Security Sector Reform Strategy of the UK's Global Conf ict Prevention Pool, London, UK. Available at: www2.lse.ac.uk

Ellis, S. (1999). *The mask of anarchy*. London, UK: Hurst.

Foucault, M. (1991). Governmentality. In G. Burchell, C. Gordon, and P. Miller (Eds.), *The Foucault effect: Studies in governmentality*. Chicago, IL: Chicago University Press, pp. 87–104.

Huband, M. (1998). *The Liberian Civil War*. London, UK: Frank Cass.

Human Rights Watch (2011). *World Report 2011: Liberia*. New York, NY: Human Rights Watch.

ICG (2009). *Liberia: Uneven progress in security sector reform*. Brussels, Belgium: ICG.

ICG (2011). *Liberia: How sustainable is the recovery?* Brussels, Belgium: ICG.

Ignatieff, M. (2003). *Empire lite: Nation-building in Bosnia, Kosovo and Afghanistan*. London, UK: Vintage.

Jaye, T. (2006). *An assessment report on security sector reform*. Paynesville, Liberia: The Governance Commission of Liberia.

Jennings, K. (2007). The struggle to satisfy: DDR through the eyes of ex−combatants in Liberia. *International Peacekeeping*, *14*(2), 204–218.

Loden, A. (2007). Civil society and security sector reform in post−conflict Liberia: Painting a moving trai without brushes. *International Journal of Transitional Justice*, *1*, 297–307.

Mkandawire, T. (1999). Crisis management and the making of choiceless democracies. In R. Joseph (Ed.), *State, conflict and democracy in Africa*. Boulder, CO: Lynne Rienner, pp. 119–136.

Nathan, L. (Ed.). (2007). *Local ownership of security sector reform: A guide for donors*. Commissioned by the Security Sector Reform Strategy of the UK's Global Conflict Prevention Pool, London, UK. Availabl at: www2.lse.ac.uk

Obi, C. (2005). Conflict and peace in West Africa. *News from the Nordic Africa Institute, 1*, 2–5.
Paris, R. (2004). *At war's end: Building peace after civil conflict.* New York, NY: Cambridge University Press.
Richmond, O. P. (2004). UN peace operations and the dilemmas of the peacebuilding consensus. *International Peacekeeping, 11*(1), 83–101.
Stadelmayer, L. (2011). *SSR Resource Centre interviews Rory Keane, UNMIL Advisor on Security Sector Reform.* New York, NY: CIGI.
Stig, K. (2009). *Promoting self-governance without local ownership: A case study of the security sector reform in Liberia.* MA thesis, University of Oslo, Oslo, Norway.
Utas, M. (2003). *Sweet battlefields: Youth and the Liberian Civil War.* Stockholm, Sweden: Lindholm & Co.
Utas, M. (2012). Introduction: Bigmanity and network governance in African conflicts. In M. Utas (Ed.) *African conflicts and informal power: Big men and networks.* London, UK: Zed, pp. 1–31.

16
MAINTAINING THE POLICE–MILITARY DIVIDE IN POLICING PEACE

B. K. Greener and W. J. Fish

This chapter begins by outlining the practical considerations that have led to military personnel being tasked with roles in peace and stability operations that, traditionally, would be squarely in the domain of civilian police. It then discusses both practical and theoretical reasons as to why this is a concerning trend. We argue that the goals of peace and stability operations are more readily achievable if the traditional police–military divide is respected as much as possible. Given this, we suggest that the urge to resign ourselves to the military being the 'least worst option' (Keller, 2010) for policing is premature. Instead, we outline some initial suggestions for practical and operationally oriented guidelines for police and military personnel that provide a way of meeting the need for policing in peace and stability operations while remaining faithful to the police–military divide.

Expanding mandates

As the mandates for peace, stability, and statebuilding missions have broadened and deepened, so has the requirement to undertake what, in the domestic environment, would be considered policing tasks. Instances of policing in such operations can involve primarily supporting roles such as monitoring, training, mentoring, capacity building, or programs to 'reform, rebuild, and restructure' existing police capabilities, through to more assertive executive policing roles where there is a mandate in place that allows for external police to have the power of arrest in situations where local law and order has broken down (Greener, 2009). However, despite these being tasks that, in the domestic environment, would be performed by civilian police, in recent operations military personnel have at times been tasked with some of these policing functions.

The United States in particular has demonstrated a willingness to utilize military personnel in undertaking policing functions. For example, in Kosovo at the turn of the twenty–first centur the US used its military police (MPs) as a constabulary–type force.[1] Though initially they were only tasked with traditional roles such as military traffic control, area security, and prisoner–of war operations, the roles of US MPs were increased to encompass deterring looting and other crimes; running police stations and detention centers; facilitating the return of refugees; and maintaining responsibility for law and order in particular sectors (Jayamaha et al., 2010: 115). Even the fundamental tasks of police training, mentoring, and institutional reform have increasingly been undertaken by US military personnel in recent years – particularly in the missions to

Iraq and Afghanistan. Here, for example, the US 2nd Stryker Cavalry Regiment unit mentored Afghan National Police (ANP) in Zabul, while MPs, Marines, Army, and Air Force personnel have undertaken similar training or mentoring roles while embedded alongside contracted civilian personnel in Iraqi Police Transition Teams (PTTs) or National Police Transition Teams (NPTTs) (Knickmeyer, 2005).[2] The involvement of MPs and other military personnel in policing roles has therefore seen the US military playing 'a key role in law enforcement and related issues, even if not specifically tasked with a law enforcement mandate' (Jayamaha et al., 2010: xii). Moreover in addition to US engagement, other national contingents such as the 1st Battalion Scots Guard have also undertaken mentoring for the ANP while military personnel in many other jurisdictions have increasingly focused on developing less than lethal and public order maintenance training to help police peace and stability operations. For example, prior to deploying to the Solomon Islands to support election security, Australian and New Zealand Defence Force personnel were given extra training in crowd control responses. Public order maintenance is now typically a part of contemporary military training for peace and stability operations.

There are a number of reasons for this trend toward the use of military personnel for policing in international peace, stability, and statebuilding operations, but there are also, as this chapter will outline, a number of both practical and normative concerns with this. This leaves us with a dilemma: how best to ensure that the policing roles in peace and stability operations are carried out in an appropriate manner. Some commentators have suggested that using the military is the 'least worst option' (Keller, 2010) when it comes to resolving this dilemma, but we will argue that this is premature.

Why military personnel have been used for policing

There are three main reasons as to why MPs and military personnel have been used to undertake policing or policing-type roles in peace operations.

Deployability issues

The issue of getting enough police on the ground in a timely manner continues to bedevil the planners of peace missions. In Africa in 2009, for example, the UN Security Council (UNSC) had authorized the use of 6,400 police for the UN–AU Hybrid Operation in Darfur (UNAMID), but less than half that number were in situ within a year of that mandate (Williams, 2009). Indeed, missions more generally often do not reach the mandated numbers of police. This is a product of the primary purpose of civilian police – policing the domestic environment – which means that such police are typically already being well employed. The decision to remove police personnel from their typical domestic roles to be deployed abroad is therefore both practically difficult in terms of the numbers available (usually there are no 'spare' police to be sent offshore without loss to capability at home) as well as politically difficult in that it may have political ramifcations if governments are not able to provide for law and order at home and/or if a police officer were to get injured or killed while overseas. Considerable resourcing and planning is required to release civilian police from their home environment, meaning that those attempting to organize deployments continue to struggle to get enough police promptly into the field. Th creation of national or regional deployment pools of international police in some areas has helped relieve some of the pressure, but quantity continues to be a factor that inhibits the use of civilian police in international operations.

This issue of 'not enough police' therefore impacts on the ability to police in peace operations with civilian police. Yet of course militaries are primed to deploy personnel in larger units with expeditionary capabilities and have such personnel ready and waiting for service.[3] The fact that military personnel can deploy quickly and in large numbers (or indeed are already in situ) has been a significant rationale for their increased involvement in policing in peace and stability operations.

Permissibility issues

The complex nature of post–conflict environments has also been a motivating factor in the increased involvement of military personnel in policing or policing–type activities. Contemporary peace operations can involve significant levels of civil disorder, often involving armed protagonists. In addition to the problem of getting enough police to deploy, then, the complex nature of peace operations has also created concerns about whether or not civilian police can in fact operate safely and successfully in more difficult or 'hotter' security situations (Bayley and Perito 2010). After all, police are civilians in uniform. Concerns over the safety of such civilian police and subsequent risk–aversion policies have at times encouraged military involvement in policing if civilian police are unable to, unwilling to, or forbidden to operate in 'non–permissive' environments.

Due to this capability gap, some military police units have begun to position themselves as possible sources of policing in difficult situations, increasingly orienting themselves toward th potential for policing in less permissive environments. For example, previously known for their main role in policing the military and for specialist capabilities such as traffic control or clos personnel protection, the Australian First Military Police Battalion's tactical briefng now asserts that 'The foundations of [the Battalion's] prof ciency are the technical aspects of policing, and the *combat survivability required to execute policing tasks where the operational uncertainty precludes or restricts operations by civilian police*' (First Military Police Battalion, 2010; emphasis added).

Military personnel are also, depending on specialization and service, well trained, equipped, and prepared for operating in non–permissive environments. In addition to this, discussions with personnel have highlighted the wide range of capabilities that exist across different services that might also be relevant to the possibility of policing less permissive environments. For example, communication and diplomatic skill sets are strong among naval personnel who must frequently host ship visits, and Air Force air security personnel may have helpful dog–handling or static protection capabilities, in addition to the more obviously tailored community–engagement skills such as those developed by Army CIMIC specialists. Indeed, the demands of contemporary military operations have encouraged the development of such a diverse array of capabilities and skills within military forces – highlighting the fact that military forces everywhere have had to undertake signif cant changes in recent years to try to meet those challenges.

Military modifications

Recent military missions have often involved concurrent humanitarian aid, disaster relief, counter–terrorism, and/or counter–insurgency (COIN) operations. Military personnel have therefore had to be increasingly flexible in their approach to these operations given their com plexity. The need to detain and question suspected combatants combined with the concurrent need to win hearts and minds in a COIN situation, for example, has meant that military personnel have had to be more nuanced in how they engage with local populations. In addition to specif operational demands, moreover, broader normative changes within international affairs have meant that there is a more general 'pressure to treat foreign civilians as individuals with rights rather than as enemies on a battlefield' (Andreas and Price, 2001: 48). Contemporary operation have therefore, among other things, necessitated a stronger understanding and application of the rule of law than in previous times (Walzer, 1992: 42). In light of this changing character of military operations General Kilcullen has therefore suggested that many contemporary military operations are 'less like conventional warfare and more like police work: cops patrolling a beat to prevent violent crime' (Kilcullen, 2009: 130).

In addition to this, many military forces are subject to additional shaping processes such as civilianization, equal opportunity policies, outsourcing, and subcontracting within a domestic setting (Caforio, 2003). These types of process have created more permeability between the military and civilian worlds, helping to demystify the role of military forces, altering how the military is perceived and received by society, and de-emphasizing traditional tenets of military life – including hierarchy (Moskos, 2000). Military forces are therefore becoming less distinct from other state agents. However, although such changes may mean that there has been some 'police-ization' of the military, this does not make military personnel into police – just as militarization of police does not make them military. Police are still the only sworn agents of the law at play, and there are therefore a number of strong conceptual reasons as to why using military personnel in policing roles is problematic.

Conceptual reasons as to why using military personnel is problematic

It is a central plank of liberal-democratic notions of statehood that militaries and police forces have different purposes. Militaries are agents of the government to be used as an instrument of statecraft; police are agents of the law to be used to secure the public interest. Police (at least in the Anglo-Peelian tradition) are personnel who operate by the principle of consent with minimum use of force; military forces, on the other hand, embody the state's coercive and lethal capacities. These differences give us the heart of the traditional police-military distinction. Using military personnel for policing tasks seriously undermines this distinction, which is why liberal-democratic states are reluctant to use the military to perform police tasks in the domestic environment. Yet these same considerations apply to the use of the military to perform police tasks internationally, particularly in situations where international statebuilding efforts are attempting to create and support liberal democratic policies and practices.

Using civilian police for internal security roles is symbolically important in a number of ways. As noted, a central feature of civilian police forces is that they operate by the principle of consent. So for liberal-democratic policing to take place, the force doing the policing needs to be seen as legitimate by those being policed. This has a number of important consequences. It is first of al important from the point of view of the outside agencies involved in peace and stability operations not being seen as being overly imperialistic by citizens of the host nation. The use of military to undertake police roles has the potential to look like a case of 'imperial policing' (as argued by Rubenstein, 2010). The use of military personnel to perform policing functions is a more overtly political statement than using police and, in post-confct environments in which these functions are played by outsiders, the regular use of the military in frontline policing runs the risk of making the population feel as though they are under occupation. Perhaps most importantly, the question of legitimacy is critical in terms of the likelihood of a local civilian police force persisting in situ, and therefore to the ability of interveners to exit from peace operations. If this legitimacy is threatened by a confusion of military and policing roles and functions in a post-conflict society by either or both the interveners and the host government, the chances for a lasting and sustainable peace are considerably diminished.

In addition to the legitimacy of the international force charged with policing during the operation, we also need to bear in mind the legitimacy of the police force that is to be left behind.

Using civilian police for policing is therefore also important from the point of view of not blurring the police–military divide in either (a) the type of policing promoted or (b) the type of police–military relationship advocated for local forces. In the first instance, for example, overl militarized approaches to training local police forces (including the mentoring of police officer by members of the military) can lead to the police force itself taking on militaristic features and militaristic priorities (Bayley and Perito, 2010; Mobekk, 2005; Sedra, 2006). In the case of Iraq, Robert Perito (2011: 13) has argued that:

> Militarization of the police will produce a force that is inconsistent with the country's long-termneeds. Assigning responsibility for training Iraq's police to the U.S. military produced a highly militarized force with little ability to enforce the rule of law.

Training by the military is likely to be 'oriented towards the elimination of an enemy threat and inherently engenders a much more militaristic attitude in civilian police bodies' (Campbell and Campbell, 2010: 331). This is problematic because more militaristic styles of policing inhibit trust and confidence, making the whole peacebuilding or statebuilding project more tenuous. Usin military personnel to carry out police tasks while attempting to deescalate and demilitarize societies therefore has the potential to be damagingly counterproductive when the long-term goals of such operations are kept in mind.

Instead, the institutionalization of a civilian police force that supports, protects and serves the local population well is key to broader democratic or human rights–centered approaches to the political and social situation at hand. Mercedes Hinton and Tim Newburn (2009) have noted in their work on policing developing democracies that those who have conf dence in rules and public authorities are likely to be more willing to be voluntarily compliant with the laws of the state. Questions of who can or should undertake policing tasks therefore relate to fundamental political issues regarding the nature of democracy and society. A key impediment to implementing democratic policing in post conflict countries has been the effort to utilize police to assist militarie in such a way that ignores the division of labor between security forces in democratic societies (Wiatrowski and Goldstone, 2010: 82).

Most fundamentally, then, the police service in situ, in addition to not being overly militarized in its approach, needs to be kept distinct from the military for significant political reasons. Def nitions of modern liberal democratic statehood rest on a number of assumptions. One of these is that, if there are military forces in situ, there is to be a clear separation of internal and external security. Internal, domestic security is to be provided for by civilian police forces while external, international security is to be provided for by military forces (Greener and Fish, 2011). There has been some blurring of this boundary through the processes of militarization of police and 'police-ization' of the military, but this distinction remains an important indicator of a liberal democratic polity. This is because the military is, in such liberal democratic entities, to be kept distant from internal matters – from political affairs in particular – to ensure that political decisions are not made on the basis of violence or coercion. Fostering public trust in civilian policing requires strong limits on the role of the military in internal security (Friesendorf, 2012).

There are therefore a number of weighty conceptual reasons to be wary of international military personnel playing a wider role in training and mentoring police forces, or in encouraging or allowing for a close working relationship between local police and military forces. There are also a number of relevant additional practical concerns.

Practical concerns over military undertaking police roles

In discussions with military, military police and civilian police personnel from Australia and New Zealand, significant disquiet regarding the use of military in law enforcement–type tasks was expressed from all sides. While the military may be in situ with useful capabilities, policing activities are *not* their core business. In addition to broader normative concerns, then, there are very practical reasons to be concerned about military personnel undertaking policing tasks.

Policing skills and mindsets are developed over time and then consolidated on a daily basis through the activities, interactions and ongoing training of police personnel – such skills or mindsets cannot be internalized quickly; rather this process takes some time to embed in order to result in a maturity of approach toward complex issues. Indeed, as Friesendorf (2012) has noted, military personnel and civilian police remain distinct in at least six main ways: material, educational, cultural, legal, organizational, and operational. Most relevant here are the differences in educational and operational characteristics, as military personnel focus on combat and how to deal with hostile foes versus police who focus on prevention, the investigation of crime, and the differences in legal characteristics. As the UN DPKO (2009: 64) notes:

> Military and police use force for different purposes in peacekeeping operations. The military uses force to deter or remove a security threat from armed forces or groups, while the police use force to arrest civilians and address criminal behaviour. The use of force by military and police are therefore also governed by different sources of law (the military is governed by humanitarian law and the police by human rights and domestic criminal law).

In addition to these general sites of difference, there are specific skills or foci that police utiliz in the field that are particularly relevant in post–conflict peace operations and that military personnel do not have. The military experience in Afghanistan, for example, demonstrated that some basic policing skill sets are simply lacking, with military personnel 'especially weak in the areas of monitoring, procedures, and record–keeping or continuity' (Fishstein, 2010: 28). These types of consideration suggest that there remain difficulties for the military in undertaking certai active policing roles if these are not their routine or core tasks.

Such considerations have led US Deputy Judge Advocate General Charles J. Dunlap Jr to claim that there are 'surprisingly few synergies between law enforcement and military missions,' and to suggest that 'using military forces for tasks that are essentially law enforcement requires a fundamental change in orientation' (Dunlap, 2005: 790–791). Likewise, General Wesley Clark contends that 'experience in peace operations has proven that good soldiers, no matter how well equipped, trained, organised and led cannot fully perform police duties among local populations' (cited in Smith, 1999: A17). Military officers in the European context and elsewhere around th world have expressed additional practical concerns about military personnel undertaking policing roles, worrying that this will 'detract from more critical missions, degrade military capabilities and morale, and create situations for which soldiers are not trained and equipped' (Friesendorf and Penska, 2008: 677).

The dilemma

As we have seen, there are technical and political problems with attempts to get enough civilian police into the field in a timely manner to undertake international policing tasks. Yet militar personnel are available in larger numbers in good time, with expeditionary capabilities to be able to move as required. Moreover, they are also increasingly training for and focusing on dealing with complex environments. This has led some authors, such as Keller, to suggest that using military personnel for policing tasks is the 'least worst option' (for the US at least).

Keller recognizes that 'using military personnel to train and advise civilian police is being justifiably criticized. Military personnel, even military police, are not prepared to train and advise civilian police in most tasks' (Keller, 2010: viii). However, given that the US does not have the capability to field enough civilian police for international deployments, he has argued (2010: vii that:

> the U.S. military must be prepared to support stability operations at regional level and below by assessing, advising, and even training police units [and that] instruction in such normative principles as responsiveness to the community, accountability to the rule of law, defense of human rights, and transparency to scrutiny from the outside, must be institutionalized.

Yet we have also seen reasons to think that encouraging an increased use of military personnel in such roles is far from an ideal solution to this dilemma, and may even be damagingly counter–productive. An alternative solution – a solution that is more in tune with general liberal–democratic ideals and principles – would be to (a) investigate ways in which the deployability problems outlined above might be lessened, and (b) work out a clearer division of responsibility between police and military in post–conflict environments to ensure that we make the best, an safest, use of those civilian police that are able to be deployed.

In the remainder of this chapter, we focus on investigating the second of these two dimensions. Given the permissibility issues discussed above, we recognize that some military involvement might be required to *support* law enforcement, but believe that these roles need to be clearly defined and understood prior to deployment, and any doctrinal developments must reflect a understanding that military and police roles and taskings are different for a reason.

Doctrinal developments

The UN has recently developed clearer guidelines for police and military taskings in UN operations. UN guidelines for its peace operations state that both troop contributing countries (TCCs) and police contributing countries (PCCs) should be guided by the tasks assigned by the Security Council mandate, the concept of operations (CONOPS) and accompanying mission Rules of Engagement (ROE) for the military component, and the Directives on the Use of Force (DUF) for the police component in order to establish a suitable police–military operational relationship (UN DPKO, 2008: 14; 2009: 25).

ROE and DUF should clearly outline the different levels of force that can be used in various circumstances, how each level of force should be used, and any authorizations that must be obtained by commanders, and mission leadership should ensure that these ROE and DUF are well understood by all relevant personnel in the mission and are being applied uniformly such that the 'credibility and freedom of action' of the UN field mission is upheld in the implementation of its mandate (UN DPKO, 2008: 35). These ROE and DUF evolve out of separate military and police CONOPS, which are strategic planning documents that outline the 'key security objectives, requirements and tasks' of military and police as per their role in fulfihg the UN mandate, which are developed predominantly by the Military Planning Service and the Police Division of DPKO, and which may be augmented by additional documentation such as a Military Operations Plan ('Operation Order') (UN DPKO, 2009: 26).

In terms of command and control, military and civilian police remain under established command and control – the Secretary General's Special Representative/Head of Mission (HOM) must approve the use of military and civilian police for non-security-related tasks, although efforts to plan and coordinate with regard to humanitarian needs rests with the Humanitarian Coordinator. More specifically, the Head of Military Component (HOMC) exercises 'UN operational control,' may delegate 'UN tactical control' of military personnel to subordinate military commanders, and may also be the HOM in 'traditional' missions. The Head of Police Component (HOPC) similarly exercises 'UN Operational Control,' may delegate specific authority to individual officers and to FPUs through their commanding officer, and is 'normal appointed' as the mission Police Commissioner (UN DPKO, 2009: 42). Significantly, recen UN peacekeeping training material stresses the importance of military, police, and civilian personnel *all* understanding the 'main tasks and functions of the different components in a mission' (UN DPKO, 2009: 46). The main tasks of military and police, the training material suggests, can be described as in Table 16.1.

More specifically, military functions and activities have been denoted as security sector involvement and provision of secure environment (through patrolling, establishing and operating checkpoints, securing major routes to facilitate mobility, securing key facilities such as hospitals and power plants). Police functions and activities have been described as restoration of the rule of law; reform of host country police services; vetting, training, and mentoring of host police; providing public order and responding to public security challenges (through static guards and close protection for dignitaries, preventive patrols and checkpoints, tactical support for high-risk operations, security for demonstrations, etc); and provision of executive policing when an established national police force is not present (UN DPKO, 2009: 57).

The development of such policies for coordinating military and policing efforts in peace operations highlights a number of things. First of all they underscore the increasing importance of utilizing a comprehensive approach to the security aspects involved in peacekeeping and peacebuilding. Second, they recognize the increased role of police in peace operations. Third, they represent an effort to identify a clearer division of responsibility between police and military. This final point is vital as it brings us back to the argument that fundamental divisions betwee police and military still do exist, as argued above, and, moreover, that these divisions are in fact very useful in the f eld and should be retained for a number of normative and practical reasons.

As can be seen, however, existing doctrine is still fairly general and glosses over the fact that such spheres of activity may overlap. Drawing on discussions with military, military police and

Table 16.1 Military and police tasks in contemporary UN peace operations (adapted from UN DPKO, 2009: 47–56)

Military component	Traditional PK operations	Monitor or supervise military arrangements that parties to a conflict have agreed upon
	Multidimensional operations	Create a secure and stable environment for other elements of the peace process to be implemented.
Police component	Can be deployed either as individual UNPOL or as formed police units to either traditional or multidimensional peace operations	Play a role in establishing public safety and preventing crime as well as facilitating rule of law. Collaborate closely with civilian components such as human rights, judicial and civil affairs, and corrections.

civilian police personnel from Australia and New Zealand, we are beginning to develop a more specific division of responsibilities

A four-fold typology for guidelines for action

In considering how best to demarcate roles for police, military police and military personnel in undertaking activities that may be considered policing–type tasks, we suggest that utilizing a four-fold typology as follows might best help policy makers develop future operating guidelines.

> *Police-only:* These are tasks that it is only appropriate for police to perform. If police are either unavailable or incapable of performing these tasks for any reason, it is better that they go unperformed. Examples include the power of arrest, and criminal investigation activities. Having said this, it is assumed that, in the performance of police–only tasks, the police may need to call on the *support* of the military. An example of a supporting role for the military may be the use of military as a general deterrent to resisting arrest in the case of high–risk arrests, though the ability to arrest remains solely in the purview of police personnel.
>
> *Police-First:* These are tasks that police should do if this is appropriate, but that could be performed by other agencies *under police guidance and supervision* if not. Again it is assumed that the police may need to call on the support of the military in the performance of these tasks. Public order maintenance is an example of where this might be appropriate. This is reinforced by the fact that military aid to the civil power remains a possibility with liberal democracies as long as particular procedures and legal constraints are abided by.
>
> *Collaborative:* These tasks could be performed by either police or military, or possibly even by both agencies together. In collaborative tasks, the lead agency would need to be determined on a case–by–case basis. An example here could be patrolling. When the situation is less permissive military might lead, as in the case of the initial months following significant civil violence in Timor–Leste in 2006. When the situation improved, police then led.
>
> *Military-only:* These are tasks that it is only suitable for military forces to perform. Reciprocally, however, there may be situations in which the military might call for *support* from the police to perform these tasks. An example of police support here might be for police to be ready to take custody of those suspected of crimes post instances of military contact.
>
> *(Greener and Fish, forthcoming)*

Conclusions

Due to problems met in deploying civilian police abroad, the nature of the operating environment, and changes within military forces, military personnel have increasingly been utilized in policing or policing–type roles in recent peace and stability operations. However, there are significant concerns about this. In addition to material, educational, cultural, legal, and organizational differences between police and military personnel, there are a number of broader ramifications that might emerge from such a trend. In particular, a major goal of most peace operations is the demilitarization and de-escalation of the local environment, as well as the embedding of particular political values and practices, therefore the use of military for policing functions can blur the democratic ideal of military as external actor and police as internal actor. Even military involvement in activities such as training of police risks a more militarized approach which has potential consequences for the long-term legitimacy of the police force and, more generally, the successes of international efforts to embed general liberal-democratic institutions.

There is, therefore, a significant dilemma. There are not enough civilian police to deploy and such civilian police cannot operate in non-permissive environments. To completely cast aside any role for military personnel in supporting or undertaking policing tasks may therefore prove impractical and unworkable. However, to fall into accepting the idea that using military for policing purposes is the 'least worst' option is also far from ideal, both from the short-term perspective of successfully policing during the operation and from the long-term perspective of setting the scene for successful and lasting peace. This chapter has therefore emphasized the need to begin to engage more concretely with this dilemma, and began this task by sketching ways in which we might arrive at a clearer division of responsibility, which would enable best use to be made of available police personnel.

Recent policy efforts by the UN have begun to sketch out appropriate generic roles for police and military personnel in peace operations and these constitute important contributions to the f eld. However, more detailed planning needs to consider how military forces might support policing efforts within clearly circumscribed boundaries, and how police may be better supported to carry out international roles, in order to avoid the current push to use military forces in policing-typeroles when they are not suited to the task at hand. The above four-fold typology drawn from Australasian experiences constitutes an initial attempt to redraw the boundaries between police and military operating in peace and stability missions while taking account of the need for these two services to work together toward common goals.

Much more could be done to develop such ideas. In particular, more work needs to be done in asking how more militarized formed police units (FPUs) or private contractors may also fi into the equation. Also as noted here, more could be done to tackle the deployability issue. This is to some degree being addressed with the development of national deployment pools, but there is room for consideration of other mechanisms that will help deliver civilian police offshore. One possibility might be to utilize a system akin to that of the Army reservists in freeing up bureaucratic processes.

The debate over the practical and ethical issues of military personnel undertaking civilian policing in peace and stability operations looks set to continue until a more ideal division of labor can be clearly identif ed, internalized by the agencies involved, adequately resourced and, most importantly of all, sited within a more general conversation about the broader ethical and normative shifts that this trend embodies. Consent, not coercion, embodies the type of political and social values to be encouraged in domestic and international affairs – particularly in international statebuilding efforts following on from or accompanying peace and stability operations – and the police-military distinction is important in identifying which of these is to prevail.

Acknowledgments

Research for this chapter was carried out as part of an Asia-Pacific Civil Military Centre of Excellence (now the Australian Civil Military Centre) funded project on 'Civil-Military Interaction in Peace Operations.' This chapter draws on research undertaken for this project and the guidelines noted here are to be published by the Centre as a working document. However, the views expressed in this piece are those of the authors alone and do not represent the position of this institution. The authors would like to acknowledge and thank all of those serving police and military personnel that gave so willingly of their time to help us undertake this research. Particular thanks are due to those who attended a June 2011 workshop in Queanbeyan to help us discuss some of these ideas in more detail as the project progressed: Senior Sergeant Peter Davis, Inspector Mal Schwartfeger, Major Tim Hind, Colonel Brian Cox, Wing Commander Wendy Horder, Major Josh Wineera, Lt Col Nick Floyd, Lt Col Andrew Combes, and Dr Tony Murney, as well as to Inspector Roly Williams, Inspector Paul Sindlin, Dr Jim Rolfe, and Lt Col Vern Bennett.

Notes

1 The term 'constabulary' may at times refer to civilian non-paramilitary police units but more often refers to continental styles of policing which are still considered to be police but are more paramilitary in nature, organized along military lines. The term is used here with reference to the latter.
2 The military heavy environment is underscored by the fact that the Multi National Security Transition Council–Iraq (MNSTC–I) is the US military organization responsible for the training, mentoring, and equipping of all Iraqi security forces. However, these PTTs/NPTTs in Iraq typically have an International Police Liaison Officer present, which brings a civilian policing view to those deployments
3 This issue has also encouraged the use of more militarized forms of police in the form of Formed Police Units (FPUs) such as *gendarmerie* which can function under military chains of command. Although this particular chapter is concerned with military personnel only, the use of FPUs in policing roles is another fertile area for future research.

References

Andreas, P., and Price, R. (2001). From war–fighting to crime fighting: Transforming the American nation security state. *International Studies Review*, 3(3), 31–52.
Bayley, D., and Perito, R. (2010). *The police in war: Fighting insurgency, terrorism and violent crime*. Boulder, CO: Lynne Rienner.
Caforio, G. (Ed.). (2003). *Handbook of the sociology of the military*. New York, NY: Kluwer Academic.
Campbell, D., and Campbell, K. (2010). Soldiers as police officers/police officers as soldiers: Role evoluti and revolution in the United States. *Armed Forces and Society*, 36(2), 327–350.
Dunlap C. J., Jr. (2005). The thick green line: The growing involvement of military forces in domestic law enforcement. In T. Newburn (Ed.), *Policing: Key readings*. Cullompton, UK: Willan, pp. 786–796.
First Military Police Tactical Policing CONOPS Brief. (2010). PowerPoint for delivery to Australian Defence Forces personnel.
Fishstein, P. (2010). *Winning hearts and minds? Examining the relationship between aid and security in Afghanistan's Balkh Province*. Boston, MA: Feinstein International Center.
Friesendorf, C. (2012). *International intervention and the use of force: Military and police roles*. Geneva, Switzerland: Geneva Centre for the Democratic Control of Armed Forces.
Friesendorf, C., and Penska, S. E. (2008). Militarised law enforcement in peace operations: EUFOR in Bosnia and Herzegovina. *International Peacekeeping*, 15(5), 677–694.
Greener, B. K. (2009). UNPOL: Police as peacekeepers. *Policing and Society*, 19(2), 106–118.
Greener, B. K., and Fish, W. J. (2011). *The development of civilian policing: Lessons for contemporary post conflict operations*. Asia Pacific Civil Military Centre of Excellence Civil Military Occasional Papers, 4/2011 Canberra, Australia: APCMCoE.
Greener, B. K., and Fish, W. J. (forthcoming). *Police–military interaction in international peace and stability operations: Working towards guidelines for action*. Queanbeyan, Australia: Australian Civil–Military Centre.
Hinton, M., and Newburn, T. (2009). Introduction: Policing developing democracies. In M. S. Hinton and T. Newburn (Eds.), *Policing developing democracies*. Abingdon, UK: Routledge.
Jayamaha, D., Brady, S., Fitzgerald B., and Fritz, J. (2010) *Lessons learned from US Government in international operations*. Carlisle, PA: Strategic Studies Institute, US Army War College.
Keller, D. (2010). *US military forces and police assistance in stability operations: The least-worst option to fill the US capability gap*. Carlisle, PA: Strategic Studies Institute, US Army War College.

Kilcullen, D. (2009). *The accidental guerrilla: Fighting small wars in the midst of the big one*. New York, NY: Oxford University Press.

Knickmeyer, E. (2005, December 30). US troops to mentor Iraqi Police. *Washington Post*.

Mobekk, E. (2005). *Identifying lessons in United Nations international policing missions*. Policy Paper No. 5. Geneva, Switzerland: Geneva Centre for the Democratic Control of the Armed Forces.

Moskos, C. (Ed.). (2000). *The postmodern military: Armed forces after the Cold War*. Oxford, UK: Oxford University Press.

Perito, R. (2011). The Iraq Federal Police: US Police—Building under Fire, Special Report, United States Institute of Peace. Washington, DC: USIP.

Rubenstein, R. A. (2010). Peacekeeping and the return of imperial policing.*International Peacekeeping*, *17*(4), 457–470.

Sedra, M. (2006). Security sector reform in Afghanistan: The slide towards expediency. *International Peacekeeping*, *13*(1), March, 94–110.

Smith, R. J. (1999, June 26). Marines kill another gunman in Kosovo. *Washington Post*, A17.

UN DPKO. (2008). *United Nations peacekeeping operations: Principles and guidelines*. New York, NY: United Nations Department of Peacekeeping Operations.

UN DPKO. (2009). *UN Peacekeeping PDT Standards, Core pre-deployment training materials*. Unit 2 – Part 1: Establishment and Operationalization of Security Council mandates in PKOs. New York, NY: United Nations Department of Peacekeeping Operations.

Walzer, M. (1992). *Just and unjust wars: A moral argument with historical illustrations* (2nd ed.). New York, NY: Basic Books.

Wiatrowski, M. D., and Goldstone, J. A. (2010). The ballot and the badge: Democratic policing.*Journal of Democracy*, *21*(2), April, 79–92.

Williams, P. (2009). Peace operations in Africa: Seven challenges, any solutions?*Conflict Trends*, *3*. Available at: www.isn.ethz.ch

17
NATURAL RESOURCE GOVERNANCE AND HYBRID POLITICAL ORDERS

Gilles Carbonnier and Achim Wennmann

Since the commodity price boom that started a decade ago, an increasing number of poor countries have become resource-rich – or rather mineral-dependent – in that more than a quarter of their exports of goods consist of fossil fuels and minerals. By 2010, 61 low- and middle-income countries were mineral-dependent, many of these being in sub-Saharan Africa. This is a one-third increase in just 14 years (Haglund, 2011: 3). Resource dependence tends to be associated with weak governance indicators. Hence, natural resource management (NRM) in general, and the governance of extractive resources in particular, has become a critical issue in many weak states undergoing complex peacebuilding and/or statebuilding processes.

Over the past decade there has been a proliferation of normative frameworks and practical guides on business and conflict, or more specifically related to extractive industries operating weak states. Because of the inadequacy of intergovernmental, global governance mechanisms in the energy sector to address these issues, many of these efforts have been carried out in the context of voluntary multi-stakeholder processes such as the Extractive Industries Transparency Initiative (EITI), the Voluntary Principles on Security and Human Rights, and others driven by industry associations or non-governmental organizations (NGOs) (Carbonnier, 2011: 135–137). These multi-stakeholder regimes have the merit of including non-state actors such as civil society organizations and the industry. Yet they still tend to overlook a critical point: the actual governance realities on the ground. Instead, they tend to take as a starting assumption the classic – or Weberian – state model. For instance, the EITI Articles of Association, Article 5, specifes that EITI members can comprise:

> a) Implementing Countries, meaning states, that have been classified by the EITI Boar as either Candidate Countries or Compliant Countries; and b) Supporting Countries, meaning states or union of states, that support the objective of the EITI Association.
>
> *(EITI, 2009)*

This somehow presupposes the participation of states that can – or wish to – provide security, welfare, and representation to the resident populations (Schwarz, 2005: 433–436).

Many scholars have adopted a critical stance toward the liberal view of the state in conflict affected and fragile settings. The major donor countries released a long overdue but welcome 'political endorsement' of this critique under the Development Assistance Committee of the

Organization for Economic Cooperation and Development (OECD): the 2011 *Policy Guidance on Supporting Statebuilding in Situations of Conflict and Fragility* underlines that 'the majority of states in the global South can . . . be described as hybrid political orders' (OECD, 2011: 25). While obvious for those living in these states or for the frequent visitors, this statement is nevertheless remarkable in the sense that a policy document by and for official donors emphasizes what state 'are' – rather than focusing exclusively what they 'should be.'

Hybrid political orders are characterized by the coexistence and overlap of competing forms of order, conflicting claims to legitimacy and economic resources, and a weak social base. Suc orders underscore that the state is not necessarily the only provider of security, welfare, and representation. It shares authority, legitimacy, and capacity with a variety of networks, strongmen, or traditional institutions. The term 'hybrid' captures different non–state forms of order and governance, including customary arrangements, and how they permeate each other into 'a different and genuine political order' (Boege et al., 2009: 606). Hybrid political orders are sometimes applied to so–called 'ungoverned spaces'; but at a closer look, there is usually no lack of governance – rather a lack of official or recognized governance by the state (Felbab–Brown 2010: 175).

While official development assistance has been slow in acknowledging the presence of hybri political orders in the Global South, extractive industries are intrinsically pragmatic and prone to deal with the polity as it is – rather than as it ought to be – in order to operate on the ground and make a profit out of it. Yet oil, gas, and minerals often lie at the heart of war economies an state fragility, be it as the cause of violent rent–seeking competition or as a way to finance th armed conf ict, both for the rebels and for the elite in power.

This chapter presents an exploratory analysis about the management of natural resources in the context of hybrid political orders. The chapter consists of three parts: the first reviews curren trends in the governance of oil, gas, and minerals; the second sets out to better understand hybrid political orders; and the third links the two previous parts together. The chapter closes by pointing to research challenges ahead that connect NRM, the global governance of oil, gas, and mining, and the hybrid political orders.

The governance of oil, gas, and minerals

Energy has played a pivotal role in the rise and transformation of civilizations. With the thermo–industrial revolution of the mid–19th century, access to fossil fuels and, to a lesser extent, fissil material, has become a key driver of the world's economic and demographic growth as well as of geopolitical tensions (Carbonnier and Grinevald, 2011: 5–7). Yet the global architecture for managing these extractive resources remains worryingly weak and patchy: it is not f t for the purpose of managing increasing tensions in a world characterized by mounting scarcity. The international and regional organizations in the energy sector only address the specific concern either of net importing or net exporting countries. The only truly global organization is the International Energy Forum, which suffers from a low level of institutionalization (de Jong, 2011: 39–41). Until recently, the World Trade Organization has tended to neglect the energy sector. This is changing with the accession of the major oil producing nations and trade disputes related to Chinese export restrictions on strategic minerals and rare earths.

Constitutional rights determine the key principles related to the ownership and custody of sub–soil assets in each producer country. In the vast majority of cases, resource ownership lies with a country's people while resource custody is entrusted to the state and exerted by the government. Viñuales (2011: 197–212) highlights that, from a public international law per–spective, resource ownership derives from the principle of permanent sovereignty of peoples and nations over their natural resources. Even when their government misuses the revenues accruing from extraction, the means provided under international law to a people despoiled of its natural resources by its own government remain very limited. Recent legal developments may offer some avenues worth pursuing, such as considering grand corruption as a violation of human rights. Yet, at present, seeking redress under international criminal law does not offer much scope for change to the extent that misappropriating natural resources and diverting funds may not qualify as an international crime because of the high threshold required for an offence to qualify as such.

International and regional organizations and existing institutions are not meant to address the so-called 'resource curse' in resource-rich fragile states. In other words, they are not concerned with mitigating the negative impact of resource extraction on economic performance and politico-institutional outcomes in developing countries. Besides, resource dependence has been identifed as a major contributor to the outbreak – or continuation – of civil wars (LeBillon, 2012). The explanation does not reside so much in the economic dynamics associated with the so-called 'Dutch disease' – domestic currency appreciation, a lack of economic diversification and budget deficits associated with extractive boom-and-bust cycles – but rather in the politica processes underlying rentier-state and rent-seeking dynamics. The exploitation of extractive resources produces a *rent* or an 'excess return on investment.' The latter results from the gap between the cost of extraction plus a 'normal return' (e.g., $20 for a barrel of oil), and the price of oil, gas, and minerals on world markets, which may be several times higher (e.g., $120), in particular during price booms associated with soaring demand, as has been the case since the turn of the millennium as a result of China's and other emerging economies' thirst for raw materials.

The struggle to get and retain a share of the extractive rent is a critical issue, which ought to be considered as a matter of priority when looking at NRM. Investment regimes and contractual arrangements between the producer state and foreign investors largely determine the share of the rent that accrues to the state. Liberal investment regimes introduced during the 1980s and 1990s under the guidance of the International Monetary Fund and the World Bank favoured foreign investors. Conversely, resource nationalism, which became more salient in South America during the 2000s, seeks to retain much of the rent in the producer country. The type of contractual arrangements, such as concessions or production-sharing agreements, and the role and capabilities of the state-owned oil or mining company in the producer country are further variables that wield a direct influence on the actual governance of extractive resources in developing countries

A critical issue is how and where the share of the rent that remains in the producer country is eventually allocated. The rentier-state model highlights the tendency of mineral-rich states to use extractive revenues to generously reward political allies and harshly repress opposition, without having to build a proper administrative capacity to levy taxes from the citizenry since extractive revenues cover most of the budgetary requirements of the ruling elite. The latter tend not to feel accountable to its own people as a result (Beblawi and Luciani, 1987). The interests of the economic and politico-military elites may easily coalesce against attempts to enhance revenue transparency and introduce a fairer redistribution scheme, which may be further reinforced by regulatory capture by industry and economic interests investing in political lobbying (Mitnick, 1980). Under these circumstances, rent-seeking easily turns violent when specific groups feel that they do not get their fair share of the 'pie' – or simply want a greater share of it.

Extractive resources can be exploited to sustain and finance the war effort. They arguabl represent a major stake in armed conflicts and may be or become the main object of contention thus contributing to the perpetuation of war and chronic violence, and rendering peacebuilding more arduous. Several studies concluded that high resource dependence heightens the probability of an outbreak of a civil war, primarily since 'greedy' rebel groups may be tempted to resort to armed violence to extract profits from the 'illegal' exploitation of natural resources (Blattma and Miguel, 2010). In this context, the UN Security Council established a series of expert panels mandated to examine and report on the exploitation of natural resources in resource-rich war-torn countries such as Angola, the Democratic Republic of Congo (DRC), Liberia, and Sierra Leone. Over the past decade, a series of reports by the Panel of Experts on the Illegal Exploitation of Natural Resources and Other Forms of Wealth of the Democratic Republic of the Congo repeatedly stressed the direct implication of foreign firms, armed forces, and political leaders i plundering the eastern DRC's natural capital (de Ville, 2008; LeBillon, 2012).

Extractive resources featured in two main ways in peace agreements. They became a critical component of some peace deals though, for example, wealth- and revenue-sharing provisions. In other cases, political economy constraints meant that the parties to the negotiations did not want to put the issue on the table. For instance in Sudan, the 2004 Agreement on Wealth Sharing became an important step toward the 2005 Comprehensive Peace Agreement. As a result, the Government of Southern Sudan received payments amounting to US$5.4 billion between 2007 and 2009 (Wennmann, 2011: 82). To the contrary, during the 2002 peace negotiations related to DRC conflict, none of the belligerents nor associated third parties wanted to openly acknowledge the conflict's economic dimensions in order to avoid exposure of their economi agendas. Instead, the parties focused on power-sharing arrangements which – in their view – would regulate the control of resources once the armed confict was over (Grignon, 2006: 72–77; Nest, 2006: 55).

The DRC example places the spotlight on the political economy constraints of NRM in settings where the state is either absent or failing. This leaves 'the governance space' open for capture by whoever holds the actual levers of power. This means that NRM in practice is under the control of non-state armed actors who *de facto* control thousands of artisanal diggers (Gansor and Wennmann, 2012: 11) and maintain close links with business and state actors abroad. This example underlines the urgency to better understand the governance that does exist in these governance spaces in which local power-brokers establish *de facto* governance arrangements. This inquiry leads us back to asking how we understand 'the state' in developing countries.

Understanding hybrid political orders

The term 'conflict-affected and fragile state' is the current label used to characterize the natur of states in the developing world. It can manifest itself at the state level through a state's inability to deliver basic services to its citizens (state failure) or the continuous erosion of political institutions (state collapse) (Milliken and Krause, 2002).

In the broadest sense, perspectives on 'fragile states' can be distinguished in two ways (Di John, 2008: 2–3). The f rst emphasizes the role of markets and their need for transparent and accountable states as a necessary input for economic development, which is limited in developing countries by corrupt and patrimonial state structures. State failure is a deviation from an ideal type that is usually associated with a functioning bureaucracy, the monopoly over the legitimate use of force, and the capacity to deliver a series of basic services to the populations living within it. From this perspective, addressing the failings of the state focuses on a 'top-down' implementation of a specific state model

The alternative perspective considers client and patrimonial states as purposefully constructed entities that serve local elites and/or foreign interests and strengthen monopolized capital accumulation and the maintenance of political power. This conceptualizes state failure as a strategy to manage resources, territory, people, and power. It places armed violence in the context of social transformation, and the historical conditions of state formation. It further recognizes alternatives to a specific state model that involve traditional figures of authority, or strongme that are perceived by local populations as a legitimate authority (Rodgers, 2006: 316–318). In this framework, hybrid political orders connect to a 'functional' perspective of the state they serve, local elites, or foreign interests, strengthen monopolized capital accumulation, and ensure the maintenance of political power, thus helping to recognize that 'disorder' can have political and economic logics (Di John, 2008: 30–31).

Early work on hybrid political orders relates to the processes of African state formation by which local elites adapted governance structures to local realities, and external incentives and pressures (Chabal and Daloz, 1999: 1–2). A central problem for African state formation was the projection of authority over inhospitable territories with a low population density. With decolonization, the leaders of newly independent states claimed full sovereignty over distant hinterlands without ever having established full control. The fact that there was no external challenger also meant that there were no incentives to build taxation systems in order to defend the borders and build meaningful state–society relations, which was compounded by rentier–state dynamics in resource–rich countries. Society viewed the state as a predator or oppressor, or as simply something that occurred somewhere far away that just happened to be in the same country (Herbst, 2000: 11, 74, 254).

The logics of governance captured by the historical experience of many African states led to a diverse set of conceptualizations including for example 'closed' and 'open' access orders, the 'political marketplace,' the 'mediated state,' 'pockets of effectiveness,' and the so–called 'ungoverned spaces.'

In 'closed–access orders,' authorities limit access to valuable political opportunities and economic resources. Such barriers to entry allow governments to create a credible commitment among elites not to fight each other because they are better off participating in a patrimonia network than by challenging the authorities violently. They also build a relationship with a larger constituency of supporters through the provision of protection, welfare, and justice. The concept is contrasted to 'open–access orders' that structure access to political and economic opportunities in competitive terms through markets, elections, and merit (North et al., 2009: 18–25).

Referring to the 'political marketplace,' Alex de Waal argues that 'a certain degree of patronage is normal and normative, but there is an excess amount that is considered unethical' (de Waal, 2010: 12). Patronage can also have important transformative functions based on expectations that political leaders will use patronage to structure political power and reward followers. As people adjust, they have more confidence in patronage politics (that they know) than formal state institutions (that they mistrust). What is more, patronage sometimes dispenses resources more rapidly and fairly than international assistance or formal state services. Finally, patronage arrangements are far more resilient in times of crises and when formal systems fail because of an armed conflict or other event (de Waal, 2010: 2).

Drawing on his work in Somalia and Kenya, Ken Menkhaus shows that when a ruler or government has little capacity to impose control over a given territory, existing power realities foster governance arrangements based on deal–making, cooption, and subcontracting whatever local non–state authority wields actual power in a particular locality. Such 'mediated states' are 'intrinsically messy, contradictory, illiberal, and constantly renegotiated deals – not ideal choices for governments but often the best of bad options for weak states' (Menkhaus, 2006: 78).

The fact that the capacity of governments in conflict–affected and fragile states is not equall distributed across the country is neither surprising nor new (O'Donnell, 1993: 1359). Indeed, a brief excursion into the field of public administration suggests that spaces with functioning stat capacity called 'pockets of effectiveness' are 'public organisations that are reasonably effective in carrying out their functions and in serving some conception of the public good despite operating in an environment in which most public organisations are ineffective and subject to serious predation [or] patronage' (Leonard, 2008: 8).

The state's inability or unwillingness to deliver justice or welfare services evenly to a population does not mean that these are not provided. In many contexts, state functions have been assumed by gangs, private networks, local militias, guerrilla armies, or customary authorities as a consequence of country splintering into different zones of autonomy (Rapley, 2006: 95). Of course these actors create their own insecurities and inefficiencies, but 'partly due to their success in providing security, these sub—state groups often become the most legitimate political authority in areas that they control' (Reno, 2008: 143). Thus 'imperfectly effective state authority can viably and normatively coexist territorially with more localised non—state forms of social regulation' (Rodgers, 2006: 317).

There is also an ever—growing research effort that uncovers the workings of the 'ungoverned' space (Clunan and Trinkunas, 2010). For example, even in illicit markets there is some degree of predictability and assurance of property rights. In Southern Italy, for example, the role of the Mafia was not necessarily the provision of absent or illegal goods, but rather regulation and enforcement in the absence of social trust (Felbab—Brown, 2010: 179). What is more, Somalia has witnessed the evolution of an 'economy without state' and is one of the main cattle exporters globally. Despite the absence of a government, local actors were able to negotiate agreements and adhere to phytosanitary rules so as to ensure the quality required for exports to the Middle East (Little, 2003).

In sum, a variety of conceptual tools are available to make sense of the workings of hybrid political orders. Coming to grips with hybrid political orders is not a natural tendency for policy makers, aid workers, and diplomats pursuing a career within apparatuses that conform to the archetypal Weberian state. It is, therefore, time to take hybrid political orders out of the shadows, understand their particularities and commonalities, and explore 'how best to manage, exploit, and coexist with them to provide human and national security to their populations' (Clunan, 2010: 12). It is in this spirit that this chapter explores the implications of hybrid political orders for natural resource governance.

Natural resource management in the context of hybrid political orders

A starting point for looking at NRM in hybrid political orders is to recognize that not all natural resources are the same, and not all have the same link to hybrid political orders. The classificatio of natural resources in conflict—affected and fragile states distinguishes between 'point' and 'diffuse resources as well as between capital—intensive and labour—intensive activities (LeBillon, 2011: 573). Diffuse resources are typically spread over a large area. They are rather labour—intensive and relatively easy to loot by small groups of individuals equipped with shovels and sieves. This is for instance the case of alluvial diamond or gold mining as discussed in the example of the DRC above, whereby the tracing of gold from the mines to the global markets is virtually impossible (Cuvelier, 2010). Other examples can be found of cattle breeding or cocoa plantations. The link to hybrid political orders is very strong partly because of government difficulty in controlling vast stretches of inhospitable territory and the *de facto* control of non—state actors. In Colombia between the mid—1980s and late 1990s, the Revolutionary Armed Forces of Colombia (FARC) could legitimize themselves in the eyes of the local population as a *de facto* state because they provided the conditions that made a livelihood for local coca farmers possible (Metelits, 2010: 100–102).

Point resources are capital—intensive and geographically concentrated. They tend to require large investments by state—owned or private firms, domestic or foreign. This is, for instance, th case with oil and gas, or deep-shaft mining. These situations place the state – and especially the rentier state – into the centre of attention, and less so political orders established parallel to and at the exclusion of the state. Because of the level of capital investments needed and the greater ease to physically control point resources, it is the formal and informal redistribution of income from natural resources that is at the heart of the hybrid political order. The most enormous adjustment of such a rentier state could be followed in Sudan. The decision by Southern Sudan to cancel all oil exports through the oil pipeline to Port Sudan led to Khartoum losing an estimated 40 per cent of its budget, and South Sudan losing nearly 100 per cent of its budget. This in turn led to great pressures on the governance system in both Sudan and South Sudan because both systems were premised on the income from oil. While Southern Sudan can offset lost revenues (to some extent) through development assistance, Khartoum faced a very real risk of state collapse (De Waal, 2012).

In the context of decentralization processes, South American countries have promoted schemes to devolve a large share of extractive revenues to the producing areas. The central Peruvian state for instance redirects half of the extractive revenues to the producing provinces and districts. While this may respond to grievances expressed by local communities who feel dispossessed of their natural wealth and left only with the environmental damage, it may also fuel existing or new local conflicts (Arellano-Yanguas, 2008).

These examples suggest that we are facing different kinds of hybrid political orders depending on whether we are dealing with diffuse or point resources. In the context of point resources, hybrid political orders are located within rentier state-like orders. Such orders are also reminiscent of what William Reno called 'warlord states' in which rulers control markets and areas of resource exploitation without relying on state institutions while at the same time receiving support from international donors (Reno, 1998: 21–22, 72). In the contexts of diffuse resources, informal micro-entrepreneurs operate in highly volatile environments and successively wrest control from the state, or fill a vacuum if the state was absent in the first place. Such orders can in their ultima manifestation develop into '*de facto* states' in which power holders become the new political authorities and are recognized as such by local populations (Lynch, 2004: 16).

While the above typology is admittedly crude and merits the caveat that more research is needed to fll the shades of gray and identify overlaps, it nevertheless makes us think about some of the issues at hand when implementing NRM in contexts of hybrid political orders. For example, such implementation entails the acknowledgement of existing power structures outside the state apparatus as well as the informal network within the state that are characteristic of rentier states. It also leads to the question of whether NRM can be used as a strategy of driving transformative negotiations toward a (slightly) better future for a greater segment of societies in fragile states. Such transformations are often driven through multi-stakeholder, political processes, and 'inclusive enough' coalitions (World Bank, 2011: 120–127). This approach stands in contrast to merely wishing hybrid political orders away (or acting as if oblivious to their existence) and placing a blind faith in whatever formal structure may exist, with the result being the creation of a parallel governance system without any link to realities on the ground.

In recent years, the international community has had painful experiences in Afghanistan, Iraq, Somalia, and Sudan, partly due to underestimating the power of hybrid political orders. This is especially evident in Somalia, where international mediators have failed to understand and deal with 'the apparent contradictions between centralized state-based authority and a traditionally egalitarian political culture, in which legitimacy of force is not vested in a centralized institution of a state but in a diffuse lineage system, regulated by customary law and other institutions' (Bradbury and Healy, 2010b: 106). As a result all international mediation efforts focusing on 'the state' have collapsed while there have been an estimated 128 local peace processes since 1991 focusing on reconciliation, security, and economic exchange between Somali communities (Bradbury and Healy, 2010a: 8).

These experiences also provide a backdrop to a multi-year process among donors within the OECD's International Network on Conflict and Fragility (INCAF) on supporting statebuildin in situations of conflict and fragility. INCAF Policy Guidance highlights that even if 'variou sources and forms of state legitimacy are unlikely to reinforce each other,' it is only in extreme cases that such hybrid orders lead to sustained violence or state collapse (OECD, 2011: 25). Outside this extreme, hybrid political orders are neither inevitably fragile nor ridden by violence and conflict

> Societies continue to function, to form institutions, to negotiate politically, and to set and meet expectations. Traditional forms of authority are not necessarily inimical to the development of rules-based political systems . . . In fact, the challenge is to understand how traditional and formal systems interact in any particular context, and to look for ways of constructively combining them.
>
> *(OECD, 2011: 25)*

For NRM, such 'ways of constructive combination' mean exploring the feasibility of a bottom-upapproach of working toward effective NRM systems. This means that NRM is *not* about replacing a particular governance order with a more 'effective' order*immediately*. It is also *not* about the export of a specific governance model. Rather, it is about the coalitions betwee local stakeholders and communities, central governments, domestic and multinational companies, and the international community that nurture a fusion of traditional, informal, and new governance components through a *progressive transformation process*. Such efforts focus not so much on what is lacking, and more on existing capacity at the municipal and district levels, and recognize that informal governance arrangements can provide 'classic' state services (such as protection, justice, or welfare), sometimes even more effectively than the state itself (Wennmann, 2010: 19–20).

Better understanding of 'ways of constructive combination' also needs to be related to the impacts on hybrid political orders of exogenous changes. A telling example is the Dodd-Frank Wall Street and Consumer Protection Act of 2010, whose Section 1502 requires all publicly traded companies to report to the US Security and Exchange Commission and on their website about any 'conflict minerals' that they source from the DRC or from neighbouring countries This results from what is, a priori, a laudable effort by advocacy groups to cut down conflic f nance in the Eastern DRC. Yet, even as the measure has not yet been implemented as of March 2012, it has resulted in a ban of certain mineral exports from the DRC, arguably putting 'from tens of thousands up to 2 million Congolese miners out of work in the eastern Congo' while doing 'little to improve the security situation or the daily lives of most Congolese' (Seay, 2012: 1). Since the illegal exploitation of 'conf ict minerals' is also part of the survival economy for thousands of miners, they should be offered an alternative to sustain themselves and their families. This may not be a realistic option in today's DRC. A more viable option may be to implemen: section 1502 in an incremental manner in conjunction with humanitarian and technical assistance to compensate for the loss of livelihood. Local civil society leaders and miners should be at the forefront of the traceability and monitoring schemes (Seay, 2012). That is, existing skills and sources of authority should be brought into a pact to help implement a potentially highly transformational scheme.

Finding the right level of inclusiveness in these settings will remain the art of politicking and also of a sense of reality as to what is possible on the ground. An all-inclusive transition process is something that is certainly worth aspiring to, but remains unrealistic in many contexts. The *World Development Report 2011* emphasizes the issue of inclusivity by distinguishing between 'elite pacts' and 'collaborative, inclusive–enough coalitions.' Elite pacts are understood 'to contain violence and to secure the property and economic interests and opportunities of pact members'; collaborative, inclusive–enough coalitions involve a greater segment of society 'to restore confidence and transform institutions and help create continued momentum for positive change' (World Bank, 2011: xv, xvii). There is a fine line between ensuring that a pact is small enoug to make key decisions possible, and inclusive enough so that these decisions can be implemented in practice.

Conclusion and future research

This exploratory analysis on NRM, governance mechanisms, and hybrid political orders raises more questions than it offers definitive answers. Overall the chapter is an invitation to thin through what a 'context–sensitive approach' or development assistance based on 'local ownership and leadership' actually means in the context of the fluid, overlapping, and contested governanc arrangements; and what this means in an environment where high–value natural resources represent a critical stake in weak states. The OECD/DAC has now acknowledged that 'hybrid political orders' may be the norm rather than the exception. Policy makers and researchers still have to come to grips with what this implies for issues such as NRM in fragile states and violent settings.

The relationship between hybrid political orders and NRM differs in the context of capital–intensive and geographically concentrated resources versus diffuse, labour–intensive ones: the former points towards hybrid political orders that are related to, or integrated into, rentier–state structures; the latter relates to orders that largely evolve outside formal institutional state structures. In this context, NRM offers an entry point to engage hybrid political orders into forward–looking transformation processes. One challenge is to form the 'collaborative and inclusive enough' coalitions that are necessary to drive forward–looking transformation at the national and local levels. At the international level, specific provisions of the Dodd–Frank Act illustrate the potentia outreach of regulations and incentives provided via the global f nancial markets. Yet they also highlight the harm that such endeavours can cause on the ground when the sanctions and incentives are based on incomplete or fraught assumptions regarding the conflict dynamics

Further research is necessary to better grasp the nexus between NRM and hybrid political orders. First, there is a gap to close in terms of exploring the benefits of adopting a more positiv appreciation of hybrid political orders, thus changing the optics from a mere understanding of these orders as something def cient, undesirable, and dangerous. Concretely, there is a lack of knowledge about (a) the patterns and evidence of engagements in hybrid political orders, (b) the conflict management and prevention functions of hybrid political orders, and (c) the practical trade–offs inherent when embarking on negotiations with stakeholders that are entrenched in hybrid political orders.

Second, there is a need for better understanding of how to fnd a workable balance between the parties' requests for informality to manage their own internal transformation (e.g., from former rebel group to political party) and external requests for immediate transparency, accountability, and compensation. Portraying transparency issues as the outcome of a temporally defined tran sition process – and not as an immediate demand – can help bridge these competing requests. Insisting on transparency and accountability right from the outset is often an unrealistic option that can jeopardize an entire long–term transformation process. More case studies would provide much needed empirical evidence.

Finally, recent research has highlighted the fact that effective checks-and-balances mechanisms constraining the power of the executive are of the essence to counter the resource curse. Voluntary multi-stakeholder regimes such as the EITI and the Voluntary Principles seek respectively to increase transparency and put some constraints on the management of security – or the exercise of violence – in and around extractive sites. But these initiatives have so far fallen short of strengthening effective checks in weak states blessed with abundant extractive resources, either taking the presence of a functioning state as a given or calling for the rapid 're-establishment' of such a state even if it never existed in the first place

References

Arellano-Yanguas, J. (2008). *A thoroughly modern resource curse? The new natural resource policy agenda and the mining revival in Peru*. IDS Working Paper No. 300. Brighton, UK: Institute of Development Studies.

Beblawi, H., and Luciani, G. (Eds.). (1987).*The rentier state: Nation, state and the integration of the Arab World*. London, UK: Croom Helm.

Blattman, Ch., and Miguel, E. (2010). Civil war. *Journal of Economic Literature*, 48(1), 3–57.

Boege, V., Brown, A., Clemens, K., and Nolan, A. (2009). Building peace and political community in hybrid political orders. *International Peacekeeping*, 16(5), 599–615.

Bradbury, M., and Healy, S. (2010a). Introduction. In M. Bradbury and S. Healy (Eds.), *Whose peace is it anyway? Connecting Somali and international peacemaking*. Accord 21. London, UK: Conciliation Resources, pp. 6–9.

Bradbury, M., and Healy, S. (2010b). How does it end? Towards a vision of a Somali state. In M. Bradbury and S. Healy (Eds.), *Whose peace is it anyway? Connecting Somali and international peacemaking*. Accord 21. London, UK: Conciliation Resources, pp. 105–107.

Carbonnier, G. (2011). The global and local governance of extractive resources. *Global Governance*, 17(2), 135–147.

Carbonnier, G., and Grinevald, J. (2011). Energy and development. In G. Carbonnier (Ed.), *International development policy: Energy and development*. London, UK: Palgrave Macmillan, pp. 3–20.

Chabal, P., and Daloz, J.-P. (1999).*Africa works: Disorder as political instrument*. Oxford, UK: James Currey

Clunan, A. L. (2010). Ungoverned spaces: The need for a reevaluation. In A. L. Clunan and H. A. Trinkunas (Eds.), *Ungoverned spaces: Alternatives to state authority in an era of softened sovereignty*. Stanford, CA: Stanford University Press, pp. 3–13.

Clunan, A. L., and Trinkunas, H. A. (Eds). (2010). *Ungoverned spaces: Alternatives to state authority in an era of softened sovereignty*. Stanford, CA: Stanford University Press.

Cuvelier, J. (Ed.). (2010). *The complexity of resource governance in a context of state fragility: The case of Eastern DRC*. London, UK: International Alert.

De Jong, S. (2011). 'Toward global energy governance: How to patch the patchwork. In G. Carbonnier (Ed.), *International development policy: Energy and development*. London, UK: Palgrave Macmillan, pp. 21–43.

De Ville, J. (2008). *An outline of trade flows of legally and illegally extracted mineral resources from fragile states: The case of coltan in the Kivus, DRC*. Institute for Environmental Security. Available at: www.envirosecurity.org

De Waal, A. (2010). *Fixing the political marketplace: How can we make peace without functioning state institutions?* The Chr. Michelsen Lecture 2009. Available at: www.cmi.no/news/?557=fixing-the-political-market place

De Waal, A. (2012, January 24). South Sudan doomsday machine. *New York Times*.

Di John, J. (2008). *Conceptualizing the causes and consequences of failed states: A critical review of the literature*. Working Paper No. 25, Crisis States Working Paper Series 2. London, UK: London School of Economics.

EITI (Extractive Industry Transparency Initiative). (2009). *Articles of association*. Available at: http://eiti.org/articles

Felbab-Brown, V. (2010). Rules and regulations in ungoverned spaces: Illicit economies, criminals, and belligerents. In A. L. Clunan and H. A. Trinkunas (Eds.), *Ungoverned spaces: Alternatives to state authority in an era of softened sovereignty*. Stanford, CA: Stanford University Press, pp. 175–192.

Ganson, B., and Wennmann, A. (2012). *Safe communities, resilient systems: Towards a new action framework for business and peacebuilding.* Unpublished background document for a multi-stakeholder retreat, Geneva, Switzerland.

Grignon, F. (2006). Economic agendas in the Congolese peace process. In M. Nest (Ed.), *The Democratic Republic of Congo: Economic dimensions of war and peace.* Boulder, CO: Lynne Rienner, pp. 62–98.

Haglund, D. (2011). Blessing or curse? The rise of mineral dependence among low- and middle-income countries. Oxford, UK: Oxford Policy Management.

Herbst, J. (2000). *States and power in Africa: Comparative lessons in authority and control.* Princeton, NJ: Princeton University Press.

LeBillon, P. (2011). The political ecology of war: Natural resources and armed conflict.*Political Geography*, 20, 561–584.

LeBillon, P. (2012). *Wars of plunder: Conflicts, profits and the politics of resources.* New York, NY: Columbia/Hurst.

Leonard, D. K. (2008). *Where are 'pockets' of effective agencies likely in weak governance states and why? A propositional inventory.* Working Paper 306. Brighton, UK: Institute of Development Studies.

Little, P. D. (2003). Somalia: Economy without state. Oxford, UK: James Currey.

Lynch, D. (2004). *Engaging Eurasia's separatist states: Unresolved conflicts and the de facto states.* Washington, DC: USIP Press.

Menkhaus, K. (2006). Governance without government in Somalia: Spoilers, state building, and the politics of coping. *International Security*, 31(3), 74–106.

Metelits, C. (2010). *Inside insurgency: Violence, civilians, and revolutionary group behavior.* New York, NY: New York University Press.

Milliken, J., and Krause, K. (2002). State failure, state collapse, and state reconstruction: Concepts, lessons and strategies. *Development and Change*, 33(5), 753–774.

Mitnick, B. (1980). *The political economy of regulation.* New York, NY: Columbia University Press.

Nest, M. (2006). The political economy of the Congo War. In M. Nest (Ed.), *The Democratic Republic of Congo: Economic dimensions of war and peace.* Boulder, CO: Lynne Rienner, pp. 31–62.

North, D. C., Wallis, J. J., and Weingast, B. R. (2009). *Violence and social orders: A conceptual framework for interpreting recorded human history.* Cambridge, UK: Cambridge University Press.

O'Donnell, G. (1993). 'On the state, democratization and some conceptual problems: A Latin American view with glances at some postcommunist countries. *World Development*, 21(8), 1355–1369.

OECD (Organization for Economic Cooperation and Development). (2011). *Supporting statebuilding in situations of conflict and fragility: Policy guidance.* DAC Guidelines and Reference Series. Paris, France: OECD.

Rapley, J. (2006). The new Middle Ages. *Foreign Affairs*, 85(3), 95–105.

Reno, W. (1998). *Warlord politics and African states*, Boulder, CO: Lynne Rienner.

Reno, W. (2008). Bottom-up statebuilding? In C. T. Call and V. Wyeth (Eds.), Building states to build peace. Boulder, CO: Lynne Rienner, pp. 143–161.

Rodgers, D. (2006). The state as a gang: Conceptualizing the governmentability of violence in contemporary Nicaragua. *Critique of Anthropology*, 26(3), 315–330.

Schwarz, R. (2005). Post-conflict peacebuilding: The challenges of security, welfare and protection.*Security Dialogue*, 36(4), 429–446.

Seay, L. (2012). *What's wrong with Dodd-Frank 1502?* CGD Working Paper No. 284. Washington, DC: Center for Global Development.

Viñuales, J. (2011). The resource curse: A legal perspective. *Global Governance*, 17(2), 197–212.

Wennmann, A. (2010). *Grasping the strengths of fragile states: Aid effectiveness between 'top-down' and 'bottom-up' statebuilding.* CCDP Working Paper 6. Geneva, Switzerland: Graduate Institute of International and Development Studies.

Wennmann, A. (2011). *The political economy of peacemaking.* London, UK: Routledge.

World Bank, The. (2011). *World Development Report 2011: Conflict, security and development.* Washington, DC: The World Bank.

18
THE POLITICAL ECONOMY OF STATEBUILDING
Rents, taxes, and perpetual dependency

Berit Bliesemann de Guevara and Florian P. Kühn

How states are fnanced, or to be more historically accurate, how they fnance themselves, is the most complex of affairs. This contribution disentangles the interwoven problems of legitimacy, economic reproduction, and sustainable fnancing of states and their institutions, personnel, and policy. The main idea of this chapter is to sketch the functional logics of state fnancing and the financing of statebuilding. In order to address this puzzle, the state of Bosnia and Herzegovina will be compared with that of Afghanistan in order to demonstrate how both formal and informal structures of power are constituted and reproduced through mechanisms of official and institutionalized domination. We ask how these are fnanced and which opportunities local and external actors have for subverting and adopting these fnancial patterns. To this end, we propose a spectrum of state finances ranging from a tax–funded state to a rentier state. Examining ho they are intermingled with the international political economy is vital to understand how interveners and intervened interact with, shape, and resist each other.

Financing statebuilding, financing states?

Countless books have been published in economics about how states can or ought to be financed. What is called public economics, however, focuses primarily on consolidated, liberal, Western states; in short: the states of the OECD world. This reveals an uncritical assumption of 'stateness,' an extrapolation of a specifically European version of social organization and structure of domination writ large to a global context. In 1968, J. P. Nettl asked for a qualification of what the state is, pointing to the distinct role the Party played in shaping Soviet society in comparison to the relatively 'stateless' societies of the Anglo–Saxon world. This indicates how a state may play different roles in different societies, but also illustrates how understanding the state changed over time. But even this historicization is already a naturalization of states, as societies are implicitly taken to be separated and enclosed within national boundaries. In the face of these very apparent differences, for example in the federal or centralized structure of states, the puzzle of the workings of 'statehood' remains – and any explanation of this puzzle needs to develop a 'useful concept of state as the institutionalisation of power' (Nettl, 1968: 563). Whether practices within sovereign space are predatory or cooperative depends on a number of factors (Bonney, 1995, 1999: 4). Tilly (1992: 30) calls the resultant forms *coercion-intensive* or *capital-intensive* modes, respectively.

One key factor here is the international system, which developed alongside the permeation of society by capitalism and its expansion (Siegelberg, 2000: 51). Most states followed the demand derived from the international norm of statehood rather than achieving stateness as a purely internal process. Even in European state development, excluding domestic contenders from competition for state domination was less important than state elites gaining international recognition from 'like' others to bolster claims for domestic legitimacy (Tilly, 1985: 171–173). A second key, and linked, factor is the ability to derive some financial means for institutionalize forms of domination. Unless one abides with mythological contractualist models, which inevitably involve some sort of consent to establish and institutionalize domination, a historically informed, functional model highlights the inherent coercion of states. Most of the institutions evolved not by design but rather 'as more or less inadvertent by-products of efforts to carry out more immediate tasks, especially the creation and support of armed force' (Tilly, 1992: 26).

The main challenge for power is to institutionalize mechanisms of domination, namely to balance 'cultivating' and 'vulgarizing' tendencies (Bliesemann de Guevara, 2012: 5). Besides creating input legitimacy (by opening spaces for participation in decision making) as well as output legitimacy (by provision of public goods and services), the state requires a sufficient amount of ideational legitimacy. This entails a commonly shared assumption that *a* state is the adequate form of domination and that *this* state is the adequate version thereof. In other words, the state ought to be 'in the minds' of people (Bourdieu, 1998: 99), so that they accept that, for example, regulation of orders of violence is the state's domain, not tribes' or ethnic or religious groups' (Elias, 1997: 151–168).

From a political economy point of view, it is the mode of economic reproduction that counts for the state's legitimacy. Broad taxation encourages broad participation; if corporate interests reign, then the majority is likely to be excluded from political decision-making. The state – its functioning as well as its acceptance – is, therefore, contingent upon the constant and processual struggle between the ideal of broad participation and representation on one hand, and the power that underpins particular interests (which may be well incorporated into state institutions or try to appropriate such functions) on the other.

For Rokkan, the state consists of two parallel worlds, one of them legitimizing the state by some sort of participative decision-making, which he calls *plebiscitarianism*, based on the inclusion of all persons living on a limited territory. Decisions are contingent upon the other world, *corporatism*, requiring 'the consent and participation of corporate groups controlling key resources' (Rokkan, 1999: 261). While those worlds are opposed in terms of interests and functional logics, decisions in one area inevitably influence the other. However, the respective weight of each sid may differ, ref ecting political institutionalization of plebiscitarian influences, political channel of accountability, and forms corporatist inf uence may take – from lobbyism, to the funding of political parties or election campaigns, to support for drafting laws or producing the knowledge these rest upon. More concealed forms can easily be conceived given the social bonds that corporate actors have as a distinct class.

What Rokkan has described for European states is, however, applicable for states under intervention and statebuilding regimes as general themes. In the Rokkan model of corporate vs. plebiscitarian interests, states under intervention acquire a third set of interests – that of the intervening actors. Declaratorily, intervening outsiders support the plebiscitarian aspects; however, considerations of exit strategies, sustainability, and a reluctance to take on long-term commitments or external trusteeship often prevail. They have to rely on local elites, often part of the corporate side. External statebuilding, in its attempt to redesign social structures and state institutions, provides funding to actors under intervention, and thus reshapes the balancing process of corporate and plebiscitarian interests.

This is all the more true where economic patterns have been transformed by war or subverted to support large-scale violence in so-called war economies (see Berdal, 2009: 77–85; also Keen, 2012). Conversely, violence remains an asset in peace to influence economic interaction (Giustozzi, 2009: 87–98). External funding bodies never remain outside political struggles. Discourses of the impartiality of external interveners that operate on the basis of romanticizing local agency and mystifying the 'power, capacities, and technologies' of the externals (Richmond, 2011: 151) do not prevent us from tracing the interactions between elite and popular interests and the policies and actions of external interveners. Often dominant policy discourse operates to depoliticize negotiation processes, which deal with funding of policy (see Duffield, 2005: 88–107; 2007: 170–172). However, the historicity of the intervention indicates that former experiences and practices of state funding inform and prescribe modes of interventionist repertoires of action; likewise, older modes of interventions define the methods intervening actor are willing and, indeed, able to apply. The result is a highly politicized local–international space (Heathershaw and Lambach, 2008), which defies its own myths of impartiality and neutrality i ethical matters.

The financial side of statebuilding

The financial side of statebuilding has not received the same attention as other issues of international interventionism. It seems clear that interventions have to be financed and that ai is part of the peacebuilding and statebuilding business. The questions of how the amounts, modes, and logics of international fnancing affect the capacity and legitimacy of the states built, however, have not figured center-stage in academic accounts. There are two main arenas that need close reflection to understand the dynamics of the financial side of statebuilding: the 'metropolita arena,' where aid commitments are negotiated and disbursements authorized (Veit and Schlichte, 2012: 169–171), and the arena of the intervention itself, where international donors and their agencies interact with 'local stakeholders' and with each other (Veit and Schlichte, 2012: 172–175; Bliesemann de Guevara and Kühn, 2010: 185–192).

In the metropolitan arena, Suhrke and Buckmaster (2006: 352–353) identify three main patterns of donor behavior. First, donors have a strong interest in stabilizing and consolidating the peacebuilding and statebuilding processes, for instance because they view peace as 'theirs' or because they favor the post-war regime. In these cases 'aid acquires great political and symbolic value' (Suhrke and Buckmaster, 2006: 352; also Veit and Schlichte, 2012: 170). Soaring aid levels during the first post-war years are characteristic, but successively decrease when the exceptionalit of the situation withers away and intervention normalizes. A second pattern can be observed where 'major donors have reservations about a peace agreement.' Due to these reservations, or because of fears of a lack of absorptive capacity, aid levels are low and bound to conditionality. In the third pattern, aid levels start at average levels to be reduced consequently following concerns about the progress of peacebuilding and statebuilding.

In any of these patterns, the amount of money being pledged rests not on assessments about what might be required. Also, insights into how modes of aid influence unfolding political processes in the countries under intervention have little impact on commitment and disbursement levels. Rather, they predominantly depend on donors' interests and the logics of political and symbolical interaction among them. Over time, financing statebuilding becomes increasingl problematic when results fail donors' expectations and/or attention moves to other conflict areas

Given the conceptual merger of development and security that has developed over the past two decades, stating that the two goals are mutually dependent, one might expect the two aspects in international interventions to receive similar levels of commitment (Tschirgi et al., 2010: 407).

Yet, in reality, and more so in view of low or sinking aid levels, security always trumps, sidelining development considerations while radicalizing aims of social modernization (see Duffield, 2005 258; Kühn, 2010: 224; Spear and Williams, 2012). Consequently, only a fraction of the overall money pledged eventually finds its way into the statebuilding mechanism

Contradictions and problems do not end once money is disbursed; modes of aid delivery also impact on political processes. One central question is whether aid money should be spent through local authorities or donors' agencies and projects. While the latter presumably helps donors to ensure that the money is used for intended purposes, it undermines the state to be built by creating a 'dual public sector' (OECD, 2010: 61–86). This not only deprives the state of opportunities to gain capacity and output legitimacy, it also negatively affects the labor market, as skilled workers choose to work for the intervention agencies rather than the state, the local NGO scene, or the local private sector. Nonetheless, such individual dependencies help in mainstreaming (neo)liberal values with cooperating elites.

The OECD recommends a 'mix of aid instruments' balancing between different modes of aid delivery, with the goal of increasingly getting aid 'on budget'; that is, spending it through the state.[1] In a 'virtual public sector,' ideally, donors and the state jointly strive to manage and oversee funds (OECD, 2010: 14–15). Whether such partnerships could really help to overcome the core dilemma is not clear, however. As Andersen shows for the GEMAP programme in Liberia, such forms of 'tacit trusteeship' might just as well lead to unintended results: 'Rather than being a transparent programme that was open for public scrutiny, the programme appeared convoluted and ambiguous, and therefore open to multiple interpretations – and exploitations – by political actors inside and outside Liberia' (Andersen, 2012: 134). The main questions with regard to the political economy of statebuilding thus remain: what incentives are produced by aid flows, how do they impact on the state, and what mechanisms help check on those spendin the money – be they local or international actors?

In any statebuilding intervention, the search for an exit strategy, not only militarily but also financially, ultimately boils down to one question: how to organize the transformation from aid dependency to self–sustainable state financing. The type of a state's material reproduction offer specific possibilities and challenges to statebuilders. The spectrum of ideal–types of state financin is marked by the tax state on the one end, and the rentier state on the other.

A tax state ideal–typically acquires its revenues from economic activities on its national territory; that is, from direct and indirect taxation and customs duties. Direct taxes and social contributions on the income of citizens and businesses are the royal way of taxation, yet their establishment is demanding: the state needs to make its society 'legible' (Scott, 1998: 65–71) in order to be able to collect, process, and store tax–relevant information, often against corporate actors' resistance, and to build up capacity to enforce tax levying. Once established, however, resource extraction by broad taxation potentially creates 'f scal bonds' between state and society (Schlichte, 2005: 183–200): the state's financial dependence on its citizens gives the latter leverag to voice their demands. 'No taxation without representation,' the slogan of the American independence movement, exemplif es this ideal–typical connection.

Conversely, rentier states are f nanced through external rents; that is, income received without investment (for detail see Beck, 2009; Kühn, 2008; Luciani, 1987: 73–75). The classical form of economic rent is the oil rent, but other highly valued natural resources also qualify. Another type is political rents; that is, transfer payments by international sponsors or in the form of development aid. Preconditions for the functioning of the ideal–typical rentier state are the monopolization of the rent by the state, relative autonomy from the rent–givers, and ideally also price control to avoid variations in rent levels. State–society relations in rentier states are shaped by a top–down mode of resource distribution, which favors the creation of patron–client relationships. This does not exclude the state's provision of welfare; however, its social logic differs from that of welfare provision in tax states, giving intermediaries between state and citizens large leverage.

In the following, we use the examples of Bosnia and Herzegovina (a tax state) and Afghanistan (a rentier state) to illustrate how the political economy of statebuilding impacts on the state and its material reproduction between the two ends of the spectrum. Most strikingly, despite considerable differences of mechanisms and outlook of the respective political economies, both cases show tendencies of a solidifying dependency on external actors.

Bosnia and Herzegovina

Following patterns of state financing in the socialist Yugoslavia, Bosnia and Herzegovina's (BiH) material reproduction is based on indirect taxes and customs duties. The civil war from 1992 to 1995 caused infrastructural destruction and economic decay. In 1995, gross domestic product (GDP) had sunk by 80 per cent as compared to 1990; industrial production was a fraction of its pre-warlevel. Ninety per cent of the population depended on humanitarian assistance. Western donors invested large sums into reconstruction and the implementation of 'their' Dayton Peace Agreement, trying to secure their investments and hoping to compensate for mistakes made during the war. Furthermore, the World Bank suggested front-loading aid as a jump-start for the country's economy (Suhrke and Buckmaster, 2006: 343–345). In terms of physical and infrastructural reconstruction, this strategy was quite successful.

With regard to its effects on political structures of power and domination, however, the economic intervention caused effects that were diametrically opposed to the goal of creating a unifed Bosnian state. In the first years, Bosnian politics and economy were a 'continuation of war wit other means': the state remained divided along ethno–nationalist lines into three separate systems of (para–state) rule. Strengthening the federal state of BiH seemed a long way away. Due to the weakness and permanent political blockades of central state institutions, most donors spent directly via BiH's two ethno–nationally controlled entities, cantons or municipalities, or with the help of NGOs.

The bureaucratic pressure to disperse aid quickly rendered spending an end in itself. The f nancial intervention thus created an 'economy sui generis, the extreme version of an economy characterised by "rent–seeking", in which the appropriation and transformation of external funds into local rents becomes the most attractive form of economic activity' (Ehrke 2003: 142; present authors' translation). Local elites used rents to consolidate their power, e.g., by channelling aid to local communities or by deciding on the distribution of humanitarian assistance. However, from 1997 on, the intervention worked toward dismantling the parallel structures of rule and creating a unif ed economic and financial space. While it eventually succeeded in 'politicall expropriating' ethno–nationalist elites, creating a better basis for statebuilding, this did not yet entail a stronger institutionalization of the central state. Rather, in interveners' 'tacit complicity' (Bliesemann de Guevara, 2012, forthcoming), some economic reforms directly strengthened the state's competitors.

A central example is the privatization process of socially owned assets, which was seen as an indispensable step in the creation of a liberal market economy and in boosting economic growth as a basis for sustainable peace (Donais, 2002; Pugh, 2002). Privatization was supposed to trigger the modernization of ailing enterprises and to increase state income needed to finance budge deficits, pay back international liabilities, and counterbalance sinking external aid. Another goal was to wrench the economy from politicians' grip. In reality, however, local elites used formal and informal ways to ensure their influence over privatized businesses or appropriate them. Thi guaranteed personal enrichment while local elites used gains and jobs to build up or keep a loyal clientele. Despite audit processes, which the intervention made mandatory to hinder informal relations between political and economic actors, informal channels created or strengthened during this phase remain effective to date (Bliesemann de Guevara, 2009: 131–144; 2012; forthcoming).

The first intervention phase brought to light the inherent problems of economic liberalizatio in an institutional vacuum. The state remained weak, as international actors either consciously circumvented its institutions or marginalized them by the collateral effects of their reforms. Local power–brokers, by contrast, quickly adapted to the new internationalized conditions and contrived ways and means to secure privileges and benefices. In 2000, the intervention's economic strategy changed. One improvement was a statement of intent that the international agencies would henceforth channel aid money through (central) state institutions, which they would have to build up and strengthen in the first place. Additionally, the international financi institutions (IFIs), such as the IMF and World Bank, and Western donors replaced reconstruction aid successively by development aid tied to structural adjustment demands. The European Union further conditioned negotiations by formulating requirements for a stabilization and association agreement. The neoliberal core of economic reform policies – growth, macroeconomic stability, and structural adjustments – remained untouched (Pugh, 2002: 473). The goal was to make the Bosnian state financially sustainable, thus creating an exit option for donors

Financially, the strategic change consisted in a decrease in international budget aid from more than 25 per cent to less than 10 per cent of the state budget. Yet BiH remained uncreditworthy and thus dependent on conditioned international aid and loans by donors to finance budget deficits, debt services, and public investments. Conditionality opened up opportunities for international actors to impose reforms of the state and its spending and to interfere with economic, fiscal, and financial politics. The aim of such reforms was inclusion into European and worl market structures, for which moves by Bosnian politicians to regulate trade, such as imposing temporary customs on imported rural produce to protect local farmers, had to be prevented.

An important reform to ensure stable federal state finances was the centralization of indirec taxes. With Dayton, the prerogative to collect taxes had fallen within the jurisdiction of the entities, cantons and municipalities, and until 2004, the central state depended on the entities' financial transfers. With their amount open to negotiations, the entities held enormous power and a quasi–statecharacter. Putting the Indirect Taxation Authority (ITA) in charge of collecting and administering indirect taxes thus meant a qualitative breakthrough in terms of state capacity, and for the first time provided the Bosnian state with a secured income and some limite financial independence (Bliesemann de Guevara, 2009: 152–154)

Nonetheless, the Bosnian tax state remains unable to finance its expenditures, as its financi base cannot be broadened signif cantly. The state's macroeconomic development prospects are slim. Since 1996, growth rates have lagged behind even the most pessimistic projections, and BiH has not yet reached pre–war economic levels. By lowering income taxes and social security contributions, the intervening agencies aimed at creating a business–friendly environment to stimulate economic growth. They hoped to reduce the shadow economy, which amounts to over 40 per cent of total employment, contributing to low state income. Yet the strategy has proved unable to lower unemployment and poverty (Pugh, 2007; UNDP, 2007). This way, not only is state income limited, but also the legitimacy the state can derive from a functioning national economy remains low. That this has not transposed into social unrest may be due to high yields for the population stemming from remittances sent by migrating relatives.

The international agencies also restructured state expenditure, criticized as excessive and socially unjust. They demanded decreasing public wages and downsizing the public sector as well as reforms to the welfare system. However, these neoliberal core instruments had contrary effects in the Bosnian post–war society. Lacking measures to enhance their social acceptability – especially improvement of employment opportunities – social system reforms provoked deep resentments. International dependency limits the Bosnian state's spending maneuverability (Bliesemann de Guevara, 2008). Regarding institution–building, the reforms had ambiguous effects. The quickly rising number of federal ministries and state agencies, accompanied by soaring costs, collided with the IFI's austerity program. In view of the federal ministries' and state agencies' notorious lack of resources, the mixture of austerity and growing costs has hindered the strengthening of state capacity. This in turn has had negative effects on the legitimacy of state institutions among Bosnian citizens who, based on historical Yugoslav experiences, expect a comparably comprehensive state performance.

In summary, the main problem for tax–state building has been the neoliberal statebuilding intervention itself. The idea of free markets, realized through trade liberalization (Willett, 2011) and business growth incentives, and based on donors' ideologies and interests, has dominated the economic agenda. Yet trade liberalization failed to increase customs revenues, while business growth based on tax exemptions contributed neither to sustainable state financing nor to jo creation or poverty reduction (Pugh, 2011). The Bosnian state's remaining dependence on budget aid caused by such external limitations to the expansion of its tax base, however, has solidifie its political dependence.

Afghanistan

Afghanistan has historically relied on external funds for financing the state. As a buffer betwee the Tsarist and British Empires, dependence on income from changing alliances coupled with very low levels of what is commonly referred to as 'development' shaped the state in the modern era. Politically, Afghanistan had put its bet on the axis powers, and had to rely on external funding during the Musahiban period.[2] The Cold War after the 1950s allowed for playing the superpowers against each other in the quest for money. The fully fledged rentier state was masterfully engineered by the Musahiban and even better orchestrated by the communists (who, however, had to rely on one donor rather than playing donors against each other). Domestic production stagnated at around 10–15 per cent of domestic demand – the economy rested mainly on subsistence; advanced goods had to be f nanced externally (Barf eld, 2010: 204). Political stagnation was the norm; frequent revolts rose against social modernization attempts. Development projects and the security apparatus used up most revenue, not to mention patronage to secure elite support for rulers. When in 2001 US warplanes supported remaining Northern Alliance troops to rid Afghanistan of the Taliban, international goodwill tied in with older rentier structures.

Despite its appalling human rights record, Taliban monopolization of violence after 1996 was undisputed (Rashid, 2010; Kühn, 2010: 285). They concentrated on gaining control of the whole country against Ahmed Shah Massoud's fierce resistance in the North (Dorronsoro, 2005: 254 256). Otherwise, they minimized state action, reserving money for weapons and logistics, lacking revenue other than opium. Massoud's resistance was itself financed by secular regimes in Central Asia, Iran (which viewed the Taliban as part of US encirclement plans), and India (which saw the strategic balance tilting towards Pakistan) (Saikal, 2006: 221–230). Also, Massoud monopolized revenues from lapis lazuli gems (Rubin, 2002: xxv). The pursuit of rents, in other words, was the prime mode of politics, and so it remains to this day.

Rent dependency shaped political and patronage relations. When money was available, rulers could strengthen ties with politically influential groups. Such relations were notoriously unstable disintegrating when funds were running low. Indeed, disintegration and integration have been the main dynamics of Afghan politics: while the central state disintegrated, local and regional, ethnic and religious, tribal— and kinship—based relations integrated to sustain economic exchange and foster people's survival. After 2001, hence, integrating factions into the state seemed to be the mission. Hamid Karzai, as the Bonn Process unfolded, was tasked with integrating power holders into the institutions (Suhrke, 2011: 33—35; 74—85). Co-opting some of those mostly military elites turned them into economic elites – while their commitment to the state remained dubious (Giustozzi, 2009: 87—100).

Donors tried to influence the statebuilding process, although, paradoxically, the rent paid t the Afghan state foreclosed decisive leverage. Politically, rent payments allow for the recipients to isolate themselves against demands by the population. The simple mechanism that whoever pays can claim some voice in decision—making is suspended. Public support for the state, thus, remained low. Economically, as rent flows require no constant reinvestment of revenue to kee the inflow, as would be the case in a capitalist cycle of production, rents are economically unsustainable, spin-off effects are limited. Like in BiH, many payments by—pass institutions, leaving only a small share of public funds; however limited, because the public sector is paid for by this rent, its political impact is enormous (Kühn, 2010: 314—330; Beck, 2009; Luciani, 1987).

In a rentier state, a 'state—class' is likely to develop, who, like classes in general, have distinct interests of their own (Elsenhans, 1974). Within the Afghan state, structures of dependency structure politics. Personal relations of patronage tend to solidify vertically rather than horizontally: bureaucratic and administrative tasks, as well as communication channels, work up and down hierarchies; cooperation on like levels of institutions hardly takes place. Consequently, state action remains slow and inefficient (Kühn, 2010: 316). This puts the Afghan president into a hing position between donors, busily beef ng up a credible terrorist threat to keep the rent flowing Synchronously, he must keep influential groups such as Islamic clerics, affiliated businessme and the security apparatus happy. Following this logic, Karzai denounces military raids while cleverly playing his cards at donor conferences. Downstream of money flows, the state class need to incorporate the most verbal groups potentially infringing on the ruling elites' influence – cooptation of ex—Taliban and influential commanders illustrates this. Groups furthest away fro the state in social and geographical terms as well as those least able to voice political dissent lose out.

In Afghanistan, opium rents are critical. Unlike other economic rents, such as oil rents in Arab countries, where scarcity yields high returns, rents from the opium trade exist because opium is illegal. A few families control the drug trade in Afghanistan and military support for statebuilding has fostered the concentration and professionalization of opium trading, filling the coffers of few. Although border guards and policemen as well as informants and others need to be bribed, capital saturation moved ref ning closer to production: while formerly heroin was produced out of raw opium elsewhere on its way to global markets, it is now increasingly refied in Afghanistan. As clean water is required for that, paradoxically, heroin makers prof from development projects providing such better living conditions (Kühn, 2011: 123–124).

Statebuilding efforts in Afghanistan have been hampered by the logics of local rentier groups and their interaction. Where drug rentiers and state rentiers cooperate to secure future rent ows and marginalize contenders, they dominate political agendas serving their interests (Kühn, 2008: 323; 2012). From a development perspective, the rent—dominated economy is far from being self—sustainable.Instead, as pledges for sustained donor payments until 2024 show, Afghan elites have managed to gain further funding, through hinting at the dangers of underdevelopment and potential security threats. The security–development—nexus approach of Western donors has perpetuated the conditions for underdevelopment, building an overdeveloped but underachieving state that shuts itself off from the population, cooperating mainly with those violently able to undermine its position – the drug rentiers.

Rentier–statebuilding, as in Afghanistan, is a variant of the political economy of statebuilding with distinct structures of dependency (Suhrke, 2011). These are likely to prolong underdevelopment while increasing economic hindrances to market evolution, inducing 'Dutch disease'[3] and other distortions. Politically, conditionality clauses are meaningless where the threat of (others') violence or terrorism is credible – the Afghan state remains able to mobilize donor payments while reducing their external influence

Conclusion: Beyond the money-drip?

From these cases, it becomes clear that the often cited narratives about 'more time' or 'more money' are misleading. The structural hindrances to statebuilding, partly established by inter – vention itself, remain as long as the intervention continues. Even if transformative policies were to be continually applied in the depoliticized contexts of international statebuilding, they would just as continually produce dysfunctional effects: adaptive and sometimes subversive tactics by local and international corporate interests competing for infuence persist. Similarly, more money available would not mean that positive impacts would outweigh negative, and unintended, consequences of a political process distorted by competition over external funding. Beyond continuous dependency and the structural faults established regarding responsiveness and effectiveness in rentier environments, the problems of bypassing state institutions or a lack of capacity to efficiently absorb external funds would remain. As most of these problems stem from the very fact of an external presence in the political post–conflict space, these stay in place wit the intervention.

Given the interventions' economic potential, they inadvertently impact economic patterns: goods imported by the intervention f nd their way to the market, will be sold and resold, may displace local produce or open new demand. Much of this activity goes unregulated. Given that, as has been shown, taxation is 'high art' for a state because it requires the measuring and counting of complex social situations, in post–conflict environments it may be very hard to have state implement comprehensive taxation. Lack of knowledge and manipulation by infuential groups are likely to subvert such efforts. However, dependency on rents or credits may not solve the problem of the lack of funds either: large funds create incentives to appropriate the state and distributive structures, including the potential to exacerbate conflict for resources rather tha help create peace. In an extreme case such as in Afghanistan, this turns into a question of responsibility for the effects of 10 years of statebuilding: having trained thousands of members of security forces, can the West afford not to pay these individuals and continue with some oversight after 2014, risking that they would turn into 'insecurity forces' inclined to bribe the population for their own survival?

Essentially, the financing of statebuilding and, in the process, transforming the political economy of these societies is a governance effort of managing risks and development along a presumably predestined path. The main economic contradiction is that in statebuilding efforts, the spaces that are intended to be opened for liberal development are beset on all sides by disruptive effects, which undermine those very efforts. Marketization, as in the case of Bosnia and Herzegovina, as well as eternal (rent) dependency, as in Afghanistan, have not proved to have lasting effects for peace and state consolidation. Rather, the political economy of statebuilding has perpetuated potentialities of conflict. While integration into capitalist worl markets and gradual integration into a Western security community have been the long–term goals, statebuilding efforts have not managed to replace social rifts and inequity with mechanisms to fairly balance individuals' and groups' interests. Financing continually dysfunctional polities is just as problematic as withdrawing support. In effect, external interventions have to face the responsibility for statebuilding results while being unable to steer the effects of their financial support. The money–drip reproduces its own conditions.

Notes

1 This approach, however, does not account for the fact that donors' aid pledges usually contain clauses that ensure that considerable parts of the aid money flow back to businesses in the donor country (Herti et al., 2004: 337).
2 The Musahiban family were the *de facto* rulers after Nadir Shah's death in 1933. His son, Zahir Shah, took the throne aged 19 as a figurehead under his reigning uncles. He forced Mohammad Daoud, hi cousin, to resign 30 years later. His monarchy ended another 10 years later, when Daoud retook power and proclaimed the republic in 1973 (Dupree, 2005). However, as Daoud was also Musahiban, this family's rule claiming traditional legitimacy continued despite its autocratic style until 1978, when a violent communist coup brought the People's Democratic Party of Afghanistan (PDPA) to power, killing Daoud (Barfield, 2010: 211)
3 'Dutch disease' describes a sharp rise in prices for services and immovables, as the supply of these goods cannot be increased. Skilled administrators as well as property are scarce in capital cities, where most of the capital inflow takes places. Hence, prices rise

References

Andersen, L. (2012). Statebuilding as tacit trusteeship: The case of Liberia. In B. Bliesemann de Guevara (Ed.), *Statebuilding and state-formation: The political sociology of intervention*. Abingdon, UK: Routledge, pp. 132–148.
Barfield, T. (2010). *Afghanistan: A cultural and political history*. Princeton, NJ: Princeton University Press.
Beck, M. (2009). Rente und Rentierstaat im Nahen Osten. In M. Beck et al. (Eds.), *Der Nahe Osten im Umbruch*. Wiesbaden, Germany: VS Verlag, pp. 25–49.
Berdal, M. (2009). *Building peace after war*. London, UK: International Institute for Strategic Studies.
Bliesemann de Guevara, B. (2008). Material reproduction and stateness in Bosnia and Herzegovina. In M. Pugh, N. Cooper, and M. Turner (Eds.), *Whose peace? Critical perspectives on the political economy of peacebuilding*. Basingstoke, UK: Palgrave, pp. 373–389.
Bliesemann de Guevara, B. (2009). *Staatlichkeit in Zeiten des Statebuilding. Intervention und Herrschaft in Bosnien und Herzegowina*. Frankfurt am Main, Germany: Peter Lang.
Bliesemann de Guevara, B. (2012). Introduction: Statebuilding and state-formation. In B. Bliesemann de Guevara (Ed.), *Statebuilding and state-formation: The political sociology of intervention*. London, UK: Routledge, pp. 1–19.
Bliesemann de Guevara, B. (forthcoming). A 'black hole' in Europe? The social and discursive reality of crime in Bosnia–Herzegovina and the international community's tacit complicity. In R. Schönenberg and A. V. Schönfeldt (Eds.), *Transnational organized crime (TOC) and the future of a democratic world*.
Bliesemann de Guevara, B., and Kühn, F. P. (2010). *Illusion statebuilding. Warum sich der westliche Staat so schwer exportieren lässt*. Hamburg, Germany: Edition Körber-Stiftung.
Bonney, R. (1995). Introduction: Economic systems and state finance. In R. Bonney (Ed.)*Economic systems and state finance*. Oxford, UK: Oxford University Press, pp. 1–18.
Bonney, R. (1999). Introduction: The rise and fall of the fiscal state in Europe, c.1200–1815. In R. Bonney (Ed.), *The rise and fall of the fiscal state in Europe, c.1200–1815*. Oxford, UK: Oxford University Press, pp. 1–17.
Bourdieu, P. (1998). *Praktische Vernunft. Zur Theorie des Handelns*. Frankfurt am Main, Germany: Suhrkamp.
Donais, T. (2002). The politics of privatization in post–Dayton Bosnia.*Southeast European Politics*, 3(1), 3–19.
Dorronsoro, G. (2005). *Revolution unending. Afghanistan: 1979 to the present*. London, UK: Hurst.
Duffeld, M. (2005). *Global governance and the new wars. The merging of development and security*. London, UK: Zed Books.
Duffield, M. (2007). *Development, security and unending war: Governing the world of peoples*. Cambridge, UK: Polity Press.
Dupree, L. (2005). *Afghanistan* (4th impression). Karachi, Pakistan: Oxford University Press.

Ehrke, M. (2003). Von der Raubökonomie zur Rentenökonomie. Mafia, Bürokratie und internationale Mandat in Bosnien. *Internationale Politik und Gesellschaft, 2,* 123–154.
Elsenhans, H. (1974). Die Überwindung der Unterentwicklung. In D. Nohlen and F. Nuscheler (Eds.), *Handbuch der Dritten Welt. Band 1: Theorien und Indikatoren von Unterentwicklung und Entwicklung.* Hamburg, Germany: Hoffmann und Campe, pp. 162–189.
Elias, N. (1997). *Über den Prozess der Zivilisation. Gesammelte Schriften, Band 3–2.* Frankfurt am Main, Germany: Suhrkamp.
Giustozzi, A. (2009). *Empires of mud: War and warlords in Afghanistan.* London, UK: Hurst.
Heathershaw, J., and Lambach, D. (2008). Introduction: Post–conflict spaces and approaches to statebuilding *Journal of Intervention and Statebuilding, 2*(3), 269–289.
Hertić, S., Šapčanin, A., and Woodward, S. L. (2004). Bosnia and Herzegovina. In S. Forman and S. Patrick (Eds.), *Good intentions.* Boulder, CO: Lynne Rienner, pp. 315–366.
Keen, D. (2012). Greed and grievance in civil war. *International Affairs, 88*(4), 757–777.
Kühn, F. P. (2008). Aid, opium, and the state of rents in Afghanistan: Competition, cooperation, or cohabitation? *Journal of Intervention and Statebuilding, 2*(3), 309–327.
Kühn, F. P. (2010). *Sicherheit und Entwicklung in der Weltgesellschaft. Liberales Paradigma und Statebuilding in Afghanistan.* Wiesbaden, Germany: VS Verlag.
Kühn, F. P. (2011). Deutschlands (Nicht–)Drogenpolitik in Afghanistan. *Zeitschrift für Außen- und Sicherheitspolitik (ZFAS), 4*(Sonderheft 3), 115–129.
Kühn, F. P. (2012). Risk and externalisation in Afghanistan: Why statebuilding upends state–formation. In B. Bliesemann de Guevara (Ed.), *Statebuilding and state-formation: The political sociology of intervention.* Abingdon, UK: Routledge, pp. 23–39.
Luciani, G. (1987). Allocation vs. production states. A theoretical framework. In H. Beblawi and G. Luciani (Eds.), *The rentier state.* London, UK: Croom Helm, pp. 63–82.
Nettl, J. P. (1968). The state as a conceptual variable. *World Politics, 20*(4), 559–592.
OECD. (2010). *Do no harm: International support for statebuilding.* Paris, France: OECD.
Pugh, M. (2002). Postwar political economy in Bosnia and Herzegovina: The spoils of peace. *Global Governance, 8*(4), 467–482.
Pugh, M. (2007). *Limited sovereignty and economic security: Survival in Southeast Europe.* Paper presented at the Harriman Institute, Columbia University, New York, NY, 1 March.
Pugh, M. (2011). Employment, labour rights and social resistance. In M. Pugh, N. Cooper, and M. Turner (Eds.), *Whose peace? Critical perspectives on the political economy on peacebuilding.* Basingstoke, UK: Palgrave, pp. 141–158.
Rashid, A. (2010). *Taliban: The power of militant Islam in Afghanistan and beyond.* London, UK: I.B. Tauris.
Richmond, O. (2011). *A post-liberal peace.* London, UK: Routledge.
Rokkan, S. (1999). *State formation, nation-building, and mass politics in europe.* Oxford, UK: Oxford University Press.
Rubin, B. (2002). *The fragmentation of Afghanistan: State formation and collapse in the international system* (2nd ed.). New Haven, CT: Yale University Press.
Saikal, A. (2006). *Modern Afghanistan: A history of struggle and survival.* London, UK: I.B. Tauris.
Schlichte, K. (2005). *Der Staat in der Weltgesellschaft.* Frankfurt am Main, Germany: Campus.
Scott, J. C. (1998). *Seeing like a state.* New Haven, CT: Yale University Press.
Siegelberg, J. (2000). Staat und internationals System – ein strukturgeschichtlicher Überblick. In J. Siegelberg and K. Schlichte (Eds.), *Strukturwandel internationaler Beziehungen.* Wiesbaden, Germany: Westdeutscher Verlag, pp. 11–56.
Spear, J., and Williams, P. D. (2012). Conclusion: The comparative conversations between security and development. In J. Spear and P. D. Williams (Eds.),*Security and development in global politics.* Washington, DC: Georgetown University Press, pp. 313–318.
Suhrke, A. (2011). *When more is less: The international project in Afghanistan.* New York, NY: Columbia University Press.
Suhrke, A., and Buckmaster, J. (2006). Aid, growth and peace: A comparative analysis*Conflict, Security and Development, 6*(3), 337–363.
Tilly, C. (1985). War making and state making as organized crime. In P. B. Evans, D. Rueschemeyer, and T. Skocpol (Eds.), *Bringing the state back in.* Cambridge, UK: Cambridge University Press, pp. 167–191.
Tilly, C. (1992). *Coercion, capital, and European states, AD 990–1990.* Cambridge, UK: Blackwell.
Tschirgi, N., Lund, M. S., and Mancini, F. (2010). Conclusion. In N. Tschirgi, M. S. Lund, and F. Mancini (Eds.), *Security & development: Searching for critical connections.* Boulder, CO: Lynne Rienner, pp. 387–412.

UNDP. (2007). Social inclusion in Bosnia and Herzegovina. *National Human Development Report 2007*. Sarajevo, Bosnia: UNDP BiH.
Veit, A., and Schlichte, K. (2012). Three arenas: The conflictive logic of external statebuilding. In B. Bliesemann de Guevara (Ed.), *Statebuilding and state-formation: The political sociology of intervention*. Abingdon, UK: Routledge, pp. 167–181.
Willett, S. (2011). Trading with security: Trade liberalisation and conflict. In M. Pugh, N. Cooper, an M. Turner (Eds.), *Whose peace? Critical perspectives on the political economy on peacebuilding*. Basingstoke, UK: Palgrave, pp. 69–86.

19
POLITICAL ECONOMY OF POST-CONFLICT STATEBUILDING IN CENTRAL AMERICA

Aaron Schneider[1]

The current chapter suggests that statebuilding, especially in war–torn developing countries, is rooted in the way in which emerging elites reinsert themselves in the international economy. As new sectors emerge to meet the opportunities of international insertion, statebuilding is the task of finding accommodations between emerging sectors, established elites, and popular actors, mediated through state institutions. As a lens into this process, taxation provides a critical indicator, as it measures not only an aspect of state capacity but also the degree to which emerging elites are brought into a national political community to contribute to public goods.

The current chapter focuses on the challenges of raising revenues in the Central American countries of El Salvador and Guatemala. The greatest improvements in capacity and universality of tax have occurred in El Salvador, while Guatemala has raised revenues only marginally and failed to address problems of horizontal inequity across sectors. As an explanation for these patterns, and to trace broader lessons for statebuilding, the project focuses on the political economy of emerging sectors and the state in the two post–conflict countries

In El Salvador emerging transnational elites are led by financial sectors with investments sprea throughout the Central American region. For 20 years they were dominant over other sectors and cohesive in their sectoral and partisan articulation to the state, and they advanced a coherent strategy to use state power to project their activities. In marked contrast, transnational elites in Guatemala have been neither dominant nor cohesive, accommodated to traditional sectors within a single peak business association, and poorly articulated to the state through a fragmented and volatile party system. Between rival factions of transnational and traditional, urban and rural elites, no Guatemalan statebuilding project attains coherence, and competitors appear content to ensure that rival factions cannot use the state to impose dominance over the rest. The differences in the two configurations of elite are evident in taxation, with broader implications for statebuilding

The next sections describe the fiscal sociology approach to post–conflict statebuilding th orients this study. After describing in more specific detail the variations in the structure of emerging elites, the chapter explores the two cases described above, El Salvador and Guatemala. The two countries display a range of variation on statebuilding patterns, with Salvadoran elites building a state slightly more capable than Guatemala's, but the conclusion ref ects on what is further missing for a more progressive state to be built in either case.

Political economy of post-conflict statebuilding

The 1980s crisis in Central America was triggered at least in part by the exhaustion of previous patterns of international insertion and the breakdown of the authoritarian states they supported. During a decade of war, economic actors were driven to new sources of dynamism more appropriate to a changed international political economy, and they were driven to design statebuilding projects that would produce the policies and institutions to complement their new patterns of accumulation.

The current international economy includes far more integrated stages of production, as productive chains cross borders to extract raw materials, transform them into intermediate goods, assemble them into finished products, and distribute them to final markets. These processes ne not occur in close geographic proximity, and firms have reorganized themselves to locate stage of production in the locations that provided the greatest returns (Kaplinsky, 2005; Dicken, 2007; Gereff and Wyman, 1990). Many observers of globalization have commented on the uniqueness of the contemporary moment, but neither liberal nor critical approaches to globalization pay adequate attention to the implications for statebuilding. Liberal observers posit that the transnational character of emerging actors would eclipse the nation state, as they outgrow state institutions as either unviable or unnecessary (Williamson, 1990).[2] Critical globalization scholars hold that owners of capital have removed their obligations to the state or to other members of society, and simply pursue accumulation wherever and however they want (Robinson, 2003).[3]

This stateless and apolitical version of globalization misses the continued relevance of national political patterns. In many national contexts, the legacy of prior institutional arrangements has proved durable (Evans, 1997; Hall and Soskice, 2001). In addition, there remain unique historical functions necessary to manage global integration (Rodrik, 1996).[4] This is particularly true in countries that must build states to deal with new global economic patterns at the same time as they rebuild after conflicts. The functions of states have not so much disappeared as transformed and the question to ask concerns the nature of the states being built in the context of post-conflict globalization.

For Central America, the homogenizing external pressure of international integration and the persistence of national particularities are both evident. Changes associated with globalization accelerated in 1980s debt crisis and revolutionary upheaval, ushering in governments favoring neoliberal reforms. With slight variations, the region followed the rest of Latin America in adopting the liberalization, deregulation, and privatization policies that characterized structural adjustment. These were locked into trade arrangements, such as the Caribbean Basin Initiative of the 1980s and the Central American Free Trade Agreement of 2006, which gave producers in Central America privileged access to the US market.

These processes attracted Central American entrepreneurs into new export activities and attracted US and third-country investors to locate in the region, creating and empowering those emerging elites who could advance transnational processes of production. Governments of Central America competed to enhance their attractiveness to these sectors by creating special tax and regulatory regimes that held down production costs while offering geographical proximity and trade access to developed country markets.

This process has played out in Central America in specific ways. The sectors most attractiv to US markets have been tourism, final assembly manufacturing, non-traditional agriculture, an remittances. In addition, financial sectors and other services have prospered by acting as intermediaries between local interests and transnational firms (Segovia Caceres, 2005). As thes sectors expand, emerging elites seek access to the state and the institutional and policy changes that can facilitate their efforts at accumulation.

As a window into these statebuilding patterns, the public finances of Central American state offer powerful evidence. In the context of post–conflict state–building, public finances are bo causal and symptomatic. In more successful cases, revenues build state capacity; the act of gathering revenues restructures societies; and productive societies and capable states generate revenues. In less successful cases, failure to raise revenue handicaps states; the absence of revenue infrastructure leaves state and society disconnected; and weak economies and weak tax capacity coincide with weak states.

There are two underlying logics that link revenues and statebuilding, rooted in the concepts of capacity and consent (Levi, 1989: 121; Brautigam et al., 2008). Capacity arguments focus on the bureaucratic, technical, and authoritative capacity of state elites. Their capacity emerges over time and is defined in part by bureaucratic effectiveness, military power, and the degree of autonomy from social pressures (Evans et al., 1985).[5] Where states are sufficiently capable, the can extract funds from social actors, even wealthy ones whose political leverage might be significant (Tilly, 1975) [6]

Not all state efforts to expand revenues are successful, however; they depend on the consent of the governed. Consent arguments come in two forms, either suggesting that states enter into direct bargaining relationships with contributors or that tax is a result of collective action among social groups. According to bargaining arguments, legislatures and other sites of state–society communication allow for the negotiation of a f scal contract in which social groups negotiate with the state over obligations and benefits. Under this model, states will vary significantly the services they provide, depending on the groups from whom they mobilize revenue (Timmons, 2005). Tax is akin to an exchange – contributions for benef ts – in which the state 'sells' services to citizen 'consumers,' who provide tax payments.

Some see this exchange as a more diffuse transaction, in which governments must overcome collective action constraints to provide universal public goods, such as democratic participation, transparent decision–making, and effective implementation. Such goods are public because they are non–exclusive and non–rivalrous; once they are established, everyone benefits, whether o not they contributed to establishing them (Olson, 1966; Ostrom, 1990). According to this view, taxation is a collective action problem of getting individual taxpayers to pool resources to pursue social ends (Lieberman, 2003).[7]

Taxation offers a useful way into post–confct statebuilding, as it highlights both the challenges of post–conflict consolidation and more general challenges of strengthening developing countr states in the context of globalization. The sections below explore revenue regimes in El Salvador and Guatemala since the end of their conflicts in the 1990s. Both countries were faced with statebuilding challenges after civil war and in the presence of dynamic transnationalized sectors. Distinct patterns of emerging elite cohesion and relationships to other groups left the two countries with quite different tax regimes, and ultimately quite different post–corifct statebuilding results.

Tax regime outcomes

Tax regime outcomes in El Salvador and Guatemala display marked contrasts. El Salvador has increased its tax capacity by almost 40 per cent while Guatemala has barely increased its tax capacity at all – it increased only around 10 per cent during the period. Figure 19.1 displays the change in tax capacity in terms of revenue as a percentage of GDP with 1992 set to 100.

What explains these differences in tax regimes? The current chapter suggests that these, and other, differences in taxation are the product of contrasting statebuilding projects of emerging elites. In the two countries, emerging elites occupied relatively similar positions in international

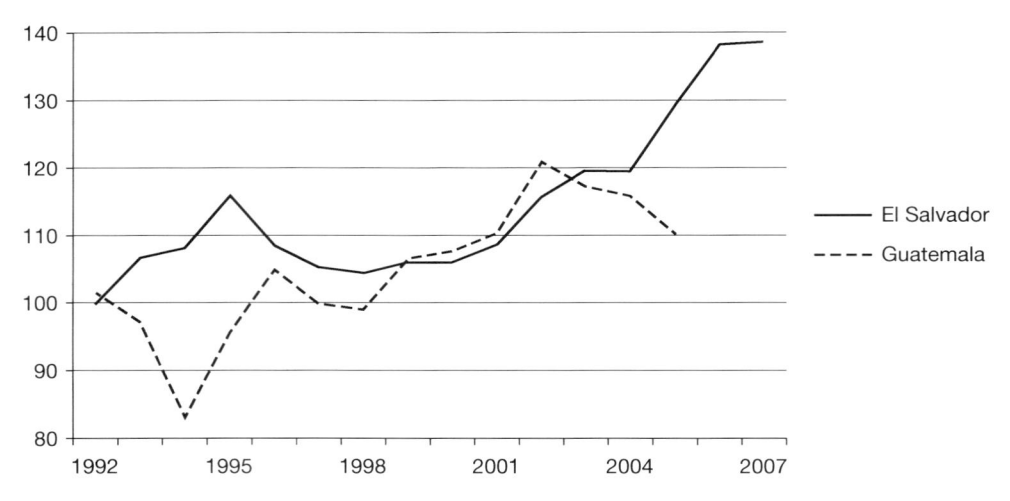

Figure 19.1 Change in tax capacity in terms of revenue as a percentage of GDP, with 1992 set to 100.
Source: Author calculations based on CEPAL data, www.cepal.org/ilpes

capitalism, but they have done so with different strategies of accumulation, distinct patterns of cohesion and dominance, and unique institutional and policy adaptations of the state. [8] These differences have played out in the tax regimes that have been established, and call into question the adequacy of the statebuilding processes that have occurred since the end of conflict

El Salvador: Inside-out statebuilding

The statebuilding project that has emerged in El Salvador has to be placed in the context of the civil war of the 1980s. With the Peace Accords of 1992, the Left gained access to electoral politics and the military reduced its presence (Torres–Rivas, 1989: 9). At the same time, the war provoked a change among private sector actors, as a new segment of elites emerged, active within dynamic sectors integrated in transnational processes of production such as assembly manufacture, non-traditional agriculture, tourism, and f nance. They were equipped with sectoral institutions to coordinate different factions of capital and to develop a statebuilding program, and they formed a business–orientedparty, the National Republican Alliance (ARENA), to carry their state-building program into the political arena. They were victorious for two decades of presidential struggles, and they were largely able to impose the statebuilding program they had devised (Blanco, 1998; Segovia Caceres, 2004). It was reflected in a pattern of taxation that mobilize new revenues and even applied tax law relatively evenly. To make sense of this combination of dominance, cohesion, tax capacity, and universality, the following paragraphs describe the political and fiscal changes that have occurred in El Salvador over the past 20 years

Diverse capitalist factions emerged during the civil war of the 1980s, and they were coordinated through family networks, political and intellectual institutions, and especially through economic conglomerates peaked by financial consortiums (Paige, 1997). They entered politica power with the government elected in 1989, led by ARENA president and banking mogul Alfredo Cristiani. The Cristiani government lowered trade barriers, prioritized stable monetary policy, liberalized domestic prices, privatized the banking system, opened a portion of the social security system to private coverage, and established the autonomy of the Central Reserve Bank (Wood and Segovia, 1999). ARENA President Calderón Sol (1994–1999) followed by privatiz-ing sugar refineries, telecommunications and electricity distribution, and pensions

These policies opened space for the financial sector to seize the reins of the economy, bot as a major source of growth and as the organizer of productive activities, allocating Salvadoran capital to transnational production. Banking interests brought together producers, service providers, construction firms, and commercial outlets in conglomerates that quickly looked beyond Salvadoran consumers and targeted the international market.

Towards the latter half of the 1990s, the consumption boom and capital influx of the imme diate after-war period began to slow, and financial sector leaders, enriched by the liberalizatio of the economy and the concentration of productive assets in their conglomerates, sought to extend their field of accumulation. They reorganized Salvadoran capital once again, this time t spread it through the region, taking advantage of the economic integration that had occurred in the aftermath of the Central American Common Market (Moreno, 2000).

To facilitate their extension into other territories, ARENA President Flores (1999–2004) adopted the dollar as the Salvadoran currency in 2001.[9] This strengthened the currency, which hurt exporters, but dollarization ensured access to credit at low interest rates, allowing banks to absorb productive activities in the rest of the region, buying up existing assets and making new investments (Towers and Borzutzky, 2004).

Salvadoran capital came to operate in the transnational sectors of other countries, coordinating those transnational processes that integrated productive activities across the countries of the region. By operating in multiple countries, non-traditional agricultural producers insured themselves against bad seasons; hoteliers and shopping mall owners replicated their investments; and manufacturing assembly firms in multiple export processing zones could share inputs and contracts. This degree of integration required coordination, and it was led by Salvadoran fiance capital, which allocated investments to ensure the compatibility of activities across territories.[10]

In addition to the economic changes this outward investment implied, it also indicated changing power relationships among factions of capital. Before the war, the Salvadoran elite had been identified as the 'most authentic oligarchy of Latin America,' reputedly dominating th economy through 14 families whose wealth rested on landholding and agricultural exports (Johnson, 1993).[11] The war prompted emerging elites to coordinate their activities in business associations and think-tanks, articulated to the ARENA party. The Salvadoran Foundation for Economic and Social Development (FUSADES) emerged in 1983 with the explicit goal of promoting a new national economic model (Rosa, 1993: 80). Beginning in 1989, members of the FUSADES Executive Committee put themselves forward and won candidacies to the presidency of the country through the ARENA party, and they carried with them FUSADES' influence [12]

In part, their impressive cohesion was reinforced by the slimness of their hold on power. Slim margins of victory over the former guerrilla opposition, FMLN, forced ARENA to purchase legislative majorities with the cooptation of smaller 'taxi' parties, as smaller conservative parties are known. Constantly threatened with the possibility it could lose power, ARENA behaved as though every election could be its last, and resisted any attempt to soften its stance during elections or to moderate its policy proposals while in off ce. The threat of losing might not have been so meaningful if the two parties were not so polarized. A survey of legislators, conducted by the University of Salamanca, exhibits differences between the FMLN and ARENA on political economy questions. On a scale from Left to Right from 0 to 10, the average score of FMLN legislators was 1.65 and the average among ARENA legislators was 8.13 (Schneider, 2008) – the most polarized party system in the Americas.[13]

Conditions of dominance and cohesion among emerging elites have played out in the tax regime in a pattern of reform in which ARENA leaders impose the reforms they desire by fiat Still, the threat of losing power to the Left led them to refrain from creating instruments that might create progressive taxation or tap into the most dynamic transnational sectors. The changes that occurred increased Salvadoran tax revenues at the fastest rate of any country in the region. In 1989, total taxes were around 9.1 per cent of GDP; they increased to 11.2 per cent by 2000 and 13.9 per cent by 2007. While this was still below the average for Latin American countries of 15.1 per cent, it was among the highest in Central America, and marks a 52.7 per cent change over the period.[14]

Most of this increase has occurred by tapping into relatively few bases. Indirect taxes have maintained their share, at 70 per cent of the total, but their allocation has shifted away from trade taxes and stamp taxes and toward the value added tax (VAT). The VAT has been applied to most services and to most commonly consumed products, and is now the most important tax in the country, responsible for more than 50 per cent of the total.

The increase in capacity and the shifting tax structure has spread the burden of taxation to a broader base, making the system more universal. In particular, in replacing the costly and inefficient sales tax and the stamp tax, the VAT has been especially productive.[15] El Salvador collects a high percentage of the tax it is due relative to the amount of economic activity that is taxable, with a rate of productivity of the VAT in 2006 that was the second highest in Latin America, behind only Chile, at 54.4 per cent. This rate also represented a 10 percentage point increase over the 15 years in which the VAT has been in existence (Artana and Navajas, 2008: 8).

Still, the Salvadoran tax regime has failed to tap into the plurinational income streams of financial elites. According to a 2008 study by the Central American Institute of Fiscal Studies, 'in El Salvador, there is not a system of taxation to tap into global income, so there are few legal instruments that can monitor payment of taxes in the context of the most signifcant changes in the national economy' (ICEFI, 2008: 22). While the system has increased capacity and universality, it has fallen short on progressivity, the ability to tax wealthy sectors at higher rates. This shortcoming will be addressed in the conclusion, as it reflects on the type of state-buildin that has occurred, and who has advanced it.

Salvadoran economic actors have advanced a strategy of accumulation focused on regional activity, extending their financial interests into the transnational activities of multiple neighborin countries. They have been dominant politically and cohesive in advancing their agenda, and they

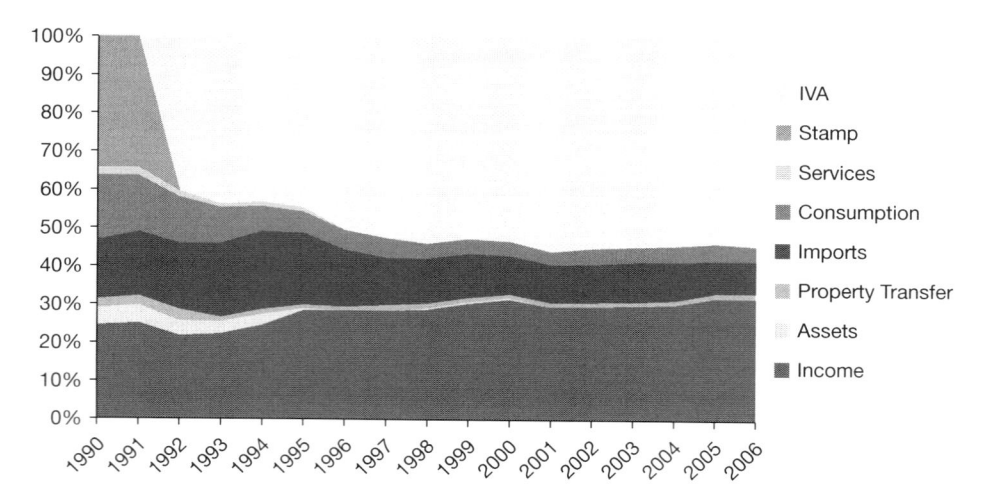

Figure 19.2 Tax trends in El Salvador.
Source: Author calculations based on data from the Ministry of Finance – General Treasury Directorate, El Salvador

have adapted the state to fit their needs. This has resulted in significant advance for tax capaci and universality, with revenues increasing and being applied across contributors. One sector that has been spared, international finance, is also the most dynamic, as it has come to coordinat transnational activities across the region. While emerging elites have largely structured a state to facilitate their strategies of accumulation, they have not been willing to pay for the state they have designed, even as they have supported efforts to secure more revenues and even to collect some revenues relatively universally. While inadequate, this statebuilding pattern and tax regime impact stands in contrast to those witnessed in Guatemala, where emerging elites have remained more divided and less dominant, with far lower changes to the capacity and universality of tax regimes.

Guatemala: Crisis in statebuilding

Unlike in El Salvador, the civil war and the economic crisis of the 1980s did not significantl weaken traditional elites, nor did the revolutionary Left emerge as a viable electoral force in the post−conflictperiod. As a result, emerging transnational elites were both subordinate and divided in their statebuilding activism, with little post−conflict change in institutions or policies, and temporary and stop−gap measures have been suffcient only to save the state from collapse. For taxes, this has produced cyclical movement in which short−term f xes respond to fiscal emer gencies but eventually reach their time limit or are rolled back, forcing governments to begin the process anew. The result is consistently poor revenue mobilization, failure to tax those with more wealth, and exemptions and incentives that complicate the tax regime. In short, Guatemalan statebuilding remains in crisis.

This condition may seem surprising, as Guatemalan business elites are impressively organized and remarkably united within a single peak business association, CACIF. Yet within CACIF there has been little turnover in terms of new elites displacing old ones, and traditional exporters have skillfully incorporated newly transnationalized sectors into existing networks. With the intensification of conflict in the 1980s and the opening of new commercial opportunities wit the Caribbean Basin Initiative in the 1980s, transnational elites attempted to create their own think−tanksand sectoral associations to articulate an independent statebuilding agenda with some autonomy from CACIF. Nevertheless, 'the transnational fraction did not achieve the amount of influence over state policy as it did, for instance, in El Salvador and Costa Rica. The Guatemalan state and its policies continued to be influenced by rival fractions of capital and competing elite and the old guard' (Robinson, 2000: 102).

New sectors gained space economically, and clothing assembly manufactures are now the single largest export, equal to 13.9 per cent of all exports; fruit accounts for 3.41 per cent of exports; and tourism receipts in 2007 totaled $965.4 million (US), equal in foreign exchange earnings to 13.48 percent of exports.[16] Still, these activities did not completely replace traditional exports, buoyed in recent years by the resurgence in commodity prices, and preserving their space within exports to the rest of the region. Coffee, sugar, and bananas remain the second, third, and fourth most important export products, joined in the top 10 by precious stones, oil, and cardamom (Economist Intelligence Unit, 2008 – eiu.com).

Equally important to their continued export relevance, traditional sectors have preserved their influence through family and financial networks that link them to transnational sectors. Surplu from traditional exports has been a source of capital for investments in new export sectors, tying them together in family−run financial conglomerates (Robinson, 2003: 102–118). The bankin sector has led this transformation, partnering with Salvadoran financial interests to integrate regional operations as well as concentrate control of banking in Guatemala (Segovia Caceres,

2004). This has resulted in the consolidation of a limited number of family networks, especially traditionally powerful families, such as the Castillo, Novella, Saravia, Herrera, and Botrán families. These families, which predate the rise of commercial elites, successfully absorbed rising sectors and maintained interests in traditional exports, industry, and agribusiness (Dosal, 1995). In one study of these networks, Marta Casaús suggests that there is 'a permanent and persistent set of family networks that operate as autonomous entities but which develop through webs or groups based on kinship' (cited in Valdez, 2003: 126).

Factions of capital are coordinated through family and financial networks and articulated politically through CACIF (Rettberg, 2007), but the failure of any one group to assert dominance has left their political activism truncated at the level of pressure group with veto power over rival programs.

No political party sustainably articulates the interests of transnational elites, and the party system remains fragmented, volatile, and inchoate. Political parties in Guatemala tend to be short-lived, emerging and disappearing from election to election, rooted in the personalities and political aspirations of their leaders, and with only loose control over deputies once in office. Parties hav only rudimentary organizational structures and limited links to groups within civil society, making it almost impossible to count on political parties to coordinate policy making or draw together a platform for statebuilding reform.

One indicator of the weakness of political parties is the level of volatility and fragmentation in party representation. Volatility examines the degree to which support for different parties stays relatively the same over time, indicating a predictable pattern of partisan competition. Where volatility is higher, with parties rapidly increasing or decreasing their support and even disappearing, they have difficulty performing their representative functions and do a poor job of connecting citizens to the state. One measure of volatility is the Pedersen index, which calculates the average percentage change in party representation from one election to the next (Pedersen, 1979). The Guatemalan party system shows extremely high volatility, with an average election-to-election swing of 62.6 per cent compared to a regional average of 21.3 (Achard et al., 2006).

Guatemala also tops the league in party system fragmentation, an indicator of the effective number of parties earning votes or winning seats in Congress (Laakso and Taagepera, 1979). The country averaged 3.64 effective parties in the legislature since 1990, peaking in 2009 with 5.05 effective parties. New parties appear and disappear from election to election, few of which survive for any length of time. In the elections of 1985, five parties captured 92 per cent of the seats i Congress, but in the 1999 election these same parties obtained only 1.8 per cent. More than 50 parties have appeared and disappeared in the past 20 years, and their average lifespan has been less than 10 years (Porras, 2005).

The combination of multiple parties with volatile bases and shifting representatives makes legislation extremely difficult. Executives face the challenge of constantly rebuilding a governin majority, something that requires repeated negotiation with party leaders and individual deputies, pursuing agreements with each on an individual basis (Eraso and Núñez, 2008; Mack, Donis, and Castillo, 2006).

These problems in the party system might be manageable if emerging elites had other institutional mechanisms through which to implement a coherent statebuilding program. They do not. In fact, most institutions of the state are left over from the 1985 Constitution, written in the context of ongoing conflict, by a traditional elite and a military loath to lose their prerogatives in a transition to democracy. State institutions are characterized by informal practices and multiple veto points, allowing powerful opponents to block long-term policy or institutional reforms. Perhaps the most important veto player is the Constitutional Court.

The Constitutional Court has carefully guarded against changes to the rules in place at the time of the transition to democracy. Among the articles used most often to oppose tax reforms, Article 243 of the Constitution prohibits confiscatory tax and double or multiple taxation, nonretroactive application of the law, and the right not to self-incriminate. These have been labeled 'fiscal padlocks' by Guatemalan observers, who note that fiscal padlocks put 'severe limi on the tax powers of Congress and [make] the courts an additional battlefield on tax legislation (CEPAL, 1996). The Constitution further allows any citizen, with legal assistance, to present a complaint to the Court, which holds the power to suspend in whole or in part a law considered unconstitutional (Fuentes Knight and Cabrera, 2006).

During the past 20 years, bridging six administrations, the Court has heard more than 100 complaints about tax reforms, ruling on 88 of them. On average, complaints were successful 43 per cent of the time (38 of 88), with 61 per cent of the complaints reviewed during the Cerezo government found meritorious and 46 per cent under Portillo. Successful complaints carried class, state, and partisan implications. The Court responded directly to pressure from CACIF, which staged media campaigns, capital strikes, and presented a flood of complaints. This had th effect of starving governments of resources, as most of their complaints were against the stop-gap measures meant to address fiscal crisis

Many Court decisions were also overtly partisan, as the Court denied funds to governments controlled by political rivals of the parties who had named the justices. One illustrative example related to tax is the overturning of the Tax on Mercantile and Agricultural Businesses. The Court received the complaints in 2001 and 2002 but waited until the final days of the sitting FRG government, in December 2003, to issue its decision. By this point, the GANA party had won the next election, and the decision denied resources to the incoming government, thereby handcuffing the new administration with a new fiscal emergenc

The Court is a typical example of both the constraints on meaningful reform and the incentives to powerful actors. As a body with significant veto power to overturn legislation on the basis o a highly specific and detailed Constitution, the Court can limit statebuilding efforts and thereb influence both the structure of the tax system and the amount of revenue enjoyed by different governments. At the same time, a poorly regulated selection process and great discretion in the interpretation of the Constitution means that powerful actors apply pressure for nomination of justices favorable to their cause, secure the decisions they desire, and make use of judicial decisions to influence partisan and governmental fortunes

Guatemalan transnational elites have remained divided and subordinate to traditional interests, and lack mechanisms to carry their interests into the state. As a result, Guatemalan revenues are the lowest in Central America and second lowest in Latin America. They are regressive, falling more heavily on poorer income brackets, and they are applied in particularistic fashion, with activities in different sectors facing different tax rules. The country mobilizes too little revenue to meet its commitments, fails to draw revenues from the wealthiest sectors, and applies tax law in a piecemeal fashion across economic actors. Capacity increased over the past two decades, but this increase was the lowest in the region and prone to frequent fictuation, as multiple stop-gap efforts patched f scal holes but quickly lapsed. State reformers are constantly running just to stand still.

Like El Salvador and the rest of the region, taxes in Guatemala have diversified but remaine concentrated on indirect bases. VAT taxes replaced trade taxes and stamp duties, but direct taxes on property, assets, and income have not increased significantly and have even deteriorated ove time. The most important indirect tax, the VAT, was introduced during the 1980s and at the moment has a 12 per cent rate. VAT is paid on purchases of goods and services and is pocked with a number of exemptions, including low-priced fresh food, smaller houses, generic medicines, financial services, and sectoral memberships. A complication for both collection and compliance with the VAT is that it can be deducted from income tax, leading individuals to report their tax number with every purchase. VAT revenues increased with administrative reforms in 2006 and remain the most important source of revenues, but they continue to show limited productivity.

Among other indirect taxes, excise taxes are among the most important, especially taxes on crude oil and petroleum derivatives. Other excises are applied to distilled alcohol, beer, and other fermented drinks, as well as tobacco products. Specific rates are applied to cement, vehicles, an stamp duties on particular protocols. Although increases in the price of oil drove up excise revenues somewhat, they have largely held steady as a proportion of total revenues.

In Guatemala, the income tax is complicated, full of exemptions, and poorly adapted to a changing economy. Taxable income is defined according to national sources, 'territorially,' leaving out the external activities of Guatemalan investors. Also, the system is 'schedular,' meaning that different rates are applied to incomes derived from different sources. This leads to signifant tax planning, as economic agents shift their activities to minimize obligations, receiving further encouragement from a plethora of exemptions granted to different sectors. The system is further complicated by two regimes in which individuals can opt into the general regime of 5 per cent applied to all nonexempt income or a regime for salaried employees (with a minimum exemption) with progressive rates on higher income brackets reaching a top rate of 31 per cent (ICEFI, 2007). Typical of the limited types of reform possible with respect to direct taxes, the past 12 years have seen three increases in income tax, each one temporary, producing only a small increase in the proportion of revenues coming from direct taxation. The result of this extremely imperfect structure of income tax is that direct taxes are the smallest proportion of total revenues of any country in the region, and the wealthiest sectors pay a smaller portion of their income in tax than poorer sections.

The evolution of different direct and indirect taxes is displayed in Figure 19.3. Tax revenues have increased, from 7.62 per cent of GDP in 1990 to 12.3 per cent in 2007, only to drop back below 10 per cent with the expiration of temporary revenues and the global economic slowdown that began in 2008. The VAT has increased its share of total revenues from 32 to 49 per cent, while specific taxes have stayed steady between 10 and 12 per cent, and income taxes have falle slightly from 22 to 20 per cent. Property taxes are negligible, while trade taxes fell steadily from 22 per cent of the total in 1990 to 8 per cent in 2007.

One weakness of the tax system, especially affecting direct taxes, is the plethora of exemptions, exonerations, and special regimes. Over the past 20 years, the Law for Promotion of Exports and Maquila (Dto. 28–89) and the Free Trade Zone Law (Dto. 65–89) have been presented as important attractions to foreign investment. These incentives target businesses located in designated free trade zones, which import raw materials for assembly and export or export nontraditional products. They offer exemptions to direct taxes, and tax holidays and reduced rates exist for indirect taxes (ICEFI, 2007).

The cost of incentives has been measured in tax expenditures, the amount of tax the state fails to collect as a result of these special treatments. According to the superintendent of Tax Administration and Ministry of Finance, tax expenditure amounted to between 14 and 16.3 per cent of GDP between 2000 and 2005, outpacing the actual tax collected. Using more conservative assumptions, the cost of tax expenditure has been calculated between 3.3 and 7.3 per cent – still a significant loss (ICEFI, 2007: 77)

Guatemalan statebuilding has remained in crisis for at least the past two decades. The country has experienced the end of civil war, a transition to democracy, and the expansion of newly transnationalized sectors. To an even greater degree than the other countries in the region, however, traditional sectors have remained dominant, able to absorb newly emerging sectors or

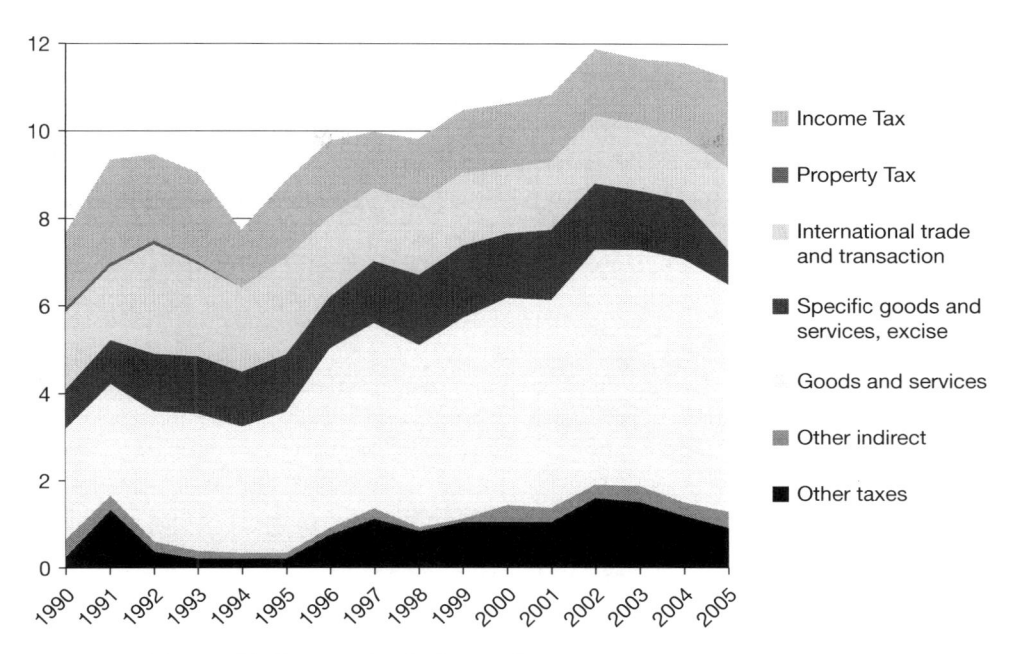

Figure 19.3 Direct and indirect taxation in Guatemala.
Source: Author calculations based on CEPAL data, www.cepal.org/ilpes

block their efforts at articulating a coherent statebuilding project. Without a statebuilding project to advance, political parties have remained chaotic and volatile, vulnerable to the institutional obstacles that preserve existing institutions and policies. These institutional obstacles include informality and multiple veto points, preserving privilege but preventing efforts to advance a coherent statebuilding project. As a result, there is a notable absence of a coherent statebuilding project, evident in the failure to increase taxes or address confusing exemptions, exceptions, and rebates, which undermine the tax regime and weaken capacity. Guatemalan statebuilding remains in a condition of 'crisis.'

Conclusion

This chapter suggests that patterns of statebuilding in post–conflict contexts can be understood in terms of the structure of emerging elites and their connection to state institutions. It also argues that tax regimes and changes to tax regimes are traceable to these state–society constellations and are indicative of broader statebuilding patterns. In El Salvador, cohesive and dominant emerging elites have coordinated their interests through think–tanks and advanced their agenda through an ideological party. They have advanced policies and institutions to project their economic activities throughout the region, led by financial sectors, coordinating transnational processes tha operate in various countries. This is an 'inside–out' statebuilding project, and it has been accompanied by important gains in tax capacity and universality that have expanded certain aspects of state f scal affairs.

In Guatemala, emerging elites have been neither dominant nor cohesive, forced to accom– modate themselves within networks, firms, and associations they share with established elite operating in traditional sectors and dominant during previous patterns of insertion in the international economy. The party system that reflects this structure is poorly suited to coordinating politics, with partisan vehicles appearing from election to election and largely devoid of ideological coherence or programmatic agendas. As a result, statebuilding remains in 'crisis' in Guatemala, a condition that is mirrored and perpetuated by the tax regime, which continues to raise few resources, and is full of exceptions and exemptions.

Several findings are relevant from this comparison of El Salvador and Guatemala. First, it i notable that essentially the same sectors have emerged as dynamic in the two countries as a result of international insertion under current forms of capitalism. As small, poor countries located close to the US, they share similar comparative advantages in terms of the kinds of products they can offer to international markets and the opportunities these present to emerging elites in dynamic sectors. Second, despite the similarity of international, economic structures, elites in the two countries are organized quite differently in their cohesion and dominance, and this helps explain the divergence in their statebuilding outcomes. This finding is important as others consider th places to look for explanations of statebuilding patterns in other post–conflict situations

Also, despite the fact that El Salvador would appear to have achieved far more improvements in tax capacity and universality, neither country has made much progress in tax progressivity. Both are among the most unequal countries in the world in the distribution of wealth, and in neither country have state elites been able to secure more significant contributions from wealth actors. Even in El Salvador, where the emerging elites are both dominant and cohesive, they have been unwilling to provide a significantly larger amount of their own resources toward publi goods, even as they use the state to restructure their economic activities and project them throughout the region.

This deserves further comment, as it refects more broadly on the kind of statebuilding project that gets advanced. It is certainly the case that cohesive and dominant elites in El Salvador have been an important ingredient to expanding a variety of areas of state capacity and rebuilding state institutions after conflict. On the other hand, as in Guatemala, emerging elites have failed t mobilize or incorporate popular sectors, thereby leaving out an important constituency of post–conflict statebuilding. Popular sectors are an important constituency not only because they are likely an important guarantor of long–term post–conflict peace, but also because they are the onl voice for a more progressive statebuilding project, in which policies such as tax can be used to address development shortcomings such as the concentration of wealth and investment in the human capital that will allow more sophisticated patterns of international insertion. It would appear that newly dominant elites may be suffcient to build capable states after conflict, but just states require the conscience and political weight of popular sectors.

Notes

1 Leo Block Associate Professor, Korbel School of International Studies at the University of Denver. Comments, suggestions, and critiques welcome at aaron.schneider@du.edu
2 Shifts in the international regime, in the form of treaties and new institutions such as the WTO, appeared to confirm the increasing constraint on regulatory power and the role of states, while structural adjustment programs imposed limits on the policy space of individual governments.
3 'Economic integration processes and neoliberal structural adjustment programs are driven by transnational capital's campaign to open up every country to its activities, to tear down all barriers to the movement of goods and capital, and to create a single unifed f eld in which global capital can operate unhindered across all national borders' (Robinson, 2008: 19).
4 The World Bank acknowledged a new set of requirements of the 'State in a Changing World' in its 1997 *World Development Report* (World Bank, 1997).
5 Many place war at the heart of greater tax efforts; militarist theory 'argued that military competition and the development of taxation went hand in hand . . . taxation furnished the resources that allowed states to make war and eliminate their competitors' (Martin et al., 2009: 9–10).

6   Public choice theories simply assume that rulers maximize revenues (Brennan and Buchanan, 2006). In some cases, this is a matter of duping taxpayers, to 'conceal the burden of taxation and exaggerate the benefits of public spending' (Martin et al., 2009: 8–10; Buchanan, 1987)
7   Over time, a culture of tax can develop, in which citizens identify tax payment with their membership in a society, their acquiescence and participation in representative government, and the pursuit of collective goods (Slemrod, 1990; Torgler, 2005).
8   Victor Bulmer–Thomas, in observing Central American economic history over the past century, makes a similar observation: 'although Central America has had no political unity . . . it has had a certain "economic unity" as a result of its subjection to common external influences. These have filtered throu domestic institutions to affect each economy in slightly different ways. Thus, the region exhibits both conformity and diversity and the problem facing an author is to see the one without losing sight of the other' (Bulmer–Thomas, 1987).
9   He also adopted the last of the privatizations, including the airport and lesser public services.
10 From 1999 to 2003, average Salvadoran investment in Costa Rica, for example, was almost $20 million per year; and between 1997 and 2004, 85 per cent of all intraregional investment in Central America came from El Salvador (Segovia Caceres, 2005).
11 Under the current international insertion, some have argued that concentration is even more severe, with an economy controlled by no more than four or five families atop financial empires (Blanco, 199 Casaús Arzú, 1992).
12 One of the first directors of FUSADES who was also the first ARENA president and is once again president of the ARENA party, Alfredo Cristiani, took with him no fewer than 17 FUSADES allies to fill ministerial and bureaucratic posts
13 Unfortunately, because of their small size, the survey did not include a sufficient number of legislator from the PDC and CD, though both would be located more toward the center of the continuum.
14 Fiscal deficits hover around 2.5 per cent of GDP, and debt has increased from 27 per cent of GDP i 1998 to 40.5 per cent in 2004, falling only slightly to 39.9 per cent in 2006. Author calculations based on data from the Central Reserve Bank of El Salvador (www.bcr.gob.sv).
15 Sales taxes, in particular, have been criticized for having an inefficient 'cascading' effect as they are passe down a production chain with each transaction. This causes particular distortions to longer production chains, in which there are more transactions. The VAT, by taxing only value added, removes the distortion caused by cascading, especially if it is applied with relatively few exemptions (Tanzi, 1991).
16 www.mineco.gob.gt/Presentacion/BibliotecaVirtual.aspx

References

Achard, D. (2006). *Un desafío a la democracia: Los partidos políticos en Centroamérica, Panamá y República Dominicana.* San José, Costa Rica: BID–IDEA–OEA–PNUD.

Artana, D., and Navajas, F. (2008).*Politica tributaria en El Salvador. Propuestas para el financiamento del desarrollo.* San Salvador, El Salvador: FUSADES.

Blanco, M.–D. A. (1998). *El conde de Aranda: Los laberintos del poder (Coleccion Mariano de Pano y Ruata).* Zaragoza, Spain: Caja de Ahorros de la Inmaculada de Aragon.

Brautigam, D., Fjeldstad, O. H., and Moore, M. (2008). *Taxation and state-building in developing countries: Capacity and consent.* New York, NY: Cambridge University Press.

Brennan, G., and Buchanan, J. M. (2006). *The power to tax: Analytic foundations of a fiscal constitution.* New York, NY: Cambridge University Press.

Buchanan, J. M. (1987). *Public finance in democratic process: Fiscal institutions and individual choice.* Chapel Hill, NC: University of North Carolina Press.

Bulmer–Thomas,V. (1987). *The political economy of Central America since 1920.* New York, NY: Cambridge University Press.

Casaús Arzú, M. E. (1992). *La estructura social de Centroamerica (historia de las Americas).* Madrid, Spain: Ediciones Akal.

CEPAL. (1996). *Economía política de las reformas tributarias en Costa Rica, El Salvador y Guatemala, 1980–1994.* Mexico City, Mexico: Naciones Unidas Comision Economica El Caribe.

Dicken, P. (2007). *Global shift: Mapping the changing contours of the world economy* (5th ed.). London, UK: Guilford Press.

Dosal, P. J. (1995). *Power in transition: The rise of Guatemala's industrial oligarchy, 1871–1994.* New York, NY: Praeger.

Eraso, M. A., and Núñez, D. (2008). *Partidos políticos y jugadores con veto: Un estudio del Congreso y la legislación en Guatemala*. Cuadernos FLACSA. Guatemala City, Guatemala: FLACSO.

Evans, P. (1997). The eclipse of the state? Reflections on stateness in an era of globalization. *World Politics*, *50*(1), 62–87.

Evans, Pe., Rueschemeyer, D., and Skocpol, T. (Eds.). (1985). *Bringing the state back in*. New York, NY: Cambridge University Press.

Fuentes Knight, J. A., and Cabrera, M. (2006). Pacto fiscal en Guatemala: Lecciones de una negociación *Revista de la CEPAL*, *88*, 153–165.

Gereffi, G., and Wyman, D. (1990). *Manufacturing miracles: Paths of industrialization in Latin America and East Asia*. Princeton, NJ: Princeton University Press.

Hall, P. and Soskice, D. W. (2001). *Varieties of capitalism: The institutional foundations of comparative advantage*. New York, NY: Oxford University Press.

ICEFI. (2007). *La política fiscal en la encrucijada (el caso de C.A.)*. Guatemala City, Guatemala: ICEFI.

ICEFI. (2008). *Incidencia de los impuestos sobre la equidad en Guatemala*. Guatemala City, Guatemala: ICEFI.

Johnson, K. (1993). *Between revolution and democracy: Business elites and the state in El Salvador during the 1980s*. Master's thesis, Tulane University, New Orleans, LA, USA.

Kaplinsky, R. (2005). *Globalization, poverty and inequality: Between a rock and a hard place*. Malden, MA: Polity.

Laakso, M., and Taagepera, R. (1979). 'Effective' number of parties: A measure with application to West Europe. *Comparative Political Studies*, *12*(1), 3–27.

Levi, M. (1989). *Of rule and revenue*. Berkeley, CA: University of California Press.

Lieberman, E. (2003). *Race and regionalism in the politics of taxation in Brazil and South Africa*. Studies in Comparative Politics. New York, NY: Cambridge University Press.

Mack, L. F., Donis, J. G., and Castillo, C. (2006) *Redes de inclusión: Entendiendo la verdadera fortaleza partidaria*. Guatemala City, Guatemala: FLACSO.

Martin, I. W., Mehrotra, A. K., and Prasad, M. (2009). *The new fiscal sociology: Taxation in comparative and historical perspective*. New York, NY: Cambridge University Press.

Moreno, R. (2000). *Reforma fiscal en El Salvador: Una exigencia impotergable*. San Salvador, El Salvador: FUNDE.

Olson, M. (1966). *The logic of collective action*. Cambridge, MA: Harvard University Press.

Ostrom, E. (1990). *Governing the commons: The evolution of institutions for collective action*. Cambridge, UK: Cambridge University Press.

Paige, J. M. (1997). *Coffee and power: Revolution and the rise of democracy in Central America*. Cambridge, MA: Harvard University Press.

Pedersen, M. N. (1979). The dynamics of European party systems: Changing patterns of electoral volatility. *European Journal of Political Research*, 7(1), 1–26.

Porras, G. (2005). *Instituciones políticas, proceso de formulación de políticas públicas y resultados de las políticas en Guatemala*. Guatemala City, Guatemala: ASIES.

Rettberg, A. (2007). The private sector and peace in El Salvador, Guatemala, and Colombia *Journal of Latin American Studies*, *39*(3), 463–494.

Robinson, W. I. (2000). Neoliberalism, the global elite, and the Guatemalan transition: A critical macrosocial analysis. *Journal of Inter-American Studies and World Affairs*, *42*(4), vi, 89–107.

Robinson, W. I. (2003). *Transnational conflicts: Central America, social change, and globalization*. London, UK: Verso.

Robinson, W. I. (2008). *Latin America and global capitalism: A critical globalization perspective*. Baltimore, MD: Johns Hopkins University Press.

Rodrik, D. (1996). *Why do more open economies have bigger governments?* NBER Working Paper 5537. Cambridge, MA: National Bureau of Economic Research.

Rosa, H. (1993). *Aid y las transformaciones globales en El Salvador*. Managua, Nicaragua: Cries.

Schneider, A. (2008). Socio–economic change and fiscal politics in Central America. In I. W. Morgan an D. Sánchez–Ancochea (Eds.), *The political economy of the public budget in the Americas*. London, UK: Institute for the Study of the Americas, pp. 163–200.

Segovia Caceres, A. E. (2004). *Modernización empresarial en Guatemala, ¿cambio real o nuevo discurso?* Guatemala City, Guatemala: F&G Editores.

Segovia Caceres, A. E. (2005). *Integración real y grupos de poder económico en América Central: Implicaciones para el desarrollo y la democracia de la región*. San José, Costa Rica: Friedrich Ebert Stiftung; Fesamericacentral.

Slemrod, J. (1990). Optimal taxation and optimal tax systems *Journal of Economic Perspectives*, *4*(1), 157–178.

Tanzi, V. (1991). *Public finance in developing countries*. Brookfield, VT: Edward Elgar

Tilly, C. (1975). *The formation of national states in Western Europe*. Princeton, NJ: Princeton University Press.
Timmons, J. F. (2005). The fiscal contract: States, taxes, and public services. *World Politics*, 57(4), 530–567.
Torgler, B. (2005). Tax morale in Latin America. *Public Choice*, 122(2), 133–157.
Torres–Rivas, E. (1989). *Repression and resistance: The struggle for democracy in Central America*. Boulder, CO: Westview Press.
Towers, M., and Borzutzky, S. (2004). The socioeconomic implications of dollarization in El Salvador. *Latin American Politics & Society*, 46(3), 29–54.
Valdez, J. F. (2003). *El ocaso de un liderazgo: Las elites empresariales tras un nuevo protagonismo*. Guatemala City, Guatemala: FLACSO.
Williamson, J. (1990). What Washington means by policy reform. In J. Williamson (Ed.), *The progress of policy reform in Latin America*. Washington, DC: IIE.
Wood, E. J., and Segovia, A. (1999). Macroeconomic policy and the Salvadoran peace accords. *Peace Research Abstracts*, 36(1), 2079–2099.
World Bank, The. (1997). *World Development Report*. Washington, DC: World Bank.

20
SHARING POWER TO BUILD STATES

Anna K. Jarstad

Sharing power between warring parties has become a standard arrangement to end civil wars during the post-Cold War era. One reason is that peace agreements have become significantl more common. After 1989, peace agreements have been signed in close to half of all civil wars. Before 1989, peace agreements were quite rare, and many conflicts ended in the victory of on party. After a victory, the life and liberty of defeated groups were often endangered. Peace agreements seek to prevent such oppression. The vast majority of peace agreements include provisions for the sharing of power to balance the influence of actors in the country. During th period 1989 to 2004, 70 out of all 83 agreements signed provided for power-sharing (Jarstad and Nilsson, 2008: 215).

Power-sharing becomes a platform for building new, more inclusive state institutions. But statebuilding is an arduous task anywhere, and it is even more difficult in societies shattered b civil war. One reason is that even after a peace deal is signed, former enemies have to learn how to live side by side and cooperate in building a common state while the country often remains divided along the conflict lines. Under such circumstances power-sharing can ease the way b guaranteeing all parties a share in the new or reformed state institutions. Some of the most pressing issues for statebuilding after civil war involve creating new or reformed institutions for political governance, territorial control, the security sector, and economic development. Such institutions are not developed from scratch. Rather peace agreements often include provisions for different types of power-sharing, most commonly political, territorial, military, and economic power-sharing. These arrangements can form the basis of the new institutions and thereby shape the new state. How does power-sharing influence statebuilding? Is it a constraint or does it facilitat statebuilding?

Consociational democracy: the background to contemporary research on power-sharing

Arend Lijphart coined the concept 'consociational democracy' in 1968 to denote an institu – tionalized form of democratic conflict management for divided societies, which he found in the Netherlands. At that time the country was deeply divided along religious and class lines which separated the population into distinct, isolated, and self-contained groups. There was minimal communication across these groups and each group had its own newspapers and radio and television organizations. Each group also had its own political parties, labor unions, and schools. Such a fragmented society would appear to foster antagonism and extremism. Surprisingly, Lijphart found that the group leaders solved the conflicts peacefully and thereby promoted a stable democracy for a divided society. This challenged the conventional wisdom at the time, as ethnic division was not seen as compatible with stable democracy (Lijphart, 1968b). In his later research, Lijphart found that several other countries also had the experience of consociationalism: Austria 1945–1966, Belgium since 1970, Canada 1840–67, Colombia 1958–74, Cyprus 1960–63, Czechoslovakia 1989–93, India, Israel, and Lebanon 1943–1975 and since 1989, Malaysia on and off since 1955, South Africa 1994–1999, and Suriname and Switzerland since 1943 (Lijphart, 1977; 1985: 89–90; 1996: 259; 1998: 101–102). In this way, Lijphart demonstrated that consociationalism was not unique to the Netherlands, but a more commonly existing practice of democratic governance in divided societies.

Lijphart describes consociational democracy as 'government by elite cartel designed to turn a democracy with a fragmented political culture into a stable democracy' (Lijphart, 1969: 216). Here the moderate attitudes of the leaders and their cooperative behavior is key. In the Netherlands a consensus on who should belong to the state already existed before consociationalism was introduced. Lijphart further defines consociationalism by four institutions designed to accommodate conflicts in deeply divided societies: grand coalition, proportionality, autonomy, and veto. All important rival groups should be included in a grand coalition, according to strict proportionality or by deliberate over-representation of minorities. Such allocation should also apply to the bureaucracy and the distribution of economic revenues. Autonomy for each group should be provided for by decentralization of all matters not of common concern. Mutual veto rights in central government are central to block regulations and reforms that could alter fundamental conditions of physical and cultural survival of the group (Lijphart, 1993: 188–189). Lijphart suggests that these institutions can develop out of a consensual culture, but the institutions as such can also contribute to such a culture (1999; for a critique see Jarstad, 2001: 42–64).

Lijphart's work has inspired several research fields. One is the field of constitutional engineering, a term coined by Giovanni Sartori, which aims to design constitutions with the purpose of changing the political behavior of elites (Sartori, 1994, ix). The main debate in this field has evolved around the choice between majoritarian and proportional electoral systems. Three of the most prominent works on this matter are *Comparative Constitutional Engineering: An Inquiry into Structures, Incentives and Outcomes* (Sartori, 1994), *Seats and Votes: The Effects and Determinant of Electoral Systems* (Taagepera and Shugart, 1989), and *Electoral Laws and Their Political Consequences* (Grofman and Lijphart, 1977). These works primarily discuss various techniques from a democratic point of view. However, in a divided society, elections reflect demographic relations. Political parties representing minorities have no chance of ever forming a majority. Shifting majorities in parliament – a healthy sign of democracy – are therefore unlikely in divided societies. Instead, minorities are in practice excluded from political influence. Under such circumstances, there is a risk that minority groups see secession as their only option to survive as a distinct group, whereas the majority believes that oppression is the only way to prevent such separatist tendencies. Robert Dahl has captured the dilemma in divided societies as follows: 'the price of polyarchy may be the break-up of the country. And the price of territorial unity may be a hegemonic regime' (Dahl, 1971: 11). Consociationalism is put forward as a way to avoid these two undesirable outcomes.

In addition to Lijphart's consociational model, Donald Horowitz, Tim D. Sisk, Benjamin Reilly, and Andrew Reynolds have developed integrative models for constitutional engineering in divided societies (Horowitz, 1985; Reilly, 2001; Reynolds, 2002; Sisk, 1996). Horowitz suggests a system that makes 'moderation rewarding by making politicians reciprocally dependent on the votes of members other than their own' (Horowitz, 1991: 196). He has suggested the alternative vote (AV) or the single transferable vote (SVT) as methods for conflict management However, there are few empirical cases of success of these systems. While the integrative models seek to prevent the emergence of ethnic parties, Lijphart suggest that recognition of existing ethnic cleavages, and political representation of such groups, better provide for moderate politics.

In New Zealand, a system has developed to allow voters to change ethnopolitical affiliation In 1993, a referendum was held to change the voting system from first−past−the−post to mixe member proportional representation (MMP). Each voter has two votes: a party vote and an electoral vote (depending on where you live). Ahead of each election, every voter enrolls on either the indigenous Maori roll or the General roll. The Maori quota depends on the share of registered voters on the Maori roll. In addition, because it is in the interest of all parties to attract Maori voters, all main political parties include Maori among their top candidates. This means that some Maori members of parliament hold a general seat as a result of the party votes, whereas others hold a Maori electoral seat (Jarstad, 2001).

Power-sharing after civil war

Another research field that builds on Lijphart's work centers around the question of how to promote democratization, statebuilding, and peacebuilding after civil war. In quantitative research on conflict management it has become common to talk about four types of power−sharing: political, territorial, military, and economic. Political power−sharing is similar to Lijphart's grand coalition, while territorial power−sharing corresponds to Lijphart's autonomy criteria. Military and economic power−sharing builds on Lijphart's proportionality principle for allocation for positions in the state administration and distribution of funds. In conflict management research the main function of power−sharing is to end violence. To lay down arms, warring groups often demand a share of power.

Barbara Walter further understands power−sharing as a mechanism for solving the commitment problem in a context of severe distrust and vulnerability (Walter, 1999). The concession involved in peace agreements leaves the parties vulnerable to each other. The parties may fear that the other party will take advantage of them and exclude them from power. Under this condition, guaranteed shares of power can reduce distrust and vulnerability. Consequently, Walter also fids that warring parties are much more likely to sign an agreement if it includes guaranteed positions in the new government (Walter, 2002: 80). Caroline Hartzell and Matthew Hoddie (2003) found that settlements that include several forms of sharing or dividing political, territorial, military, and economic power are more likely to see peace prevail. However, when including the implementation of the power−sharing provision, Anna Jarstad and Desirée Nilsson find no evidence that more power−sharing is better. It is also found that both implemented territorial and military power−sharing increase the chances of peace, while political power−sharing has no effect on peace (Jarstad and Nilsson, 2008).

Political power-sharing: Former enemies in joint government

Democracy is a system for managing conflicts peacefully. There is also strong empirical evidenc for the so−called 'democratic peace,' which means that democratic states do not engage in warfare against each other (Oneal and Russett, 1999). To promote democracy has therefore become a central task for international organizations. But the road to democracy – democratization – is often paved with gross human right violations and violent conflicts. One reason is that democrac builds on the notion of free political competition and uncertain electoral outcome, which is seen as a threat to some political actors. The opening up of political space and liberalization of media also introduce new actors and new motives for violence. During election campaigns candidates are more visible than usual, and voters may become targets of violence from actors who seek to affect the electoral outcome. Hence, violence often peaks around election times and can even trigger a return to war. Under such circumstances, a period of political power–sharing – inclusion of vital parties in a broad coalition government – can ease the transition from war to democracy. Such power–sharing is identical to Lijphart's grand coalition. The main function of power–sharing is here to reduce the uncertainty of actors who fear losing power when democracy is introduced. Second, power–sharing has also been described as a school in democracy (Tocqueville, 2000) by socializing new political actors into the game of democracy. This can be particularly useful when warring actors are transformed into political parties. Third, under the best circumstances power–sharing buys time to build strong institutions which can sustain the dangers of elections. In this way, it is believed that power–sharing can contribute to statebuilding.

However, the track record of political power–sharing is poor; there is no statistical evidence that it provides for durable peace. Despite the fact that half of the political power–sharing agreements have failed and resulted in resumed conflict, such power–sharing is still very common Since 1989 political power–sharing agreements have been signed in 19 states: Afghanistan, Angola, Bangladesh, Bosnia–Herzegovina, Burundi, Cambodia, Comoros, Democratic Republic of Congo, Guinea Bissau, Ivory Coast, Liberia, Mali, Mexico, Rwanda, Sierra Leone, Somalia, Sudan, Tajikistan, and Uganda (Jarstad, 2009).

In Rwanda in 1994, genocide took place after a power–sharing agreement was signed. The Hutu extremists in government feared that they would be excluded from power and misused the new rights of information for propaganda where Tutsi and moderate Hutus were labeled as cockroaches that should be exterminated. After three months, when Tutsi rebels overpowered the government forces, more than 500,000 people had been killed. This example points to the danger in excluding heavily armed groups from a power–sharing arrangement. Barbara Walter argues that third–party security guarantees are vital for successful settlements of civil wars. She suggests that it was the lack of credible commitment of the UN that caused the settlement to break down: 'a false hope of international intervention is worse than no hope at all' (Walter, 2002: 159). However, there are cases where agreement on political power–sharing has been followed by elections and peace was kept the year after the election without third–party guarantees. Such agreements include Burundi 2003 and Comoros 2003 (Jarstad, 2009). This means that third–party security guarantees are not always necessary for political power–sharing to enable peace. One of the cases that are considered to be most successful is South Africa, where political power–sharing was agreed upon and carried out without any third–party guarantee. This example points to the importance of local ownership of the peace process. Despite the many predictions in the 1970s and 1980s of inevitable racial war in South Africa, the many local initiatives to unite the country after apartheid and years of violent conflicts were successful

Territorial power-sharing: devolution and decentralization

Lijphart suggest that 'no state can exist without some degree of consensus on matters of fundamental concern . . . [namely] the desire to preserve the existing system.' This minimal consensus is based on 'the feeling of belonging to a common nation as well as to one's own block' (Lijphart, 1968a: 78–79). In many countries undergoing simultaneous statebuilding and peacebuilding, the political structure is constructed while the question of who constitutes the *demos* (the people) is still a source of conflict. This is what Juan J. Linz and Alfred Stepan hav called the 'stateness problem' (Linz and Stepan, 1996: 29). Territorial power–sharing seeks to solve this issue, by devolving some power to local government or by autonomy for a certain region. This can provide for separate education systems and separate laws in parts of the country to enable cultural diversity. Malaysia applies a dual justice system with sharia law limited to Muslims and secular criminal and civil law for the rest of the population. Also in Nigeria and in Sudan, sharia is the law in parts of the country.

The majority in the country may fear that territorial power–sharing is a stepping–stone toward partition. Historically, there are such cases. In Cyprus, before independence 1960, the Greek Cypriots wanted to unite the island with Greece while the Turkish Cypriots favored a division of the island. This is a typical case where power–sharing was applied in an attempt to solve the stateness problem. The 1960 constitution for the newly independent country provided for consociational democracy. Before agreement was reached, there was an intense debate on the criteria for belonging to the respective Greek and Turkish communities. While the Turkish side stressed language as the most important criterion, the Greek side insisted that religion should define which community individuals belonged to. Each community was then to enroll on separate electoral rolls. Turkish Cypriots were to be overrepresented in government posts as well as in the bureaucracy, the judiciary, the police, and the army (Jarstad, 2001: 133–137).

In addition, the Turkish Cypriots had extensive autonomy. While Greek and Turkish Cypriots had lived intermingled all over the island, at least since the millet system under the Ottoman era there was a tradition that each community attended to its own business. During colonial rule, separate Turkish Cypriot municipalities had existed *de facto* since 1958. However, the decision to formally accept these municipalities as provided in the constitution was blocked. Turkish Cypriots became increasingly isolated as they were not allowed to enter Greek Cypriot areas. In December 1963 interethnic violence broke out, and UNIFICYP was deployed in March 1964. Many positions reserved for Turkish Cypriots were taken over by Greek Cypriots, and Turkish Cypriots became more and more isolated and forced into ghettos. Under these harsh conditions Turkish Cypriots had to rely on their own administrative system for registration of births etc. They also became gradually dependent on the UN and Turkey for supply of food. In 1974 Turkey invaded the island, and since then Cyprus is divided into a northern Turkish Cypriot part (recognized as a state only by Turkey) and the Republic of Cyprus, with territorial control over the southern Greek Cypriot part. The Kof Annan plan on a new power–sharing agreement was put to a referendum in 2004, but Greek Cypriots rejected it, and the island remains divided. Hence, the stateness problem is still not solved and no peace agreement has been signed.

Also in a few other cases, referenda have been stipulated for the purpose of settling the state–ness problem. In Papua New Guinea in 2001 an agreement created autonomy for the island Bougainville. At a later stage a referendum on independence is supposed to be held. In Sudan, the Machakos process included peace agreements on political power–sharing as well as territorial power–sharing by autonomy for Southern Sudan. It was also agreed that a referendum on inde – pendence was to be held. In July 2011 the new state was proclaimed, but the violence did not end. This indicates that referenda do not seem to promote reconciliation and cooperation for a joint state, but rather strengthen the perception of vulnerability and insecurity. A planned referendum also tends to put statebuilding on hold. It is difficult to build institutions when no one knows where the future borders will be and who will fall under the jurisdiction of the future state.

However, referenda on independence are unusual and division after a period of territorial power–sharing is rare. Rather, many groups striving for autonomy seem to settle for rather minor forms of self–government. Territorial power–sharing has contributed to ending large–scale violent conflict in countries such as Angola, Croatia (Serbian Republic of Krajina), Bosnia–Herzegovina, Comoros, Djibouti, Georgia (Abkhazia), India (Bodoland), Indonesia (Aceh), Macedonia, Mali, Mexico, Moldova, Papua New Guinea, and the UK (Northern Ireland). Statistical studies also show that territorial power–sharing is conducive to durable peace and that such power–sharing is almost as common as political power–sharing (Jarstad and Nilsson, 2008). But does it contribute to statebuilding?

In Bosnia and Herzegovina, the territorial power–sharing arrangement keeps the state formally together. However, the state is divided and the institutions are weak. According to David Chandler, the 1995 Dayton agreement created a high degree of international dependence. Democracy was further undermined by the extended mandate for the Office of the High Representative, which granted him the right to enact laws and to remove elected politicians (Chandler, 1999; Knaus and Martin, 2003). However, few other autonomy arrangements have attracted such international involvement. A more common problem is that the new entities have few resources to develop strong local institutions. In many cases the national government is still in control of collection of taxes. Economic power–sharing could assist in achieving a more even distribution of resources.

Economic power-sharing: distributing incomes of natural resources

The relationship between economic inequality and violent conflict is at the center of a larg discourse. Statistically, income inequality does not contribute to the probability of civil war (Collier, 2000). However, great inequalities between regions or groups can create tensions and have negative consequences for statebuilding. Sometimes the richer region wants to secede. This was the case in Yugoslavia, where the wealthiest republic, Slovenia, was the first to proclaim it independence. Perceived economic discrimination often gives rise to grievances and can fuel riots (Gurr, 2000). Issues related to economic inequality, such as land distribution and control over natural resources, often contribute to the conflict. In an effort to settle such issues, economi power–sharing is part of several peace agreements, for instance in the Philippines, where the regional government was granted control over finance and a share of the profits from minin Other cases include Colombia, Costa Rica, El Salvador, Guatemala, Nicaragua, Mali, Moldova, Rwanda, and Zimbabwe (Hartzell and Hoddie, 2007: 47–49, 128).

In Sudan there have been several conflicts between the Arabs in the north and the black Africans in the south. In Sudan between 2002 and 2004, the parties agreed on provisions for political, territorial, military, and economic power–sharing during a transitional period of six years. The political power–sharing agreement stipulated two governments: a Government of National Unity at the central level and a Government of Southern Sudan. The territorial power–sharing was an agreement on some parts of the south/north boundary and provisions for a referendum on secession after the end of the transition period. Militarily power–sharing took the form of creation of some Joint Integrated Units in southern Sudan, Khartoum, the Nuba Mountains, and the Blue Nile during the interim period, while the rest of the army remained divided (Sriram, 2008).

Economic power–sharing was provided for by an agreement on wealth sharing. The oil revenues from southern Sudan should be shared on a 50–50 basis between the two governments during the interim period. In addition, the revenues from the Abyei area should be shared, with 50 per cent to the National Government, 42 per cent to the Government of Southern Sudan, and the rest to the local population (Brosché, 2009, 17–19). The agreements also included provisions for non–oil revenues, stipulating that 50 per cent of all taxes collected in South Sudan by the National Government would be allocated back to the Government of Southern Sudan (Rogier, 2005: 40).

After the independence of South Sudan, there are a lot of unsettled issues regarding the border and the land allocation for the returned refugees. In addition, new arrangements need to settle the issues of oil revenues, as the two countries depend on each other if they are to reap continued benefits of the oil. About three-quarters of the old oil reserves are located in the South, while the infrastructure to exploit it, such as pipelines, refineries, and export terminals, is in the Nort (ICG, 2011). This shows that continued negotiations are necessary.

Military power-sharing: integrating armed forces

Military power is at the heart of security relations, as it provides security for its group at the same time as it poses the greatest threat to its adversaries. Agreements regarding military power are very painful for the parties, as they risk leaving them vulnerable. For this reason, agreements often include security guarantees or a share of the military power. Military power-sharing usually means integrating the warring parties into a joint army. An example is the Bosnian case where, following the Dayton peace agreement in 1995, the Bosnian and Croat forces completed a merger in 1997. Military power-sharing was also an important part of the peace agreement reached by the Philippines government and the Moro Islamic Liberation Front in 1996. Four years after the signing, a large number of the soldiers called for in the agreement had been integrated into special and auxiliary units of the armed forces and the national police. As stipulated in the 1992 peace agreement in Mozambique, the government and Renamo merged their armed forces and formed a new national army with equal numbers of troops from each side. In all of these three cases, military power-sharing has contributed to peace (Hartzell and Hoddie, 2007: 129–135).

In Nepal in 2011, an agreement was made to integrate the Maoist rebel forces into the national army. Military power-sharing agreements have also been struck in countries such as Angola, Bosnia, Cambodia, Chad, El Salvador, Lebanon, Nicaragua, Rwanda, Sierra Leone, and South Africa. In addition, Matthew Hoddie and Caroline Hartzell include division of military forces, or permission for antagonists to remain armed or retain their own armed forces, in a study on implementation of agreements on military provisions. Among the 16 agreements on military power that they identify during the period 1980–1996, there are only three agreements that do not require any integration of the militaries. These cases of military power division are Azerbaijan, Chechnya, and Georgia–South Ossetia (Hartzell and Hoddie, 2003: 308, 312). In addition there are cases where some parties are allowed to retain their own armed forces; for instance, the 1989 Taif Accord which allowed Hezbollah to retain its military wing, while all other militias integrated into the Lebanese reformed security force (Hartzell and Hoddie, 2007: 175). In their article, Hoddie and Hartzell demonstrate that implementation of agreements on dividing or sharing military power is important for durable peace. They suggest that the reason is that implementation involves great costs for the parties, and the fact that they do implement agreements sends a signal of their genuine commitment to peace (Hartzell and Hoddie, 2003). This hypothesis was statistically tested in a study including the implementation of other types of power-sharing arrangements, spanning a longer time period and including agreement after less deadly conficts. In line with Hartzell and Hoddie, it was found that most integrative military power-sharing agreements are at least partially implemented and that complete implementation of such agreements improves the prospects for lasting peace (Jarstad and Nilsson, 2008).

Military power-sharing is often paired with broader security sector reforms as well as demobilization, disarmament, and reintegration (DDR) programs. In South Africa, a number of the armed forces associated with the ANC and Inkatha were integrated into the new national defense force. A British Advisory Training Team assisted in this relatively successful integration. Nevertheless, there were some problems. For instance discontented former fighters left their bases and complained to President Nelson Mandela about their poor treatment. They were paid less than regular government forces and were denied the ranks that they had when fighting for th ANC. Other fighters were not allowed to join the new force and remained unoccupied in camp during long periods without training or education to enable reintegration into the post-apartheid society. Some of them retained their 'profession' by joining mercenary companies (Spear, 2002: 147–148). Other former fighters have been employed as body guards. The level of political violence is still rather high in some areas in South Africa, especially around election times (Höglund and Jarstad, 2011). This is partly a legacy of the conflict and points to the consequence of inadequate DDR.

How can power-sharing facilitate statebuilding?

Power-sharing freezes the power balance and thereby reduces uncertainty. This creates a space that can be used to build strong institutions and plan for eff cient statebuilding, given that the former warring parties can cooperate. It is noteworthy that many peace processes entail several peace agreements before peace eventually holds. There is reason to expect that the parties gradually learn what can be achieved during negotiations. But negotiations must also continue during and after power-sharing in order for peace to be maintained.

Previous experience of power-sharing points to many directions, and no ideal type of power-sharing emerges. Many states that have implemented power-sharing after civil war are facing huge challenges including weak institutions, fragile peace, and poor economic development. We know more of what does not work with regard to power-sharing than what is working in order to facilitate statebuilding. Power-sharing not only may fail to end the violent conflict, but it ca also work contrary to statebuilding. Does this mean that power-sharing should be removed from the toolbox of statebuilders?

In reality, after civil war there are few alternatives to power-sharing. Power over political, territorial, military, and economic issues is at the heart of many armed conflicts. A preconditio for warring parties to sign an agreement is that they believe that they no longer can win militarily and that they have more to gain from a peace agreement. The promise of guaranteed shares of power may be necessary to end such civil wars. Thus, the main function of power-sharing is short-term peace, not statebuilding. At the same time, when power-sharing is deemed necessary to end the war, it should be designed in such a way that longer processes such as statebuilding are facilitated. Policymakers are advised to acknowledge tradeoffs involved in different solutions. It is vital that the power-sharing agreement be designed in such a way that the worst pitfalls and risks are reduced. Power-sharing should at least not undermine statebuilding; at best it can even contribute to building functional institutions. This means that policymakers must look ahead and analyze the long-term consequences of different power-sharing arrangements and also make use of innovative ideas to improve power-sharing.

- *Including extremists.* Peace is made between enemies, not friends. Warring parties that are excluded from a power-sharing arrangement have an incentive to continue fighting. Therefor power-sharing should aim to include all strong actors, including the most hardline extremists. This choice entails certain tradeoffs. Including warring parties always involves the risk that they continue to use violent tactics in parallel to politics. In addition, such inclusion can be viewed as rewarding violence. However, transitional power-sharing arrangements can buy time to integrate former fighters into society. Ideally, during the period of political power sharing the former enemies should be exposed to democratic methods of solving conflicts an socialized into democrats.

- *Including non-violent parties.* It is important to make use of the local capacity for peace. Aim to include non-violent representatives in the power-sharing government, for instance existing political parties and civil society representatives. This can provide for a broader form of local ownership of the peace process. The challenge in this regard involves identifying local actors that are seen as legitimate representatives who want elections.
- *Continued dialogue.* Several rounds of peace agreements are often needed before lasting peace is achieved. Even when a power-sharing agreement is reached there is a need for continued dialogue and negotiation to solve remaining issues. International mediators and local religious leaders can play a pivotal role to facilitate such talks.
- *A monopoly of violence.* The state must seize a monopoly of violence. In exchange for inclusion, the warring parties must refrain from illegal violence. A period of power-sharing allows time for DDR and security sector reform (SSR) to develop rule of law and respect for human rights. Military power-sharing can provide for reform and incorporation of the warring forces into a united national army and training to abide by international conventions.
- *Decentralization and devolution.* In conflicts where territorial control is contested, territorial power-sharing can be appropriate. To avoid the risks involved in secessions, territorial power-sharing can relieve the central government from some contested issues and devolve power to more or less autonomous local governments. A tradeoff is that new minorities may emerge in the new entity and if they feel discriminated against, a new conflict may rise. This is a particularly important point to consider if the new entity is allowed to have separate laws. In addition, local leaders do not always enjoy greater legitimacy than national ones.
- *Economic power-sharing.* Economic power-sharing can reduce uneven development in the country by ensuring that all parties share revenues from natural resources such as oil and mines. Economic power-sharing can also entail land reforms. An overlooked issue in peace agreements is often how to improve the tax base and the institutions for tax collection. As resources are essential in order to build strong institutions, this is an issue that needs to be addressed in future peace agreements.
- *A transitional measure.* It is important that the transitional period allows sufficient time to begi building capable state institutions (not least rule of law), carry out DDR and SSR, and prepare for democratic elections. Power-sharing arrangements tend to be based on the power relations at the end of the war. Over time, there are changes in power relations, demography, and economy. While power-sharing ensures inclusion for the parties to the agreement, the political space needs to open up to include also other political parties. In addition, power-sharing does not allow for accountability and replacement of the government. Therefore power-sharing should be a temporary provision, and ideally be followed by elections within a five-year period.
- *Integrative electoral system.* If power-sharing needs to be retained after the transitional period to secure the peace, design a system that allows for existing moderate groups and new actors to stand for elections. This can be done by reserving only part of the seats in parliament and leaving some open for electoral contestation outside of the quotas. Ensure that voters have a choice of candidates in each election, also for the quota seats. Reserve seats for political parties, not for individual candidates.
- *Conflict-sensitive international engagement.* It is not certain that international assistance provides for more successful power-sharing arrangements. Rather, there is a risk of international dependency and a lack of local ownership. However, some conflicts cannot be ended withou international involvement. Under such circumstances, it is important that third parties do not promise to act as guarantors unless they can follow through on their promise. Equally important is that the developments are closely monitored, and that mediation facilitates

continuing difficult negotiations to solve remaining conflict issues and preclude new conflic Finally, conflict sensitivity is always essential during peace operations. It is particularly important to assess how assistance affects the power relations in society and to prevent new tensions from turning violent.

References

Brosché, J. (2009). *Sharing power – Enabling peace? Evaluating Sudan's Comprehensive Peace Agreement 2005*. Uppsala, Sweden: Uppsala University and New York, NY: Mediation Support Unit, Department of Political Affairs, United Nations.

Chandler, D. (1999). *Bosnia: Faking democracy after Dayton*. London, UK: Pluto Press.

Collier, P. (2000). Doing well out of war: An economic perspective. In M. Berdal and D. M. Malone (Eds.), *Greed and grievance: Economic agendas in civil wars*. Boulder, CO: Lynne Rienner.

Dahl, R. A. (1971). *Polyarchy: Participation and opposition*. New Haven, CT: Yale University Press.

Grofman, B., and Lijphart, A. (Eds.). (1977). *Electoral laws and their political consequences*. New York, NY: Agaton Press.

Gurr, T. R. (2000). *Peoples versus states: Minorities at risk in the new century*. Washington, DC: United States Institute of Peace Press.

Hartzell, C., and Hoddie, M. (2003). Institutionalizing peace: Power sharing and post–civil war conf ict management. *American Journal of Political Science*, 47(2), 318–332.

Hartzell, C., and Hoddie, M. (2007). *Crafting peace: Power-sharing institutions and the negotiated settlement of civil wars*. University Park, PA: Pennsylvania State University Press.

Höglund, K., and Jarstad, A. (2011). Towards electoral security: Experiences from KwaZulu–Natal. *Africa Spectrum*, 1: 33–59.

Horowitz, D. L. (1985). *Ethnic groups in conflict*. Berkeley, CA: University of California Press.

Horowitz, D. L. (1991). *A democratic South Africa? Constitutional engineering in a divided society*. Berkeley, CA: University of California Press.

ICG. (2011). Politics and transition in the new South Sudan *Africa Report*, 172, April 4. Juba, South Sudan: International Crisis Group.

Jarstad, A. (2001). *Changing the game: Consociational theory and ethnic quotas in Cyprus and New Zealand*. Uppsala, Sweden: Department of Peace and Conflict Research, Uppsala University

Jarstad, A. K. (2009). The prevalence of power–sharing: Exploring the patterns of post–election peace *Africa Spectrum*, 44(3), 41–62.

Jarstad, A. K., and Nilsson, D. (2008). From words to deeds: The implementation of power–sharing pacts in peace accords. *Conflict Management and Peace Science*, 25(3), 206–223.

Knaus, G., and Martin, F. (2003). Travails of the European Raj. *Journal of Democracy*, 14(3).

Lijphart, A. (1968a). *The politics of accommodation: Pluralism and democracy in the Netherlands*. Berkeley, CA: University of California Press.

Lijphart, A. (1968b). Typologies of democratic systems. *Comparative Political Studies*, 1(April): 3–44.

Lijphart, A. (1969). Consociational democracy. *World Politics*, 21(2), 207–225.

Lijphart, A. (1977). *Democracy in plural societies*. New Haven, CT: Yale University Press.

Lijphart, A. (1985). *Power-sharing in South Africa*. Berkeley, CA: Institute of International Studies, University of California.

Lijphart, A. (1993). Consociational democracy. In J. Krieger (Ed.), *The Oxford companion to politics of the world*. Oxford, UK: Oxford University Press.

Lijphart, A. (1996). The puzzle of Indian democracy: A consociational interpretation. *American Political Science Review*, 90(2), 258–268.

Lijphart, A. (1998). Consensus and consensus democracy: Cultural, structural, functional, and rational–choice explanations. *Scandinavian Political Studies*, 21(2), 99–108.

Lijphart, A. (1999). *Patterns of democracy: Government forms and performances in thirty-six countries*. New Haven, CT: Yale University Press.

Linz, J., and Stepan, A. (1996). *Problems of democratic transition and consolidation*. Baltimore, MD: Johns Hopkins University Press.

Oneal, J. R., and Russett, B. (1999). The Kantian peace: The pacific benefits of democracy, interdependence, and international organizations, 1885–1992. *World Politics*, 52(1), 1–37.

Reilly, B. (2001). *Democracy in divided societies: Electoral engineering for conflict management*. Cambridge, UK: Cambridge University Press.

Reynolds, A. (Ed.). (2002). *The architecture of democracy: Constitutional design, conflict management, and democracy.* Oxford, UK: Oxford University Press.

Rogier, E. (2005). *Designing an integrated strategy for peace, security and development in post-agreement Sudan.* The Hague: The Netherlands: Netherlands Institute of International Relations Clingendael.

Sartori, G. (1994). *Comparative constitutional engineering. An inquiry into structures, incentives and outcomes.* London, UK: Macmillan.

Sisk, T. D. (1996). *Power sharing and international mediation in ethnic conflicts.* Washington, DC: United States Institute of Peace Press.

Spear, J. (2002). Disarmament and demobilization. In S. J. Stedman, D. Rothchild, and E. M. Cousens (Eds.), *Ending civil wars: The implementation of peace agreements.* Boulder, CO: Lynne Rienner.

Sriram, C. L. (2008). *Peace as governance: Power-sharing, armed groups, and contemporary peace negotiations.* Basingstoke, UK: Palgrave Macmillan.

Taagepera, R., and Shugart, M. S. (1989). *Seats and votes: The effects and determinants of electoral systems.* Yale, CT: Yale university Press.

Tocqueville, A. De (2000). *Democracy in America.* New York, NY: Perennial Classics. (Original title *De la démocratie en Amérique,* London, UK: Saunders and Otley, 1838.)

Walter, B. (1999). Building reputation: Why governments fight some separatists but not others. *American Journal of Political Science, 50*(2), 313–330.

Walter, B. F. (2002). *Committing to peace: The successful settlement of civil wars.* Princeton, NJ: Princeton University Press.

21
ELECTIONS AND STATEBUILDING AFTER CIVIL WAR
Lurching toward legitimacy[1]

Timothy D. Sisk

On July 7, 2012, just nine months after the death of former dictator Muammar Gaddaf ended the country's civil war on the battlefield of Sirte, Libyans went to polls to elect a new transitiona government that would ultimately, in a constitutional assembly (General National Congress), negotiate a new relationship between the people and the state. In the elections, some 274 political parties registered to contend for the 80 party seats in the new assembly, and there were more than 2600 candidates for the 120 candidate–based seats. While there was violence, particularly in the Benghazi region – and a staged boycott by major local parties – the poll was remarkably peaceful for an initial post–civil war electoral process. Perhaps equally remarkably, the Libyans conducted the elections with a high degree of 'local ownership,' with a small–footprint size UN political mission giving, primarily, technical, logistical, and capacity development assistance. Few analysts doubted, at the end of the day, that the Libyan elections imbued the new transitional government with a new sense of internal, local legitimacy to inherit the deeply disabled Libyan state.

As a post–conflict election, the Libyan poll of 2012 was unusual in that it went against leadin theories, and indeed some degree of empirical evidence, that prior to meaningful elections in post–warcountries is the need for an extended period of disarmament and security sector reform, such that – absent international administration of the election, together with commensurate security guarantees – elections without security reform are highly risky. The International Crisis Group warns, correctly, that despite a relatively successful process, building a Libyan state, and the sealing of a new social contract, remains elusive: Libya's elected–but–weak government continues to struggle with providing security, especially in the restive eastern regions of Benghazi[2].

That the Libyan election of 2012 appears, initially, to have contributed to post–conflict statebuilding in the country – despite its being an anomalous example when seen comparatively from the literature which sees elections as inherently problematic in post–war states – raises the principal argument of this chapter: there is no single sequence of success in electoral processes' ability to contribute to the legitimacy needed for post–war elites to 'build' a state after civil war. While in some cases, such as Libya, elections seemed to be a necessary earlier step in post–war recovery, in other cases, such as the Democratic Republic of Congo (DRC) in 2005 and 2011, they seemed to be somewhat ill–advised as a strategy for successful statebuilding; in the DRC elections, prolific problems and deep–seated election violence have meant that elections hav little to do with conferring regime legitimacy and creating a foundation for building a new state.

Indeed, the literature suggests that in most cases electoral processes in post–war countries have been deeply troubled; such processes can lead to war recurrence, be troubled by widespread electoral violence, or create the conditions for ethnic reification or state capture by a narro faction or clique.

The success of the statebuilding enterprise itself is thus predicated on an electoral process that generates exceptionally broad legitimacy for the immediate, post–war ruling coalition; absent the contingent consent of all parties with the military capacity and ideological or power–seeking interest to spoil the post–war peace, progress toward effective statebuilding remains elusive. The implication is that those in the international community involved in the peacebuilding–as–statebuilding projects must directly confront the difficulties, contradictions, and dilemmas tha post–warelectoral processes pose and see them as the principal instrument for defining ane mutually empowering relations between states and societies after civil conflict. The task for effective statebuilding is thus not whether or even when to have elections to build effective states for sustainable peace after civil war, but how and how long to stay engaged once the first electio has passed.

This chapter explores four critical conceptual and practical themes for evaluating post–war electoral processes. The first is the path dependency of war termination and how this affects th nature and sequencing of post–war elections. The second is the electoral system and the ways in which its choice ref ects patterns of power and analytical imagination of elites and the effects of electoral system choice on the political party system . . . both critical factors for state–society relations. The third theme is the electoral administration and the relative autonomy of election–management bodies. And, in conclusion, the chapter explores the implications for external assistance to post–war electoral processes.

Pathways of politics: electoral processes and sequencing in post-war contexts

Elections – for better or for worse –*are* an essential step in the process of reconstituting political order after civil war, despite the clear and evident risks they impose for reigniting violent conflic in the heat and passion of the contest for power. While it might be ideal to delay post–war elections for up to 10 years after a civil war – to allow for statebuilding, for reviving the economy and improving human development, for changing incentive structures of elite predation, and for fostering trust and reconciliation (as the World Bank's Paul Collier argues in Collier et al., 2003) – practical political imperatives demand faster action.

Electoral processes in post–conflict countries are invariably a critical step in transition processe from war to re–legitimating of the state through reference to the ballot box. Although each situation is unique, there are common characteristics of elections held in the wake of civil war that can point the way to understanding the conditions under which they are relatively successful in establishing legitimacy for the post–war state, or when they might serve instead to stimulate new fears, provoke new violence, and set back statebuilding rather than advancing it. As Ben Reilly (2003: 174) appropriately observes, 'In any transition from conflct to peace, the creation or restoration of some form of legitimate authority is paramount .. . the support of the citizenry must be tested and obtained . . . The overarching challenge of peacebuilding is to construct a sustainable democratic state that can function without international involvement.'

The sequence pathway for an electoral process finds its antecedents, path–dependently, in th prior stage of conflict de–escalation, where the formula for settlement of the war – and the wa out – is codified. Often, international mediators have significant influence on the nature of settlements, specific sequences of events, and in some instances specific detail such as the elector system or the creation of a pre–election power–sharing pact.

The question of sequencing equally involves issues of 'what' and 'when.' What needs to occur prior to a relatively free and fair election, such as the review or drafting of an electoral law, voter registration, and the disarmament, demobilization, and reintegration of armed forces, among other desiderata? When, following the end of fighting, should elections be held (with the understanding that they may be too early or too late)? Most observers agree that the November 1996 elections in Bosnia, just a year after the guns fell silent, were too soon. But waiting too long can also be problematic, as interim or transitional administrations inherently lack legitimacy. Also, it might make sense to consider local elections first then move to national elections (as i Kosovo), rather than the now somewhat standard practice of sequencing national elections firs and having local elections thereafter (as in Sierra Leone). In other situations, however, local elections might have deleterious results for peacemaking; each situation needs to be carefully considered in terms of how the sequencing of elections in the post–war environment may affect the prospects for peace and for subsequent democratization (Risley and Sisk, 2005).

Indeed, elections are critical turning points that often mark passing through a phase in which post–warelites take power in the wake of war–ending peace agreements or in the aftermath of military victories: politics is 'demilitarized' (Lyons, 2002). Other observers acknowledge that electoral processes are fraught with problems but argue that they are a necessary ingredient to 'validating' peace agreements and for providing sorely needed legitimacy for post–war governance.[4] In some circumstances, electoral processes *are* the critical turning point that ends an uncertain, and usually turbulent, transition period and may in fact be the key ingredient in moving beyond the vulnerabilities of post–war settings to ongoing political violence. For example, it was the transition–culminating elections in South Africa in April 1994 that set the stage for a national unity government that drafted a new constitution, restructured apartheid–era bureaucracies, and allowed for support from society for state development initiatives: in this view, the electoral moment must come prior to meaningful progress on forging a new social contract as a prerequisite of post–conflict statebuilding (Sisk, 1995; Reynolds, 1994)

Most civil wars today end in negotiated settlements, and in most instances an essential part of such agreements is agreement on a defined political pathway through which a transitional proces to consolidate peace is to unfold. These transition paths often feature the formation of transitional governments, sometimes constitution–making processes, and, at some point, an electoral process and event to give post–war governance a new sense of legitimacy.[5] The transition sequences and institutional choices made in war–settlement negotiations often determine the nature and timing of initial post–war elections; in turn, these electoral processes deeply affect the nature of the state that emerges for years to follow. In sum, elections are the principal means by which war–terminating peace agreements are democratically legitimated by the affected population, and they determine initial control of state institutions by either aff rming existing patterns of power or ushering in new elites and by rearranging state–society relations.

Generally, those processes that are broadly inclusive and that pair proportionality with accountability have the best chance of creating the legitimacy needed for effective post–war governance because they create the conditions for mutually empowering state–society relations. Many scholars and analysts investigating recent experiences of civil war termination are deeply skeptical of electoral processes in the immediate post–war environment: elections occur in troubled circumstances with deeply fragmented political structures, war–ravaged societies, and, usually, widespread deprivation. Added to this difficult political climate are problems includin population displacement, captured or disabled states that are parties to war, and practical challenges such as the absence of a voters' roll or the presence of landmines. This school of thought argues that statebuilding should come first, putting into place a viable structure of authority to provid basic security and enhancing service–delivery capacities and economic revival before electoral competition takes place. Statebuilding first approaches focus on improving economic condition in post-war environments as a higher priority than fostering political competition (Collier et al., 2003).

Likewise, many observers suggest that post-war electoral processes introduce new uncertainties and that they make war-torn, fragile societies deeply vulnerable to relapse into civil war (Mansfiel and Snyder, 2005). Clearly, the problems associated with immediate post-war elections are acute, suggesting that electoral processes held in the wrong circumstances following civil war do inhibit the building of a functional, capable state because power is distributed along the political lines over which war was fought instead of lines that would contribute to the national integration necessary for long-term state survival. Related are concerns that indeed democratization itself is an inherently conflict-inducing enterprise, fundamentally at odds with the imperatives of conciliation implicit in peacebuilding.

Because election *contests* are just that – a competitive game for political power – they heighten social divisions and enhance differences in the political community in a process through which the people choose among alternative views and leaders. Elections are contests over the governance of the state and nature (often the boundaries) of the 'nation.' This fact about elections is essentially a paradox for conflict management in those societies that are already deeply divided along ethnic racial, or religious lines: a popular mandate through an electoral process is necessary to produce a government able to govern with a high degree of legitimacy, but the very way in which the population is required to choose often gives rise to or heightens already deep differences (Lyons, 2002). The potentially contradictory aims of potentially divisive, competitive elections and peacebuilding have been pointed out by insightful observers who have looked at efforts to use democratization processes to settle civil strife in deeply divided societies? Thus, one of the most vexing challenges facing policy makers in the international community, and protagonists in societies deeply divided by internal conflict alike, is the special set of circumstances that occu in immediate post-war elections. From Namibia in 1989 to Libya in 2011, there have been many instances in which after a civil war a new government is inaugurated in first-ever, post-war elections.[7]

Evaluating electoral systems

Electoral system choices have strong influences on a variety of outcome variables critical to evaluating critical aspects of statebuilding (Reynolds et al., 2005), among them the *structure of the party system*, such as how many parties form, whether and when they may coalesce, their prospects for gaining power, and potentially their very makeup in terms of the various social divisions that might exist within any given political community (e.g., municipality, region, or country).

In some situations, it may be possible to induce certain kinds of candidates for offe to adopt certain types of appeals (Reilly, 2001; Lijphart, 2004). A common example is requirements for a presidential winner to carry a certain minimum percentage of the votes in a very large, and often diverse set of regions. With this rule, it is almost essential that any winner will have had to appeal to at least some voters throughout the country. As a result, it is hoped that presidential candidates will be unifiers, not dividers, of society

Finally, election systems can affect the overall character of the contest in terms of what the competition is for. The electoral system, which in more technical terms translates votes into particular 'seats' or positions, is about determining how a ruling coalition is put together. Winner-take-allsystems, including plurality/majority systems, give the winners of a certain threshold of votes – say, 50% in strict majority-rule systems – all the power to make decisions for the entire community. Other systems, such as the alternative vote or two-round systems, can have similar winner–take–all effects. Proportional systems give various political parties an equal share in political power for an equal share of overall votes cast. In the first type of system, candidates and partie are competing for unbridled rule, trying to form coalitions of people and groups to garner the magical threshold with a given system that produces a majority.

Election-related violence

Election–relatedviolence is prompted by a broader concern that violent elections have devastating effects on the subsequent legitimacy of the regime, and thus undermines the role of governance in providing security and fostering development in 'fragile states' (OECD–DAC International Network on Conflict and Fragility, 2010). As well, it is widely recognized that electoral moment can become crises that present 'windows of vulnerability' during which conflict escalation ma be more likely (Mansfeld and Snyder, 1995). With this knowledge, as well, both the United Nations Development Program and the United States Agency for International Development have commissioned analyses and lesson–learned stocktaking on the causes of election–related violence in an effort to develop conflict prevention approaches and to improve election securit (UNDP, 2009; USAID, 2010; see also Fisher, 2002).

It is clear that elections run under conditions where some parties have the capacity to return to widespread violence present special dangers of war recurrence, and that elections conducted in conditions of grave insecurity with regard to street–level political violence are unlikely to produce legitimate or widely accepted results. In the first instance, the 1992 presi dential elections in Angola are an oft–cited case of the problems of hasty electoral processes conducted without sufficient disarmament or containment of forces: when the UNITA factio under Jonas Savimbi appeared likely to lose in the second round of voting for the presidency, it returned 'to the bush' and the war dragged on for another seven years at a cost of some 150,000 lives.

As in Angola in 1992, much depends on actual or expected exclusion of key protagonists in terms of electoral outcomes. That electoral processes produce winners and losers is an indicator of their capacity to catalyze or to open 'windows of vulnerability' to violence: when a highly insecure party or faction expects to be systematically excluded from political power, it may well turn to violence either to prevent its exclusion or to prevent the election's success (Höglund, 2004). Thus, it is likely that at least some of the insurgent violence in Iraq following the US–led coalition's occupation there after 2003 can be explained by the expectations of the Sunni minority of ethnic–census voting in elections and thus the likelihood of a Shi'a–dominated government that, in coalition with Kurdish parties, would overwhelmingly dominate as far as the eye could see.[8]

Among the common challenges are the following.

- Low trust exists among protagonists for power, because often there is no external force (such as UN peace operation) capable of enforcing the outcome of elections: parties lack a sense of credible commitment by their opponents to the peace deal and fear cheating or rejection of legitimate election results.
- Post–warelections feature high stakes for winning, particularly in situations of 'lootable' commodities: loss of power may endanger economic fortunes.
- Post–warenvironments may be vulnerable to the emergence of wily elites who will mobilize on divisive nationalist, ethnic, or racial themes in their quest for power;
- After civil wars, political parties are often weak, and the party system is either underdeveloped or untested: there is high uncertainty regarding relative strengths of the factions, which heightens tensions and fears about winning and losing.[9]

- Civil society is weak and populations are traumatized by the effects of war: weak civil society and affected populations are less able to stand up to political forces led by extremists or ideologues.
- Basic state capacities are compromised, with governments often unable to ensure proper preparation for elections or to meet other higher−level human needs, rendering elections somewhat surreal as voters vote in conditions that are otherwise fraught with insecurity and destitution (for an overview, see Kumar, 1999).

Typical accounts of structural grievances underlying election−related violence are found in land or chieftaincy disputes, political, cultural, or economic marginalization along identity lines, and state fragility and the politics of 'neo−patrimonialism.' Unpacking the incentives for violence during electoral processes requires carefully thinking about the conditions under which election violence may be instrumentally useful to elites: as noted above, when a highly insecure party or faction expects to be systematically excluded from political power, it may well turn to violence either to prevent its exclusion or to prevent the election's success (Höglund, 2004).

Theories of election−related violence often highlight the perpetuation of highly personalistic or patronage politics or a system in which politicians are gang−like 'warlords' that control resources (such as access to jobs and income) and dispense public services such as housing, health care, or lucrative government contracts (Schwartz, 2001). In Africa, these approaches related directly to state capture, and the close association of presidentialism with clientelistic approaches to governance (van de Walle, 2003).However, there is a need to understand these conditions at both national and local levels, and how state power affects the distribution of public goods and the exploitation or use of private resources (van de Walle, 2002). Thus, the stakes of elections are often seen as opportunities to engage in corruption and economic rent−seeking. This in turn leads to highly factionalized politics, often along religious, sectarian, or ethnic lines or along party−politicaldivides, where control of the state leads to the reinforcement of class divisions or economic opportunity along lines of social difference. Scholars have pointed to the existence and perpetuation of the overlap between control of the state, economic opportunity, and identity politics – known as 'horizontal inequalities' – as strongly contributing to the likelihood of violent encounters (Stewart, 2008). Bates' work on state failure in Africa and the challenges of political violence emphasizes the critical role of top state elites engaged in predation as a driver of corift, whereas others emphasize the challenges of 'disruption from below' from aggrieved or mar−ginalized groups (Bates, 2006).

What are the minimal conditions necessary for a 'good' election in high−conflict settings, on that produces a legitimate, stable, and effective government that can make progress toward social goals of human development, human security, and social reconciliation? Can a government created in a process that is essentially confictual lead a society in a manner that prevents, manages, or transforms social conflict? The answer to these questions is crucial for understanding the conditions under which electoral processes contribute to conflict management and thus statebuilding. Electoral processes require a prior degree of progress on the security front: disarmament of independent armed forces by factions and political parties, basic safety and security for electoral administration personnel, the elimination of 'no−go' zones for campaigning by all parties, and measures to ensure that there is no illegitimate, violent opposition to the outcome. How much security is enough? When is a 'bad' election good enough? Elections are not an end of the post−war transition, a definitive green−light for an international exit strategy or the sol solution to peacebuilding; yet they are a critical turning point of the transition with considerable (if not determinative) implications for statebuilding.

Building autonomous state institutions

Conversely, perceptions of fraudulent or stolen elections are a strong predictor of violence; thus, a key element of electoral processes for long-term statebuilding is the creation of neutral, autonomous electoral management bodies.[10] At the same time, the presence of extensive international election monitoring missions has likewise been key to address concerns of stolen, managed, or manipulated elections.[11] When domestic capacities for electoral management and monitoring are insufficient, the UN has at times stepped in to oversee polls through UN transitional administrations; while such 'trusteeship' appears necessary in failed states, it introduces the paradox of the world body introducing democracy through neo-imperial suzerainty (see Chesterman, 2004).

Electoral management in post-war environments occurs in essentially three different ways. First is the full conduct of the election by outsiders, in most instances the United Nations (as in Cambodia) or other international organizations such as the Organization for Security and Cooperation in Europe (as in Bosnia). A second model is joint administration by UN and local electoral management bodies (as in Afghanistan), involving international oversight but with official authority residing in the national electoral commission. Finally, there are some post-war instances in which the entire electoral process is run by insiders (as in South Africa), albeit with the participation of international experts. These choices affect statebuilding in that they seek to balance the need for professionalized capacity to run an electoral process in a volatile post-war environment with the imperatives of state capacity-building over the long term.

State capacity – particularly in the area of electoral administration, election dispute resolution, and policing and security – is *the* pivotal variable in determining whether underlying vulnerabilities become violent encounters. Collier finds that the greatest constraint to democratizatio in Africa is the 'three illicit electoral tactics' of bribing voters, intimidating voters, and deliberate, pervasive electoral fraud (Collier, 2009). This fundamental appreciation that peacebuilding is about democratic statebuilding is coupled with a stark recognition that international efforts to build peace have failed to devote sufficient attention to the local level. Neçla Tschirgi (2003: 1) argues, for example, that 'Despite lip service being paid to the centrality of local ownership of peacebuilding, it is not clear that international actors have developed effective strategies for assessing local needs, setting priorities, allocating resources, or establishing accountability.'

The key components of a legitimate electoral process are that it be free and fair in both political and administrative terms, inclusive of all elements of society through a well-considered law of citizenship and of voter registration, and offering meaningful choices to the population (Pastor, 1999). Capacities to monitor compliance with international professional best practices, legal requirements, and to deter fraud and intimidation are essential. Election observation refers to evaluations of internal and external neutral organizations on all aspects of the electoral process; verification is more extensive, and occurs when such organizations actually oversee and verify that the electoral management body has run the election fairly. The role of international observers has emerged in the 1990s and 2000s as an essential element in post-war elections precisely because domestic observer capacities are weak. Extensive electoral observation in post-war elections is a necessary component if the results are to be accepted both internally and externally as the outcome of a process that is free and fair in both procedural and substantive terms. Likewise, the capacity for electoral dispute resolution is seen as a key component.[12]

Implications for international engagement

The linkage between elections and statebuilding is rooted in the desperate need for governing elites emerging in post–war contexts to find their base of legitimacy in reference to popular support. But using electoral processes to find legitimacy is both risky for conflict recurrence a quite ambiguous as to the conditions under which elections can lend legitimacy to newfound governing elites. Several integrated findings emerge from the look at the nexus between electora processes and statebuilding outcomes. First, electoral processes – despite myriad well–founded concerns leveled against them – are essential to statebuilding because they give a modicum of legitimacy and credibility to post–war regimes, as the case of Libya illustrates. In any situation, electoral processes are pivotal moments of transition processes linked to a broad sequence of events. Despite a plethora of sensible and well–founded concerns with conducting elections after civil war, there remains no alternative, feasible mechanism to test for the legitimacy of a state.

Second, much depends on how elections are sequenced in terms of the providing of security, how they are related to power–sharing pacts that limit state capture, and how they are designed in terms of institutional choice. The most important variables in the viability of elections are the provision of security (usually, but not always, by external forces) and the extent of inclusivity in electoral outcomes. The creation of legitimacy and the promotion of mutually reinforcing state–society relations in post–war settings depend on whether new ruling elites are involved in processes widely perceived as being free and fair. In situations where electoral processes return elites to power who have engaged in war (as in Cambodia, but also in Bosnia and Timor–Leste), they garner less legitimacy. Throughout the entire electoral process – from creation of the electoral management body, to evaluation of statutes on political party registration, to voter registration, candidate certification, laws on press freedoms, to design and distribution of ballots to management of security, to election day itself, and certification of results, the entire proces must be considered reasonably legitimate for elections to be legitimate and fair.

Third, the choice of electoral system is a critical consideration, not just for the f rst election but in subsequent polls as well. There is a *de facto* 'default option' of closed–list PR as an electoral system choice among UN circles in post–war environments (used in Cambodia and South Africa, and in many other settings as well): they tend to produce inclusivity in parliamentary outcomes, they do not prejudice the emergence of a relatively strong presidency, they are more amenable to facilitating the participation of displaced persons, they may strengthen party systems, and they do not require the delimitation of boundaries or even a fully f nalized voters' roll. But list–PR may not be conducive to further democratization that strengthens the state in the long run. The concern about list PR suggests there is a longer–term need for combining proportionality with accountability, either through opening up lists or through moving toward candidacy–based systems or, more commonly (as in the Libya case), a mixed system.

Finally, there is strong reason for the international community to stay a strongly engaged actor well beyond the initial elections in an unflinching effort to help create the autonomous capacitie of the electoral management body as the principal state institution for managing future free and fair electoral processes. This focus on institution–building must be coupled with building up other areas of autonomy and accountability within state institutions, most important of which are legal institutions most likely to be involved in election dispute resolution. Like other areas of statebuilding, however, focusing on the state alone to manage the electoral process is not enough: because elections reside at the interface between state and society, statebuilding as such requires a concomitant focus on the capacity of non–state institutions to manage credible processes of elections as a pathway toward legitimating the state.

Notes

1. This chapter builds from the author's work 'Pathway of the political: Electoral processes and statebuilding after civil war,' in R. Paris and T. D. Sisk (Eds.)*The dilemmas of statebuilding: Confronting the contradictions of postwar peace operations*, London, UK: Routledge, 2009.
2. *Divided we stand: Libya's enduring conflicts.* International Crisis Group Middle East/North Africa Report No. 130, 14 September 2012, at www.crisisgroup.org
3. Conflict−exacerbating election outcomes can be mitigated by a pre−election pact that determines the fate of the election well before the ballots are cast; negotiation of pre−election pacts is strongly encouraged when there are significant spoiler challenges to elections or when an especially powerful party or factio seeks to boycott an election. Pre−election pacts are a form of power−sharing. For analysis, see Roeder and Rothchild, 2005.
4. On the function of immediate post−war elections as 'validating' peace agreements, see Reilly, 2003.
5. An electoral process is the entire sequence, from the design of the election (e.g., presidential or parliamentary, or proportional or majoritarian) and launch in the campaigns through the long lead−up to election day (the electoral 'event'), any run−offs that may occur, and including the eventual resolution of post−election disputes.
6. For a further articulation of this argument, see Snyder (2000) and Mansfeld and Snyder (1995).
7. For a comprehensive evaluation of the UN role in promoting democracy, see Newman and Rich (2004) and Brown (2003).
8. For an analysis of the Iraq imbroglio, see Diamond (2005). For a broader analysis of the issues of ethnic census voting, expectations in electoral contests, and the effects of electoral system choice in such considerations, see Horowitz (1985).
9. Paradoxically, election−related violence is found in situations where the outcome of the election is wholly uncertain (when power is up for grabs) and when there is a high degree of certainty about the outcome (when a particular party or faction is expected to win). Much depends on the motivation of prospective losers to do everything they can, including wage a violent struggle, to prevent themselves from losing political power through an electoral process.
10. For comprehensive information on electoral administration, see ACE: The Electoral Knowledge Network at www.aceproject.org
11. As Eric Bjornlund (2004: 304–305) writes, 'The involvement of multilateral organizations in election monitoring has helped them to strengthen their commitment to promoting genuine democracy among member states. Meanwhile, non−partisan domestic election−monitoring groups in developing countries have not only deterred fraud and improved public confidence in important elections but have also encouraged citizen involvement in political life more generally.'
12. Procedures for handling electoral disputes through impartial, efficient, and legally valid and widely accepted mechanisms are crucial even in the most advanced democracies. Accidents happen, mistakes are made, and trust is low: the institutions and procedures for dispute resolution need to be established and tested early in the electoral process, such that by the time voting day arrives there is trust in the fairness of the mediation and arbitration process. Without such institutions and mechanisms for dispute resolution, parties may well turn to violent means to press their interests in an election dispute.

References

Bates, R. H. (2006). *When things fell apart: State failure in late-century Africa.* Cambridge, UK: Cambridge University Press.

Bjornlund, E. (2004). *Beyond free and fair: Monitoring elections and building democracy.* Baltimore, MD: Johns Hopkins University Press.

Brown, M. M. (2003). Democratic governance: Toward a framework for sustainable peace. *Global Governance*, 9, 141–146.

Chesterman, S. (2004). *You, the people: The United Nations, transitional administration, and state-building.* Oxford, UK: Oxford University Press.

Collier, P. (2009). *Wars, guns and votes: Democracy in dangerous places.* New York, NY: Harper Collins.

Collier, P., Elliott, V. L., Hegre, H., Hoeffler, A., Reynal−Querol, M., and Sambanis, N. (2003)*Breaking the conflict trap: Civil war and development policy.* Washington, DC: The World Bank and Oxford, UK: Oxford University Press.

Diamond, L. (2005). Building democracy after conflct: Lessons from Iraq. *Journal of Democracy, 16*(1), 9–23.

Fisher, J. (2002). *Electoral conflict and violence: A strategy for study and prevention*. IFES White Paper 2002–01. Washington, DC: International Foundation for Election Systems.

Horowitz, D. (1985). *Ethnic groups in conflict*. Berkeley, CA: University of California Press.

Höglund, K. (2004). *Violence in the midst of peace negotiations: Cases from Guatemala, Northern Ireland, South Africa, and Sri Lanka*. Research Report No. 69. Uppsala, Sweden: Uppsala University Department of Peace and Conflict

Kumar, K. (Ed.). (1999). *Post-conflict elections, democratization, and international assistance*. Boulder, CO: Lynne Rienner.

Lijphart, A. (2004). Constitutional design for divided societies. *Journal of Democracy, 15*(2), 96–109.

Lyons, T. (2002). Post conflict elections, war termination, democratization, and demilitarizing politics. Working Paper 20. Arlington, VA: George Mason University Institute for Conflict Analysis and Resolution.

Mansfield, E., and Snyder, J. (1995). Democratization and the danger of war (Correspondence)*International Security, 20*(4), 197.

Mansfield, E., and Snyder, J. (2005). *Electing to fight*. Cambridge, MA: MIT Press.

Newman, E., and Rich, R. (2004). *The UN role in promoting democracy*. Tokyo, Japan: United Nations University Press.

OECD−DACInternational Network on Conflct and Fragility. (2010). *The state's legitimacy in fragile situations*. Paris, France: OECD−DAC.

Pastor, R. A. (1999). A brief history of electoral commissions. In A. Schedler, L. Diamond, and M. F. Plattner (Eds.), *The self-restraining state: Power and accountability in new democracies*. Boulder, CO: Lynne Rienner.

Reilly, B. (2001). *Democracy in divided societies: Electoral engineering for conflict management*. Cambridge, UK: Cambridge University Press.

Reilly, B. (2003). Democratic validation. In J. Darby and R. Mac Ginty (Eds.), *Contemporary peacemaking: Conflict, violence and peace processes*. London, UK: Palgrave.

Reynolds, A. (Ed.), (1994). *Election '94 South Africa: An analysis of the campaign, results and future prospects*. New York, NY: St Martin's Press.

Reynolds, A., Reilly, B., and Ellis, A. (Eds.). (2005). *Electoral system design: The new international IDEA handbook*. Stockholm, Sweden: International IDEA.

Risley, P., and Sisk, T. D. (2005). *Democracy and peacebuilding at the local level: Lessons learned*. Stockholm, Sweden: International IDEA.

Roeder, P. G., and Rothchild, D. S. (2005).*Sustainable peace: Power and democracy after civil wars*. Ithaca, NY: Cornell University Press.

Schwartz, R. (2001). *Political and electoral violence in East Africa*. Working Papers on Conflict Managemen No. 2. Nairobi, Kenya: Friedrich Ebert Stiftung and Centre for Confict Research.

Sisk, T. D. (1995). *Democratization in South Africa: The elusive social contract*. Princeton, NJ: Princeton University Press.

Snyder, J. (2000). *From voting to violence: Democratization and nationalist conflict*. New York, NY: W.W. Norton.

Stewart, F. (Ed.). (2008). *Horizontal inequalities and conflict: Understanding group violence in multiethnic societies*. London, UK: Palgrave.

Tschirgi, N. (2003). Peacebuilding as the link between security and development: Is the window of opportunity closing? New York, NY: International Peace Academy Policy Report.

UNDP. (2009). *Elections and conflict prevention: A guide to analysis, planning, and programming*. Oslo, Norway: Bureau for Development Policy, Oslo Governance Center.

USAID. (2010). *Electoral security framework: Technical guidance handbook for democracy and governance officers*. New York, NY: USAID.

Van de Walle, N. (2002). Africa's range of regimes. *Journal of Democracy, 13*(2), 66–80.

Van de Walle, N. (2003). Presidentialism and clientelism in Africa's emerging party systems*Journal of Modern African Studies, 41*(2), 297–319.

PART III
Policy implementation

22
INTERVENTION AND STATEBUILDING IN KOSOVO

Jens Stilhoff Sörensen

Kosovo is the most controversial case of statebuilding in contemporary Europe and the question of recognition continues to divide the EU as well as UN member states. NATO's intervention in 1999, which paved the way for it, was itself the most controversial in the organization's post–Cold War history. As it has divided states, so has it divided scholars. The controversial issue around Kosovo's status came from the outset to shape the character of international administration and statebuilding efforts in Kosovo, and an analysis of these must be placed within the context of this protracted conflict. Moreover, as argued elsewhere (Sörensen, 2012), international statebuilding measures are profoundly conditioned by local structures and agents with which they interact, and the relative relations of power and legitimacy within competing local elite formations, in relation to which they have to form allies, contest, and compete. Thereby the local–domestic political dynamic prior to intervention, and how this is affected by intervention, is central to the analysis. In Kosovo the most crucial issue aside from evolving Serbian–Albanian relations has been the *intra*–Albaniancompetition between the moderate (and initially hegemonic) political party LDK (Democratic Alliance of Kosovo) and the radical faction KLA (Kosovo Liberation Army), with its gradual consolidation during the second half of the 1990s and, especially, how the latter attained international support both intentionally and unintentionally. This process, primarily shaped in the 1990s, came to profoundly influence the nature and direction of statebuilding after 2000. Here, institution–building has also to a large extent been developed upon structures shaped during the 1990s.

Aside from the direct effects on political and institutional organization in the protectorate, the protracted unresolved issue of Kosovo's status had consequences for any development–related work that ideally should have followed an initial post–war recovery phase. Typically most development–relatedwork, for example credits from the World Bank, is dependent on the resolution of legal issues that require reference to a state as partner, guarantor, and provider of a clear judicial framework. The lack of resolution of status issues prevented international policy interventions from taking a technical or purely administrative form, above local conflict dynamics In this way, political issues remained in the foreground, effectively blocking many programs (or hopes thereof), which in turn generated further tensions and continuing social frustration which fed back into the contested political dynamic.

This chapter analyzes statebuilding in Kosovo in this historical and political context, thereby aiming to avoid any conceptual 'point–zeros' after intervention. It first outlines the regional an internal political dynamics in the 1990s, which moved toward escalating violence, then proceeds to the context of the Rambouillet agreement, which paved the way for military intervention, and then discusses the main developments and problems of the international UN administration (UNMIK) and policies from its setup in 1999 to the declared independence in 2008. The fina section critically discusses and highlights some remaining outstanding issues.

Politics and conflict dynamics during the early 1990s: building proto-state structures

The crisis that started in 1981 in Kosovo played a crucial role in the breakup of Yugoslavia. Since the late 1960s Kosovo had received increasing autonomy as a Serbian province within the Yugoslav federation and was constitutionally guaranteed the same rights as other republics with some minor exceptions, notably the right to secession. In 1981 student protests for better conditions at the University of Pristina spread and escalated into wider demonstrations with demands that Kosovo's status should be elevated to that of a separate Yugoslav republic. This wave of Albanian nationalism calmed down by the mid-1980s, but had ignited a much more explosive Serbian reaction, and tensions were escalating between the Albanian majority (about 82 per cent in 1981) and the Serbian minority (about 10 per cent in 1981). In 1988 the Serbian party branch of the League of Communists annexed its counterpart in Kosovo, which was a visible contrast to the pluralism that seemed to be emerging in Slovenia and Croatia. This was followed by *de facto* abolishment of Kosovo's autonomy within Serbia in 1989–1990.

Like elsewhere in Eastern Europe, intellectuals organized the Albanian opposition in various associations, with the writers' association, with Ibrahim Rugova as president, taking a lead after it had presented a national program in April 1988 (Maliqi, 1998: 26). Several political parties and councils were established in winter 1989–1990, but the LDK, again with Rugova as president, immediately became the dominant force. Rather than just being a political party the LDK projected itself as a national movement. In response to Kosovo's abolished autonomy, the Albanians boycotted all (Serbian) state institutions and opted for a strategy of non-violent resistance. This remained the dominant, albeit disputed, strategy throughout the first half of th 1990s even as the Yugoslav federation collapsed with violent conf ict in Croatia and Bosnia–Herzegovina. The result was a deeply divided society with all formal institutions dominated by Serbs and with the Albanians organizing completely separate institutions. These institutions were largely built on structures existing prior to 1990. To a large extent they simply took over the organization of the 'socialist alliance' from the Kosovo branch of the League of Communists and ref ned it into quite separate underground networks of institutions, especially during 1990–1992. Complete or partial networks were developed to cover a range of sectors such as social, health, school, media, culture, and sport activities, and a rudimentary social welfare system based on solidarity funds was developed to provide aid for the most impoverished and to support the unemployed miners of Trep ča mining complex. The solidarity funds were established with diaspora remittances from Western Europe, the US, Croatia, and Macedonia, as well as through contributions collected within Kosovo (Maliqi, 1998: 110). The network was f nanced by a 3 per cent tax for all Albanians, including those working abroad, through diaspora remittances and, to a lesser extent, international aid, with donors supporting 'independent media' or what they perceived as 'civil society' in the making. Solidarity, reduced salaries, voluntary work, barter, and subsistence farming also played an important role in the economy in dire conditions and it should be noted that the private and informal sectors, as well as subsistence farming, had been extensive in Kosovo throughout the Yugoslav period. In Kosovo some 80 per cent of the population, and perhaps more among the Albanians, had been confined to the private sector thereby working outside socially owned enterprises (see Woodward, 1995: 342). In addition, there was an extensive parallel and black economy, such as the drug trade, which could expand in the wake of the international sanctions placed on Serbia in 1992, and which particularly financed some radical networks (Sörensen, 2006; 2009: Chapter 7). Some sources have suggested that the income from smuggling, especially drugs, together with diaspora remittances, was the most important in financing the parallel institutions throughout the 1990s (SELDI, 2002: 13)

In September 1990, the Albanians passed a constitution and proclaimed independence and in 1992 they elected a parliament and president (Ibrahim Rugova). To avoid arrest, several of the leaders fled the country and formed a government in exile. From Switzerland the Prime Ministe Bujar Bukoshi organized a military organization, FARK (the armed forces of Kosovo), gathering former Albanian officers of the JNA (Yugoslav People's Army). Kosovo thereby increasingl came to resemble an organized and independent state although the proclaimed independent republic was symbolic, since the territory was fully controlled by Serbia.

The choice of non-violence as a strategy toward the goal of independence involved a calculation that it would attract international goodwill and support, and thereby a way to seek external alliances. The LDK's success in mobilizing support was based on solidarity in opposition to the Serbs, but they also directed much energy to fighting political rivals within the Albania community. The concept of a common enemy in Serbia and the Serbs became instrumental in unifying the Albanian clans, and in 1990 the phenomenon of blood-feud, regulated in Albanian customary law, was addressed through a special campaign resulting in a successful reconciliation of some 2,000 families and enabling 20,000 people to be released from house confinement (Maliqi 1995: 242; Clark, 2000: 60–64; Vickers, 1998: 248). Still, the LDK strategy was not undisputed and opposition and divisions both within the party and with other smaller parties, such as the Liberals and the Peasants' Party, grew especially from autumn 1994. This led to a split with a breakaway moderate faction of those who were willing to settle for autonomy within the new Yugoslavia (now consisting only of Serbia and Montenegro). The split was also notable across the diaspora, especially in Germany, Switzerland, and the US, and there was an accompanying growing opposition toward LDK's dominance in local government (Vickers, 1998: 281).

Within the diaspora there were some radical groups such as the 'Popular Movement for the Republic of Kosovo' (LPRK), which had been founded in 1982. In 1990 most of its members joined the LDK, but the most militant faction founded the 'Popular Movement of Kosovo' (LPK) (Judah, 2000b). This group had members in the diaspora in Germany, Sweden, and Switzerland, and out of this grew the KLA, which was formed during 1992–1993. The KLA's objective was an independent Kosovo and unification of all Albanians in a Greater Albania (Janji c, 2009). It had members mainly in the diaspora and in a few clans in the Drenica area, which was the home area of Hashim Thaqi, one of its co-founders and leaders. The group remained marginal until autumn 1995.

The Dayton effect in Kosovo and escalation of violence, 1995–1999

During the second half of the 1990s there were growing internal divisions and a change in strategy in the Albanian movement in Kosovo. This came partly as a result of a perception shock from the Dayton Agreement for Bosnia and Herzegovina (BiH), which had ignored the issue of Kosovo. The realization that the international community intended to address the issue of violent conflict in BiH, whereas Kosovo was treated only in terms of human rights concern (although Rugova explicitly had stated that the Albanian aim was independence), led many Albanians to conclude that the non-violence strategy was a failure. The Albanians also interpreted Dayton as legitimizing ethnic cleansing as a method for statebuilding, since the entities in BiH had been created through ethnic cleansing and since a precondition for Dayton had been the Croatian ethnic cleansing of Serbs from Krajina (Janjić, 2009; Maliqi, 1998). Ibrahim Rugova's strategy was now openly challenged and the political spectrum widened with divisions into three positions, the pacifist, the activist, and the militant. The 'activist' implied various forms of active resistance from demonstrations and occupations to the more militant strategy of a Kosovo *intifada*. There were also alternative political and confederal ideas, such as the construction of a Balkan confederation suggested by the respected writer Adem Demaqi, and there was increasing disagreement within the various factions. In 1997 Demaqi and another leading intellectual, Rexhep Quosja, together with the Syndicate of Trade Unions of Kosovo, founded Democratic Forum as a counterweight to LDK. Another consequence of the Dayton Agreement was the relaxation of the UN sanctions, which affected the black market and smuggling networks in the whole region. A direct effect was a suddenly shrinking market for smuggling, especially of oil/petrol from Albania, which contributed to the collapse of the pyramid schemes and the subsequent political unrest and fall of the government in Albania in 1997 (Sörensen, 2009; Racsmány, 1998). The anarchical situation then created a space for obtaining weapons from Albanian military depots, through which the KLA and other networks could arm themselves.

Violent resistance now grew, with attacks on individual Serbs, on refugees, on Serbian police and on Albanians who were considered too moderate or as collaborating with Serbs. From November 1997 masked KLA guerrillas started displaying themselves at funerals to read statements (Salihu et al., 2004). They also targeted LDK supporters and members of FARK, and many Albanians began to fear the KLA. It did not have heavy weaponry or a trained military organization, but its strategy was that by provoking violence, as had been done in BiH, it would attract international attention for its cause (Thaqi, 2000). This strategy would prove successful. An incident in early 1998, labeled the Drenica massacre, placed Kosovo at the center of international attention and strengthened the KLA considerably. In two operations, on 28 February and 4 March, Serbian forces attacked a few extended families connected to the KLA in the Drenica area and killed 26 people in the first operation and then, in the second, 58 people in th compound of the guerrilla leader Adem Jashari (Magnusson, 1999: 69; Judah, 2000b). This had two important consequences: f rst, it provoked outrage among Albanians throughout Kosovo and in the diaspora, and the clan elders in various regions now began supporting the military uprising; second, the Albanian–American community, which had been supporting the LDK, now shifted its support to the KLA, politically and financially (Nazi, 2000: 152). This was a considerable victory for the KLA, which could now grow, launch further attacks, and even take territory in Drenica. When Serbian forces responded, the KLA simply vanished in the forest or among the population.

The international reaction was to condemn both the excessive use of force by Serbia and all 'terrorist action' by the KLA, and to insist that the parties negotiate a peaceful solution. [1] This message rang hollow to the KLA, which saw its strategy working. A weakened LDK made attempts to open negotiations with Belgrade, but since it could not control the KLA it could not deliver and discussions broke down in May, when Serbian forces took new measures against the KLA. The latter was still labeled a terrorist organization at this time, but within a few months the US would come to radically change its position in favor of the KLA. [2] Serbian troops continued their operations in the summer, and in July 1998 they attacked and burned villages in the Drenica area, displacing tens of thousands of civilians. The international reaction was widespread condemnation and demands that Serbia withdraw its forces from Kosovo and allow an OSCE Kosovo Verification Mission (KVM) to monitor the situation, while simultaneousl starting negotiations. The US and NATO threatened air strikes unless Serbia agreed. The idea with the KVM was to monitor the withdrawal of Serbian forces while negotiations took place between Belgrade and the LDK. The problem was that the LDK was now sidelined by the KLA and had no control over the situation. For the KLA, the altered position of the US meant that its strategy was successful (Thaqi, 2000). The KLA was not even bound by the KVM agreement, as the Yugoslav government was, which in effect meant that the KVM was doomed to fail. Slobodan Milošević agreed to the KVM but when Serbian forces withdrew, the KLA reclaimed territory, to which Serbian troops then responded. In mid-January an incident in the village of Račak ignited political condemnation and the US repeated its threats of military action.[3]

The US policy change to drop the LDK and support the KLA came during the second half of 1998 and was completed by spring 1999. It has been argued that this shift was due to heavy lobbying in Washington, especially by the NGO/think-tanks International Crisis Group (ICG), the Balkan Institute (later the Balkan Action Council), and the United States Institute for Peace (USIP) (see Magnusson, 1999). These organizations accommodated support for the Albanian position, for the most radical claims and the KLA. Important in the lobby was the US Ambassador Morton Abramowitz, who had a close relationship to Secretary Albright. The KLA strategy of pursuing radical demands and provoking violence had thereby proved superior to Rugova's strategy of non-violent resistance as a means to gain international support. While it did not have the majority support of the Albanian population, it had succeeded in gaining organized support from the diaspora, then in strategically outflanking the LDK and gaining the support from the most important international actors, first the US and then NATO

The Rambouillet intervention

The KLA was given an important role at Rambouillet in February 1999, whereas the LDK was marginalized. The Rambouillet negotiations had the character of a non-negotiable and politically impossible ultimatum presented to the Serbs by the Americans, and both the process and the substance of the agreement suggest that it was a pro forma arrangement to legitimize a NATO intervention (for details see Magnusson, 1999; Dauphinee, 2003; Sörensen, 2009, 2013). [4] NATO's bombing campaign followed on 24 March 1999 and lasted 78 days. The campaign spurred a massive Serbian assault inside Kosovo, both as preparation for a NATO invasion and as pure revenge on Albanians. In the face of the subsequent humanitarian disaster it became evident that new negotiations were necessary to break the deadlock. A renegotiation, now involving Russia, was opened and the crucial problem points from the February version of Rambouillet were dropped or altered, after which Serbia agreed to what in effect became a UN protectorate in Kosovo (Magnusson, 1999; Dauphinee, 2003; Sörensen, 2009). UN Security Council Resolution 1244 formalized the mandate, which officially guaranteed Serbia's sov - ereignty over Kosovo but placed it under UN administration.

Problems in creating the protectorate governing structures

The UN administration had from the outset a diffcult task in that it was to build institutions and provide the conditions for self-government, reconstruct society, and help promote a political process that could be a foundation for the future definition of status, while the region formall was to remain part of Serbia. The mission both inherited and was erected upon the highly explosive issue of Kosovo's status. Moreover, despite the presence of almost 50,000 NATO troops to help secure UNMIK's (UN Mission in Kosovo) establishment, it took some six to nine months, from June 1999, to obtain international control. During this period the KLA consolidated its position by taking power of local administration and declaring a government with Hashim

Thaqi as Prime Minister. Although the UN considered this illegal, it was unable to prevent it and had to cooperate with these actors for practical reasons. Moreover, the KLA and Albanian radicals engaged in a wave of ethnic cleansing of Serbs, Roma, and other minorities. During this period, in the midst of NATO and formal UN rule, some 230,000 people fled and 1,200 wer killed.[5] Private property and hundreds of medieval orthodox monasteries were looted and burned. Violence then spread first to South Serbia, with an Albanian population in Medv de, Preševo, and Bujanovac, and then in 2001–2002 into Macedonia, where branches of the KLA took control over border areas and parts of the town of Tetovo. These events created from the very beginning a deep mistrust of the UN among the Serbian population.

International control and an agreement on institutional organization came in early 2000, under the first Special Representative Bernard Kouchner. In order to create legitimacy and prepar self–governing institutions, a Joint Interim Administrative Structure (JIAS) was organized, consisting of an Interim Administrative Council (IAC) and a Kosovo Transitional Council (KTC). The IAC had eight members: four UNMIK representatives, three Albanians, and one Serbian minority representative who could only be an observer. The KTC had 35 members, consisting of the IAC, various minority, political, and religious leaders, and members from some NGOs. On a local level each of 30 municipalities was to have an appointed UNMIK governor, who in turn selected representatives for a municipal board, which would act as a local executive, and a municipal council to advise on policy.

UNMIK further legitimized the transition of the KLA into the Kosovo Protection Corps (KPC), which was to be a kind of fire brigade and rescue service, and a Kosovo Police Servic (KPS). As expected, this was met with deep suspicion among the Serbian minority, but for UNMIK it provided a formula for legitimizing and relating to the KLA. To provide the ground for a legitimate local administration it was necessary to develop an international police force and judiciary that could train and work alongside a local structure. This was established gradually after about one year but was accompanied by a number of practical and legal problems; the judiciary had to combine some pre–1989 Yugoslav laws with selected international laws, which created legal confusion.

As a means to legitimize local representations UNMIK, pressured by the US, wished to organize elections at an early stage. This strategy came with serious setbacks regarding the legitimacy of the process. First municipal elections were held in October 2000, and again in 2002. Parliamentary elections were held in November 2001, and again in 2004. An immediate trend was established with decreasing voter turnout, beginning with 79 per cent in 2000 and down to 51 per cent by 2004, and with decreasing minority participation. Gradually the Serbs would almost completely boycott the elections. The quality of elections, especially the first municipal ones, was questionable. They were pushed forward by the US, but there were problems with voter registration, since there had been no census in Kosovo since 1981 (the 1991 Yugoslav census was useless for Kosovo as it was boycotted by the Albanians) and because many documents had been lost during the war. The problem with documentation was addressed in an ad hoc manner. There was also legal and procedural confusion, with many of the local staff not knowing the rules, defective provisional voter lists, and in the case of the Turkish minority a lack of registration forms in Turkish (in the Yugoslav 1974 Constitution Turkish had been given the status of minority language). Other conspicuous issues were the apartheid–like situation for minorities, the existence of secret voter lists, highly restricted access for election monitors, mono–ethnic polling station committees, intimidation, biased media, less than 10 per cent participation at some polling stations, and a general lack of transparency.

The elections provided the basis for establishing municipal assemblies in 27 out of 30 municipalities. The LDK gained control over 20 municipalities, indicating the relative popular support it still had *vis-à-vis* the KLA. The intra—Albanian power struggle was visible in considerable tensions during the formation of some municipalities, and a lack of will to compromise among the parties; in 10 of the municipalities the opposition boycotted the assemblies. In the three remaining municipalities the Serbian boycott made it impossible to establish the results and instead UNMIK appointed the assemblies.

During this initial period, with Bernard Kouchner as Special Representative, the Serbian minority was alienated. Most of its demands were rejected while Albanian demands were met, and the wave of ethnic cleansing and violence, the slow set—up of international control, and the eventual introduction of a provisional self—government signaled to the radical elements among the Albanians that their objective of an ethnically pure and independent Kosovo was, at least passively, sanctioned by the international administration. To the Serbs, and to the minorities that had fled, this signaled that to return to, or stay in, Kosovo was neither welcome nor safe

Political structures: institutions and parties

Increased attempts to involve the Serbian minority came with Hans Haekerup, the next Special Representative who took over in 2001. The fall of the Slobodan Milošević regime in Serbia in October 2000 also opened a possibility to seek increasing cooperation from Belgrade, but this would eventually enrage the Albanians and force Haekerup to leave his post (Janfi, 2009). During his mandate the local institutional governing structure was further established and he signed a 'Constitutional Framework' for 'Provisional Institutions of Self—Government' (PISG); in November 2001 elections were held for a National Assembly. Some 25 political parties registered, with the main Albanian parties being LDK and a new party led by Hashim Thaqi called the 'Democratic Party of Kosovo' (PDK, initially PPDK). This party was a political outgrowth of the KLA and primarily populated by KLA members. Another KLA outgrowth was Ramush Haradinaj's 'Alliance for the Future of Kosovo' (AAK). There were also minority parties and coalitions, such as a block of Serbian parties forming the 'Return Coalition' (Povratak). A major fault line was opening within the Serbian community with disputes regarding representation and whether to participate at all in elections. The Serbian National Council (SNV), founded in 1999 by, among others, Momčilo Trajković, had split within a year and was now led by Bishop Artemije. The Serbian community was divided between the Serbs in Mitrovica and those in Gračanica and the villages outside Pristina. In Mitrovica Belgrade supported and had direct influence in the administrative structures and in party politics as well as in the local village guards, or so—called 'bridge watchers,' that had been formed in 1999. Serb participation in the elections was thereby partial and many considered them illegitimate. The general voter turnout was 64 per cent, but among the Serb population only 50 per cent and in some polling stations less than 10 per cent. The LDK won 46 per cent of the votes, the PDK 25 per cent and the AAK just below 8 per cent. The Serbian bloc received some 11 per cent.

Kosovo now had a governmental structure with a national assembly with 120 seats (20 guaranteed for the minorities) and 30 municipalities. The presidential cabinet was formed with seven members and one seat reserved for a Serb representative and one for 'other minorities.' Electoral procedures had been established with closed lists for the parties, promoting party instead of candidate votes, and with one—third of the lists reserved for women. Kosovo is constituted as a single electorate, which works against the principle of geographic representation, of some significance in an agricultural society with traditional and regionally based loyalty structures. In effect the system favors the capital, while some municipalities have had no assembly candidate at all (UNDP, 2004: 59). Clearly the principle of geographic representation was sacrificed i favor of ethnic and gender quotas. The political parties were essentially vehicles for the elite to legitimize their positions in the new framework. They had no real ideological basis and there were no bridging or communication links to social groups or citizens. The parties were based first on ethnicity and then on other traditional loyalty structures, such as clan and family alliances. The PDK and AAK typically reflected this extension of patron–client relations into party politic and both had strong regional anchoring (Sörensen, 2009: Chapter 7; Cocozzelli, 2004; Andersen, 2002). The 2001 elections were followed by months of deadlock and disputes among the Albanians, but in February 2002 the three main Albanian parties agreed to a coalition government. The ten ministries were divided between the parties. The institutions received increasing responsibilities from 2002. In April 2002 the next Special Representative, Michael Steiner, presented a 'Standards before Status' checklist to be fulfilled before any discussion over Kosovo' future status could begin. This, along with a detailed 'Standard Implementation Plan' the following year, was accepted by the Albanians since they perceived the gradual transfer of powers to PISG as a move toward independence. In November an agreement followed with Serbian Prime Minister Zoran Đinđić, in which Belgrade handed over 'parallel Serbian institutions' to UNMIK and gave consent to the introduction of the Kosovo Police Service. Thereby Belgrade interrupted the support for some Serbian institutions in Mitrovica, but continued to finance others including the health sector and administrative structures.

Steiner pursued a shifting policy whereby he tried to balance various factions. This brought him at odds with the EU and in July 2003 he was replaced by Harri Holkeri. During Holkeri's mandate the UNMIK system was brought to near collapse. The beginning of his period saw an increased incidence of ethnically motivated violence, and on 18–19 March 2004 it erupted in a well-organized Albanian attack on Serbs throughout Kosovo, with 22 Serbs killed, some 600 wounded and some 4,000 forced from their homes. International UNMIK personnel were also targeted, with around 150 wounded. The riots demonstrated UNMIK's relative impotence and signaled that it had seriously misjudged the situation in Kosovo.

From UNMIK crisis to independence

After the March riots UNMIK effectively lost credibility among Serbs and Albanians alike and tensions increased between UNMIK and PISG. This prompted the EU and NATO to create separate information channels and appoint their own special representatives. The UN commissioned a review of the policies in Kosovo, which resulted in strong criticism with UNMIK described as lacking direction and cohesion, and as having become a static, inward-looking routine operation with policies lacking credibility (UNSC S/2004/932). The review resulted in the restructuring of UNMIK and accompanying policy change. Holkeri was replaced by Soren Jessen-Pedersen, who started to adjust to Albanian requests. Combined with the fear instilled during the March riots, this frustrated the Serbs, who boycotted the parliamentary election held in October 2004. UNMIK continued to be tainted by critique, internal UN revision, and charges of corruption. Jessen-Pedersen showed no interest in addressing the situation and was replaced by Joackim Rücker in 2006. After a second UN review in 2005 the former Finnish President Martti Ahtisaari was appointed to mediate on Kosovo's status. Negotiations began in 2006 but immediately ran into deadlock. In March 2007 Ahtisaari submitted a report in which he concluded that independence was the best option. Meanwhile Albanian radicals continued to put pressure on UNMIK with violent demonstrations, and attacks on the UN headquarters in Pristina in November 2007. Negotiations remained at a deadlock. Belgrade considered its sovereignty guaranteed in international law, and in UN Security Council Resolution 1244, while the Albanians saw no reason to compromise on the claim to full independence. On 17 February 2008 they (again) declared independence and were recognized by the US and about two-thirds of the EU, but not by Russia, China, or most of the states in Africa, Asia, or Latin America.

Privatization as development

During the initial years of international administration a rapid physical reconstruction of houses, roads, and public buildings led to a visible economic recovery. The international presence required local staff, as well as cafés and hotels, and previously underground small-scale activities now surfaced. Humanitarian assistance was also considerable. The visible change nurtured optimistic miscalculations among many internationals, including UNMIK, about overall progress in the region. But a number of problems related to international aid soon became apparent, and by 2003 a decline and growing social frustration were visible. Kosovo's uncertain status and accompanying legal concerns blocked most development work and, for example, prevented the World Bank from giving credits to Kosovo, which could not even obtain BIC/SWIFT codes. For this reason, the World Bank had only marginal influence for years. Other problems include a lack of census data and accompanying statistics on which policy planning depended. The various ministries in Kosovo operated with different estimates of such basics as the size of population, which ranged from 1.7 to 2.4 million. There was a clear contrast in development visions between Albanians and internationals, with the former placing hopes in a revival of heavy industry such as the Trepča mines, while the latter focused on privatization and the promotion of small- and medium-scale enterprise, without the context of larger industry or companies to support it. Privatization programmes were pushed heavily by the US but became tainted by legal problems, initially ignored by UNMIK but then occasionally interrupted on legal grounds. Micro-financ as a development strategy to promote individual entrepreneurship has also been attempted but, as in neighboring Bosnia-Herzegovina, it seems to have merely reproduced problems of individual debt traps and deepening poverty (Drezgi´ et al., 2011; Cipruš et al., 2011; Bateman, 2010, 2011). A decade after international intervention, Kosovo remains one of Europe's poorest countries (along with Moldova), with an aid-dependent economy that esentially can be divided into five segments: (i) pure aid, which inevitably has been decreasing; (ii) the market created b the international presence, which is ultimately unsustainable; (iii) remittances from the diaspora, which are in decline both because of the f nancial crisis and because individuals migrating form their own families to support; (iv) subsistence and barter; (v) a widespread black market, which has been highly adaptable and consolidating. The Serbian minority in Mitrovica has in turn been completely dependent on Serbia.

Critical issues

The international mission in Kosovo was from the outset caught in the locally and internationally explosive issue of independence. The UN Mission was premised on a Security Council Resolution (1244) that guaranteed Serbian sovereignty, in line with international law, but the Albanians interpreted the intervention and institution-building measures as gradual steps toward full independence. Thereby all supposedly 'technical' issues, whether judicial, institutional, or economic reform, were always embedded in the most deep-rooted political conflict. Under suc conditions policies tended to change with each new Special Representative in a constant search for balance between Albanian and Serbian and various international demands. One of the theoretical debates in the statebuilding literature has been the question of building an institutional framework before democratic inclusion, that is 'institutionalization before liberalization' as prescribed by Roland Paris (2004), versus the problem of institutionalization as imposed peacebuilding and statebuilding without local participation (see Chandler, 2006). In Kosovo this dichotomy appears as a 'false choice,' highlighting the lack of options, with both avenues leading into deadlock. Here, the first avenue was directly related to the core of the inter−ethnic confli and gradually provoked frustration among the majority population, which became increasingly impatient and hostile, thereby threatening to end in a situation where the UN and NATO simply would have taken over Serbia's role in the 1990s as an oppressor while facing similar parallel state structures as Serbia did. The second option would instead play into the hands of the majority population and the road to independence, formally in violation of international law and the UNSC 1244, with wide−ranging international as well as local and regional ramifications, an effectively confine the Serbian minority to enclaves

These questions of institutionalization and 'democratic involvement' revolve around a Weberian concept of the state. While a useful concept (and influential within the literature i this area), this offers, as discussed by John Heathershaw, a limited perspective on processes of statebuilding (Heathershaw, 2012). Weberian−based conceptions of statebuilding, such as 'constructing or reconstructing institutions of governance' (Chesterman, 2004: 1) and 'establishing institutions of government in society' (Zaum, 2007: 16), can be contrasted and complemented by a more historical–sociological approach focusing on the networked character of states and the structuring of political practice as producing 'state effects,' and where the 'idea' and vision of autonomy and statehood itself is crucial (see Abrams, 1988). As highlighted here, the 1990s was a formative period of consolidating networks and institutions, as well as a 'state idea,' and in structuring society in Kosovo, which largely conditioned international institution−building measures. Nevertheless, judicial−related questions of statehood constantly permeated the daily practices of reform and aid, such as the privatization of socially owned enterprises, which from the Serbian perspective was considered pure theft and contested as illegal. When the inevitable question of independence was addressed it would split the international community. While rejected by Russia, China, and other states with their own potential breakaway regions or minority concerns, for example Spain, and by precarious post−colonial states in Africa and Asia, it was recognized by the US and most of the EU. It was a challenging precedent, closely monitored by minorities and central governments worldwide; to the former it signaled that independence was a possibility given the right formula of violence and international alliances, and to the latter it warned against granting autonomy to minorities, since this could be trans − formed into independence. It opened questions for Bosnia−Herzegovina, where a contradictory principle had been imposed to prevent Republika Srpska from breaking off, and beyond the Balkans the list seemed endless: Transnistria, the Kurds in Iraq, Tibet, Taiwan, etc. Six months later it also provided arguments for the Russian−backed breakaway of South Ossetia and Abkhazia from Georgia.

While independence for Kosovo has been a source of self−confidence for Albanians, the critical problems remain: ethnic tension with the Serbian minority, economic underdevelopment, unemployment, and a deep−rooted black economy. For the international community, Kosovo and the Balkans in general have illustrated the lack of instruments to deal with inter−ethnic confict. Perhaps the best contributions to the subject from political science have been models of consociational or consensus democracy (for example, Lijphart, 1984). However, when the 'ethnie' is mobilized and people still don't want to live within the same state, it offers a weak prospect with the only alternative being separation.

Notes

1. This was repeated by the Contact Group and in a series of UN Security Council Resolutions starting with SCR 1160 and later that year SCR 1199.
2. Both Madeleine Albright and the spokesman James Rubin made such statements during 1997, repeated by US ambassador Robert Gelbard during a visit to Belgrade in February 1998 (see Magnusson, 1999: 69–70).
3. The event has been disputed, with the US and NATO claiming that 45 Albanians, primarily civilians, were massacred, while some KVM monitors, and a French journalist present at the time, claimed the incident was staged by the KLA and a US team (references, especially to German and French articles, are collected in Pumphrey and Pumphrey (n.d.); see also Loquai, 2000). The latter claim is that Serbian troops killed 15 KLA f ghters, but that the KLA then collected bodies from elsewhere and arranged them to look like a massacre. Tim Judah (2000a: 193) builds a scenario based on the claim of a massacre.
4. Space limits preclude all but this cursory overview of the Rambouillet intervention, but see the referenced works (including Sörensen, 2009, 2013).
5. These figures were referred to by international organizations, including the Danish Refugee Counci and the Yugoslav Red Cross, while the Orthodox Church stated a higher figure of some 360,000 Serb expelled from their homes (see further Sörensen, 2009: 222).

References

Abrams, P. (1988/1977). Notes on the difficulty of studying the state. *Journal of Historical Sociology*, 1(1), 58–89.
Andersen, A. (2002). *Transforming ethnic nationalism: The politics of ethno-nationalistic sentiments among the elite in Kosovo*. Unpublished thesis, University of Oslo, Oslo, Norway.
Bateman, M. (2010). *Why doesn't microfinance work?* London, UK: Zed Books.
Bateman, M. (2011). Introduction: Looking beyond the hype and entrenched myths. In M. Bateman (Ed.), *Confronting microfinance: Undermining sustainable development*. West Hartford, CT: Kumarian Press, pp. 1–21.
Chandler, D. (2006). *Empire in denial: The politics of statebuilding*. London, UK: Pluto Press.
Chesterman, S. (2004). *You the people: The United Nations, transnational administration and state-building*. Oxford, UK: Oxford University Press.
Cipruš, V., Hughes, L., and Vukojević, M. (2011). Gender and microfinance in Southeastern Europe. I M. Bateman (Ed.), *Confronting microfinance: Undermining sustainable development*. West Hartford, CT: Kumarian Press, pp. 207–227.
Clark, H. (2000). *Civil resistance in Kosovo*. London, UK: Pluto Press.
Cocozzelli, F. (2004). Political parties in Kosovo, 2003.*Global Security and Cooperation Quarterly (GSC)*, 11. New York, NY: Social Science Research Council, Program on Global Security and Cooperation.
Dauphinee, E. A. (2003). Rambouillet: A critical (re)assessment. In F. Bieber and Ž. Daskalovski (Eds.), *Understanding the war in Kosovo*. London, UK: Frank Cass.
Drezgić, S., Pavlović, Z., and Stoyanov, D. (2011). Microfinance saturation in Bosnia and Herzegovina. I M. Bateman (Ed.), *Confronting microfinance: Undermining sustainable development*. West Hartford, CT: Kumarian Press, pp. 175–205.
Heathershaw, J. (2012). Conclusions: Neither built nor formed – The transformation of post–conflict state under international intervention. In B. Bliesemann de Guevara (Ed.), *Statebuilding and state-formation: The political sociology of intervention*. London, UK: Routledge.
Janjić, D. (2009). *Kosovo under the reign of Slobodan Milošević*. Belgrade, Serbia: Forum for Ethnic Relations, Institute of Social Sciences.
Judah, T. (2000a). *Kosovo: War and revenge*. New Haven, CT: Yale University Press.
Judah, T. (2000b). A history of the Kosovo Liberation Army. In J. B. Buckley (Ed.), *Kosovo: Contending voices on Balkan interventions*. Grand Rapids, MI: Eerdmans, pp. 108–115.
Lijphart, A. (1984). *Democracies: Patterns of majoritarian rule and consensus government*. New Haven, CT: Yale University Press.
Loquai, H. (2000). *Der Kosovo-Konflikt: Wege in einen vermeidbaren Krieg*. Baden–Baden,Germany: Nomos Verlag.
Magnusson, K. (1999). Rambouilletavtalet: Texten, förhandlingarna, bakgrunden. *Current Issues*, No. 1, Centre for Multiethnic Research, Uppsala University, Uppsala, Sweden.

Maliqi, S. (1995). Demand for a new status: The Albanian movement in Kosovo. In D. Janjić (Ed.), *Serbia – Between the past and the future*. Belgrade, Serbia: Forum for Ethnic Relations, Institute of Social Sciences.

Maliqi, S. (1998). *Kosova: Separate Worlds*. Pristina, Kosovo: Dukagjini.

Nazi, F. (2000). Balkan diaspora 1: The American–Albanian community. In W. J. Buckley (Ed.), *Kosovo: Contending voices on Balkan interventions*. Grand Rapids, MI: Eerdmans.

Paris, R. (2004). *At war's end: Building peace after civil conflict*. Cambridge, UK: Cambridge University Press.

Pumphrey, D., and Pumphrey, G. (n.d.). The "Racak massacre": Casus belli for NATO. Available at: www.aikor.de/Artikel/gp-rac-e.htm

Racsmány, Z. (1998). Conflict prevention and early action in Albania: Too little, too late? In P. Wallenstee (Ed.), *Preventing violent conflicts: Past record and future challenges*. Uppsala, Sweden: Department of Peace and Conflict Research Report No. 48, pp. 100–135

Salihu, A., Hajrullahu, M., and Xharra, J. (2004). Radicals test the ground in Drenica.*Balkan Crisis Report*, No. 498, May 20. London, UK: Institute for War & Peace Reporting.

SELDI – South–East European Legal Development Initiative. (2002). *Anti-corruption in Southeast Europe: First steps and policies*. Sofia, Bulgaria: Center for the Study of Development

Sörensen, J. S. (2006). The shadow economy, war and state–building. *Journal of Contemporary European Studies*, *14*(3), pp. 317–351.

Sörensen, J. S. (2009). *State collapse and reconstruction in the periphery: Political economy, ethnicity and development in Yugoslavia, Serbia and Kosovo*. Oxford, UK: Berghahn Books.

Sörensen, J. S. (2012). War makers and state makers. In B. Bliesemann de Guevara (Ed.), *Statebuilding and state-formation*. London, UK: Routledge

Sörensen, J. S. (2013). Reconstituting crisis: Revisiting the Dayton and RambouilletAgreements and their impact in Kosovo. In M. Eriksson and R. Kostic (Eds.), *Mediation and liberal peacebuilding: Peace from the ashes of war?* (forthcoming).

Thaqi, H. (2000). The KLA brought NATO to Kosova. In J. W. Buckley (Ed.), *Kosovo: Contending voices on Balkan interventions*. Grand Rapids, MI: Eerdmans, pp. 282–290.

UNDP. (2004). *Human Development Report Kosovo 2004: The rise of the citizen: Challenges and choices*. New York, NY: United Nations Development Programme.

UNSC. (United Nations Security Council) S/2004/932. New York, NY: United Nations.

Vickers, M. (1998). *Between Serb and Albanian: A history of Kosovo*. London, UK: Hurst.

Woodward, S. (1995). *Socialist unemployment: The political economy of Yugoslavia 1945–1990*. Princeton, NJ: Princeton University Press.

Zaum, D. (2007). *The sovereignty paradox: The norms and politics of international state-building*. Oxford, UK: Oxford University Press.

23
BOSNIA: BUILDING STATES WITHOUT SOCIETIES?
NGOs and civil society

Roberto Belloni

This chapter critically assesses the internationally led statebuilding experience in Bosnia–Herzegovina (hereafter Bosnia). It shows how the structural contradictions embodied in the 1995 Dayton Peace Agreement (DPA), together with the related difficulties in implementing the agreement led international actors to focus increasingly on the development of domestic civil society. This new effort, however, has been driven from the top down, with international agencies providing the resources and often the blueprint for civil society development. As a result, rather than providing the space for a new social contract, civil society has become an arena for the implementation of a technocratic governance agenda. The gradual phasing out of bilateral donors, and the related growing role of the European Union (EU) in the country since the early 2000s, has not significantly altered this pattern of intervention

This chapter is structured as follows. First, it briefly reviews the structural contradictions o the DPA and the international community's attempt to overcompensate for these contradictions by creating a *de facto* protectorate. Second, it shows how this interventionist approach went hand in hand with an exploration of alternative statebuilding avenues, and in particular with an increasing focus on civil society development. Third, the chapter discusses the top–down, NGO–focused, technocratic nature of civil society building and its limitations. Finally, the chapter considers the increasing EU role in the country, showing how – despite the rhetoric on participation, inclusion, and domestic ownership – such a role furthers a narrow vision of civil society, instrumentally focused on NGOs. As a whole, Bosnia remains a state where inter – nationally propped–up institutions are both inefficient and considered illegitimate by a large segment of the population.

The Dayton Peace Agreement and its contradictions

The DPA, signed on 21 November 1995, terminated the bloodiest war in Europe since the end of World War II. The agreement created a byzantine institutional structure composed of two federal units, or 'entities': the Federation of Bosnia–Herzegovina, dominated by Croats and Bosniaks (Muslims), and the Republika Srpska (RS), controlled by the Serbs. At Dayton, it was decided that the Federation would be internally divided into 10 cantons, each with its own constitution, an assembly elected by the Federation voters, a prime minister, and ministries. By contrast, the RS constitutional structure was conceived in a much more centralized way. The central government, standing above the two entities, was granted only limited powers; only three ministries were created (Foreign Affairs, Foreign Trade, and Civil Affairs and Communications) – a number that increased over time to the current nine ministries. Despite this growth, the Bosnian state remains rather weak, leaving much political power at the level of the entities, which maintain wide legislative prerogatives. The post–Dayton increase in the number of state ministries and the related transfer of competences from the entities to the state has not removed real power from the sub–state level (FPI BH, 2008). The most significant indicator of the weakness of centra institutions lies in their budget, which is not only significantly smaller than that of the entities but also largely dependent on transfers from them (see Belloni, 2007: Chapter 3; Bieber, 2005: Chapter 3).

This decentralized political structure was supposed to facilitate the achievement of some key liberal objectives identified by the agreement's international midwives. Not unlike other post conf ict states, Bosnia was expected to benefit from the key tenets of the liberal peace, includin democratic institutions and a market economy. Accordingly, the Bosnian Constitution, which is included in the DPA as Annex 4, affirmed that 'Bosnia and Herzegovina shall be a democrati state,' operating 'under the rule of law and with free and democratic elections,' ensuring the 'highest level of internationally recognized human rights and fundamental freedoms' and promoting, among other things, 'the general welfare and economic growth through the protection of private property and the promotion of a market economy.' From the beginning of the peace process, however, progress toward these ambitious liberal–democratic goals and market principles was hindered by at least three major structural weaknesses underpinning the agreement (for further analysis of the DPA's contradictions see Caplan, 2000).

First, the DPA established political institutions that were not intended to create the conditions for effective government but to prevent each group from imposing its own views on the others (FPI BH, 2008). The nationalist leadership of each ethnic group obtained almost exclusive control over its own national constituency, as well as the possibility of vetoing decisions affecting its own 'national interest.' In practice, central institutions have been constantly deadlocked. Since 1996, the veto has been placed on over 160 legal acts and proposals (Džihić and Wieser, 2011: 1812). Meanwhile all other institutional levels, from the entities to the municipalities, came to be dominated by wartime leaders – who skillfully ensured their political survival by depicting the other groups as an existential threat while simultaneously proposing themselves as the solution to that threat. The use of patronage and access to post–war reconstruction funds further consolidated their grip on power. As a result, the peace process moved forward at a glacial pace, and sometimes not even that. Since the mid–2000s, in particular, nationalist rhetoric has been increasing, while the working of democratic institutions has 'deteriorated signif cantly' (BTI, 2009: 3). In spring 2006 a constitutional reform package was turned down by Parliament by two votes. In the aftermath of these failed reform efforts, Serbs have accentuated their separatist demands by threatening to hold a referendum on secession. Croat hardliners have been toying with their wartime idea of establishing a third Croatian entity. Bosniaks, for their part, have reacted by calling for further centralization – thus incentivizing further secessionist demands (Belloni, 2009).

Second, not only did Bosnia's constitution create inefficient institutions prone to nationalis manipulation, but also it elevated ethnic discrimination as a principle of law, with important consequences for individual human rights. By granting each of the three main ethnic groups a special status as a 'constituent people' of Bosnia, the constitution created the conditions for the ethnicization of state institutions (Mujkić, 2007). Bosnia's three–member presidency consists of one Croat, one Bosniak, and one Serb. Membership to the Upper House of the state parliament is also restricted to representatives of the same three 'constituent' peoples. In practice, the DPA prohibits members of ethnic minorities (identified in the constitution as 'others') – about half million Bosnians, out of a total of about 4 million – from holding major state posts.

In addition to openly discriminating against individuals who do not belong to the three main ethnic groups, the DPA's prioritization of group rights has created an obstacle to the pursuit of other goals of the peace agreement, in particular the commitment to support the conditions for the postwar re–establishment of a degree of multi–ethnicity. Annex 7 of the DPA stated that Bosnian refugees and displaced persons have 'the right freely to return to their home of origin.' However, the simultaneous presence of a collective right to exclusive self–government for the three main ethnic groups and the right of individuals to return to the places from which they were expelled during the war through multiple campaigns of ethnic cleansing proved hard to reconcile. While pushing for return, prominent international officials had to recognize how th re–creation of the celebrated multi–ethnic character of the country has always been wishful thinking (see, for example, Petritsch, 2001: 331–333). While tens of thousands took advantage of the possibility to return, the majority of them did so only to sell their properties and leave again for those areas where their group constitutes a numerical majority (Toal and Dahlman, 2011). As a result, despite localized returns, Bosnia is made up of three de facto mono–ethnic entities.

The DPA's third main structural weakness involves the role assigned to international actors in peace implementation. The civilian head of the peace operation, the High Representative of the International Community and its Office (OHR), was given the task to supervise the implementation of the DPA but was not granted any authority over the military component. Local ethno–nationalists exploited this enforcement gap in order to hinder or delay the implementation of various terms of the agreement. After little progress in peace implementation, the OHR's limited powers were increased in late 1997, when the institution was granted extensive executive prerogatives such as the possibility of imposing legislation and removing elected officials. These new powers were used extensively and have led to the establishment o a de facto protectorate. According to Sumantra Bose (2002), most positive results in the implementation of the DPA were achieved primarily through the presence, assistance, pressure, and, above all, the assertiveness of the international community. On the down side, extensive international intervention stimulated the development of a 'dependency syndrome' (Ashdown, 2007: 238), as local actors often refused to implement signif cant political, economic, and social reforms on the expectation that the OHR would intervene and assume the political costs of change. In addition to undermining domestic political responsibilities, the external imposition of policy has created the superficial impression that the system is 'working,' thus alleviating pressures for structural reforms (FPI BH, 2008: 42; Belloni, 2007: 32).

In sum, while the DPA proved successful in ending the war, it failed to create the foundations for a functioning polity. However, although the constitutional structure created at Dayton is greatly responsible for the difficulties Bosnia continues to face, such a structure is also a r ection of the deep divisions existing within Bosnian society. Indeed, little or no sense of common identity and purpose exists among the three main ethnic groups. This lack of a sense of common belonging among citizens is ref ected in the public sphere. For example, the national anthem cannot be sung and is only instrumental because Bosnians could not agree on the wording. Even public holidays are divisive: while November 25 is celebrated in the Federation as Bosnia's National Day (in memory of the 1943 Anti–Fascist Assembly which is considered to have set the foundations for Bosnia's present–day independence), RS authorities fail to commemorate it. By contrast, they celebrate November 21, when the DPA was signed, a day perceived by the Federation as a day of defeat and division of the country (Bos'ković, 2011; Hunt, 2001). These differences signal how citizens do not have common values to celebrate.

Thus, at the societal level, division remains the fundamental characteristic of the country. Bosnians may maintain a good degree of inter−ethnic interaction in the cities but the level of mutual mistrust and suspicion remains considerable (O'Loughlin, 2010; Hakånsson and Sjöholm, 2007). A major UNDP study on social attitudes concluded that trust between people is 'virtually non−existent'(UNDP, 2007). Especially in the countryside, ethnic homogenization is apparent and divisions are rife in all sectors of life (BTI, 2009). Everything from greetings to soccer shirts is utilized to identify one's ethnic belonging and religious persuasion. Religious divisions are frequently carried over to the political sphere, with each group claiming the superiority of its own worldviews and practices, and religious leaders have repeatedly sought to influence electio results in favor of the main nationalist parties. Education policy perpetuates ethnic separation through the adoption of separate curricula, teaching languages and religious education. Crucially, education policy also fails to provide young people with practical skills to improve their employability in a country where offcial unemployment is approximately 40 per cent and poverty has reached alarming levels. In this context, tens of thousands of young people, frequently the most skilled ones, have left the country, and many more are hoping for an opportunity to do the same (UNDP, 2007).

The rise of civil society building

Confronted by an unworkable political system, dominated by wartime ethnic leaders, and a deeply divided citizenry, from 1998 onward international donors increasingly began to turn their focus to the development of civil society. Although the civil society realm is undoubtedly a key component of the liberal peace, such a realm was ignored by the DPA. Rather, the agreement relied on the post−war cooperation of wartime ethnic leaders in progressing toward ambitious democratization and marketization goals. However, the structural contradictions of the agreement, with the related Sisyphean difficulties in peace implementation, led donors to revis their intervention strategy to include an important civil society component. Civil society building came to be interpreted as a way to address, and possibly resolve, the weaknesses embedded in the deal that ended the war (Belloni, 2001).

Rather than directing their attention exclusively to the building of state institutions, international actors have increasingly focused on cultivating and promoting the 'right' kind of democratic culture from the bottom up. Research on civil society's contribution to both democracy and peace seems to confirm the possibility that civil society can bring important practical benefits to post−war transitions. In particular, the presence of a robust civil society i strongly correlated to that of a functioning democracy, leading some scholars to claim that civil society and democracy reinforce each other (Putnam, 1993; Edwards, 2009). In addition, civil society is frequently credited for its positive contribution to the development of peaceful, non−violent relationships among citizens and groups (Varshney, 2002).

Needless to say, civil society's positive impact on both democracy and peace could require a long time to take root, and cannot be taken for granted (Belloni, 2008; Paffenholz, 2010). Civil society organizations may also have a negative inf uence on post−war political transitions, since some of these organizations can, and sometimes do, perpetuate societal divisions, breed sectarianism and, in the most extreme cases, even participate in violence. Nonetheless, international donors hold a generally positive view of civil society organizations and the role they can play in advancing a democratization agenda. To begin with, by directing resources to civil society organizations, international donors can sidestep, at least in part, unpalatable domestic nationalist elites. Moreover, donors widely believe that the non−governmental sector provides a cheaper and more efficien alternative to government service provision, thus removing the responsibility of the state (and more broadly of international organizations) for such a task. At the same time, civil society organizations are perceived as closely connected to the grassroots and therefore able to reach the most marginalized and disadvantaged. Thus, civil society organizations can provide a channel for both expressing and meeting citizens' needs, and a means to favor local 'ownership' of the peace process, at least on paper. Finally, and perhaps too optimistically, civil society organizations are thought to be an antidote against widespread corruption (Belloni, 2012).

Overall, by refocusing their intervention on civil society development, international organizations have hoped to turn complex political, social, and economic processes into manageable issues of governance and policy. The emphasis on civil society development implicitly allows international actors to set aside the structural contradictions embedded in the peace agreement and to focus on local conditions as matters requiring technical and mechanistic approaches rather than political solutions. Crucially, the difficulties in peace implementation are located at the leve of domestic factors (such as underdevelopment, post–war trauma, lack of democratic traditions, and scarce technical capacities). The Bosnian people themselves are thought to lack the capacities to fully gain from the benefits offered by the presence and work of international organization and thus have themselves become targets of international attention.

International organizations' understanding of Bosnians' electoral behavior, and ways to change it, provides an example of the technocratic approach adopted by international actors. For international policy–makers it has always been puzzling that, despite their record, nationalist parties have been regularly voted into power (Hulsey, 2010). This electoral behavior has not been explained as a rational response to persisting conditions of insecurity. Rather, Bosnians have been seen as apathetic and/or lacking civic virtues because of the infience of a supposed 'Bosnian mentality' shaped by decades of totalitarianism and war. Accordingly, the reform of Bosnians' mentality in the direction of greater moderation and civility has been considered necessary to foster the emergence of a democratic ethos, convince Bosnians to vote for moderate political parties, and thus to ground the building of democratic institutions on better foundations (Belloni, 2001). Voter education programs, typically provided by NGOs, have provided the supposed technical solution to the political conundrum presented by Bosnians' electoral behavior.

Such a solution has failed to take proper account of the complexity of Bosnian political life. It has downplayed both the responsibilities of domestic elites, who have built political consensus by exploiting ethnic divisions, and those of international organizations, which have frequently failed to present a workable strategy to further the goals of the peace agreement. One is reminded of Berthold Brecht's mocking of the communist government's stance in East Germany during the Cold War: if the people did not do better, the government would have to fire the peopl and elect a new one. Similarly, in order to overcome the post–Dayton impasse, international organizations have symbolically 'fired the Bosnian people,' interpreting their behavior as problematic and not as a rational response to conditions of insecurity, while attempting to reshape the social order via education and, crucially, civil society building programs.

The ambiguities of civil society building

From these assumptions, international donors have provided considerable resources to civil society building projects. This international support has led to important quantitative achievements (Belloni and Hemmer, 2010). More than 12,000 organizations are registered in the country, although it is estimated that only about 55 per cent of them (around 6,600) are active. More than 70 per cent of active organizations are member benefit organizations (MBOs), established to work in the interests of their members, while the remaining ones are so–called public benef t organizations (PBOs), whose purpose is to work in the general public interest (TACSO, 2010:

17–18). While MBOs are generally small and financially dependent on local authorities, whic tend to direct the bulk of their economic support toward sports clubs and veterans' associations, PBOs are professional, well-developed organizations, located in Bosnia's major towns, with more or less regular access to international donors.

Despite the significant numerical presence of civil society organizations, their overall impac has been rather modest. There are two sets of reasons for this. The first is the domination o ethnic affiliation over civic consciousness. Because political representation depends on ethni belonging, bottom-up, citizens-based, ethnic-blind initiatives tend to be discouraged. Rather than aggregating and expressing citizens' interests, the public space tends to be channeled via ethnic representation (Mujkić, 2007). The legal framework, which reflects the divided nature o the Bosnian state, further hinders civil society activities. There exist four different laws to regulate the civil society sector, one at the level of the state, one for the Federation, one for the RS, and one for the Brcko District in the north-east corner of the country. The place of registration of an association makes its ethnic character immediately apparent, thus hindering the possibility of conducting activities in areas controlled by another ethnic group (Žeravćić and Bišćević, 2009: 9). In this context, civil society organizations have been unsuccessful in their efforts to aggregate across ethnic lines, to engage with the general public, and to influence domestic political processes The second has to do with international policy-making. Rather than engaging with the complexities of the social, political, and economic context and the constraints and opportunities it could offer to civil society development, international donors have adopted a rather technical approach based on the focus on and sometimes even the obsession with, the quantifiable, numerical growth of NGOs.

The international approach to civil society building has been criticized on several grounds. To begin with, the attempt to 'export' civil society in the shape of NGOs has been described as a benevolent form of colonialism (Sampson, 2002). Rather than supporting the development of indigenous, locally rooted resources, the civil sector has been seen as colonized by international actors and 'their frameworks, assumptions, meanings and practices' (Stubbs, 2001: 24). Frequently, international intervention is seen to have led to the creation of organizations that are virtual clones of their Western counterparts and that contribute to the imposition of exogenous agendas on local communities. These agendas, in turn, have only a limited connection with local needs. Among the many possible examples, suffce it to mention international donors' focus on projects aimed at post-war 'reconciliation' between former warring parties. While this focus is intuitively understandable, in reality one would be hard pressed to find any genuine interest among Bosnian of different ethnic backgrounds in this theme (Belloni and Hemmer, 2010: 147).

Second, and consequently, international organizations have been seen to have boosted an artif cial non-state sector with little or no connection with the local reality. Bosnian organizations, and above all PBOs, are largely dependent on the desires and interests of their donors (Žeravćić and Bišćević, 2009: 93). As David Chandler (1999: 151–152) put it, 'the unintended consequence of creating civil society NGOs which are reliant on external support has been that they are never forced into building their own base or popular support or take on the arguments or political programmes of the nationalists.' Unsurprisingly, this lack of connection with the local reality has had significant negative repercussions. Local organizations are frequently seen by the populatio at large as either opportunistic or rent-seeking – or both (TACSO, 2010: 16). At the same time, local, donor-driven organizations have tended to be seen by domestic authorities as either a nuisance or a potential threat and they therefore act to discredit them and keep them at the margins of political life.

Third, this externally driven process has focused on the development of 'projects' rather than 'programs'; that is, on well-defined, short-term initiatives (usually lasting between six month and one year) with a clear beginning, implementation, and completion, rather than broader and more ambitious schemes with greater potential to make a difference (TACSO, 2010: 23). A syndrome described as 'projectomania' (Sejfija, 2006: 135–136) has been seen to overwhelm loca organizations, which have become obsessed with the goal of developing 'projects,' meeting donor criteria and expectations rather than the needs of the communities where the projects are implemented. Project-obsessed organizations, in Bosnia as elsewhere, are easily caught in an endless, self-referential process of proposal writing, tenders, and reports, until a project is completed and a new proposal is to be written. Missing in this process is a clear sense of the organization's mission in the community.

Fourth, the beneficiaries of Western moneys typically are individuals and PBOs based in Bosnia's bigger towns and cities and embodying the middle-class values, interests, and objects that best resonate with the priorities of international donors. Smaller and more recently established organizations have received only limited attention from donors. Perhaps more importantly, international support has overlooked organizations that do not fit the liberal parameters establishe by international actors. These organizations include a wide range of groups, such as those linked to Bosnia's communist past (including cultural and sports organizations) and non-liberal groups (such as religious communities, veterans' groups, and even labor organizations), some of which occasionally undertake initiatives against aspects of the liberal peace. For their part, these organizations have shown a remarkable ability to simply ignore, adapt to, or subvert international initiatives (Kappler and Richmond, 2011).

Among these organizations, veterans' groups stand out for both representativeness and political importance. Veterans' groups enjoy a membership estimated at 4.4 per cent of the entire Bosnian population (Živanović, 2006: 39). Some of them are linked to nationalist groups or political parties and have taken a stand against the internationally driven post-war liberal agenda. Rather than being supporters of the peace process, they are frequently considered to be 'spoilers,' blocking the possibility of cooperation between the three main national groups. In the RS, for example, the Serb Movement of Independent Associations (SPONA), a diverse group composed of 11 nationalist NGOs and war veteran groups, has been very vocal in opposing internationally led reforms while supporting calls for a referendum on the RS's secession from Bosnia (Belloni and Hemmer, 2010: 145). By neglecting groups such as these, international intervention has failed to take account of the articulation and expression of significant local needs, while promoting an artificial civil society with limited connections with the local reality

In sum, international organizations have supported and reinforced a distinction between 'two Bosnias,' separated by their relation to liberal, civic values and norms. While a 'first Bosnia' i made up of educated professionals who speak foreign languages, live in the major urban areas and receive the lion's share of international attention and funding, the 'second Bosnia' does not necessarily endorse donor discourses, or agree with all the tenets of the liberal peace, and thus is largely neglected by the Western aid system. Crucially, there can appear to be an inverse relationship between the ability of Bosnian organizations to attract foreign donor support and their ability to mobilize local constituencies around an agenda close to the needs of the local population. To put it another way, rather than strengthening civil society, international support has frequently widened the gap between domestic organizations and their social constituencies, in particular by making civil society agendas sometimes irrelevant for the majority of the population.

Toward a European future?

Since 2002, OHR has been 'double hatted' and also performs the role of the European Union Special Representative – signaling the increasing presence and importance of European institutions in the country. From roughly the same time, many bilateral donors began to phase out their activities. The international spotlight, and financial resources, gradually moved to Kosovo and later to Afghanistan and Iraq. As a result of the decreasing availability of funding, competition among local organizations increased, leading to the closure of some organizations or their *de facto* disappearance even though they may continue to exist on paper. The decreasing presence of bilateral donors went hand in hand with a growing EU influence over Bosnian affairs The EU has furthered the liberal peace agenda with less blatantly top−down means as compared with previous international practices. While the OHR has intervened directly in state con− struction, the EU has recognized that external imposition is in contradiction with the rule of law and democratic governance (Venice Commission, 2005). It has adopted a softer approach based on a set of procedural measures, grounded on contractual relationships, asymmetrical cond− itionalities, and the need to enhance the domestic ownership and democratic participation of Bosnian citizens in the EU integration process. The emerging 'EU peacebuilding framework' (Richmond et al., 2011) is based on the 1993 Copenhagen criteria involving the promotion of democratic governance, a market economy, and respect for human rights.

While attempting to foster the adoption of a set of institutional reforms compatible with liberal−democraticprinciples, in Bosnia as in other candidate and acceding states, the EU has also placed great emphasis on assisting the development and strengthening of civil society organizations (Fagan, 2010: 9). In 2005, the European Commission explained how a comprehensive and sustained dialogue between societies from EU member states and EU candidate states represented an essential component of the EU involvement in neighboring states. In addition, it affirme that civil society must play a fundamental role in developing mutual understanding and integration between different peoples and in favoring the harmonization of different policies and economic systems (European Commission, 2005). In order to turn this vision into reality, the EU has attempted to enhance the coherence and effectiveness of its aid program. In 2006 it rationalized its pre−accession financial support into a single framework, through the establishment of an Instrument for Pre−Accession Assistance (IPA). IPA funds for the entire south−eastern European area for the 2007–2013 period amount to €11.46 billion and include a significant civil societ building component. Armed with such a considerable financial leverage, the EU developed country−specifc assistance papers for both candidate and potential candidate states.

In the Bosnian case, the EU stressed the need to develop the relationship between civil society organizations and state authorities, in particular foreseeing the possibility that local organizations will 'become better "watchdogs" and also stronger partners of the Government' (European Commission, 2007: 14). Similar to the approach adopted by bilateral donors, the EU has privileged support to NGOs rather than other civil society actors such as community groups, grassroots organizations, religious groups, veterans' associations, and trade unions. NGOs have been deemed as important for a number of reasons. Not only can they provide a link with grassroots and community−based groups but also, and more importantly, they can support the EU's access to f rst−handinformation on democratization processes in Bosnia, they can act as multipliers in circulating information about EU policies, and they can advocate in favor of reforms required by the process of EU accession (TACSO, 2010: 10).

Thus, despite the rhetoric on domestic ownership of reforms and citizens' democratic participation, in engaging with Bosnian civil society the EU has not put forward an agenda genuinely open to domestic inputs, but rather it has conceived of civil society development instrumentally. In particular, the focus on developing civil society actors, and above all NGOs, has been rationalized as a way to prepare aspiring members, such as Bosnia, for integration into EU governance structures. Indeed, the EU has managed civil society building with a functional, output−orientedapproach, which values civil society because of its contribution to political problem—solving. In this context, citizens' opportunities to participate depend on the resources they introduce into the political process (Finke, 2007: 6) and not, despite EU rhetoric, on a democratic right deriving from membership in a political community. For some critics, the EU approach is post—liberal in that, rather than supporting individual and collective self—government, it reflects the desire to directly regulate Bosnian governance (Chandler, 2010)

This approach has led to some formal progress toward Bosnia's accession to European institutions. In 2008, the Bosnian government signed a Stabilization and Association Agreement, accepting the obligation of a number of institutional and economic reforms on the way to European integration, including that of establishing a social dialogue with civil society (Gordon, 2009). However, progress toward these reforms has been minimal. The EU has identified broade principles, such as those embodied in the Copenhagen criteria, but has failed to adopt a clear list of statebuilding conditions that Bosnia has to fulfill in order to progress toward membership i European institutions. This failure, which is due to a lack of agreement among member states and EU actors on what kind of democracy should be promoted by the European Union, has lessened the EU's influence and slowed down the pace of reform (Aybet and Bieber, 2011). Furthermore, a certain 'enlargement fatigue' has further enfeebled the EU's ability to impact on developments on the ground (Schimmelfennig, 2008). After 2004, when 10 states were admitted simultaneously, the EU progressively tightened its conditions, complicating the accession process for its neighbors. Among the post—Yugoslav states, Croatia will join the Union in 2013, while all other states, including Bosnia, are thought to be many years away from admission. This long—term admission prospect gives rise to political problems: politicians are expected to adopt politically risky reforms that are likely to undermine their domestic support, while the rewards of such reforms will be reaped at least several years on, if ever. Needless to say, the EU's ability to influence political events is thereby greatly undermined

Civil society development and the promotion of better civil society—state relationships are areas where the EU has struggled to implement positive changes. The EU welcomed the signing, in May 2007, of a Memorandum of Understanding between the Council of Ministers and representatives of Bosnian NGOs. However, little progress has been made toward implementing the agreement (TACSO, 2010: 13). Civil society continues to not be consulted by Bosnian authorities and its input and views are not taken into account in the policy—making process. The ability of civil society organizations to participate in the formulation and implementation of public policies is 'almost negligible' (Žeravčić and Biščević, 2009: 145). The Parliament has been ignoring the demands coming from citizens and their associations, thus providing additional grounds for citizens' apathy and dissatisfaction (Dzˇihić and Wieser, 2011: 1818). Overall, cooperation between the governmental and non—governmental sectors in Bosnia is 'still in its infancy' (Žeravčić, 2008: 8).

Even the EU's instrumental expectations in supporting civil society organizations have proved to be misplaced. While the EU expected local organizations to disseminate information about the EU itself, its policies and enlargement mechanisms, the vast majority of domestic organizations continue to have scant knowledge of the process of EU integration and its signif cance (TACSO, 2010: 21). Moreover, rather than broadening the reach of international assistance beyond a relatively small number of organizations based in Bosnia's bigger cities, EU assistance has confirmed an approach based on top—down, project—based intervention focuse on more developed organizations. Indeed, only a small proportion of organizations have the technical capacity to apply for IPA or other European funding (Fagan, 2010: 98). These more developed organizations are easily caught in a version of the project obsession described above with reference to other bilateral donors. The adoption of the logical framework (log frame) project management system for EU projects encourages NGOs to focus on activity—based initiatives leading to quantifiable and isolatable effects. These service–oriented activities are implemented at the expense of the promotion of more explicitly political and structural types of change (Kurki, 2011: 361).

Conclusion

After many years of internationally led statebuilding efforts, Bosnia continues to suffer from 'an acute case of virtual statehood' (FPI BH, 2008: 9). Political institutions designed at Dayton are both discriminatory and dysfunctional, and are frequently deadlocked; many citizens do not recognize state institutions as legitimate and, if given a choice, would prefer stronger ties with neighboring Croatia and Serbia; a lack of educational and economic opportunities encourages many citizens, especially the young and skilled ones, to leave; there is little sense of common belonging or mutual trust between members of the three main ethnic communities.

In order to address the Bosnian conundrum, international organizations have placed great emphasis on civil society building, but with limited results. Instead of supporting the development of indigenous democratic and peaceful resources, international support has ultimately reinforced the existence of 'two Bosnias,' separated by their attitude to liberal, civic values: while a 'firs Bosnia' is primarily located in bigger cities and enjoys international donor support but lacks a connection with the grassroots, a 'second Bosnia' is largely excluded from the international aid system but remains much more representative of domestic needs and expectations than internationally supported civil society.

The EU's growing presence in Bosnia has not fundamentally changed this pattern of intervention. The EU had hoped to replace direct statebuilding with softer forms of conditionality but has ultimately failed to develop an effective alternative strategy. Even in the civil society realm, the EU has substantially followed in the steps of other international donors, investing instrumentally in civil society rather than broadening the opportunities for citizen participation. On balance, the results have been disappointing. As the European Commission acknowledged, the 'overall pace of reform has been very limited' (European Commission, 2011: 1). Despite almost two decades of international statebuilding efforts, Bosnia is widely considered to be institutionally vulnerable and possibly even unsustainable.

References

Ashdown, P. (2007). *Swords and ploughshares: Bringing peace to the 21st Century*. London, UK: Weidenfeld & Nicolson.
Aybet, G., and Bieber, F. (2011). From Dayton to Brussels: The impact of EU and NATO conditionality on state building in Bosnia & Herzegovina. *Europe–Asia Studies*, *63*(10), 1911–1937.
Belloni, R. (2001). Civil society and peacebuilding in Bosnia–Herzegovina.*Journal of Peace Research*, *38*(2), 163–180.
Belloni, R. (2007). *State building and international intervention in Bosnia*. London, UK: Routledge.
Belloni, R. (2008). Civil society in war–to–democracy transitions. In A. Jarstad and T. Sisk (Eds*From war to democracy: Dilemmas of peacebuilding*. Cambridge, UK: Cambridge University Press, pp. 182–210.
Belloni, R. (2009). Bosnia: Dayton is dead! Long live Dayton! *Nationalism & Ethnic Politics*, *15*(3–4), 355–375.
Belloni, R. (2012). Part of the problem or part of the solution? Civil society and corruption in post–conflic states. In D. Zaum and C. Cheng (Eds.),*Selling the peace: Post-conflict peacebuilding and corruption*. London, UK: Routledge, pp. 220–238.
Belloni, R. and Hemmer, B. (2010). Bosnia–Herzegovina: Building civil society under a semiprotectorate. In T. Paffenholz (Ed.), *Civil society and peacebuilding: A critical assessment*. Boulder, CO: Lynne Rienner, pp. 129–152.
Bieber, F. (2005). *Post-war Bosnia: Ethnicity, equality and public sector governance*. Basingstoke, UK: Palgrave.

Bose, S. (2002). *Bosnia after Dayton: Nationalist partition and international intervention*. Oxford, UK: Oxford University Press.

Bošković, N. (2011). Happy holidays for whom: Ethnic diversity and politics of regulation of public holidays in BiH. In E. Sarajlić and D. Marko (Eds.), *State or nation? The challenges of political transition in Bosnia and Herzegovina*. Sarajevo, Bosnia: Center for Interdisciplinary Postgraduate Studies, pp. 127–150.

BTI (Bertelsmann Stiftung). (2009). *BTI 2010 – Bosnia and Herzegovina country report*. Gütersloh, Germany: Bertelsmann Stiftung.

Caplan, R. (2000). Assessing Dayton: The structural weaknesses of the General Framework Agreement for Peace in Bosnia and Herzegovina. *Diplomacy & Statecraft*, 11(2), 213–232.

Chandler, D. (1999). *Bosnia: Faking democracy after Dayton*. London, UK: Pluto Press.

Chandler, D. (2010). The EU and Southeastern Europe: The rise of post–liberal governance. *Third World Quarterly*, 31(1), 69–85.

Džihić, V., and Wieser, A. (2011). Incentives for democratisation? Effects of EU conditionality on democracy in Bosnia & Herzegovina. *Europe–Asia Studies*, 63(10), 1803–1825.

Edwards, M. (2009). *Civil society* (2nd ed.). Cambridge, UK: Polity Press.

European Commission. (2005). *Civil society dialogue between the EU and candidate countries*, 29 June. Brussels, Belgium: EC.

European Commission. (2007). *Multi-annual indicative planning document 2007–2009 for Bosnia and Herzegovina*. Brussels, Belgium: EC.

European Commission. (2011). *Bosnia & Herzegovina 2011 progress report*, SEC(2011) 1206 final, 12 October Brussels, Belgium: EC.

Fagan, A. (2010). *Europe's Balkan dilemma: Paths to civil society or state-building?* London, UK: I. B. Tauris.

Finke, B. (2007). Civil society particpation in EU governance, *Living Review in European Governance*, 2(2).

FPI BH (Foreign Policy Initiative Bosnia Herzegovina). (2008). *Governance structures in BiH: Capacity, ownership, EU integration, functioning state*. Sarajevo, Bosnia: FPI BH.

Gordon, C. E. (2009). The stabilization and association process in the Western Balkans: An effective instrument of post–conflict management?*Ethnopolitics*, 8(3), 325–340.

Hakånsson, P., and Sjöholm, F. (2007). Who do you trust? Ethnicity and trust in Bosnia–Herzegovina. *Europe–Asia Studies*, 59(6), 961–976.

Hulsey, J. (2010). 'Why did they vote for those guys again?' Challenges and contradictions in the promotion of political moderation in post–war Bosnia and Herzegovina.*Democratization*, 17(6), 1132–1152.

Hunt, W. (2001). Bosnia: Two days in November. In G. H. Cornwell and E. Walsh Stoddard (Eds.)*Global multilateralism: Comparative perspectives on race, ethnicity and nation*, Lanham, MD: Rowman & Littlefield pp. 239–262.

Kappler, S., and Richmond, O. P. (2011). Peacebuilding in Bosnia and Herzegovina: Resistance or emancipation? *Security Dialogue*, 42(3), 261–278.

Kurki, M. (2011). Governmentality and EU democracy promotion: The European instrument for democracy and human rights and the construction of democratic civil societies. *International Political Sociology*, 5(4), 349–366.

Mujkić, A. (2007). We, the citizens of ethnopolitics. *Constellations*, 14(1), 112–128.

O'Loughlin, J. (2010). Inter–ethnic friendships in post–war Bosnia–Herzegovina. *Ethnicities*, 10(1), 26–54.

Paffenholz, T. (Ed.). (2010). *Civil sociey and peacebuilding: A critical assessment*. Boulder, CO: Lynne Rienner.

Petritsch, W. (2001). *Bosna i Hercegovina: Od Daytona do Evrope*. Sarajevo, Bosnia: Svjetlost.

Putnam, R. (1993). *Making democracy work: Civic traditions in modern Italy*. Princeton, NJ: Princeton University Press.

Richmond, O., Björkdahl, A., and Kappler, S. (2011). The emerging EU peacebuilding framework: Confirming or transcending liberal peacebuilding? *Cambridge Review of International Affairs*, 24(3), 449–469.

Sampson, S. (2002). Weak states, unicivil societies and thousands of NGOs: Western democracy export as benevolent colonialism in the Balkans. In S. Resic and B. Tornquist–Pewa (Eds.),*Cultural boundaries of the Balkans*. Lund, Sweden: Lund University Press, pp. 27–44.

Schimmelfennig, F. (2008). EU political accession conditionality after the 2004 enlargement: Consistency and effectiveness. *Journal of European Public Policy*, 15(6), 918–937.

Sejfija, I. (2006). From the civil sector to civil society? Progress and prospects. In M. Fischer (Ed.)*10 Years after Dayton: Peacebuilding and civil society in Bosnia and Herzegovina*. Berlin, Germany: Lit, pp. 125–140.

Stubbs, P. (2001). 'Social sector' or the diminution of social policy? Regulating welfare regimes in contemporary Bosnia−Herzegovina. In Open Society Fund BiH (Ed.)*International support policies to SEE countries − Lessons (not) learned in Bosnia-Herzegovina*. Sarajevo, Bosnia: Open Society Fund, pp. 95–107.

TACSO (Technical Assistance for Civil Society Organizations). (2010). *Bosnia & Herzegovina: Needs assessment report*, 4 January. Sarajevo, Bosnia: TACSO.

Toal, G., and Dahlman, C. T. (2011). *Bosnia remade: Ethnic cleansing and its reversal*. Oxford, UK: Oxford University Press.

UNDP (United Nations Development Programme). (2007). *The silent majority speaks: Snapshots of today and visions of the future of Bosnia-Herzegovina*. Sarajevo, Bosnia: UNDP.

Varshney, A. (2002). *Ethnic conflict and civic life: Hindus and Muslims in India*. New Haven, CT: Yale University Press.

Venice Commission. (2005). *Opinion on the constitutional situation in Bosnia and Herzegovina and the powers of the High Representative*, CDL−AD (2005) 004, 11 March. Available at: www.venice.coe.int

Žeravčić, G. (2008). *Analysis of insitutional cooperation between governmental and non-governmental sectors in BiH*, Sarajevo, Bosnia: Kronauer Consulting.

Žeravčić, G., and Bišćević, E. (2009). *Analysis of the civil society situation in Bosnia and Herzegovina*. Sarjevo, Bosnia: HTSPE Ltd UK and Kronauer Consulting.

Z[V]ivanović, M. (2006). Civil society in Bosnia and Herzegovina: Lost in transition. In W. Benedek (Ed.), *Civil society and good governance in societies in transition*. Belgrade, Serbia: Centre for Human Rights, pp. 23–53.

24
IRAQ
US approaches to statebuilding in the twenty-first century

David A. Lake

Iraq is the crucible in which post–Cold War theories of statebuilding were destroyed and then, in the heat of battle, forged anew. During the 1990s, a neoliberal statebuilding paradigm emerged that emphasized democracy and free markets as the primary means toward rehabilitating public authority (for a summary and critique, see Paris, 2004). This paradigm was implemented in Iraq between 2003 and 2007 by the administration of President George W. Bush in extreme form, almost in caricature. The insurgency that followed the initially successful military invasion laid bare the inadequacy of neoliberal statebuilding. Small islands of apparent success in Iraq, in turn, directly informed a new paradigm on 'counter–insurgency' (COIN) statebuilding, which emphasizes winning the hearts and minds of the local population. This new model was the centerpiece of US statebuilding efforts from the announcement of the Bush 'surge' in Iraq in January 2007 to the withdrawal of US forces from Iraq in December 2011. Continuing instability and tensions in Iraq, however, reflect the incomplete nature of statebuilding in that country and suggest additional lessons that follow, perhaps ironically, from the neoliberal approach rejected in the early years of the Iraq War. Political reconciliation, an essential part of statebuilding, requires not just an effective state but also constraints on state power, best achieved through democracy and economic liberalism.

Statebuilding seeks to strengthen weak or failed states such that they can exercise a monopoly of the legitimate use of violence within their territories. States become fragile or fail for many reasons, usually because rent–seeking by leaders 'hollows out' the state so that it loses its capacity to provide security and other public goods necessary for social order; in such cases, the political void is then filled by pre–existing social groups who become competitors with the state for legitimate authority over their members, often leading to a vicious circle of strengthened social forces and weakened states. In some cases, as in Iraq, a consolidated state that does effectively control its territory is intentionally destroyed by outside powers through 'regime change.' Although the paths by which they fail are wholly different, these states share attributes of failed states more generally: they lack a legitimate central authority and possess multiple sectarian groups often reinforced by widespread violence. Just as patients can rarely perform surgery on themselves, fragile states suffering from weak authority can rarely rebuild their own legitimacy. Thus, statebuilding is typically undertaken by external actors, usually states, supported more or less by the international community. Would–be statebuilders, in turn, aim to re–create central authority in the face of social forces that do not share a vision of the future or preferences over alternative institutions and policy.

The United States declared war on Iraq in 2003 for many reasons, including Iraq's threats to American allies in the region, human rights abuses, weapons of mass destruction programs and the possibility – however vague – that it might share the products of these programs with terrorists, and potential power on international oil markets, as well as the desires of at least some Americans to set an example of successful democratization in the Middle East and possibly settle old scores from the 1991 Persian Gulf War (see Lake, 2010–2011). No one reason was decisive, but together for the Bush administration and many Americans they justified the invasion. Centra to all of these reasons, however, was the goal of 'regime change' and the removal of Saddam Hussein and his Bathist supporters from political power. Having removed Saddam and his regime, however, the United States then confronted the need to build a new state that could govern effectively and legitimately.

Unlike other cases discussed in this handbook, the case of statebuilding in Iraq is almost entirely a story of US policy and practice. The Iraqi state was quite literally 'made in the USA.' As is well known, the United States in the Iraq War and afterwards operated largely outside the United Nations and its imprimatur. The United States also thoroughly dominated the ad hoc coalition that fought the war, and responsibility for postwar statebuilding passed entirely to Washington. President Bush, for instance, appointed Ambassador L. Paul Bremer as head of the Coalition Provisional Authority (CPA) without consultation with his coalition partners. In turn, the failure or success of the effort rests almost entirely on the scholars and policy makers who advanced the neoliberal theory of the 1990s, and the Bush administration that interpreted it through its own ideological lens.

This chapter proceeds in three steps. The first section examines the Iraq war and its aftermath, with a focus on the theory and practice of statebuilding between 2003 and 2006. The second section outlines the surge and the change in doctrine that began in late 2006 through the withdrawal of US forces in late 2011. The third and final section draws lessons from the tw phases for statebuilding more generally.

The Iraq War and its immediate aftermath: US statebuilding 2003–2006

During the Cold War, statebuilding efforts were limited. Each superpower intervened in fragile states only to balance the other, often creating political stalemate. Throughout, the emphasis was on supporting loyal clients, often autocrats, rather than promoting effective and legitimate states *per se*. In the 1990s, freed from the shackles of Cold War competition, the United States engaged in new statebuilding efforts in Somalia, Haiti, Bosnia, Afghanistan, and elsewhere. This was an 'end of history' moment in which liberalism prevailed, with corresponding emphasis on democracy as the sole legitimate form of government and free markets as the sole effective source of economic prosperity. US statebuilding practice fully embraced these 'neoliberal' beliefs, as they became known. In all of its statebuilding efforts, the United States promoted rapid move‒ments to new, more democratic constitutions and broad‒based elections and pressed for market‒oriented reforms (Paris, 2004; Lake, 2010).

Even before Iraq, problems with this neoliberal approach to statebuilding were evident. Democracy and free markets were not necessarily embraced by all societies, especially those with no history of liberalism. Social groups empowered and advantaged under the old regime also resisted broadening political participation and freeing commerce. Nonetheless, neoliberalism was the prevailing orthodoxy that the Bush administration inherited. Having decided on a preemptive war against Iraq, the administration then implemented an extreme version of this strategy, leading to one of the worst statebuilding failures in modern history and ultimately undermining the orthodoxy on which it was built.

The statebuilding plan

There is considerable debate over whether there was adequate planning within the Bush administration for postwar Iraq. Opinions about the administration's planning vary from the charitable conclusion that it was 'not well thought out' to the more critical assessment that it was 'mired in ineptitude, poor organization and indifference.'[1] The debate is hard to resolve, as the major players within the administration have attempted to fix the blame for the post-war fias on each other.[2] It now appears that there was a significant planning effort before the war, led b the State Department, that was subsequently ignored by the civilian and military leadership who regarded it as inadequate. David Kay, a CIA weapons inspector on the initial team of the Offic for Reconstruction and Humanitarian Affairs (ORHA, see below), described the State Department's 'Future of Iraq Study' as 'unimplementable,' more 'a series of essays to describe what the future could be' than a plan that would have made a difference (Gordon and Trainor 2006: 159; see also Isikoff and Corn, 2007: 191–200). Meanwhile, having wrested control of reconstruction from other agencies, the Pentagon carried out a parallel planning effort under the supervision of Secretary of Defense Donald Rumsfeld and Undersecretary of Defense for Policy Douglas Feith. This plan was also not well developed and rested on a series of erroneous assumptions (discussed shortly).

The lack of a thorough plan was not an accident. As summarized by journalist George Packer (2005: 147), 'if there was never a coherent postwar plan, it was because the people in Washington who mattered never intended to stay in Iraq,' at least as an occupying or nation–building force (see also Robinson, 2008: 20). The Bush administration entered office hostile to the notion o nation–building. During the campaign, candidate Bush bluntly declared, 'I don't think our troops ought to be used for what's called nation–building' (Washington, 2004). Consistent with this view, the administration consistently set itself the goal of liberating Iraqis to rebuild their own country, not occupying them. By April 15, 2003, Bush was already meeting with his top aides to plan the withdrawal of US forces from Iraq, a task expected to be begun within 60 days (Gordon and Trainor, 2006: 457–460). Embodying this view of the US as a liberating as opposed to an occupying or transformational force, former UN Ambassador John Bolton subsequently said that the administration's only mistake in the war was not turning the country over to the Iraqis sooner, giving 'them a copy of the *Federalist Papers*,' and saying 'good luck.'[3]

The planning effort, such as it was, rested on fve ultimately naïve and incorrect assumptions. First, buying fully into neoliberal orthodoxy, administration officials assumed that inside the hear of every Iraqi was a 'small d' democrat yearning to be free (Daalder and Lindsay, 2003: 125). As Vice President Richard Cheney stated, 'I really do believe that we will be greeted as liberators' (Packer, 2005: 97). In explaining why few occupation troops would be needed, Chair of the Defense Advisory Board Richard Perle similarly observed that there will 'be no one fighting fo Saddam Hussein once he is gone' (Ricks, 2006: 65; see also Feith, 2008: 415). As described by Carl Strock, a two–star general from the Army Corps of Engineers, the dramatic ouster of Saddam was expected to create a '*Wizard of Oz* moment' in which 'after the wicked dictator was deposed, throngs of cheering Iraqis would hail their liberators and go back to work' (Gordon and Trainor, 2006: 463).

Second, both the State Department and Pentagon plans relied heavily on expatriate Iraqis, some of whom had spent most of their lives and careers in the West, and assumed these pro–American leaders would be immediately welcomed into the new democratic regime. The Pentagon's ties to Ahmed Chalabi are, of course, well known. A darling of the neoconservatives even while they were in exile during the Clinton years, Chalabi was Director of the Iraqi National Congress (INC), an umbrella group of anti–Saddam exiles. Distrusted by the CIA, the State Department, and many uniformed military, Chalabi nonetheless had broad support within DoD and was expected to head a new Iraqi government after Saddam's fall. Indeed, belying his serious intent, Feith once joked with Garner that when OHRA got to Iraq, 'we could just make Chalabi president' (Ricks, 2006: 104). INC fighters were even flown into southern Iraq on US milita planes to assist in fighting Saddam's fedayeen, a move widely interpreted as aimed to give Chalab a leg up on both internal and external rivals for the presidency. Even the State Department relied heavily on expatriates in the Future of Iraq study group that produced its massive if inadequate report (Packer, 2005: 124–125). Given relations between the US and Iraq under Saddam, and the authoritarian nature of the Iraqi government, there were few lines of communication between US officials and potential Iraqi leaders. Nonetheless, the Bush administration assumed that it interlocutors could figuratively 'parachute' into Iraq and gain popular support. This was naïve at best. As one prominent Iraqi politician later assessed the exiles and, indirectly, the US government, 'The exiles – they made a big mistake, thinking that because they have the Americans on their side, they . . . can ride an American tank into Baghdad, they can gain legitimacy. It just doesn't work that way' (Allawi, 2007: 140).

Third, the plan for the postwar period failed to anticipate the decrepit state of Iraq's infrastructure. According to Ali Allawi (2007: 114), Iraq's first postwar minister of defense an minister of finance, the country 'was in an advanced state of decay.' Under international sanction and threatened by domestic unrest throughout the 1990s, Saddam had withdrawn from detailed management of the economy, focusing on his immediate survival. Large areas of Southern Iraq were deliberately starved of basic services, with Sunni areas north of Baghdad faring only marginally better. Overall, 'the standard of living had precipitously crashed' after the Persian Gulf War. Much of the country's economic infrastructure, including its oil pipelines, was allowed to deteriorate radically. Yet officials in Washington optimistically predicted that Iraq could easil pay for its own reconstruction.

Fourth, the plan did not anticipate the tensions that would be released between religious groups once the Sunni–dominated government was defeated. In a joint news conference with British Prime Minister Tony Blair before the war, Bush remarked that it was 'unlikely there would be internecine warfare between the different religious and ethnic groups' in Iraq, and Blair agreed (Isikoff and Corn, 2007: 180). Likewise, Wolfowitz testified before Congress tha postwar force requirements might be low because 'there's been none of the record in Iraq of ethnic militias f ghting one another' (Isikoff and Corn, 2007: 194). Nonetheless, other observers foresaw severe problems. As early as 1999, Central Command chief General Anthony Zinni, concerned about the stability of a post–Saddam Iraq, conducted a classifed war game that 'brought out all the problems that have surfaced' after the invasion. Although 'it shocked the hell' out of him, he was unable to interest other parts of the government in preparatory work (quoted in Ricks, 2006: 20). As Allawi (2007: 12) concludes, 'none of this should have come as a surprise.'

Finally, the plan was premised on the expectation that the Iraqi military and police forces would remain intact to provide political stability after the war. Encouraged by the mass desertions during Desert Storm in 1991, the CIA predicted that Iraqi forces would simply switch sides *en masse* with their equipment. The plan was that these army units would then control the country's borders and take on other tasks that overstretched US troops could not. Instead, as US forces moved closer to Baghdad, the Iraqi military dissolved before their eyes. As Gordon and Trainor (2006: 89) observe, 'Rarely has a military plan depended on such a bold assumption.'

The failure of neoliberal statebuilding

The postwar statebuilding effort, limited though it was, was originally embodied in the minimalist but appropriately named ORHA, headed by Lt General Jay Garner (retired), who had led the relief effort in northern Iraq in 1991. The ORHA team arrived in Baghdad on April 21, 2003 – three weeks late, small and poorly staffed, and grossly underfunded. Tellingly, Garner had a budget of just $25,000 to resurrect the devastated Iraqi government ministries (Packer, 2005: 143). Designed largely as a humanitarian effort, OHRA was immediately overwhelmed by the outbreak of violence in Baghdad. At a first meeting with locals in Baghdad on April 28, whic focused on the need for a liberal constitution to protect individual rights, a tribal sheikh stood up and complained 'I have no running water, no electricity, no security – and you are talking about a constitution?' Another demanded 'Who's in charge of our politics?' To which Garner revealingly replied, 'You're in charge' (Packer, 2005: 144).

The charge to OHRA was to undertake minimal changes in the political system of Iraq. Accordingly, it drew heavily on the expatriates and their allies, even as it reached out to local Iraqis (Rice, 2011: 209). Central to its reconstruction effort was a proposed Interim Iraqi Authority, discussed at the Nasiriya conference where Garner made his f rst public appearance (Allawi, 2007: 101–102). Impediments arose immediately, however, from Iraqis who were not yet ready to take charge of their country, and Chalabi and other expatriates who, supported by the Pentagon, wanted to keep the leadership council small to maximize their influence. Littl progress resulted.

As violence swept through Iraq, Garner was informed three days after his arrival that he and ORHA would be replaced by Bremer and the new CPA, an announcement that was made public on May 6. The CPA under Bremer took the occupation in a completely new direction, one not anticipated in any of the previous planning exercises. On May 12, four days after his arrival, Bremer declared the CPA to be the supreme authority in Iraq and assumed sovereignty over its people and territory, overturned plans for the creation of a provisional Iraqi government, disbanded the Iraqi army, began a purge of Baath Party officials, announced plans to reform th economy, and in general took up the previously denigrated task of nation–building. Like ORHA, the CPA was inadequate to the task, though not this time understaffed or underfunded. Rather, the mistakes now were more of policy than of resources.[4]

Bremer's disbanding of the army and policy on de–Baathification were the most controversia of these new directions. Although most troops had simply melted away during the war, formally dissolving the army ended any lingering hopes that the Iraqi military would take responsibility for defense in the near future. Yet the Bush administration still proceeded with planning to reduce the American 'footprint' in Iraq over the summer. Disbanding the army and expelling high–ranking officials also ended any hopes on the part of Iraqi soldiers and those with close ties t Saddam that they might have a place and job in the future Iraq, driving at least some of these individuals and their weapons into the growing insurgency (Robinson, 2008: 3). Although less controversial at the time, the decision to abandon the promised provisional government had a larger long–run effect by undercutting indigenous forces supporting democratization (Galbraith, 2006: 118–124; Isikoff and Corn, 2007: 225). This also undermined the credibility and hopes of those Iraqi elites with whom 'the USA had been engaged, with varying degrees of enthusiasm, for the better part of a decade' (Allawi, 2007: 110).

Nonetheless, despite the centralization of authority within the CPA, Bremer and his team followed the neoliberal script and focused on moving rapidly toward a new constitution and democratic elections, as well as economic reform. An Iraqi Interim Government was formed and the CPA itself disbanded in June 2004, returning full sovereignty to Iraq. Following elections in January 2005 to draft a new constitution, an Iraqi Transitional Government was finally forme in May 2005. The constitution was ratified in October and a National Assembly was elected i December 2005. After months of negotiations, a coalitional government was finally formed unde Prime Minister Nouri al–Maliki in May 2006, completing the initial transition to democracy. In this process, the balance of political power was shifted dramatically from the Sunni minority, which traditionally ruled Iraq but had boycotted the vote, to the Shiite majority. The expatriates were also essentially sidelined in favor of locals who were willing to work with the United States. This drove Chalabi and his supporters into the opposition, where he allied with Moqtadr al-Sadr, a radical Shiite cleric, and Iran, which eventually lost him even his supporters in the Defense Department. As Major General David Fastabend reflected, 'We needed elections in the wors kind of way in 2005—and we got them' (Ricks, 2009: 31).

Along with democratization, the CPA began a massive liberalization of the previously state-owned socialist economy, dramatically opening the country to foreign investment and trade (Foote et al., 2004). These moves were extremely destabilizing, both economically and politically. The minority Sunnis, with no oil resources in their region of the country, were nonetheless economically privileged and the wealthiest group in pre-war Iraq. The economic reforms championed by the CPA stripped the Sunnis of their base of power and prosperity and redirected it to the Shiites in the South and Kurds in the North of Iraq. It should have been no surprise that the new politically and economically empowered Shiite majority would attempt to consolidate its power, or that the politically and economically weakened Sunni minority would have a very different vision of Iraq's future. Yet Bremer regarded the economic reform effort as his biggest accomplishment in Iraq even though it created a 'fearsome' backlash from the Iraqi business community (Chandrasekaran, 2006: 70, 134, 328; Allawi, 2007: 198).

Despite this apparent success in meeting various institutional 'benchmarks' central to the Bush administration, neither legitimacy nor political stability followed as hoped. By 2006, after a massive bombing at the al-Askari Mosque, rising violence between sectarian groups exploded into civil war. In 2007, coalition casualties rose to their highest levels of the war. Iraqi military and civilian casualties skyrocketed as well, into the thousands per month. As Secretary of State Colin Powell had famously warned in his 'Pottery Barn rule,' the United States had broken Iraq and it now owned it – but, despite the prescient warning, it did not know what to do with the pieces. The neoliberal paradigm of statebuilding in Iraq had failed miserably, much to the consternation of its proponents in the Bush administration and, more importantly, to the Iraqis who were its victims.

The surge in Iraq: US statebuilding, 2006–2011

The 'surge' announced by President Bush in January 2007 is often portrayed as simply an increase in the number of US troops deployed in Iraq, a move aimed primarily at reversing the under-deployment that had plagued US efforts since 2003. It is also frequently depicted as a singular event and, in retrospect, a turning point in the war. In actuality, it was a series of at least four interconnected changes in American strategy that played out in late 2006 and early 2007, of which the 20,000 additional troops were perhaps the least important (Ricks, 2009: 165). Central to the greater success of US statebuilding efforts in Iraq starting in 2008 was the Anbar Awakening, the shift to the new COIN strategy by the US military, and political reconciliation. These three developments together embodied a new theory and practice of statebuilding that departed radically from the neoliberal paradigm. Unlike its predecessor, the new approach eschews democracy and free markets and emphasizes instead the provision of essential goods and services. If the mantra of neoliberal statebuilding was 'democracy first,' the new paradigm proclaims 'public security first' – with democracy and economic reform relegated to distant priorities (see Lake, 2010).

The Anbar Awakening began slowly in mid-2006, months before the surge was announced (Ricks, 2009: 59–72). Anbar is one of the few almost entirely Sunni provinces in Iraq and was the cradle of the insurgency and a haven for al—Qaeda in Iraq. Encouraged by their US military liaisons, the moderate Sunni sheikhs in Anbar decided to throw their future in with the Americans for two primary reasons (Robinson, 2008: 252). First, the sheikhs were increasingly put off by the agenda of the foreign religious extremists and jihadists who flooded Anbar after the fall o Saddam. The sheikhs slowly realized that the foreign fighters who dominated the insurgency i Anbar were not fighting for Iraq but were playing a larger international game that did not coincid with their own interests. Second, the sheikhs were persuaded that the political process was in fact open and that the Shiite—led government they had so feared would be restrained in practice by the Americans (Ricks, 2009: 66). As a result, the sheikhs turned their own militias against the foreign insurgents and joined the political process then unfolding in Baghdad. The United States reinforced this turn by redeploying more troops to Anbar to assist the militias and secure the gains they were achieving. The awakening thus became the 'foundation' of the surge, even before the surge had begun (Robinson, 2008: 324; Rice, 2011: 590). This same strategy, along with often substantial cash payments or other targeted benefits, was later extended to 'turn' much o the Sunni—based insurgency (Ricks, 2009: 202).

The second and perhaps most important step was the introduction of the new COIN strategy. COIN was a long time coming. Following Vietnam, the Army intentionally forgot nearly everything it had learned about counter—insurgency warfare (Packer, 2005: 201; Ricks, 2006: 226, 267). The Persian Gulf War of 1991, in turn, reinforced the military's desire to f ght tank battles rather than lightly armed insurgents in urban settings (Ricks, 2006: 132). Yet several commanders in Iraq did try innovative counter—insurgency strategies, especially the 101st Airborne Division deployed in Mosul until February 2004 and led by General David Petraeus. The general was subsequently brought home from Iraq in September 2005 to rewrite the *US Army/Marine Counterinsurgency Field Manual* (CFM) (2007) (Robinson, 2008: 76). Armed with his new fiel manual, Petraeus then returned to Iraq to lead the surge and moved quickly to impose the new COIN doctrine on the military even as the extra troops were pouring into the country. [5] It is unlikely that the additional troops by themselves would have changed the dynamics on the ground. Central to the success of the surge was the way both old and new forces were used.

The CFM outlines a very different approach to warfare and, in turn, statebuilding. Recognizing that you 'can't kill your way out of an insurgency,' COIN aims to win the hearts and minds of the local population (Robinson, 2008: 97). It begins with the core insight that the struggle between insurgents and counterinsurgents is over political power, a battle in which 'each side aims to get the people to accept its governance or authority as legitimate' (CFM, 2007: 2, see also 3 and 15). Essential here is the competition for the 'uncommitted middle,' which lies between 'an active minority supporting the government and an equally small militant faction opposing it' (CFM, 2007: 35). Legitimacy, in turn, is expected to follow from the ability of an actor – be it the insurgents or the state – to provide essential public services, especially security. As the CFM (2007: 16) states, 'a government that cannot protect its people forfeits the right to rule. Legitimacy is accorded to the element that can provide security, as citizens seek to ally with groups that can guarantee their safety.' Explicitly recognizing that legitimacy can follow from many sources, including tradition and religion, the feld manual nonetheless leaves no doubt that 'the ability of a state to provide security—albeit without freedoms associated with Western democracies—can give it enough legitimacy to govern in the people's eyes, particularly if they have experienced a serious breakdown of order' (CFM, 2007: 37). Clearly downgrading democracy as a basis for legitimacy, the CFM makes clear that security is a necessary and possibly sufficient condition for a legitimate state

By providing security and other basic collective goods such as potable water, sanitation, and heath services, COIN seeks to gain the loyalty of locals who, in turn, are more likely to provide the intelligence necessary to identify and defeat the insurgents. It does not attempt to defeat the enemy directly by breaking its ability and will to fight, but rather to win over the local populatio and thereby deny insurgents the safe havens they require to operate. It is, in part, a confidenc game. By providing locals with essential public services that make them better off, and especially security against retaliation, and convincing them that victory is likely, COIN aims to draw citizens into the new regime and turn them against the insurgents – much as had happened somewhat more spontaneously in Anbar province. Using an 'oil spot' strategy of pacifying one area and then proceeding to its neighbor, COIN progressively chokes off the ability of the insurgents to hide within sympathetic populations.

Interestingly, COIN explicitly reverses the priorities of the neoliberal orthodoxy that dominated previous thinking on statebuilding, even in Iraq. That model presumes that democratization and economic reform will lead to a consolidated state that will then 'step up' and take control of the war, and then defeat any remaining insurgents. COIN focuses on the provision of goods and services to earn the loyalty of the public and demotes democracy and freer markets to the lowest priority and last steps in statebuilding (see CFM, 156, Figure 5–2 (Dobbins et al., 2007: xxiii)).

The third and final step in the new approach to statebuilding – and still the most fragile – wa political reconciliation. According to Secretary of Defense Robert Gates, 'The purpose of the surge was to create enough space that the process of reconciliation could go forward in Iraq' (Ricks, 2009: 261). After the passage of the Transitional Administrative Law in March 2004, elections for a national assembly, the drafting of a new constitution, and another round of elections, al–Maliki was finally inaugurated as Prime Minister in May 2006. Yet, widely perceived by Sunnis as a Shiite partisan, Maliki's rise to power did more than perhaps anything else to stoke the insurgency in 2006 (Robinson, 2008: 17). Perceived as politically weak by the United States, Maliki was supported almost unconditionally by the Bush administration (Robinson, 2008: 23; on fissures within the Shiite community, see 145). Without other viable leaders, the United States was the dog that was wagged by the proverbial Iraqi tail. Rather than insist that Maliki be a national statesman, he was allowed to pursue support exclusively from within his Shiite community. In the end, the government of Iraq was not a neutral arbiter between antagonistic social forces but, as in many other failed states, became a partisan in the sectarian conf ict (Robinson, 2008: 123).

Critical to the Anbar Awakening was a changed perception among the Sunni sheikhs that the United States was an 'honest broker,' even if the government was not. With the surge and return of Petraeus, moreover, the United States placed new pressure on Maliki to play a less partisan role, including incorporating substantial numbers of Sunnis into the new Iraqi military and reining in the National Police, the latter of which 'at times was indistinguishable from a Shiite militia' (Ricks, 2009: 177). By 2008 Maliki was f nally willing to turn the nascent powers of the Iraqi state against his own Shiite community, demonstrated most visibly by his launching operations in Basra, described as a 'major turning point in the war' and US–Iraq relations (Ricks, 2009: 278–283). By 2009, Maliki had consolidated himself as 'a national leader who commanded respect across sectarian lines.' Some moderate Sunnis even began considering a joint electoral ticket with Maliki for the 2010 elections (Visser, 2011).

Nonetheless, political reconciliation, such as it is, remains fragile. National elections in 2010 failed to deliver a clear winner, and it then took Maliki nine months to form a new coalition government, ultimately composed mostly of pro–Iranian Shiite Islamists (Shanker et al., 2011). In December 2011, as the final US troops were withdrawing, one of Maliki's new coalition partners – the radical cleric Moktada al–Sadr – threatened to withdraw and force a new election, even as Maliki issued an arrest warrant for his Sunni Vice President, Tariq al–Hashimi, for running a death squad (Schmidt and Healy, 2011). Attacks, suicide bombings, and general violence recur daily (Arango, 2012). The Iraqi state the US leaves behind still faces an uncertain future.

Despite these continuing challenges, the second statebuilding effort in Iraq must be judged at least a partial success. The violence began to drop dramatically by July 2007, allowing for a graduate withdrawal of US forces. The Bush administration negotiated a Status of Forces Agreement (SOFA) that specified all US troops would be withdrawn by the end of 2011. Although few expected that deadline to be achieved, the Maliki government steadfastly maintained that all US forces that remained would have to be subordinate to Iraqi sovereignty, a position the United States could not accept. As a result, US troops were withdrawn on schedule in December 2011. Although the new regime faces serious challenges, the United States–led effort did, in the end, create a political space within which the Iraqis can try to build a future for themselves.

Conclusion: lessons from Iraq

The Iraq case suggests several important lessons for future statebuilding efforts. First, regime change requires statebuilding. An external power cannot topple an existing state without replacing it with something else. This is especially true for autocratic states that have, over time, decimated civil society so as to preserve their own power. Although it may be possible for cooperation to emerge spontaneously from the anarchy that is created when political authority is removed, it is by no means guaranteed (Axelrod, 1984). The biggest mistake in the Iraq War was in not anticipating the costs of statebuilding after removing Saddam Hussein and his regime (Lake, 2010–2011). Had these costs been properly assessed, the United States might not have chosen to go to war on weak evidence of Iraq's supposed weapons programs. Regardless of this counterfactual, adequate planning for the necessary postwar statebuilding effort would have spared the Iraqi people tremendous and entirely unnecessary suffering in a barely contained civil war.

Second, on its own, neoliberalism is a failed paradigm. Democracy and free markets are laudable goals, but they necessarily alter the balance of political power within societies and challenge interests vested in the *ancien régime*. All political institutions privilege some social interests over others. In autocratic regimes, the military, individuals with personal ties to the leadership, or industries that share their economic rents with politicians tend to have political influence disproportionate to the number of votes they control, as did the Sunnis under Saddam. Democracy shifts political power from these interests toward the majority of citizens, in Iraq from Sunnis to Shiites and Kurds. For its proponents, this is one of democracy's key benefits. Yet, by disrupting the political equipoise, democracy can be extremely destabilizing (Mansfeld and Snyder, 2007), and initially drove many Sunnis into the insurgency. Economic reform has a similar effect. Markets necessarily strip away economic protections and reduce the rents of those individuals and industries that had prospered through their connections to the old regime and shift returns toward industries and entrepreneurs that can compete effectively in domestic and international markets. Again, liberals see this process of economic and political change as one of the benefts of market reform. Yet these economic reforms also disrupt existing interests. The economic losers will seek to block reforms, and if they fail will likely judge the state that caused their new 'plight' as illegitimate. Oil wealth remains a tremendous source of contention within Iraq.

Third, winning hearts and minds is necessary for building a new state, but it may not be sufficient. A central problem with all states is that any government effective enough to enforce the rule of law is also strong enough to abuse its power, at least in the short run. Granting coercive power to a ruler to create and enforce a social order necessarily gives that ruler the ability to use coercion in her own self-interest as well. In turn, the fear of future exploitation prevents groups from subordinating themselves to a new central authority, and thus they are reluctant to permit the state to gain significant legitimacy either by denying their support or by actively fighti against it. Such fears of abusive central authority are still critical impediments to political reconciliation in Iraq today.

This suggests that, although disruptive, democracy and market reforms must also be part of the new statebuilding paradigm. Although not sufficient for successful statebuilding, these elements of a liberal state may be essential and should be accorded a higher priority than they now receive. Democracy has, historically, been one of the most effective ways of controlling state power. By diffusing authority and ensuring that popular preferences are represented in the policy process, democracy ties 'the sovereign's hands,' in North and Weingast's (1989) classic rendition of this problem. Freer markets and private property rights also limit state power. Although providing essential public services is important, limiting potential abuses by the regime may be equally essential to building new, legitimate states.

Notes

1 Ricks (2006: 179), quoting an anonymous general involved in postwar planning at the Pentagon; Allawi (2007: 83). See also Packer (2005: 114, 116–117) and Chandrasekaran (2006: 35, 59).
2 For retrospective defenses of the planning efforts, see Feith (2008: 274–298), Bush (2010: 248–250), and Rice (2011: 188–195).
3 Interview with Jeremy Paxman on the BBC show *Newsnight*, 'Iraq 4 Years On,' Wednesday, March 21 2007. For a transcript of the interview and link to the televised interview, see Bob Fertik, 'John Bolton's Astonishing Neo-Neo-Con Rewrite of History,' April 17, 2007, www.democrats.com/bolton-rewrites-history
4 For his reflections on these mistakes, see Bush (2010: 259–260) and Rice (2011: 238). An under-reported problem was the incompetence of many CPA officials, at least some of whom were picked for thei party credentials and past work on Bush's election campaign. See Chandrasekaran (2006: 103–104).
5 Success has many fathers. Robinson (2008) largely credits the surge and COIN to Petraeus while Ricks (2009: esp. 107) highlights the roles of General Jack Keane (retired) and Lt General Raymond Odierno.

References

Allawi, A. A. (2007). *The occupation of Iraq: Winning the war, losing the peace*. New Haven, CT: Yale University Press.
Arango, T. (2012, April 19). Iraq insurgency asserts presence with wave of attacks. *New York Times*.
Axelrod, R. (1984). *The evolution of cooperation*. New York, NY: Basic Books.
Bush, G. W. (2010). *Decision points*. New York, NY: Crown.
Chandrasekaran, R. (2006). *Imperial life in the Emerald City: Inside Iraq's Green Zone*. New York, NY: Vintage.
Daalder, I. H., and Lindsay, J. M. (2003). *America unbound: The Bush revolution in foreign policy*. Washington, DC: Brookings Institution Press.
Dobbins, J., Jone, S. G., Crane, K., and DeGrasse, B. C. (2007). *The beginner's guide to nation-building*. Santa Monica, CA: RAND Corporation.
Feith, D. J. (2008). *War and decision: Inside the Pentagon at the dawn of the War on Terrorism*. New York, NY: Harper.
Foote, C., Block, W., Crane, K., and Gray, S. (2004). Economic policy and prospects in Iraq. *Journal of Economic Perspectives*, 18(3), 47–70.
Galbraith, P. W. (2006). *The end of Iraq: How American incompetence created a war without end*. New York, NY: Simon and Schuster.
Gordon, M. R., and Trainor, B. E. (2006). *Cobra II: The inside story of the invasion and occupation of Iraq*. New York, NY: Pantheon.
Isikoff, M., and Corn, D. (2007). *Hubris: The inside story of spin, scandal, and the selling of the Iraq War*. New York, NY: Three Rivers Press.

Lake, D. A. (2010). The practice and theory of U.S. statebuilding. *Journal of Intervention and Statebuilding*, *4*(3), 257–284.

Lake, D. A. (2010–2011). Two cheers for bargaining theory: Rationalist explanations of the Iraq War. *International Security*, *35*(3), 7–52.

Mansfield, E., and Snyder, J. (2007). The sequencing 'fallacy'. *Journal of Democracy*, *18*(3), 5–9.

North, D. C., and Weingast, B. R. (1989). Constitutions and commitment: The evolution of the institutions of public choice in 17th century England. *Journal of Economic History*, *49*(4), 803–832.

Packer, G. (2005). *The assassins' gate: America in Iraq*. New York, NY: Farrar, Straus and Giroux.

Paris, R. (2004). *At war's end: Building peace after civil conflict*. New York, NY: Cambridge University Press.

Rice, C. (2011). *No higher honor: A memoir of my years in Washington*. New York, NY: Crown.

Ricks, T. E. (2006). *Fiasco: The American military adventure in Iraq*. New York, NY: Penguin.

Ricks, T. E. (2009). *The gamble: General David Petraeus and the American military adventure in Iraq, 2006–2008*. New York, NY: Penguin.

Robinson, L. (2008). *Tell me how this ends: General David Petraeus and the search for a way out of Iraq*. New York, NY: Public Affairs.

Schmidt, M. S., and Healy, J. (2011, December 27). Powerful Iraqi bloc calls for new elections in blow to government. *New York Times*, A8.

Shanker, T., Schmidt, M. S., and Worth, R. F. (2011, December 16). Pentagon declares end to a war, despite mixed legacy and fresh attacks. *New York Times* (National Edition), A19.

US Army/Marine Corps Counterinsurgency Field Manual. (2007). Chicago, IL: University of Chicago Press.

Visser, R. (2011, December 16). The Iraq we're leaving behind. *New York Times*, A43.

Washington, W. (2004, March 2). Once against nation–building, Bush now involved. *Boston Globe*.

25
'LIBERAL' STATEBUILDING IN AFGHANISTAN

Péter Marton and Nik Hynek

The international statebuilding effort in Afghanistan followed in the wake of the autumn 2001 military intervention which removed the Taliban regime. Regime-changing intervention was not the consequence of the Taliban's blockade of Hazara villages or of its excesses there, nor of the Taliban's harsh rules and conduct in the enforcement of its interpretation of Islam. Even the East Africa Embassy bombings of 1998, the attack in October 2000 in Aden on the US warship *USS Cole*, or, for that matter, the thwarted millennium bombing plot against Los Angeles were not enough to bring it about. It took the magnitude of the September 11, 2001 attacks on New York and the Pentagon for a US-led coalition of the willing to be interested enough to decisively intervene and to try to fundamentally transform local conditions in the hope of sustainable change and the exclusion from the area of unwanted elements, namely al-Qaeda and its local hosts, allies, and beneficiaries, the Taliban. It is the efforts since then that the present chapter reviews in detail providing an overview of what the extensive literature on the subject may tell or reveal to the observer about statebuilding in Afghanistan.

Two blind spots are identified in this process. The first relates to the argument that some the existing literature on statebuilding in Afghanistan fails to transcend the key problem of the generalist literature on statebuilding; i.e., a one-size-fits-all approach based on liberal wishfu thinking. In Afghanistan, the latter has never fully been translated into actual policy. The second blind spot that is highlighted and rectifed concerns the paucity of analyses on possible *motivations* of countries/international organizations statebuilding in Afghanistan. This is surprising considering the high prominence of the related international efforts and highly problematic, as those motivations have profoundly shaped the types of commitments various countries have had as a part of the International Security Assistance Force (ISAF) efforts. For that reason, a theoretically based typology of coalition contributions is offered and political and/or security concerns of selected countries involved are discussed.

An analysis of the literature on statebuilding in Afghanistan

General criticism of statebuilding

More than 10 years after the post-9/11 Western-led intervention in Afghanistan, a review of the literature that is critical of the general performance of Western statebuilding also lends itself to an understanding of the problems here. There is the focus, for example, on how 'ownership' of the statebuilding effort may itself be practiced in ways that are not conducive to sustainable locally managed structures that would be to the liking of the interveners – how liberal absolutism may breed local subversion and deviation from expected results (Chopra, 2002; Bliesemann de Guevara, 2008; Chandler, 2002; Hoehne, 2009). Others point out that the liberal statebuilding paradigm is aiming for a bridge too far as its strategic objective, claiming that liberalism will fall short of its target, especially when ill-suited in terms of material conditions and cultural context to its environment, and partly because the push toward it is excessive under the circumstances (Coyne, 2006; Eriksen, 2009; Belloni, 2006; Fukuyama, 2005). Yet others point to practices that are inconsistent with liberalism but stem from interests of the interveners – how the liberal project suffers from its inconsistent implementation (Chandler, 2002; Bliesemann de Guevara, 2008; Piiparinen, 2007).

It is noteworthy of course that these critiques of the contemporary statebuilding paradigm may clash with each other, or be differentiated as agent- and structure-focused, or problem-solving versus critical and *longue-durée*-oriented approaches (Goetze and Guzina, 2008: 320–321; Piiparinen, 2007: 355). They may even cancel each other out: for example, when claiming that the inconsistency and the rigidity of a liberal approach to statebuilding may be problems at the same time. However, a simple analytical distinction may produce a clearer picture. If inflexibility and inconsistency are present on the side of the external agents, and resistance and insurgency are partly the response and partly the default behavior of local agents – illustrating thereby a great difference between external and local agents in terms of the view of the legitimacy of key elements of the statebuilding vision – the difficulties are bound to be enormous.

The literature on Afghanistan

The literature dealing specifically with Afghanistan reflects the above general patterns of observations but naturally transcends these in specific ways given the subject in focus. The following overview may be best imagined as structured around a number of circles within circles. At the core of the statebuilding effort is, as usual, the provision of security, including the introduction of stabilization forces, a program of demobilization, disarmament, and reintegration (DDR) of former combatants, and reorganization or reconstruction of the key security institutions in the process of security sector reform (SSR). This is supposed to provide the necessary conditions for institution-building (the second circle). DDR and SSR as well as the larger aim of institution-building in general are typically externally assisted – in Afghanistan's case even externally shaped – processes, which makes inquiry about the role of external agents very important (the third circle). Finally, in cases where subversion and resistance are observed, as is the case in Afghanistan, it is important to study how external agents, through the processes of DDR, SSR, and institution-building, come into conflict with actors locally (not necessarily onl with 'local' actors as such). The sections of the ensuing overview follow this sequence below.

DDR, SSR, and warlordism

In 2001, a governing regime, and what passed for its security forces, was defeated and pushed across the border into Pakistan by a combination of US air power, US and other Western special operations troops, and local militias, such as Abdul Rashid Dostum's Junbesh-e-Milli and the forces of the late Ahmed Shah Massoud's Shura-e-Nazar faction.

Disarmament of these armed groups was delayed and finally negotiated down to a lesser figu of just above 60,000 former combatants. The leaner effort was rationalized as not benefiting th 'warlords' – that is, the anti-Taliban allies – too much, given how they were expected to profi from using the DDR process as a form of patronage to those who eventually underwent the program, as was indeed eventually the case (Giustozzi, 2008a). Mac Ginty emphasizes that the program was thought to result in a 'diluted warlordism' of sorts, but certainly in 'no instant transformation [of warlords] into model citizens' (Mac Ginty, 2010: 578). The signs are that the implementation of the program was procedurally deeply flawed at various points, and especiall the reintegration of many ex-combatants suffered from implementing organizations' lack of knowledge about Afghanistan (Giustozzi and Rossi, 2006).

The Afghan state, and Hamid Karzai at its head, was in a 'Catch-22' situation where, in Mac Ginty's words, 'in order to survive it required the support of a small number of powerful warlords. Yet, in order to make a transition to a meritocratic "modern" state, it needed to decommission those same warlords' (2010: 592). In Mac Ginty's account, Karzai and the West were at firs forced to reckon with the raw battlefield strength of various Northern Alliance commanders and other strongmen, and only after a certain time had passed could the Afghan president engage in the selective cooptation and/or marginalization of these actors – a process partly reversed as the insurgency started gaining strength, once again forcing the Afghan government and its international partners to turn to these strongmen for assistance (Mac Ginty, 2010: 588). New strongmen appeared as well, albeit on a smaller scale, at the lead of village militias, armed, trained, and supported as counterinsurgency proxy forces usually by Western special operations troops.

Western forces themselves started directly cooperating with local and regional strongmen right in the wake of the 2001 intervention. Giustozzi (2007: 75) points out that 'the Bush administration believed that its priority was to ensure stability, even if this should come at the expense of the process of state building.' The US and its partners accepted that strongmen would have 'in-builtsafety valves' in the security sector and that, at least informally, the new Afghan National Army would be built primarily on the human resources of their militias, resulting in 'shadow ownership' of the SSR process (Giustozzi, 2008b).

Nevertheless, the term 'warlord' itself is problematic, and with strategic implications at that. Giustozzi notes that this supposedly 'catch-all' term tries to collect under one category people who do not have only their proficiency as military leader to thank for their position, but ar fundamentally political and often also economic actors at the same time. Political party heads, 'ethnic mobilizers,' 'violent entrepreneurs,' oligarchs of oligopolistic market structures and much else, in one (Kühn, 2012; Giustozzi, 2007). Post-2001 they were actors seeking to transform a factionalized war economy into an equally factionalized peace economy (Giustozzi, 2007: 77–78), conserving their social positions within it. In the process, they all developed, or in some cases kept, a share in the illegal economy (Giustozzi, 2007: 83) as well as acquired varying degrees of access to state resources. Through coming into contact with state structures some eagerly experimented with 'self-cooptation' to secure strategic positions within the central institutions of the state (as was the case with Rashid Dostum, who became the interim government's Minister of Defence); others were coopted by Karzai later down the road (as was the case with Ismail Khan). For some, this came with a primacy of political considerations; for others the state was a treasure trove of positions that could be captured and, opportunistically and corruptly, exploited, not unlike what Engvall talks of in the context of Kyrgyzstan as the problem of the state being seen and approached as 'an investment market' (Engvall, 2011: 23–25).

Strongmen, or in other words Afghanistan's politico-economic overlords, certainly pose a challenge to the statebuilding process, but this may be similar to the resistance of different magnates to the centralization of power in medieval European polities. For one, Kühn shows some long-term optimism regarding their role (2012). He problematizes how the international community's easy assumption of war-ravaged Afghanistan being in a fully deinstitutionalized condition in 2001 resulted in 'disregarding existing social structures' (p. 24), and he reckons with the possibility that the interaction of warlord and statebuilding politics may breed a pro–state transformation of the elite in the future, through the Weberian institutionalization of former strongmen's informal exercising of power into gradually formalized authority and rule, also helped by the potential 'economic connector' of the illicit economy. Needless to say, as Kühn's conceptualization of the role of the illicit economy is not shared by Western decision–makers and publics, the Western strategy of statebuilding did not explicitly try to build on this assumption. Nevertheless, one may have an example of an implicit attempt at bringing the illicit economy under strategic control in how the late Ahmed Wali Karzai [1] is said to have moved into the emerging vacuum on the drugs market in around 2005; interestingly, he may at the time have been on the payroll, receiving regular pay–outs, of the US Central Intelligence Agency (Filkins et al., 2009).

Institution-building

In terms of the weak traditions of the institution, the planned creation of a centralized state was a 'high risk strategy' decided on at the first Bonn/Petersberg Conference in 2001, as Nixon an Ponzio refer to it (2007: 28). A Loya Jirga or grand assembly of various political figures was thought to be necessary to sanctify the interim political process and the constitutional framework devised to lead to such an outcome. Sometimes remembered as a positive example of what could work in Afghanistan, as a mix of traditional and popular representation, the decision–making process of the Loya Jirga was, in fact, greatly influenced and even shaped by a coalition of Afghan and external actors (Rashid, 2008). Noelle–Karimi (2002) and Buchholz (2007), among others, point out how this external manipulation was in line with previous uses of the Loya Jirga by Afghanistan's rulers.

Nixon and Ponzio's assessment of the key problems of the post–2001 Afghan polity is shared by many observers and largely stands to this day. The authors list several key issues from 'the re–establishment of the National Assembly elected through an inappropriate voting system and creation of Provincial Councils without substantive responsibilities and administrative support, to community–level governance without fundamental debates about formal/informal justice systems, the role of religion, and decentralization settled' as the central challenges that any future rethinking of these institutions should deal with (2007: 26). They deem the current parliament (i.e., its Lower House, the Wolesi Jirga) 'unlikely to allow organized parliamentary action and likely to hamper the development of stable parliamentary groupings and eventually political parties' (p. 35), at the same time as they consider Provincial Councils as not really representative of realities on the key local (district, valley, village, etc.) levels of Afghan politics (p. 32).

The formal world of national–level politics is thus characterized by the constant deal–brokering of a constitutional–competence–wise strong president related to whom there was 'a perceived need to preserve [his ability], through the process of cabinet and provincial governor appointments and other means, to co–opt or defuse tensions with regional power–holders' (Nixon and Ponzio, 2007: 30). Hence a parliament with only independent members. The disorganization of the latter was also a goal with Afghanistan's strongmen in mind – it was their parties, the 'mujahedeen parties,' that were not supposed be able to organize too strongly through action in the legislature. In fact, in Afghanistan's polity where the informal can quite meaningfully counterbalance the formal, this proved to be an invitation to struggle at times, rather than a setting in which 'tensions' could be 'defused.' A good example is Baghlan province, where the security institutions were largely in the hands of the predominantly Tajik local strongmen belonging to the Shura–e–Nazar faction while Karzai challenged their control by appointing Pashtun governors, sometimes from outside the province, sometimes even from opposing factions, e.g., from the legally operating parliamentary–party faction of Gulbuddin Hekmatyar's Hizb–i–Islami (Foschini, 2010; Marton and Wagner, 2011: 198–201). Karzai similarly challenged Rashid Dostum's hold on Jowzjan province by appointing Hizb–i–Islami–affiliated Juma Khan Hamdard as governo there (Bleuer, 2007).

Crucially, this results in weak transparency, in the shade of which nepotistic corruption, or the 'investment market' mentioned earlier, can prosper across all the crucial sectors and branches of government. The justice system may be considered as a case in point. Both the formal and the informal, unofficial parallel mechanisms of justice undermine the Afghan state given the wa they operate: corruption in the justice system means gross distortion of process in a high number of cases and this pushes local demands for justice and dispute settlement to seek the supply of justice through informal mechanisms.

Thus was created the democratic polity of Afghanistan post–2001, which Nixon and Ponzio refer to as Afghanistan's second chance at democratization, after the 1960s (2007: 28). It is important to register the underlying problems in order to realistically assess criticisms of state–building in Afghanistan, which are largely focused on the imperfection one finds in today's Afgha polity compared to an ideal–type liberal democracy.

The external effort

As to the external effort, the most commonly raised concerns related to statebuilding are the size of the statebuilders' 'footprint,' the desired length of their stay, and whether their efforts should be closely coordinated by a central actor, be it the UN or the strongest state in a coalition–of–the–willing. Many pros and cons regarding a small or a bigger footprint, finite or open–ende stay, and closer or looser coordination may be found in the general literature; however, in the Afghanistan case, since very early, it was the inadequate size of the footprint – i.e., the 'light footprint approach' – along with the international community's short–termism and its poor coordination of statebuilding and other efforts that was problematized by observers. A study by the RAND Corporation (Quinlivan, 2003) noted, in a comparison that came very early into the effort in Afghanistan, how much better manned and resourced similar efforts in Bosnia, Kosovo, or even Timor–Leste had been in the past. In fact, the Afghanistan effort even at its peak reached neither those levels, nor, specifically, the minimum level of armed forces required in the face o an insurgency, proportionately to the population of an area. Marton (2009) highlighted how the sequencing of statebuilding–related tasks and the prioritization of objectives may have been fundamentally ill–arranged with the contradictory motives of the international intervention, for example in how the prerogatives and the institutional agents of counter–narcotics, counter–terrorism, counterinsurgency, humanitarian and development aid, and statebuilding regularly clashed with each other, resulting in outcomes desired by no one.

A peculiar source of complications was the perceived need on the part of the UN, its agencies, and NGOs to be impartial. Hasegawa's study (2008) of the UN Assistance Mission in Afghanistan, UNAMA, is instructive in this respect. In Donini's assessment, no matter how much UNAMA strived for the role of enlightened balancer, 'after the aid/donor/contractor juggernaut descended on Afghanistan following the Bonn Agreement in 2001, the UN became a relatively small assistance player in a very crowded and confusing field' (2007: 168)

NGOs themselves also had aspirations for an aura of impartiality that they, in fact, never fully enjoyed in Afghanistan (Donini, 2007: 161; Bleuer, 2008). Their quest for independence partly immunized them against control of their efforts by others, resulting in what Cordesman assesses as 'miserable fiscal controls' over the money pouring through them into Afghanistan (2010: 5)

Anecdotes related to this abound, including from whistleblowers from the aid community. For example, Han recounts a case where her organization received €70,000 from a donor for a project that it wanted neither to openly turn down nor to accept (Han, 2012). Efforts of internationally coordinated provincial reconstruction teams (PRTs) were no less a patchwork of large variation and inconsistency. In Piiparinen's description, 'The group of 21 PRTs could be termed a "loosely coupled system" both with regard to relations between PRTs and considering different components within a PRT' (2007: 148). While some countries may have paid insurgents for the security of their projects in certain areas (Coghlan and Bone, 2011), others such as the US suffered from inflexibility and, for example, Creighton complains of how the US Army Corps of Engineers could not deviate from US housing standards in contracting for the building of facilities with local entrepreneurs (2012).

Insufficient and highly complicated progress in the field of development occurred in the context of a gradually deteriorating security situation where the lack of resources increasingly began to show. One element of the (neo)liberal peace was nevertheless to a great extent realized in Afghanistan, namely in the economic sphere. Trade liberalization was one of the shifts swiftly, and most likely damagingly, pushed through by international institutions (Oxfam, 2007).

The conflict

In 2009, Matthew Hoh, a political officer assigned to the US-led PRT in Zabul province, resigned from his position and announced this in a letter to US Ambassador to Afghanistan Karl Eikenberry, among others. The press, starting with the *Washington Post*, carried the text of this letter, which summarized the Afghan conflict in the following way: '[The conflict here], fr at least the end of King Zahir Shah's reign, has violently and savagely pitted the urban, secular, educated and modern of Afghanistan against the rural, religious, illiterate and traditional' (Hoh, 2009: 1–2).

This understanding of the conflict lies not far from that of scholars with *longue-durée* approach. Fänge (2010) takes this kind of argument to the extreme, claiming continuity between three insurgencies in Afghanistan's history that have toppled two different governments so far: fi st that of King Amanullah in 1928 and second the communist regime, under Najibullah's rule at the time, after the long struggle of 1978–1992. The common weakness of these regimes may have been, in Fänge's view, their attempt at modernization with, at the head, 'highly centralised but weak government institutions which have used an inflexible top–down approach' (2010: 2) The prediction is that for this reason the current government of Hamid Karzai may fall as well, no matter if it is aided, just as Afghan communists were, by external allies present with their own troops at the moment.

An interesting aspect is, however, that in the case of Karzai's government of the Islamic Republic of Afghanistan, while it is certainly, to an extent, the representative of a modernization attempt, the crucial part of the drive for modernization comes from external agents def ning a vision for Afghanistan's future partly on the basis of their security interests, and partly on the basis of their normative considerations. Some, for example Schmeidl and Karokhail, criticize this as the same 'McDonaldized' form of statebuilding, seen elsewhere in the world, which the West 'tries to sell to the Global South with a "prêt–a–porter" mentality' (2009: 69). If this were the case in Afghanistan, it would be unlike the Soviet case, where the Moscow Politburo even attempted to pragmatically slow down Nur Mohammed Taraki's push for aggressive modern-ization. Here the *sui generis* hybrid nature of statebuilding in Afghanistan is observable (Debiel et al., 2009). Western actors are united neither in talk nor in practice, and if one were to characterize the nature of Western endeavors in Afghanistan with a sweeping statement, it would have to be focused on the larger than usual tolerance for the informal elements of the political process, even as on the surface Western leaders seem not to have made fundamental compromises.

The explanation for this may lie partly in a pessimistic assessment on the key external actors' side of what is realistically feasible in Afghanistan, and partly in how a very large international (or, with the inclusion of IGOs and NGOs, transnational) coalition can only be united around formally politically correct objectives in spite of that assessment. It is a very large coalition indeed which has been trying so far to generate an adequate amount of resources for its formally voiced objectives. It ought not to be a surprise therefore that the process resulted in much friction between the participant countries, with equitable burden−sharing – or rather what would be perceived as such by the relevant stakeholders – remaining a major challenge over the years.

ISAF politics

This section investigates political and/or security motivations that countries engaged in statebuilding efforts in Afghanistan have had. It shows that what has been commonly perceived as a collective effort done through the multilateral ISAF framework has in fact been a series of unilateral practices of countries involved. Deeper coordination between and among provincial reconstruction teams (PRTs), which have been chosen as the main form of Afghan statebuilding, has been non−existent. Additionally, since various ISAF countries have been in Afghanistan for different reasons, problems of collective action have also been highlighted at the political level, as the final analysis of the NATO Chicago Summit demonstrates

Political and security considerations

A simple framework of assessment, based partly on Bennett et al. (1994), reckons with alliance dependence and threat balancing as the key structural motives factoring in coalition members' Afghanistan policies. This suggests that countries entered Afghanistan and stayed there over the years either because they needed to do so themselves, or because they were compelled to do so by others who did. The former have committed more, in terms of both quantity and quality, to the coalition's mission as they have seen the need to 'balance' threats in Afghanistan, and at the same time value the NATO alliance, or the alliance of one or more key NATO countries within the NATO bloc ('strivers'). Conversely, the weakest motivation has been expected in cases where both threat perceptions and strong alliance dependence are absent ('onlookers'). Empirically interesting cases are those where either only threat balancing ('mavericks') or only alliance dependence ('servants') appears as an inf uential factor.

Empirical f ndings of a recent comparative analysis (Hynek and Marton, 2011) concerning political motives for joining ISAF confrm that the majority of the coalition have been reminiscent either of 'servants' or of 'strivers.' The notion that most countries are free−riding on US efforts is wrong. Non−NATO ISAF members Australia and New Zealand are making a comparatively proportional contribution to ISAF operations, contrary to the proposition that they may be involved only as 'onlookers' merely because they are non−NATO members. So much may be said, even if, as William Maley concludes, 'success in Uruzgan offers no guarantee of success in Afghanistan as a whole' (2011: 135), and, as Hoadley points out, 'New Zealand officers wit field experience, are inclined to [believe that] good outcomes ... reflect creative adaptations t the varied and ever−changing security and development environments that characterize Afghanistan' (2011: 150).

Experience of East–Central European NATO members' efforts, including in leading PRTs in different provinces of Afghanistan, suggest that the 'servant' characterization has been more varied than expected. In their study, Marton and Wagner conclude that 'Hungary, proud of its nominally major contribution to ISAF's efforts in Afghanistan, was never really eager to do more than just go through the motions' (2011: 208; see also Rac̆ius, 2011 on Lithuania; Kulesa and Górka−Winter, 2011 on Poland). Meanwhile, as to the Czech Republic, Hynek and Eichler posit that 'an explanation of the Czech government's motivation in this matter is that there was a successful internalization of US and NATO strategic narratives concerning the Allied necessity to reconstruct Afghanistan . . . seen as natural, right and legitimate' (2011: 238).

Foust discusses France and refers to the French approach as different from the US approach in being more 'pragmatist,' in that 'the French do not believe they can create large−scale social change.' In terms of results, however, he debates the relevance of this, and notes that 'the methods differed, but the results . . . were much the same.' Moreover, France did what it did with a view 'to remain a major actor within the alliance, but to do so in responsible, strategic manner' (Foust, 2011: 99–100). Therefore he concludes that France 'can be placed right along the boundary of the "mavericks" and "strivers" boxes ... The French military can properly be called "strivers" in the sense that it exudes a strong sense of coalition . . . the French government can be called "mavericks" in the sense that it independently sees value in participating in the war in Afghanistan' (Foust, 2011: 98). The one real maverick overall seems to be Turkey. Vamvakas (2011: 243–260) outlines why the Turkish contribution may be among those least fitting the alliance dependence/threat balancing framework, given how the ruling AKP government is just as interested in statebuilding and nation−building in Turkey through the policy it implements *vis-à-vis* Afghanistan as it is in building special ties with Afghanistan, Central Asia, and beyond, through its participation in ISAF.

Several genuine 'strivers' can also be identified. Anthony King generally confirms the hypothesis concerning the United Kingdom, while the Netherlands, and possibly even Germany – the latter sometimes misleadingly defined as a 'weakest link' in northern Afghanistan – ma qualify in this category, as Rietjens (2011) and Behr (2011) argue. It should be noted that the typology used highlights but does not fully capture important nuances in terms of motivations, such as Norway's conflicted commitment to live up to expectations as a 'peace nation' even i the Afghanistan environment. As Kristian Harpviken notes: 'The ambiguity of the [PRT] concept . . . not only [allows] divergent narratives between nations, it also allows multiple narratives to coexist within the same nation' (2011: 170).

Force scarcity and the managed withdrawal of the West

Regardless of how large this coalition's effort is, overall troop numbers were and are not enough: many, for example Rubin and Hamidzada, warned very early of there not being enough troops in Afghanistan, and noted with worry that the Bush administration was for a long time even considering a troop drawdown to deploy additional forces in Iraq. The significance of the distraction of the Iraqi confict is noted by many (Rubin and Hamidzada, 2007: 11–12; Barfeld, 2008: 411). For a long time, Western−led force generation for the Afghanistan mission was simply out of step with reality.

Given the relative scarcity of available forces, stabilizing and waging counterinsurgency by proxies was always sought as an alternative option: beyond the regional strongmen of the former Northern Alliance, local or 'village' militias began to be supported in large numbers in various programs, for example the Afghan Public Protection Force and the Afghan Local Police schemes or the now defunct Local and Community Defence Initiatives. These militias are often mentioned as *arbaki*, i.e., traditional tribal self−defence and order−enforcement forces, but in fact the institution of the *arbaki* cannot be understood as traditional in areas outside certain parts of Loya

Paktia in eastern Afghanistan, Loya Kandahar in the south, and parts of Pakistan's tribal areas (Tariq, 2008: 3). The stubborn reference to *arbaki* and Afghan traditions is what would in Western eyes lend local legitimacy to the 'liberal' statebuilding effort. However, evident in it is a misunderstanding of Afghan society as a population consisting of tribes that would function as mutually exclusive conflict groups. Even the US military's Human Terrain System documente that this is not the case, however – not even in the more tribal areas of eastern Afghanistan (HTS, 2009; see also Coburn, 2008 on *qawmiyat*, wrongly associated exclusively with tribes). Still, the idea of Afghanistan's tribal nature does not seem to weaken in Western discourse.

Beyond the problematic nature of arming mini–Leviathans in light of the statebuilding effort, the strategy also carries the risk of alienating further parts of the population, driving more as both *majbur* ('forced') and *naraz* ('unhappy') into joining the 'caravan' of the Taliban insurgency (van Bijlert, 2009: 160–161).

Conclusion

The most recent event with lasting impact on the future security situation in Afghanistan has been NATO's Chicago Summit that took place in May 2012. It has been the key event particularly for an outline of the next steps related to the transformation of the ISAF mandate in Afghanistan. In Chicago, US president Obama and fellow statesmen announced the end of ISAF's direct involvement in the (more than a decade long) war and therefore the time horizon for the so-called transition (or 'Afghanization' of the conflict) by summer 2013; i.e., a year or two earlie than previously expected. Indeed, NATO will attempt to give a semblance of the 'together in, together out' approach, despite the fact that France under the recently elected President Hollande will most probably begin pulling out its forces later this year (2012). Thus, recent thinking about the war has shifted from the transformation of the mandate to ensuring that militaries of the 28-country alliance can be brought back to their respective countries in a coordinated fashion and unharmed (Brunnstrom and Ryan, 2012).

As this chapter has demonstrated, Afghanistan is probably the most difficult case for the generalist approach to statebuilding, and the Western approach and an assessment of the motivations of Western countries certainly prevent one from speaking about sustainable success and rather point to the necessity for embracing a damage–limitation strategy.

Note

1   President Hamid Karzai's half brother, assassinated in 2011.

References

Barfield, T. (2008). The roots of failure in Afghanistan. *Current History*, December: 410–417.
Behr, T. (2011). Germany and Regional Command–North: ISAF's weakest link? In N. Hynek and P. Marton (Eds.), *Statebuilding in Afghanistan: Multinational contributions to reconstruction*. London, UK: Routledge, pp. 42–64.
Belloni, R. (2006). Rethinking 'nation–building:' The contradictions of the neo–Wilsonian approach to democracy promotion. *Whitehead Journal of Diplomacy and International Relations*, Winter/Spring, 97–109.
Bennett, A., Lepgold, J., and Unger, D. (1994). Burden–sharing in the Persian Gulf War. *International Organisation*, 48(1), 39–75.
Bleuer, C. (2007). What's behind the shooting of demonstrators in Northern Afghanistan? *Ghosts of Alexander*, 29 May. Available at: http://easterncampaign.com
Bleuer, C. (2008). The politicization and militarization of aid to Afghanistan. *Ghosts of Alexander*, 8 June. Available at: http://easterncampaign.com

Bliesemann de Guevara, B. (2008). The state in times of statebuilding. *Civil Wars*, *10*(4), 348–368.
Brunnstrom, D., and Ryan, M. (2012, May 21). NATO to endorse Afghan exit plan, seeks routes out. *Reuters*.
Buchholz, B. (2007). Thoughts on Afghanistan's Loya Jirga: A myth?' *Asien*, *104*, July, 23–33.
Chandler, D. (2002). Anti−corruption strategies and democratization in Bosnia−Herzegovina. *Democratization*, *9*(2), 101–120.
Chopra, J. (2002). Building state failure in East Timor. *Development and Change*, *33*(5), 979–1000.
Coburn, N. (2008). Qaum: Conceptualizing potters in the Afghan political arena. Available at: www.bu.edu/aias/coburn.pdf
Coghlan, T., and Bone, J. (2011, 12 August). US President Bush begged Italian PM Berlusconi to stop bribing the Taliban in Afghanistan. *The Australian*.
Cordesman, A. (2010). *How America corrupted Afghanistan: Time to look in the mirror*. Washington, DC: Center for Strategic and International Studies.
Coyne, C. J. (2006). Reconstructing weak and failed states: Foreign intervention and the Nirvana fallacy. *Foreign Policy Analysis*, *2*(4), 343–360.
Creighton, J. L. (2012). How bureaucracy impedes victory in Afghanistan. *World Policy Blog*, April 16. Available at: www.worldpolicy.org/blog
Debiel, T., Glassner, R., Schetter, C., and Terlinden, U. (2009). Local statebuilding in Afghanistan and Somaliland. *Peace Review*, *21*(1), 38–44.
Donini, A. (2007). Local perceptions of assistance to Afghanistan. *International Peacekeeping*, *14*(1), 158–172.
Engvall, J. (2011). The state as investment market: An analytical framework for interpreting politics and bureaucracy in Kyrgyzstan. Doctoral thesis, Uppsala University, Uppsala, Sweden.
Eriksen, S. S. (2009). The liberal peace is neither: Peacebuilding, state building and the reproduction of conflict in the Democratic Republic of Congo. *International Peacekeeping*, *16*(5), 652–666.
Fänge, A. (2010). *The state of the Afghan state*. Afghanistan Analysts Network, 8 January. Available at: http://aan-afghanistan.com
Filkins, D., Mazzetti, M., and Risen, J. (2009, October 28). Brother of Afghan leader said to be paid by C.I.A. *New York Times*, A1.
Foschini, F. (2010). *Campaign trail 2010 (2): Baghlan – Divided we stand*. Afghanistan Analysts Network, 7 July. Available at: http://aan-afghanistan.com
Foust, J. (2011). France in Kapisa: A combined approach to statebuilding. In N. Hynek and P. Marton (Eds.), *Statebuilding in Afghanistan: Multinational contributions to reconstruction*. London, UK: Routledge, pp. 88–103.
Fukuyama, F. (2005). *Statebuilding: Governance and world order in the 21st century*. Ithaca, NY: Cornell University Press.
Giustozzi, A. (2007). War and peace economies of Afghanistan's strongmen. *International Peacekeeping*, *14*(1), 75–89.
Giustozzi, A. (2008a). Bureaucratic façade and political realities of disarmament and demobilisation in Afghanistan. *Conflict, Security and Development*, *8*(2), 169–192.
Giustozzi, A. (2008b). Shadow ownership and SSR in Afghanistan. In T. Donais (Ed.), *Local ownership and security sector reform*. Geneva, Switzerland: Geneva Centre for the Democratic Control of Armed Forces, pp. 215–232.
Giustozzi, A., and Rossi, S. (2006). *Disarmament, demobilisation and re-integration of ex-combatants (DDR) in Afghanistan: Constraints and limited capabilities*. Crisis States Research Centre Working Paper, Series 2, No. 2. London, UK: LSE.
Goetze, C., and Guzina, B. (2008). Peacebuilding, statebuilding, nationbuilding – Turtles all the way down? *Civil Wars*, *10*(4), 319–347.
Han, S. (2012). Guest blog: Working in aid: *Donor rule, funding flows, and awkward 'no's*. Afghanistan Analysts Network, 18 April. Available at: http://aan-afghanistan.com
Harpviken, K. (2011). A peace nation in the war on terror: The Norwegian engagement in Afghanistan. In N. Hynek and P. Marton (Eds.), *Statebuilding in Afghanistan: Multinational contributions to reconstruction*. London, UK: Routledge, pp. 157–173.
Hasegawa, Y. (2008). The United Nations Assistance Mission in Afghanistan: Impartiality in new UN peace operations. *Journal of Intervention and Statebuilding*, *2*(2), 209–226.
Hoehne, M. V. (2009). Mimesis and mimicry in dynamics of state and identity formation in northern Somalia. *Africa*, *79*(2), 252–281.
Hoadley, S. (2011). The New Zealand PRT experience in Bamyan Province: Assessing political legitimacy and operational achievements. In N. Hynek and P. Marton (Eds.), *Statebuilding in Afghanistan: Multinational contributions to reconstruction*. London, UK: Routledge, pp. 139–156.

Hoh, M. (2009). Letter addressed to Ambassador Nancy J. Powell, Director General of the Foreign Service and Director of Human Resources, 10 September 2009. Available at: www.washingtonpost.com

HTS. (2009). My cousin's enemy is my friend: A study of Pashtun 'tribes' in Afghanistan. Afghanistan Research Reachback Center White Paper TRADOC G2, Human Terrain System, Fort Leavenworth, KS.

Hynek, N., and Eichler, J. (2011). Post–decisional and alliance–dependent: The Czech engagement in Logar. In N. Hynek and P. Marton (Eds.), *Statebuilding in Afghanistan: Multinational contributions to reconstruction*. London, UK: Routledge, pp. 226–242.

Hynek, N., and Marton, P. (2011). *Statebuilding in Afghanistan: Multinational contributions to reconstruction*. London, UK: Routledge.

Kühn, F. P. (2012). Risk and externalisation in Afghanistan: Why statebuilding upends state–formation. In B. Bliesemann de Guevara (Ed.), *Statebuilding and state-formation*. London, UK: Routledge, pp. 23–39.

Kulesa, Ł., and Górka–Winter, B. (2011). From followers to leaders as 'coalition servants': The Polish engagement in Afghanistan. In N. Hynek and P. Marton (Eds.), *Statebuilding in Afghanistan: Multinational contributions to reconstruction*. London, UK: Routledge, pp. 212–225.

Mac Ginty, R. (2010). Warlords and the liberal peace: Statebuilding in Afghanistan. *Conflict, Security & Development*, 10(4), 577–598.

Maley, W. (2011). PRT activity in Afghanistan: The Australian experience. In N. Hynek and P. Marton (Eds.), *Statebuilding in Afghanistan: Multinational contributions to reconstruction*. London, UK: Routledge, pp. 124–138.

Marton, P. (2009). The sequence of statebuilding and related complications in the case of Afghanistan. In M. Majer et al. (Eds.), *Panorama of the global security environment*. Bratislava, Slovakia: CENAA, pp. 507–524.

Marton, P., and Wagner, P. (2011). Hungary's involvement in Afghanistan: Proudly going through the motions? In N. Hynek and P. Marton (Eds.), *Statebuilding in Afghanistan: Multinational contributions to reconstruction*. London, UK: Routledge, pp. 192–211.

Nixon, H., and Ponzio, R. (2007). Building democracy in Afghanistan: The statebuilding agenda and international engagement. *International Peacekeeping*, 14(1), 26–40.

Noelle–Karimi, C. (2002). The Loya Jirga – An effective political tool? A historical overview. In C. Noelle–Karimi, C. Schetter, and R. Schlagenweit (Eds.), *Afghanistan – A country without a state?* Frankfurt am Main, Germany: IKO–Verlag für Interkulturelle Kommunikation, pp. 37–52.

Oxfam. (2007). *Getting the fundamentals right: The early stages of Afghanistan's WTO accession process*. Oxfam Briefing Paper No. 92, June. Oxford, UK: Oxfam

Piiparinen, T. (2007). A clash of mindsets? An insider's account of provincial reconstruction teams. *International Peacekeeping*, 14(1), 143–157.

Quinlivan, J. T. (2003). Burden of victory: The painful arithmetic of stability operations. *RAND Review*, Summer.

Račius, E. (2011). Trials and tribulations of the Lithuanian participation in the NATO ISAF mission. In N. Hynek and P. Marton (Eds.), *Statebuilding in Afghanistan: Multinational contributions to reconstruction*. London, UK: Routledge, pp. 261–277.

Rashid, A. (2008). *Descent into chaos: The United States and the failure of nation building in Pakistan, Afghanistan, and Central Asia*. New York, NY: Viking Penguin.

Rietjens, S. (2011). Between expectations and reality: The Dutch engagement in Uruzgan. In N. Hynek and P. Marton (Eds.), *Statebuilding in Afghanistan: Multinational contributions to reconstruction*. London, UK: Routledge, pp. 65–87.

Rubin, B. R., and Hamidzada, H. (2007). From Bonn to London: Governance challenges and the future of statebuilding in Afghanistan. *International Peacekeeping*, 14(1), 8–25.

Schmeidl, S., and Karokhail, M. (2009). "Prêt-a-porter states": How the McDonaldization of state-building misses the mark in Afghanistan – A response. Dialogue Series No. 8, April. Berlin, Germany: Berghof Center For Constructive Conflict Management

Tariq, M. O. (2008). *Tribal security system (Arbakai) in Southeast Afghanistan*. Crisis States Research Centre Occasional Paper No. 7, December 2008. London, UK: London School of Economics.

Vamvakas, P. (2011). Turkey's ISAF mission: A maverick with strategic depth. In N. Hynek and P. Marton (Eds.), *Statebuilding in Afghanistan: Multinational contributions to reconstruction*. London, UK: Routledge, pp. 243–260.

Van Bijlert, M. (2009). Unruly commanders and violent power struggles: Taliban networks in Uruzgan. In A. Giustozzi (Ed.), *Decoding the new Taliban*. New York, NY: Columbia University Press, pp. 155–178.

26
STATEBUILDING AFTER VICTORY
Uganda, Ethiopia, Eritrea, and Rwanda

Terrence Lyons

There has been considerable research in recent years examining patterns of post-conflict statebuilding that focused on cases of negotiated settlements where the international community had high levels of involvement through peacekeeping operations (Stedman et al., 2002; Roeder and Rothchild, 2005; Jarstad and Sisk, 2008; Paris and Sisk, 2009). This scholarship has produced important findings on the dilemmas of war-to-democracy transitions that help us understand why some peace processes collapse, some result in weak regimes, and some lead to sustainable peacebuilding. Other scholars have drawn attention to the importance of processes to 'demilitarize politics' so that the warring parties may be transformed into political parties that can participate effectively in post-conflict politics (Lyons, 2005; Kovacs, 2007; Manning, 2008; de Zeeuw, 2007). What is less clearly understood, however, is how these processes differ in cases where civil war ended in victory. While the percentage of civil wars that ended in negotiations grew dramatically in the 1990s, 40 per cent still ended in victory (Toft, 2010a, b: 6). Limited international intervention and support for liberal statebuilding in these cases allows greater focus on local actors and dynamics.[1]

This chapter outlines the distinct paths to statebuilding in cases that end in the victory of the insurgent group, and will pay particular attention to the cases of Uganda, Ethiopia, Eritrea, and Rwanda. It will not focus on cases of civil wars that end in incumbent victory as in Algeria, Chechyna, and Sri Lanka.[2] These cases are characterized more by the re-establishment of the old order and a return to the *status quo ante* rather than a transition to a new form of statebuilding.

All post-conflict outcomes are shaped by the dynamics of war and the type of war termination. There are three distinctions between cases of negotiated settlement and the cases of insurgent victory that are the focus of this chapter. First, the political transitions after rebel victory are shaped by the challenges of consolidating power, rather than powersharing and reconciliation.[3] Victorious insurgents must transform themselves from military to political organizations in order to sustain statebuilding, but do so on their own terms rather than from within a context of a negotiated settlement and external monitoring. Second, demobilization after victory is different. The security dilemmas, risks of demobilization without credible commitments, and the consequent emphasis on international peacekeeping in cases of negotiated settlements are not present when one side wins and the other side loses. Demobilization still occurs, but it is shaped more by the imperative to shift resources toward post-conflict development.

Third, the roles played by the international community are limited in cases of unilateral victory. Much of the debate in the literature on statebuilding focuses on how international intervention can best support sustainable peace. Without an internationally negotiated settlement and the ensuing deployment of peacekeepers, external powers play a much more limited role in statebuilding. The debates among scholars and practitioners of statebuilding around the size of the international 'footprint,' questions of who to include in the process, and worries about dependency on and the 'tight embrace' of international peacekeepers to maintain stability are largely irrelevant in cases of victory.[4] The winning party will seek international assistance and legitimacy but it deals with external interests from a position of more autonomy and less dependence. Local ownership in these cases is not contrasted with international ownership but rather entails the domination of one set of victorious actors at the expense of the vanquished.

Post-conflict politics and the legacies of victory

Much of the literature on statebuilding seeks to uncover how and when security and legitimacy are created after civil war in which both have failed. These two challenges, however, differ depending on how the conflict ended. In cases of a negotiated settlement, security often is shaped by international peacekeeping and legitimacy linked to postconflct elections.[5] In cases of victory, however, the winning army seizes the monopoly of force on the battlefield and does not need peacekeeping forces to separate warring parties or monitor a ceasefire. In cases of war termination by victory, legitimacy also is derived from success on the battlefield and, over time, the abilit of the winning military force to transform into an effective political party willing and able to provide public goods and open up political space. Statebuilding after insurgent victory is therefore shaped by the ability of one party to use power unilaterally to create a new regime rather than processes of bargaining and joint decision-making.

There is debate among scholars of statebuilding on whether insurgent victory or negotiated settlement is more or less likely to lead to democracy. Monica Duffy Toft argues that civil wars that end in rebel victory are inclined to produce democratic outcomes because they have both the military capability to penalize spoilers and the incentives to govern justly to gain legitimacy from both their domestic constituencies and the international community. 'Rebels are more likely to enjoy support from civilians and to have a need for international legitimacy, support, and aid; thus, when rebels win, they may be more likely to encourage, or at least tolerate, an increased degree of political competition' (Toft, 2010a: 96–97; see also Toft, 2010b; Huang, 2012). Weinstein (2007) suggests that popular mobilization by the National Resistance Army created the conditions for post-conflict democratization in Uganda

However, the case study literature of the four victorious rebel groups under examination here – the National Resistance Army in Uganda, the Eritrean People's Liberation Front, the Ethiopian People's Revolutionary Democratic Front, and the Rwandan Patriotic Front – demonstrates that each transformed into a powerful authoritarian regime. These transformations succeeded in ending the wars and creating stability but did little to advance democratization. In Uganda there was a period of 'no-party' democracy in the early 1990s and in Ethiopia and Rwanda there were a series of non-competitive elections that resulted in the ruling party winning by majorities of over 90 per cent. Each regarded dissent as illegitimate and used state power to repress local media and civil society.[6]

Post-conflictpolitics is shaped by the institutional legacies of the insurgencies. In cases where the rebels won, the 'guerrilla to government' transformation requires key operational adjustments:

> Secrecy yields to relative openness. Coercion is replaced by persuasion, although the persuasion can easily be co-optation. Ringing declarations of principle are traded for

policy analysis. Enemies are transmuted into opponents. And bureaucratic tedium becomes the new fog of battle.

(Close, 2007: 19)

Post–conflict parties based on victorious rebel movements differ in four ways from those that evolve from parties to a negotiated settlement. First, successful insurgents are more likely to have coherent leadership, high levels of solidarity, and effective command and control. Second, victorious insurgent groups often have experience in administering liberated territory and therefore opportunities to develop trained and effective cadres with the capacity to govern civilians and wartime relationships with civilian constituencies and international actors (Mampilly, 2011; on El Salvador see Allison, 2010). Military governance of liberated territory often creates non–democratic norms and precedents that shape how the party operates during peacetime. Third, victorious rebels are more likely to derive signif cant popular legitimacy from defeating the old order and ending the violence. Insurgents who fight to stalemate and negotiations ca claim a role in forcing a transition, but those claims are more ambivalent and contingent than claims of unilateral victory.

Fourth, vanquished incumbents are less likely to play important post–conflict roles in cases o insurgent victory. In some cases supporters of the losing side have shattered (as in Uganda and Ethiopia/Eritrea) or gone into exile (as in Rwanda), making reconciliation with these spent forces less imperative. The victorious rebels have greater scope to decide whether and how the defeated parties may participate in the political transition. Rather than struggling with power–sharing or the integration of rebel forces into the national military, victorious insurgents can focus on consolidating and expanding their political power and on building upon their pre–existing structures of command and control.

Postconflict elections organized under the provisions of negotiated peace agreements are part of what Ottaway has called the 'democratic reconstruction model' (Ottaway, 2003; see also Ottaway, 2002). In cases of rebel victory, postconflict elections are also common but play differen roles in the process of statebuilding. Uganda, Ethiopia, and Rwanda all held postconflict election but these polls served to consolidate the authority of the militarily victorious party. In Uganda, Museveni banned political parties as divisive and in 1989 used 'no–party' elections for local Resistance Councils to select higher levels of representation (Omara–Otunnu, 1992; Kasf, 1991). Elections for the president and parliament took place in the 1990s but the opposition had to compete as individuals against the government, with all the advantages of incumbency supporting the NRM. In Ethiopia, the opposition had difficulty in challenging rules of the game that severel disadvantaged it, and used boycotts and other methods to try to delegitimate the elections the regime organized to consolidate its rule in 1992, 1995, and 2000. The 2005 elections were an exception and offered the Ethiopian people a meaningful choice, but violent demonstration and mass arrests quickly closed this challenge to the strong authoritarian regime of the EPRDF. Elections in 2010 returned to form, with the ruling party winning 99.6 per cent of the seats in the parliament. In Rwanda, local elections in 2001 were organized on the basis of 'consensual democracy' and opposition parties were not allowed to compete (International Crisis Group, 2001). By 2003, opposition parties were banned and the RPF won the presidential election with 95 per cent of the vote but with little electoral legitimacy (Reyntjens, 2004).

Despite the lack of competition, turnout was often high in these elections. Many voters, however, went to the polls in order to avoid being characterized as an opponent of the military regime. As one Ethiopian farmer explained his 1995 vote for the ruling party, 'I was afraid. The Government said I should vote so I voted. What could I do?' (Buckley, 1995). Frightened voters can acquiesce to but not legitimate the power of military regimes. Postconflict elections followin rebel victory provide opportunities for the authoritarian party to demonstrate its power and to marginalize potential rivals, both within the ruling party and from other potential sources of opposition. The victory of over 90 per cent sends a powerful message that the ex−insurgent party remains overwhelmingly dominant and that compliance or acquiescence is necessary. When Rwandan President Paul Kagame was asked if his 93 per cent victory in the 2010 election represented the will of the people he answered, 'So, 93 per cent – I wonder why it wasn't higher than that?' (AFP, 2011).

Elections play important roles in liberal peacebuilding after a negotiated settlement, as articulated by many in the international community. In cases of insurgent victory, such polls also play important roles but are not tied to the demands for legitimacy that may be derived from competitive elections. Elections organized by winning rebel movements are part of the process of statebuilding by consolidating authoritarian regimes, not statebuilding by liberalization.

The strength and durability of a political party, Huntington notes, 'derives more from its origins than from its character' (Huntington, 1968: 324; see also Huntington and Moore, 1970). Not surprisingly, some of the strongest authoritarian parties have their origins in victorious insurgencies or national liberation struggles (Levitsky and Way, 2010: 62). The intense social−ization and solidarity of the armed struggle serves as the basis of collective identities that are vital to success on the battlefeld and are often sustained during peacetime. Secrecy is fundamental to the survival of clandestine mobilization and is refected in the use of *noms de guerre* and cellular structures to limit the risk of infiltration and betrayal in Ethiopia and Eritrea. The winning partie often recall their origins in small, highly dedicated groups. The Eritrean People's Liberation Front started with 11 men, the National Resistance Movement in Uganda with 27, and the Tigray People's Liberation Front (TPLF) with 100 fighters (Herbst, 2004; on the TPLF see Young 1997). These narratives of secret, tightly knit groups that grew into victorious rebellions are powerful.

Trust and loyalty among political leaders who faced death and imprisonment together are compelling bases for strong solidarity. To defect from the political party in crisis is perceived by many to be as unthinkable as desertion on the battlefield. Political parties that originated in labo unions, non−violent social movements, or identities groups have different legacies and hence different institutional structures and patterns of behavior than those with their origins in insurgent organizations (LeBas, 2011). The transformation of movements into parties emphasizes fexible structures that encourage broad participation. In contrast, effective insurgent groups tend to be structured as vertical command organizations (Close and Prevost, 2007).

Political leaders who gained power through rebel victory also draw upon their links to the coercive apparatus of the insurgency, especially the instruments of internal intelligence and discipline and the defeat of rival internal factions. Military intelligence is key to clandestine mobilization and 'a fghter's every single move was under surveillance,' according to a key rebel leader in Ethiopia (Aregawi Berhe, 2009: 96). Ruth Iyob argues that Eritrea was marked by 'clandestinity and an endemic culture of public silence' during the war and that a 'cult of secrecy' remained even after liberation (Iyob, 1997; see also Makki, 1996). Secrecy is crucial to a rebel movement but makes the transformation into an open, democratic political party more difcult.

A victorious insurgent group will have a set of leaders with experience in using violence against its enemies within the armed opposition as well as the old regime. [7] Insurgent forces often go through internal crises as factions challenge top leadership and lose. Factionalism is endemic within rebel movements (Woldemariam, 2011). The divisions between the Eritrean Liberation Front and the Eritrean People's Liberation Front and between the Tigray People's Liberation Front and the Ethiopian People's Revolutionary Party resulted in violence within the insurgency as part of the process of consolidation by the winning faction[8]. Rivals are defeated militarily and dissent is not tolerated, creating precedents and expectations that shape post–conflict politics

During protracted armed struggles, insurgent groups must manage relationships with the civilian population, particularly in liberated areas under rebel control. Rebel recruitment, according to Weinstein, is shaped by the insurgent group's initial endowment of economic resources. Access to resources often leads to opportunistic rebellions where recruits are motivated by short–term incentives and often lack discipline. When an insurgent group lacks material resources, as in Uganda, Ethiopia, and Eritrea, it must rely on social endowments and collective incentives, resulting in an activist rebellion where recruits are committed for the long term and tend to be more disciplined (Weinstein, 2007). Rebel engagement with civilians during wartime shapes politics during post–conflict statebuilding. Successful activist rebellions such as those i Ethiopia, Eritrea, Rwanda, and Uganda begin the war–to–peace transition with committed troops, disciplined cadres, and strong social networks of mobilization.

In Ethiopia, the TPLF (the core party in the victorious Ethiopian People's Revolutionary Democratic Front [EPRDF] coalition) engaged in a protracted civil war from its base in the northern Tigray region (Young, 1997; Hammond, 1999). It liberated significant territory withi Tigray in the 1980s, seized the regional capital Mekele in 1989, and had deep ties to the population during the armed struggle. The TPLF deployed political cadres with its military unit to insure discipline and organize regular self–criticism sessions known a*gimgema*.[9] Local councils known as *baito* ('peoples' council') worked under TPLF guidance to administer liberated zones. The *baito* provided a mechanism for top–down wartime governance and served to implement the TPLF's war policies and 'generate the maximum contribution to the movement's project'.[10] During the mid–1980s famine, the TPLF had the capacity and local legitimacy to organize a massive movement of the population from Tigray to TPLF–controlled camps in Sudan (Hendrie, 1991). The movement had its own very impressive humanitarian wing, the Relief Society of Tigray (REST), its own trading company, the Endowment Fund for the Rehabilitation of Tigray (EFFORT), and relationships with neighboring insurgents in Eritrea as well as a range of international actors and organizations.[11] As a result, the rebels began the transition in 1991 with not only a large and battle–hardened military but also cadres in every village in Tigray who were well integrated into a region–wide political network, and with experience in managing liberated territory and building relationships with the peasantry.

Similar patterns of military governance during wartime are seen in other cases of insurgent victory. In Uganda, the National Resistance Army established village–level National Resistance Councils, particularly in the war–torn Luwero triangle where most of the war was fought. The RPF occupied portions of northern Rwanda along the border with Uganda from 1990 to 1994 and many of its leaders had fought in Uganda's NRA (Reed, 1996). Kagame, the RPF leader, said 'At the beginning of the war we started with an army that we stole from Uganda,' indicating the debt the RPA owed to the Ugandan army (Misser, 1993, cited in Reno, 2011: 144–145). Liberated territory in Eritrea had highly organized systems of control by the EPLF, and many of the local mechanisms for mobilization continued to shape post–confict politics.[12]

Winning national liberation movements can draw upon considerable reservoirs of popular legitimacy and authority when they transform their organizations into political parties. 'We rule because we won' is a more credible and instantly recognizable claim to legitimacy than the more ambivalent claims of successfully forcing a negotiated settlement and winning subsequent post–conflict elections. In Ethiopia, for example, the EPRDF's early political mobilization benefite from the public's appreciation that the movement had succeeded in removing the brutal military dictatorship. The sacrifices made by martyrs during the liberation struggle in Eritrea or the defea of the genocidal forces by the Rwandan Patriotic Front similarly provided substantial initial endowments of legitimacy. These legacies of victory are different than parties that fought the old regime to a stalemate and then accepted a negotiated settlement. The FMLN in El Salvador, Renamo in Mozambique, or UNITA in Angola, for example, made appeals on the basis of their roles in forcing the old single–party regimes to open up and hold elections. Such appeals, however, may not resonate across a war–weary population in the same way as victory.

Rebel victory also alters the challenges of incorporating groups that were not part of the insurgent movement. The need for reconciliation among warring parties is central to many peace processes but does not arise in the same way following insurgent victory. In Ethiopia and Eritrea, for example, there was little need to reconcile with the defeated government, as most of the old leadership had fled into exile, its party disintegrated, and its military collapsed almost overnight The consolidation of power and the incorporation of constituencies that were not engaged in the armed struggle shape post–conflict politics after victory rather than the relationship with th old regime. Insurgent groups that negotiated their way into power necessarily made bargains along the way, while those that won unilateral victory, as in Uganda, Ethiopia, Eritrea, and Rwanda, came to power with fewer hindrances (Dorman, 2007).

The victorious EPRDF had to move beyond its base in northern Ethiopia to draw in the many populations of southern Ethiopia that had been less involved in the liberation struggle. It structured the transition around ethnically def ned parties and regions that allowed the original core of the party rooted in the armed struggle in Tigray to bring in new constituencies mobilized on the basis of ethnicity from the Oromo and southern region. Structuring politics around ethnicity allowed the TPLF to draw upon ethnic affinities along with wartime solidarity an ideology to position itself to lead in Tigray. This framework also provided an avenue to mobilize affiliated parties with at least putative claims to ethnic affinities, if not wartime solidarity (Keller 1995; 'Ethiopia: From Rebels to Rulers', 1991; 'Ethiopia: Majorities and Minorities', 1991).

Museveni, the leader of the victorious National Resistance Army, identified multi–party politics where parties typically mobilized on the basis of ethnicity as one of the culprits in the violence of the old order. He responded by institutionalizing 'no–party politics.' The early years of the transition were characterized by efforts to foster reconciliation and broad–based support for human rights. The NRM was most active in Buganda and recruited from the South while it engaged in more brutal tactics to impose its order in northern Uganda (specif cally Acholi), where previous regimes and their armies had been recruited (Brett, 1995).

While the victorious insurgent forces sought to reintegrate the rank–and–file soldiers of thei former antagonists, top officials fared differently. The EPRDF created a Special Prosecutor's Office in 1992 to hold trials of many of the old leaders (Tronvoll et al., 2008). In Rwanda, both the international community through the International Criminal Tribunal for Rwanda based in Arusha, Tanzania and the victorious RPF government held trials for top off cials. In addition, Rwanda organized a system of local judicial processes known ag*acaca* to manage lesser offenders. Transitional justice mechanisms in these cases may be seen as a victor's justice and serve the exigencies of authoritarian statebuilding rather than reconciliation (on Rwanda see Waldorf, 2006).

Demobilization after victory

The relationships among demobilization, security, and successful peace implementation have been central to scholarship on statebuilding (Berdal, 1996). Spoilers, security dilemmas, and the inability of warring parties to make credible commitments to demobilize often derail peace and sometimes reignite new cycles of violence. Stedman has stated: 'By signing a peace agreement, leaders put themselves at risk from adversaries who may take advantage of a settlement, from disgruntled followers who see peace as a betrayal of key values, and from excluded parties who seek either to alter the process or to destroy it' (1997: 5; see also Spear, 2002: 147). Many analysts regard third–party peacekeeping and security guarantees as essential. Walter, for example, is categorical on this point: 'If an outside state or international organization is not willing or able to provide such guarantees, the warring factions will reject a negotiated settlement and continue their war' (Walter, 1999: 139; see also Walter, 1997).

Demobilization after insurgent victory does not face the same security dilemmas or needs for third–partysecurity guarantees. Rivals to the winning army have been defeated and the rebel force's ability to manage threats has been demonstrated by its victory. The victorious insurgent force does not need a third party to overcome the security dilemmas among belligerent parties because its dominance was settled on the battlefield. Demobilization after victory follows a different set of imperatives. First, the winning army often wants to demobilize to reduce the expense of a large army and, by creating a smaller, often more professional army, shift resources toward economic reconstruction and development. Second, security sector reform may be used to incorporate new recruits from ethnic groups or regions that had not been engaged in the civil war. In Ethiopia, for example, the EPRDF military sought to decrease the number of soldiers from Tigray while recruiting more soldiers from southern Ethiopia so that the national army more closely refected national diversity.

The demobilization of Mengistu's defeated army in Ethiopia/Eritrea was not a matter of a negotiated agreement that needed external monitoring but rather related to budget resources and the welfare of ex–combatants (Quehl, 2002). The shattered military of the old regime in Ethiopia and Eritrea wanted to demobilize and the new regime saw threats from ex–combatants without livelihoods or community ties. The EPRDF recognized that keeping the ex–combatants in the army was too expensive and allowing them to drift away would result in large numbers of dislocated young men with weapons that would threaten domestic security. In addition, most of the soldiers had been conscripted, often forcibly, and were anxious to return home. Reintegrating them into communities therefore was imperative (Colletta et al., 1996a). The new regime set up the Commission for the Rehabilitation of Members of Former Army and Disabled War Veterans to manage the process. The Commission's goal was to contribute to security and stability by restricting the movement of ex–combatants rather than to manage the security dilemmas characteristic of security sector reform after a negotiated settlement. In the end 475,000 were reintegrated with some minimal assistance, with a total budget of $200 per demobilized soldier.[13]

The NRA in Uganda demobilized 33,000 soldiers, reducing the size of the military budget without putting the regime's stability at risk (Colletta and Ball, 1993). In Rwanda, some 60,000 individuals were demobilized from the ex–Forces Armées Rwandais (FAR, the pre–1994 government army) (Edmonds et al., 2009). The Eritrean Department of Reintegration for Demobilized Fighters demobilized some 48,000 fighters (about half of the force) in a move t shift resources to peacetime development priorities (Colletta et al., 1996a: 67). While demobilization and security sector reform are often seen as central to liberal peacemaking, these cases demonstrate that they can just as readily be subordinated to the demands of authoritarian statebuilding.

Another motivation for security sector reform following insurgent victory is to absorb units of the old regime's military into the new rebel–led army and to build a post–conflict army tha incorporates groups not active in the civil war. In Uganda, for example, the National Resistance Army absorbed large numbers of government soldiers as it took control over more and more territory (Mudoola, 1991; Kiyaga–Nsubufa, 2004). The EPRDF army also recruited additional members from southern Ethiopia at the same time as it was reintegrating some Tigrayan soldiers to civilian life in order to create a national army that better reflected the population at large. Some 20,000 to 30,000 EPRDF soldiers were demobilized in 1994 to make way for recruits from under-represented regions and populations (Colletta et al., 1996b: 28). The victorious RPF merged elements of the ex-FAR into what became the Rwandan Defence Force. Donors provided resources for the demobilization exercise but ended this support in 1997 after Rwanda invaded Congo (Takeuchi, 2011). Part of demobilization included participation in *ingando* camps that some claimed were re-education camps to disseminate pro-RPF ideology (Mgbako, 2005). While the victorious armies absorbed recruits from the losing forces and populations not engaged in the struggle, officers and key units such as intelligence and presidential guards remained firm in the hands of the ruling party.

Victorious insurgents may still have dangerous enemies. In Rwanda, many of the perpetrators of the genocide and large portions of the ex-Armed Forces of Rwanda fled across the border into Zaire (later the Democratic Republic of Congo). Kigali remained highly militarized and engaged in operations in eastern Congo after its victory in Rwanda. Eritrea also remained highly militarized with a sense of itself as vulnerable to the predatory intentions of its neighbors. In Uganda, after the NRA seized power in 1986, internal conflict persisted through 1991, leading to an expansion of military expenditures during the first five years 'post-victory.' Demobilization in Uganda did not begin until 1992. While the Eritrean Peoples Liberation Front (EPLF) demobilized in the mid-1990s, its command and control remained intact and had the ability to re-mobilize rapidly, as it did during its border war with Ethiopia (1998–2000).

International roles and the strong post-conflict state

As in other areas, the roles played by international actors are distinctly different in cases of insurgent victory than in cases of negotiated settlement. There is a considerable literature on the wisdom and efficacy of the international community imposing liberalism as a mechanism for statebuilding (Paris and Sisk, 2009; Campbell et al., 2011). While in some cases Barnett and Zürcher (2009) argue that the relationships between the international community and local actors result in a 'peacebuilding contract,' in cases of rebel victory the international community plays a decidedly secondary role. Statebuilding after insurgent victory, of course, is shaped by the international context in which it takes place. But the new leaders are able to negotiate with the external world from a position of autonomy rather than from a position where UN peacekeepers are already on the ground in their territory. Victorious insurgents relate to the international community in a manner similar to other weak but sovereign and autonomous states. Regimes controlled by ex-rebels look to the bilateral and multilateral donors for support but have less need for international peacekeeping or internationally sponsored post-conflict elections to validate their rule.

In Eritrea and Rwanda, the post-conflict governments had deep distrust of the international community. The EPLF had few supporters among the major powers or international organizations and prided itself on its autonomy. EPLF leader Isaias Afewerki said in his inaugural speech in 1993 to the Organization of African Unity that joining it 'was not spiritually gratifying' because it was a 'nominal organization that has failed to deliver on its pronounced goals and objectives' (AFP, 1993.). In Rwanda, the RPF continuously criticized the United Nations and the United States for their failure to stop the 1994 genocide and has accused France of complicity (Barnett, 2003). Kigali has been enormously successful in retaining international support even while intervening in eastern Congo, a process that Reyntjens (2011) labels the 'domestication of the world.' Rather than seeking some kind of accommodation with international interveners, victorious insurgents sometimes are able to stand in moral outrage against the establishment that did little to support them.

In some cases the winning party has specific needs for the international community, such a Eritrea's desire to have the United Nations deploy a mission to verify the referendum that led to the recognition of the new state's independence. Ethiopia welcomed international observers to its local elections in 1992 in order to project its legitimacy to the global community. The victorious leaders in these cases enjoyed favorable international treatment in the years after assuming power. In Washington, Museveni, Isaias, and Meles were regarded by the administration of President Bill Clinton as an 'impressive new generation of African leaders' (Rosenblum, 2002; Ottaway, 1999). A sense of guilt over the international community's failures in Rwanda led Clinton to make a special trip to Kigali to meet with genocide survivors and apologize (Powers, 2001).

Conclusions

Statebuilding after insurgent victory differs in key ways from statebuilding after negotiated settlement. As illustrated by the cases of Uganda, Eritrea, Ethiopia, and Rwanda, rebel movements that win civil wars are not constrained by peace treaties or by the interests of international interveners. They more often control the war-to-peace transition from a position of strength. The transformation of victorious insurgency to ruling party can build on the legacies of the war and often produce strong authoritarian parties. Victory rather than internationally sponsored post-conflict elections settles who will form the post-conflict government, and the initiative rests wit local rather than international actors. Post-confict politics is less focused on power-sharing and reconciliation and more on power consolidation and the expansion of the insurgency to incorporate groups that had not been part of the wartime front. Demobilization is part of post-conflict statebuilding in cases of victory as it is in cases of negotiated settlement. When rebels win the war, however, demobilization serves to reduce military expenditures and to make the new national army more representative of the entire state rather than a key element in managing security dilemmas during peace implementation. Without third-party leadership in negotiating the peace agreement, cases of rebel victory have much more limited roles for the international community.

Cases of statebuilding after rebels win the war indicate how the goals of liberal peacebuilding may be subordinated to statebuilding and the consolidation of strong authoritarian regimes. This dynamic is more clearly drawn in these cases of war termination by victory but is related to the larger dilemmas of stability and liberalization. Many analysts have pointed to the tensions between the international community's interests in stability and its interests in democratic elections, human rights, and independent civil society. Winning rebel movements engage in post-confict state-building by building on their wartime institutions and patterns of behavior to consolidate power, create authoritarian orders, and maintain stability. Uganda, Ethiopia, Eritrea, and Rwanda are therefore not exceptions but rather a set of cases that prioritize the stability side of the core statebuilding dilemma.

Notes

1 Sending (2011: 56) similarly argues that 'studies of peacebuilding would benef from a shift in analytical and empirical focus that does not a priori privilege the power and behavior of external actors.'
2 For an important account of peacebuilding after government victory in Sri Lanka see Goodhand et al. (2011).
3 On power-sharing see Hartzell and Hoddie (2007).
4 Paris and Sisk (2009). The image of the 'tight embrace' is from Suhrke (2009).
5 Lake (2010). On postconfict elections see Lyons (2005), Kovacs (2007), Manning (2008), and de Zeeuw (2007).

6 On Uganda see Kasfir (1998). On Ethiopia see Lyons (2010). On Rwanda see Reyntjens (2006)
7 Successful insurgents have a history of brutal and violent reactions against defectors. On the principal–agent models to understanding defection and discipline, see Gates and Nordås (2010).
8 Factionalism also characterized the Sudan People's Liberation Movement and the ZANU–ZAPU conflict during the liberation struggle in Zimbabwe
9 Similar structures existed within the EPLF during the civil war. See Pool (2001).
10 Aregawi Berhe (2009: 252). Aregawi was one of the founders of the TPLF.
11 The TPLF worked with a number of Scandinavian humanitarian organizations that provided relief supplies through the TPLF during the Ethiopian famine of the mid–1980s. See Prendergast and Duffield (1994).
12 Pool (2001). Connell (1993) provides a sympathetic account of EPLF–liberated territory.
13 While integration was relatively successful, ex–soldiers faced the same levels of poverty as the larger communities they joined. See Dercon and Ayalew (1998).
14 Donors raised concerns about indoctrination in EPRDF demobilization camps but the World Bank found little evidence. See Colletta et al. (1996a: 46).

References

AFP. (1993, June 28). *OAU summit opens to criticism from newest member Eritrea*.
AFP. (2011, June 7). *Rwandan president: 93 percent of the vote was not enough*.
Allison, M. E. (2010). The legacy of violence on post–civil war elections: The case of El Salvador. *Studies in Comparative International Development*, 45(1), 104–124.
Aregawi Berhe (2009). *A political history of the Tigray People's Liberation Front (1975–1991): Revolt, ideology, and mobilization in Ethiopia*. Los Angeles, CA: Tsehai.
Barnett, M. N. (2003). *Eyewitness to genocide: The United Nations and Rwanda*. Ithaca, NY: Cornell University Press.
Barnett, M., and Zürcher, C. (2009). The peacebuilder's contract: How external statebuilding reinforces weak statehood. In R. Paris and T. D. Sisk (Eds.),*The dilemmas of statebuilding: Confronting the contradictions of postwar peace operations*. London, UK: Routledge.
Berdal, M. R. (1996). *Disarmament and demobilisation after civil wars*. Adelphi Paper no. 303. London, UK: International Institute for Strategic Studies.
Brett, E. A. (1995). Neutralising the use of force in Uganda: The rôle of the military in politics. *Journal of Modern African Studies*, 33(1), 129–152.
Buckley, S. (1995, June 18). Ethiopia takes new ethnic tack: Deliberately divisive. *Washington Post*, A21.
Campbell, S., Chandler, D., and Sabaratnam, M. (Eds.). (2011). *A liberal peace? The problems and practices of peacebuilding*. London, UK: Zed.
Close, D. (2007). From guerrillas to government to opposition and back to government: The Sandinistas since 1979. In K. Deonandan, D. Close, and G. Prevost (Eds.), *From revolutionary movements to political parties: Cases from Latin America and Africa*. New York, NY: Palgrave/Macmillan.
Close, D., and Prevost, G. (2007). Transitioning from revolutionary movements to political parties and making the revolution 'stick'. In K. Deonandan, D. Close, and G. Prevost (Eds.), *From revolutionary movements to political parties: Cases from Latin America and Africa*. New York, NY: Palgrave/Macmillan.
Colletta, N. J., and Ball, N. (1993). War–to–peace transition in Uganda. *Finance and Development*, June. Washington, DC: The World Bank.
Colletta, N., Kostner, M., and Wiederhofer, I. (1996a).*The transition from war to peace in Sub-Saharan Africa*. Washington, DC: The World Bank Directions in Development.
Colletta, N. J., Kostner, M., Wiederfoer, I. (1996b). Case studies in the war–to–peace transition: The demobilization and reintegration of ex–combatants in Ethiopia, Namibia, and Uganda. Discussion Paper no. WDP331. Washington, DC: World Bank.
Connell, D. (1993). *Against all odds: A chronicle of the Eritrean Revolution*. Trenton, NJ: Red Sea Press.
Dercon, S., and Ayalew, D. (1998). Where have all the soldiers gone? Demobilization and reintegration in Ethiopia. *World Development*, 26(9), 1661–1675.
de Zeeuw, J. (Ed.). (2007).*From soldiers to politicians: Transforming rebel movements after civil war*. Boulder, CO: Lynne Rienner.
Dorman, S. R. (2007). Born powerful? Authoritarian politics in postliberation Eritrea and Zimbabwe. In K. Deonandan, D. Close, and G. Prevost (Eds.),*From revolutionary movements to political parties: Cases from Latin America and Africa*. New York, NY: Palgrave/Macmillan, pp. 157–179.

Edmonds, M., Mills, G., and McNamee, T. (2009). Disarmament, demobilization, and reintegration in the Great Lakes: The experience of Rwanda, Burundi, and the Democratic Republic of Congo. *African Security*, *2*(1), 29–58.
'Ethiopia: From rebels to rulers'. (1991, May 31). *Africa Confidential*, 1–3.
'Ethiopia: Majorities and minorities'. (1991, July 12). *Africa Confidential*, 1–2.
Gates, S., and Nordås, R. (2010). Recruitment and retention in rebel groups. Presented at the Annual Meeting of the American Political Science Association, Washington, DC, September 2–5.
Goodhand, J., Spencer, J., and Korf, B. (Eds.). (2011). *Conflict and peacebuilding in Sri Lanka: Caught in the peace trap?* London, UK: Routledge.
Hammond, J. (1999). *Fire from the ashes: A chronicle of the revolution in Tigray, Ethiopia*. Lawrenceville, NJ: Red Sea Press.
Hartzell, C. A., and Hoddie, M. (2007). *Crafting peace: Power-sharing institutions and the negotiated settlement of civil wars*. Pennsylvania State University Press, 2007.
Hendrie, B. (1991). The politics of repatriation: The Tigrayan refugee repatriation 1985–1987. *Journal of Refugee Studies*, *4*(2), 200–218.
Herbst, J. (2004). African militaries and rebellion: The political economy of threat and combat effectiveness. *Journal of Peace Research*, *41*(3), 357–369.
Huang, R. (2012). *The wartime origins of postwar democratization: Civil war, rebel governance, and political regimes*. PhD dissertation, Columbia University, New York, NY.
Huntington, S. P. (1968). *Political order in changing societies*. New Haven, CT: Yale University Press.
Huntington, S. P., and Moore, C. H. (Eds.). (1990). *Authoritarian politics in modern society: The dynamics of established one-party systems*. New York, NY: Basic Books.
International Crisis Group. (2001). *'Consensual democracy' in post-genocide Rwanda: Evaluating the March 2001 district elections*. Brussels, Belgium: ICG.
Iyob, R. (1997). The Eritrean experiment: A cautious pragmatism.*Journal of Modern African Studies*, *35*(4), 658.
Jarstad, A. K., and Sisk, T. D. (Eds.). (2008). *From war to democracy: Dilemmas of peacebuilding*. Cambridge, UK: Cambridge University Press.
Kasfir, N. (1991). The Ugandan elections of 1989: Power, populism, and democratization. In H. B. Hansen and M. Twaddle (Eds.), *Changing Uganda: The dilemmas of structural adjustment and revolutionary change*. London, UK: James Currey.
Kasfir, N. (1998). 'No party democracy' in Uganda. *Journal of Democracy*, *9*(2), 49–63.
Keller, E. J. (1995). Remaking the Ethiopian states. In I. W. Zartman (Ed.)*Collapsed states: The disintegration and restoration of legitimate authority*. Boulder, CO: Lynne Rienner, pp. 133–135.
Kiyaga-Nsubufa,J. (2004). Uganda: The politics of 'consolidation' under Museveni's regime, 1996–2003. In T. M. Ali and R. O. Matthews (Eds.), *Durable peace: Challenges for peacebuilding in Africa*. Toronto, Canada: University of Toronto Press.
Kovacs, M. S. (2007). *From rebellion to politics: The transformation of rebel groups to political parties in civil war peace processes*. Uppsala, Sweden: Department of Peace and Conflict Research, Uppsala University
Lake, D. A. (2010). Building legitimate states after civil wars. In C. Hartzell and M. Hoddie (Eds.), *Strengthening peace in post-civil war states: Transforming spoilers into stakeholders*. Chicago, IL: University of Chicago Press, 29–51.
LeBas, A. (2011). *From protest to parties: Party-building and democratization in Africa*. Oxford, UK: Oxford University Press.
Levitsky, S., and Way, L. A. (2010).*Competitive authoritarianism: Hybrid regimes after the Cold War*. Cambridge, UK: Cambridge University Press.
Lyons, T. (2005). *Demilitarizing politics: Elections on the uncertain road to peace*. Boulder, CO: Lynne Rienner.
Lyons, T. (2010). Ethiopian elections: Past and future.*International Journal of Ethiopian Studies*, *5*(1), summer.
Makki, F. (1996). Nationalism, state formation and the public sphere: Eritrea, 1991–1996.*Review of African Political Economy*, *23*(70), December.
Mampilly, Z. C. (2011). *Rebel rulers: Insurgent governance and civilian life during war*. Ithaca, NY: Cornell University Press.
Manning, C. (2008). *The making of democrats*. Basingstoke, UK: Palgrave Macmillan.
Mgbako, C. (2005). Ingando solidarity camps: Reconciliation and political indoctrination in post–genocide Rwanda. *Harvard Human Rights Journal*, *18*(205), 201–224.
Misser, F. (1993, July). Kagame speaks. *New African*, 17.
Mudoola, D. M. (1991). Institution building: The case of the NRM and the military in Uganda, 1986–1989. In H. B. Hansen and M. Twaddle (Eds.), *Changing Uganda: The dilemmas of structural adjustment and revolutionary change*. London, UK: James Currey.

Ottaway, M. (1999). *Africa's new leaders: Democracy or state reconstruction?* Washington, DC: Carnegie Endowment for International Peace.

Ottaway, M. (2002). Rebuilding state institutions in collapsed states. *Development and Change, 33*(5), 1001–1023.

Ottaway, M. (2003). Promoting democracy after conflict: The difficult choices. *International Studies Perspectives, 4*(3), 314–322.

Omara-Otunnu, A. (1992). The struggle for democracy in Uganda. *Journal of Modern African Studies, 30*(3), 443–446.

Paris, R., and Sisk, T. D. (Eds.). (2009). *The dilemmas of statebuilding: Confronting the contradictions of postwar peace operations.* London, UK: Routledge.

Pool, D. (2001). *From guerrillas to government: The Eritrean People's Liberation Front.* London, UK: James Currey.

Powers, S. (2001, September). Bystanders to genocide. *The Atlantic.* Available at: www.theatlantic.com

Prendergast, J., and Duffield, M. (1994). *Without troops and tanks: The emergency relief desk and the cross border operation in Eritrea and Tigray.* Trenton, NJ: Red Sea Press.

Quehl, H. (Ed.). (2002). *Living in wartimes – Living in post-wartimes.* Proceedings of an International Workshop on the Horn of Africa, held in Melsungen, Germany, January 29–31.

Reed, W. C. (1996). Exile, reform, and the rise of the Rwandan Patriotic Front. *Journal of Modern African Studies, 34*(3), 479–501.

Reno, W. (2011). *Warfare in independent Africa.* Cambridge, UK: Cambridge University Press.

Reyntjens, F. (2004). Rwanda, ten years on: From genocide to dictatorship. *African Affairs, 103*(April), 177–210.

Reyntjens, F. (2006). Post–1994 politics in Rwanda: Problematising 'liberation' and 'democratisation' *Third World Quarterly, 27*(6), 1103–1117.

Reyntjens, F. (2011). Constructing the truth, dealing with dissent, domesticating the world: Governance in post–genocide Rwanda. *African Affairs, 110*(438), 1–34.

Roeder, P. G., and Rothchild, D. (Eds.). (2005). *Sustainable peace: Power and democracy after civil wars.* Ithaca, NY: Cornell University Press.

Rosenblum, P. (2002). Irrational exuberance: The Clinton Administration in Africa. *Current History, 101*(655), 195–202.

Sending, O. J. (2011). The effects of peacebuilding: Sovereignty, patronage, and power. In S. Campbell, D. Chandler, and M. Sabaratnam (Eds.), *A liberal peace? The problems and practices of peacebuilding.* London, UK: Zed, p. 56.

Spear, J. (2002). Disarmament and demobilization. In S. J. Stedman, D. Rothchild, and E. M. Cousens (Eds.), *Ending civil wars: The implementation of peace agreements.* Boulder, CO: Lynne Rienner.

Stedman, S. J. (1997). Spoiler problems in peace processes. *International Security, 22*(5), Fall.

Stedman, S. J., Rothchild, D., and Cousens, E. M. (Eds.). (2002). *Ending civil wars: The implementation of peace agreements.* Boulder, CO: Lynne Rienner.

Suhrke, A. (2009). The dangers of a tight embrace: Externally assisted statebuilding in Afghanistan. In R. Paris and T. D. Sisk (Eds.), *The dilemmas of statebuilding: Confronting the contradictions of postwar peace operations.* London, UK: Routledge.

Takeuchi, S. (2011). *Gacaca and DDR: The disputable record of state-building in Rwanda.* Tokyo, Japan: Japan International Cooperation Agency Research Institute.

Toft, M. D. (2010a). *Securing the peace: The durable settlement of civil war.* Princeton, NJ: Princeton University Press.

Toft, M. D. (2010b). Ending civil wars: A case for rebel victory? *International Security, 34*(4), 7–36.

Tronvoll, K., Schaefer, C., and Aneme, G. A. (Eds.). (2008). *The Ethiopia, Red Terror trials: Transitional justice challenged.* London, UK: James Currey.

Waldorf, L. (2006). Mass justice for mass atrocity: Rethinking local justice as transitional justice. *Temple Law Review, 79*(1), 1–87.

Walter, B. F. (1997). The critical barrier to civil war settlement. *International Organization, 51*(3), Summer.

Walter, B. F. (1999). Designing transitions from civil war: Demobilization, democratization, and commitments to peace. *International Security, 24*(Summer), 139.

Weinstein, J. M. (2007). *Inside rebellion: The politics of insurgent violence.* New York, NY: Cambridge University Press.

Woldemariam, M. H. (2011). *When rebels collide: Factionalism and fragmentation in African insurgencies,* PhD dissertation, Princeton University, Princeton, NJ.

Young, J. (1997). *Peasant revolution in Ethiopia: The Tigray People's Liberation Front, 1975–1991.* New York, NY: Cambridge University Press.

27

POST-STATEBUILDING AND THE AUSTRALIAN EXPERIENCE IN TIMOR-LESTE AND SOLOMON ISLANDS

Julien Barbara[1]

This chapter considers Australia's divergent statebuilding experiences in East Timor and Solomon Islands. An important sponsor of formal interventions in both countries following periods of violent conflict, Australia's participation – under United Nations auspices in East Timor (Timor Leste) and a Pacific regional mandate in Solomon Islands – saw it become a leading practitione of the statebuilding paradigm.

As a major underwriter of statebuilding missions in East Timor and Solomon Islands, Australia's intervention set it on a new policy trajectory. Intervention through statebuilding changed the tenor of Australia's bilateral relationships with its two near neighbors, bringing Australia closer to key governance and security challenges facing each country. Australia assumed significant, long–term security and development obligations in each country. Intervention also raised expectations of institutional reform and the reconstitution of state–society relations in the subject states.

This chapter is interested in the issue of *post*–statebuilding. How do states reconstitute their bilateral relations after intervention? What inf uences the process of 'normalization,' whereby interventionary mandates are gradually rescinded in favor of orthodox modes of diplomatic, development, and security cooperation? What is the legacy of intervention and how does this impact on the quality of the post–interventionary relationship? These are important questions as the timeframe for state reconstruction has in practice proven much longer than the inter – ventionary appetite and mandate of statebuilders and subject communities. The basis on which statebuilders 'depart' will impact on the prospects for 'success' over the long term and the nature of the interventionary tail.

Australia's experience in East Timor and Solomon Islands provides interesting case studies in post–statebuilding. Compared to more prominent international interventions in Iraq and Afghanistan, the normalization process in each has been notable for its relative equanimity; a managed and negotiated process, conducted in the context of mutual expectations of long–term cooperation. Nevertheless, the demand and supply factors shaping the normalization process in each have been significantly different, leaving different post–statebuilding legacies. In East Timor a confident political elite enjoys development options from its burgeoning oil revenues, giving it greater room to dictate post–statebuilding relations. In Solomon Islands, continued state weakness and limited development prospects have resulted in weak demand for 'transition' with statebuilders themselves driving the normalization agenda.

The chapter considers how the significantly different context and statebuilding experience i each country have framed the policy imperatives and options for Australia and its post-statebuilding relationships, as the formal statebuilding missions draw to an end. The chapter concludes with a consideration of the challenges for statebuilders who have invested considerable resources to build viable states when the formal statebuilding mission ends but the process of state reconstruction is only partially complete.

The interventionary political cycle and the normalization of inter-state relations

The early 21st century has been notable for the emergence of the statebuilding paradigm as an extraordinary response to state failure. Beginning with Kosovo and East Timor, the period was notable for the proliferation of formally sanctioned statebuilding interventions operating under a variety of 'mandates' (East Timor, Kosovo, Iraq, Afghanistan). Characteristic of all has been the suspension of 'normal' forms of bilateral and multilateral engagement in favor of more intrusive intervention, deemed necessary to comprehensively reconstruct failed or fragile nation-states, consistent with western expectations of contemporary statehood. Intervention was justified because governance was deemed to have so completely broken down in subject states that 'normal' forms of engagement would be ineffective in restoring human security.

Formal statebuilding interventions have been notable for their ambition and the early enthusiasm of interveners. Mandates of varying legitimacy have vested interveners with comprehensive reform powers focused on security sector reconstruction, democratic governance, and market liberalization. In East Timor, UNTAET was granted broad sovereign powers to build a new state. In Iraq, the US-led coalition sought to build a liberal-democratic exemplar as a regional model.

Looking back one decade on, the degree to which international enthusiasm for ambitious intervention has waned is notable. Statebuilders have discovered the enormous complexities involved in state formation, the protracted timeframes for state reconstruction, the enormous resource implications accompanying what inevitably become long-term statebuilding obligations, and the limited prospects for 'success.'

Technocratically informed attempts to build modern institutions have foundered against the profound challenges in reconstructing state-society relations. Subject populations have proved surprisingly 'ungrateful' for interventionary effort. Anticipated peace dividends fail to materialize as a basis for state viability, requiring long-term international subsidization. Democratic elections have become sites of perverse political contestation and instability. Statebuilders have struggled to support effective nation-building as a necessary corollary to functional statebuilding.

Statebuilders have found it particularly diff cult to reconstruct polities as a basis for effective institution-building. As a response to political disorder, political stabilization has been a core but elusive measure of statebuilding success. Efforts to institutionalize political moderation through the introduction of Western-style democracy have foundered as political elites compete for influence. Rebuilt police and military institutions have become sites of political contestation. Prospects for the return of violent conflict to resolve political difference remain high (Collier 2010). Difficulties in brokering enduring political settlements have necessitated prolonged interventions as statebuilders need to remain to preserve uneasy peace.

Statebuilding interventions have been characterized by an *interventionary political cycle* in which the decades-long realities of comprehensive state reconstruction clash with the much shorter tolerance thresholds of statebuilders and subject governments and communities for the costs and strictures associated with the intervention. Political elites who are the beneficiaries of an intervention initially welcome the prospects for peace and development, accepting a loss of sovereignty as the price for future independence and stability. Statebuilders take this initial support for granted and embark upon ambitious state re-engineering programs. Slow progress in institutional reconstruction pushes out the timeframe for intervention and results in increasing frustration within subject communities. Faced with the prospect of protracted intervention, statebuilders look for opportunities to cut costs, reduce the burden of their statebuilding obligations, and transition support to less costly bilateral relationships.

The interventionary political cycle manifests in acute pressure for 'normalization' of relations between statebuilders and subject communities. But the process of normalization is itself complicated by the unfinished business of state reconstruction and the lingering obligations thi vests in statebuilders. The act of intervention forges 'special relationships' marked by new obligations. The cost of intervention leaves statebuilders anxious to protect their statebuilding investments through security and development guarantees and raises questions of dependency as core institutions remain partially built. Intervention itself results in new habits of engagement, with interveners becoming used to exercising considerable influence in support of preferred security and development policies. Intervention itself can create dependency and crowd out indigenous statebuilding efforts. Interveners and newly sovereign counterparts may find themselves with competing visions of the nation-state, complicating prospects for post-statebuilding cooperation.

Australian statebuilding in East Timor and Solomon Islands

Australia became a prominent statebuilding practitioner in the early 21st century with its central involvement in East Timor and Solomon Islands, and coalition participation in Iraq and Afghanistan. The emerging statebuilding paradigm aligned closely with Australia's national interests (Barbara, 2008a). In the case of its close neighbors, East Timor and Solomon Islands, it helped legitimate new forms of engagement in response to extraordinary security and development challenges: in East Timor, responding to the devastation that followed the 1999 independence referendum; in Solomon Islands, responding to the cost of prolonged civil confct in an already fragile small island state. As an important regional power in the south Pacific regio notable for the preponderance of fragile states in an 'arc of instability,' Australia has clear security and development obligations. Statebuilding, with its distinctive interventionary modalities, provided a new mechanism through which Australia hoped to better engage with the regional challenges of confict and fragility.

Australia's support for statebuilding in East Timor and Solomon Islands was framed by an acute awareness of the sovereign sensitivities implicit in such radically new forms of engagement. Intervention was only countenanced following strong representations from local leaders. Great store was placed on the securing of legitimate international mandates as a precondition for intervention – from the UN in the case of East Timor and from the Pacifc Islands Forum (PIF) supplemented by enabling legislation from the national parliament, the Facilitation of International Assistance Act, in the case of Solomon Islands. Successive Solomon Islands prime ministers pleaded for Australian intervention to halt the grinding conflict that began in 199 before eventual agreement to intervene in 2003.

In both cases, Australia could be described as a reluctant intervener, fully aware of the sovereign sensitivities and resource costs. In the case of East Timor, intervention marked a radical departure from Australia's decades-long policy regarding Indonesia's occupation and resulted in a major thawing of a key bilateral relationship with Indonesia. In the case of Solomon Islands, intervention played into regional criticisms of Australia as a pushy metropolitan power. Australia was also conscious that as one of the few developed regional nations, it would likely shoulder the burden of military and development support in any prolonged statebuilding mission.

The path to normalization in East Timor

The UN–led mission in East Timor is a 'critical exemplar of international contemporary statebuilding' (Leach and Kingsbury, 2012: 3). Invested in 1999 with a broad Security Council mandate, the United Nations Transitional Administration in East Timor (UNTAET) enjoyed full sovereign powers to support a comprehensive statebuilding programme and prepare the country for independence. UNTAET ran East Timor's indigenous security forces and the international peacekeeping mission.

Australia was a leading contributor to UNTAET, reflecting its regional obligations as a pros perous near–neighbor, its specific national interests stemming from East Timor's decolonization and the strong moral expectations from its own citizens to support East Timor following the egregious atrocities committed there. Australia led and was the major contributor to the multilateral peacekeeping force for East Timor (INTERFET), with 5,500 personnel, and a lead contributor to UNTAET's subsequent Peacekeeping Force and civilian police operations. It was also a key development partner through its own bilateral programs, which included significan immediate humanitarian assistance and subsequent, long–term development support through a signif cantly increased bilateral aid program (Australia's aid contribution to East Timor, administered by AusAID, was estimated at AU$235 million from 1999–2000 to 2003–2004; Australian National Audit Office (ANAO), 2003: 11) and sizable contributions to multilateral trust fund established by the international community. Australia has maintained its military and development support in various guises including through ongoing contributions to UN policing operations, support for the International Stabilisation Force (ISF) from 2006, and through a substantive bilateral development program.

Australia's support for the UN–led mission was recognized by Australian policy–makers as a major policy shift. Australia's prominent role in it meant that Australian policy–makers came to see the success of the statebuilding mission in East Timor as a measure of success for its own regional policy. UN leadership was a fundamental prerequisite for Australia's participation, giving Australia the diplomatic cover necessary for it to be able to provide substantive support. The UN mission also encouraged broad burden–sharing across the international community, allaying Australian fears it would be left carrying the burden of intervention.

UNTAET worked to a tight timeframe to return sovereignty to the East Timorese, recog – nizing Timorese expectations for a speedy transition and donor preferences to normalize support as quickly as practicable. UNTAET established a joint UN–Timorese Cabinet and began the process of constructing new military and police institutions and the full panoply of state institutions required to run a modern state. A transnational government was established following national elections in August 2001 with independence achieved in May 2002. Following independence, UN support was transferred to the United Nations Mission of Support to East Timor (UNMISET, May 2002–May 2005) and UNOTIL (May 2005–August 2006). Successive mandates reduced the UN's security sector and development footprints, reflecting optimisti judgments in progress made in statebuilding. 'By early 2006, Timor–Leste was widely seen as a UN success story' (Leach and Kingsbury, 2012: 3).

Normalization efforts proved premature. The outbreak of tensions between East Timor's police and military forces in April–May 2006 heralded a period of significant instability and highlighted the fragility of new institutions built on unstable socio–political foundations. The crisis required the revamping of international support through the UN Integrated Mission in Timor–Leste(UNMIT) in August 2006. UNMIT reinstituted the UN's peacekeeping mandate with an emphasis on security sector reform. Assassination attempts on President Ramos–Horta and Prime Minister Gusmão in early 2008 saw the return of Australian troops and the ISF (operating in parallel to but outside of a UN mandate), and underlined again the need for sustained international intervention to guarantee stability.

The 2006 crisis pointed to the long–term nature of the statebuilding project in East Timor and underscored the need for sustained international engagement. One decade on, the East Timorese state remains only partially built and the nation not fully cohered. Timorese administrative capacity remains weak, with state institutions bequeathed by the UN remaining fragile and dependent on international support. Notwithstanding East Timor's burgeoning petroleum revenues, broad–based economic development has not materialized to provide the much–anticipatedpeace dividend. While the country has enjoyed a period of political stability with Prime Minister Gusmão's premiership (Arnold, 2011), an enduring political settlement, capable of underpinning long–term peace and security, has not yet been struck. Significant fault lines remain within Timorese society over national identity and language.

Statebuilding since the 2006 crisis has occurred against a backdrop of increasing tension between Timorese leaders and statebuilders as the former lose confdence in the latter's capacity to manage an orderly normalization process. Challenges faced by donors in supporting the construction of viable institutions (see, for example, IEG World Bank, 2011) have underlined East Timorese concerns about a protracted interventionary tail and the self–serving nature of the intervention. Institution building in the security sector has been particularly fraught and, given the sector's central importance to long–term stability, has complicated prospects for an orderly UN withdrawal. Differences between the UN and East Timorese over police reform have become irreconcilable, leading the International Crisis Group (ICG) to recommend the UN's withdrawal from the sector (ICG, 2010). The UN's release of a draft development report in 2011, which was highly critical of the government's employment record, became a lightning rod for Timorese frustrations with the UN's continued presence (Murdoch, 2011). Gusmão has been highly critical of the self–serving nature of development assistance reflected in highly paid international advisers absorbing too much of East Timor's limited development budget. East Timor has sought to lessen Australia's dominance as a bilateral partner by courting bilateral relationships with China and other Southeast Asian nations, while recognizing the fundamental importance of the relationship (Babo–Soares, 2011).

Tensions have also centered on competing visions of the Timorese state and the national development model being sponsored by statebuilders. The statebuilding template in East Timor sought to institutionalize a neoliberal economic development model (Barbara, 2008b) but has failed to generate broad–based economic growth. Timorese leaders have become increasingly aggrieved that the country's sizable petroleum fund – US$6.9 billion in December 2010 (Ministry of Finance, 2011: 1) – has not been used more proactively to improve living standards. Gusmão's political ascendancy since 2008 has been secured in part by his determination to use Timor's petroleum revenues to construct a 'grand alliance' incorporating disparate social forces (NGOs, gangs, veterans, business) into a stable patronage network (Jones, 2010: 568). Under Gusmão, Parliament's approval of 'exceptional' government spending from the petroleum fund, in support of Timor's National Strategic Development Plan for 2011–2030, has raised concerns among the donor community that East Timor is straying from a 'good governance' statebuilding path. But it has also been seen to contribute to Timor's relative political stability since 2008 (Arnold, 2011: 218).

The ongoing nation–building process in East Timor has also complicated the country's relationship with its statebuilding partners. Despite the unifying impact of a decades–long resistance struggle, Timor is a nation not fully formed. Ethnic, social, and regional differences remain important sources of political instability. Statebuilders have been inevitably embroiled in the process of Timorese nation–building, reflected in an emerging nationalism. As Leach and Kingsbury (2012: 22–23) observe: 'In the years leading up to the 2012 elections, East Timorese political leaders expressed increasingly pointed observations that Timor–Leste was a sovereign state that no longer needed or desired a high level of external involvement in its internal affairs.' Nationalist tensions have been most apparent around perceived Australian obstructionism in the joint development of petroleum revenues from the Timor Sea and the apparent economically unviable option of petroleum processing on Timor itself.

It is against this backdrop that normalization is proceeding. UNMIT is scheduled to depart in December 2012, subject to the orderly conduct of national elections and formation of a new government, at the request of the East Timorese Government (United Nations Security Council, 2011). A transition planning and implementation mechanism overseen by a joint high–level steering group was established in 2010. The ISF has stated its intention to withdraw at around the same time, subject to conditions on the ground (Murdoch, 2010).

A key post–statebuilding challenge for Australia in East Timor centers on how to protect its not inconsiderable investments in good governance and security as a basis for long–term stability. The declining efficacy of the UN mission in East Timor as a basis for effective statebuilding ha seen Australia progressively shift the focus of its support toward orthodox bilateral and multilateral support mechanisms. This was exemplifed in Australia's decision to provide ISF troops under a bilateral agreement operating outside UNMIT's mandate following the 2006 violence, which reflected 'Australian government dissatisfaction with UN command structures in earlier missions' and 'a growing [Australian] commitment to direct roles in regional peacekeeping where Australian "security interests" were seen to be at stake' (Leach and Kingsbury, 2012: 4).

The Australian Government's Independent Review of its aid program (2011a) noted the importance of East Timor as a focus for Australian aid. Australia has progressively increased bilateral support (Australian Government, 2009, 2011b), with bilateral aid totaling some AU$130 million in 2011–12, and consolidated its bilateral military and police cooperation arrangements (Kingsbury, 2011). But the review notes that aid effectiveness in East Timor is constrained by poor governance and on this basis argues that there is a weak case for future expansion which will be dependent on the 'reform orientation' of Timorese governments (Australian Government, 2011a: 131). Responding to the review, the Australian Government (Commonwealth of Australia, 2011: 44) noted its 'deep interest in the future prospects of East Timor' and that the 'international community expects that Australia will play a leadership role in fostering stability and development.' It is committed to 'increase aid ... in sectors where we assess the development benefits are highest' (Commonwealth of Australia, 2011: 44)

The Independent Review's recommendation points to one of the key legacies arising from Australia's central role in statebuilding efforts in East Timor. Support for intervention gave rise to a 'special relationship' with substantive long–term security and development obligations. But the experience of the intervention has made East Timor a more sceptical and demanding partner, not averse to criticizing its development partners, including Australia. Timorese scepticism will make it more difficult for Australia to influence the direction of East Timor's development a security policies. Timorese assertiveness in the use of its petroleum revenues will diminish the relative significance of Australia's not insubstantial bilateral support. It is telling that, in 2010 East Timor's President Jose Ramos–Horta criticized the effectiveness of Australian support since 2000 for being 'all over the place' (Kelly and AAP, 2010), while recognizing the ongoing importance of the bilateral relationship. As East Timor enters a challenging period around the 2012 national elections, Australia finds itself with less traction on key governance and securit issues.

The path to normalization in Solomon Islands

The Regional Assistance Mission to Solomon Islands (RAMSI) arrived in Solomon Islands in July 2003 at the request of its government to help end the violent conflict that had beset th country since 1998 (Braithwaite et al., 2010). As a statebuilding mission, RAMSI is both an exemplar and an anomaly. As an exemplar, RAMSI came to embody the ambitious statebuilding aspirations of the period. Its principal objective was restoration of law and order through a police–led security operation, but it also came to take on a broad statebuilding role. RAMSI's three developmental 'pillars' sought to reconstruct core state institutions in the areas of law and justice (formal justice system and police administration), economic governance (treasury and finance) and the machinery of government (parliament, democratic elections, public service, accountability institutions). RAMSI's influence in Solomon Islands has derived from its scale, with funding o around AU$250 million per year (covering development and security), and the deployment of strategically placed 'in–line' advisers in key state institutions, which has allowed it to exercise administrative authority (Barbara, 2008a).

RAMSI's mandate was open–ended in the sense that its statebuilding objectives were recognized from the start as long–term. It is subject to regular review by the PIF to gauge its statebuilding progress. Solomon Islands' own Facilitation of International Assistance Act, which provides the legal basis for the RAMSI mission in Solomon Islands, must be renewed annually, providing an important check on RAMSI's activities. RAMSI's participating nations have consistently focused on the 'conditions–based' nature of any RAMSI draw–down (Foreign Relations Committee, 2009: 33).

Formally a Pacific regional mission of 14 countries, RAMSI is substantively an expression o Australian policy (Commonwealth of Australia, 2007: 11). Australia provides around 95 per cent of RAMSI's funding and many of the security and development personnel. The RAMSI Special Coordinator is an Australian diplomat. In developing RAMSI, Australian policy–makers were acutely aware of the signif cance of the intervention as a major shift in Australia's Pacif c policy and the long–term security and development obligations Australia's commitment entailed. RAMSI was deployed at the apogee of the statebuilding paradigm and arguably represented a distinctively antipodean version of the dominant statebuilding paradigm (Barbara, 2008a). Australian support for RAMSI was couched as a clear commitment to the Pacifc region and an aff rmation of Australia's special responsibilities as a regional power.

RAMSI has had mixed success as a statebuilding mission (Braithwaite et al., 2010; Barbara, 2008a). It was undoubtedly successful as a peacekeeping and stabilization mission; violent conflic was suppressed immediately and basic governance restored. Progressing long–term state recon–struction objectives has been more challenging. The quality of public administration has improved in key areas such as economic governance but 'rebuilt' state institutions remain dependent on RAMSI support. RAMSI has made an important contribution in the area of fiscal strengthenin and economic reform (Braithwaite et al., 2010: 136–137). But evidence of sustainable institution–building is patchy, with capacity gains fragile and dependent on continued adviser support (Independent Experts Team, 2011). Braithwaite et al. (2010: 153–164) argue that RAMSI has suffered from a rigid, state–centric approach to the post–conflict challenge in Solomon Islands while acknowledging concerns about 'mission creep' and that RAMSI has become more effective in adapting its support in the latter phases of its mission. Riots following the 2006 national elections required a heightened police response and underlined the deep social fragilities that have yet to be satisfactorily addressed (and were not part of RAMSI's mandate). Almost a decade after the intervention, RAMSI has arguably struggled to shift the focus of support from stabilization to development as a basis for its own departure.

RAMSI has been an anomaly for the way in which discussion of its mandate in Solomon Islands has not conformed to the political interventionary cycle described above. A decade after its arrival, there has been remarkably little pressure from Solomon Islanders for RAMSI's departure. Notwithstanding the crisis that occurred during the premiership of Manasseh Sogavare in 2006–2007, when the prime minister sought to harness nationalist sentiment to restrict RAMSI's influence, national debates have been supportive of a prolonged RAMSI presence. Fo example, Francis Fukuyama, following a visit in 2008, noted the absence of 'strong political pressures for a wholesale exit,' and that the 'sharing of responsibility for sovereign functions is largely accepted' (2008: 21). A parliamentary review of the Facilitation of International Assistance Act 2003 (Foreign Relations Committee, 2009) conducted by Solomon Islands' Foreign Affairs Committee largely affirmed in 2009 the focus of RAMSI's work and the basis of the engagement An annual People's Survey conducted by RAMSI has consistently reported very high levels of community support for RAMSI's continued intervention (ANU Enterprise, 2012). Public debate on RAMSI within Solomon Islands is notable for its supportive tone, with criticisms leveled at specif c aspects of the mission rather than the substantive principle of intervention. The RAMSI Special Coordinator has consistently sought to allay Solomon Islander concerns about a precipitous departure (RAMSI Public Affairs, 2011).

Muted pressure for normalization ref ects the distinctive context in which statebuilding in Solomon Islands is occurring. Here, Solomon Islands' fragile economy and limited development prospects loom large. Solomon Islands has a very narrow economic base with few sustainable economic development options (World Bank, 2010). Economic fragility has reinforced state weakness, with resource constraints severely limiting the capacity of the Solomon Islands state to deliver services to its citizens. Solomon Islands ranks second–lowest of all Pacific nations i the UN's Human Development Index. Economic growth has been significant since RAMSI' arrival but its reliance on unsustainable logging is a long–term problem (World Bank, 2010). As one of the most aid–dependent countries, Solomon Islanders recognize their dependency on donor support. This recognition arguably dampens national enthusiasm for the departure of RAMSI, which forms a significant part of total donor support to Solomon Islands

Whereas in East Timor indigenous frustration with the statebuilding ineffectiveness of interveners has been an important push factor for normalization, in Solomon Islands RAMSI's *relative* effectiveness has underpinned continued community support. Here, Solomon Islands' post–colonial history is instructive. Solomon Islands had independence thrust upon it in 1978 and its leaders have repeatedly acknowledged the country's unpreparedness for it. Colonial indifference meant that the independent state was incompletely built. To this day, the state has very little presence beyond the capital Honiara and arguably enjoys limited legitimacy outside it. For all its challenges, RAMSI has provided Solomon Islanders with one of the f rst examples of state effectiveness since the end of the colonial period and they are, understandably, reluctant to relinquish perceived improvements in order and governance. The People's Survey has consistently highlighted limited public confidence in the capacity of national and provincial governments in Solomon Islands to deliver core services and concerns about the prospect of RAMSI's departure.

Solomon Islands arguably suffers from a lack of political leadership tied to a coherent national development vision. A Westminster–style parliamentary democracy fused onto a pre–modern tribal system, Solomon Islands' post–colonial history has been notable for its political volatility.

National elections are characterized by high representative turnover, with some 50 per cent of incumbent MPs losing their seats in the 2010 elections. Political fragmentation is significant i Solomon Islands; there is no substantive party political system and the first−past−the−post electora system returns MPs with very small electoral bases. Political incentive structures are highly localized, based on 'big man' politics, making it difficult for the political system to articulate inclusive and collective 'national interests' as a basis for an agreed national development agenda. Former Solomon Islands Prime Minister Mamaloni reputedly described his country as a 'nation conceived but never born' and successive governments have struggled to articulate a compelling national vision capable of mobilizing broad−based support. Occasional opportunistic attempts to use nationalist sentiment to mobilize political support against RAMSI have been largely ineffectual. The 2011 People's Survey reports low levels of trust in national representatives. At the level of individual agency, Solomon Islands' peaceful colonial transition deprived it of a strong leadership cadre born from revolutionary resistance. In the absence of strong and strategic local leadership, RAMSI itself may be seen to fill a political void by underwriting a degree of politica order.

Without strong demand for normalization, the 'transition' debate in Solomon Islands has been notable for being supply−driven by interveners. Relative stability since 2006 has allowed donors to contemplate a 'gradual withdrawal' in favor of bilateral and multilateral programs (Allen, 2011: 1). Agreement of the SIG−RAMSI Partnership Framework in 2009, following the recom− mendations of the Forum RAMSI Review Task Force, set clear parameters for RAMSI activities and identified 'specific and ver able targets and indicative timeframes for their achievement' (Partnership Framework, 2009). Progress reports against Partnership commitments are given annually to the PIF, documenting institution−building developments and prospects for transition.

The Solomon Islands government's own engagement with the transition process can be characterized as reluctant and cautious. The Foreign Relations Committee review noted the then CNURA's Government Policy Statement which stipulated in 2008: 'When RAMSI completes the work it was requested to do, Forum leaders will meet to consider whether the Mission should eventually withdraw or set up a permanent military and police presence as police backup support service and continue to act as an avenue through which economic development assistance can be channelled' (2009: 211). There has been a rhetorical commitment to transition since the signature of the Partnership Framework but little in terms of specific action to progress arrangements. It was only in December 2011 that the Solomon Islands Cabinet endorsed a Cabinet paper setting out a process to determine 'the gradual and phased−out transition of RAMSI's work in Solomon Islands' (*The Island Sun*, 2011). The government's public pro− nouncements on transition have been most notable for the degree to which they have sought to allay public concerns that RAMSI will depart prematurely.

As in East Timor, Australia's normalization interests have centered on the consolidation of RAMSI's statebuilding gains to prevent the return of violence, while shifting support modalities to more sustainable forms of development and security cooperation over the long term. In Australia, the public debate on RAMSI's 'transition' has been framed by an awareness of the unf nished nature of the statebuilding project and Solomon Islands' long−term dependency on donor support. For example, Allen (2011) argues that Solomon Islands is entering a 'high−risk period for conflict . . . [which] means that an external "security guarantee" will need to be maintained' based on a recognition that '*acomplete* transition of Australian support from the very particular vehicle that is RAMSI isn't a credible option' (2011: 2; emphasis in original). Allen argues for the retention of RAMSI's security mandate because: 'Maintaining a credible security guarantee for Solomon Islands isn't something that can be done via regular bilateral aid and foreign relations' (2011: 14).

While RAMSI has constantly evolved since its inception in 2003 (Foreign Relations Committee, 2009), it is now entering a more significant and substantive 'transition' phase. Discussions have begun between the Solomon Islands Government and RAMSI about the timing and nature of transition. Central to these discussions has been the premise that RAMSI will not end abruptly but in a staged and appropriately calibrated manner. In the first instanc transition will center on the normalization of civilian support and development assistance, from mid-2013. Reports around Solomon Islands Cabinet's endorsement of RAMSI's transition noted that 'going forward, some selected [RAMSI] development programs in high priority areas can be redesigned and transitioned to AusAID ... as appropriate, but not in their current form. That also means that while current funding that comes under RAMSI will decrease funding for the same areas under bilateral donor partners will increase' (*The Island Sun*, 2011: 1). RAMSI will continue in a truncated form as a regional police mission with oversight from the PIF (Coppel, 2012).

The Australian government has signaled its commitment to provide substantive long-term development support through its bilateral Partnership for Development, and many of RAMSI's current institution-building programs will be transferred in some form to the bilateral program. However, as with East Timor, prospects for significant increases over the long term will remai dependent on the reform orientation of future governments. The Australian Government's Independent Review (2011a: 131) noted the 'aid program is critical for stability, but under current settings a large expansion would not be effective.' As with East Timor, responding to the Review, the Australian government affirmed its 'deep interest' in Solomon Islands and international community expectations that Australia would play a leadership role in future support (Commonwealth of Australia, 2011: 44).

Set against a backdrop of long-term donor dependency, the supply-driven nature of the transition dialogue raises questions about the prospects for effective normalization and a shift in donor support away from an *interventionary* model to an orthodox post-statebuilding *partnership* model based on bilateral and multilateral assistance. Fukuyama observed of Solomon Islands in 2008 that the predominant kinship basis for social relations provided an unstable foundation for the creation of a modern state, required for effective governance. He argued that because of this underlying reality, 'RAMSI is thus operating under rather fictional premises, namely, that at some point the country's capacity will improve across the board to the point that RAMSI can be withdrawn' (Fukuyama, 2008: 21). He proposed a long-term form of intervention based on a shared sovereignty model with the international community committing itself 'to playing key governance functions on a continuing basis' in select areas such as security, while supporting 'sequenced capacity-building on other well-defied areas where there is reasonable chance that the Solomon Islands government will be able to create self-sustaining institutions in some reasonable time frame' (Fukuyama, 2008: 21).

The transition debate in Solomon Islands underscores the difficulties faced by statebuilders i reconciling their long-term obligations arising from intervention with their appetite for providing intensive support over the long term. If, as Fukuyama suggests, RAMSI has been an important backstop to a profoundly weak state, normalization of international support risks removing key institutional supports underpinning state functionality in post-conflict Solomon Islands. The reluctance of Solomon Islands' political elites to engage robustly with the transition debate suggests that they recognize their country's dependence on donor support. Given the consistently high levels of public support for RAMSI in Solomon Islands, in the context of a donor-dependent fragile state, it is notable that interveners have taken the lead in trying to normalize relations, rather than build on the interventionary model introduced with RAMSI.

Post-statebuilding and the 'normalization' of relations

Formal intervention to rebuild failed states constitutes an extraordinary form of international engagement to address profound development and security problems in fragile or failed states. Australia's participation in statebuilding missions in East Timor and Solomon Islands constituted a significant departure from its prevailing regional policy, in recognition of the exceptional human security circumstances in each. The experience of intervention has had important implications for Australia's subsequent relationships with its near neighbors. It has cemented 'special relationships' with enduring obligations – in 2009, Australian support for East Timor and Solomon Islands accounted for 12 per cent of its overseas development assistance (Australian Government, 2011a: 129) – while introducing new sensitivities around sovereign encroachment.

International experience has shown that the timeframes for state reconstruction accompanying ambitious intervention are not aligned with international appetites for sustained engagement, nor for subject community tolerance for intervention. Supply and demand pressures for normalization quickly manifest, often in the form of overt violence, as in Iraq and Afghanistan. However, the process of normalization has proved fraught. Subject communities, keen to assume greater sovereign control, remain conscious of capacity limitations and state–society fragilities. Statebuilders are keen to scale down their interventionary obligations while remaining anxious about relinquishing power to protect their interventionary investments.

Different supply and demand pressures have shaped the process of normalization in East Timor and Solomon Islands. In East Timor, an assertive political elite with development options arising from its petroleum riches, coupled with mounting dissatisfaction with what was perceived to be an ineffectual statebuilding approach, resulted in strong normalization pressures. Australia has responded to Timorese demands by refocusing its bilateral support while trying to remain engaged with the long–term statebuilding process. In Solomon Islands, limited development prospects and dependency on donor support have required Australia, through RAMSI, to encourage 'transition' discussions as a basis for more sustainable engagement.

The interplay of these competing supply and demand pressures has in turn shaped the parameters of Australian post–statebuilding support. In East Timor, the intervention legacy for Australia is a substantial bilateral relationship and a more demanding bilateral partner. Australia's substantial bilateral program will not necessarily give it traction over the continuing statebuilding process in East Timor. In Solomon Islands, the interventionary legacy will be different. Normalization will also bequeath Australia a substantial bilateral relationship and expectations for significant long–term development support. But the supply–driven nature of the normalization process may result in weak national ownership of the transition and the normalized development partnership. In the context of continued high donor dependency in Solomon Islands, Australia, as a major donor partner, will be faced with the obligations of substantial support, without the interventionary legitimacy that came with RAMSI to infuence Solomon Islands security and development directions.

Note

1 The views in this chapter are the author's private views and do not reflect the views of the Austral an government.

References

Allen, M. (2011). Long–term engagement: The future of the Regional Assistance Mission to Solomon Islands. *Strategic Insights*, Australian Strategic Policy Institute, Canberra, March.

ANU Enterprise. (2012). *The People's Survey 2011*. Regional Assistance Mission to Solomon Islands, February. Available at: www.ramsi.org

Arnold, M. A. (2011). Timor–Leste in 2010. *Asian Survey, 51*(1), 215–220.
Australian Government. (2009). *Australia–Timor-Leste Country Strategy 2009 to 2014.* Available at: www.ausaid.gov.au./publications
Australian Government. (2011a). *Independent Review of Aid Effectiveness,* April. Available at: www.ausaid.gov.au/publications
Australian Government. (2011b). *Strategic Planning Agreement for Development between the Government of Timor-Leste and the Government of Australia,* November. Available at: www.ausaid.gov.au/publications
Australian National Audit Office (ANAO). (2003). *Aid to East Timor: Australian Agency for International Development.* Audit Report No. 20 2003–04, Performance Audit. Available at: www.anao.gov.au
Babo–Soares,D. (2011). The future of Timor–Leste's foreign policy. In Australian Strategic Policy Institute, *A reliable partner: Strengthening Australia–Timor-Leste Relations,* Special Report – Issue 39. Canberra, Australia: Australian Strategic Policy Institute.
Barbara, J. (2008a). Antipodean Statebuilding: The Regional Assistance Mission to Solomon Islands and Australian intervention in the South Pacific', *Journal of Intervention and Statebuilding, 2*(2), 123–149.
Barbara, J. (2008b). Rethinking neo–liberal state building: Building post–conflict development states. *Development in Practice, 18*(3), 307–317.
Braithwaite, J., Dinnen, S., Allen, M., Braithwaite, V., and Charlesworth, H. (2010). *Pillars and shadows: Statebuilding as peacebuilding in Solomon Islands.* Canberra, Australia: ANU E Press.
Collier, P. (2010). *Wars, guns & votes: Democracy in dangerous places.* London, UK: Vintage.
Commonwealth of Australia. (2007). *Australia's Aid Program in the Pacific: Joint Standing Committee on Foreign Affairs, Defence and Trade.* Canberra, Australia: Commonwealth of Australia.
Commonwealth of Australia. (2011). *An effective aid program for Australia: Making a real difference – Delivering real results.* Canberra, Australia: Commonwealth of Australia.
Coppel, N. (2012). *RAMSI set for significant change next year.* Interview with RAMSI Special Coordinator Nicholas Coppel, Radio Australia, 1 August. Available at: www.ramsi.org
Foreign Relations Committee. (2009). *Inquiry into the Facilitation of International Assistance Notice 2003 and RAMSI Intervention.* Committee Report No. 1, November. Available at: www.parliament.gov.sb
Fukuyama, F. (2008). *Statebuilding in the Solomon Islands,* 9 July, memo. Available at: www.sais–jhu.edu/faculty/fukuyama
IEG World Bank. (2011). Evaluation of World Bank Group Program, Timor–Leste Country Program Evaluation, 2000–2010. Available at: http://ieg.worldbankgroup.org
Independent Experts Team. (2011). *Annual Performance Report 2010: A Report on the Performance of the Regional Assistance Mission to the Solomon Islands.* Available at: www.ramsi.org
International Crisis Group (ICG). (2010). Timor–Leste: Time for the UN to step back. *Asia Briefing No. 116,* 15 December. Available at: www.crisisgroup.org
Island Sun, The. (2011, December 6). Cabinet endorses RAMSI's transition. Issue 1074.
Jones, L. (2010). (Post–)colonial statebuilding and state failure in East Timor: Bringing social confict back in. *Conflict, Security & Development, 10*(4), 547–575.
Kelly, J., and AAP. (2010, June 23). Australian aid all over the place, says East Timor President Jose Ramos–Horta. *The Australian.* Available at: www.theaustralian.com.au
Kingsbury, D. (2011). The ADF and Timor–Leste: Looking towards 2020. In Australian Strategic Policy Institute, *A reliable partner: Strengthening Australia–Timor-Leste Relations,* Special Report – Issue 39. Canberra, Australia: Australian Strategic Policy Institute.
Leach, M., and Kingsbury, D. (2012). Introduction: East Timorese politics in transition. In M. Leach and D. Kingsbury (Eds.), *The politics of Timor-Leste.* Ithaca, NY: Cornell Southeast Asia Program Publications.
Ministry of Finance. (2011). *Petroleum Fund Annual Report: Financial Year 2010.* National Directorate of the Petroleum Fund, Ministry of Finance, Democratic Republic of Timor–Leste, August.
Murdoch, L. (2010, November 4). ADF troops to leave East Timor in 2012. *The Age.* Available at: www.theage.com.au
Murdoch, L. (2011, January 3). East Timor leaders scathing about crucial UN report *Sydney Morning Herald.* Available at: www.smh.com.au
Partnership Framework between Solomon Islands Government and Regional Assistance Mission to Solomon Islands. (2009). Available at: www.ramsi.org
RAMSI Public Affairs. (2011). *RAMSI will still be here in 2013: Special Coordinator reassures Premiers.* Available at: www.ramsi.org/news/ramsi–will–still–be–here–in–2013–special–coordinator–reassures–premiers.html
United Nations Security Council. (2011). *Adoption by the Security Council at its 6487th meeting, on 24 February 2011,* Resolution 1969 (2011). New York, NY: United Nations.
World Bank, The. (2010). *Solomon Islands growth prospects: Constraints and policy priorities,* Discussion Note, October. Washington, DC: The World Bank.

28
STATEBUILDING IN PALESTINE
Caught between occupation, realpolitik, and the liberal peace

Mandy Turner

In 2013, it was the twentieth anniversary of the signing of the Declaration of Principles on Interim Self–GovernmentArrangements (otherwise known as the Oslo Accords). This, and subsequent agreements, led to the creation of the Palestinian Authority (PA) as an interim administration in the West Bank and Gaza Strip. But even with the assistance of billions of dollars of aid, the creation of a sovereign and independent Palestinian state was no closer. This chapter critically assesses the reasons for this. It takes as its starting point that the PA offers a unique case study of neoliberal quasi–statebuilding in the highly securitized context of the Israel–Palestine conflict, a the foundation of which is a process of colonization. It then proceeds to undertake three tasks through which the chapter is structured.

First, it analyzes the context for this quasi–statebuilding project – including Israel's colonization practices, US unconditional support for Israel, and the role of external actors and international aid. It argues that the PA's experience of statebuilding – or rather 'quasi'–statebuilding – has been framed by a situation of quasi–autonomy (negotiated with Israel) supplemented with a form of contingent autonomy (negotiated with the donors). Second, it critically reflects on two alternativ perspectives provided for the PA's role and reason for existence: the 'occupation subcontractor' thesis and the 'transitional client quasi–state' approach. It then goes on to assess two different explanations for why the PA failed to become a fully independent state: the 'facts on the ground' perspective that focuses on the external Oslo framework and the context of occupation, and the 'elite disunity' approach that focuses on internal Palestinian political rivalry. Third, it offers up the 'partners for peace' paradigm as the ideological discursive framework to explain how Israel has managed to dictate the terms of the peace settlement, why donors (outside of the US, who needed little persuading) and the UN largely accepted these diktats, and the context for Palestinian political elites to variously be manipulated, bought off, coopted, or frozen out of the peace negotiations as well as the intra–political struggles that this occasioned. The chapter concludes by arguing that the pursuit of statebuilding and national liberation in the occupied Palestinian territory (oPt) has been caught between occupation, realpolitik, and the liberal peace.

Quasi-statebuilding and contingent statebuilding in the oPt

In 1994, the PA was established as an interim administration in the West Bank and Gaza Strip by the Oslo Accords and subsequent agreements. Peace processes, as Jan Selby characterizes them, should largely be regarded as 'inter—elite political accommodations whose aim is often not so much "peace" as the reconfiguration of domestic hegemony and/or international legitimacy (Selby, 2011: 13). As applied to the Oslo Accords, the peace process in this context assisted the reconfiguration of Israel's image from one of occupier to one of peacemaker and a reconstitution of its international legitimacy at a time when images of its use of force during the first *intifada* (1987–1993) had done much to damage its reputation. The Accords also helped resurrect legitimacy for the Palestine Liberation Organization (PLO) after its support for Saddam Hussein's invasion of Kuwait instituted a backlash from Gulf and Western states; and it also helped to ensure dominance over political rivals in the oPt, particularly those leading the first *intifada*.

While both sets of elites gained from signing the Oslo Accords, the power asymmetries continued to be vast and this went unchallenged due to US unconditional support for Israel. The reasons for this support lie in a combination of what Ilan Pappe calls the 'strategic relationship' (Pappe, 2007) and what John Mearsheimer and Stephen Walt refer to as the 'Israel lobby' (Mearsheimer and Walt, 2006). These two factors ensure that if US presidents appear to be stepping off—message, they are quickly reminded of their ally's position by both US and Israeli politicians, as indicated in the 2011 spat between US President Barack Obama and Israeli Prime Minister Benjamin Netanyahu, over references to the 1967 borders – a disagreement that was rapidly resolved in Israel's favor (Mualem and Khoury, 2011).

After Oslo was negotiated and signed, the bilateral peace process, overseen by the US, was based on the principle that any change in the Palestinians' status depended entirely on Israel's consent. In this context, Israel was able to dictate the terms of 'peace.' Borders, Jewish settlements, the status of East Jerusalem, and the (re)settlement of Palestinian refugees were to be left to final status negotiations whereas international consensus up to that point had favored a complete Israeli withdrawal from Gaza and the West Bank (including East Jerusalem) and the right of Palestinians to an independent state in these areas (Hovdenak, 2009; Waage, 2005). In this context, therefore, the PA's experience of quasi—statebuilding was framed by a situation of quasi—autonomy (negotiated with Israel) supplemented with a form of contingent autonomy (negotiated with the donors). The PA's quasi—autonomy meant that it seemed more like a municipal authority than a prototype for a sovereign state. It was granted limited autonomy over the municipal affairs of the majority of the Palestinian people in the West Bank and Gaza (but not over the land) as Israel formally withdrew from Palestinian high—density population areas while continuing to control access to and from them (and making frequent incursions and arrest raids into them). Israel retained overall control over more than 70 per cent of the West Bank (Aronson, 2000) as well as retaining territorial rights which gave it control over key factors of production (including land, labor, water, and capital) and external borders. Furthermore, the oPt was still ruled by Israeli military law (Roy, 2007: 81).

Geographically, the oPt was divided into administrative parcels: in the West Bank into Area A (under PA civilian and security control), Area B (under PA civilian control and Israeli military control), and Area C (under Israeli control); in Hebron into H1 (akin to Area A) and H2 (akin to Area C); and in Gaza into Yellow and White Areas. As well as controlling borders, land, water, movement, and access, Israel also had control over key Palestinian statebuilding resources including fiscal revenue and trade as enshrined in the Paris Economic Protocol (PEP) (Khan e al., 2004: 5). This meant that Israel could withhold revenue transfers, which constituted two—thirds of the PA's revenue in 2010 (IMF, 2011), whenever it felt like it, which has been a particularly useful weapon used on frequent occasions.

Despite these obstacles and restrictions, the PA was to involve itself in the task of institution—building and creating a viable economy in preparation for statehood, with assistance from international donors, the aid from which has risen year on year from US$178.74m in 1993 to

US$2.519bn by 2010 (OECD database). The dominant overall framework for donor activities in the oPt was to 'support the peace process,' which largely meant adhering to Israel's security interests while at the same time supporting the PA – contradictory goals that pulled in opposite directions. The atypical structures, mandates, and roles created for the UN and the World Bank underlined the extreme degree of politicization of aid to the Palestinians (Le More, 2008). And yet, despite the highly securitized context, the Western donor policy framework (which has been the dominant one followed by the PA) was also guided by liberal peacebuilding assumptions. The usual coterie of Western peacebuilding practices were therefore promoted, including neoliberal policies of open markets, privatization, and fiscal restraint, and governance policie focused on enhancing instruments of state coercion, 'capacity building' and 'good governance' (Cooper et al., 2011). It is often assumed that the Palestinian case does not 'fit' as an example o liberal peacebuilding because of the occupation and the centrality of US support for Israel which, in effect, has allowed a 'victor's peace' to be imposed. However, it is the practice and interaction of these very factors – occupation, realpolitik, and liberal peacebuilding – that has framed the statebuilding experience for the Palestinians in the oPt. Palestinian political elites have variously had to decide whether and how to accept, adapt, or resist these practices (and this has varied during the time period since Oslo and between the different political parties).

Aid dependency and the complex aid coordination structures set up to monitor and support the PA meant that the quasi–autonomy it had to continually negotiate with Israel was supplemented with contingent sovereignty negotiated with the donors. While an astonishing number of donors and multilateral agencies have been involved in the oPt since Oslo – around 42 donor countries and 20 UN and other agencies – an 'aid politburo' made up of the US, the EU, the UN, and the World Bank has dominated (Brynen, quoted in Le More, 2008: 37). The World Bank was the leading multiparty actor in donor coordination: it dominated the key positions in nearly every committee and was the administrator of the multi–donor trust funds (Le More, 2008: 106–108). This ensured that, right from the start, the PA had a far more open economy than any of its Arab neighbors. The Palestinian Investment Law, for example, ensured that no restrictions were put on foreign ownership or the transfer of net profits. These structure and the PA's dependency on external actors meant that the IMF and World Bank could put pressure on the PA to restructure public investment through privatization (Hilal and Khan, 2004: 89–90) – particularly after the PA's bankruptcy in the wake of Israel's 2002 destructive military campaign, Operation Defensive Shield.

While these 'Oslo coordination structures' were initially conceived as bilateral between donors and the PA, they quickly became trilateral: involving donors, the PA, and Israel (Le More, 2008: 34). At f rst glance, these structures appear to offer an example of Krasner's concept of 'shared sovereignty' (Krasner, 2004), Harrison's concept of the 'governance state' (Harrison, 2004), or even a form of 'provisional statehood' (Bolton and Visoka, 2010) akin to that which initially existed in Kosovo after its declaration of independence in February 2008. And yet the inclusion of Israel (the other more powerful party to the conf ict and peace process) in this coordination structure was unprecedented. It meant that the two methods of control – that exercised by Israel and that exercised by the donors – became mutually constitutive.

In this context it is therefore hardly surprising that Palestinian national self–determination and independent statehood have remained elusive and the fragmentation of the Palestinian body politic has continued apace. Indeed, by 2012 the PA had shrunk both politically and geo–graphically: i.e., it was not representative (as its mandate had expired in 2010) and it covered only Palestinians resident in the West Bank (after the split with Gaza in June 2007, which thereafter was ruled by Hamas). There are, of course, different explanations for why the PA failed to become a fully independent state – two of the main ones are explored below.

The Palestinian Authority: subcontractor to the occupation or transitional quasi-state?

There are a number of perspectives about the role and rationale for the PA, two of which will be reviewed here. The first approach, here labeled the 'occupation subcontractor' thesis, posit that the PA was never designed to be a viable entity promoting and building Palestinian statehood. On the contrary, it was created to be a 'subcontractor' to Israel's occupation (Said, 1994, 2000; Roy, 2007; Gordon, 2008). Associated with the work of Edward Said, Sara Roy, Neve Gordon, and many others, the Oslo process was regarded as a capitulation to the needs and wants of Israel. Indeed, Said's response to the PLO signing the process was: 'it was a betrayal of our history and our people' (Said, 1994: xxxii). Agreeing with Said, Roy argued that the Oslo Accords allowed Israel to continue colonizing Palestinian land and were an extension of the 1967 Allon Plan and the 1978 Drobless Plan, both of which proposed a framework for Israeli colonial expansion, land annexation, and 'native' control (Roy, 2007: 324). For Roy, this meant that

> The Oslo process, therefore, did not represent the end of Israeli occupation but its continuation, albeit in a less direct form. The structural relationship between occupier and occupied, and the gross asymmetries in power that attend it, were not dismantled by the accords but reinforced and strengthened.
>
> *(Roy, 2007: 236)*

'Outsourcing' responsibility for the population to the PA was, argued Gordon (2008: 169), an 'ingenious idea' that allowed real power to be reorganized, sustained, and concealed.

The second perspective, here labeled the 'transitional client quasi–state' approach and associated with Jamil Hilal and Mushtaq Khan, focuses on the external limitations placed on Palestinian statebuilding (Hilal and Khan, 2004). While this looks similar to the fst perspective, there are important differences. First of all, this perspective characterizes the PA as an interim institution stuck in an indefinite transition period, not a 'subcontractor' to a different phase o Israel's occupation. And second, the main problem is considered to be located *within* the Oslo process and the PEP, which gave Israel control over key Palestinian statebuilding resources including f scal revenue and trade (Khan et al., 2004: 5). According to Khan et al. (2004: 47), 'Since Israel believed that it was unlikely that a sovereign Palestinian state would put the security of Israel at the top of its agenda, it insisted on controlling a range of rents that were critical for the survival of the emerging Palestinian state.' The Palestinian leadership, argued Khan, accepted the necessity of a temporary form of client status and compromises on sovereignty, yet this 'could only remain politically viable if the emerging state could provide the PA's internal constituency with substantial new economic opportunities' (Khan et al., 2004: 53). But Israel's policy of asymmetric containment, particularly restrictions on the movement of goods and people, meant that, despite an initial stable period between 1994 and 1999, the PA was likely to face economic stagnation and recurring political crises. Client status and asymmetric containment, argued Hilal and Khan (2004: 74–75), created contradictory conditions for state formation.

Khan et al. (2004: 16) also criticize the 'good governance' agenda of the 2002 Roadmap that was meant to recommit both parties to the peace process after the outbreak of the second intifada in September 2000 and Israel's 2002 military actions in the West Bank and Gaza. They argue that this agenda was deeply problematic not only because it was based on an abstract neoliberal model of how a democratic state is supposed to work, but because the direction of causation – that anti–corruption, democracy, and liberalization lead to economic prosperity – is highly questionable and contradicts the historical record of statebuilding. This, of course, applies to the whole donor statebuilding and peacebuilding discourse and implementation, but in the case of the PA this agenda was triply problematic: first, in that the Oslo process deliberately created anti democratic structures to push through a peace process that had substantial internal opposition; second, because Israel colluded in the corruption by agreeing to pay a part of the PA's money into unaudited accounts directly controlled by Yasser Arafat, chairman of the PLO and the firs president of the PA; and third, some of the PA's rent–seeking activities, such as trading monopolies, were created in an attempt to work around the constraints imposed by the PEP and Israel's closure regime (Hilal and Khan, 2004: 77–79). So if and when these examples of 'bad governance' were reduced or eradicated, argued Khan, the likely impact (in the context of no other change in the political–economic structure in which the PA operated) was not economic prosperity but 'deep de–development' (Khan, 2009).

The economic, geographic, and political restrictions on Palestinian statebuilding were such that there needed to be a swift move toward successful final status negotiations – an event tha did not transpire. What happened instead was the creation of what former Israeli prime minister, Ariel Sharon, referred to as more 'facts on the ground.' Under its 'matrix of control' (Halper, 2011) Israel's colonial practices of annexing land and settling its own population, and controlling the water resources of the West Bank, continued unabated (Messerschmidt, 2013). This meant that by 2012 the number of Israeli settlers in the West Bank (including East Jerusalem) had grown to 550,000 (Macintyre, 2012). This growth was made possible by the provision of generous Israeli state subsidies, the promise of military protection, and a substantial infrastructural support system. By 2007, the infrastructure for (and connecting) the settlements took up nearly 40 per cent of the West Bank (UNOCHA, 2007: 9). In Jerusalem the accelerated processes of colonization are also crystal clear when one observes the increase in restrictions on building permits, the increase in the number of demolition orders, the increase in the number of residency rights being revoked, and the increase in harassment of Palestinians by both settlers and the Israeli border police (UNOCHA, 2011; HRW, 2010). Meanwhile in Gaza, Israel has continuously extended the maritime restrictions and the 'buffer zone' which, by 2009, encompassed 30 to 40 per cent of Gaza's agricultural land and a significant number of water wells (Save the Children, 2009). Fro this perspective, one could conclude that the Oslo Accords have presided not over a peace process but over an acquisition process.[2] And it is this process of modern colonization through the creation of 'facts on the ground,' in which the tiny fragmented remnants of historic Palestine are being rapidly absorbed into an expanding Israeli state, that writers such as Ilan Pappe (2007, 2012) and Nur Musalha (2000) focus on as the reason for the failure of Palestinian self–determination and statehood.

For other writers, it is undeniable that the lack of sovereignty and Israel's occupation made the task of statebuilding more diff cult. But the way in which the PA developed was akin to other postcolonial states and this needs to be explained, argues Amal Jamal, by Palestinian politics itself. Jamal and Khalil Shikaki's analyses thus focus on internal competition for power and disunity among the Palestinian elite as the primary reason for the impasse in progress toward independence and statehood (Jamal, 2005; Shikaki, 2002). These divisions are categorized as being between an 'Old Guard' (i.e., the PLO exiles who returned in 1994 and took the main positions in the PA) and a 'Young Guard' (which has variously included local leaders who played key roles in the first *intifada*, Fateh Tamzin activists, and the Islamist opposition). Jamal argues that 'Elite disunity and factionalism in the Palestinian national movement since 1967 have impacted the patterns of political institutionalization and the chances of democratic Palestinian politics in general' (Jamal, 2005: xv). The return of the PLO exiles from Tunis did not break down the division between 'insiders' (leaders inside the oPt) and 'outsiders' (PLO returnees); and the latter's dominance in the governing structures has been regarded as one of the reasons for the widening disconnect between the PA and the population.

Jamal thus charts the centralization of power in the Office of the President, the developmen of neopatrimonial politics, the dominance of Fateh, the misuse of public money and corruption, and tensions between the secular elite and the Islamic elite, particularly Hamas. The fragmentation of the elite and the competition for power caused 'the Palestinian leadership to miss important opportunities to move towards independence in a sovereign Palestinian state' (Jamal, 2005: 177). According to Shikaki (2002), the power and legitimacy of the 'Old Guard' has been undermined by public anger at corruption, nepotism and the failure of the peace process. From this perspective, the Old Guard squandered this historic moment and thus the outbreak of the second intifada marked the shift in the balance of power toward the 'Young Guard' and the rise in popular support for the Islamic parties and violent resistance (Shikaki, 2002). The 'Old Guard' was also dependent on the presence and support of Arafat, thus his death in 2004 also contributed to its demise (although Arafat's successor, Mahmoud Abbas, was also part of the 'Old Guard'). Despite agreeing that there were major shortcomings in the Oslo framework, Jamal and Shikaki see the establishment of the PA as having offered real hope and space for statebuilding (Sayigh and Shikaki, 1999: 27–28; Jamal, 2005: 120–122).

International assistance toward the task of Palestinian statebuilding has been seen to be crucial in this regard, despite the problems created by bilateral relations between donors and PA departments, quangos, and NGOs, particularly rivalry for funds (Sayigh and Shikaki, 1999: 27–28; Jamal, 2005: 120–122). Within the 'elite disunity' approach, donors and international organizations are regarded as playing a supportive role through the provision of funds and foreign expertise. However, third-party actors also played a key role in the creation of a new discursive framework for peacebuilding in the oPt – here labeled as the 'partners for peace' discourse – that repackaged Israel's security discourse. The following section analyses this discourse and its impacts.

Promoting 'partners for peace'

The bilateral peace process, overseen by the United States, was based on the principle that any change in the Palestinians' status depended entirely on Israel's consent – and this was codified in the framework and structures instituted through the Oslo Accords. This granted Israel the defiing role in determining what constituted 'legitimate' and 'illegitimate' political practice for the PA (and Palestinians in general) and so helped to institute a more sophisticated form of Israel's longstanding policy of trying to gain control over, and manipulate, Palestinian political elites. Initially, after 1967, Israel had tried to control Palestinian municipalities; when this failed it introduced the Village Leagues in the late 1970s (Gordon, 2008: 96–115). And in the 1980s, in an attempt to undermine support for the PLO, Israel lent legitimacy and status to the Islamist movement, Hamas (Milton–Edwards, 1999: 151; Chehab, 2007: 20). After signing the Oslo Accords with the PLO, elite manipulation was repackaged – and 'rubberstamped' with international approval – as being about ensuring 'partners for peace.'

The phrase 'partners for peace' has become popular parlance in the context of the Israel–Palestine conflict. While it has been used by Palestinian leaders as well as by Israel and donors the ability to decide whether someone is or is not a 'partner for peace' and act on this decision is unequal. This phrase, therefore, made Israel's attempts to control Palestinian political elites seem innocuous. It also allowed donors to believe that funding and working with Palestinian elites regarded by Israel as being 'partners for peace' would assist their mission of supporting the peace process (Turner, 2011). In its application, this paradigm has variously meant Israel justifying cutting off revenue transfers to the PA, arresting and detaining democratically elected Palestinian politicians, extrajudicial executions, and military violence. It has also been used by donors to justify cutting off aid and supporting regime change. It has been, in effect, the discursive framework that has bound the two practices of control together and has given them common purpose.

While it is crucial to give due weight to the asymmetrical power relations between Israel and the Palestinians, it is also important to analyze the role of Palestinian political elites in adapting, co-opting, or rejecting the 'partners for peace' discursive framework. The concessions made by the 'Old Guard' in the signing of the Oslo Accords ensured opposition from other Palestinian resistance groups in the oPt.[3] Donors and UN agencies therefore put disproportionate effort – both financial and practical – into building up the PA's security services, including the construction of a massive covert operations programme by the CIA (Mahle, 2005). The primacy given to policing in the statebuilding (or rather, in this case, 'quasi-statebuilding') process meant that the West Bank and Gaza Strip had one policeman to every 75 civilians – one of the highest ratios in the world (Hilal and Khan, 2004: 84–85). Nevertheless, the PA (and thus the Old Guard) had to juggle contradictory roles – satisfy Israel and the United States on security issues, reward its own supporters, meet the needs of its population, and retain its position as leader of the Palestinian resistance. Command of the PA and the system of control instituted by the PA's security services gave Arafat and his supporters power over their Palestinian opponents (as well as over other sections of the Fateh movement) (Reinhart, 2006: 147). Arafat, in this regard, operated no differently to the majority of post-colonial rulers in trying to control/destroy his opponents and consolidate his rule, the main difference being that the PA was not in a post-colonial situation. Israel had the power to dictate which Palestinian elites were in favor and which were not. While it regarded Arafat as a 'partner for peace,' Israel assisted the PA in ensuring that mutually beneficial trading monopolies (beyond the control of the 'aid politburo') were institute and that these monopoly revenues, as well as official tax remittances, were transferred into Arafat' unaudited accounts (Hilal and Khan, 2004: 79–80). The collapse of the Camp David talks (July 2000) and the outbreak of the second *intifada* changed this.

Simultaneously with its 2002 military offensive (Operation Defensive Shield), Israel lobbied donors for a policy of regime change, which involved promoting reform of the PA in order to create an alternative leadership. Efraim Halevy, director of the Mossad at the time, claims it took only 10 weeks for Israel to persuade key donors to support regime change (Halevy, 2006: 209–215). In the aftermath of the September 11, 2001 attacks that destroyed the World Trade Center in New York, Israel was able to (re)frame its violence against the second intifada as an essential part of the wider US-led 'war on terror' (Baxter and Akbarzadeh, 2008: 150).

The Quartet (the EU, the US, the UN, and the Russian Federation) established in 2002 to restart the peace process pursued reform of the PA through the 'Roadmap,' which included (among other things) establishing an 'empowered' prime minister and a new Cabinet (La Guarda, 2002). That this was a sophisticated form of diluting Arafat's power and imposing a new leadership was not lost on some young Fateh activists, who suggested that the new post of prime minister be f lled by Hamid Karzai, the US-installed prime minister of post-invasion Afghanistan (ICG, 2002: 15).

Practices to institute regime change were used overtly again in the aftermath of the January 2006 Palestinian general election. The victory of Hamas, the Islamist party proscribed as a terrorist organization by the United States and the EU, indicated that the Palestinian people (when given a choice) voted for a party that rejected the Oslo Accords, advocated redistributive policies, and proposed breaking the control of Israel and the Quartet over the PA (Halpern, 2006a, 2006b). Nevertheless, the Quartet demanded that the new Hamas-led PA renounce violence, accept all previous agreements, and recognize Israel. But Hamas believed the result gave it a mandate to change the PA to reflect the needs of Palestinians in the post–Oslo era and to renegotiate previou agreements. Hamas's refusal to accede to the Quartet's demands led to the imposition of economic and political sanctions, enforced by the US Treasury using anti–terrorist legislation (ICG, 2006: 21–26). Alvaro de Soto, the UN Secretary–General's Special Envoy for the Middle East Peace Process, complained that the Quartet had 'set unattainable preconditions for dialogue,' and resigned soon afterwards (de Soto, 2007).

EU policy focused on developing a 'temporary international mechanism' to bypass Hamas and channel money through the Office of the President. Implemented for 'humanitarian purposes,' this reinstituted practices used by the PA under Arafat that the Roadmap reforms had been targeted to eradicate (Turner, 2009: 571–572). The United States resorted to cruder, more direct, methods of regime change – it poured millions of dollars into building up a presidential guard that could defeat Hamas (Rose, 2008), and it threatened the UN with loss of funding to keep it on board (Marsden, 2008: 202). Israel's response was to arrest 64 Hamas offials including cabinet members and parliamentarians (*The Independent*, 2006). Since 2006, the United States has used political and economic pressure to prevent a unity government that includes both Hamas and Fatah, while Israel has used the withholding of revenue transfers as an effective control strategy. At the elite level, therefore, there is little room for maneuverability – apart from the PA unilaterally disbanding itself – and so it is largely accepted that pressure will have to come from the grassroots.

Palestinians have experienced and negotiated over 60 years of dispossession and over 40 years of occupation in a variety of ways, including forms of resistance, collaboration, acquiescence, and migration – the usage of which has not necessarily been mutually exclusive. The everyday lives of Palestinians and their resistance strategies have been conditioned by the shifting geography and political economy of Israel's control and by the global neoliberal developmental consensus into which the PA emerged – regulated through the Oslo framework. Israel's initial strategy of 'partial integration' (1967 until early 1990s) was replaced by the pursuit of 'asymmetric containment' (early 1990s until the present day), which has ensured Israel's economic dominance and a poor developmental context for the oPt (Zagha and Zumlot, 2004). The Oslo Accords and the framework of quasi–autonomy entangled the PA in a web of control and created incentives for certain sections of the Palestinian elite to increasingly embrace neoliberal policies, which have accelerated inequality and poverty in the West Bank and increased the oPt's economic dependency on Israel. The application of liberal peacebuilding in the oPt needs to be understood in its context, particularly as part of a region–wide attempt to reconfigure Middl Eastern states, open them up and plug them into the global economy. For the Palestinians, though, in the context of their struggle for self–determination this has created a fundamental contradiction because, as Khalidi and Samour have argued, 'Crucially, the economic liberalization and new trade initiatives that have resulted are consonant with an agenda of political and economic normalization with Israel (the "New Middle East")' (Khalidi and Samour, 2011: 11).

By 2012, in the context of a moribund peace process, the creation of even more 'facts on the ground' by Israel, and the fragmentation of the PA between the West Bank and Gaza, a viable state for the Palestinians appears more remote than ever.

Conclusion

The agreements and beliefs institutionalized through the Oslo process created the framework for Palestinian statebuilding. But this was not a viable framework – largely because the three core underlying assumptions that have powered this process since 1993 were misguided. The fi st assumption was that Israel would eventually grant the Palestinians a state because it was in its interests to do so. Donors therefore considered it prudent to support Palestinian political elites that Israel endorsed as 'partners for peace' – the innocuous phrase used to justify a multitude of practices that have, at their extreme, included military violence and regime change. Similar methods of elite control are evident in other peacebuilding missions; however, in the context of the oPt, it granted Israel control over its negotiating partner – and legitimized this control. The second assumption was that the United States would act as an 'honest broker' rather than an unconditional supporter of Israel – something that the Palestine Papers, published by the Doha–based media group, al–Jazeera, in 2011, finally proved not to be the case (Swisher, 2011)

The third assumption was that successful Palestinian statebuilding required the transformation of the political economy of the oPt, regarded as having been distorted through clientelism (solved by 'good governance' initiatives) and barriers to private sector growth (solved by free market strategies). Not being plugged into the global economy was therefore regarded as a key source of the oPt's problems in addition to the structural realities of occupation and colonization. Unable to directly influence the 'external' environment (which could only be changed through the bilateral peace process), agencies such as the EU, the World Bank, and the UN focused on the PA's 'internal' environment. But rather than helping to enhance the developmental capacity of the PA, donors, transfixed by the neoliberal paradigm and a belief that this could underpin peace merely ensured, through their policies, that the 'asymmetric containment' imposed by Israel's colonial practices was enhanced.

The PA is a fascinating case study of statebuilding in a conflict–country context; it is a uniqu type of institution forged in the context of a highly politicized asymmetric conflict underpinne by naive donor assumptions about how to build peace between Israel and the Palestinians. It is clear that, whether the PA is regarded as a 'subcontractor' to Israel's occupation or a 'transitional client,' it has undertaken quasi–statebuilding tasks in a context framed by Israel's colonization practices. Without international aid and assistance the PA would not have survived, nor would it have been able to rebuild itself in 2002 and again after June 2007. But 20 years on from the signing of the Oslo Accords and the beginning of the Palestinian (quasi–)statehood experiment, the PA remains trapped in a web of quasi–autonomy (negotiated with Israel) and contingent autonomy (negotiated with the donors). Palestinian statebuilding and national liberation have thus been caught between occupation, realpolitik, and the liberal peace.

Acknowledgments

The research that informed this chapter was funded by grants from the Council for British Research in the Levant, the British Academy, and the Leverhulme Trust. The author would like to thank Neil Cooper, Tawfq Haddad, Michael Pugh, and Alaa' Tartir for comments made on an earlier version; however, any errors are the author's own.

Notes

1 The Quartet on the Middle East was established in 2002 to institute the 'Roadmap' (full title: 'A Performance–Based Roadmap to a Permanent Two–State Solution to the Israeli–Palestinian Confl') because of the escalating conflict and the breakdown of the Oslo peace process. It involves the UN, th US, the EU, and Russia.
2 I am grateful to Mike Pugh for this point.
3 This chapter uses the terms 'Old Guard' and 'New Guard'; however, the author heeds the International Crisis Group's caution about using them: that they fail to do justice to the complexities of the alliances and agendas (ICG, 2002: 2).

References

Aronson, G. (2000). *Recapitulating the redeployments: The Israel–PLO Interim Agreements*. Washington, DC: The Jerusalem Fund Information Brief 32.

Baxter, K., and Akbarzadeh, S. (2008). *US foreign policy in the Middle East: The roots of anti-Americanism*. London, UK: Routledge.

Bolton, G., and Visoka, G. (2010). *Recognising Kosovo's independence: Remedial succession or earned sovereignty*. South East European Studies Centre, St Anthony's College, University of Oxford, UK, Occasional Paper No. 11/10.

Chehab, Z. (2007). *Inside Hamas: The untold story of militants, martyrs and spies*, London, UK: IB Tauris.

Cooper, N., Turner, M., and Pugh, M. (2011). The end of history and the last liberal peacebuilder: A reply to Roland Paris. *Review of International Studies*, 37(3), 1995–2007.

de Soto, A. (2007). *End of mission report*. Available at: http://image.guardian.co.uk/sys-files/Guardian/documents/2007/06/12/DeSotoReport.pdf

Gordon, N. (2008). *Israel's occupation*. Berkeley, CA: University of California Press.

Halevy, E. (2006). *Man in the shadows: Inside the Middle East Crisis with a man who led the Mossad*. London, UK: St Martin's Press.

Halper, J. (2011). *The matrix of control*. Available at: www.mediamonitors.net/halper1.html

Halpern, O. (2006a, January 26). Document: Change and Reform Platform. *The Jerusalem Post*.

Halpern, O. (2006b, February 9). Hamas plans independent economy. *The Jerusalem Post*.

Harrison, G. (2004). *The World Bank and Africa: The construction of governance states*. London, UK: Routledge.

Hilal, J., and Khan, M. H. (2004). State formation under the PA: Potential outcomes and their viability. In M. H. Khan, G. Giacaman, and I. Amundsen (Eds.), *State formation in Palestine: Viability and governance during a social transformation*. Abingdon, UK: Routledge Curzon, pp. 64–119.

Hovdenak, A. (2009). Trading refugees for land and symbols: The Palestinian negotiation strategy in the Oslo Process. *Journal of Refugee Studies*, 22(1), 30–50.

HRW. (2010). *Separate and unequal: Israel's discriminatory treatment of the Palestinians in the Occupied Palestinian Territories*. New York, NY: Human Rights Watch.

ICG. (2002). *The meaning of Palestinian political reform*. Middle East Briefing. Brussels, Belgium: International Crisis Group, 12 November.

ICG. (2006). *Enter Hamas: The challenges of political integration*. Middle East Report No. 49. Brussels, Belgium: International Crisis Group, 18 January.

IMF. (2011). *Macroeconomic and Fiscal Framework for the West Bank and Gaza: Seventh review of progress*. Staff Report Meeting for the Ad Hoc Liaison Committee, Brussels, Belgium, April 13.

Independent, The (2006, June 29). Israeli forces arrest Hamas cabinet ministers. *The Independent* (London). Available at: www.independent.co.uk

Jamal, A. (2005). *The Palestinian National Movement: Politics of contention, 1967-2005*. Indianapolis, IN: University of Indianapolis.

Khalidi, R., and Samour, S. (2011). Neoliberalism as liberation: The Statehood Programme and the remaking of the Palestinian National Movement. *Journal of Palestine Studies*, XL(2), 6–25.

Khan, M. H. (2004). Evaluating the emerging Palestinian State: "Good governance" versus "transformation potential". In M. H. Khan, G. Giacaman, and I. Amundsen (Eds.), *State formation in Palestine: Viability and governance during a social transformation*. Abingdon, UK: Routledge Curzon, pp. 13–63.

Khan, M. H. (2009). Palestinian state formation since the signing of Oslo Accords. Unpublished background paper for the Palestinian National Human Development Report 2009, commissioned by UNDP/PAPP, Jerusalem.

Khan, M. H., Giacaman, G., and Amundsen, I. (Eds.). (2004). *State formation in Palestine: Viability and governance during a social transformation*. Abingdon, UK: Routledge Curzon.

Krasner, S. D. (2004). Shared sovereignty: New institutions for collapsing and failing states. *International Security*, 29(2), 85–120.

La Guarda, A. (2002, July 17). US wants Arafat 'kicked upstairs'. *Daily Telegraph*. Available at: www.telegraph.co.uk

Le More, A., (2008). *International assistance to the Palestinians after Oslo: Political guilt, wasted money*. London, UK: Routledge.

Macintyre, D. (2012). More than 350,000 Israeli settlers in West Bank for the first time. *The Independent*. 27 July. Available at www.independent.co.uk

Mahle, M. B. (2005). A political–security analysis of the failed Oslo process. *Middle East Policy*, XII(1), 79–96.

Marsden, L. (2008). *For God's sake: The Christian Right and US foreign policy*, London, UK: Zed Books.
Mearsheimer, J., and Walt, S. (2006, March 23). The Israel lobby. *London Review of Books*, 28(6).
Messerschmidt, C. (2013). Hydro–apartheid and water access in Israel/Palestine: Challenging the myth of water scarcity. In M. Turner and O. Shweiki (Eds.), *The Palestinian people and the political economy of development*. London, UK: Routledge.
Milton–Edwards, B. (1999).*Islamic politics in Palestine,*: London, UK: IB Tauris.
Mualem, M., and Khoury, J. (2011, May 23). Likud: Obama's AIPAC speech showed he listened to Netanyahu. *Haaretz*. Available at: www.haaretz.com
Musalha, N. (2000). *Imperial Israel and the Palestinians: The politics of expansion*. London, UK: Pluto Press.
Pappe, I. (2007). Clusters of history: US involvement in the Palestine question*Race and Class*, 48(3), 1–28.
Pappe, I. (2012). *The bureaucracy of evil: The history of the Israeli Occupation*. London, UK: Oneworld.
Reinhart, T. (2006). *The roadmap to nowhere: Israel/Palestine since 2003*. London, UK: Verso.
Rose, D. (2008, April). The Gaza bombshell. *Vanity Fair*.
Roy, S. (2007). *Failing peace: Gaza and the Israel–Palestine conflict*, London, UK: Pluto Press.
Said, E. (1994). *The politics of dispossession: The struggle for Palestinian self-determination*. New York, NY: Pantheon.
Said, E. (2000). *The end of the peace process: Oslo and after*. New York, NY: Pantheon.
Save the Children. (2009). *Gaza Buffer Zone fact sheet*. London, UK: Save the Children, October.
Sayigh, Y., and Shikaki, K. (1999). Strengthening Palestinian public institutions: Independent Task Force Report. Washington, DC: Council on Foreign Relations.
Selby, J. (2011). The political economy of peace processes. In M. Pugh, N. Cooper, and M. Turner (Eds.), *Whose peace? Critical perspectives on the political economy of peacebuilding*. Basingstoke, UK: Palgrave Macmillan, pp. 11–29.
Shikaki, K. (2002). Palestinians divided. *Foreign Affairs*, 81(1), 89–105.
Swisher, C. E. (2011). *The Palestine Papers: The end of the road?* London, UK: Hesperus.
Turner, M. (2009). The power of 'shock and awe': the Palestinian Authority and the road to reform. *International Peacekeeping*, 16(4), 562–577.
Turner, M. (2011). Creating 'partners for peace': The Palestinian Authority and the international statebuilding agenda. *Journal of Intervention and Statebuilding*, 5(1), 1–21.
UNOCHA. (2007). *The humanitarian impact on Palestinians of Israeli settlements and other infrastructure in the West Bank*. East Jerusalem, Israel: UNOCHA, July.
UNOCHA. (2011). *East Jerusalem: Key humanitarian concerns*. East Jerusalem, Israel: UNOCHA, March.
Waage, H. H. (2005). Norway's role in the Middle East peace talks: Between a strong state and a weak belligerent. *Journal of Palestine Studies*, 34(4), 6–24.
Zagha, A., and Zumlot, H. (2004). Israel and the Palestinian economy. In M. H. Khan (Ed.) with G. Giacaman and I. Amundsen, *State formation in Palestine: Viability and governance during a social transformation*. Abingdon, UK: Routledge Curzon, pp. 120–140.

29
EU POLICE MISSIONS

Giovanna Bono

Security and the rule of law are recognized as central to the success of international peacebuilding and statebuilding in fragile and post-conflict states. Introducing security and the rule of la in conflict zones or countries coming out of a conflict is understood as involving the reform building of the national armed forces, the police, judiciary and courts, including the strengthening of human rights, civil society, political parties, and parliamentary institutions. Security sector reform (SSR) policies toward fragile states are relatively new phenomena that have their origin in the transformation of UN peacekeeping practices in the late 1990s, with the development of the concept of 'peacebuilding' and the growth of UN involvement in running international administrations (Ahmed et al., 2007). The European Union (EU) – together with the United Nations (UN), North Atlantic Treaty Organization (NATO), and Organization for Security and Co-operation in Europe (OSCE) – is at present one of the leading international organizations undertaking SSR policies in fragile states (Spence and Fluri, 2008). In the immediate post-Cold War period, the European Commission had run training programs for police reform in the former communist countries of Eastern Europe and in Latin America, but in 2003 the nature of its engagement changed. With the development of the Common Security and Defence Policy (CSDP – formerly the European Security and Defence Policy, ESDP), the EU assumed the role of reforming police forces in conflict zones in its neighborhood and beyond by sending polic off cers through new command structures controlled by the European Council. In fact, under the ESDP from 2003 to 2011, the EU conducted 15 police missions in Asia, the Balkans, the Middle East, and sub-Saharan Africa.

Within EU circles, the issue of SSR gave rise to a protracted internal debate about how and whether EU security and development policies should become closely interlinked and the geographical scope of such engagements. For example, the British and Dutch governments, with the strong support of some NGOs, along with officials in NATO, favored mainstreaming SS activities across all EU areas of external policy-making. In other words, they advocated a stronger linkage between the activities undertaken by the European Commission in external affairs and the security and military activities of the European Union. By so doing, this collaboration called for a deeper commitment of the EU in international statebuilding practices.

This chapter has three aims: f rst, to provide a brief overview of EU police missions and to examine how they have been conceptualized by academics and policy-makers. I will argue that police missions are most commonly defined as an integral part of the EU peacebuilding effort and are described as having unique features because they are not driven by the pursuit of a specifi national interest; rather they are based on normative principles – the export of good governance, ownership, and accountability. Second, I will explain the challenges of implementation commonly identified as being located in the inability of the EU to put forward sufficient resources, the lack of coordination as well as the resistance of local actors. In the final section, will provide a critique of some aspects of this analysis.

The record of EU police missions and their conceptualizations

Since 2003, the EU has conducted 15 police missions under the CSDP – in Afghanistan, the Balkans (Bosnia, Kosovo, Former Republic of Macedonia), Middle East (Iraq, Palestine), and sub–SaharanAfrica (Democratic Republic of Congo (DRC), Guinea–Bissau, Sudan, and Somalia) and in Moldova. As Table 29.1 shows, the missions have been different in size and duration: the oldest mission has been that undertaken in Bosnia (the EUPM) and the largest mission that in Kosovo (the EULEX Kosovo, with over 1,900 police and other civilian officers deployed). Wit the exception of EULEX Kosovo, which officially has a mandate to take over some securit functions from the local authorities, all the other missions have been in an advisory role: they involve the deployment of EU police off cers to advise and train the local police. The missions also differ according to whether they were deployed prior to or during an ongoing armed coriêt or soon after a ceasefire was agreed. Some of the missions have worked closely with other international organizations, such as the UN, NATO, and the OSCE; others have worked more closely with missions undertaken by individual EU countries or an ad hoc coalition of the willing. Internally, in order to generate these EU police missions, the EU first set up new institution and a process to generate civilian capabilities: the Civilian Headline Goals and Action Plan for Civilian Aspects of Crisis Management. The Civilian Headline Goals, established in 2000, envisaged that EU member states were to commit to putting at the disposal of the EU 5,761 police, 631 rule of law experts, 562 civilian administrators and 4,988 civilian protection staff for EU civilian missions (Nowak, 2006; Jakobsen, 2006; Chivvis, 2010: 6–9).

The emerging conceptualization

Although the EU engagement in international police missions and other SSR activities, under the second pillar, began in 2003, it was only in 2006 that the European Commission and the European Council decided to work together on a conceptualization of their activities in this field as part o its 'civilian aspects of crisis management' and 'security sector reform,' which aim to contribute to bringing peace and democracy to conf ict zones or other countries in transition. Initially there were some differences in the approach taken by the European Council and the European Commission (EC). To simplify, the European Council provided a vision of its external activities in this area as more 'narrow in scope' because from its point of view such activities involved an intervention by an external actor or group of actors to strengthen, reform, restructure, or construct a branch of state activity that had a formal mandate to ensure the safety of the state and its citizens, such as the armed forces, paramilitary forces, intelligence services, and the police. The EC provided a wider definition of SSR. In its perspective, the SSR is not restricted to the bodies that provid security to citizens but rather focuses on the overall functioning of the public sector, as well as the strengthening of democracy, the rule of law, and the protection of human rights. It advocated that SSR should not purely involve the reform of 'security state institutions' but should also lead international actors to 'mainstream' security concerns in the development and economic programs that they run, including development cooperation; enlargement; the stabilization and association

Table 29.1 EU police missions, 2003–2011

ESDP mission name	Aims	Date mission agreed and current status	Strength	Country/Region
EUPM (EU Police Mission in BiH)	Monitor, mentor and inspect Bosnian police in order to establish sustainable policing arrangements under BiH ownership in accordance with best European and international practice.	1 January 2003; ongoing	440 police officer [1]	Bosnia–Herzegovina
EUPOL Proxima	Monitor, mentor, and advise the country's police, thus helping to fight organized crime as well as promoting European policing standards.	15 December 2003; ended 15 December 2005	200 police officer	FYROM
EUPOL Kinshasa	Monitor, mentor, and advise on the setting up and the initial running of an integrated police unit (IPU) in Kinshasa.	December 2004; ongoing	~30 police officer	DRC
EUSEC DR Congo	Provide advice and assistance for SSR in the DRC with the aim of contributing to a successful integration of the Congolese army.	2 May 2005; ongoing	8 advisors	Democratic Republic of Congo
EUJUST Lex	Providing training for (770) high– and mid–level officials in senior management and criminal investigation duties so as to improve the capacity of the Iraqi criminal justice system.	21 February 2005; ongoing	57 advisors on police, judicial, and criminal matters.	Iraq
AMIS EUcivil –military supporting action to the African Union in the Darfur region, Sudan.	Building AMIS's civilian policing capacity	18 July 2005; ongoing	16 police off cers, mil/19 operational and logistics experts	Darfur–Sudan in support of Africa Union
EU Border Assistance Mission at Rafah	Monitor, verify, and evaluate implementation by the Palestinian Authority of the Framework Security and Customs Agreements; contribute through monitoring to building up the Palestinian capacity in all aspects of border management of Rafah Crossing Point.	15 November 2005; ongoing	60 police and customs experts	Palestine

Table 29.1 Continued

ESDP mission name	Aims	Date mission agreed and current status	Strength	Country/ Region
EC Border Assistance Mission, Moldova	Prevent smuggling, trafficking, and customs fraud, by providing advice and training to improve the capacity of the Moldovan and Ukrainian border and customs service.	30 November 2005; ongoing	60 border police and customs officer	Moldova
EU Police Advisory Team in the Former Yugoslav Republic of Macedonia EUPAT	Support the development of an efficient and professional police service; monitoring implementation of police reform in the field, police–judiciary cooperation and professional standards/internal control; monitoring and mentoring the country's police on priority issues in the f eld of border police, public peace and order, the fight against corruption and organized crime.	15 December 2005; completed 30 November 2006	30 police advisors	Bosnia
EUPOL COPPS	Assist in the implementation of the Palestinian Civil Police Development Plan, advise and mentor senior members of the Palestinian Civil Police Development Plan, advise and mentor senior members of the Palestinian Civil Police and criminal justice system and coordinate EU assistance to Palestinian Civil Police.	1 January 2006; ongoing	33 police and civilian personnel	Palestine
EUPOL Afghanistan	Contribute to the establishment of sustainable and effective policing arrangements that will ensure appropriate interaction with the wider criminal justice system under Afghan ownership.	Mid–June 2007; ongoing	~248 international and 165 local staff	Afghanistan
EU SSR Guinea–Bissau	Advice and assistance on SSR in order to contribute to creating the conditions for the implementation of the National SSR Strategy by downsizing and restructuring the armed forces and the security forces.	12 February 2008; closed 30 December 2010	8 international staff and 16 local staff	Guinea– Bissau

Table 29.1 Continued

ESDP mission name	Aims	Date mission agreed and current status	Strength	Country/Region
EUPT Kosovo and later EULEX Kosovo	Support the Kosovo authorities in their efforts to build a sustainable and functional rule of law system.	16 February 2008; ongoing	~1,700 experts working in the police, judiciary, customs and correctional services	Kosovo
EUTM Somalia	Provide military training mission in order to contribute to strengthening the Transitional Federal Government (TFG) and the institutions of Somalia. The aim is to contribute to strengthening the Somali security services through the provision of specif c military training.	7 April 2010; ongoing	150 EU staff	Somalia

Note: 1 At the highest level of engagement. The number was then reduced.

process; the European Neighbourhood Policy; conflict and crisis management; democracy an human rights; etc. The EC in fact argued that in the past, it had already supported SSR−related activities in over 70 countries. As a result of this analysis, the Commission recommended the integration of SSR in Country and Regional Strategy Papers, Action Plans, and programming tools, prioritizing SSR under the new financial instruments . (Commission of the European Communities, 2006a, 2006b; Council of the European Union, 2006).

Indeed, some experts have conceptualized EU international police activities following this 'wide' definition (Law and Myshlovska, 2008: 27) and others have described the EU police mission as part of EU peacebuilding efforts. Some scholars suggest that, although 'peacebuilding' is not easy to def ne in the EU context − given that there is no legal definition in the EU treaties of this concept − peacebuilding should be understood as a 'framework term' of a number of sub−themes, which are part of the overall conf ict prevention strategy, to include crisis management and post−conflict stabilization (Blockmans et al., 2011: 19)Moreover, it is claimed that EU SSR policies are unique. David Spence (2011), for example, asserts that in the past Western efforts in undertaking SSR in developing countries were usually linked to the strategic interests of the donor countries, which wanted to influence the military system of developing nations along Western lines for traditional reasons of national prestige and cooperation with former colonies. As he puts it, 'Security enhancement has often been a short−term for maintenance in power of often disputable governments, corrupt leaders and fragile elites' (Spence, 2011: 198). The EU efforts in SSR are viewed as fundamentally different from those previous initiatives because, although the EU might have a self−interest in preventing instability, it is mainly driven by a desire to export its own norms.

As Spence explains, 'the normative role of the EU is rapidly becoming the most heartening feature of EU policy on SSR' (2011: 215). He claims that the EU undertakes SSR missions mainly for the good of the recipient countries; that there is no 'national interest' involved because

SSR 'epitomises a general commitment to "good governance"' and indeed its focus is 'good governance' rather than security as traditionally narrowly construed (Spence, 2011: 198, 216). From this perspective, SSR is an integral part of the 'human security concept' and of the 'whole security system of a given state.' The EU police missions thereby are understood to have broadly human-centeredaims rather than the state-centered aims of traditional security policy concerns. In practice this is done by focusing not only on reforming the army and the police but also on creating 'participatory reform processes'; by prioritizing 'local ownership'; by addressing the security challenges facing the population; by devising gender-sensitive policing; and by reforming the institutions of the state involved in the security domain. The EU police missions in Afghanistan and the DRC have been analyzed as having been based on these criteria (Gross, 2011; Martinelli, 2011).

The challenges of implementation

EU police missions have faced a number of challenges of implementation that seem to cut across all operations. First, the lack of sufficient qualified and readily available personnel and financ capabilities. Second, the problem of poor logistics and various challenges of coordination: here issues are regularly raised regarding the diff culties of coordination between EU member states engaged in a country on separately run missions; also between the EU police mission and other EU or UN or NATO military operations, as well as problems of cooperation between the European Commission and the European Council in deploying and implementing the mission (Chivvis, 2010: 24, 27, 39; Jakobsen, 2006; Freire et al., 2010: 44–46). Third, resistance from local actors: many commentators emphasize the problems of implementation due to resistance from local players who have been unwilling to adopt the 'good governance' agenda proposed by the EU (Gross, 2011; Martinelli, 2011).

Critical appraisal

Conceptualization

Academics and policy-makers who conceptualize EU police missions as part of a 'framework' or a 'spectrum of activities' that span conflict prevention, crisis management, and post-conflict stabilization neglect to take into account that there is a substantial difference as to whether an EU police mission is sent when a country is not experiencing armed conf ict, when an armed conf ict is raging, or when armed groups have agreed to a ceasefire that seems to be sustainable As argued in more detail below, when EU police missions have been deployed in a war-like scenario or when the peace was still highly contested – such as in Afghanistan, the Democratic Republic of Congo, Iraq, and Somalia – they have been part of a wider Western military engagement that could be conceptualized as a form of 'statebuilding' rather than 'peacebuilding.' This is because Western powers, either in a coalition of the willing or through UN operations, were involved in using coercive force to settle the conflict

In the academic literature, the definition of all kinds of recent external engagements as 'peacebuilding' has in fact been hotly contested and there have been various attempts to clearly define the distinction between the terms 'peacebuilding' and 'statebuilding.' For example, Paris and Sisk (2008: 1) define peacebuilding as 'post-conflict peacebuilding' and argue that state-building can be conceptualized as a subcomponent of peacebuilding. As they explain, 'statebuild-ing is a particular approach to peacebuilding, premised on the recognition that achieving security and development in societies emerging from civil wars partly depends on the existence of capable, autonomous and legitimate governmental institutions.' In contrast, Oliver Richmond argues that Paris and Sisk problematically combine the two concepts: that despite attempts at keeping them distinct, they conflate statebuilding with liberal peacebuilding and the latter is quite differen from 'peacebuilding.' As Richmond explains, 'rather than being focused on grassroots, human needs, civil society and sustainability emanating from the most marginalized and their problems . . . liberal peacebuilding focuses on institutions in liberal−democratic markets and rule of law modes' (Richmond, 2010: 169–170). To simplify complexity, it could be argued that one key difference between 'peacebuilding' and 'statebuilding' has to do with the extent to which Western governments allow for ownership processes from below and seek to achieve consent between external and local players (Richmond, 2007).

'Local ownership,' 'human rights,' and 'good governance'

What is the evidence that EU police missions have implemented the principle of 'local owner−ship,' prioritized human rights, and successfully exported 'good governance'? At present there has been no systematic comparative study of EU police missions across all geographical regions that assesses the implementation of the principle of 'local ownership' or the implementation of human rights. There has been one comparative study that has sought to evaluate all ESDP−type missions (military and civilian) in terms of effectiveness for short− and long−term crisis manage−ment (Asseburg and Kempin, 2009). Another study has brought together all the different insights from separate individual case studies and has demonstrated that at present there is no systematic evaluation built on a rigorous methodology (Freire et al., 2010: 40–41). There is thus insufficien evidence to suggest that the goal of local ownership has been achieved. On the contrary, in the cases of EUPM (Bosnia−Herzegovina), EUPOL Afghanistan, EUSEC COPPS (Palestine), and EULEX (Iraq), some argue that the missions were implemented with little regard for the needs of local citizens (Freire et al., 2010: 47; Merlingen and Ostrauskaite, 2008). A study that has analyzed the implementation of human rights in the case of the EU police missions in Afghanistan and Iraq has delivered a rather negative verdict (Van Genderen, 2010). Most of the analyses that have sought to address the issue of impact have been single case studies and some of them have been unable to overcome some of the diff culties in analyzing the complex interaction of local, regional, and international factors. Internally, within the EU and other international organizations, the emphasis has been to evaluate police missions through benchmarking methods that involve assessing how many police officers were trained, the disbursement of funds and the opinion poll of citizens' perception of the forces. These methods are limited in nature because they prevent a systemic analysis of impact on the local, regional, and international dynamics of conf ict and prospects for sustainable peace.

From the current literature, it appears that in some cases the missions did not achieve the objective of creating 'good governance.' This has been particularly the case when the missions were deployed on the territory of states that were in a war situation or in which a struggle for state power was still ongoing, as has been the case in Afghanistan, the DRC, Iraq, Somalia, and West Gaza. In all of these cases, the missions resulted, perhaps involuntarily, in direct financial training, and diplomatic support for particular factions that were struggling for state power despite clear evidence that these factions were not willing to use their control over sections of the local police forces to stop them from perpetrating human rights abuses, such as the practice of torture or indiscriminate arrest and killing of civilians. For example, in West Gaza, the EU, along with the United States, has been heavily involved in building the security sector of the government, ruled by Prime Minister Fayyad. As Sayigh (2011) has demonstrated, far from leading to a successful reform of the police, the international missions contributed to the emergence of authoritarianism. After five years of effort, the West Bank security forces lack a clear chain o command and unambiguous civilian control and are far from being coherent or autonomous from donors. Moreover, police officers and security agents employed by the Ministry of the Interior have not refrained from using torture, which in the period from January to September 2010 gave rise to 106 complaints. Indeed, the Palestinian Authority in West Gaza has been rather lax in prosecuting security officials for torture and ill−treatment of detainees. In Afghanistan, th EU and US efforts have been unsuccessful because Afghan police forces have continued, up to the present, to commit extensive human rights abuses (Harding, 2011; Koring, 2010).

Normative power Europe? The lack of a common political and security strategy

The argument that there is a unique feature to EU police missions because they are not driven by traditional state interests but rather by normative purpose underestimates the fact that EU external policy appears as ethical or normative precisely because of the internal inability to devise its own high−level consensus on collective external purpose, either as for the good of humanity or for itself. As an assessment of ESDP missions and operations points out:

> In many cases missions and operations have been initiated by one of the major EU member states. In itself that does not have to be a problem. But the case studies show that sometimes deployments are approved even when one or more member states have strong reservations or there is little enthusiasm outside the initiating state.
> *(Asseburg and Kempin, 2009: 153)*

It is this unique feature of EU external policy – its inability to develop internally a high level of consensus about external purpose – that has led to all kinds of policy and geographical concerns being added to the EU agenda for external action, without any well−thought−out strategy.

In fact, EU external policy is driven by the particularistic interests of some of the member states, or a grouping of them, and in some cases by those of external powers, particularly the United States (Zielonka, 2006: 52–141; Hyde−Price, 2008; Keukeleire, 2007). These groupings and external players seek to upload to the EU level their own concerns so as to obtain support for a redirection of EU external efforts toward specific regions of the world. Moreover, some o these players are so doing not for the good of humanity but rather to seek to assert control over post−colonialterritory or zones considered dangerous for their own internal security, albeit in a less geostrategic manner than in the past. A misguided military strategy for combating international terrorism has also shaped the decision to send EU police off cers to Afghanistan, as explained below. Clear evidence for these particularistic interests is the EU decision to launch a police mission to Guinea−Bissau, where the EU did not have any strong diplomatic engagement or geostrategic objective. The decision was driven by the concerns of the former colonial power, Portugal (Blocking, 2010: 3). A similar pattern was present in Iraq, where the United Kingdom, with the support of Denmark and the Netherlands, called for the establishment of EULEX Iraq in 2004 and 2005 in order to seek to reengage EU member states in the post−war reconstruction of the country after the disagreement over the invasion of Iraq that had occurred in 2003 (Steinberg, 2009: 125–127).

The idea that EU police missions should be deployed at all stages of a conflict is a highly problematic development. At times an EU police mission is sent to a conflict zone as a substitut for working out differences among EU member states about their vision of how to deal with the conflict. For example, in the case of the EU engagement in the DRC in 1999–2005, the EU did not have a common political strategy because Britain, along with the United States, was unwilling to put pressure on Rwanda to stop supporting various armed rebel movements that sought to conquer Congolese territory for economic and security reasons. France and Belgium took sides with L.-D. Kabila and later his son, Joseph Kabila, whose coming into power they helped legitimize by paying for the elections, even if he had been initially promoted to his presidential role in a less than democratic manner. Rather than seeking to find a common diplomatic stance toward the warring parties, the EU deployed the EU police missions, along with the disarmament and demobilization initiative (EUSEC DR Congo) and financed the elections, as a substitute for a common strategy, which could have, for example, put more pressure on Rwanda and Uganda to stop meddling in the affairs of the DRC. It was approximately fiv years later, in the 2009–2010 period, that such a strategy was adopted, with some success (Bono, 2011).

The same use of EU police missions, as a substitute for an alternative diplomatic approach, is evident in the case of the decision to send the EU police mission to Afghanistan – EUPOL Afghanistan – in mid-June 2007. The mission was, in fact, never meant to be purely about the training of Afghan police, or about peacebuilding, as Eva Gross has argued (2011). Rather, from the initial impetus in October 2006, some EU countries, as well as the US government, perceived the mission as a way to ensure that the EU put forward additional civilian resources for the newly devised military strategy, the 'popular centric' or 'comprehensive' approach. However, the EU police mission did not become operational until the end of March 2008 because of the unfolding of the war and reluctance on the part of EU member states to risk the lives of their police officer and civilians. Let us look at this in some detail.

Prior to 2007, the US government followed a military strategy that relied on air superiority, the deployment of special forces, and the buy-in of a number of warlords so as to stay clear of deep engagement in 'nation-building.' Following the 9/11 attack, by early October 2001 until the end of February 2002, the US government used air bombardments on a vast scale, dropping 18,000 bombs in less than five months, and left the fighting on the ground to be undertaken warlords of the Northern Alliance and a small group of US-led special forces. The US government, together with other Western powers, then sponsored the coming into power of Karzai and then executed the long-planned strategy to move the theater of war to Iraq. It thus sought to outsource its military commitment to the International Security Assistance Force (ISAF) and to undertake 'mop-up' military operations through, for example, Operation Enduring Freedom, with the aim to then quickly reduce its special forces in the region. The United States gave the EU and the UN the task to undertake statebuilding. The EU, in fact, made available a substantial share of the development aid for Afghanistan and led in aspects of the 'democratization' strategy, but it did so without questioning the overall political and security strategy pursued by the United States.

However, officials in Brussels and Washington totally misjudged the political and militar situation on the ground. Between 2003 and 2006, the Taliban – with the support of Pakistan Inter-ServiceIntelligence Agency and elements of al-Qaeda reorganized itself on a larger scale, partly because of the failure of Western nations, including the EU, to seek a diplomatic solution and the extensive impact that the reliance on air power had on the civilian population in the Pashtun-populated areas. Widespread military activities restarted in early 2006. Officials in Washington thus realized that they had to reengage the military in Afghanistan, and did so by basing their approach on 'winning the hearts and minds' of the local population – the population-centric or comprehensive approach – which focused on counter-insurgency (Tomsen, 2011: 634). This approach sought to bring together civil and military capabilities to win the war and was to be implemented through the Provincial Reconstruction Teams (PRTs), composed of a mixture of civilian and military personnel working closely with local and international NGOs (William, 2011: 103–108). This is one of the reasons why the British and US officials lobbie for the EU to send police officers to the PRTs as part of the mandate of EUPOL. But, as thei efforts were ongoing, the situation on the ground deteriorated and the first PRTs in the sout were caught in wide–scale fighting with the Taliban and al–Qaeda elements, for which they wer not prepared and that resulted in a high levels of civilian casualties. As Bird and Marshall (2011: 153–216) note, the British and US military strategy failed to take account of the extent of penetration and organization of the Taliban's network and the system of alliances that the Taliban had created with local leaders. Thus, as the British and US military strategy was faced with a highly organized resistance during autumn and winter of 2006, many EU countries opposed a quick deployment of EUPOL personnel. At the same time, evidence seems to suggest that although some EU diplomats advocated a more differentiated diplomatic strategy, which would have allowed negotiations to take place between certain sections of the Taliban and the Afghan leadership, there was insufficient consensus to push fully for this vision in high–level meeting with US officials. The deployment of EU police officers acted again as a substitute for a forwar looking diplomatic strategy.

Even in the Balkans, where the EU has been more willing to coordinate a range of external instruments to shape a post–conflict environment, the EU police missions became the subject of competing intra–EU, as well as EU–US, visions about the future of the region. As a result, despite more than nine years of engagement, the Bosnian police forces are yet to be fully autonomous. The EUPM mission did not suffer from a lack of resources or personnel and it undertook substantial efforts to train and reform the Bosnian police forces (Merlingen and Ostrauskaite, 2006: 52–78). However, by 2006, the EU involvement in Bosnia substantially increased because it took over the NATO–ledStabilisation Force (SFOR), which resulted in the launching of EUFOR Althea. In addition, High Representative Paddy Ashdown became double–hatted as the EU Special Representative, in preparation for the EU taking over additional responsibilities in the region. From 2006 to 2008, Ashdown politicized his control over the instrument of policing, which in turn led to controversy among EU ranks about the best way to move Bosnia–Herzegovina toward European integration and gave rise to locally organized resistance. Ashdown sought to put into question the fundamentals of the delicate ethno–political power–sharing device that was the result of the war and was embodied in the Dayton Agreement. He attempted to use the issue of police reform to abolish the Ministry of the Interior of Republika Srpska, and by so doing change the constitutional framework and put into question the territorial integrity of Republika Srpska while giving extra power to the Bosnian Muslim community. Since Ashdown did not have a strong political case, he was ultimately forced to back down and to adjust his position (Muehlmann, 2008).

Similarly, in the case of Kosovo, the EU launched its largest ever police mission and the challenges it faces in deploying the mission are mainly due to lack of coherent political strategy: they have to do with differences of opinion over the recognition of Kosovo as an independent state (Dijkstra, 2011). Some of the EU member states that have supported independence perceive the mission as a way to consolidate the take–over of the Kosovo Albanians of disputed territory – the North region and enclaves where the Kosovo Serbs are a majority – while some of those countries that had rejected independence (Cyprus, Romania, Spain, and Slovakia) backed a compromise (Bono, 2010).

Conclusions

EU police missions are an example of the growing role that the EU has assumed in international statebuilding practices. Although the official discourse, supported by some academics and polic analysts, defines EU police efforts as having unique features because of the EU commitment t the principle of 'local ownership,' human rights, and 'good governance,' there is at present insufficient evidence, across the full spectrum of missions, to substantiate this analysis

The description of EU police missions as an integral part of 'EU normative power' confuses the ideational aspects of EU external policy with the internal dynamics of power projection. This chapter has, in fact, suggested that EU police missions are an example of the way in which EU internal decision−making processes – an expression of its own internal culture – prevent it from developing its own strategic vision, which could facilitate the emergence of long−term policy for conflict resolution and the building of a sustainable peace in fragile states. At present, EU police missions are an example of how EU external policies represent the 'uploading' of concerns of some member states and the United States. This inability to work out its own interest, and articulate a clear strategic approach to conflict management, is one of the most important cause of the challenges of implementation that the EU has experienced in deploying EU police missions.

Acknowledgment

The research for this chapter was made possible thanks to a Marie Curie Intra−EU Fellowship obtained by the European Research Agency: Grant Agreement PIEF−GA−2009−252015, Project Acronym: EU peacebuilding.

References

Ahmed, S., Keating, P., and Solina, U. (2007). The United Nations and peacebuilding: Prospects and perils in international regime (trans)formation. *Cambridge Review of International Studies*, 20(1), 11–28.

Asseburg, M., and Kempin, R. (Eds.). (2009). *The EU as a strategic actor in the realm of security and defence? A systematic assessment of ESDP missions and operations.* SWP Research Paper. Berlin, Germany: German Institute for International and Security Affairs.

Bird, T., and Marshall, A. (2011). *Afghanistan: How the West lost its way.* New Haven, CT: Yale University Press.

Blocking, S. (2010). EU SSR Guinea−Bissau: Lessons identified. *European Security Review*, No. 52.

Blockmans, S., Wouters, J., and Ruys, T. (2011). *The European Union and peacebuilding: Policy and legal aspects.* The Hague, The Netherlands: T.M.C. Asser Press and University of Leuven.

Bono, G. (2010). Explaining the international administration's failures in the security and justice areas. In A. Hehir (Ed.), *Kosovo, intervention and statebuilding: The international community and the transition to independence.* London, UK: Routledge, pp. 132–148.

Bono, G. (2011). *The European Union 'peace-building' and 'statebuilding' policies in sub-Saharan Africa.* Paper presented at the 3rd Global Studies Conference, August 17–20, University of Porto, Porto, Portugal.

Chivvis, C. S. (2010). *EU civilian crisis management: The record so far.* Santa Monica, CA: RAND.

Commission of the European Communities. (2006a). Communication from the Commission to the Council and the European Parliament, *A Concept for European Community Support for Security Sector Reform*, May 24. Brussels, Belgium: European Commission.

Commission of the European Communities. (2006b). 'Commission Staff Working Document' Annex to the Communication from the Commission to the Council and the European Parliament, *A Concept for European Community Support for Security Sector Reform* (COM(2006) 253 final, SEC(2006), SEC(2006 658). Brussels, Belgium: European Commission.

Council of the European Union. (2006). *Draft EU Concept for Support of Disarmament, Demobilisation and Reintegration (DDR).* Brussels, Belgium: CEU.

Dijkstra, H. (2011). The planning and implementation of the rule of law mission of the European Union in Kosovo. *Journal of Intervention and Statebuilding*, 5(2), 193–210.

Freire, M. R., Lopes, P. D., Cavalcante, F., Gauster, M., Lucianetti, L. F., Pereira, P. S., et al. (2010). *Mapping research on European peace missions.* The Hague, The Netherlands: Netherlands Institute of International Relations 'Clingendael.'

Gross, E. (2011). The EU in Afghanistan: Peacebuilding in a conflict setting. In S. Blockmans, J. Wouters and T. Ruys, *The European Union and peacebuilding: Policy and legal aspects*. The Hague, The Netherlands: T.M.C. Asser Press and University of Leuven, pp. 295–308.

Harding, T. (2011, May 10). Charity accuses Afghan police of torture and child sex abuse. *The Daily Telegraph*, 14.

Hyde–Price, A. (2008). A 'tragic actor'? A realist perspective on 'ethical power Europe'.*International Affairs*, *84*(2), 29–44.

Jakobsen, P. V. (2006). The ESDP and civilian rapid reaction: Adding value is harder than expected.*European Security*, *15*(3), 299–321.

Keukeleire, S. (2007). *EU Core Groups: Specialisation and division of labour in EU foreign policy*. Leuven, Belgium: Faculty of Social Sciences of the University of Leuven.

Koring, P. (2010, March 12). U.S. report offers damning picture of human rights abuses in Afghanistan. *The Globe and Mail*, 4.

Law, D., and Myshlovska, O. (2008). The evolution of the concepts of security sector reform and security governance: The EU perspective. In D. Spence and P. Fluri (Eds.),*The European Union and security sector reform*. London, UK: John Harper, pp. 2–27.

Martinelli, M. (2011). Strengthening security, building peace: The EU in the Democratic Republic of Congo. In S. Blockmans, J. Wouters, and T. Ruys,*The European Union and peacebuilding: Policy and legal aspects*. The Hague, The Netherlands: T.M.C. Asser Press and University of Leuven, pp. 221–247.

Merlingen, M., and Ostrauskaite, R. (2006). *European Union peacebuilding and policing*. London, UK: Routledge.

Merlingen, M., and Ostrauskaite, R. (2008). The implementation of the ESDP: Issue and tentative generalizations. In M. Merlingen and R. Ostrauskaite (Eds.), *European security and defence policy: An implementation perspective*. London, UK: Routledge.

Muehlmann, T. C. (2008). Police restructuring in Bosnia–Herzegovina: Problems of internationally–led SSR. *Journal of Intervention and Statebuilding*, *2*(1), 1–22.

Nowak, A. (2006). Civilian crisis management within ESDP. In A. Nowak (Ed.),*Civilian crisis management the EU way*. Paris, France: Institute for Security Studies, pp. 15–36.

Paris, R., and Sisk, T. S. (2008). Understanding the contradictions of postwar statebuilding. In R. Paris and T. S. Sisk (Eds.), *The dilemmas of statebuilding: Confronting the contradictions of postwar peace operations*. London, UK: Routledge.

Richmond, O. P. (2007). *The transformation of peace*. Basingstoke, UK: Palgrave Macmillan.

Richmond, O. P. (2010). Between peacebuilding and statebuilding: Between social engineering and post–colonialism. *Civil Wars*, *12*(1–2), 167–175.

Sayigh, Y. (2011). *Policing the people, building the state: Authoritarian transformation in the West Bank and Gaza*. Washington, DC: Carnegie Middle East Center, Carnegie Endowment for International Peace.

Spence, D. (2011). The European Union and security sector reform. In S. Blockmans, J. Wouters, and T. Ruys, *The European Union and peacebuilding: Policy and legal aspects*. The Hague, The Netherlands: T.M.C. Asser Press and University of Leuven, pp. 196–217.

Spence, D., and Fluri, P. (Eds.) (2008). *The European Union and security sector reform*. London, UK: John Harper.

Steinberg, G. (2009). The European Union Integrated Rule of Law Mission for Iraq (EUJUST Lex). In M. Asseburg and R. Kempin (Eds.),*The EU as a strategic actor in the realm of security and defence? A systematic assessment of ESDP missions and operations*. SWP Research Paper. Berlin, Germany: German Institute for International and Security Affairs.

Tomsen, P. (2011). *The wars in Afghanistan*. New York, NY: Public Affairs.

Van Genderen, W. T. (2010). *Human rights challenges in EU civilian crisis management: The cases of EUPOL and EUJUST Lex*. Occasional Paper 84. Paris, France: EU Institute for Security Studies.

William, M. J. (2011). *The good war: NATO and the liberal conscience in Afghanistan*. New York, NY: Palgrave Macmillan.

Zielonka, J. (2006). *Europe as empire*. Oxford, UK: Oxford University Press.

30
EU STATEBUILDING THROUGH GOOD GOVERNANCE

Wil Hout

At the launch of the newly established European External Action Service, the service's Chief Operating Officer indicated that 'promoting human rights and good governance' would be 'th silver thread running through everything we do' (O'Sullivan, 2011: 7). 'Good governance' has been part of the vocabulary of the European Union since, roughly, the turn of the century.The term was adopted by the EU in the wake of more general attention for governance among international aid agencies. Following the World Bank, many donors embraced the idea that the quality of governance is an important determinant of the success of aid programs (see World Bank, 1998).

This chapter focuses on one specific aspect of the EU's development policy, namely its attention to fragile states. As is the case for many other international aid donors, the EU started to take an interest in state fragility as part of more general security considerations spurred by the terrorist attacks of '9/11.' The EU's High Representative for the Common Foreign and Security Policy, Javier Solana, included a concern with 'state failure' as a key security threat in the 2003 European Security Strategy (European Council, 2003a: 4). The EU's policy on fragile states, published roughly four years after the security strategy, emphasized a broader set of policy instruments that link development, humanitarian, military, and security aspects – referred to as a 'whole–of–EUapproach' (European Commission 2007a: 7). Within this framework, the governance dimension is emphasized – indeed, as is argued below, the EU defines fragile states largely in terms of weak governance structures – but the way in which the agenda regarding those fragile states is implemented has strong security overtones (Youngs, 2008: 435).

This chapter suggests that the EU's approach to governance in fragile states has a rather technocratic character, with a strong emphasis on public sector reform and the reconstruction of state capacities. This approach contrasts with the increasing awareness in the donor community of the political–economic dimensions of governance reforms. In particular, a major World Bank report on so–called 'low–income countries under stress' (LICUS) stressed already in 2005 the desirability of performing 'political economy and conflict analysis' when selecting and sequencin priorities for the rebuilding of fragile states (World Bank, 2005: 8). Similarly, the World Bank's Independent Evaluation Group (2006: 21) emphasized the need for 'commissioning and consuming' good political analysis regarding countries where the Bank is actively involved. Against the background of the lessons formulated by the World Bank, the EU's failure to incorporate political economy and conflict analysis is rather surprising

This chapter presents an analysis of recently adopted EU policies on fragile states. The next section contains a brief discussion of the EU's approach to (good) governance in the context of its development policy. The following section gives an overview of diverging interpretations of fragile states, and discusses the concept of fragile states as applied in the EU context. There then is provided an analysis of several Country Strategy Papers for fragile states in the context of European development assistance, and specifically of the way in which concerns regarding governance rehabilitation have entered these documents. The final section presents some conclusions.

The EU and (good) governance

The aid relationship between the European Union and partner developing countries is structured by the so-called Country Strategy Paper (CSP). The CSP contains the EU's medium-term strategy for the provision of development assistance on the basis of a country's official nationa policy priorities. The latter have usually been laid down in a Poverty Reduction Strategy Paper (PRSP), required for support from the World Bank and the IMF.

The first steps toward including a governance dimension in EU development assistance wer set in 2003. A communication drafted by the European Commission, as well as ensuing conclusions formulated by the European Council, stressed the centrality of proper governance arrangements to securing positive development outcomes. The Commission, which interpreted governance primarily in terms of rules and processes guiding interest articulation, resource management, and the exercise of power, argued that

> [the] way public functions are carried out, public resources are managed and public regulatory powers are exercised is the major issue to be addressed in that context. The real value of the concept of governance is that it provides a terminology that is more pragmatic than democracy, human rights, etc.
>
> *(European Commission, 2003: 3)*

The Commission and the Council agreed that good governance policies should not be 'one-size-fts-all,' but rather should recognize the distinction between 'effective partnerships' where conventional tools for governance reform would be feasible and 'difficult partnerships and post conflict situations' (fragile states) that would necessitate the adoption of more targeted approaches (European Commission, 2003: 18; European Council, 2003b: 4).

The 'European Consensus on Development,' adopted by the European Council, Parliament, and Commission in December 2005, is generally seen as a landmark in the EU's take on development assistance, as it signaled agreement among member states and Union institutions (Carbone, 2007: 55–56). The European Consensus contained a reaffirmation of the EU's orientation to governance: it emphasized the promotion of 'democracy, human rights, good governance and respect for international law, with special attention given to transparency and anti-corruption' (European Parliament, Council and Commission, 2006: C46/9).

As a follow-up to the European Consensus, the European Commission published a communication in which it announced a more 'incentive-based approach' to governance in the context of its most important development relationship, namely its partnership with the group of African, Caribbean, and Pacific (ACP) countries. The Commission introduced a 'governanc incentive tranche' as part of the 10th round of the European Development Fund (EDF), amounting to €2.7 billion, or roughly 12 per cent of the funds made available for the 2008–2013 period. The funds were distributed as 'additional financial support to countries adopting or read to commit themselves to a plan that contains ambitious, credible measures and reforms' (European Commission, 2006b: 10). In a similar vein, the European Neighbourhood and Partnership Instrument (ENPI) for the 2007–2010 period contained €50 million for a 'governance facility' (European Commission, 2008: 5). In order to monitor the state and progress of governance reform in partner countries, and allocate funds, the Commission established a 'governance profile consisting of indicators on aspects such as democratic governance, rule of law, control of corruption, government effectiveness, economic governance, and internal and external security (European Commission, 2006a: 13–29).

Fragile states

Fragile states: concepts and approaches

The term 'fragile states' has gained general currency since the adoption of the Paris Declaration on Aid Effectiveness in 2005 and gradually replaced concepts that were applied earlier, such as difficult partnerships, countries at risk, failing states, and low income countries under stress (World Bank, 2005: 1). The broad acceptance of the term has not, however, produced consensus as to its meaning. Cammack et al. (2006: 16–18) have distinguished three types of definition in the literature, as follows.

- Definitions emphasizing *state functions* understand fragile states in terms of the lack of capacity or will to contribute to the security and wellbeing of a country's citizens.
- Definitions focusing on *state outputs* see fragile states as the source of problems (including poverty, violent conflict, terrorism, refugees, organized crime, epidemic diseases, and environmental degradation), which may spread to neighboring countries or across a whole region.
- Definitions concentrating on the difficult *relationships with donors* see the cause of fragility in 'factors that have more to do with the relationship (e.g., a particular shared history) than with the nature of the state itself.'

On the basis of this distinction, the approach of international aid agencies to fragile states can be understood in relation to three objectives: the promotion of human security, basic needs, and peace by providing humanitarian aid and peacebuilding; the furthering of development and improvement of governance; and the provision of global security (Cammack et al., 2006: 25–26). Underlying this variety of objectives, some commentators have argued, is a focus on the inadequate functioning of the state, and most remedies consequently revolve around the strengthening of government institutions (see, for example, Van der Borgh, 2008).

Although there is a desire in the donor community to develop clear–cut models of state fragility and differentiate fragile from stable developing countries, several important caveats have been formulated with regard to the implementation of policies on fragile states. The Organisation for Economic Co–operation and Development's Development Assistance Committee (DAC) has pointed out that state fragility is not an either–or issue, but rather a 'spectrum . . . found in all but the most developed and institutionalised states' (Organisation for Economic Co–operation and Development, 2008: 12). The DAC argued that the understanding of fragility as a continuum instead of a single condition highlights the need for a political response to fragility and leads to a focus on resilience ('the ability to cope with changes in capacity, effectiveness, or legitimacy') rather than stability as the opposite of fragility: 'Resilience . . . derives from a combination of capacity and resources, effective institutions and legitimacy, all of which are underpinned by political processes that mediate state–society relations and expectations' (OECD, 2008: 12).

The emphasis on the political aspects of state fragility led to a call by the OECD and World Bank for context–specific action. The first of the 'Principles for good international engageme in fragile states and situations,' adopted by OECD countries in April 2007, emphasized the need to differentiate whether problems derive from a lack of capacity, political will, or legitimacy. Moreover, the principles point out that policies on fragile states need to be tailored to the dynamics of the countries concerned. In line with similar conclusions reached earlier by the World Bank, the OECD argued that it is crucially important to recognize whether countries are going through a phase of political transition, are in a situation of deteriorating or rather improving governance, or have become locked into a political impasse (World Bank, 2005: 13; OECD, 2008: 6). The World Bank, reflecting on its experience with the LICUS framework, emphasize that the implementation of institutional reform in fragile states should recognize local dynamics instead of adopting a one–size–fits–all approach

> In most fragile state contexts, developing technical suggestions for institutional reform is easy; managing the political process of reform is much more difficult. It is therefor important that institution–building initiatives avoid purely technocratic approaches, devoting considerable attention to the process of decision–making and implementation, and to well–designed participation and widespread communication of reform initiatives.
> *(World Bank, 2005: 5)*

The EU and fragile states

The European Security Strategy, adopted in 2003, included 'state failure' as a key threat, which could be a threat in itself as well as a possible contributing factor to other types of threat. State failure was seen as a policy challenge, because

> Bad governance – corruption, abuse of power, weak institutions and lack of account–ability – and civil conflict corrode States from within . . Collapse of the State can be associated with obvious threats, such as organised crime or terrorism. State failure is an alarming phenomenon, that undermines global governance, and adds to regional instability.
> *(European Council, 2003a: 4)*

The strategy argued that the European Union should apply a variety of instruments in its response to impending or actual state failure, ranging from military force to diplomatic engagement, trade, development aid, and humanitarian assistance. In relation to developing countries, the strategy argued that 'Security is the first condition for development' (European Council, 2003a: 13). Further to this, the European Consensus on Development called for a 'comprehensive prevention approach to state fragility, conflict, natural disasters and other types of crises' (European Parliament, Council and Commission, 2006: C46/14).

European Council conclusions of November 2007 understood state fragility in reference to

> weak or failing structures and to situations where the social contract is broken due to the State's incapacity or unwillingness to deal with its basic functions, meet its obligations and responsibilities regarding the rule of law, protection of human rights and fundamental freedoms, security and safety of its population, poverty reduction, service delivery, the transparent and equitable management of resources and access to power.
> *(European Council, 2007: 2)*

An earlier communication issued by the European Commission referred to fragility as a feature of low- and middle-income countries that are faced with structural weaknesses of the economy, and are vulnerable to crises, external shocks, epidemics, drug trafficking, natural disasters, environmental degradation, and endangered cultural diversity. Governance deficits, however, were see as the main cause of state fragility: 'Fragility is often triggered by governance shortcomings and failures, in form of lack of political legitimacy compounded by very limited institutional capacities linked to poverty' (European Commission, 2007c: 8).

In order to start addressing the issue of state fragility at the level of EU development policy, the Council requested the Commission to 'test' the EU response in several cases. Burundi, Sierra Leone, Guinea Bissau, Haiti, Timor-Leste, and Yemen were selected as pilot countries for this purpose (European Commission, 2010), and the experience in these countries was supposed to feed into an *Action Plan for Situations of Fragility and Conflict*, which was expected to result in a more comprehensive approach at the level of the EU. At the time of writing, however, the preparation of the action plan had stalled, as the European External Action Service appeared to have little direct interest in taking forward the fragile state agenda (Castillejo, 2011: 169).[3]

Analysis of EU Country Strategy Papers

This section contains an analysis of governance-oriented responses in the six 'pilot' countries selected by the European Commission. The analysis is performed on the basis of the CSPs that were concluded by the Commission and the countries concerned in the context of the Development Cooperation Instrument (for non-ACP countries) or the 10th European Development Fund (for ACP countries) for the period between 2008 and 2013.

Burundi

In the framework of the 10th EDF, the allocation for Burundi amounted to €188 million for programmable activities and another €24 million for unforeseen purposes (République de Burundi–Communauté européenne, 2007: 23). Burundi's poverty reduction strategy of 2006 had included improvement of governance and security as one of four central elements, and mentioned it as a *sine qua non* for national reconciliation and economic development. Security sector reform figured as a prime element, with strengthening of the rule of law and the figh against impunity as important components of governance improvement (République de Burundi–Communauté européenne, 2007: 10–11).

The CSP 2008–13 selected rural development and health as the concentration areas for EU support. Good governance issues, most notably public finance management, were mentioned as a component of the programs in each of the concentration areas, as well as part of budget support (République de Burundi–Communauté européenne, 2007: 20–21). Other governance-oriented activities, included among so-called 'non-focal areas,' would be supported with €10 million. These funds were meant for state reform (in particular, justice, civil service reform, and security); strengthening of oversight institutions such as the auditor's off ce and anticorruption services; adoption of international human rights norms into national legislation; decentralization; and support of elections (République de Burundi–Communauté européenne, 2007: 22).

The CSP for Burundi discussed the country's political situation in terms of a continuing violation of human rights and the rule of law despite the apparent 'political will' among contestants to improve the situation. The failure to bring an end to the armed struggle between the government and the rebel Hutu party was ascribed to the lack of experience and capacity of the armed forces and the police. The CSP argued that relations between rival Hutus and Tutsis had improved as a result of constitutional guarantees on the respect for ethnic and religious diversity and power—sharing arrangements relating to state institutions and state—owned enterprises. Consolidation of the fragile democratic process was felt to require better cooperation between the majority party, political opposition, and civil society (République de Burundi–Communauté européenne, 2007: 3–4).

It is striking that the CSP, in contrast to the scholarly literature on Burundi, did not refer to other than ethnic and religious causes for the tensions between the Hutus and Tutsis. Scholars analyzing Burundi have pointed at deeper structural political–economic causes of the conflict i the country that are related to the unequal distribution of and access to resources, in particular land (for example, Jooma, 2005: 1).

Guinea-Bissau

The CSP agreed between the European Commission and Guinea–Bissau for the 2008–2013 period resulted in an allocation of almost €103 million to the country, €27 million of which was designated for programs aimed at strengthening the rule of law and democracy (République de Guinée–Bissau–Communauté européenne, 2007: 36).

The CSP 2008–2013 allocated €24 million to measures aimed to support central state organs, public sector reform and reform of the security sector, including the reintegration of former soldiers. Next to this, support of the National Authorising Officer and electoral support amounte to another €3 million. Budget support to the tune of €32 million should assist Guinea–Bissau in the establishment of 'good economic governance' and public finance management (République de Guinée–Bissau–Communauté européenne, 2007: 31, 37–8).

The CSP saw the elections of 2004 and 2005 as a step toward a normalized political situation, despite the fact that relations between the president and the parliamentary majority remained fragile, thus being a potential threat to stability. The main governance issues were identified i the limited control of the government over the armed forces, the presence of arms among the population, and the weakness of public administration, notably the public control institutions (République de Guinée–Bissau–Communauté européenne, 2007: 5–6). The low degree of transparency in resource management and public finance were noted as a serious problem, as these had led to corruption, fraud, money laundering, and tax evasion. Weakness of the legal framework was seen as a severe limit to access to justice for the population and as a cause of the unfavorable business environment (République de Guinée–Bissau–Communauté européenne, 2007: 6–7).

The CSP's analysis of Guinea–Bissau's political situation focused on the country's history of political violence and military coups. The causes of the political problems, according to the CSP, are diverse and include the country's weak economic basis, the lack of social cohesion produced by ethnic cleavages, as well as the recent military conflict (République de Guinée–Bissau–Communauté européenne, 2007: 29). Analysts of Guinea–Bissau have, however, emphasized several 'structural conditions' brought about by the country's unequal distribution of wealth and the grip on the country's resources by the political group in power, which rules by maintaining profound clientelist networks. The structural conditions include deep divisions within the political elite and the military, incapacity of public institutions to provide basic social services, corruption, poverty, and dependence on foreign aid (for example, Magalhães Ferreira, 2004).

Haiti

As the single pilot country in the Western hemisphere, the EU allocated Haiti €291 million for programmable activities and almost €14 million for unforeseen purposes over the 2008–2013 period (République d'Haïti–Communauté européenne, 2008: 2). From the former amount €36 million would be made available for the improvement of the country's governance (République d'Haïti–Communauté européenne, 2008: 37).

The CSP 2008–2013 agreed between the EU and Haiti focused on two main governance programs. In the first place, the CSP emphasized decentralization and deconcentration, including the strengthening of spatial planning capacities. It was argued that more attention for decentralization and deconcentration would be needed in order to improve service delivery as a contribution to poverty reduction, food security and economic growth. Next to this, strengthening of the judiciary would be aimed at enhancing its independence, improving the level of training and expertise and restoring integrity (République d'Haïti–Communauté européenne, 2008: 28–29).

The political and institutional analysis in the CSP of Haiti focused on issues of domestic security and the lack of capacity to implement proper governance. In particular, the CSP addressed the governance *problématique* of the country in terms of an incomplete process of decentralization and deconcentration, and the relative frailness of the rule of law, epitomized in the country's weak judiciary (République d'Haïti–Communauté européenne, 2008: 8–9). Strengthening of governance structures would, according to the CSP, contribute to the return to the rule of law, enhance support for development policies among the population, and mobilize foreign investment.

In contrast to the focus of the Haitian CSP, scholars have emphasized the structural problems characterizing the country. Analyses have highlighted the endemic weakness of the Haitian neo-patrimonial state, fuelled by the activities of rival elites that seek to build their own power bases and extract rents instead of contributing to the country's development (for example, Gros, 2000: 215–218). Such analyses point to the long-standing 'privatization' of the state and question whether decentralization would lead to better state performance or would, rather, produce independent power centers that are even less committed to state performance (Gros, 2000: 223; 2011: 152).

Sierra Leone

Under the 10th EDF, Sierra Leone received an allocation for programmable activities of €242 million and an additional €26.4 million for unforeseen purposes. Approximately 15 per cent of the former amount was to be spent on good governance and institutional support (Sierra Leone–European Community, 2007, part 2: 1).

The EU and UK adopted a Joint Country Strategy for Sierra Leone in 2007, focusing *inter alia* on governance, peace, and security. Measures to support good governance and institutional reform fell into four categories: electoral assistance, in particular through voter and civic education, political registration, and awareness-raising; support of decentralization; assistance with civil service reform, aimed at restructuring and 'right-sizing', and capacity-building within the bureaucracy; and civil society support (Sierra Leone–European Community, 2007, part 2: 3–4).

According to the CSP, Sierra Leone's political situation was still shaped by the impact of the civil war (1991–2002), which had destroyed the country's infrastructure and political institutions and led to a massive outflow of refugees. The roots of the civil war were traced to centralization of power, the absence of accountability in the civil service, and widespread corruption. The EU's assessment was that the country 'remains an extremely "fragile state", with a poorly resourced civil service that lacks capacity, operates inefficiently and lacks even the basic facilities to deliver adequate services to the majority of its citizens' (Sierra Leone–European Community, 2007: 6). The regular occurrence of elections since 2002, according to the CSP, had produced neither democratic and effective governance nor effective oversight mechanisms (such as parliament and the judiciary). Local social networks were felt to be major sources of political allegiance, and potential causes of internal instability (Sierra Leone–European Community, 2007: 6–7).

In contrast to this assessment, analysts have pointed to the more deeply rooted causes of the conflict in Sierra Leone, related to the underdevelopment of the country's economy and the pervasiveness of social exclusion. Keen (2004: 289–296), among others, has argued that lack of education, unemployment, and failure of local justice led to grievances among all participants in the Sierra Leone conflict, and that the violence that swept the country in the 1990s can be explained largely in terms of group efforts to draw attention to these grievances.

Timor-Leste

In 2007, Timor–Leste received an allocation of approximately €64 million as part of the 10th EDF multi–annual agreements, almost all of which was for programmable activities (Timor–Leste–European Community, 2007: 2). EU assistance under the 10th EDF was targeted at supporting the government's National Development Plan in three main areas, one being 'institutional capacity building.' Support in this domain amounted to €13 million, or 21 per cent of the funds provided, focused on fve main activities: capacity building of the judiciary; support of the civil service and of decentralization; strengthening of the national parliament; support of communication media; and support of the National Authorising Officer to improve implementation of aid (Timor–Leste–European Community, 2007: 70–77). Next to these activities, the CSP contained support for non–state actors and for governance–related joint initiatives with Portuguese–speaking African countries.

The CSP for Timor–Leste emphasized the impact of the country's violent road to independence in 1999. It also noted the instances of violent unrest, most recently in 2006. The causes of the 2006 crisis were analyzed in terms of the resurfacing of divisions that predated 1999 – in particular the failure to do justice in view of the crimes preceding independence – and poverty among youth and the urban population, resulting in a legitimacy crisis of the government. Peaceful elections in 2007 did not, according to the CSP, succeed in removing all sources of instability, such as the widespread possession of weapons among the civilian population, the vast number of displaced persons and the general discontent among members of the security forces (Timor–Leste–European Community, 2007: 9–12).

Analysts have pointed at the limits of the model of 'liberal peacebuilding' that was applied in the case of Timor–Leste. The danger of the model, according to such analysts, is that democratization is narrowed down to the electoral process, and that elections are held prior to the establishment of effective institutions. In such a context, certain groups proved to be able to 'hijack' the state under the pretext of establishing liberal democracy, while effectively excluding large parts of the population from the political process (for example, Richmond and Franks, 2008: 192–198).

Yemen

As one of two non–ACP members within the group of pilot countries, Yemen was allocated €60 million in the 2007–2010 period in support of programmes aimed at promoting good governance and fighting poverty (European Commission, 2007b: 3–4). Governance–oriented activities, whic received €19.5 million, were aimed at strengthening the electoral framework, parliament, and political parties, and at supporting the judicial system in order to improve the rule of law and human rights. Specifically, the governance program contained the following components: suppor of the Supreme Election Committee to deliver credible free and fair elections; assistance to members of parliament in order to develop their capacity to represent citizens' interests and to link with civil society; training of judges in various commercial, civil, and penal courts; and mainstreaming of human rights in penal courts and the security forces (European Commission, 2007b: 6–8).

The political analysis of the CSP for Yemen emphasized the lack of reform of the country's political system despite the need to address serious political problems. Notably, the document highlighted the weak role of the legislative and judiciary institutions *vis-à-vis* the executive, the existence of widespread corruption in the country (referred to as a 'deal–killer' of many initiatives), continued human rights issues and discrimination against women, and security issues springing from the presence of terrorist groups in the country and the use of the country as a transit point for militants and weapons (Yemen–European Community, 2007: 12–14). Despite its analysis, the CSP argued that 'by regional standards, democracy is reasonably well–developed in Yemen' (Yemen–European Community, 2007: 12).

Analysts focusing on the country's governance situation tend to address more fundamental issues relating to Yemen's social and political structures. For instance, Hill (2008: 6) has argued that the Yemeni government has over the years lost its tribal power base that had been built on a 'web of personal loyalty through the distribution of oil rents.' The political–economic dynamics brought about by the fall of oil revenues accruing to the government have led to a loss of control over the country, leading to increasing risk of civil war in the north, the rise of separatist movements in the south, and increased activities of terrorist groups.

CSPs and the EU's response to fragile states

The discussion of the Country Strategy Papers agreed by the European Commission with the six pilot countries has illustrated some of the challenges inherent in the formulation of a strategy to deal with state fragility. As all CSPs follow the same format, it has been possible to compare the political–economic analyses that are underlying the Commission's approach to the different fragile states, as well as the main components of its response strategy for these countries.

The analyses of the political–economic situation in the cases described above illustrate the resolve of the European Commission to ground its response strategy in an understanding of the local dynamics of the countries concerned. From a methodological point of view, one could question the transparency and reliability of the analyses, which do not provide an insight into the sources on the basis of which judgments are made, and have apparently not involved independent analysts from outside the Commission. The Commission's account of political–economic problems in the countries concerned demonstrates, however, the wish to present a substantively sound and policy–relevant comprehension of the main causes of state fragility.

Previous sections have shown, with reference to some independent accounts, that the Commission's analyses did not seem to dig deep enough to uncover the structural or root causes of the problems experienced by the countries concerned. Yet, despite this criticism, it is clear that the Commission's analyses refect a general agreement about the *manifestation* of the problems in the pilot fragile states.

The content of the response strategies for the fragile states shows, however, a clear gap between the political–economic analyses and the measures adopted in the EU support packages. The various measures are compared in Table 30.1, which illustrates the dominance of certain types of response to the problems in fragile states: public sector reform, decentralization, support of electoral processes, and reform of the justice sector are key to the EU's approach in a majority of cases analyzed above. Next, public finance management, security sector reform, and suppor

Table 30.1 EU support strategies in six pilot countries

	Burundi	Guinea-Bissau	Haiti	Sierra Leone	Timor-Leste	Yemen
Public sector reform	•	•		•	•	
Decentralization	•		•	•	•	
Public finance managemen	•	•		•		
Electoral support	•	•		•		•
Security sector reform	•	•				•
Support/reform of justice sector	•	•		•	•	•
Support of parliament and central state organs		•			•	•
Anti-corruption	•					
Civil society support				•	•	

Sources: République de Burundi–Communauté européenne (2007: 20–22); République de Guinée–Bissau–Communauté européenne (2007: 31–38); République d'Haïti–Communauté européenne (2008: 28–29); Sierra Leone–European Community (2007, part 2: 3–4); Timor–Leste–European Community (2007: 70–77); European Commission (2007b: 6–8).

of parliament and other central state organs show up as a measure in half of the fragile states studied. Finally, anti–corruption and civil society support show up only in one or two cases.

The listing of priority areas in Table 30.1 illustrates that the general approach of the European Commission is to assist in *reconstructing* state capacities in fragile states through essentially technical and managerial measures. In a good number of the cases analyzed in this paper, such technocratic measures do not seem to square with the analysis of the problems made either in the CSPs or by independent analysts. Issues raised in the analyses of state fragility relate to problems of state capture, including patronage and clientelism, violent resistance of groups against central government, ethnic divisions, human rights violations, weak socioeconomic basis, and extreme inqualities and social exclusion or marginalization of particular groups. The failure to address the fundamental problems underlying state fragility raises serious questions about the effectiveness of the EU's policy on fragile states.

Conclusions

This chapter has attempted to interpret the current focus of EU development policy on the issue of state fragility. The chapter argues that the EU's concern with the issue has had strong security overtones, and that the EU response fits in with the overall trend of 'securitizing' development In this respect, the role played by fragile states in the supply of energy, raw materials, and drugs, as well as their role in the 'global war on terror,' may have been an important factor for the EU, similar to the US, in terms of engaging with such countries (Briscoe, 2008: 9).

The EU's approach to fragile states has concentrated on governance issues: the def nition of state fragility that was adopted by the European Council in 2007 ref ects this focus. The EU's understanding is that state fragility implies a breakdown of the social contract due to a state's failure to perform its major functions, such as safeguarding the rule of law, security, poverty reduction, service delivery, and resource management.

Recent discussions on governance and fragile states in policy–making circles have produced various lessons for development agencies. Assessments of earlier interventions have led the World Bank and the OECD to emphasize context–specific action, based on thorough knowledge o the local situation, and political analyses of processes and events spurring state fragility. The EU's approach to governance and state fragility does not seem to pay sufficient attention to these insights. The analysis of six CSPs demonstrated that the European Commission's 'response strategy' for the pilot fragile states shows a disparity between the understanding of political–economic dynamics and the support measures adopted. In particular, the CSPs' concern with the reconstruction of state capacities by technical and managerial means creates the serious risk of overlooking more fundamental political–economic problems in the countries concerned.

It seems safe to conclude that the EU's approach to reconstructing fragile states reflects th view that the real problem of these countries stems from the inadequate functioning of the state – i.e., inadequate when looked at from prevalent Western conceptions of the 'modern' state. This approach overlooks the fact that the state is an institution that is embedded in local social, political, and economic realities, and that its functioning (or dysfunctioning) needs to be understood in relation to specific social, political, or economic interests. In this vein, Chabal an Daloz's argument, that judgments on the 'failure' of the state in Africa are essentially a function of the Weberian approach to the state, is highly pertinent. The dominance of the 'fundamentally instrumental concept of power' has given rise to an 'informalization of politics' and an 'instrumentalization' of the state (Chabal and Daloz, 1999: 4). The question, therefore, is not so much whether the fragile state 'works,' but rather *for whom* it works. Attempts to reconstruct fragile states need to be grounded in an understanding of the political–economic realities of the countries concerned, in particular of the incentives, challenges, and opportunities faced by various actors (see further Fritz and Rocha Menocal, 2007: 44). Policies that do not take account of the local political economy of fragile states are bound to fail.

Notes

1. Probably the f rst use of the term was in a statement of 10 November 2000 by the European Council and the European Commission on development policy (European Council and Commission, 2000: point 6).
2. Apparently these pilot countries were chosen under the Portuguese Presidency of the European Council, and this may explain why countries such as Guinea–Bissau and Timor–Leste were included. Yet no formal statements on the selection process have been uncovered.
3. Despite some general references to EU policies on fragile states, the conclusions on confct prevention of the European Council meeting held in June 2011 contained no indication that the Council would place the issue high on its agenda in the foreseeable future (European Council, 2011).

References

Briscoe, I. (2008). The EU response to fragile states, *European Security Review*, 42, 7–10.
Cammack, D., McLeod, D., Rocha Menocal, A., and Christiansen, K. (2006). *Donors and the 'fragile states' agenda: A survey of current thinking and practice*. London, UK: Overseas Development Institute.
Carbone, M. (2007). *The European Union and international development: The politics of foreign aid*. London, UK: Routledge.
Castillejo, C. (2011). Improving European policy towards fragile states, *Interdisciplinary Political Studies*, 1(2), 169–172.
Chabal, P., and Daloz, J.–P. (1999). *Africa works: Disorder as political instrument*. Oxford, UK: James Currey.
European Commission. (2003). *Governance and development*, 20 October, COM(2003) 615 f nal. Brussels, Belgium: European Commission.
European Commission. (2006a). *Commission staff working document accompanying the communication 'Governance in the European Consensus on Development: Towards a Harmonised Approach within the European Union'*, 30 August, SEC(2006) 1020. Brussels, Belgium: European Commission.
European Commission. (2006b). *Governance in the European Consensus on Development: Towards a harmonised approach within the European Union*, 30 August, COM(2006) 421 final. Brussels, Belgium: European Commission.

European Commission. (2007a). *EU response to situations of fragility in developing countries: Engaging in difficult environments for long-term development*, report of the external debate. Brussels, Belgium: European Commission.

European Commission. (2007b). *Multiannual indicative programme (Yemen, 2007–2010)*. Brussels, Belgium: European Commission.

European Commission. (2007c). *Towards an EU response to situations of fragility: Engaging in difficult environments for sustainable development, stability and peace*, 25 October, COM(2007)643 final. Brussels, Belgium: European Commission.

European Commission. (2008). *Principles for the implementation of a governance facility under ENPI*. Brussels, Belgium: European Commission.

European Commission. (2010). *Addressing situations of fragility*, 31 December. Brussels, Belgium: European Commission.

European Council. (2003a). *A secure Europe in a better world: European security strategy*, Brussels, 12 December. Brussels, Belgium: European Council.

European Council. (2003b). *Governance in the context of development cooperation*, Council Conclusions, 19 November, No. 14453/03. Brussels, Belgium: European Council.

European Council. (2007). *An EU response to situations of fragility*, 19 November, No. 15118/07. Brussels, Belgium: European Council.

European Council. (2011). *Council conclusions on conflict prevention*, 20 June. Brussels, Belgium: European Council.

European Council and Commission. (2000). *The European Community's development policy*, 10 November, No. 12929/00. Brussels, Belgium: European Council and Commission.

European Parliament, Council and Commission. (2006). The European consensus on development*Official Journal of the European Union*, 24 February, C46/1–19.

Fritz, V., and Rocha Menocal, A. (2007). *Understanding state-building from a political economy perspective: An analytical and conceptual paper on processes, embedded tensions and lessons for international engagement*, London, UK: Overseas Development Institute.

Gros, J.-G. (2000). Haiti: The political economy and sociology of decay and renewal*Latin American Research Review*, *35*(3), 211–226.

Gros, J.-G. (2011). Anatomy of a Haitian tragedy: When the fury of nature meets the debility of the state, *Journal of Black Studies*, *42*(2), 131–157.

Hill, G. (2008). *Yemen: Fear of failure*. Chatham House Briefing Paper MEP BP 08/03. London, UK: Roya Institute of International Affairs.

Jooma, M. B. (2005). *'We can't eat the constitution': Transformation and the socio-economic reconstruction of Burundi*, ISS Paper 106. Pretoria, South Africa: Institute for Security Studies.

Keen, D. (2004). *Conflict and collusion in Sierra Leone*. Oxford, UK: James Currey.

Magalhães Ferreira, P. (2004). Guinea–Bissau: Between conflict and democracy, *African Security Review*, *13*(4), 45–56.

Organisation for Economic Co-operation and Development. (2008).*Concepts and dilemmas of state building in fragile situations: From fragility to resilience*. Paris, France: OECD.

O'Sullivan, D. (2011). Setting up the EEAS, speech at Institute of International and European Affairs, Dublin, Ireland, 14 January.

République de Burundi–Communauté européenne. (2007). *Document de stratégie pays et programme indicatif national pour la période 2008–2013*, Lisbon, Portugal, 9 December.

République de Guinée–Bissau–Communauté européenne. (2007). *Document de stratégie pays et programme indicatif national pour la période 2008–2013*, Lisbon, Portugal, 9 December.

République d'Haïti–Communauté européenne. (2008). *Document de stratégie pays et programme indicatif national pour la période 2008–2013*, Port au Prince, Haiti, 5 December.

Richmond, O. P., and Franks, J. (2008). Liberal peacebuilding in Timor Leste: The emperor's new clothes? *International Peacekeeping*, *15*(2), 185–200.

Sierra Leone–European Community. (2007). *Country Strategy Paper and National Indicative Programme for the Period 2008–2013*, Lisbon, Portugal, 9 December.

Timor–Leste–EuropeanCommunity. (2007). *Country Strategy Paper and National Indicative Programme for the Period 2008–2013*, Lisbon, Portugal, 9 December.

Yemen–European Community. (2007). *Strategy Paper for the Period 2007–2010*. Available at: http://ec.europa.eu

Van der Borgh, C. (2008). A fragile concept: Donors and the fragile states agenda. *The Broker Online*, 28 July.

World Bank, The. (1998). *Assessing aid: What works, what doesn't and why*. New York, NY: Oxford University Press.
World Bank, The. (2005). *Fragile states: Good practice in country assistance strategies*. Washington, DC: World Bank Operations Policy and Country Services.
World Bank Independent Evaluation Group. (2006). *Engaging with fragile states: An IEG Review of Work Bank support to low-income countries under stress*. Washington, DC: The World Bank.
Youngs, R. (2008). Fusing security and development: Just another Euro-platitude? *Journal of European Integration, 30*(3), 419–437.

31
THE SECURITY COUNCIL, R2P, AND STATEBUILDING

Thomas G. Weiss

Whether a state is partially intact or to be rebuilt completely after being torn apart by war, a new geopolitical reality is the necessity for that state to behave 'responsibly' toward its own citizens. The bar is not set very high because a responsible sovereign means at least not committing mass atrocities (genocide, war crimes, crimes against humanity, and ethnic cleansing).

This chapter traces the development of the changing nature of the definition used by the Security Council to reflect a modicum of respect for human rights in addition to the other characteristics (territory, people, authority, and independence) spelled out in the 1934 Montevideo Convention on the Rights and Duties of States. It revisits the unfinished journey of 'the responsibility to protect' from the ad hoc actions of the 1990s, to the 2001 report by the International Commission on Intervention and State Sovereignty (ICISS),[1] to the 2005 decision by the World Summit, to the 2011 decision to enforce a no-fly zone in Libya (see Weiss, 2011). There ar limits to a state's autonomy, or it loses the claim to the protective shield of non-intervention that accompanies sovereignty. However, the World Summit watered down the ICISS's original conception in two ways: by making the Security Council's agreement a show-stopper and by eliminating the third part of the original three-part responsibility to protect (to prevent, to react, *and* to rebuild). The conclusion points to the need to return to the original logic for international efforts to help improve the chances for sustainable peace in war-torn societies.

The responsibility to protect

Friends and foes alike have pointed to the commission's central conceptual contribution, namely reframing state sovereignty as contingent rather than absolute. The commissioners aimed to halt mass atrocities by invoking a three-pronged responsibility – to prevent, to react, and to rebuild. Prevention and rebuilding were not ICISS afterthoughts, but the main motivation for convening the commission in fall 2000 was to break new ground and reach consensus about reacting to mass atrocities. Its comparative advantage, at least in comparison with other international blue-ribbon groups, was a narrow focus – what used to be called 'humanitarian intervention.' After divisive and inconsistent instances of military humanitarianism in the tumultuous 1990s, states genuinely sought guidance about intervening across borders to protect and assist war victims. Nonetheless, the logic of the ICISS's work was to do everything possible to prevent mass atrocities but to react and halt them if prevention failed; and after a successful reaction, it was incumbent on the interveners to do everything possible to help reconstitute a state and re-knit the society that would need to recover from outside intervention.

The R2P norm has taken root in today's international normative landscape, which leads us to trace its move from the prose and passion of a group of eminent individuals toward a mainstay on the international public policy agenda since the release in December 2001 of the ICISS's *The Responsibility to Protect*. The UN's High-Level Panel on Threats, Challenges and Change issued its 2004 report titled *A More Secure World: Our Shared Responsibility*, which endorsed 'the emerging norm that there is a collective international responsibility to protect.' Shortly thereafter former UN secretary-general Kofi Annan also endorsed it in his 2005 report, *In Larger Freedom*.

The ICISS coined the term 'R2P' (rendered later in uglier UNese as 'RtoP') in order to move beyond the pitched battles of 'humanitarian intervention,' and more than 150 heads of state and government at the September 2005 World Summit took a giant step in that direction. Paragraphs 138–140 in the intergovernmental agreement on the occasion of the UN's 60th anniversary are appropriately interpreted as a turning point in the norm's crystalization, albeit falling short of 'an international Magna Carta' – hyperbole from the State Department's former director of policy planning, Anne-Marie Slaughter (Slaughter, 2011).

The main motivation for Canada to convene the independent commission in fall 2000 was to break new ground and reach consensus about reacting to mass atrocities. As mentioned above, its demand-driven character helped focus the mind, but the ICISS's original formulation of R2P sandwiched military force between the sliced-white-bread of prevention and post-conflict peacebuilding. These popular issues made 'military intervention for human protection purposes' (the mouthful coined by the commission) somewhat more palatable than it had been, especially to critics in the global South. Both the bread and the meat were essential to the concept's appeal. Nonetheless, sovereignty remained paramount, the deployment of such military force objectionable and rare, and R2P contested.

Why is halting mass atrocities not always on the side of the angels? Beginning with the international response in northern Iraq in 1991, the moniker of 'humanitarian intervention' had resulted in largely circular tirades about the agency, timing, legitimacy, means, circumstances, consistency, and advisability of using military force to protect human beings. Reticence at best and hostility at worst is understandable to those familiar with the number of sins justified by colonial powers with a 'humanitarian' veneer. Countries that gained their independence only in the second half of the 20th century are unlikely to welcome outside interference, especially military intervention, merely because of a qualifying adjective. The Iraq War illustrated this reality when the justifications coming from London and Washington morphed into 'humanitarian' claims after the original justifications (links to al-Qaeda and weapons of mass destruction) evaporated as governmental fabrications with collusion from national intelligence services. That war without the Security Council's imprimatur was temporarily a conversation stopper for R2P. Contemporary foreign adventurism and imperial meddling in humanitarian guise were not more acceptable at the outset of the 21st century than earlier incarnations.

As mentioned, the central insight and main tactical advantage of the responsibility to protect is that state sovereignty is viewed as conditional rather than absolute; it entails duties, not simply rights; and it permits a conversation (although many have been *dialogues de sourds*) about the limits of repressive state power even with the most ardent defenders of sovereign inviolability. After centuries of largely looking the other way, sovereignty no longer provides a license for mass murder in the eyes of legitimate members of the international community of states. Hence, every state has a responsibility to protect its own citizens from mass killings and other gross violations of their rights. If any state, however, is manifestly unable or unwilling to exercise that responsibility, or actually is the perpetrator of mass atrocities, its sovereignty is abrogated. Meanwhile the responsibility to protect civilians in distress devolves to other states, ideally acting through the UN Security Council.

This creative notion of a dual responsibility – internal and external – drew upon Francis Deng and Roberta Cohen's pioneering work about 'sovereignty as responsibility' in reframing the thorny requirements for the protection of internally displaced persons. [2] They, along with the ICISS, Annan, and the World Summit, emphasized the need – indeed, the responsibility – for the international community, embodied by the United Nations and mandated since its creation to deliver 'freedom from fear' to do everything possible to prevent mass atrocities. Deploying military force is an option after alternatives have been considered and proved patently inadequate. Military intervention to protect the vulnerable is restricted, however, in the summit's agreed paragraphs to cases of 'genocide, war crimes, ethnic cleansing and crimes against humanity' – or the shorthand, 'mass atrocities' or the redundant 'mass atrocity crimes.'

By the time that the 2005 consensus materialized, the message was clear: R2P was ref ned from a broad framework to a focus on preventing and halting mass atrocities; and the consistency of the norm's interpretation was bolstered by restricting the number of agreed triggering crimes. As such, the responsibility to protect provides a range of possible responses to the most gross and systematic violations of human rights that deeply offend any sense of common humanity. R2P – like human rights more generally – seeks to cross cultural boundaries and ultimately aspires to universality. By restricting the norm to the most heinous and conscience-shocking crimes rather than the garden variety of abuses, the 2005 agreement added to the norm's clarity and thereby advanced its potentially universal aspirations and applicability.

Most observers agree that R2P's potential strength, like other norms, is demonstrated by its legitimate use; but its misuse also shows potential power because normative imitation is a sincere form of flattery. As such, abuse of the norm – for instance, by the United States and the Unite Kingdom for Iraq in 2003, by Russia for Georgia in 2008, and by France for Burma in 2008 – also helped to clarify what it was not (Badescu and Weiss, 2010). R2P certainly was not an acceptable rationalization for the war in Iraq; nor for the imperial aims of Moscow in its weaker neighbor; nor for intervention after a hurricane when the local government was dragging its feet but not murdering its population.

R2P breaks new ground in coming to the rescue because in addition to the usual attributes of a sovereign state that students encounter in international relations and law courses, there is another: a modicum of respect for the most basic of human rights – life. The interpretation of privileges for sovereigns has made room for modest responsibilities as well. When a state is unable or manifestly unwilling to protect the rights of its population – and especially when it abuses its own citizens – that state's sovereignty evaporates, and it loses the accompanying claim to the right of non-intervention. The traditional rule of non-interference in domestic affairs does not apply in the midst of mass atrocities.

Moreover, and in terms of multilateral diplomacy perhaps the most crucial development, the outdated discourse of humanitarian intervention is turned on its head and transformed from that properly detested in parts of the global South. The merits of particular situations should be evaluated objectively rather than blindly given an imprimatur as 'humanitarian.' For anyone familiar with the number of sins previously justified by that qualifying adjective, this change marks a profound shift away from the rights of outsiders to intervene toward the rights of populations at risk to assistance and protection and the responsibility of outsiders to come to the rescue, or at least be embarrassed by not acting.

Whither R2P?

The potential for normative backpedalling has always been present – in all states, and none more so than former colonies that jealously guard their sovereign prerogatives and remain on their guard against any measure that smacks of neo–imperial meddling. The red herring of imperialism is often tossed into the debate pool as a distraction; and support by countries in the Arab League for outside intervention in both Libya and Syria is noteworthy and perhaps a harbinger. 'Though some critics fret that RtoP could prove to be a humanitarian veneer by which powerful states could justify military intervention in the development world, more often the problem has been the opposite,' Edward Luck commented. 'They have looked for excuses not to act, rather than for reasons to intervene' (Luck, 2010: 361). Or as the moral philosopher Michael Walzer echoed, 'It is more often the case that powerful states don't do enough, or don't do anything at all, in response to desperate need than that they respond in imperialist ways' (Walzer, 2011: 77).

The follow–up debate after the Security Council's authorization in 2011 to take action in Libya – especially the theatrical huffing and puffing about 'regime change' not having been authorized by the no–flight zone – was reminiscent of high–voltage and high–decibel criticis that confronted the emergence of R2P 10 years earlier. For many critics, seeking to make 'never again' more than a slogan was not necessarily progress. For instance, on the eve of the first interactive dialogue on the topic in the General Assembly in August 2009 *The Economist* reported that opponents of the responsibility to protect 'have been busily sharpening their knives.' Critics painted R2P in imperialistic hues, including the opening jeremiad by the then president of the General Assembly, a Nicaraguan former Maryknoll priest, Miguel d'Escoto Brockmann, who dubbed it 'redecorated colonialism' and invited Noam Chomsky to harangue fellow delegates (Brockman, 2009).

But to date, acquired normative territory has been defended. Moreover, the R2P norm has substantial potential to evolve further in customary international law and contribute to ongoing conversations about contingent state responsibilities. Despite ongoing dissent and contestation, R2P's normative agenda has continued to advance, and doubts about the transnational resonance of the responsibility to protect have continued to diminish although not disappear.

The ICISS's contention in 2001 was that R2P was an 'emerging' norm. Would the journey since then permit us to characterize it as having 'emerged'? On one hand, the consensus appears to be widening and deepening across the North as well as the global South (Serrano, 2010a). On the other hand, that R2P resonates better among states and the political tone is less acrimonious than a few years ago is scant solace to victims in Darfur or Sri Lanka. Moreover, reluctance, skepticism, and even hostility continue to characterize the positions of naysayers who regularly appear on the international conference circuit. After all is said and done, we still confront the operational challenge of how R2P can move from soothing statements to meaningful state action.

As he began his first term as UN secretary–general, Ban Ki–moon placed his personal prestig behind this normative construct, including appointing both a special advisor for the prevention of genocide (Francis M. Deng in 2007–2012, and Adama Dieng from mid–2012) and a special advisor tasked with promoting R2P (Edward C. Luck in 2007–2012). The secretary–general referred to R2P as one of his priorities and in January 2009 released *Implementing the Responsibility to Protect*. In August 2009 the General Assembly's first interactive debate took place in order t discuss that report and reaffrmed the norm, which a month later was encapsulated in resolution 63/308.[3] In August 2010, another constructive informal interactive dialogue addressed a second report by the Secretary–General, *Early Warning, Assessment, and the Responsibility to Protect*. In December 2010 the General Assembly approved resolution 64/245, which established the joint office for the prevention of genocide and the promotion of R2P and approved UN staff positions for the regular budget.

Whether international action in Libya has definitively accelerated or slowed down the internalization of the norm is difficult to say at this juncture. It is worth noting that with bombin still under way, 'focal points' from capitals and New York gathered in May 2011 at the invitation of the foreign ministers from Denmark and Ghana (later joined by Australia and Costa Rica). In spite of the dispute over the intended results in Libya, the conversation at the third interactive dialogue in July 2011 was less heated than in the previous summers, with fewer of the usual suspects trying to torpedo consensus. The focus of the secretary-general's report on regional organizations was timely in that they had been so crucial in securing widespread political backing for the Libyan intervention – by the Arab League, Gulf Cooperation Council, Islamic Conference, and African Union (AU). In Côte d'Ivoire, the AU's diplomacy was ultimately unsuccessful; but more traction came from the Economic Community of West African States (ECOWAS) (Bassett and Straus, 2011).

The fourth interactive dialogue in September 2012 focused on Ban Ki-moon's 'third pillar' or R2P's coercive dimensions, a topic that also was central to the Focal Points Network later that month although it had a different focus in keeping with Ban's 'year of prevention.' The secretary-general's earlier repackaging of ICISS recommendations had sought to avoid coercion in favor of his other two pillars: the responsibility of states themselves to protect their citizens; and international assistance to help them be able to exercise that protection effectively. According to Ramesh Thakur, the secretary-general's reformulation 'did not retreat from the necessity for outside military action in some circumstances but it diluted the central defining feature of R2P' (Thakur, 2011:150). I would be harsher: the secretary-general sought to avoid the third pillar, the sharp end of the R2P stick of using or threatening to use military force to stop mass atrocities. Indeed, by proceeding gingerly, as Aidan Hehir argues, R2P may represent a regression of sorts from the unfashionable humanitarian intervention by diverting attention away from reaction (Hehir, 2012).

The debate was intriguing in light of the impasse in Syria, where coercion was required but any resort to muscle was blocked by Russian and Chinese vetoes even for watered-down measures if Bashar al-Assad were identified as responsible for Syria's civil war

The 2012 gatherings afforded occasions to turn up the volume of lingering buyer's remorse, especially Brazil's proposal at the 66th session of the UN General Assembly in fall 2011 that 'the international community, as it exercises its responsibility to protect, must demonstrate a high level of responsibility while protecting' ('Letter Dated 9 November 2011 . .'). Albeit tautological, the framing also was another intriguing indication of the norm's perceived pertinence and power. An emerging Brazil was obliged to have a foreign policy unequivocally supportive of human rights; hence, Brasilia could not be among R2P spoilers. At the same time, a resident in America's 'backyard' also felt compelled in its new leadership role to communicate uneasiness about the use of military force for regime change.

Hence, the annual interactive dialogues, combined with work within the UN system by Deng and Luck, helped keep the norm's advance on track, and this reality was complemented by a number of state and non-state initiatives (Serrano, 2010b). Most prominent were the informal group of like-minded countries in New York known as the 'Group of Friends for R2P'; the partnership to promote national R2P focal points; the International Coalition for the R2P; and the Global Centre for the R2P whose bi-monthly watchdog is *R2P Monitor* (see Bellamy, 2010: 146–148; Luck, 2010).

'R2P lite' and statebuilding

The intergovernmental decision by over 150 heads of state at the 2005 World Summit certainly has made a difference to the internalization of the R2P norm beyond that of an 'emerging' norm, the ICISS's contention in 2001. It may not as yet be customary international law, but it certainly frames increasingly the way that diplomats, international civil servants, nongovernmental organizations, and scholars examine the range of options to halt mass atrocities.

At the same time, paragraphs 138–140 also can be considered 'R2P lite' in comparison with the commission's original thinking for two distinct reasons, both of which bear directly on the tasks of rebuilding states after armed conflicts. The first is the contrast between roles for the Security Council. Rather than making approval by the Security Council highly desirable but not an absolute necessity, the World Summit makes council approval a *sine qua non* for the implementation of R2P. Paragraph 139 is clear:

> In this context, we are prepared to take collective action, in a timely and decisive manner, through the Security Council, in accordance with the Charter, including Chapter VII, on a case-by-case basis and in cooperation with relevant regional organizations as appropriate, should peaceful means be inadequate and national authorities manifestly fail to protect their populations from genocide, war crimes, ethnic cleansing and crimes against humanity.

ICISS, in contrast, argued that 'There is no better or more appropriate body than the United Nations Security Council to authorize military intervention for human protection purposes.' Using the council – which ideally should be reformed and in which the P–5 'should agree not to apply their veto power . . . to obstruct the passage of resolutions authorizing military intervention for human protection purposes' – was clearly the most desirable outcome in the view of the commissioners. But they also were not so wedded to the ideal that it became the enemy of the good. Hence, the commissioners left open the door to action when the Security Council was paralyzed because 'if it fails to discharge its responsibility to protect in conscience-shocking situations crying out for action, concerned states may not rule out other means to meet the gravity and urgency of that situation' (ICISS, 2001, xii–xiii).

On the one hand, the World Summit's emphasis on the sanctity of the Charter's Chapter VII provisions would have made Hedley Bull and Robert Jackson and other members of the English School happy about respecting the most fundamental rule of international society. On the other hand, not being held hostage to the lowest common denominator in the council in the face of mass atrocities should have been obvious before Syria. If not, then it certainly should be crystal clear now. For the same reason that the Kosovo Commission judged NATO's use of military force there to be 'legitimate' even if it was 'illegal' without Security Council approval, that option should be available if individual rights truly trump state sovereignty. Otherwise, we return to the narrowest of interpretations of Charter Article 2(7), according to which all actions, even mass atrocities, fall within the prerogative of a sovereign state; and responsibilities for the welfare of citizens stop at national boundaries.

To state the obvious, the longer one waits to intervene, the more signifant the statebuilding tasks once peace is established or a post-conflict transition begins. The case of Rwanda's 1994 genocide is the most often cited illustration of this reality, but the more recent case of Côte d'Ivoire is a poignant reminder that fewer, not more, barriers should be in the way of potential military interveners. The absence of a meaningful threat to actually deploy military force in 2010–2011 to oust Laurent Gbagbo and install Alassane Ouattara also illustrates what happens when the Security Council dithers, Chapter VII is held hostage to the whims of major powers, and a viable military option is absent from the international tool-kit.

The installation of Ouatarra and the surrender of former president Gbagbo followed a half-year of dawdling as Côte d'Ivoire's unspeakable disaster unfolded before our eyes. The turmoil accompanying the electoral campaigns even before the ballots were cast was a harbinger of uglier events to come. The country's first election in 10 years in December 2010 led to an overpowerin wave of renewed violence when Gbagbo refused to step down from his decade-long rule after losing to Outtara, who was universally recognized as the winner.

Action in Libya was swift and robust, but in Côte d' Ivoire it was not. The UN Operation in Côte d'Ivoire (UNOCI) was a traditional peacekeeping force deployed earlier by the world organization at the request of the Gbagbo government. The United Nations refused to withdraw in spite of Gbagbo's demand that it leave because of the violence against peaceful protestors that already had prompted the flight of tens of thousands. For three months and in a fashion far mor typical than its pace in Libya, the UN Security Council dragged its collective feet. The result of taking no decisive action was predictable: refugees, massacres, full-scale civil war, and a ruined economy.

The eventual ouster of incumbent Ggagbo fnally followed after six months of saber rattling. The linchpin was robust action from the 1,650-strong French Licorne force as the avant-garde of the UN peace operation. The contrast with what happened in Libya as a result of Resolution 1973, which specifically justified military strikes to avoid the massacre of civilians, suggests w military humanitarianism is a necessary, if insufficient, component of the responsibility to protect The unwillingness to apply armed force abetted Gbagbo's intransigence as Côte d'Ivoire's humanitarian catastrophe took place. And this sequence speaks directly to a counter-factual pertinent for statebuilding after an armed conflict. Was it really necessary to sustain war crimes crimes against humanity, a million refugees, and a ravaged economy? Obviously, international military action could and should have been deployed earlier so that the task of rebuilding the Côte d'Ivoire state would have been far more manageable.

The second reason for labeling the 2005 agreement as 'R2P lite' is as or perhaps even more relevant for this book. The World Summit's decision to exclude post-intervention peacebuilding as an integral part of the responsibility to protect was a step backwards from the compelling logic of the ICISS's original formulation. In addition to citing Chapter VII's necessity for intervention to stop mass atrocities, paragraph 139 goes on to specify 'helping States build capacity to protect their populations from genocide, war crimes, ethnic cleansing and crimes against humanity and to assisting those which are under stress before crises and conf icts break out.' No mention is made, however, of the requirement to help war-torn societies mend after an intervention, which the ICISS made central to the international responsibility to protect. While some, including this author at the outset, argued that such a commitment was making even less likely the use of military force for human protection purposes, state-rebuilding remains compelling as a necessary element of an international commitment to moving beyond mass atrocities.

Why? Because without such rebuilding, the original decision to intervene may prove to be myopic. Mustering the cross-cultural political will to give concrete and consistent protection to civilians is never going to be easy (Mani and Weiss, 2011), but Libya is pivotal for what Shannon Beebe and Mary Kaldor call 'human security intervention' (Beebe and Kaldor, 2010). Clearly Libya's people were protected from the kind of murderous harm that Muammar Gaddafinf icted on unarmed civilians early in March 2011 and continued to menace against those 'cockroaches' and 'rats.' Gaddafi's rhetoric was usually theatrical, but this usage served as a wake-up call t those who were aware that the same vile descriptions were used in 1994 by Rwanda's murderous Hutu regime.

As the situation in Tripoli and elsewhere across the Middle East unfolds, acute dilemmas remain for humanitarians and policymakers (Barnett and Weiss, 2011). If the post-intervention operation fares reasonably well, the R2P norm will be strengthened. If it goes poorly, future decision making undoubtedly will be more problematic. All decisions and actions, especially interventions, have unintended and perverse consequences; and it is unreasonable to think that R2P action entails fewer than other types.

What comes to mind is Colin Powell's reported warning to George W. Bush in February 2003 on the eve of the War in Iraq: 'You break it, you own it' (Woodward, 2004: 150). The wisdom of this so-called Pottery Barn rule is also directly relevant for the responsibility to protect. The commitment to post-conflict peacebuilding is an essential component of a responsible decision to come to the rescue in the first place

Whether using the original ICISS conception or the 2005 World Summit version, two specifi challenges remain for the responsibility to protect. First, it should not become synonymous with everything that the United Nations does. In addition to reacting and protecting civilians at risk, the value added of R2P consists of proximate prevention and proximate peace-building – that is, efforts to move back from the brink of mass atrocities that have yet to become widespread or efforts after such crimes to ensure that they do not recur. International action is required before the only option is the US Army's 82nd Airborne Division; and additional commitments to help mend societies are also essential in order to avoid beginning anew a cycle of settling accounts and additional mass atrocities.

In short, the responsibility to protect is not about the protection of everyone from everything. Broadening perspectives has opened the foodgates to an overfow of appeals to address too many problems. For example, part of the political support at the World Summit ref ected an under-standable but erroneous desire to mobilize support for development to overcome root causes of conflict. As bureaucrats invariably seek justifications for pet projects, we run the risk that everything may f gure on the R2P agenda. It is emotionally tempting to argue that we have a responsibility to protect people from HIV/AIDS and small arms, and the Inuit from global warming. However, if R2P means everything, it means nothing.

Second and at the other end of the spectrum, the responsibility to protect also should not be viewed too narrowly. In spite of earlier supportive arguments, it is essential to underline that R2P is not *only* about the use of military force. The responsibility to protect begins long before the dispatch of bombers or troops for military humanitarianism. As we have seen, the responsibility to prevent and the responsibility to rebuild are essential elements of R2P.

That said, however, the responsibility to react and halt mass atrocities provides the teeth to make the entire R2P norm a serious policy option. Halting genocide and other mass atrocities occasionally requires deploying military force and always the threat to do so if negotiations are to succeed, preventive measures to be credible, and civilians ultimately to be safe. For instance, the mere consideration of military force for Libya undoubtedly made the initial decision on other Chapter VII measures easier. Security Council resolution 1970 contained a package of an arms embargo, assets freeze, travel bans, and an inquiry by the International Criminal Court. These relatively robust stances, for the UN at least, were agreed unanimously in late February 2011 instead of being the most that might have been expected after months or years of protracted deliberations.

The international military action against Libya that began in March 2011 marked a turning point in the post-9/11 intervention slump – other than modest efforts by the United Kingdom and France in West and Central Africa, respectively, there had been no serious military operations for human protection purposes since NATO's 1999 intervention in Kosovo. Hence, the Security Council's willingness to authorize 'all necessary means' against Tripoli's rogue regime as it mowed down protestors may mark a new dawn for the responsibility to protect. Indeed, members of the 22-memberArab League called on the world body to impose a no-fly zone against Libya. An France, the United Kingdom, and the United States immediately gave meaning to council resolution 1973 to protect civilians with overwhelming air power.

Military force is not a panacea, to be sure, but its use or threatened use is essential. As James Pattison pointedly reminds us, 'humanitarian intervention is *only one part* of the doctrine of the responsibility to protect, but . . . it *is* part of the responsibility to protect' (Pattison, 2010: 250; emphasis in original). Otherwise, we are obliged to accept the judgment by Gary Bass in his history of efforts to halt mass atrocities: 'We are all atrocitarians now – but so far only in words, and not yet in deeds' (Bass, 2008: 382).

The international response against Libya was not about bombing for democracy, sending messages to Iran, implementing regime change, keeping oil prices low, or pursuing narrow geopolitical interests. They may have resulted, but the dominant motivation for military force was to protect civilians. Is Syria the default option, and thus will Libya be an aberration? Is assertive liberal interventionism of the 1990s ancient history? At that time 'sovereign equality looked and smelled reactionary,' Jennifer Welsh wrote. 'But as the liberal moment recedes, and the distribution of power shifts globally, the principle of sovereign equality may enjoy a comeback' (Welsh, 2010: 428). Let us hope that Libya proves her partially wrong. At the very least, it reinforces Jarat Chopra's and my 1992 argument that 'sovereignty is no longer sacrosanct' (Chopra and Weiss, 1992).

Conclusion

The secretary-general's former special advisor with the R2P portfolio, Edward Luck, aptly reminds us that the lifespan of successful norms is 'measured in centuries, not decades' (Luck, 2011: 387), but R2P already is firmly embedded in the values of international society and occasionally in policies and tactics for humanitarian crises. And it certainly has the potential to evolve further in customary international law and to contribute to ongoing conversations about the qualifications of states as legitimate, rather than rogue, sovereigns

The political and military roller-coaster ride of R2P's move from the periphery to the center of public policy debate has taken place in what Gareth Evans calculates as 'a blink of the eye in the history of ideas' (Evans, 2008: 28). Libya is the most significant recent precedent that show the importance of the norm's move from the printed pages of a blue-ribbon commission's report to the center of public policy discourse and occasionally decision-making. With the exception of Raphael Lemkin's advocacy and the 1948 Convention on the Punishment and Prevention of the Crime of Genocide, no idea has moved faster or farther in the international normative arena than the responsibility to protect.

At the same time, this chapter has also indicated that the 2005 UN World Summit's decision about R2P represents a step backwards from the recommendations of the International Commission on Sovereignty and Intervention. The watered-down version, or 'R2P lite,' is so characterized because of the two missing elements that are essential for readers of this volume and their concerns with statebuilding. The intergovernmental text that governs the application of the responsibility to protect is weaker than the original recommendations not only by the ICISS but by the High-level Panel on Threats, Challenges and Change as well.

Both shortcomings are directly relevant to this handbook's focus on statebuilding. The first is that the application of R2P is held hostage to the lowest common denominator of the Security Council, which means that outside muscle (sanctions, juridical pursuit, or military force) may take longer than it should to be approved and deployed. Thus, statebuilding will face additional challenges in the form of unnecessary destruction and still more accounts to be settled. Syria is the current Exhibit A and its president Assad is the poster child of the need to take action when a council decision is unfeasible or feeble, in this case because of Russian and Chinese threatened or actual vetoes.

The second shortcoming could be remedied by returning to the ICISS's three-part responsibility (to prevent, to react, *and* to rebuild). The World Summit shortchanged the third, which is absolutely crucial to international efforts to help improve the chances for sustainable peace in war-torn societies. That the responsibility to rebuild a country after the use of military force for human protection purposes is not viewed as an integral component of making a decision to use Chapter VII intervention to halt mass atrocities is a definite lacuna. As Mohamed Sahnoun one of the ICISS co-chairs, summarized, 'R2P's peace building pillar is not as prominent as it should be on the international agenda ... Moreover, genuine and substantial support for peace building, healing traumatic memories, and resolving past problems adds credibility to the entire R2P enterprise' (Sahnoun, 2011: 21–22).

Syria demonstrates the extent to which normative advances are necessary but insufficient; an it also shows why continued normative efforts are worthwhile. The international actions (or, to date, rather inactions) in Syria indicate that a robust R2P response is not automatic. The gruesome death toll continued to mount in 2012, it is true; but a historical perspective perhaps provides a note of encouragement at the end this chapter. A deafening silence greeted the 1982 massacre by Hafez al-Assad of what may have been 40,000 people in an artillery barrage of Hama, but his son's machinations have encountered hostile reactions from a host of critical actors: the UN's Joint Off ce on the Prevention of Genocide and R2P called for a halt to crimes against humanity; the Human Rights Council condemned the crimes by a crushing vote and published a thorough report detailing extensive crimes; the United States, the European Union, and other states imposed sanctions and recalled ambassadors; the Arab League has unequivocally condemned Assad's actions, formulated a peace plan, sent human rights monitors, and sponsored a resolution in the Security Council; and the UN General Assembly initially condemned the violence and supported the peace plan with a two-thirds majority and subsequently even more overwhelmingly (only 12 of 193 states voted against) condemned Bashar al-Assad's unbridled crackdown on his population and specif cally called for his resignation.

The anemic response to Syria's plight confirmed the growing ability of the international community of states to condemn abhorrent state conduct but far more limited ability to agree on a common course of action even in the face of mass atrocities. While of little solace to the victims and their families, the responsibility to protect is a principle and not a tactic. That principle remained intact in Syria even if international action was considerably slower and less forceful than in Libya and Côte d'Ivoire. But it still may result; and if it does, it can be attributed to the evolving power of the R2P norm.

Notes

1 See also Weiss and Hubert (2001). For interpretations by commissioners, see Evans (2008) and Thakur (2006). The author's version of the normative itinerary is Weiss (2012).
2 See, for example, Deng et al. (1996) and Cohen and Deng (1998a, 1998b). This story is the basis for the analysis by Weiss and Korn (2006).
3 Accounts of the 2009–2012 debates and the meetings by focal points are reported by the Global Centre for the Responsibility to Protect and are available at: http://globalr2p.org/advocacy/index.php
4 See especially Bull (1977) and Jackson (2001). Another member of the English School, Nicholas J. Wheeler, would be more supportive; see Wheeler (2000).

References

Annan, K. A. (2005). *In larger freedom: Towards development, security and human rights for all*. New York, NY: United Nations.

Badescu, C., and Weiss, T. G. (2010). Misrepresenting R2P and advancing norms: An alternative spiral? *International Studies Perspectives*, *11*(4), 354–374.

Ban Ki-moon. (2010). *Early warning, assessment, and the responsibility to protect*. Report of the Secretary-General, UN document A/64/864, 14 July. New York, NY: United Nations.

Ban Ki-moon. (2012). *The responsibility to protect, Pillar III: Timely and decisive response*. Report of the Secretary-General, UN document S/2012/578, 24 July. New York, NY: United Nations.

Barnett, M., and Weiss, T. G. (2011). *Humanitarianism contested: Where angels fear to tread*. London, UK: Routledge.

Bass, G. J. (2008). *Freedom's battle: The origins of humanitarian intervention*. New York, NY: Knopf.

Bassett, T. J., and Straus, S. (2011). Defending democracy in Côte d'Ivoire. *Foreign Affairs*, *90*(4), 130–140.

Beebe, S. D., and Kaldor, M. (2010). *The ultimate weapon is no weapon: Human security and the new rules of war and peace*. New York, NY: Public Affairs.

Bellamy, A. J. (2010). The responsibility to protect—Five years on. *Ethics & International Affairs*, *24*(2), 143–169.

Brockmann, M. E. (2009). Statement by the President of the General Assembly, Miguel d'Escoto Brockmann, at the Opening of the 97th Session of the General Assembly, 23 July. New York, NY: United Nations.

Bull, H. (1977). *The anarchical society: A study of order in world politics*. New York, NY: Columbia University Press.

Chopra, J., and Weiss, T. G. (1992). Sovereignty is no longer sacrosanct: Codifying humanitarian intervention. *Ethics & International Affairs*, *6*, 95–117.

Cohen, R., and Deng, F. M. (1998a). *Masses in flight: The global crisis of internal displacement*. Washington, DC: Brookings Institution.

Cohen, R., and Deng, F. M. (Eds.). (1998b). *The forsaken people: Case studies of the internally displaced*. Washington, DC: Brookings Institution.

Deng, F. M., Kimaro, S., Lyons, T., Rothchild, D., and Zartman, I. W. (1996).*Sovereignty as responsibility: Conflict management in Africa*. Washington, DC: Brookings Institution.

The Economist. (2009, July 23). An idea whose time has come—and gone? Available at: www.economist.com

Evans, G. (2008). *The responsibility to protect: Ending mass atrocity crimes once and for all*. Washington, DC: Brookings Institution.

Hehir, A. (2012). *The responsibility to protect: Rhetoric, reality and the future of humanitarian intervention*. Basingstoke, UK: Palgrave Macmillan.

High-LevelPanel on Threats, Challenges and Change. (2004). *A more secure world: Our shared responsibility*. New York, NY: United Nations.

International Commission on Intervention and State Sovereignty. (2001).*The responsibility to protect*. Ottawa, Canada: International Development Research Centre.

Jackson, R. (2001). *The global covenant: Human conduct in a world of states*. Oxford, UK: Oxford University Press.

Letter Dated 9 November 2011 from the Permanent Representative of Brazil to the United Nations Addressed to the Secretary-General. UN document A/66/551–S/2011/701, 1. New York, NY: United Nations.

Luck, E. C. (2010). The responsibility to protect: Growing pains or early promise? *Ethics & International Affairs*, *24*(4), 349–365.

Luck, E. C. (2011). The responsibility to protect: The first decade. *Global Responsibility to Protect*, *3*(4), 387–399.

Mani, R., and Weiss, T. G. (Eds.). (2011). *Responsibility to protect: Cultural perspectives from the Global South*. London, UK: Routledge.

Pattison, J. (2010). *Humanitarian intervention and the responsibility to protect: Who should intervene?* Oxford, UK: Oxford University Press.

Sahnoun, M. (2011). Foreword. In R. Mani and T. G. Weiss (Eds.), *Responsibility to protect: Cultural perspectives from the Global South*. London, UK: Routledge, pp. 21–22.

Serrano, M. (2010a). The responsibility to protect: True consensus, false controversy*Development Dialogue*, *55*, 101–110.

Serrano, M. (2010b). Implementing the responsibility to protect: The power of R2P talk. *Global Responsibility to Protect*, *2*(1–2), 167–177.

Slaughter, A.-M. (2011). A day to celebrate, but hard work ahead. *Foreign Policy*, 18 March. Available at: www.foreignpolicy.com

Thakur, R. (2006). *The United Nations, peace and security: From collective security to the responsibility to protect*. Cambridge, UK: Cambridge University Press.

Thakur, R. (2011). *The responsibility to protect: Norms, laws and the use of force in international politics*. London, UK: Routledge.

Walzer, M. (2011). On humanitarianism. *Foreign Affairs*, *90*(4), 69–80.

Weiss, T. G. (2011). RtoP alive and well after Libya. *Ethics & International Affairs*, *25*(3), 1–6. This article is part of a symposium, 'Special Roundtable on Libya and Humanitarian Intervention'.

Weiss, T. G. (2012). *Humanitarian intervention: Ideas in action* (2nd ed.). Cambridge, UK: Polity Press.

Weiss, T. G., and Hubert, D. (Eds.). (2001). *The responsibility to protect: Research, bibliography, background*. Ottawa, Canada: International Development Research Centre.

Weiss, T. G., and Korn, D. A. (2006). *Internal displacement: Conceptualization and its consequences*. London, UK: Routledge.

Welsh, J. (2010). Implementing the "responsibility to protect": Where expectations meet reality. *Ethics & International Affairs*, *24*(4), 415–430.

Wheeler, N. J. (2000). *Saving strangers: Humanitarian intervention in international society*. Oxford, UK: Oxford University Press.

Woodward, B. (2004). *Plan of attack*. New York, NY: Simon & Schuster.

World Summit Outcome. (2005). UN document A/60/1, 24 October 2005, paragraphs 138–140. New York, NY: United Nations.

32
AID AND FRAGILITY
The challenges of building peaceful and effective states

Alina Rocha Menocal

Fragile states have been a leading priority in international development thinking and practice starting in the 1990s. This concern with fragility emerged from the confluence of a variety o factors, including (i) an emphasis on human security and peacebuilding; (ii) the emergence of new states (the Balkans, the former Soviet Union, Timor–Leste, and, most recently, South Sudan), some of which have remained weak and unstable; (iii) closely linked to this, a concern with poor development performance and state effectiveness; and (iv) a belief that underdevelopment, insecurity (individual, national, and global), and conflict are related (Cammack et al., 2006). focus on fragile states gained increased prominence in policy-making circles in the aftermath of the terrorist attacks on the United States on September 11, 2001, which placed renewed emphasis on the linkages between development and governance on one hand and security on the other.

Today, fragile states are the home of the 'bottom 1.5 billion' of the world's population (Collier, 2007). Fragility is also severely exacerbated by conflict. According to Paul Collier (2007), 73 pe cent of the people living in fragile settings have recently been through a civil war or are still in one. Moreover, conflict tends to be recurring: since 2000, 90 per cent of new conflicts ha occurred in countries with a previous conf ict (World Bank, 2011).

This chapter looks at how donor thinking on the concept of fragility has evolved and how the statebuilding agenda emerged. It explores some frameworks that the international assistance community has developed to foster more peaceful states and societies, as well as at the proposals that have been developed by a growing group of fragile states known as the g7+ toward that same goal. The chapter then analyzes some of the tensions and dilemmas that are embedded in statebuilding processes. By way of conclusion, the chapter asks whether current international engagement in fragile states is fit for purpose, and what some of the challenges in ongoing dono practices are to promote more effective statebuilding efforts.

Evolving thinking on 'fragility' in international development circles

The concept of 'fragility' is complex and multifaceted, and there is as yet no set defi ition of the term. Nevertheless, the understanding of the term has evolved considerably over the past decade, and there is a growing consensus within the international development community regarding some of its key characteristics.

Early definitions and their limitations

Early definitions of fragility in international development circles fell into two overlapping categories: where fragility was defined in terms of the functionality of states, or of their outputs In the first instance, fragile states are those that lack the capacity and/or will to perform key cor functions that are necessary to ensure the wellbeing and security of the population, especially the poor. Early definitions also focused on their outputs – poverty, violent conflict, and instabili – and their undesirable spill–over effects across borders, including terrorism, global security threats, refugees, organized crime, etc. (Cammack et al., 2006).

Such definitions of fragility had considerable limitations. Definitions based on functionali or outcomes are not sufficiently fine–grained. Among other things, such definitions fail to distinguish sufficiently between the particular conditions of 'fragility' and the general condition of 'underdevelopment' (Putzel, 2010). After all, most poor countries tend to lack the capacity to reduce poverty and to promote development. The key analytical challenge is thus to understand why countries with similar poor development outcomes have followed markedly different trajectories in the development and consolidation of their state institutions, and why they are more or less vulnerable to (violent) conflict. But early definitions of fragility tended lump together countries as diverse as Haiti and North Korea into a single, all–encompassing label, in ways that were not particularly helpful or illuminating (Call, 2011; Putzel, 2010; Bertoli and Ticci, 2012).

Early definitions were also problematic because they were static and based on a notion of th state that is highly normative and Western–centric (Bertoli and Ticci, 2012; Pritchett and de Weijer, 2010). This made the term 'fragility' very contentious and contested. Especially among countries considered 'fragile,' it led to perceptions of an externally imposed label based on the failure of the country in question to follow development priorities imposed by the outside (e.g., pro–poorpolicies, the Millennium Development Goals, human rights) (Bertoli and Ticci, 2012). Aid recipient countries also feared that the 'fragility' label could generate stereotypes and stigmatization that put their international image and development prospects in jeopardy (Faria and Magalhães Ferreira, 2007; Collier, 2007; Bertoli and Ticci, 2012).

Toward a new understanding of fragility grounded in internal processes of change and contestation

The need to refne understandings of fragility has led to a progressive shift in international thinking toward a definition that is less driven by (external) standards of what the state ought to be/do and more grounded on internal processes of contestation and bargaining between state and society. There is a growing consensus that fragility is a deeply political phenomenon: at its core, a fragile state is one where effective political processes that can bring state capacities and social expectations into equilibrium are lacking (Jones et al., 2008; OECD, 2011a). In a fragile setting, the quality of the political settlement – or of the underlying agreements and arrangements establishing the rules of the game – is deeply flawed, is not resilient, and/or has become signif cantly undermined or contested. A social contract binding state and society in mutually reinforcing ways is missing (see DFID, 2010; Rocha Menocal, 2011a; and OECD, 2011a, among others).

There is also a growing appreciation that fragility is a multifaceted and dynamic phenomenon. Rather than being binary, fragility can best be understood as a continuum: some countries represent entrenched and systemic state fragility, while others exhibit local and temporary fragile characteristics. Fragility thus has different drivers and finds different expressions and degrees o intensity in different settings – hence the recognition by the OECD DAC and others that there are not only fragile states, but also *fragile situations* within otherwise stable states (Putzel, 2010).

An emerging body of academic literature has proved useful in understanding fragility along three key dimensions of the state – capacity, authority, and legitimacy (see Box 32.1). These different dimensions are conceptually distinct, though they often overlap (Call, 2011; Stewart and Brown, 2009). The most fragile of states are those where the state suffers considerable weaknesses or gaps in all three of these dimensions, which reinforce and feed on one another. These states lack the fundamental capacity, authority, and/or legitimacy to mediate relations between citizen groups and between citizens and the state, or to channel conflict through peaceful mechanisms (e.g., Democratic Republic of Congo (DRC), South Sudan). These cases are qualitatively very different from states that may have a gap only in one dimension and may be stagnant developmentally but remain relatively stable and peaceful (e.g., Bangladesh) (Putzel, 2010). The main point is that fragility comes in many shades and varieties, and understanding these multiple dimensions and combinations is essential because they present different challenges.

Box 32.1 *Key dimensions of the state*

Capacity refers to the state's ability to provide its citizens with basic life chances. These include protection from curable diseases; basic education; social protection; and a basic administration that regulates social and economic activities sufficiently to increase collective gains and avoid massive negative externalities. Capacity is not only technical but also political, institutional, administrative, and economic.

Authority has two essential components. One is security and relates to the extent to which a state faces an organized challenge to its monopoly of violence. The other refers to the extent to which the state controls its territory and national law is recognized. While institutional multiplicity to varying extents exists in all states, the question is the degree to which these are competing and overlapping in ways that undermine rather than complement formal state rules.

Legitimacy refers to the normative belief of key political elites and the public that the rules regulating the exercise of power and the distribution of wealth are proper and binding. Historically, states have relied on a combination of different methods to establish their legitimacy, including legitimacy based on performance, legitimacy based on rules and procedures, and legitimacy based on international recognition, among others.

Sources: Putzel, 2010; Call, 2011; Stewart and Brown, 2009; Rocha Menocal, 2011a.

Part of this newer understanding of fragility still hinges on the capacity of the state to perform basic functions. However, at least in principle, fragility is not meant to be assessed against externally determined benchmarks, but rather in relation to domestically driven processes of contestation and bargaining, and to the state's ability to mediate and address different needs, expectations and claims emerging from different levels of the social structure. Thus, this more nuanced interpretation of fragility is less normative, and it also recognizes much more explicitly that pathways out of fragility must come from within and cannot be imposed from the outside.

Has a focus on fragility made a difference in international development?

The identification of fragility as a leading priority in development has been welcome in several key respects. Among other things, during the 1990s, with the rise of the good governance agenda, there were many arguments to allocate aid to 'best performers.' But the focus on fragile states was important in directing a larger share of international development assistance toward countries that may not perform as well but are most in need (Putzel, 2010).

As Louise Anten et al. (2012) have put it, 'despite ongoing debate on whether the label "fragile" is a valid, appropriate, or fair description for these states, the concept of a group of ... countries where the structures of power and authority fail to deliver basic public goods is one that has proven extremely resonant.' Over time, 'fragility' has become a rallying point for action for the international donor community – at least in principle and despite considerable limitations in actual practice (more on this below).

This growing concern with fragility has reflected a recognition that aid in fragile states is no 'business as usual' – states that are fragile face development challenges that are qualitatively different and more profound than those confronted by more mainstream developing countries. As a result, a different international approach may be needed that goes beyond an exclusive focus on the Millennium Development Goals (MDGs) and the 2005 Paris Declaration on Aid Effectiveness. Both of these frameworks, which have been the linchpins of development efforts over the past decade, are based on the expectation that national development strategies will provide a strategic policy framework that donors can support. But they do not address how greater ownership of a development agenda is to be achieved in the first place, and they assume to easily that most countries already have development-oriented political leaderships at the helm of (relatively) effective and capable states. However, this cannot be taken for granted in fragile settings (Fritz and Rocha Menocal, 2007a; Booth, 2011; Bertoli and Ticci, 2012) – and in fact most fragile states are not on track to achieve a single MDG by 2015 (World Bank, 2011).

Hence, a focus on fragility has put statebuilding and the need to build peaceful and more effective, inclusive, and responsive states [1] at the top of the international development agenda. This was clearly articulated in the OECD's Principles for Good International Engagement in Fragile States that were endorsed in 2007 and seek to provide a more grounded and coherent international response to fragility (OECD, 2010). Principle 3 in particular stresses that statebuilding should be 'the central objective' of engagement. A wide diversity of external actors has become involved in statebuilding efforts, including bilateral and multilateral aid agencies, security organizations, humanitarian bodies, civil society organizations, and military and diplomatic actors. Today, almost every major donor identifies statebuilding as a priority, with flows of resources to fragile states accounting for 30 per cent of total annual development aid from OECD countries (OECD, 2011a).

Statebuilding

What does the international community mean by 'statebuilding'?

In its simplest formulation, statebuilding refers to a set of actions undertaken by national and/or international actors to establish, reform, and strengthen state institutions where these have been seriously eroded or are missing (Caplan, 2005), often, though not always, as a result of violent conflict. Yet, like understandings of fragility, the concept of statebuilding has also evolved considerably over time. Based on a more dynamic appreciation of fragility and its root causes, there is now growing recognition within the international assistance community that statebuilding is not purely a technical exercise but rather an inherently political one. From a narrow preoccupation with building/strengthening formal institutions and state capacity across various dimensions (e.g., security or public financial management), there has been an important shift toward recognizing that the state cannot be treated in isolation and that the dynamic capacity of state and society to negotiate mutual demands and obligations and manage expectations without resorting to violence is central to the process of building more peaceful and effective states (see for example Jones et al., 2008; DFID, 2010; and OECD, 2011a and also discussion above on fragility).

This shift has rightfully placed the concept of legitimacy – both as a means to building state capacity and as an end in itself – at the center of the statebuilding agenda (Wyeth and Sisk, 2009). According to the World Bank, for example, legitimate institutions constitute the 'immune system' of a properly functioning and resilient state (World Bank, 2011). The political process linking state and society is fundamental here: at the heart of statebuilding efforts lies the challenge to strengthen/revitalize the linkages between the state and different groups in society. So statebuilding is not simply about 'top–down' approaches of institution–strengthening (i.e., those focusing on state actors and/or national elites) but also about 'bottom–up' approaches (focused on civil society) and – crucially – about bringing these together (see also OECD DAC Principle 3).

Building on the above, different international organizations and initiatives (e.g., the OECD DAC's International Network on Conflict and Fragility (INCAF), DFID, Institute for State Effectiveness, the International Dialogue on Peacebuilding and Statebuilding, the World Bank's 2011 *World Development Report*[2]) have developed frameworks outlining what the key areas for supporting the building of peaceful and effective states and societies should be. While each of these varies in some respects, giving different weight to different areas and assigning different characteristics/functions to the state, they all share fundamental similarities (see Box 32.2 for examples from the OECD and the World Bank). Current thinking on what is needed to rearticulate the linkages between state and society and foster legitimacy centers around the following:

- making political settlements and political processes more inclusive, especially in terms of incorporating women and other groups that have traditionally been excluded or marginalized;
- strengthening key core functions of the state (however narrowly or broadly these are defined);
- helping the state meet public expectations;
- nurturing social cohesion and a society's capacities to promote reconciliation and/or re–weave the social fabric.

Box 32.2 *Examples of international frameworks to support the building of peaceful and effective states*

OECD StateBuilding Framework (OECD, 2011a)

The OECD StateBuilding Framework focuses on three dimensions of state–society relations that influence the resilience or fragility of states. These dimensions are meant to be understood within a larger regional and global policy environment and as operating at multiple levels – national and sub–national – within the domestic polity:

- the political settlement, which reflects the implicit or explicit agreement (among elites principally)

> on the 'rules of the game' and how power is distributed, and the political processes through which state and society are connected;
> - the capability and responsiveness of the state to effectively fulfill its principal functions and provid key services, in relation to
> - broader social expectations and perceptions about what the state should do, what the terms of the state–society relationship should be, and the ability of society to articulate demands that are 'heard.'
>
> At the heart of the interaction between these three dimensions lies the matter of legitimacy, which provides the basis for rule by primarily non-coercive means.
>
> ### The 2011 World Development Report's roadmap to move beyond conflict and fragility and secure development (World Bank, 2011)
>
> The WDR argues that institutional transformation sits at the heart of successful transitions out of fragility, and that legitimate institutions, both formal and informal, are a country's 'immune system' against external and internal shocks. The WDR avoids defining legitimacy in terms of narrow normative commitments to democratic principles and acknowledges that states can rely on a combination of different methods to establish their legitimacy.
>
> Critical early steps in breaking the cycle of conflict and fragility and building legitimacy include
>
> - restoring confidence on crucial institutions through the development of 'inclusive enough coalitions' that should include not only state actors but also community leaders, NGOs, the private sector, as well as informal actors and institutions
> - 'getting the basics right' by focusing on the provision of citizen security, justice, and jobs.
>
> Progress along these priorities is essential in order to give everyone a stake in the (new) social order, improve the nature of state–society relations, and foster a sense of collective belonging.

The rise of the g7+ and the New Deal on aid

While much of the statebuilding agenda has been developed by the international donor community, over the past several years, developing countries themselves have begun to play a much more active role. One of the most significant outcomes to emerge from the Third Hig Level Forum on Aid Effectiveness held in Accra, Ghana in 2008 was the establishment of the International Dialogue on Peacebuilding and Statebuilding (Wyeth, 2012). The Dialogue is intended to bring together donors (including traditional bilateral and multilateral donors but also emerging ones such as China and Brazil), recipient countries, and civil society actors to address the root causes of conflict and fragility in a more realistic and effective manner.

Led by Timor-Leste and the DRC, a small group of countries affected by conflict and fragilit – including in addition Afghanistan, Sierra Leone, Central African Republic, Haiti, and Côte d'Ivoire – became deeply involved in the process of establishing the Dialogue. Originally known as the g7, this group has continued to expand, and the g7+ now includes 17 countries (see www.g7plus.org). The g7+ has called for a New Deal for Engagement in Fragile States that was endorsed at the Fourth High Level Forum on Aid Effectiveness in Busan, Korea at the end of

2011. This New Deal elaborates a series of Peacebuilding and Statebuilding Goals (PSGs) that are deemed to be essential preconditions for development in fragile contexts. They include the following.

- *Legitimate Politics:* Foster inclusive political settlements and conflict resolution
- *Security:* Establish and strengthen people's security.
- *Justice:* Address injustices and increase people's access to justice.
- *Economic Foundations:* generate employment and improve livelihoods.
- *Revenues & Services:* Manage revenue and build capacity for accountable and fair service delivery.

As can be seen from the discussion above, these objectives and priorities are very similar to those espoused by the international community. But the g7+ is particularly significant and ha gained considerable recognition because it is the f rst such forum to bring together the world's most fragile and conflict-afflicted states around a common purpose and to give them a voice putting forward an agenda for change in aid practice (Denney, 2011; Wyeth, 2012).

Tensions embedded in the statebuilding agenda

The building of peaceful, more capable and more accountable states has emerged as a critical strategic priority for the international aid community. Yet, thus far, despite all the important shifts in thinking outlined above, the proliferation of political declarations, multi-stakeholder dialogues and networks, high-level official meetings, and commitments to make aid better suited to the particular needs confronting fragile states, the international response to fragility has remained weak and ineffective. A survey monitoring the Fragile States Principles in 13 countries has found that the implementation of these principles is seriously off-track and that, thus far, the principles have stimulated relatively limited change in international engagement at the country level (OECD, 2011b).

Weaknesses in international support include the persistence of technocratic and 'one size fit all' approaches, in spite of a rhetorical commitment to take context as the starting point; an aversion to the risks embodied in institution building, which leads donors to privilege institutional form over function and to support the establishment and/or strengthening of formal institutions that may be hollow; inflexible and cumbersome aid mechanisms; and a lack of engagement wit national stakeholders, with resulting deficits in country ownership (Pritchett and de Weijer, 2010 Wyeth, 2012; Rocha Menocal, 2011b). As different studies have shown, aid can also 'do harm,' especially in terms of undermining state capacity and legitimacy in fragile settings (OECD, 2010; Fukuyama, 2004).

In addition, international statebuilding efforts continue to be characterized by a distressing lack of coherence and coordination (Wyeth, 2012). New and important sources of aid, particularly from emerging Southern powers, have added to the diversity of approaches and fragmentation of efforts (Anten et al., 2012). Aid remains highly volatile and seemingly dependent on the short-term interests and imperatives of a plethora of donor countries and organizations.

The rise of the g7+ can be seen as a response to such persistent shortcomings. The g7+ countries have declared their intention to work together and develop national strategies to address crucial governance challenges. Among other things, they are in the process of developing locally grounded indicators for the PSGs and monitoring progress. They have agreed to establish country-ledplans based on joint fragility assessments and political dialogue, and to develop new ways of engaging with donors that are based on mutual trust and the achievement of better results in fragile states (Naudé, 2012).

However, as welcome as the arrival of the g7+ is, this initiative should not be seen as a panacea to the challenges besetting fragile states. The task ahead, both for the international community and for domestic actors committed to change, is daunting. As Roland Paris and Timothy Sisk (2008) have noted, the enterprise to build more peaceful and effective states has the quality of an enormous experiment, especially given the magnitude and scale of the transformations being sought, and how complex and uncertain this transformational process is likely to be. Statebuilding is ultimately about fundamentally reshaping values, principles, interests, and power relations, and not just about 'bricks and mortar' (Engberg–Pedersen et al., 2008).

This is an endeavor that remains full of internal contradictions and diffcult trade–offs and dilemmas, and not a linear sequence of cumulative or mutually reinforcing steps. A growing body of literature explores some of these tensions (see, for example, Call, 2008; Paris and Sisk, 2008; World Bank, 2011). The analysis below focuses on a few of the most prominent ones.

Statebuilding may not automatically lead to peace

The current vision of the international donor community, as well as that of the g7+, on statebuilding seems to be based on the assumption that the process can be remarkably consensual, inclusive, bottom–up, and democratic (see Principle 3 of the OECD DAC as well as the PSGs). However, historical experiences with state formation and statebuilding suggest otherwise. State formation and statebuilding have emerged as long–term, non–linear, tumultuous, inherently conflict–riddenprocesses often associated with violence and war (see Tilly, 1992 in particular). Such efforts have frequently been top–down, heavily driven, and controlled by national elites, and concern for human rights and justice has been minimal. In cases in which social mobilization has played a formative role in statebuilding processes, the relationship between state and society has more often than not been contentious and conflict–ridden[3]

Clearly, contemporary statebuilding efforts are qualitatively and contextually different from earlier state formation processes. The current devastation within which fragile states are attempting to transform themselves offers a crucial window of opportunity for more inclusive and peaceful statebuilding processes. Given the weakness and/or lack of legitimacy of much of the state apparatus, there is a signifcant opportunity for civil society actors (NGOs, religious organizations, indigenous groups, women's organizations, social movements, etc.) to become key interlocutors in the rearticulation of a social pact that is more legitimate and inclusive. In addition, as leading actors in contemporary statebuilding attempts, international players (and for the purposes of this chapter donors in particular) have come to assume particular responsibilities, and they are committed, at least in principle, to fomenting peace and constructing a domestic basis of legitimacy in different fragile settings.

Nevertheless, statebuilding remains deeply political in nature. Again, this is something that the international community has become less reluctant to acknowledge more openly over the past few years – at least in principle. But the practical implications of this still need to be more fully internalized: in the measure that statebuilding in the 21st century continues to create winners and losers, it has the potential to spark further conflict rather than simply reinforce a consensual process through a virtuous circle linking state and society.

Statebuilding and democratization are not one and the same thing

There has been a tendency in international development circles to equate efforts to build peaceful and effective states with efforts to democratize, and the PSGs embedded in the New Deal reflec similar thinking. However, it is essential to recognize that these two are distinct processes, and they can pull in different (if not opposite) directions (Rocha Menocal, 2011d). For instance, democratization often entails establishing checks and balances mechanisms, and diffusing power more evenly across a greater number of actors both within and outside government, while strengthening state capacity may call for greater autonomy and centralization of power. The case of contemporary Rwanda is a vivid illustration of the kinds of tensions that exist between state capacity and democracy, and of the problem of conflating the two

Numerous scholars have highlighted the perils of promoting political liberalization and democratization too quickly in fragile settings (Snyder, 2000; Paris, 2004), before institutions are in place that are strong and effective enough to channel new rights and freedoms peacefully. However, it is also clear that postponing democratic openings until perfect institutions emerge is unrealistic, especially given the acute need to build a state that is perceived as legitimate in the eyes of its population. There are no answers here, and a fine balance needs to be achieved tha draws on existing experiences and insights.

Steps that may be necessary to consolidate peace and arrive at an agreement on the (new) rules of the game or political settlement may undermine the creation of a capable and effective state in the longer term

This can manifest itself in a number of different ways. For instance, especially in post–conf ict settings where a peace settlement needs to be negotiated, a significant challenge lies in the fac that there are no clear winners and losers, so that difficult compromises need to be made. Amon other things, there may be a need to include unsavory actors responsible for considerable human rights atrocities at the negotiating table. This happened in Liberia during the time of the National Transitional Government from 2003 to 2006, with consequences that are still being felt today in terms of an unfinished process of national reconciliation and a political settlement that is no f rm and remains subject to manipulation by a variety of actors in ways that could be destabilzing (United Nations Development Programme and World Bank, 2009; Rocha Menocal, 2011c).

In addition, confidence–building measures, including provisions such as power–sharing arrangements and compromise, come with advantages and drawbacks that need to be taken into account. Such measures may be necessary to overcome the distrust of the state and to foster the legitimacy of the peace settlement and the post–conflict political order in the short run, but they can also have a negative impact on the capacity and effectiveness of state institutions in the medium and long terms. One of the basic tensions in this respect is to over–privilege the pursuit of peace over state coherence and effectiveness (London School of Economics and PricewaterhouseCoopers, 2009). A drive toward inclusiveness and broad representation can lead to such a dispersion of power and authority that the political system becomes paralyzed and unable to carry out critical governance reforms. In Afghanistan, for example, the central state remains weak and thoroughly ineffective, in large part as a result of the need to accommodate potential spoilers and preserve internal peace (Call, 2008).

There is also a danger that different parties will refuse to enter into negotiations unless a general amnesty is granted.[4] In some contexts, bringing individuals to account too early may compromise a political settlement. Conversely, failing to bring individuals to justice may undermine people's trust in the political process. Thus, it is not always clear that the goals of achieving peace and those of achieving justice can be easily reconciled – and a careful and context–sensitive balance between these twin needs is an essential component of (and challenge to) successful statecraft. Different societies have attempted to experiment with different methods and mechanisms in search of such a balance. South Africa's use of so–called 'restorative justice' and Rwanda's *gacaca* tribunals offer creative, if not entirely unproblematic, examples of this.

Aid undermines statebuilding when it bypasses state institutions, even though doing so may make a lot of sense in the short term

There are multiple manifestations of this. Michael Carnahan and Clare Lockhart (2008), for example, have been critical of donor practices that channel funds outside the domestic system of public finance. They and others (e.g., Manuel, 2011) have argued that international assistanc needs to run through state institutions and rely on the formal budget process. This is essential to build the capacity of these institutions to perform basic functions, as well as to strengthen legitimacy by enhancing the state's ability to address citizen expectations and demands.

While relying on country systems may be risky, especially if the state in question lacks legitimacy, donors need to think about the long–term impact of their actions and seek to identify ways in which they can allow greater reliance on country systems in the future, even while substituting for these in the short run. The Governance and Economic Management Program (GEMAP) in Liberia is an innovative example of creating safeguards (a dual signatory system) to mitigate the risk of using country systems. Rwanda is another example where early reliance on country systems proved instrumental in helping to build state institutions (and make considerable progress in domestic tax collection, for example) (Manuel, 2011).

The provision of basic social services, such as health, water, and electricity, provides another, powerful illustration of this issue of undermining statebuilding efforts in the long term to address short–termimperatives. Confronted by a persistent (and profound) lack of state capacity in fragile contexts, donors have often put service delivery in the hands of international and local NGOs to generate quick and visible improvements in everyday conditions. The creation of such 'peace dividends' is an extremely valid concern, especially given the decrepitude, if not outright absence, of state institutions that can fulfill basic functions. And yet it has to be managed very carefully the temptation to bypass the state can have potentially negative consequences on longer–term statebuilding priorities, and undermine the legitimacy of the state in the eyes of its population (Fritz and Rocha Menocal, 2007b). In the DRC, for example, schools and clinics are being built without the authorization of the local administration (which would normally oversee these processes), and such initiatives have contributed to the weakening of the state and its linkages to society (LSE and PwC, 2009).

'Multiple accountabilities' can generate pressures that undermine statebuilding

Related to the point above, a narrow focus on short–term and visible results – which donors tend to emphasize as part of a 'results–based agenda' so that they can be accountable to their home publics – does not always provide the foundations to support effective, resilient, and responsive states in the long term (see for example World Bank, 2011) . That endeavor is by nature more difficult to quantify and measure, and also more uncertain. In effect, many of the pathologies of aid, including an emphasis on formal institutions without due concern about their actual substance and viability, and a reluctance to engage in riskier institution–building, are grounded in this tension between competing accountabilities to taxpayers on one hand and to the governments and people of recipient countries on the other. Accountability to taxpayers is obviously desirable. But the challenge is how to make domestic expectations fit with the needs and realities of assistance on the ground in a more realistic and honest manner. This task has become even more difficult in the context of the ongoing global economic crisis, with taxpayers unconvinced about the wisdom of promoting international development within the current fiscal environment. (Rocha Menocal, 2011b)

Are current donor practices fit for purpose in fragile states?[5]

Over the past decade, donor thinking on issues related to fragility and statebuilding has evolved considerably. As discussed above, there is now much more open and explicit recognition that many of the challenges besetting fragile states are inherently political in nature, and that technocratic, 'one size fits all' approaches cannot adequately address them. Political economy i now at the heart of the work of a growing number of donors (including DFID, the EU, The Netherlands, the OECD DAC, and the World Bank, among others), who have committed to develop more sophisticated analysis on the dynamics and complexities of statebuilding and to take context as the starting point. Yet it has proved very challenging for donors to translate the insights from such analysis into operational practice (Unsworth, 2010). Moreover, it has remained extremely difficult for the international assistance community to act on lessons that have bee drawn from cumulative years of experience of statebuilding, as well as scholarly literature on this subject, many of which are embodied in the OECD DAC principles of engagement in fragile states and multiple other declarations and donor policy guidance notes. Much of this may be because the ways donors currently work do not facilitate this kind of uptake.

To begin with, donor time horizons are not sufficiently focused on the long term. Three— t five—yeartimeframes are not enough when considering that the changes being sought in fragile states are likely to take generations. In addition, in order to engage with the political dimensions of statebuilding, donors need to be able to act as facilitators and conveners of reform and change – bringing together domestic stakeholders, supporting them in identifying problems and solutions, etc. – rather than simply as providers of funds or implementers. And it also requires greater donor tolerance, not only in principle but also in practice, for the 'messiness' of statebuilding, which is likely to be uncomfortable, risky, and resource—intensive. This is especially true in terms of well— qualified staff, both in—country and at the headquarters level. However, for the most part, this is not how organizations that support statebuilding efforts tend to operate. Much statebuilding work continues to be short—term, risk—averse, and focused on technical aspects of development, a tendency that is exacerbated by ongoing pressures to do 'more with less' (i.e., disburse more funds with fewer staff to provide needed support and guidance).

In addition, staff, especially at the country level, face perverse incentives to working in a more politically informed manner. There is a strong preference in donor agencies toward continuous fluctuation and rapid turnover rates. This poses considerable problems for the development of in—depthcountry knowledge, the building of long—term relationships with in—country partners that are based on mutual trust, and the maintenance of institutional memory, all of which are essential to successful statebuilding efforts.

Hence, what may be needed to make international statebuilding efforts more effective is a better understanding of the political economy not only of fragile states, but of donors as well. Until international actors change ongoing practices (for example, developing longer—term horizons, a greater tolerance to risk, and openness/competence to engage in the more political aspects of statebuilding work, greater continuity of personnel in the field), effective engagement will continu to be the exception and assistance will continue to fail to have a significant and sustained impact

Notes

1. While it is essential to acknowledge that these two processes are mainly driven from within, the focus of this chapter is primarily on the role of donors in supporting them.
2. See OECD, 2010; DFID, 2010, the Institute for State Effectiveness's list of the ten key functions of the state (http://www.effectivestates.org/ten.htm), and International Dialogue on Peacebuilding and Statebuilding, 2010.

3   For a good example of such processes, see K. Polanyi's (1957) analysis of the 'Great Transformation' that entailed the collapse of 19th-century civilization in Europe and the emergence of the welfare state (in England for example) and fascism (in Germany). Other, more recent examples of the confrontational/antagonistic relationship between state and society in statebuilding are provided by the struggle against apartheid in South Africa, and the overthrow of authoritarian rulers and ensuing challenges to establish democratic systems in Arab Spring countries.
4   By way of illustration, as Sara Pantuliano, a Research Fellow in the Humanitarian Policy group at ODI and an expert on Sudan, has put it, warring factions in Sudan may disagree about everything except calling for a general amnesty (personal communication with the author in October 2008).
5   The analysis below is taken from Rocha Menocal and O'Neil (2012).

References

Anten, L., Briscoe, I., and Mezzera, M. (2012). *The political economy of state-building in situations of fragility and conflict: From analysis to strategy*. The Hague, The Netherlands: Netherlands Institute of International Relations (Clingendael).

Bertoli, S., and Ticci, E. (2012). A fragile guideline to development assistance. *Development Policy Review*, 30(2), 211–230.

Booth, D. (2011). *Aid effectiveness: Bringing country ownership (and politics) back in*. ODI Working Paper 336. London, UK: Overseas Development Institute.

Call, C. (2008). Conclusion: Building states to build peace? In C. Call with V. Wyeth (Eds.)*Building states to build peace*. Boulder, CO: Lynne Rienner.

Call, C. (2011). Beyond the 'failed state': Toward conceptual alternatives. *European Journal of International Relations*, 17(2), 1–24.

Cammack, D., McLeod, D., and Rocha Menocal, A., with Christiansen, K. (2006). *'Fragile states' agenda: A survey of current thinking and practice: Report submitted to the Japan International Cooperation Agency*. London, UK: ODI (unpublished).

Caplan, R. (2005). *International governance of war-torn territories: Rule and reconstruction*. Oxford, UK: Oxford University Press.

Carnahan, M., and Lockhart, C. (2008). Peace-building and public finance. In C. Call with V. Wyeth (Eds.), *Building states to build peace*. Boulder, CO: Lynne Rienner.

Collier, P. (2007). *The bottom billion: Why the poorest countries are failing and what can be done about it*. Oxford, UK: Oxford University Press.

Denney, L. (2011). The g7 who? Fragile states set the agenda for aid effectiveness. ODI Blog, October 14. Available at: www.odi.org.uk

DFID. (2010). *Building peaceful states and societies: A DFID Practice Paper*. London, UK: DFID.

Engberg-Pedersen, L., Andersen, L., Stepputat, F., and Jung, D. (2008). *Fragile states on the international agenda*. DIIS Report. Copenhagen, Denmark: Danish Institute for International Studies.

Faria, F., and Magalhães Ferreira, P. (2007).*Situations of fragility: Challenges for an European Response Strategy*. Maastricht, The Netherlands: European Centre for Development Policy Management.

Fritz, V., and Rocha Menocal, A. (2007a). Developmental states in the new millennium: Concepts and challenges for a new aid agenda. *Development Policy Review*, 25(5), September.

Fritz, V., and Rocha Menocal, A. (2007b). *Understanding state-building from a political economy perspective: An analytical and conceptual paper on processes, embedded tensions and lessons for international engagement*. Report prepared for DFID's Effective and Fragile States Teams. London, UK: DFID.

Fukuyama, F. (2004). *State-building: Governance and world order in the 21st century*. Ithaca, NY: Cornell University Press.

Jones, B., and Chandran, R., with Cousens, E., Slotin, J., and Sherman, J. (2008).*From fragility to resilience: Concepts and dilemmas of state-building in fragile states*. Report prepared for the OECD by the Center on International Cooperation at New York University and International Peace Academy, New York, NY.

Manuel, M. (2011). *Getting better results from assistance to fragile states*. ODI Working Paper 70. London, UK: ODI.

Naudé, W. (2012). *What is the (new) deal with fragile states? Policy Brief 1*. Helsinki, Finland: United Nations University and UNU-WIDER.

OECD. (2010). Do no harm: International aupport for atatebuilding. Paris: OECD. Available at: http://www.oecd.org/dac/conflictandfragility/donoharminternationalsupportforstatebuilding.htm

OECD. (2011a). Supporting statebuilding in situations of conflict and fragility: Policy guidance. Paris: OECD DAC.

OECD. (2011b). *International engagement in fragile states: Can't we do better?* Paris, France: OECD DAC.

Paris, R. (2004). *At war's end: Building peace after civil conflict.* Cambridge, UK: Cambridge University Press.

Paris, R., and Sisk, T. (Eds.). (2008). *The contradictions of state building: Confronting the dilemmas of post-war peace operations.* London, UK: Routledge.

Pritchett, L., and de Weijer, F. (2010). *Fragile states: Stuck in a capability trap?* Background Paper, World Development Report 2011. Washington, DC: World Bank.

Putzel, J. (2010). *Why development actors need a better definition of state fragility.* Policy Directions. London, UK: Crisis States Research Centre.

Rocha Menocal, A. (2011a). 'State−building for peace' – A new paradigm for international engagement in post−conflict fragile states? *Third World Quarterly, 32*(10), 1715–1736.

Rocha Menocal, A. (2011b). Wanted: Smarter aid to support political and institutional reform in Africa. ODI Blog, July 25. Available at: www.odi.org.uk

Rocha Menocal, A. (with Kenneth Sigrist) (2011c). *Centres of government: Liberia case study.* Paris, France: OECD DAC (unpublished).

Rocha Menocal, A. (2011d). Analysing the relationship between democracy and development: Definin key concepts and assessing key linkages. *Commonwealth Good Governance 2011/12* (November). London, UK: Commonwealth Secretariat.

Rocha Menocal, A., and O'Neil, T. (2012). *Mind the gap: Lessons learned and remaining challenges in parliamentary development assistance – A Sida Pre-Study.* Stockholm, Sweden: Sida.

Snyder, J. (2000). *From voting to violence: Democratization and nationalist conflict.* New York, NY: Norton.

Stewart, F., and Brown, G. (2009).*Fragile states.* CRISE Policy Paper 51. Oxford, UK: Centre for Research on Inequality, Human Security and Ethnicity (CRISE).

Tilly, C. (1992). *Coercion, capital and European states, AD 990–1992.* Cambridge, MA: Blackwell.

United Nations Development Programme and World Bank. (2009).*Report of the Technical Mission to Liberia on State Building in Fragile and Post-Conflict Contexts.* New York, NY: UNDP.

Unsworth, S. (Ed.). (2010). *An upside down view of governance.* Brighton, UK: Centre for the Future State, IDS.

World Bank. (2011). *World Development Report – Conflict, security and development.* Washington, DC: The World Bank.

Wyeth, V. (2012). Knights in fragile armor: The rise of the 'g7+'. *Global Governance, 18*, 7–12.

Wyeth, V., and Sisk, T. (2009). *Rethinking peace-building and state-building in war-torn countries: Conceptual clarity, policy guidance, and practical implications.* Discussion Note for the OECD DAC International Network on Conflict and Fragility (draft).

INDEX

Locators in *italics* are to tables. The letter 'n' indicates a reference to the end notes of the chapter.

Abramowitz, Morton 273
accountability 191, 396
Action, John, 1st Baron 68
Action Plan for Situations of Fragility and Conflict (EU) 366
Adivasi Janajatis (indigenous peoples) 150
Afewerki, Isaias 322
Afghanistan 21, 42, 304–12; *arbaki* 311–12; cash transfers 20n6; corruption 18, 23, 308; democratization 308, 358; foreign forces 77; Najibullah regime 24, 309; nationalism 76; peace formation 135; policing 201, 357, 358; Provincial Reconstruction Teams (PRTs) 309, 358–9; rentier state 225–7; security 181; weak state 70, 309–10, 395; women 31, 33, 38
Afghan National Police (ANP) 197
Africa: elections 262, 263; hybridity 97, 212; nationalism 70, 71, 72; peacekeeping 163; political clientelism 95
African National Congress (ANC) 252–3
African Union (AU) 164, 379
Afrobarometer 15
'Agenda for Democratization' (UN) 145
Ahmed, Salman 159, 161
Ahtisaari, Martti 276
aid: Australian review 332, 336; Bosnia and Herzegovina (BiH) 223; corruption 24–5; delivery 222; East Timor 330; EU 363; fragile states 387–97; humanitarian responses xix; Kosovo 277; Mozambique 111; Palestinians 341 *see also* donors
aid dependency 222, 277, 334, 336–7, 341, 347 *see also* dependency
aid donors *see* donors

Ake, C. 94
al–Askari Mosque 298
Albanians (Bosnia and Herzegovina (BiH)) 270–7
Albright, Madeleine 4n2
alienation 109, 186, 191, 192
Alkatiri, Mari 45
Allawi, Ali 296
Allen, M. 335–6
'Alliance for the Future of Kosovo' (AAK) 275, 276
al–Qaeda 299, 304
America *see* US
Anbar Awakening 298–9, 300
ANC (African National Congress) 252–3
Andersen, L. 222
Angola 21, 159, 261, 320
Annan, Kofi 159, 170, 376, 377
Annual Review of Global Peace Operations (CIC) 157
anomie, logics of 10
Anten, Louise 390
Arab Awakening 72
Arab League 379
Arafat, Yasser 343, 344, 345
arbaki (tribal self–defence) 311–12
ARENA (National Republican Alliance) 234, 235
armed forces of Kosovo (FARK) 271, 272
Armed Forces of Liberia (AFL) 187, 188–9, 192
Armed Forces of Rwanda 322
Armenian diaspora 72
armies: deployment of 8; integration 320, 321–2
Artemije, Bishop 275
Ashdown, Paddy 359
Askari Mosque, al– 298
Assad, Bashar al– 384

Assad, Hafez al– 384
Asseburg, M. 357
assimilados ('assimilated') 107
Association for the Study of Nationalities 64
asymmetrical hybrid formations 100
'asymmetric containment' 342, 346, 347
Ataturk, Kamal 69
Athor, George 47
Australia 59–60, 310, 327–37
Australian Defence Force (ADF) 197
Australian Federal Police (AFP) 60
Austria 70
authoritarian regimes 316, 318
authority, state 43, 169, 389, *389*
autonomous electoral management bodies 263
autonomous rational individuals 87–8
'autonomous state' 7–8

Baath Party 297
'bad governance' 343, 345, 365 *see also* 'good governance'; governance
Badie, Bertrand 67
Baghdad 297
baito ('peoples' councils') 319
Balkan Institute 273
Balkans 278, 359
Bangladeshi peacekeepers 164
bargaining arguments 233
Barnett, M. 322
Bass, Gary 383
Bates, R. H. 262
Beebe, Shannon 381
Beetham, David 5, 10
Behr, T. 311
Beira corridor 109
Belgium 121–2, 358
benchmarking 52, 185, 298, 356
Bennett, A. 310
Berghof Report 96
Berlin Conference (1884–1885) 121
Berlin Conference (1889) 107
Berlin, Isaiah 64, 79
Berman, B. 121
Bickerton, C. J. 56
'big tent' approach 48
BiH (Bosnia and Herzegovina) *see* Bosnia and Herzegovina (BiH)
bilateral development assistance organizations 55
bilateral relationships 327–37
biopolitics 7, 87
Bird, T. 359
Bjornlund, Eric 263n11
Blair, Tony 296
Blau, Peter 5
Bøås, M. 191–2
Boege, V. 56, 97, 98, 102
Boko Haram 74

Bonn Agreement 21, 226, 307, 308
borders 6, 68, 340
Bose, Sumantra 283
Bosnia and Herzegovina (BiH) 22, 270, 281–90; armed forces 178, 252; elections 260, 285; interim authorities 177; nationalism 76; peace formation 135; police 359; Stabilization and Association Agreement (2008) 289; tax state 223–5; territorial power–sharing agreement 251 *see also* Dayton Peace Agreement (DPA); Republika Srpska
Bosniaks 281, 282
Boutros–Ghali, Boutros 4n2, 5, 145
Brahimi, Lakhdar 44, 159, 161
Brahimi panel on peacekeeping reform, Report of (UNSG) 146
Braithwaite, J. 333
Bratton, Michael 101
Brazil 379
Breaking the conflict trap: Civil war and development policy. (Collier) 72
Brecht, Berthold 285
Bremer, L. Paul 55, 294, 297
Breuilly, J. 76
Britain *see* UK
Brubaker, Rogers 66, 76
Bryden, A. 190
Bukoshi, Bujar 271
Bull, Hedley 380
Bureau of Crisis Prevention and Recovery (BCPR) 149
Burundi: EU strategies 366–7, *371*; nationalism 70; patronage 21–2, 37; peace agreement 249; police reform 35; security sector reform (SSR) 176; UN peacekeeping 159; women 31, 35
Bush administration 295–6, 297, 298, 301, 306, 311
Bush, George W. 293, 294, 295, 298, 382
Bushra, J. El– 35
business elites 237–8
Buzan, Barry 9

CACIF 237, 238
Calhoun, Craig 75
Call, Charles 21
Cambodia 21, 95, 97, 98, 100–1
Camdessus, Michael 147–8
Cammack, D. 364
Camp David 345
capability model 42, 43–4, 45
capacity 54–7, 233, 242, 389, *389*
capital, control of 45
capital-intensive modes 219
Carayannis, Tatiana 125–6
Carnahan, Michael 396
Carothers, Thomas 92, 100–1
Casaús, Marta 238

Castillejo, C. 36
Cavour, Camillo 68
Center on International Cooperation (CIC) 157, 162
Central American Institute of Fiscal Studies 236
Central American trade agreements 232, 235
Central Intelligence Agency (CIA) 67, 307
Chabal, Patrick 100, 372
Chalabi, Ahmed 295–6, 297, 298
Chandler, David 56, 151, 192, 251, 286
Cheney, Richard 295
Chesterman, Simon 79, 190
China 123, 160, 379
Chissano, Joaquim 112
choiceless democracy 112, 190
Chomsky, Noam 378
Chopra, Jarat 383
Christopher, Warren 71
Civilian Headline Goals (EU) 351
civilian police *see* police
civilian population 319, 358–9
civil society 35–7, 83–93, 133–4, 284–7, 290
civil society organizations (CSO's) 35, 36–7, 285–6, 288
civil wars: Iraq 298; Liberia 186–7; relapses 260; resource dependence 210; settlements 259; Sierra Leone 368–9; South Sudan 47; victory in 315–23
clans 19–20, 276
Clark, Wesley 201
client states 342
Clinton, Bill 323
Close, D. 316–17
'closed–access orders' 212
CNURA 335
Coalition Provisional Authority (CPA) (Iraq) 294, 297
coalitions 247, 249
coercion-intensive modes 219
Cohen, Roberta 377
COIN (counter–insurgency operations) 198, 293, 298–300, 311 *see also* insurgencies
Cold War: civil society interventions 92; peacebuilding 21, 97; post–colonial world 85–6; post–war state failure 67; statebuilding 293, 294 *see also* post–Cold War
Cole, USS 304
collapsed states xx, 5, 8, 10–11
Collier, Paul 72, 89–90, 263, 387
Collins, Randall 7
colonial states 68, 107–8, 109, 111, 112, 121–2 *see also* post–colonial states; states
colonization 84–5, 97, 339, 343, 347
combatants: demobilization 315, 320–2; integration 176–7, 178, 252, 320, 321–2 *see also* disarmament, demobilization, and reintegration (DDR)

Commission for the Rehabilitation of Members of Former Army and Disabled War Veterans (Ethiopia) 321
Common Security and Defence Policy (CSDP) (EU) 350, 351
community identity 36
Comoros 249
Comparative Constitutional Engineering: An inquiry into Structures, Incentives and Outcomes (Sartori) 247
competing elites 101, 237, 343, 344
Comprehensive Peace Agreements (CPA): Liberia 186; Sudan 46, 47, 211 *see also* peace agreements
Comprehensive Proposal for Kosovo Status Settlement 31
concept of operations (CONOPS) 202
confidence–building measures 39
conflict–affected states 15, 2
'confict minerals' 215
conflict prevention 149–5
confict resolution 90, 91, 134, 144
conficts 86, 89–90, 339
conflict–sensitive international engagement 254–
Congo 22, 118–28; China 160; 'conflict minerals 215; economic partnerships 126–7, 160; elections 257; European Union (EU) 127, 357–8; national unity 70, 126; natural resources 211, 213, 215; and Rwanda 124–5; statebuilding 121–2, 396; UN peacekeeping 156, 158, 162, 165; women 35 *see also* MONUC (UN Organization Mission in the Democratic Republic of the Congo)
Congo Free State 121
Connolly, William 90
Connor, Walker 66, 68, 69
Conseil National pour la Défense du Peuple (CNDP) 123, 124
'consensual democracy' 317
'consociational democracy' 246–7
consolidated states 293
constitutional assistance 143–52
constitutional market democracy 151
constitutional reform 31, 33–4, 247–8, 283
constitutions: Bosnia and Herzegovina (BiH) 282; Iraq 297, 300
Convention on the Punishment and Prevention of the Crime of Genocide (UN) 383
coordinated transnational spaces 59
Copenhagen criteria 289
Cornwall, A. 36
corporatism 220
corruption 15–26; Afghanistan 18, 23, 308; Côte d'Ivoire 23; elite factionalization *20*; Guinea–Bissau 367; Liberia 23, 187; mogul–type 19, 24; neo–patrimony 100; Palestinian 343, 344; women 33

Corruption Perception Index (CPI) 15
Côte d'Ivoire 23, 161–2, 164–5, 189, 380–1
Counterinsurgency Field Manual (CFM) 299
counter–insurgency operations (COIN) 198, 293, 298–300, 311 *see also* insurgencies
Country Strategy Papers (CSPs) (EU) 363, 366–72; Burundi 366–7; Guinea–Bissau 367; Haiti 367–8; Sierra Leone 368–9; Timor–Leste 369; Yemen 369–70
courts 7, 38, 238–9, 382
Creighton, J. L. 309
Cristiani, Alfredo 234–5
'critical agency' 135
Croatia 270, 272
Croats (Bosnia and Herzegovina (BiH)) 252, 282
cultural assimilation 107
culture 84–9
customary institutions 38
Cyprus 250
Czech Republic 311
Czech Sudetenland 70

Dahl, Robert 247
Daloz, Jean–Pascal 100, 372
Darfur 164, 165, 197 *see also* Sudan
Davidheiser, Evelyn 7
Dayton Peace Agreement (DPA) 223, 251, 252, 271–3, 281–4 *see also* Bosnia and Herzegovina (BiH)
debt cancellation 110
debt crises 54, 232
debt relief 110, 149
decentralization 254, 368
decolonization 71, 85, 144, 145, 212
defeated parties 317
Demaqi, Adem 272
demobilization *see* combatants; disarmament, demobilization, and reintegration (DDR)
democracy: Afghanistan 308; choiceless 112, 190; civic nationalism 71; conflict resolution 90 248; consensual 317; consociational 246–7; and elites 98, 101, 247; European Union (EU) strategy 358, 363; and hybridity 95, 98–9; Iraq 294, 297–8, 301, 302; Kosovo 278; legitimate state 299; Middle East 294; Mozambique 112; rationalist approaches 90–1; rebel victories 316–17; security sector reform (SSR) 169, 171, 190–1; South Sudan 47, 48; statebuilding 90, 394–5; UN Charter 150–1; women 32 *see also* elections
Democratic Alliance of Kosovo (LDK) 269, 270, 272–3
Democratic Forum (Kosovo) 272
'Democratic Party of Kosovo' (PDK) 275, 276
Democratic Republic of Congo (DRC) *see* Congo
democratic transition xxii, 86
Deng, Francis 377, 379

dependency xxi, 77, 192–3, 210, 227 *see also* aid dependency
d'Escoto Brockmann, Miguel 378
de Soto, Alvaro 346
Deutsch, Karl 66, 78
development 48, 85, 111–12, 139, 171, 221–2
development assistance 55, 147, 148–9, 336, 363
Development Cooperation Instrument (EU) 366
devolution 254
diasporas 72
diffuse resources 213
Di John, J. 44
Đinđić, Zoran 276
direct tax 240, *241*
disarmament, demobilization, and reintegration (DDR): Afghanistan 305–7; Congo 358; post–conflict security 172–3, 176, 188, 254, 320–2; risks 315; and women 35 *see also* combatants, integration of; security sector reform (SSR)
discrimination 34, 36, 192
Doe, Samuel 186, 187
'domestic legitimacy' 74 *see also* legitimacy
Donais, Timothy 100
Donini, A. 308
donors: Afghanistan 226–7, 308–9; Bosnia and Herzegovina (BiH) 287, 288; civil society organizations (CSO's) 284–5; Palestine 347; peacebuilding 133; Solomon Islands 336–7; statebuilding 221–2, 396, 397; women's movements 36–7 *see also* aid; Western donors
Doss, Alan 156, 160–1
Dostum, Abdul Rashid 305
Doyle, Michael 8
DPA (Dayton Peace Agreement) *see* Dayton Peace Agreement (DPA)
DPKO (UN Department of Peacekeeping Operations) 159, 201, 202
DRC (Democratic Republic of Congo) *see* Congo
Drenica (Kosovo) 271, 272
Drenica massacre 272
drugs trade 226, 307
Duffield, M. R. 11
Dunlap Jr., Charles J. 201
Durkheim, Emile 9, 10, 73, 106
Durkheimian sociology 4, 9–10, 11, 73, 74 *see also* statebuilding; Weberian States
'Dutch disease' 227
DynCorp 188–9

Eastern Congo 122
East Jerusalem 340, 343
East Timor *see* Timor–Leste
economic and social poverty–reduction programs 149
economic barriers 39–40

Economic Community of West African States (ECOWAS) 379
economic power-sharing 251–2, 254
economic reforms 289, 298, 301
economic rents 222, 223, 301
economy: and international norms 96; Mozambique 108–9; Palestinian 340–1, 343, 346; Solomon Islands 334; Yugoslavia 270–1
Edelstein, David 76, 77
education 284
Egypt 32
Eichler, J. 311
Eikenberry, Karl 309
Einstein, Albert 66
Ekman, Joakim 100–1
elections 257–64; Bosnia and Herzegovina (BiH) 285; disputes 263; El Salvador 235; Ethiopia 317; Guinea–Bissau 367; Iraq 261, 300; Kosovo 274–5, 276; monitoring 263; Mozambique 110; Palestinian 345; Rwanda 317, 318; Solomon Islands 333–4, 335; South Sudan 47; Timor–Leste 332, 369; Uganda 317; UN peacekeeping 159; violence 248–9, 261–2 *see also* democracy; voting systems
'electoral assistance' 144
Electoral Laws and Their Political Consequences (Grofman and Lijphart) 247
elite bargains 44–8, 48
elite factionalization 20
elite networks 124, 238, 276
'elite pacts' 216
elites 42–9; business 237–8; competing 101, 237, 343, 344; and democracy 98, 101, 247; fnancial 236–7; local 25, 132, 211–12, 223–4; and peace settlements 48; political 76, 328–9, 336–7, 344–5, 347; post-war 259; religious 344; ruling xxi, 187; state 113, 233; transnational 237, 239
elite settlements 21–2, 25, 42–3, 48–9
El Salvador 231, 234–7, 320; Peace Accords 234; tax revenues *234*; tax trends *236*
emerging elites 237, 241–2
Endowment Fund for the Rehabilitation of Tigray (EFFORT) 319
Enduring Idea of the Congo, The (Weiss and Carayannis) 125–6
Enlightenment, the 87
'environmental variables' 88–9
Eritrea 315–23
Eritrean People's Liberation Front (EPLF) 316, 318, 322
Essay on the History of Civil Society (Ferguson) 87
Ethiopia 315–23
Ethiopian People's Revolutionary Democratic Front (EPRDF) 316, 320, 321, 322
Ethiopian People's Revolutionary Party 318

ethnic cleansing 271–2, 274 *see also* genocide; mass atrocities
ethnic divisions, Bosnia and Herzegovina (BiH) 282–4, 286, 287
ethnic groups 68, 150
ethnicity, and nationalism 71, 72, 126
ethnic violence: Balkans 278; Cyprus 250; Kosovo 271–2, 274, 276
ethnopolitical affiliations 248, 28
EUFOR Althea 359
EULEX (Iraq) 356, 357
EUPM (Bosnia and Herzegovina) 356, 359
EUPOL Afghanistan 356, 358–9
European Commission (EC) 351, 354
European Consensus on Development (EU) 363, 365
European Council 351
European Development Fund (EDF) 363–4, 366, 368
European External Action Service 366
European Security and Defence Policy (ESDP), missions 356, 357
European Security Strategy (2003) 362, 365
European Union (EU): Afghanistan 359; Bosnia and Herzegovina (BiH) 287–90, 359; Common Security and Defence Policy (CSDP) 350, 351, *371*; Congo 127, 158; Country Strategy Papers (CSPs) 363, 366–72; debt crises 54; enlargement 289; external policy 357, 360; 'good governance' policies 362–72; Kosovo 276; Palestine 341, 346; police missions 350–60, *352–4*; Sierra Leone 368; supranationalism 72
EUSEC COPPS (Palestine) 356
EUSEC DR Congo 358
Evans, Gareth 383
exit strategies 222
export trade 232, 237
external funding bodies 221
external intervention 90–1
external security 172
Extractive Industries Transparency Initiative (EITI) 208, 217
extractive rents 210
extractive revenues 214
extremists 253

factionalism 318–19, 343–4
failed states 4, 7, 119, 121, 293, 337 *see also* fragile states; weak states
'Failed States Index' (*Foreign Policy*) 122–3
failing states *see* fragile states
family alliances 238, 276
Fänge, A. 309
FARC (Revolutionary Armed Forces of Colombia) 213
FARK (armed forces of Kosovo) 271, 272

Fastabend, David 298
Fateh 344
Federally Administered Tribal Areas (FATA) 38–9
federal states 59, 281–2
Feith, Douglas 295, 296
Ferguson, Adam 87
Fierlbeck, Katherine 101
final status negotiations (Israel–Palestine) 340, 343
financial elites 236–
First Military Police Battalion (Australia) 198
first–past–the–post voting system 248, 33
fiscal contract, state–society 222, 23
FMLN 235, 320
force, legitimate use 169, 380
Forces Armées de la République Démocratique du Congo (FARDC) 123
Forces de Libération du Rwanda (FDLR) 123, 124
foreign adventurism *see* imperialism
foreign investments 240
foreign ownership 341
Foreign Policy 122–3
Forum RAMSI Review Task Force 335
Foucault, Michel 7, 87–9, 119–20
Fourth High Level Forum on Aid Effectiveness 392–3
Foust, J. 311
FPUs (militarized formed police units) 205
fragile states xx–xxii, 5, 9, 67, 364–6; Africa 212; aid 387–97; corruption 15–16; election violence 261; inequality 29; natural resources 213; nature of 211–12; *reconstructing* state capacities 371; statebuilding xx, 52–3, 58, 390–7 *see also* failed states; weak states
Fragile states: Good practice in country assistance strategies (World Bank) 362, 365
Fragile States Principles 393
France 69, 162, 311, 312, 358
Franck, Thomas 150
free markets 294, 298, 300, 301, 302
Frelimo movement 108, 109, 112
French Licorne force 381
Fretilin 45
Friedrich, Carl 5–6
Friesendorf, C. 201
Fukuyama, Francis 6, 8, 52, 86, 334, 336
FUNCINPEC 67, 100
FUSADES (Salvadoran Foundation for Economic and Social Development) 235
'Future of Iraq Study' (US State Department) 295

Gacaca tribunals 320, 395
Gaddaf, Muammar xx, 257, 381
Gadet, Peter 47
Gai, Gatluak 47

Gambino, Tony 125
Garang de Mabior, John 46
Garner, Jay 296–7
gas 209, 214 *see also* natural resource management (NRM)
Gates, Robert 300
Gaza Strip 339–47
Gbagbo, Laurent 161–2, 164, 380–1
Gellner, Ernest 66, 70, 76, 78
gender inequality 29–40, 148
genocide 146, 249, 282 *see also* ethnic cleansing; mass atrocities
Georgia 377
Germany 8, 69, 311
Giddens, Anthony 8
Gilbert, Andrew 65
Giustozzi, A. 306
Global Centre for the R2P 379
global interventions xxii
globalization 232
Global Values Survey 15
Goetz, A. M. 32, 36
gold mining 213
Goma (Congo) 125, 164
'good governance' 59, 149, 331, 342–3, 356–7, 362–4 *see also* 'bad governance'; governance
Gordon, M. R. 296
Gordon, Neve 342
governance: breakdown 6, 328; Burundi 366–7; 'conservatorship' 9; corruption 15; fragile states 58, 364–6; Guinea–Bissau 367; Haiti 367–8; 'incentive–based approach' 363–4; Palestine 340–1; security sector reform (SSR) 169; Sierra Leone 368–9; South Sudan 47–8; structures 59; Timor–Leste 47–8, 369; Yemen 369–70 *see also* 'bad governance'; 'good governance'
Governance and Economic Management Assistance Program (GEMAP) 222, 396
Governance in the Context of Development Cooperation (EC) 363
Government of Southern Sudan (GoSS) 47 *see also* South Sudan
governments: elite cartel 247; Kosovo 275; legitimacy 5; power–sharing 248; transitional 259
Gračanica (Kosovo) 275
Grafstein, Robert 6
grand assembly (Loya Jirga) 307
grand coalition 248
?grassroots peacebuilding' 133
'greed and grievance' framework 89
Greek Cypriots 250
Greek diaspora 72
Greenfeld, Liah 66, 71
Grofman, B. 247
Gross, Eva 358

'Group of Friends for R2P' 379
g7+ 392–3
Guatemala 31, 33, 231, 233–4, 237–41; Constitutional Court 239; Free Trade Zone Law 240; Law for Promotion of Exports and Maquila 240; Tax on Mercantile and Agricultural Businesses (IEMA) 239; tax revenue *234*
Guebuza, Armando 112
Guéhenno, Jean–Marie 162, 163
guerrillas 316–17
Guidance note of the Secretary General: UN Assistance to constitution-making projects (UN) 150
Guinea–Bissau 179, 357, 367,*371*
Gulf Cooperation Council 379
Gusmão, Xanana 331

Habermas, Jürgen 6
Haekerup, Hans 275
Haiti 76, 158, 163, 367–8, *371*
Halevy, Efraim 345
Hamarskjöld, Dag 122
Hamas 344, 345–6
Hama (Syria) 384
Hamidzada, H. 311
Hänggi, H. 190
Haradinaj, Ramush 275
Harpviken, Kristian 311
Hartzell, Caroline 248, 252
Hasegawa, Y. 308
Hashimi, Tariq al– 300–1
health care 126
hearts and minds 293, 299, 301–2, 358
Heathershaw, John 278
'heavier footprint' SSRs 174, *174*, 177–8
Heavily Indebted Poor Country (HIPC) (IMF) 110, 149
'heavy footprint' SSRs 174, *174*, 175–7
Hegel, G. W. F. 67
Hehir, Aidan 379
Hekmatyar, Gulbuddin 308
Helmand Province (Afghanistan) 22
Helman, Gerald 3, 4, 9
Herbst, Jeffrey 70
Hezbollah 74, 158–9, 252
High Level Panel on Threats, Challenges, and Change, Report on the (UN) 152, 376
Hilal, Jamil 342
Hill, G. 370
Hinton, Mercedes 200
Hintze, Otto 69
Hobbes, Thomas 67
Hobsbawm, Eric 66, 76
Hobson, John 7
Hoddie, Matthew 248, 252
Hoeffler, Anke 8
Hoffman, B. 98

Hoh, Matthew 309
Holkeri, Harri 276
Hollande, François 312
Holsti, Kalevi 86
Homem Novo (New Man) 108
Hooghe, L. 59
'horizontal inequalities' 262
Horowitz, Donald 247–8
humanitarian aid *see* aid
Humanitarian Coordinator 203
humanitarian intervention 55, 86, 375–6, 377, 379, 383
human rights 147, 169, 189, 248, 271, 370
Hungary 311
Hun Sen 21n8, 101
Huntington, S. P. 318
Hussein, Saddam 294, 295, 296, 301
Hutus 122, 249, 366–7
hybridity 84, 94–104, 136 *see also* states
hybrid political orders 97, 98, 209, 212, 213, 216–17
Hynek, N. 311

ICISS (International Commission on Intervention and State Sovereignty) 375, 378, 380, 381, 382, 384
Ignatieff, Michael 71, 192
IMF (International Monetary Fund) 147–8
imperialism 85, 96–7, 376
Implementing the Responsibility to Protect (UNSG) 378
'imported state' 67
incentives 43
independence: Kosovo 271, 276–7, 278; Mozambique 108–9, 112; Palestine 341; Solomon Islands 334; South Sudan 46–7; Timor–Leste 46, 330
indígenato system 107
indigenous peoples (*Adivasi Janajatis*) 150
individual rights 380
Indonesia 330
industrialization 66, 108–9
inequalities 29, 86, 251
influence 25, 31, 37–
informal power 37, 40
informal practices 102
ingando camps 322
Inkatha 252–3
In Larger Freedom (UN) 376
insecurity 23, 29 *see also* security sector reform (SSR)
institutional approaches 3–11
institutional multiplicity 95, 103, 104
institution–building 87, 180, 264; Afghanistan 305, 307–8; Bosnia and Herzegovina (BiH) 225; Palestinian Authority 340–1; post–conflict 161 Solomon Islands 329, 333

institutions: corruption 19; customary 37; hybrid regimes 101; legitimate 148
insurgencies 109, 293, 299, 309, 315–23 *see also* counter–insurgency operations (COIN)
integration, of combatants 176–7, 178, 252, 320, 321–2
integrative electoral systems 254
integrative models 247–8
'integrative' nationalism 69
inter–ethnic conflict *see* ethnic violence
Interim Iraqi Authority 297
internal displacement 125
internal security 172, 173, 199–200
'internal sovereignty' 68
international approaches 135, 286
International Coalition for the R2P 379
International Commission on Intervention and State Sovereignty (ICISS) 375, 378, 380, 381, 382, 384
international community 78, 160–1, 193, 264, 315–16, 322
International Criminal Court 382
International Crisis Group (ICG) 257, 273
International Dialogue on Peacebuilding and Statebuilding (IDPS) 77, 392
international–domestic interactions xxii
international donors *see* donors
international election monitoring 263
International Energy Forum 209
International Financial Institutions (IFIs) 147–8, 149
International Force for East Timor (INTERFET) 330, 332
international funding amounts *127*
international intervention xxii; civil society 86–9; and dependency 283; footprint 76, 174–80, *174*, 190; neo–Weberian 56; R2P 375–83; security sector reform (SSR) 173–5; statebuilding 328–9
international law 378
international mediators 258
International Monetary Fund (IMF) 147–8
International Network on Conflict and Fragility (INCAF) (OECD) 215
international security xix
International Security Assistance Force (ISAF) 304, 310–11, 312, 358
international system xix, 220
inter–scalar power relations 59
inter–state conflicts 8
inter–state relationships 328–37
intervention *see* international intervention
interventionary political cycle 328–9
intervention regimes 60
intifada 272, 342, 345
intra–state conflicts 8
Iraq 293–302; foreign forces 77; insurgency 181, 261; police 197; R2P (responsibility to protect) 376, 377; statebuilding 70, 178, 296–8; Transitional Administrative Law 300
Iraqi army 297
Iraqi Interim Government 177, 297
Iraqi National Congress (INC) 295–6
Iraqi Transitional Government 297
Iraq War 376
irrational antagonistic conflict 9
irredentist nationalism 70–1
Isaias, Afewerki 323
Ishakzai tribe (Afghanistan) 22
Islam 250, 281
Islamic Conference 379
Israel 158–9, 339–47 *see also* Oslo Accords; Palestinians
Italy 69, 70, 213
Ivory Coast *see* Côte d'Ivoire
Iyob, Ruth 318

Jackson, Robert 68, 100, 380
Jamal, Amal 343–4
Japan 8
Jarstad, Anna 248
Jashari, Adem 272
Jayasuriya, K. 58
Jennings, K. 191–2
Jerusalem 340, 343
Jessen–Pedersen, Soren 276
Jessop, B. 57
Jewish settlements 340
JNA (Yugoslav People's Army) 271
Johnson Sirleaf, Ellen 160, 186
Johnstone, Ian 157, 158, 159–60, 166
Johnston, Michael 18
judicial systems 34, 250, 368, 369, 370
Junbesh–e–Milli militia 305
'juridical sovereignty' 68
justice, delivery of 213

Kabbah, Ahmad Tejan 160
Kabila, Joseph 122–5, 158, 160, 165, 358
Kabila, Laurent 122, 358
Kagame, Paul 318, 319
Kaldor, Mary 86, 89, 381
Kandiyoti, D. 31
Kaplan, Robert 71
Kappler, Stephanie 90
Karlsrud, J. 161
Karokhail, M. 309
Karzai, Ahmed Wali 307
Karzai, Hamid 226, 306, 309
Katangan rebels 122
Kay, David 295
Keen, D. 369
Keller, D. 202
Kelsall, Thomas 101–2

Kempin, R. 357
Kenya 31, 38, 212
Keynes, John Maynard 11
Khan, Mushtaq 44, 75, 342, 343
Kiir Mayardit, Salva 46
Kilcullen, D. 199
Ki-moon, Ban 150, 165, 378, 379
King, Anthony 311
Kingsbury, D. 332
kinship 336
Kivu (Congo) 123, 124, 125
Kloeck-Jenson, S. 114
Kof Annan plan, Cyprus 250
Kongo kingdom 121
Kosovo 42, 269–78; Joint Interim Administrative Structure (JIAS) 274; nationalism 76; policing 196, 359; security sector reform (SSR) 177; status negotiations 31, 36, 276; women 31, 36, 37
Kosovo Commission 380
Kosovo Liberation Army (KLA) 269, 272–5
Kosovo Police Service (KPS) 274, 276
Kosovo Protection Corps (KPC) 274
Kosovo Security Council 35
Kosovo Verification Mission (KVM) 272–
Kouchner, Bernard 274, 275
Krajina (Croatia) 272
Krasner, S. 67, 341
Kühn, F. P. 306–7
Kurds 68, 261
Kymlicka, Will 71
Kyrgyzstan 306

laissez-faire 88
land rights 31, 38, 343
Latin America 68, 71, 163
law enforcement 60, 172 *see also* police
LDK (Democratic Alliance of Kosovo) 269, 270, 272–3
Leach, M. 332
leadership 33, 193, 317
League of Communists (Kosovo) 270
Least Developed Countries (LDCs) 152
Lebanon 74, 158–9, 252
legitimacy: Congo 123; counter-insurgency operations (COIN) 299; Durkheim approach 9–11, 73–4; electoral processes 258, 259, 263, 264; fragile states xxi, 389, *389*, 394; ideational 220; international 178; intervention mandates 328, 329; liberal hegemony 103; liberation movements 319–20; local 99, 138, 319; peacebuilding 99, 101, 134–5, 138; PLO 340; political 86; post war 316; soft norms 43; statebuilding 99, 138, 391; UN built state institutions 148; use of force 169, 380; Weberian approach 3, 5–6, 97
Lemay-Hébert, Nicolas 73–4, 79

Lemkin, Raphael 383
Leopold II, King of the Belgiums 121
liberal democracy 87, 90–2, 99
liberalization 110–11, 112–13, 298
liberal market-based relations 55
'liberal nationalism' 72
Liberal Party (Kosovo) 271
liberal peace 96
liberal peacebuilding: Bosnia-Herzegovina 288; external support 138; hegemony 103; Palestine 346; and statebuilding 56–7, 131, 132; Timor-Leste 369
liberal statebuilding 111, 131, 138, 170–1, 181, 305
liberal statebuilding paradigm *see* statebuilding paradigm
Liberia 185–93; civil war 21, 186–7; corruption 21, 23, 187; customary institutions 38; gender-based violence 35; Governance and Economic Management Program (GEMAP) 222, 396; police training 176; reconciliation 395; Truth and Reconciliation Commission 72
Liberian National Police (LNP) 187, 189–90, 192
Libya: elections 143, 257; fragile states xx; R2P (responsibility to protect) 378–9, 381–3
'lighter footprint' SSRs 8, *174*, 175, 178–80, 190
Lijphart, Arend 246–7, 248, 249
Linz, Juan J. 249
Lipset, Seymour 6
literacy programmes 109
local agency 135–6, 305
local cultures 95, 96
local elites 25, 132, 211–12, 223–4
local government 222, 250
local legitimacy 101–2 *see also* legitimacy
local organizations 286–7, 289
local ownership: EU police missions 356; and international ownership 316; legitimacy 99, 138, 319; Libyan elections 257; natural resources 215–16; security sector reform (SSR) 189, 190, 191, 193
Locke, John 87
Lockhart, Clare 396
logical framework 289–90
Lomé Peace Accord 21, 110, 149
Lonsdale, J. 121
'low-income countries under stress' (LICUS) 67, 362, 365
low pay 22n9
Loya Jirga (grand assembly) 307
LPK ('Popular Movement of Kosovo') 271
LPRK ('Popular Movement for the Republic of Kosovo') 271
Luba kingdom 121
Luck, Edward 146, 378, 379, 383
Luhmann, Niklas 6
Lumumba, Patrice 122

Index

Lunda kingdom 121

Macedonia 270, 274
Mac Ginty, R. 95–6, 306
Machar, Riek 46
Machel, Samora 108, 113–14
Mafia 21
Mahoney, M. 111
Making States Work (von Einsiedel) 5
maladjusted societies 84–5
Malawi 149
Malaysia 250
Maley, William 310
Maliki, Nouri al– 297–8, 300, 301
Mallet, Richard 103
Mamaloni, Solomon 335
managed inclusion 48
Mandela, Nelson 252
Mann, Michael 7
Mano River region (Liberia) 189
Mano River Women's Peace Network 36
Maori 248
marginalized groups 48
maritime restrictions 343
market economy 111, 139, 147, 151, 227
Marks, G. 59
Marshall, A. 359
Marshall, J. M. 109
Marton, P. 308, 311
Marxism 8, 72
mass atrocities 282, 376, 377, 384 *see also* ethnic cleansing; genocide
Massoud, Ahmed Shah 225, 305
materialist state theory 57
Mazzini, Giuseppe 72
'McDonaldized' statebuilding 309
Mearsheimer, John 340
'mediated states' 212
mediators 258
Mekele (Ethiopia) 319
Meles Zenawi Asres 323
member benefit organizations (MBO) 285–6
Menkhaus, Ken 212
Menocal, A. 98, 101
Merelman, Richard 6
Mexico 133
micro–finance 27
Middle East 294 *see also* named countries
Migdal, Joel 7, 74, 96
militarized formed police units (FPUs) 205
military: civilian population 319, 358–9; elites 47; logistics 163; post–conflict policing 196–205 *203*; power–sharing 251, 252–3; R2P (responsibility to protect) 379; UN peacekeeping 162, 202–3
militias 311–12
Millennium Declaration (UN) 145

Millennium Development Goals (MDGs) 110, 112, 390
Millennium Development Villages 114
Mill, John Stuart 68
Milošević, Slobodan 275
mineral resources 18, 123–4, 209 *see also* natural resource management (NRM)
minorities 147, 247
MINURCAT (UN Mission in Central African Republic and Chad) 179–80
Mitchell, Audra 90
Mitchell, Timothy 120
Mitrovica 275, 277
mixed member proportional representation (MMP) 248
Mkandawire, T. 112, 190
Mobutu Sese Seko 120–1, 122, 126
mogul–type corruption 19, 24
money–drip 227–8 *see also* aid dependency
monopolies 112–13
Monrovia 192
Montevideo Convention on the Rights and Duties of States (1934) 375
MONUC (UN Organization Mission in the Democratic Republic of the Congo) 122n1, 127, *127*, 158, 160, 163–4 *see also* Congo
MONUSCO (UN Organization Stabilization Mission in the DR Congo) 122n1, 127, *127*
'more is better' approach 3, 8–9, 11
More Secure World: Our Shared Responsibility, A (UN) 376
Moro Islamic Liberation Front 252
Mouffe, Chantal 90
Mozambique 106–15, 252, 320; Five Year Plan (*Plano Quinquenial do Governo*) 114; Organic Charter (1933) 107–8
Mozambique Aluminium (Mozal) 113
Mudrooroo, Nyoongah 94
Mukhopadhyay, Dipali 23
multilateral development assistance organizations 55
Musahiban period 225
Musalha, Nur 343
Musembi, C. N. 32
Museveni, Yoweri 317, 323
Muslims 250, 281
Mutesa, Fred 100
Myanmar 18

Nairn, Tom 72
Najibullah regime 24
Namibia 97
Nathan, I. 190
nationalism 64–79, 210
Nationalities Papers (Association for the Study of Nationalities) 64
nationalization 108

National Patriotic Front of Liberia (NPFL) 187
National Republican Alliance (ARENA) 234, 235
National Resistance Army (Uganda) 316, 319, 321
National Resistance Movement (Uganda) 318
national self−determination 69, 341
National Transitional Council (Libya) 143
nation−building 7, 11
nations, concepts of 66–8
NATO: Bosnia and Herzegovina (BiH) 359; Chicago Summit (2012) 310, 312; ISAF members 310–11; Kosovo 273, 276, 380; led missions 77
natural resource management (NRM) 208, 209–11, 213–17, 320 *see also* gas; mineral resources; oil
natural resources xxi, 208–17, 222
Ndaywel è Nziem, I. 121
negotiated settlements 315, 320
neoliberal economic development model 331
neoliberal institutionalism 54, 55–6
neoliberal statebuilding 60–1, 225, 293, 294, 298, 301
neo−patrimony 17, 96, 99–100, 187, 344
neo−Weberian state 6, 7–8, 54, 56, 60–1 *see also* Weberian state
Nepal: military power−sharing 252; paralegal committees 34; parliamentary quotas 32; women 29, 31–2, 36, 150
nepotistic corruption 102, 308
Netanyahu, Benjamin 340
Netherlands 246–7, 311
Nettl, J. P. 219
Newburn, Tim 200
'New Deal for Engagement in Fragile States' (IDPS) 30, 77
Newman, Edward 10
New Man (*Homem Novo*) 108
New Public Management (Mozambique) 111
New State (*Novo Estado*) 107–8
'New Wars' (Kaldor) 86, 89
New Zealand 248, 310
New Zealand Defence Force (NZDF) 197
NGOs 92, 286, 288, 308–9
Nigeria 74, 250
Nilsson, Desirée 248
9/11 attacks 181, 304–5, 345, 387
Nixon, H. 307, 308
Nkunda, Laurent 122, 124
non−Western societies 84
'no−party' elections 317
normalization 327, 329, 330–1, 334, 337
normative agenda 181, 357, 378
North, Douglass C. 44, 85, 302
Northern Alliance 225, 306, 311
North Sudan 31, 36 *see also* South Sudan; Sudan
Novo Estado (New State) 107–8
Ntaganda, Bosco 122, 156, 160, 165

'nuisance groups' 21–2

Obama, Barack 312, 340
'occupation subcontractor' thesis 342
occupied Palestinian territories (oPt) 339–47, 346
OECD 30, 222
OECD/DAC: guidance on fragile states 5, 73, 75, 208–9, 364–5, 397; hybrid political orders 216; statebuilding 16
OECD StateBuilding Framework (OECD) *391–2*
Office for Reconstruction and Humanitaria Affairs (ORHA) (US) 296
Office of the High Commissioner of Huma Rights (OHCHR) (UN) 146
'official mogul' corruption 1
oil 209; East Timor 331–2, 337; Iraq 301; rents 222; Sudan 214, 251–2 *see also* natural resource management (NRM)
'oil spot' strategy 300
oligarchic corruption 19–20, 23–4
101st Airborne Division (US) 299
ONUB (UN Operation in Burundi) 159
operational overstretch 163–5
Operation Defensive Shield 341
Operation Enduring Freedom 358
opium rents 226
opposition parties 100–1
oPt (occupied Palestinian territories) 339–47, 346
Organization of African Unity 322
ORHA (Off ce for Reconstruction and Humanitarian Affairs) (US) 296, 297
Orientalism (Said) 7, 84
OSCE Kosovo Verification Mission (KVM) 272–3
OSCE (Organization for Security and Cooperation in Europe) 263
Oslo Accords 339, 341, 342–3, 345, 346 *see also* Israel; Palestinians
Ottaway, Marina 56, 92, 99, 317
Ouattara, Alassane 164, 380–1
ownership 113, 305

Pacific Islands Forum (PIF) 32
Pakistan 32, 38–9, 358
Palestine Liberation Organization (PLO) 340, 344
Palestinian Authority (PA) 339–47
Palestinian Investment Law 341
Palestinians 339–47 *see also* Israel; Oslo Accords
Pappe, Ilan 340, 343
Paris Declaration on Aid Effectiveness 364, 390
Paris Economic Protocol (PEP) 340
Paris Peace Accord (1991) 21n8
Paris, Roland xxiii, 65, 73, 76–7, 77, 277, 355–6, 394
Park, Robert Ezra 84–5

parliamentary quotas 32
patronage: Bosnia and Herzegovina (BiH) 282; corruption 21–4; East Timor 331; election violence 262; hybrid regimes 95; political 60, 212; rentier states 226
patronage politics 42
Pattison, James 383
PDK ('Democratic Party of Kosovo') 275, 276
peace 95–6, 134, 136, 137–8, 395
peace agreements: elections 234, 259; and elites 48; human rights 147; implementing 175–6; Liberia 186; post–Cold War 21; power–sharing 248–9, 253–4; risks 248, 320–1; Sudan 46, 47, 211 *see also* named countries
peacebuilding 100–3, 130–9; and colonization 97; institutionalization 103, 277–8; insurgent victories 322; legitimacy 99, 102, 134–5, 138; local frameworks 100, 103, 135; post–intervention 381–2; statebuilding 103–4, 132–5, 355–6; terminology 133; and UN 145, 160; women's groups 36, 133
Peacebuilding and Statebuilding Goals (PSGs) 393
peacekeeping xix, 156–66, 331, 333
peace processes: Israel–Palestinian 339–40, 343, 344–5, 347 *see also* Oslo Accords
Peasants' Party (Kosovo) 271
Pempel, T. J. 58
'peoples' councils' (*baito*) 319
People's Survey (Solomon Islands) 335
Perito, Robert 200
Persian Gulf War (1991) 294, 299
Peru 214
Petraeus, David 299, 300
petroleum revenues *see* oil
Pfaff, William 71
Philippines 36, 251, 252
Piccolino, G. 161
Piiparinen, T. 309
Pitcher, M. A. 112, 113
Pitkin, Hanna 5
Plato 67
plebiscitarianism 220
point resources 213–14
police: EU 350–60; military 197–205, *203*; security sector reform (SSR) 35, 351–5; transnational forces 60; UN 187, 189–90, 202–4 *see also* law enforcement
police training: EU police missions *352–4*, 356; Liberia 176, 187, 189–90; militarized 198, 200; US 196–7
Policy Guidance on Supporting Statebuilding in Situations of Conflict and Fragility (OECD) 30, 208–9
political accountability 149, 191
political clientelism 95
political corruption 22, 25–6
political economy 55, 112–13, 227–8, 397
political elites 47, 76, 328–9, 336–7, 344–5, 347
Political Instability Task Force (Rotberg) 6
political leadership 318, 335
political mobilization 138
political moderation 328
political orders 99, 212, 258
political participation 37, 149
political parties: Guatemala 238, 241–2; Kosovo 271, 275–6; Mozambique 112; power–sharing 249; and rebel victories 318; Solomon Islands 335; women 33
political power structures 131
political practices, Palestinian 344
political reconciliation 300
political rents 222
political representation 86, 286
political settlements xxi, 30–2, 44–5, 48, 75, 388, 395
political society 87–8
political stability 298, 328
political violence 33, 253, 261, 262, 367
politics: and aid 341; post–conflict countries 162; security sector reform (SSR) 181; and women 33, 36
Politics of poverty: Elites, citizens and states. Findings from Ten Years of DFID-funded research on governance and fragile states (DFID) 75
Ponzio, R. 307, 308
'Popular Movement for the Republic of Kosovo' (LPRK) 271
'Popular Movement of Kosovo' (LPK) 271
Portugal 107, 357
positivist approach 7
post–Cold War 21, 42, 97 *see also* Cold War
'post–colonial nationalism' 71
post–colonial societies 86, 87, 89
post–colonial states 68, 334 *see also* colonial states; states
post–colonial world 85–6
post–conflicts: constitutional frameworks 148–9; contexts 36; elections 159, 257–9, 317–18; institution–building 161; planning 84–5, 295–6; policing 197–205, 355–6; politics 97, 316–20, 395; public finances 233 reconstruction 147; social framework 92; South America 231–42
post–9/11 intervention 181, 304–5, 345, 387
post–statebuilding 327
post–war elites 259
'Pottery Barn rule' (Powell) 298, 382
Poulantzas, N. 57
poverty 29, 114, 139, 149
Poverty Reduction Strategy Papers (PRSPs) 110, 112, 127, 148, 363
Povratak ('Return Coalition') 275
Powell, Colin 298, 382

power: asymmetrical 340; competing elites 98, 101, 343; corruption 21, 25–6; expansion of 66; and hybridity 75; informal 31, 37; local elites 25; political 59, 131
power–sharing 132, 246–54, 395
Prevention of Armed Conflict, The (UNSG) 151–2
'principle of intelligibility' (Foucault) 119
Principles for Good International Engagement in Fragile States (OECD) 390
Pristina 275
private contractors 25, 188–9, 205
privatization 112–13, 223, 277, 368
property ownership 107
proportional representation 248, 261
prosecutions 320, 357
protect, responsibility to *see* R2P (responsibility to protect)
Provincial Councils (Afghanistan) 307
'Provisional Institutions of Self–Government' (PISG) 275
'provisional statehood' (Bolton and Visoka) 341
public administration 113–15
public benef t organizations (PBOs) 285–6
public economics 219
public finances 224–5, 23
public order *see* police; security sector reform (SSR)
public servants 22n9
public services 16–17, 22–3, 42
Putzel, J. 44

Qaeda, al– 299, 304
Quartet, The 345–6
'quasi–states' 68, 339
Quosja, Rexhep 272

Račak (Kosovo) 273
race 83–93
Rambouillet negotiations 273
Ramos–Horta, Jose 331, 332
RAMSI (Regional Assistance Mission to Solomon Islands) 59, 333–7
RAND study (Quinlivan) 8, 308
Rassemblement Congolais pour la Démocratie (RCD) 123, 124
rational agonistic contestation 91
Ratner, Steven 3, 4, 8, 9
rebel movements 122, 123, 124, 317, 318–19
rebel victories 315–23
reconciliation 320, 395
reforms: economic and political 110–11; security sector reform (SSR) 181, 188–93; Timor–Leste 332
refugees 283, 340
regime change 293, 301, 345–6
Regional Assistance Mission to Solomon Islands (RAMSI) 59, 333–7

regions 250–1
Regulating Statehood (Hameiri) 53, 61
regulatory statebuilding 52–61
Reilly, Benjamin 247, 258
reintegration *see* combatants, integration of
Reisinger, Christian 95
Relief Society of Tigray (REST) 319
religious elites 344
religious nationalism 74
Renamo 109, 110, 252, 320
Renan, Ernest 66
Reno, William 214
rentier states 46, 210, 222–3, 225–7
Republic (Plato) 67
Republika Srpska (RS) 278, 281, 287, 359 *see also* Bosnia and Herzegovina (BiH)
Resilience of an African giant (World Bank) 123
'resource curse' 210
resource management 42
responsibility to protect (R2P) *see* R2P (responsibility to protect)
responsibility to protect, The (ICISS) 375
'restorative justice' 395
'results–based agenda' 396
'Return Coalition' (Povratak) 275
revenues 42, 233, 346
Revolutionary Armed Forces of Colombia (FARC) 213
Revolutionary United Front (RUF) 21
Reynolds, Andrew 247
Rhodesia 109
Richmond, O. P. 56, 57, 192, 356
Rietjens, S. 311
risk management 58
'*Risorgimento* nationalism' 69
'Roadmap' (Israel–Palestinian) 345
Roadmap to move beyond conflict and fragility and secure development (WDR) *392*
Rokkan, S. 220
Roma people 274
Rosberg, Carl 100
Rosser, A. 58
Rotberg, Robert 4, 6, 8, 52, 56
Roy, Sara 342
'R2P lite' 379–84
R2P Monitor (Global Centre for the R2P) 379
R2P (responsibility to protect) 146, 375–84
Rubin, B. R. 159, 311
Rücker, Joackim 276
Rugova, Ibrahim 270, 273
rule of law 33–4, 145, 169, 199, 203
Rules of Engagement (ROE) 202
ruling elites xxi, 187
Rumsfeld, Donald 295
Russia 377, 379
Rwanda: aid 396; and Congo 124–5, 322; demobilization 321–2; elections 317; *Gacaca*

tribunals 320, 395; genocide 122, 249, 322; international community 322, 358; sub–state nationalism 70; women 29, 32
Rwandan Arusha Agreement 147
Rwandan Defence Force 322
Rwandan Patriotic Front (RPF) 316, 319–20, 322

Sadr, Moqtadr al– 298
Sahnoun, Mohamed 384
Said, Edward 7, 84, 342
Salazar, António de Oliveira 113–14
Salvadoran Foundation for Economic and Social Development (FUSADES) 235
Sambanis, Nicholas 8
sanctions 296, 346
Sankoh, Foday 21
Sartori, Giovanni 247
Savimbi, Jonas 261
SBIs (statebuilding interventions) 48, 52–61
Scharpf, Michael 74
Schatzberg, Michael 120, 122
Schmeidl, S. 309
Schoofs, S. 35
Schoplfin, George 7
Schori, Pierre 161
Scots Guards (UK) 197
Scott, J. C. 133
Seabrooke, Leonard 7
Seats and Votes: The Effects and Determinant of Electoral Systems (Taagepera and Shugart) 247
secessionists 70, 282
Second Treatise of Government (Locke) 87
sectarian conflicts 300
secular laws 250
security: and corruption 23–4; and development 221–2; fragile states 58; Israel and Palestinians 345; post war 316
security sector reform (SSR): Afghanistan 305–7; and elections 257; European Union (EU) 350, 351, 354; gender issues 34–5; Liberia 188–9, 190, 191–3; outsourcing 188–9; statebuilding 168–81, *174*, 179; technical approaches 191; Timor–Leste 331; Western interests 181, 354–5 *see also* disarmament, demobilization, and reintegration (DDR)
Selby, Jan 339
self–determination 69, 341
Sena Sugar Estates 113
September 11 2001 181, 304–5, 345, 387
Serbia 270, 271
Serbian communities: ethnic cleansing 272, 274; Kosovo 274, 275, 276, 277; Republika Srpska (RS) 281
Serbian forces 272–3
Serbian National Council (SNV) 275

Serb Movement of Independent Associations (SPONA) 287
sexual violence 35
'shared sovereignty' (Krasner) 341
sharia law 34, 250
Sharon, Ariel 343
Sherman, Jake 156–7
Shiite Muslims 261, 298, 299
Shikaki, Khalil 343, 344
Shugart, M.S. 247
Shura–e–Nazar militia 305
Sierra Leone: elite settlements 21; EU support strategies 368–9, *371*; reforms 149; UN peacekeeping 158, 163; women 33, 34, 38
SIG–RAMSI Partnership Framework Agreement (2009) 335
Sisk, Timothy 65, 73, 76–7, 91, 247, 355–6, 394
Skocpol, Theda 7, 56
Slovenia 251, 270
Smith, Adam 87
Smith, Anthony 66, 78
Smits, R. 35
social barriers 39–40
social contract 16, 29, 75
socialism 108–9
social justice 134
socially constituted development 48–9
social movements 394
social orders 49
social services 396
social stability 58
social structures 87, 96–7
society 7–8, 16–17, 56, 89, 247
socioeconomic development 171
soft norms, of legitimacy 43
Sogavare, Manasseh 334
Solana, Javier 362
soldiers *see* combatants
Solomon Islands 59, 197, 327–37
Somalia 4, 42, 212, 213, 214–15
South Africa 32, 249, 252–3, 259, 395
South America 231–42
Southern Rhodesia 109
south Pacific region 32
South Serbia 274
South Sudan: Agreement on Wealth Sharing 211; 'capable state' model 43–4, 45; civil wars 47; governance 47–8; independence 46–7; oil revenues 214, 251–2; referenda 165; women 30–1, 36 *see also* North Sudan; Sudan
South Sudan Defence Forces 46
sovereign capacity 160
sovereignty 68, 86, 151–2, 162, 341, 376–7, 383
Soviet states 86
Special Representative/Head of Mission (HOM) (UNSG) 203

Spence, David 354–5
SRSG (UN Special Representative of the Secretary-General) 156, 159, 161
Staatsvolk (founding ethnic group) 68
Stabilisation Force (SFOR) 359
Stalin, Joseph 66
'Standards before Status' checklist (Kosovo) 276
standard-setting, and constitution-making 146–7
state authority 43, 169, 389, *389*
'state autonomy' theory 7
statebuilding: approaches 132; definition 11, 143 fragile states xx, 52–3, 390–7; gender equality 29; 'horizontal' 21; institutional approach 3, 4–5, 7, 10; legitimacy 99, 138, 391; and nationalism 64–5; political basis 42 *see also* Durkheimian sociology; Weberian States; Western states
statebuilding interventions (SBIs) 48, 52–61
statebuilding paradigm: and Australia 329, 333; good governance 170–1, 181; Iraq 293, 298; liberalism 305; post-conflict 88; response to state failure 328; social conflicts 90
statebuilding policy framework 89
state capacities xxi, 16, 54–7, 262, 263, 371
state destruction 109
state elites 113, 233
state failure *see* failed states
State Failure Task Force (Rotberg) 6
state formation 73–4, 132, 136–8, 212, 328
state fragility *see* fragile states
'state-in-society' model 7n3
state institutions 263, 288, 396
state-led nationalism 69–70, 78
'stateness problem' 249–50
states: collapse xx, 5, 8, 10–11; concepts 4; control of 75; creation 69–71; failed by design 130–1; financing 219–28; homogeneity 68; 'polis' 78 *see also* colonial states; hybridity; post-colonial states
state–society relations 16, 73–5, 115, 212–13, 222–3, 328
Stedman, S. J. 320–1
Steiner, Michael 276
Stepan, Alfred 249
stolen elections 263
Stonequist, Everett 85
Straw, Jack 6–7
Strock, Carl 295
Stryker Cavalry Regiment (US) 197
sub-state nationalism 70, 77, 78
Sudan: Agreement on Wealth Sharing 211; Comprehensive Peace Agreement (CPA) 46, 47, 211; Darfur 164, 165, 197; domestic violence 35; oil income 214; power-sharing agreements 251–2; sharia law 250; women 34, 35 *see also* North Sudan; South Sudan

Sudan People's Liberation Army (SPLA) 30n3, 46
Sudan People's Liberation Movement (SPLM) 46–7
Suhrke, Astri 76
Sunni Muslims 261, 298–300
supranationalism 72–3, 78
Sutherland, Clair 78
Syndicate of Trade Unions of Kosovo 272
Syria 165, 379, 383, 384

Taagepera, R. 247
'tacit trusteeship' 222
Taliban 22, 76, 225, 304, 306, 358–9
Tamir, Yael 72
Tanzi, Vito 102
Taraki, Nur Mohammed 309
taxation: Bosnia and Herzegovina (BiH) 224; capacity 233; El Salvador 236, 242; Guatemala 239–40, *241*; participation 220, 222
'taxi' parties 235
Taylor, Charles 186, 187
technocratic approaches 285, 393
territorial boundaries 68–9, 293
territorial power-sharing 249–51
Tetovo (Macedonia) 274
Thakur, Ramesh 379
Thaqi, Hashim 273–4, 275
Third High Level Forum on Aid Effectiveness (2008) 392
third-party security guarantees 249, 321
Tigray 319, 320
Tigray People's Liberation Front (TPLF) 318–19
Tilly, Charles: 'autonomous state' 7; centralization 47, 48; legitimacy 6; 'national' homogeneity 68–9; state formation 42, 43, 136
Timor-Leste: Australian involvement 327–37; defence forces 178; EU support strategies 369, *371*; governance 45–6, 47–8; Ministry of Health and the Ministry of Social Solidarity (MSS) 49; National Strategic Development Plan (2011–2030) 331; peace formation 135; UN statebuilding 43, 77, 177; women 32
Toft, Monica Duffy 316
Tolbert, William 187
Tortolani, Benjamin 163
trading monopolies 345
traditional structures 97
training: leaders 178; police *see* police training
Trainor, B. E. 296
Trajković, Momčilo 275
'transformatory peacebuilding' 10
'transition' *see* hybridity
'transitional client quasi-state' approach 342
transitional governments 259
transitional justice 172–3
transnational elites 237, 239

transparency 188–9, 191, 308
Transparency International 15
Trepča mines (Kosovo) 270, 277
tribal leaders 38–9
tribal self-defence (*arbaki*) 311–12
tribal systems 335, 370
True Whig Party (TWP) (Liberia) 186, 187
trust 200, 284
Tschirgi, Neçla 263
Tubman, William 187
Turkey 69, 311
Turkish Cypriots 250
Turkish (Kosovo) 274
Tutsis 249, 366–7

Uganda 32, 315–23
UK: Afghanistan 311, 358–9; Department for International Development (DFID) 5, 23, 44, 55, 75; responsibility to protect (R2P) 377; Rwanda 358; Sierra Leone 158, 162, 368; South Africa 252
UN: civilian political missions 165; Kosovo administration 273–4; led missions 77; military observers 165; overseeing elections 263, 322; Palestinians 341; peacekeeping 156–66, 202–3, *203*; policing 202–3, *203*; sanctions 272
UN Assistance Mission in Afghanistan (UNAMA) 308
UN–AU Hybrid Operation in Darfur (UNAMID) 164, 197
UN Charter 144, 380, 381, 384
UN Constitutional Assistance (UNCA) 143–53
UN Convention on the Punishment and Prevention of the Crime of Genocide 383
UN Country Teams (UNCTs) 148–9
UN Department of Peacekeeping Operations (DPKO) 159, 201, 202
UN Development Assistance Frameworks (UNDAFs) 148–9
UN Development Fund for Women (UNIFEM) 30–2, 147
UN Development Program (UNDP) 29n2, 143–4, 148–9, 261, 284
UN Directives on the Use of Force (DUF) 202
UN General Assembly 151, 379
UN Head of Military Component (HOMC) 203
UN Head of Police Component (HOPC) 203
UN High–Level Panel on Threats, Challenges and Change 152, 376
UN Human Rights Council 384
UN Integrated Mission in Timor–Leste (UNMIT) 331, 332
UN Integrated Peacebuilding Office Sierra Leon (UNIPSIL) 179
UN Interim Administration Mission in Kosovo (UNMIK) 270, 273–4, 276

UN Interim Force in Lebanon (UNIFIL) 158–9
UN Mediation Support Unit (MSU) 146
UN Military Operations Plan ('Operation Order') 202
UN Mission in Central African Republic and Chad (MINURCAT) 179–80
UN Mission in Liberia (UNMIL) 185, 190
UN Mission in Nepal (UNMIN) 150
UN Mission in Sierra Leone (UNAMSIL) 163, 179
UN Mission in South Sudan 43
UN Mission of Support to East Timor (UNMISET) 330
UN Office in East Timor (UNOTIL) 33
UN Office of the High Commissioner of Huma Rights (OHCHR) 146
UN Office of the High Representative (OHR 283, 287–8
UN Operation in Burundi (ONUB) 159
UN Operation in Côte d'Ivoire (UNOCI) 146, 161–2, 164–5, 381
UN Organization Mission in the Democratic Republic of the Congo (MONUC) 122n1, 127, *127*, 158, 160, 163–4 *see also* Congo
UN Organization Stabilization Mission in the DR Congo (MONUSCO) 122n1, 127, *127*
UN Panel of Experts on the Illegal Exploitation of Natural Resources and Other Forms of Wealth of the Democratic Republic of the Congo 211
UN Peacebuilding Commission 162
UN Peacekeeping Force in Cyprus (UNFICYP) 250
UN Police (UNPOL) 176, 187, 189–90
UN Report on the High Level Panel on Threats, Challenges, and Change 152, 376
UN Resident Coordinator (UNRC) 148
UN Secretary General (UNSG) 144–5, 152, 203
UN Security Council Resolution (1244) 273, 276, 277
UN Security Council Resolution (1325) 30, 34, 147
UN Security Council Resolution (1509) 187
UN Security Council Resolution (1970) 382
UN Security Council Resolution (1973) 381
UN Security Council (UNSC) 144, 162, 164–5, 197, 375–84
UNSG Special Representative/Head of Mission (HOM) 203
UN Special Advisers on the Prevention of Genocide and the Responsibility to Protect 146, 384
UN Special Representative/Head of Mission (HOM) 203
UN Special Representative of the Secretary–General (SRSG) 156, 159, 161
UN Support Mission in Libya (UNSMIL) 143, 257

UN Transitional Administration in East Timor (UNTAET) 43, 45, 328, 330
Underkuffler, Laura 2
'ungoverned spaces' 209, 213
'unification' nationalism 6
UNITA 261, 320
University of Pristina 270
US: Afghanistan xxiii, 25, 309, 358–9; Iraq xxiii, 293–302; Israel–Palestine 339, 340, 341, 346. 347; Kosovo 196–7; Liberia 162, 188–9; post–9/11 security strategy 178, 345; R2P (responsibility to protect) 377; statebuilding 8, 358
US Agency for International Development (USAID) 125, 261
US Army Corps of Engineers 309
US Army/Marine Counterinsurgency Field Manual (CFM) 299
US Congressional report (2010) 25
US Department of Defense (DoD) 295–6
US Dodd–Frank Wall Street and Consumer Protection Act (2010) 215, 216
US Human Terrain System 312
US Institute for Peace (USIP) 273
US Military Police 196–7
US National Security Strategy (NSS) 57
US Off ce for Reconstruction and Humanitarian Affairs (ORHA) 296, 297
US State Department 295, 296

value added tax (VAT) 236, 239–40
Vamvakas, P. 311
veterans 176–7, 287
Village Leagues, Palestinian 344
'villagization' 114
Viñuales, J. 209
violence, state monopoly 42, 254
violent conf ict: corruption 20, 23; elections 248–9, 261–2; Iraq 297, 301; Kosovo 272; Macedonia 274; political settlements 22; power–sharing agreements 249, 250–1; South Serbia 274 *see also* wars
voluntary multi–stakeholder regimes 217
Voluntary Principles on Security and Human Rights 208
von Bismarck, Otto 68
von Einsiedel, Sebastian 5
von Trotha, T. 97
voters 263, 285, 317–18
voting systems 248, 254, 261, 264 *see also* elections

Waal, Alex de 17, 21, 165, 212
Wagner, P. 311
Wall Street Journal 20n6
Walter, Barbara 248, 249, 321
Walt, Stephen 340

Walzer, Michael 378
warlords 23, 95, 305–7
'warlord states' 214
'war on terror' 345, 371
wars: Congo 122; financing 210–11; Mozambiqu 109; 'old' and 'new' 86 *see also* violent conflic
war termination 315, 316
Washington Post 164
water 299
weak states xxi, 42, 67, 293; Bosnia and Herzegovina (BiH) 224; Congo 119, 121, 123; Solomon Islands 336–7 *see also* failed states; fragile states
Weberian states 3–11, 56, 95, 97, 213, 278 *see also* Durkheimian sociology; neo–Weberian state; statebuilding
Weber, Max: 'autonomous state' 7–8; legitimacy 4, 5–6, 43, 49; on nations/nationalism 66; state formation 42; states as human communities 67; 'state–society' relations 73, 74
Weingast, B. R. 302
Weinstein, J. M. 319
Weiss, Herbert 125–6
welfare services 213
Welsh, Jennifer 383
Wendt, Alexander 10
West Bank 339–47
Western anthropological engagements 131
Western bilateral development assistance organizations 55
Western democracy 84–5, 328
Western donors 110, 226–7, 341 *see also* donors
Western states 7, 138, 191–2 *see also* statebuilding
Western superiority 85
West Gaza 356–7
West, H. G. 114
Whaites, Alan 44
Wilson, Woodrow 69
Wolfowitz, Paul 296
women 29–40; civil society organizations (CSO's) 36; human rights 147; inf uence 31, 37–8, 40; Kosovo 31, 275; Nepal 29, 31, 36, 150; Pakistan 38; peacebuilding 133; Rwanda 31; South Sudan 30–1, 36; Yemen 370
World Bank 55, 147; aid programs 362; Bosnia and Herzegovina (BiH) aid 223; Kosovo credits 277; LICUS framework 365; Palestinian aid 341; report on diasporas 72
World Development Report 2011: Background case study Democratic Republic of Congo. (World Bank) 125
World Development Report 2011: Conflict, security and development (World Bank) 44n8, 216, 392
World Summit (2005) 376, 379–80, 381, 382, 384

World Summit Outcome (UN) 145
World Trade Organization 209
World War Two, post–war planning 84–5

Yauyau, David 47
Yemen 369–70, *371*
Yugoslavia 4, 251, 270–1

Yugoslav People's Army (JNA) 271

Zaire 21
Zapatista rebellion 133
Zartman, I. W. 56
Zinni, Anthony 296
Zürcher, C. 322

Taylor & Francis
eBooks
FOR LIBRARIES

ORDER YOUR FREE 30 DAY INSTITUTIONAL TRIAL TODAY!

Over 23,000 eBook titles in the Humanities, Social Sciences, STM and Law from some of the world's leading imprints.

Choose from a range of subject packages or create your own!

Benefits for you
- Free MARC records
- COUNTER-compliant usage statistics
- Flexible purchase and pricing options

Benefits for your user
- Off-site, anytime access via Athens or referring URL
- Print or copy pages or chapters
- Full content search
- Bookmark, highlight and annotate text
- Access to thousands of pages of quality research at the click of a button

For more information, pricing enquiries or to order a free trial, contact your local online sales team.

UK and Rest of World: **online.sales@tandf.co.uk**
US, Canada and Latin America:
e-reference@taylorandfrancis.com

www.ebooksubscriptions.com

ALPSP Award for BEST eBOOK PUBLISHER 2009 Finalist

Taylor & Francis eBooks
Taylor & Francis Group

A flexible and dynamic resource for teaching, learning and research.